A History of the Council of Trent

Volume I

HUBERT JEDIN

★

A History of
the Council of Trent

Translated from the German
by
DOM ERNEST GRAF O.S.B.

★

Volume I

B. Herder Book Co.
15 & 17 South Broadway, St Louis 2, Mo.

Imprimatur:

✝ GORDON J. GRAY

*Archbishop of St Andrews
and Edinburgh*

This is the authorised translation of
Hubert Jedin

Geschichte des Konzils von Trient, Band I
Verlag Herder
Freiburg im Breisgau
1949

First published in English 1957

Translator's Preface

THE author's preface explains the nature and genesis of the present work. However, some explanation by the translator, and even an apology, may be in order—an apology, that is, for the use of certain terms that may hurt a sensitive ear, but which are inescapable if the reader is to be spared lengthy and awkward circumlocutions. The expression "conciliar theory" is generally accepted. It stands for the view that the authority of a General Council is superior to that of the Pope, so that its decisions have force of law even without the latter's approval. The Germans describe this opinion—an utterly wrong one —as "conciliarism" and also use the adjective "conciliarist".

I also use the terms "evangelicalism" and "evangelistic"; they simply designate the Lutheran or Protestant movement on the Continent.

The author, whose reading is immense, not unnaturally quotes a vast number of German writers. The works of some of these have been translated into English, for instance Pastor's voluminous history of the Popes. In these instances I have endeavoured to quote the equivalent English translation. However, in the case of Pastor, the author of this *History of the Council of Trent* quotes from the more recent editions, e.g. those of 1924 and 1926, whereas the English translation of the earlier volumes was made from the first or the second edition. So in a few instances, only the references to the German text can be given. In a few other cases the reference to the English translation is only approximate, for the reason just stated. If, therefore, in a very few instances, the reference to the English translation is not accurate, or not quite accurate, I may plead that it is due to the fact that the earlier German volumes have been retouched and enlarged so that the cross-references, when they were possible, may not be completely reliable. If English translations of French, Italian and Spanish books quoted by Jedin are not given, the reason is that very few of them seem to have been translated. In the case of *Seripando*, in which the German original is in three volumes, the English translator has made some drastic cuts, especially in the very numerous, often lengthy footnotes. I have also failed to identify some references to Ranke. For such omissions I must crave the reader's indulgence.   E. G.

v

Contents

Book One

Council and Reform from the Council of Basle to the Lateran Council

vii

CONTENTS

CONTENTS

x

List of Plates

Author's Preface

EVER since the days of Sarpi and Pallavicino, that is, for some three hundred years, the world has been waiting for a history of the Council of Trent that would be other than an accusation or a defence. Ranke thought that such a history could not be written: those who were willing to make the attempt were bound to fail because they had no access to the most important sources, while those who could write it lacked the will to do so. The first of these two difficulties was overcome when the Vatican archives were thrown open; but there remained another, one that has assumed enormous proportions since the days of Ranke. Today, more than ever before, a history of the Council of Trent is a hazardous enterprise, for the writer sees himself confronted with a problem with which a single individual can scarcely hope to deal adequately. On the one hand he is expected to assess the political issues of an agitated period of history, while on the other he must needs follow up the thought of a whole generation of divines and, besides, master the development of ecclesiastical law and discipline at the turn of the Middle Ages and their transition into the modern era.

If he is to succeed in an enterprise of this kind the writer must be at home in history, theology and canon law. But mastery of any one of these three disciplines demands a lifetime. The more perseveringly a scholar strives to equip himself for his task, the more painfully aware he becomes of the inadequacy both of his physical strength and of his actual knowledge as well as of the impossibility, for a single human mind, of encompassing the spiritual and political life of an entire epoch and giving it adequate expression. More than once I felt tempted to lay down my pen, reluctant as I was to play the pitiful role of the amateur before the experts in the above-mentioned branches of learning. If I resisted the temptation, it was because of a conviction that on their integration depends our spiritual survival, and that no institution was better qualified to strive for such a survival than the Catholic Church.

From the Church the present work borrows its standard of values: it has never stood in my way when I sought to understand and to appraise the standpoint of "the other side"; it was no hindrance even when unpleasant truths had to be uttered, and I have ever borne in mind the axiom laid down by Cicero and stressed by Leo XIII in his letter of 18 August 1883 to Cardinals De Luca, Pitra and Hergenröther: "Primam esse historiae legem ne quid falsi dicere audeat, deinde ne quid veri non audeat; ne qua suspicio gratiae sit in scribendo, ne qua simultatis." In addition to this I have presented the subject-matter in accordance with a very definite conception of the historian's duty which I have explained elsewhere ("Esame di coscienza di un storico", in *Quaderni di Roma*, 1947, pp. 206-17). Whether, and to what extent, my work conforms to this conception the critics must decide.

This book is written for discerning readers: it needs to be read, not merely dipped into. The footnotes enable the student to verify statements and to carry the examination of problems still further. Those who read merely to pick holes will find that a number of persons and incidents only briefly referred to deserve by themselves a fuller treatment. They will not fail to point to documents and papers that I have "overlooked". To these people I say that while I pay homage to their circumstantial information and am prepared to learn from them, I am unwilling to alter my general plan. It was necessary to limit myself, and to leave out a vast amount of material accumulated in my portfolios and my files, if the work was to be kept within reasonable bounds. I am well aware of the gaps; they are due, at least in part, to present-day conditions.

The reader who contents himself with a mere perusal of the book may feel that I have reached too far back; that, for instance, a short introduction would have sufficed to describe the views about Council and reform that were current in that period of transition, and that too much space has been allotted to the struggle for the Council. I must crave the indulgence of such readers. The volumes yet to follow will show the bearing of the questions discussed in the present one on the course of the Council.

Even the most impartial historical work cannot but bear the stamp of its author's personality; hence a brief account of the origin of this book may be a key to its understanding. The decision to draw up a comprehensive account of the history of the Council of Trent was taken in the spring of 1939. Thanks to the personal intervention of H.E. Cardinal Giovanni Mercati, I was able to take up residence in Rome in November of the same year. The clergy of the German Campo Santo made me an honorary member of their body and thereby provided for my maintenance. The first chapters were written amid the thunder of the guns of Anzio, the latter ones at a time when my heart was heavy with anxiety for my relatives and my Silesian homeland. A long-planned journey to Spain was delayed by the war, which also prevented me from seeing a number of German and French publications. I nevertheless venture to publish the work, conscious as I am that the original material I have exploited is so copious, and so representative of every aspect of the subject, that a substantial change in its general interpretation is hardly to be expected.

The work will be completed in 8 books. Of these, Books I and II are contained in the first volume. Books III to V will cover the two Tridentine periods 1545-7 and 1551-2, together with the Bolognese interlude, which, by their bearing on the schism in Germany and their close connexion with Charles V's religious policy, form an organic whole. Books VI and VII will deal with the great reform Council under Pius IV. Book VIII will provide a review of the impact of the Council on the life of the Church, to which will be added a survey of the relevant literature, chronological tables, and lists of the members of the Council.

The present volume appears too late to commemorate two memorable events. It should have marked the four-hundredth anniversary of the opening of the Council of Trent, and also should have been an act of homage to H.E. Cardinal Mercati on the occasion of his eightieth birthday—17 December 1946—for it was with his encouragement that the work was undertaken. Neither of these aims was realised. None the less I trust that the volume will call forth interest in the great event it describes and that the eminent patron and all who have contributed to its production by their counsel, or otherwise, will regard it as an expression of my gratitude.

Bonn   HUBERT JEDIN

12 *September* 1949

Book One

CHAPTER I

The Victory of the Papacy over the Reform Councils

STRANGE though it may sound, the history of the Council of Trent begins with the triumph of the Papacy over the reform Councils. In the course of the century between the dissolution of the Council of Basle and the assembling of the Council of Trent the notions of the Papacy, the Councils and Church reform that had taken shape in the late Middle Ages underwent a change and gave rise to tensions within the Church, and to a mental atmosphere which influenced the course and the result of the Tridentine assembly no less profoundly than the great event of the sixteenth century—the break-up of Christian unity.

True, we are here concerned chiefly with ideas, our presentation of which may seem pale and colourless, because it does not deal with the exploits of great men, and is not seasoned with the colourful details of actual life. However, like an induction-current which diverts the magnet, these ideas influenced the actions of the ecclesiastics and the politicians of the period of the Councils. If we succeed in grasping their inner content, we shall be on the way to an understanding of the history of the Council.

Up to the fateful turn of the Middle Ages, about the year 1300, the supremacy of the Papacy in the Church and in the *Respublica christiana* had remained unchallenged. Caesarism had collapsed after a long struggle, and its former universal authority was more nominal than real. A rigid centralisation of authority characterised the papal government of the Church. By reserving to themselves the right of nomination, the Popes disposed of an ever-growing number of ecclesiastical offices and benefices, and at the same time the charges on these, and the annates, were some compensation for the slowing down of the flow of income derived from the tenth everywhere demanded from the faithful for the crusade. Recently founded and centrally governed, the Mendicant Orders could be regarded as a bodyguard. The fourth Council of the Lateran, the two Councils of Lyons and that of Vienne, showed the Pope as the unquestioned head of Christendom. The teaching on the Pope's supremacy which theologians and canonists had formulated in the course of the thirteenth century was given its final sanction in the Bull *Unam sanctam*.

However, the internal strength of the Christian and universal idea that had built up the spacious yet most compact structure of the world of the early Middle Ages had long ago grown weak. The collapse of the medieval conception of the world, together with that of a universal papal monarchy, proceeded almost at an identical rate. While the systems of later scholasticism were being breached by the critics of other schools, the rising national states of the West also voiced their claims. At Avignon the Papacy was made subservient to France's power-policy, while for such theologians as Olivi the concept of the Church had become a problem. The spiritual outlook of the modern individual and that of the modern state were both entering on the road that was to lead to Luther and Machiavelli.

Was the collapse unavoidable? Must we look for its causes in the Church herself?

Neither the first nor the second of these questions can be answered with a simple denial. Not the first, because the fact that individuals and peoples come of age does not put an end to human freedom; not the second, because contemporaries did not themselves hesitate to lay their finger on the abuses, and so on the historic guilt, of the Church of the late Middle Ages. Now that it had become a factor in the advance of culture, and even a world in itself—wealthy and powerful—the ecclesiastical hierarchy was no longer wholly in harmony with its apostolic mission. The campaign for a return to the practice of poverty —heretical in the case of the Waldensians, Catholic in that of St Francis —was a reaction against this development, nor was it the only one. The call for a reform, for a return to the primitive form of Christianity which had its roots in the very nature of revelation, and whose lineaments had been stamped on it by the early Church, became ever louder.[1] This call originated in the consciousness that Christ's foundation, as

---

[1] It would be an exaggeration to claim that the notes to this chapter provide a complete survey of the vast literature about the reform Councils and about conciliar theory; they merely point to the sources on which I have drawn and the various studies and treatises that I have consulted. Among the latter, in spite of its one-sided political approach to the subject, Haller's *Papsttum und Kirchenreform*, VOL. I (Berlin 1903), still holds the first place; see especially p. 154. For the influence of Gallicanism on the general development, see V. Martin, *Les Origines du Gallicanisme* (2 vols. Paris 1939). For a good survey of the reform literature, see A. Posch, *Die Concordantia catholica des Nicolaus von Cues* (Paderborn 1930), pp. 36 ff. On the problem of the Church, from the High Church point of view, see F. Heiler, *Altkirchliche Autonomie und päpstlicher Zentralismus* (Munich 1941), pp. 283-98.

historically realised in its individual members, no longer corresponded to the ideal—in other words, that it was not what it should be; and in this respect it was no new thing but was almost as old as the Church herself. However, it must be admitted that at the close of the thirteenth century the call became louder and more general, and that it took a very definite orientation. Though for the time being the institution of papal supremacy by Christ was not attacked, the demand for reform was aimed at the worldliness of the Church's hierarchy. But it was above all the centralisation of authority in the Curia, the procedure adopted in granting benefices, and the system of taxation connected therewith, that cried out for reform.

In the tract on the scandals of the Church which he drew up for the second Council of Lyons, Gilbert of Tournai still observed some restraint when speaking of the Pope. "The Lord's anointed", he declared, "we leave to the Supreme Judge. Let him study St Bernard's book *De consideratione*; it will teach him his duty."[1] However, in the course of the conflict between Boniface VIII and Philip the Fair, the French King's supporters Nogaret, Flot and Dubois attacked the Pope's position in the Church, while the French bishops ranged themselves behind their King's appeal to a Council, thus joining him in brandishing the formidable weapon forged by the Colonna Cardinals.[2] Long before D'Ailly and Gerson, the Dominican John of Paris, "the most versatile and most striking figure of the old Thomist school of Paris",[3] had formulated the thesis that a Council, since it represents the whole Church, is above the Pope and has power to depose him should he misuse his authority. However, the time was not yet ripe for so radical a solution of the question of authority. At the Council of Vienne, at

---

[1] *Archivum Franciscanum historicum*, XXIV (1936), p. 36. So also Humbertus de Romanis, *Opus tripartitum*, VOL. III, PT ii (in Crabbe, *Concilia Omnia* (Cologne 1538), VOL. II, p. 1000): "Nemo inferior audet ponere os in ecclesiam Romanam." On the question of authorship, see B. Birckmann, *Die vermeintliche und die wirkliche Reformschrift des Humbert de Romanis* (Heidelberg 1916).

[2] H. X. Arquillière, "L'Appel au concile sous Philippe le Bel et la génèse des théories conciliaires" in *Revue des questions historiques*, LXXXIX (1911), pp. 23-55. J. Rivière, *Le Problème de l'Eglise et de l'Etat aux temps de Philippe le Bel* (Louvain 1926), pp. 109 ff. On p. 346 we read that Dubois, in his demand for a Council, "n'a rien soupçonné des théories conciliaires". On the three memorials of the Colonna cardinals in 1297, see *Archiv für Literatur- und Kirchengeschichte des Mittelalters*, v (1889), pp. 509-24.

[3] M. Grabmann, "Studien zu Johannes Quidort von Paris", in *Sitzungsberichte der bayrischen Akademie, philosophisch-historische Klasse*, VOL. III (Munich 1922), p. 3. On the tract *De potestate regia et papali*, written in 1302-03, see R. Scholz, *Die Publizistik zur Zeit Philipps des Schönen und Bonifaz VIII* (Stuttgart 1903), pp. 298 ff.; Rivière, *Le Problème*, p. 295.

which, according to Philip the Fair's original design, Boniface VIII was to have been condemned as a heretic, proceedings against the dead Pope were dropped with the King's agreement, but the assembly met his wishes in the affair of the Templars. A tract destined for this same Council of Vienne by Guillaume Durant (Durandus) the Younger is significant as witnessing to the growth of the idea of reform. The tract is entitled *De modo concilii generalis celebrandi*, and in it Durandus lays down the principle that the reform of the Church must proceed from the head, that is, from the Roman Church.[1] The Pope must be a pattern for all by his faithful observance of the "ancient law". In Durandus's mind observance of the ancient law is almost identical with a strengthening of the authority of the bishops. A regular celebration of provincial and diocesan synods as well as of General Councils—the latter every ten years—would, in his opinion, substantially promote the health of the ecclesiastical organism.

For Durandus a "reform of the head" means the proper use of papal authority; the idea of its constitutional limitation does not present itself to his mind; still less does it occur to the papal penitentiary Alvaro Pelayo when, a lifetime later, he too laments the abuses in the Church.[2] In point of fact it was precisely at this time that the Pope's supreme authority was most clearly and most comprehensively defined by Augustinus Triumphus of Ancona.[3]

But here too there was a conflict of opinions. The struggle between John XXII and Louis of Bavaria gave birth in 1324 to a work which, by its cold array of arguments, constitutes the most revolutionary attack on the medieval Papacy. Its title is *Defensor pacis* and the author's name is Marsiglio of Padua. The Paduan scholar was not content to deny Christ's institution of the papal primacy and the fact of St Peter's sojourn in Rome as its bishop; he also put bishops and priests on an equal footing in respect of their spiritual powers. Moreover, by

---

[1] G. Durandus, *De modo concilii generalis celebrandi*, VOL. III, pp. 1, 27, in *Tractatus illustrium iurisconsultorum*, VOL. XIII, i (Venice 1584), fols. 173ʳ-175ᵛ. The significance of this book for the rise of episcopalism is touched upon but far from adequately worked out by A. Posch, "Der Reformvorschlag des Wilhelm Durandus jun. auf dem Konzil von Vienne", in *M.Ö.I.G.*, *Ergänzungsband*, XI (1929), pp. 288-303. For further information see Scholz, *Publizistik*, pp. 208-23; E. Müller, *Das Konzil von Vienne* (Münster 1938), pp. 499 ff., 591 ff.; Haller, *Papsttum und Kirchenreform*, VOL. I, pp. 60 ff.

[2] N. Jung, *Alvaro Pelayo* (Paris 1931), pp. 52 ff.

[3] Scholz, *Publizistik*, pp. 32-189. Aegidius Romanus, *De potentia ecclesiastica*, ed. R. Scholz (Weimar 1929). On James of Viterbo's *De regimine christiano*, written in 1302, see D. Gutiérez, *De Jacobi Viterbiensis vita, operibus et doctrina theologica* (Rome 1939), pp. 35 ff.

applying his principle that the Church derives all her authority from the people, he ascribed to General Councils, as representing the body of the faithful, supreme authority in the Church. Authority, that is, to decide questions of faith and to alter such ecclesiastical institutions as rest on the decisions of former Councils. In his opinion, the right of appeal, and generally all coercive authority, rests with the secular power.[1]

Marsiglio did more than loosen a few stones in the structure of the universal papal monarchy—he levelled it to the ground. In its place he set up a vision of a Church deprived of authority, restricted to the purely spiritual sphere, impoverished, democratically governed, and subject to the secular state in her temporal condition and in her possessions. John XXII accordingly condemned, in 1327, this "son of Belial", in the Bull *Licet iuxta doctrinam*, without, however, ascribing any significance to his conciliar theory. For the moment, as a matter of fact, that question lacked actuality. When it did become relevant most of its advocates hesitated to appeal to the condemned work.

Much more effective was Ockham's *Dialogue*, written in 1343. Though the Friar Minor adduced most of Marsiglio's arguments in the form of a scholastic disputation, he was not interfered with by ecclesiastical authority. Ockham did not contest the Pope's right to summon a Council, but he made it a condition that no injury should accrue to the Christian faith.[2]

Sooner than might have been thought, a situation of this kind arose out of the Western Schism. The thought with which the "Venerabilis inceptor" of nominalism had merely toyed—that there might be more than one Pope at one and the same time—became a sorry reality.

It required the pitiful situation created by the Schism to bring about the alliance of conciliar theory with the demand for reform which determined the fate of both at the close of the Middle Ages. The kernel of the conciliar theory, as it has been called (though not quite accurately), may be summed up in the following propositions: Even as only a decision of a General Council is able to remedy the critical

---

[1] The decisive propositions in *Defensor pacis*, VOL. II, 18, 8, and more fully II, 20, 21 (ed. Scholz, Hanover 1933, pp. 382 f., 392-420); also Martin, *Gallicanisme*, VOL II, pp. 32-41; E. F. Jacob, *Essays in the Conciliar Epoch* (Manchester 1943), pp. 85-105. The Bull *Licet* in Raynald, *Annales, a.* 1327, Nos. 27-35.

[2] *Dialogus*, PT i, BK VII, ch. 84; *Monarchia*, VOL. II, p. 603 f.; see Martin, *Gallicanisme*, VOL. II, pp. 41-54. The *Breviloquus de potentia papae* (ed. L. Baudry, Paris 1937) of a later date takes a more positive view of the doctrine of the primacy; cf. R. Scholz, *W. von Ockham als politischer Denker und sein Breviloquium de principatu tyrannico* (Leipzig 1944).

condition of the Church, so the only way to an effective reform is the limitation of papal authority by a General Council. Such a programme implied neither more nor less than the overturning of the Church's monarchical constitution as it had developed in the course of the centuries on the basis of Christ's word.

The first champions of the conciliar theory, the theologians Konrad von Gelnhausen and Heinrich von Langenstein, could not by any means be described as revolutionaries; it would be more correct to describe them as traditionalists.[1] They remembered that at the Councils of the late Middle Ages, such as those of the Lateran, Lyons and Vienne, the whole Church, clergy and laity, had been represented; from this it was only one more step to conceive the General Council as in fact the representative of the universal Church. As theologians they knew that even the Curia had always agreed that there was one case in which the Pope would forfeit his office—namely, if he were to lapse into heresy. In that case a Council would be qualified to pronounce that such a situation was actually in being, even though it would not be entitled to judge him. John of Paris actually drew up several imaginary cases analogous to this extreme one, in which the Pope would be amenable to the judgment of a Council. Lastly, in Gratian's *Decretum* the originators of the conciliar theory thought they had at least a fragmentary relic of the synodal system of the primitive Church. Durandus's demand for a return to the ancient law was based on Gratian's *Decretum*. In his view it was binding even on the Pope. In view of the desperate situation of the Church there was no need of Marsiglio's revolutionary notions for people to hit upon a conciliar solution as a kind of Columbus-and-the-egg expedient, though as soon as they looked round for theological arguments, the speculations of the radical theorists, in particular those of Ockham, offered a welcome support for such a procedure. Above all, the two so-called originators of the conciliar theory share with the Friar Minor the responsibility for introducing the notion of a right arising out of a state of emergency. Nearly every one of the later advocates of the conciliar theory have drawn on the *Dialogue*, the radical Dietrich von Niem no less than the much more conservative Gerson.[2]

[1] This view has been strongly advocated of late by M. Seidlmayer, *Die Anfänge des grossen abendländischen Schismas* (Münster 1940), pp. 174 ff. In so doing Seidlmayer follows in the wake of Bliemetzrieder and Ritter.

[2] H. Heimpel, *Dietrich von Niem* (Münster 1932) p. 125, does not hesitate to say that "die ganze konziliaristische Theorie, und so auch die *modi* (Niem's) lebt von Ockham" (the whole conciliar theory, hence also the *modi*, derives from Ockham).

All the protagonists of the conciliar theory during the period of the Schism unanimously maintain the thesis that the universal Church, viewed by them as a society embracing all Christians, is the ultimate and supreme depositary of ecclesiastical authority, which it exercises, in certain cases, through its representative, a General Council. It matters very little, from the historical point of view, whether authority is regarded as resting with the whole body of the faithful, as Marsiglio thought, or whether it lies with the bishops as the successors of the Apostles. Nor is it decisive whether the bestowal of the primacy by Christ is flatly denied, as it is by Dietrich,[1] or whether it is retained with certain limitations, as by Gerson, who asserts that though Christ conveyed the Power of the Keys to the Apostle Peter and to his successors, that power rests in the last instance with the universal Church—that is, with her representative, the General Council, because the conveyance of authority is linked with its purpose, which is the building-up of the Church.[2] The point is that in the conciliar theory it is not the Pope, but the universal Church, that is invested with final and supreme spiritual authority, which a General Council may use even against the Pope should he be found wanting, even through no fault of his own, or if he were found misusing his pastoral authority. A General Council ranks above the Pope. Its authority is final; it controls and regulates the whole of the Church's life. Hence even the papal administration comes within its purview. Let me repeat it: these views of the Council were born of the straits created by the Schism. There seemed to be no other means to bring about a reunion between two contending Popes, two Colleges of Cardinals, and two obediences. But once the decision was taken to override them, and to fall back upon Church and Council, it was almost inevitable to submit to the same authority the earlier problem—that of the reform of the Church. As a matter of fact, Heinrich von Langenstein in his *Epistola concilii pacis* (1381) had already asserted that the reform of the Church would be one of the tasks of the Council of reunion.[3] It was reserved to the Gallicans to

---

[1] *De modis uniendi*, ch. 5, ed. Heimpel (Leipzig 1933), p. 15; cf. Heimpel, *Dietrich von Niem*, pp. 127 ff.

[2] *De potentia ecclesiastica, cons. X—XII*, in *Opera omnia*, ed. Dupin (Antwerp 1706), VOL. II, pp. 239 ff. A study of Gerson's conception of the Church, on the basis of the material accumulated since Schwab wrote, is still wanting. J. L. Connolly, *J. Gerson, Reformer and Mystic* (Louvain 1928), and W. Dress, *Die Theologie Gersons* (Gütersloh 1931), do not deal with the question. Perhaps A. Combes's studies will produce such a work; see his *Jean de Montreuil et le Chancelier Gerson* (Paris 1942) together with *Six sermons inédits de J. Gerson* (Paris 1946).

[3] Dupin, VOL. II, pp. 835 ff.

mould this idea into the formula which was to become so characteristic of the conciliar theory in its later stages.

At the French national councils of 1398 and 1406 Pierre le Roy, the father of Gallicanism, expounded the following ideas [1]: "The Schism will end when obedience is withheld from the Pope, or at least when the means and the power to win supporters are denied him by rejecting his right of nomination to benefices, and by witholding annates and procurations. Let us revert to the ancient law of the primitive Church and reassert the right of election by the ecclesiastical bodies. This right rests upon the canons of General Councils. Let us restore the rights of the ordinaries, which have been curtailed to the injury of the Church. By revoking these rights the Pope exceeded his powers, which were given him solely for the salvation of souls. He also offended against the canons of the General Councils, by which he is bound and which he cannot repeal. These things were only made possible because for a long time no General Council has been held and because the provincial synods and the general chapters of the Orders have fallen into desuetude."

Thus the aim was the healing of the Schism by means of a *reformatio capitis*, though more exactly by a curtailing of the powers of the papal government and a denial of the pecuniary charges connected with it: this was to be a return to the "ancient law". In this way the Gallicans' programme for union and reform was given its anti-curial twist. No doubt their intention in the first instance was to secure for themselves the same kind of ecclesiastical independence as that which the Church in England had won for herself in the fourteenth century. But they also provided all the malcontents with a catchword which was to be heard from that time onwards until the days of Trent and beyond.

Matthew of Cracow and Dietrich von Niem are justly regarded as the chief spokesmen of this pointedly anti-curial reform-plan. In his book—the mere title of which is a provocation—*Concerning the Filth of the Roman Curia* (1403-04), the former follows the same line of thought as le Roy, and goes even further.[2] Once again we are told that the granting of benefices by the Pope is at variance with the "ancient code"

[1] Bourgeois du Chastenet, *Nouvelle histoire du Concile de Constance* (Paris 1718), Preuves 29-36, 164-76; also Martin, *Gallicanisme*, VOL. I, pp. 280 ff., 315 ff.

[2] Ch. Walch, *Monimenta medii aevi*, VOL. I (Göttingen 1757), pp. 25, 46 ff., 79 f.; Haller, *Papsttum und Kirchenreform*, VOL. I, pp. 483 ff. For an appreciation of the man see G. Ritter, *Die Heidelberger Universität*, VOL. I (Heidelberg 1936), pp. 354 ff.

(*priora jura*). This right should be restored to the ordinaries, and care should be taken to appoint good bishops—all will then come right! The Pope is not the proprietor of the benefices, hence free to dispose of them as he pleases; he is only their steward (*dispensator*). His right of disposal is circumscribed by the canons, but above all by the very purpose of the benefices, which is the edification of the faithful. When he grants them against payment of money, as happens at this time, he incurs the guilt of simony. However subtle, all attempts to defend the existing practice are mere evasions. All those who have anything to do with these practices are simoniacs and are in a state of mortal sin. It is no use pleading that taxes and annates are required to meet the Pope's financial needs. In point of fact, the wretched financial situation of the Apostolic See is the direct result of the neglect of the Councils. If the bishops had been convened betimes, a way out of the difficult situation would have been found. The fact that these practices prove a failure may be a just judgment of God, because the Roman Church was determined to rule without reference to the other Churches.

The man who hurled these terrible accusations against the Curia died unmolested (in 1410 as Bishop of Worms), although he had made no mystery of the fact that he was one of the principal authors of the above-mentioned inflammatory pamphlet. Dietrich von Niem had been an official of the Curia for a number of years and was therefore well acquainted with its habits. His judgment is not any milder than that of Matthew of Cracow. In his great work on union and reform he lays down the axiom that if a Council intends to restore unity and to raise up the Church, it must begin by circumscribing the papal power according to the precedent established by the Fathers. Four years later he heads his *Avisamenta* for the Council of Constance with the thesis: The removal of the Schism will have no useful bearing on the reform of the Church unless it is followed by a careful limitation of the papal ruling power, the misuse of which has inflicted so many wounds on the body of the Church. Otherwise it might happen that if a saint came down from heaven to solicit a bishopric or an abbey he would not get a hearing, unless he produced cash.[1] Dietrich takes it for granted that only by regularly convened Councils could effect be given to his suggestions for a reform, and the evil of simony done away

---

[1] *De modis uniendi*, ch. 10, in Hardt, *Conc. Const.*, VOL. I, v, p. 90. The passages in the *Avisamenta* in *Acta Conc. Const.*, VOL. IV (Münster 1928), pp. 595, 601.

with. The next General Council should be held within five years.

Not all reformers spoke in the same passionate terms as Matthew and Dietrich, who had both been embittered by personal experiences. Others, though more moderate, were at one with them in their concrete demands. Characteristic of their attitude is a tract by an anonymous writer of about the year 1406. This author, a whole century before the humanists had opened out a broader vista on Christian antiquity, was able to take a comprehensive view of the problem of the reform and to see it in what one might call a truly historic perspective.[1] He shares the radicals' conviction that all the evils that have befallen the Church are due to the Curia and to the absolutism of the papal administration. He too demands a return to the "episcopalism", and to the canons, of the primitive Church. On the other hand, his conception of the ancient ecclesiastical constitution is far more accurate than theirs—and he shows acquaintance with the Greek Church. When he suggests that the synodal institutions and the patriarchal constitution of antiquity should be restored, one senses a motive that points far beyond the problems of the moment, namely, a reform that would be a return not only to the "ancient law" previous to the Schism or the decretals, but to an ideal condition which he imagines to have been realised in the primitive Church.

Every advocate of reform in the period of the Schism sounds his own particular note; but, however diverse their voices may be, they blend in one chorus. With one accord they clamour for a great Council that would unite and reform the Church. For them reform spelt Council. The assembly of Pisa convened by the cardinals was not what they wanted,[2] and it produced neither unity nor reform. Only the gathering which, after protracted efforts, at length met at Constance, and which represented the whole of Christendom, seemed destined to resolve the two great problems of the age in the sense of the upholders of the conciliar theory. Results fell short of expectation. Faced with the threat of internal collapse after the flight of John XXIII, who had succeeded the Pope elected at Pisa, the Council, on the proposal of the French Cardinal Fillastre, issued its celebrated decree *Sacrosancta* in

---

[1] R. Scholz, "Eine Geschichte und Kritik der Kirchenverfassung vom Jahre 1406", in *Papsttum und Kaisertum, Festschrift Kehr* (Munich 1926), pp. 595-621.

[2] Conciliarist ideas are found, e.g. in the anonymous memorial of the year 1408, published by J. Vincke, *Schriftstücke zum Pisaner Konzil* (Bonn 1942), pp. 410 ff. On the decree as a simple emergency measure without dogmatic significance see *R.Q.*, XLVI (1938), p. 93.

14

the fifth session, 6 April 1415,[1] to the effect that the General Council,
representing as it did the whole of Christendom, derived its authority
directly from Christ. Hence everyone, the Pope included, was bound
to obey it in all that concerns the faith, unity and general reform.
However, after the Schism had been happily disposed of, at a time when
King Sigismund and the German (and, for a while, the English)
conciliar "nation" also, pressed for a discussion of reform before the
election of a new Pope, they met with opposition both from the Latin
"nations" and from the cardinals, so that all they secured was the
decree *Frequens*, passed in the thirty-ninth session, 9 October 1417, by
which provision was made for the future convocation of General
Councils at regular intervals. The first two were to be held at intervals
of five or, if necessary, seven years, while subsequently there was to be
one every ten years. Precautions were likewise taken against a renewal
of schism. Every newly elected Pope would be obliged to make a
professio fidei by which he bound himself to observe the decisions of
the eight ancient Councils as well as those of the more recent ones,
viz. those of the Lateran, Lyons and Vienne. The fortieth session,
30 October 1417, drew up a scheme for the reform of the Curia
which would be enforced after the election of a Pope.[2]

The two decrees *Sacrosancta* and *Frequens* represented an undoubted
success for the partisans of the conciliar theory, but by no means a
complete victory, much less a final one. Victory was not complete, for
how could a Council which only met periodically assert itself against a
permanent and powerful institution such as the Papacy, firmly grounded
as that institution is in the Church's consciousness of her own nature?
It was not final, for the true conception of the Papacy was not by any

---

[1] *Sacrosancta concilia*, edd. P. Labbé and G. Cossart (Paris 1671-2), VOL. XII,
p. 22; Mansi, VOL. XXVII, p. 590 f. The preliminary proposals in *Acta Conc. Const.*,
VOL. II, pp. 701 ff. J. Hollnsteiner's attempt (*M.Ö.I.G., Ergänzungsband*, XI (1929),
pp. 410 ff.) to explain the decree as a simple emergency measure of no doctrinal import is not convincing. The assertion (p. 417) that in authoritative circles of the
Council no one thought that the supremacy of the assembly could be extended beyond
the election of a Pope is quite wrong. N. Valois's arguments, *Le Pape et le Concile*,
VOL. I (Paris 1909), pp. vii-xxvii, seem to me most to the point.

[2] Labbé-Cossart, *Sacrosancta concilia*, VOL. XII, pp. 238 ff.; Mansi, VOL. XXVII,
pp. 1159 ff.; B. Hübler, *Die Constanzer Reformation und die Konkordate von 1418*
(Leipzig 1867), pp. 118 ff. The so-called *Professio fidei* of Boniface VIII (*Acta
Conc. Const.*, VOL. II, pp. 616 ff.), on which the formula of the oath was based, was
only drawn up in 1407 according to Lulvès in *M.Ö.I.G.*, XXXI (1910), pp. 375-91.
For a comprehensive presentation of the discussions about reform on the basis of
the material available up to the year 1920 see A. Hauck, *Kirchengeschichte Deutschlands* (Leipzig 1920), VOL. II, ii, pp. 1020-49, and *Acta Conc. Const.*, VOL. II, pp. 547
ff.; VOL. IV, pp. 539 ff.

15

means disposed of. When, in the fourth session, Cardinal Zabarella, the great Paduan jurist, was called upon to read the decree of the Council's superiority over the Pope, he refused to do so, for though he favoured the notion he was nevertheless unwilling to admit the Pope's subjection to the Council in matters connected with reform, on the ground that this would be equivalent to a general subordination. In the fifth session, the bishop-elect of Posen had to deputise for Zabarella.[1] Even at Constance the papal conception never lacked champions.[2] Martin V, the Pope of unity, who was elected on 11 November 1417, refrained from a general confirmation of the decrees of the Council,[3] and on 10 May 1418 he prohibited every kind of appeal from the Pope to another tribunal in matters concerning the faith.[4] Gerson was right when he interpreted this prohibition as a rejection of the superiority of the Council. The attempts to alter the constitution of the Church proved unsatisfactory, as did the reforms of Church administration, of the clergy, and of the pastoral ministry. Events justified King Sigismund's previsions: the divergent proposals for a reform by the various "nations" gave the Pope the desired opportunity for embodying the bulk of the reform of the Curia in the concordats with the conciliar "nations", thus robbing them of their sting.

The seven decrees of the forty-third session only partially met the real demands of the convinced protagonists of the conciliar theory, while the Pope's declaration, that they had adequately discharged the obligation to initiate a reform to which he had agreed before his election, provided him with a formal means of avoiding a duty.[5] The Curia's management of provisions and taxes was brought under a measure of control, but no attempt was made to breathe a new spirit into the

---

[1] Thus John of Palomar, Döllinger, *Beiträge*, VOL. II, p. 416, confirmed by Fillastre, *Acta Conc. Const.*, VOL. II, p. 27. Cerretanus (*ibid.*, p. 299) does not mention this particularity.

[2] Among the defenders of the primacy mention must be made of Leonardus Statius, the general of the Dominicans, *Acta Conc. Const.*, VOL. II, pp. 705 ff. Others are discussed by P. Arendt, *Die Predigten des Konstanzer Konzils* (Freiburg 1933), pp. 127 ff. The majority of the preachers, especially those of the first period, upheld the conciliar theory, *ibid.*, pp. 119 ff., 238 ff.

[3] F. X. Funk, *Martin V und das Konzil von Konstanz: Kirchengeschichtliche Abhandlungen und Untersuchungen*, VOL. I (Paderborn 1897), pp. 489-98; Valois, *Le Pape*, VOL. I, p. xx f. This view coincides with the conciliar theory according to which the decisions of a Council do not require papal confirmation.

[4] Valois, *Le Pape t le Concile*, VOL. I, pp. xxii ff.

[5] The reform dec ees of the forty-third session in Mansi, VOL. XXVII, pp. 1174-94. Hübler, *Constanzer Reformation*, pp. 158 ff.; text of the concordats also in Mercati, *Raccolta*, pp. 144-68.

pastoral ministry. Everybody was tired of the protracted discussions and disputes and wanted to go home.

However, it would not be true to say that everything went on as before, as was feared by the University of Vienna's delegate to the Council, Peter von Pulka.[1] Martin V stood formally upon the decisions of Constance; in fact the validity of his election was dependent on their binding force. The Antipope Benedict XIII obstinately maintained his pretensions at Peñiscola. In spite of grave misgivings about its conciliar tendencies, Martin V sent legates to the General Council convened at Pavia in 1423 but soon transferred to Siena. When the Fathers of that feebly-attended assembly began to squabble over the question of authority and reform, he dissolved it, on 7 March 1424.[2] At the same time he sought to pacify the reformers by initiating a reform of the papal Curia. In this he was unsuccessful. By the time the Council summoned to meet at Basle in 1431 actually opened, and, after some delay, had been given a papal legate in the person of Cardinal Cesarini, the radicalism of the adherents of the conciliar theory was greatly increased and the call for reform became louder than ever.[3] It was at Basle that the decisive battle between the Papacy and the conciliar theory was fought out.[4]

After a hard and protracted struggle, during which the Church, for the last time, was rent by schism, the Papacy proved victorious. The victory was less a personal achievement of Eugenius IV than the consequence of a stronger grasp of the notion of the primacy and, we may

[1] "Pro nunc, ut timeo, non erit notabilis reformatio quantum per homines stabit", report of 10 February 1418, in *Archiv für Kunde österreichischer Geschichtsquellen*, xv (1856), p. 66.

[2] On these tensions, see John of Ragusa, *Mon. Conc. gen.*, VOL. I (Vienna 1857), pp. 20, 35 ff.; Valois, *Le Pape et le Concile*, VOL. I, pp. 1-39; Mengozzi, "Papa Martino V e il concilio ecumenico di Siena", in *Bolletino Senese*, xxv (1918), pp. 247-314; also separate print (Siena 1918).

[3] Preoccupation with the Pope's compliance with the decrees of Constance is a characteristic feature of the whole of the reform literature, cf. *Mon. conc. gen.*, VOL. I, pp. 32, 35; *Conc. Bas.*, VOL. VIII, p. 34; VOL. I, p. 215. On the German National Council planned in 1413, to be preceded by provincial synods, see *R.T.A.*, VOL. X, p. 517; K. Beer in *M.Ö.I.G.*, *Ergänzungsband*, XI (1929), pp. 432-42.

[4] For the Councils of Basle and Constance a full presentation of the material accumulated in *Conc. Bas.*, VOLS. I-VIII (Basle 1896-1939), is not yet available. Useful for our purpose are, besides Valois, the studies of P. Lazarus, *Das Basler Konzil* (Berlin 1912), and R. Zwölfer, "Die Reform der Kirchenverfassung auf dem Konzil von Basel", in *Basler Zeitschrift*, xxviii (1929), pp. 141-247; xxix (1930), pp. 1-58. On Cesarini's reform material see Dannenbauer, *Conc. Bas.*, VOL. VIII, pp. 4 ff. Wackernagel, *Geschichte der Stadt Basel*, VOL. I (Basle 1907), pp. 476-538, has a masterly description of the scene.

add, the result of the heavy blunders of the assembly of Basle. Its first conflict with the Pope, in which it was victorious, was provoked by the Bull of Dissolution dated 12 November 1431. During this contest the assembly republished, in the second session (15 February 1432) the decree of Constance on the superiority of the Council. In the eighteenth session [1] (26 June 1434), when Eugenius IV had yielded and declared it to be a legitimate Council, the assembly proclaimed once more what it regarded as a fundamental principle. Three years later, after it had finally broken with the Pope over the question of re-union with the Greeks, it went so far as to declare, in the thirty-third session (16 May 1439), that the proposition "The General Council is above the Pope" was a dogma of the Catholic faith.[2] The deposition of Eugenius IV and the election of Felix V were only the ultimate consequences of the new "dogma".

Even before this step the Council had begun to exploit in good earnest yet another axiom of conciliar theory, namely that the reform of the Church must be brought about by curtailing papal administrative powers. The abrogation (in the twenty-first session) of annates and the curial taxes deprived the Pope of one of his main sources of income while leaving him no compensation. In the twenty-third session the Council abrogated reservations and decreed a reform of the College of Cardinals. At a later date the Council of Trent reverted to the stipulations of this decree with regard to the number, composition and filling-up of the College in nearly every one of its own proposals for a reform. Preoccupation with the *reformatio capitis* did not lead to a complete overlooking of the *reformatio membrorum*. The decrees of the fifteenth session on the celebration of provincial and diocesan synods, and those of the twentieth against clerical concubinage were a first step to meet the no less pressing need of a reform of the members—and it was no more than a first step. More plainly than formal decrees, the tracts and proposals concerning reform of which parts have been preserved in Cesarini's manuscript memoranda, convey the impression that the Council was well aware of the grave injury done to ecclesiastical life everywhere, in episcopal curias, in chapters, in religious orders and in the pastoral ministry, and that it was prepared to apply a remedy to so many abuses. But the longer these measures were delayed, the more

---

[1] Labbé-Cossart, *Sacrosancta concilia*, VOL. XII, pp. 477, 540 ff.; Mansi, VOL. XXIX, pp. 21, 91.

[2] Labbé-Cossart, *Sacrosancta concilia*, VOL. XII, p. 619; Mansi, VOL. XXIX, p. 178 f.

the assembly allowed itself to be influenced by the one-sided Gallican principle for which the parliamentary councillor Gée coined the axiomatic formula: "Let but the head be reformed, the reform of the members will follow easily." [1] The representatives of the lower clergy, the chapters and the universities, and the horde of doctors, had long ago gained an overwhelming ascendancy at Basle, while the bishops were withdrawing from a Council which, after creating a curia of its own, was deeply engaged in the business of allocating prebends. Not a few of the best members of the Council went over to Eugenius IV, including Cesarini, its one-time president, Cardinal Capranica, Andrew of Escobar, and Nicholas of Cusa. In the end the assembly's energy spent itself almost exclusively in a struggle for self-preservation and for the upholding of the conciliar theory, with which it stood or fell. Furthermore, there was a suspicion that the French, who numerically were strongly represented, and who in the person of Louis d'Aleman had provided the president, were determined to recover the ascendency over the Church which they had exercised during the Avignon period. This proved prejudicial to the Council. As a matter of fact, in the very first days of the assembly the Archbishop of Tours had remarked to Aeneas Silvius Piccolomini that this time they would wrest the Papacy from the hands of the Italians or "pluck" it to such an extent that it would no longer matter where it was. [2]

While the men of Basle were engaged in a desperate struggle for their principle under the leadership of Aleman and Segovia, Eugenius IV brought to a successful issue the great task of leading back into the unity of the Church the Greeks, the Armenians and the lesser oriental Churches. In the Bull of Unity, *Laetentur coeli* (6 July 1439), the Council of Florence defined that the Pope is the successor of St Peter and the Vicar of Christ, head of the universal Church and father and teacher of all Christians and that in the person of Peter full power was conferred on him by Christ to guide and rule the whole Church. [3] This

[1] *Conc. Bas.*, VOL. VIII, p. 171. Copious material on the "reformatio membrorum" is provided by two anonymous Italians, *Conc. Bas.*, VOL. I, pp. 210 ff., and VOL. VIII, pp. 37, 143; Andrew of Escobar, VOL. I, p. 219, and the Spanish proposal, VOL. VIII, pp. 49 ff.; the Frenchmen Meynage and Maurel, VOL. VIII, pp. 61 ff., 165 ff.; an anonymous German, and Bishop Schele of Lübeck, VOL. VIII, pp. 100 ff., 119 ff. But the fact remains that as Beckmann observes, *Conc. Bas.*, VOL. VI, p. lxiv, very little was achieved after the outbreak of the second conflict.

[2] "Commentarius de rebus Basileae gestis", in Aeneas Silvius Piccolomini's correspondence, ed. Wolkan, VOL. II, p. 188.

[3] Mansi, VOL. XXXI, pp. 1030 ff. On the two versions of the text, see G. Hofmann, *Papato, conciliarismo, patriarcato* (Rome 1940), pp. 59 ff.

definition was the answer to Basle's attempt to erect the conciliar theory into a dogma. It became the *Magna Carta* of the papal restoration.

It took some time before the scales came definitely down against Basle. Powerful forces confronted each other—on the one hand the Church's consciousness of her unity which was deeply injured by the new schism, as well as the various nations' strong attachment to the successor of St Peter, and, on the other, the idea of the Council thanks to which Constance effected the removal of the schism, and the longing for a reform which it was generally thought a Council alone would carry through. But by the side of these forces, which were essentially religious, with their roots in the early Middle Ages, other forces of more recent origin also asserted themselves.

In the Pragmatic Sanction of Bourges France arbitrarily invested twenty-four decrees of the Council of Basle with the authority of a law of the State, while the German Electors took a similar decision in the *Acceptatio* of Mainz. Both measures were inspired by a determination to take the reform of the Church into their own hands. Both documents insist on a periodic holding of a General Council, the restoration to chapters and monasteries of the right of election, and a curtailing of the papal right of nomination which was at variance with these claims. Both documents are dictated by distrust of Rome. Over the question of superiority the French side with Basle while Mainz observes a cautious reserve in consequence of the Elector's policy of neutrality. Far more serious than any particular act was the principle on which both measures were based. The fact was that the two most important nations of Christendom were prepared to regulate ecclesiastical affairs in their respective territories with complete independence and without reference to either Pope or Council.[1]

In the end the defeat of the men of Basle was decided by the action of the princes. The assembly of Basle was a crowded one, one that did not shrink from the revolutionary step of deposing a legitimate Pope. But what political advantages had it to offer? For their part, the princes demanded and obtained the most far-reaching privileges in return for a declaration of obedience to Eugenius IV, viz. for Alfonso V

---

[1] The two documents collated in A. Werminghoff, *Nationalkirchliche Bestrebungen im deutschen Mittelalter* (Stuttgart 1910), pp. 33-85. On the drafting and execution of the Pragmatic Sanction see N. Valois, *Histoire de la Sanction Pragmatique de Bourges sous Charles VII* (Paris 1906), and Haller, in *H.Z.*, CIII (1909), pp. 1-51; Martin, *Gallicanisme*, VOL. II, pp. 293 ff.

of Aragon the investiture of Naples,[1] and for the Emperor Frederick III
the disposal of a large portion of the benefices of his hereditary lands.
As for the German territorial princes, they abandoned their neutrality
for a promise of a new Council and recognition of its authority, together
with certain financial concessions. The concordat with Eugenius IV's
successor, Nicholas V, concluded with Vienna, upheld precisely the
Curia's chief claims, namely the principle of reservations and the
annates.[2] France announced its willingness to put an end to the Schism,
though without renouncing the Pragmatic Sanction [3] while in return
for the abdication of Felix V Savoy was granted an extremely favourable
indult. England and Burgundy had always remained faithful to the
Pope, were it for no other motive than that of countering French
influence at Basle.[4]

Thus the Papacy had triumphed over the conciliar movement—but
at a heavy price. The chief beneficiary was the modern state which
during the period of conflict had got into the habit of independent
action in purely ecclesiastical questions. It had widened its authority
over the Church, its offices and its property within its boundaries, and
through the concordats its relations with the Papacy were based on the
law of nations.[5] In the ecclesiastical conflict between Pope and Council
both the national states of the West and the territories of the Empire
had adopted an attitude for the most part inspired by political considerations. In the sequel also they seized upon the longing for a Council in
order to render the Pope amenable to their political demands. But
when the break-up of Christian unity necessitated a new Council,
France's opposition was once more inspired by purely political
motives.

The conciliar theory had been defeated by the Papacy's skilful
policy; that institution even issued from the struggle with Basle with

---

[1] Pastor, VOL. I, p. 393 (Eng. edn., VOL. I, p. 331).

[2] The so-called princes' concordat of 5 February 1447, and the Vienna concordats
of 17 February and 19 March 1448 respectively, Mercati, *Raccolta*, pp. 168-85; *ibid.*,
the indult for Saxony dated 10 March 1452 mentioned below; cf. W. Michel, *Das
Wiener Konkordat vom Jahre 1448 und die nachfolgenden* gravamina *des Primarklerus
der Mainzer Kirchenprovinz* (Dissertation, Heidelberg 1929).

[3] Valois, *Le Pape*, VOL. II, pp. 327 ff.

[4] Haller, *Piero da Monte*, pp. 42* ff.; J. Toussaint, *Les Relations diplomatiques de
Philippe le Bon avec le Concile de Bâle* (Louvain 1942), pp. 265-81—text of the discourse
pronounced at Nuremberg in 1444 by the Bishop of Verdun in defence of Philip's
loyalty to the Roman See.

[5] W. Bertram, *Der neuzeitliche Staatsgedanke und die Konkordate des ausgehenden
Mittelalters* (Rome 1942), pp. 159 ff.

renewed internal strength, a result due in no small measure to the writings of its theologians. Although the controversial writings of both parties exist for the most part only in manuscript, so that they have not been by any means adequately studied, even so it may be said that the monarchical conception of the Papacy experienced a notable strengthening within the Church. This revulsion of feeling may be observed even in the greatest thinker of the time, Nicholas of Cusa.

Nicholas's *Concordantia catholica*, completed in 1433, is the most original product of the conciliar theory in the period that concerns us.[1] Two basic principles, and, we may add, two standpoints confront each other in this work. With pseudo-Dionysius, Nicholas views the Church as a divine cosmos from the head of which, that is, Christ, grace flows into humanity through the channel of the hierarchy. The hierarchy is the depositary of the priesthood in which the Pope, the bishops and even simple priests participate. On the other hand men are by nature free, hence it is only with their consent that ecclesiastical superiors and ecclesiastical laws may demand their obedience. It is in virtue of this consent of the subordinates that the bishop represents his diocese and the Council the whole Church.

The main lines of the Church's constitution start from these two principles: the Pope and the bishops are equally the successors of Peter and are invested, by right divine, with essentially the same authority. The gradation of powers in the Church refers only to their use, that is, their execution. This gradation exists in virtue of an enactment of the positive law, though not without divine concurrence. The Pope's authority, in particular, rests not only upon Christ's institution, when He constituted Peter the principle of unity, but likewise on a transmission by the Church embodied in the cardinals who elect the pontiff. However, the primacy of the Bishop of Rome is not a primacy of jurisdiction. The Pope is not *episcopus universalis*, he is only *super alios primus*. Like Peter he takes precedence over all the others though only as an administrator, for the good of the whole body. The doctrine of the Pope's plenitude of power over the whole Church is no more than

---

[1] It is impossible within so small a compass to develop Cusa's conception of the Church which won for him the title of "Cyprianus redivivus" (Heiler, *Altkirchliche Autonomie*, p. 299). The basic notions of Council and reform expounded in the text are to be found in *Concilia catholica*, VOL. II, pp. 13-17 and, more summarily, p. 34, *Opera* (Basle 1565), pp. 722 ff., 734 ff., 774; cf. Posch, *Concordantia catholica*, pp. 78-126. E. Bohnenstädt's *Kirche und Reich im Schrifttum des Nicolaus von Cues* (Heidelberg 1939) is little more than a mosaic of quotations in my opinion.

a discovery of base adulators. Supreme power, as well as infallibility, belong to the General Council, which derives its authority directly from Christ, while it represents at the same time the unanimous agreement of all Christians. The Council is above the Pope and may depose him, or reform him, as the case may be, not only if he falls into heresy but for any other misdemeanour. The Council is convened by the Pope but does not depend on him; its decisions do not need papal confirmation; on the contrary, they are binding on him, so that he can only dispense from them in particular cases. As a matter of fact, the difference between conciliar canons and papal decrees consists precisely in that the former have already secured the assent of the universal Church whereas the latter still require it. The canons, therefore, constitute an insuperable barrier to papal legislation. However, in order to render the misuse of papal authority impossible in time to come it is necessary to create constitutional securities, chiefly by the concession of wider powers to the College of Cardinals. The cardinals should be chosen with the consent of the bishops from all the various nations. Both the rights of metropolitans and those of patriarchal Councils should be restored.

The *Concordantia* embodies all the principles of the conciliar theory and all the demands of its adherents, such as the Council's superiority over the Pope, its right to correct him, the subjection of papal legislation and administration to the canons, the need of guarantees against misuse of the primacy and a return to the "ancient laws". These ideas are all cast into a speculative mould from which there issues a conception of the Church as a divine cosmos in which God's will and man's freedom are interlocked. The practical application of this speculative notion makes it difficult either to interpret the *Concordantia* or to account for Cusa's subsequent evolution, for when he turned his back on Basle he also changed his attitude to the question of authority. In his propositions and discourses at Mainz [1] he unequivocally traces the authority of the Council back to the Pope and attributes to him the right to dispose of all benefices. In his letter to Sánchez de Arevalo, 20 May 1442,[2] he endeavours to harmonise his new opinion with his earlier teaching by

---

[1] *R.T.A.*, VOL. XV, pp. 643 ff., 761 ff.

[2] *Opera*, pp. 825-9. G. Kallen, *Cusanustexte*, VOL. II (Heidelberg 1935), pp. 1064 ff. A definitive evaluation of Cusa's teaching on the Church will only be possible when the Heidelberg edition of his works is completed. The earlier studies by M. Birk, in *T.Q.*, LXXIV (1892), pp. 617-42, and *H.J.*, XIII (1892), pp. 770 ff., and that of P. P. Albert, *Festgabe Grauert* (Freiburg 1910), pp. 116-31, are both one-sided and antiquated. Posch, *Concordantia catholica*, pp. 163 ff., and Heiler, *Altkirchliche Autonomie*, pp. 313 ff., are too summary.

recourse to the principle of divided authority. A papalist in the customary sense of the word he never became. Thus he continued to regard as fundamental the notion that the Pope exists for the building up of the Church—*aedificatio ecclesiae*—and he would not forgo guarantees against a possible misuse of the primacy. Pius II himself has left us a description of the dramatic scene when Nicholas championed with the utmost conviction the pretensions of the College of Cardinals.[1] On the other hand his great journey through Germany as papal legate shows how seriously he took the work of reform to which the Pope was committed.

Like Nicholas of Cusa, the Portuguese Andrew of Escobar, in his work *Gubernatio conciliorum* published between 1430 and 1435, had begun as a strong advocate of the supremacy of a General Council over the Pope in all that concerns the faith and the general state of the Church, hence also general reform. However, he too ended by abandoning his opinion on the nature of the Council and his name appears among the signatories of the Florentine Bull of Unity.[2] Cesarini's former collaborator, John of Palomar, defended the attitude of the Council during the first conflict with the Pope and regarded the decree *Sacrosancta* of Constance as binding; however, after the schismatical election, when the question who should be obeyed had to be decided, he unhesitatingly pronounced in favour of Eugenius IV.[3] Aeneas Silvius Piccolomini, who had long defended the standpoint of Basle in his writings and had even acted as secretary to the curia set up by that Council, adopted at first a neutral attitude, but in the end he too went over to the party which was about to triumph. As secretary to Frederick III he worked for that Emperor's adhesion to Eugenius IV.[4]

The conciliar theory continued to find learned and convinced advocates who, unlike the author of a self-styled *Confutatio primatus*

---

[1] J. Cugnoni, *Aeneae Silvii Piccolomini Sen. opera inedita* (Rome 1883), p. 216 f.

[2] *Gubernatio conciliorum*, written in 1434, and dedicated to Cesarini, in Hardt, *Conc. Const.*, VOL. VI, ch. 4, pp. 139-334. On the question of authority and reform see Parts i-iii. For Aeneas's activities at Basle, see *Conc. Bas.*, VOL. I, p. 114. I have not been able to consult L. Walter, *Andreas von Escobar, ein Vertreter der konziliaren Theorie am Anfang des 15. Jahrhunderts* (Münster 1921). For Aeneas's role at the Council of Florence see Hofmann, *Papato, conciliarismo, patriarcato*, pp. 31 ff.

[3] Döllinger, *Beiträge*, VOL. II, pp. 414-41. With regard to the decree *Sacrosancta* he makes a reservation to the effect that the Pope was only subject to the Council in respect of reforms affecting the whole Church (p. 419).

[4] G. Voigt, *Enea Silvio Piccolomini*, VOL. I (Berlin 1856), pp. 295 ff., 340 ff. For a verdict on the *Commentarius de rebus Basileae gestis*, written in 1447, and after he had changed sides, see *Conc. Bas.*, VOL. I, pp. 15 ff.

papae, declined the cover of anonymity. The greatest canonist of the period, Niccolò Tudeschi, made a bold stand for the Council in his apologia directed against Cardinal Cesarini. To his authority it was largely due that the conciliar theory found supporters as late as the following century.[1] Notwithstanding the fact that he was a Roman and a lawyer of the Curia, Ludovico Pontano remained a supporter of the Council until the plague carried him off in the summer of 1439.[2] Even more resolutely than any of the above-named, Juan of Segovia, a theologian of Salamanca and celebrated even at this day as a historian of the Council, criticised Eugenius IV and the neutrality of the German Electors in a book on the authority of the Church, as well as in several smaller publications.[3] However, when we examine the survey of the bibliography, incomplete though it is, with which the studious Lorenzo of Arezzo prefaces his great compilation of 1440,[4] with a view to ascertaining the attitude of particular writers to the question of authority, we find that the number of the defenders of papal primacy

---

[1] Of the utmost importance is the answer to Cesarini's declaration beginning with the words "Maximum onus", written early in 1438, Mansi, VOL. XXX, pp. 1123-84; *Mon. conc. gen.*, VOL. II, pp. 1144-93. In Chapter V we shall revert to "Quaestio Episcopus et quidam rector" (*Consilia*, Venice 1578, fols. 183^r-190^v). Tudeschi's contribution to the survival of conciliarist ideas in the latter part of the fifteenth century is mainly due to his frequently reprinted commentary on the decretals (Hain, Nos. 12308-24). I have not been able to consult J. Schweitzer, *Nikolaus de Tudeschi* (Strasbourg 1927).

[2] Pontano's *Consilia* have been reprinted more than once (Hain, Nos. 13274-8). For his conciliarist opinions *Cons.* 521-3 are the most important. The *Tractatus super potestate universalis ecclesiae et generalium conciliorum* I only saw in manuscript, Vat. lat. 4118, fols. 1^r-15^r; Vat. lat. 4905, fols. 1^r-16^v, each followed by the "Sermo" mentioned in *R.T.A.*, VOL. XIII, p. 568 *n.*

[3] The long series of Segovia's writings on the Council opens with a memorial dated 1434, on the admission of papal legates. Most important is *De auctoritate ecclesiae seu de insuperabili sanctitate et summa auctoritate generalium conciliorum*, and the *Tractatus X avisamentorum*, written at the very latest in the spring of 1439. These were followed by *De tribus veritatibus fidei*, a treatise against the neutrality of the Electors, and *Justificatio sententiae contra Gabrielem*, all of them in manuscript. For their content and historical value see *Conc. Bas.*, VOL. I, pp. 20-53. For the reputation of holiness in which he died, as did Allemand and Felix V, cf. Valois, *Le Pape*, VOL. II, pp. 356 ff.

[4] Printed by Eckermann, *Studien zur Geschichte des monarchischen Gedankens im 15. Jahrhundert* (Berlin-Grünewald 1933), pp. 161-8; Grabmann, "Studien über den Einfluss der Aristotelischen Philosophie auf die mittelalterlichen Theorien über das Verhältniss von Kirche und Staat", in *Sonderband der bayrischen Akademie, philosophisch-historische Abteilung*, II, 1934 (Munich 1934), pp. 134-44, though neither is quite satisfying. There is no up-to-date survey of the controversial literature; Voigt, *Enea Silvio Piccolomini*, VOL. I, pp. 189 ff., is obsolete; B. Ziliotto has published the *Dialogus de papali potestate* by the Minorite Lodovico da Cividale, in *Memorie storiche forogiuliese*, XXXIII (1938), pp. 151-91.

already counterbalances that of its opponents. Most of the former belong to the Dominican Order.[1]

Here also voices must be weighed, not merely counted. Abandonment of the conciliar theory was indeed fostered by the flow of benefices that could be expected from Eugenius IV; but it must be admitted that the opinions of not a few divines who wrote in support of the papal primacy lacked firmness, and many continued to make far-reaching concessions to the conciliar theory. Thus the jurist Piero da Monte in his *Monarchia*, which became celebrated at a later date, borrowed from Zabarella, while in another of his works directed against Tudeschi, he drew upon a treatise by the Dominican Raphael de Pornaxio.[2] Yet the same man, whom the next generation was to regard as a pillar of the Papacy, still grants in the first of these two works that the Power of the Keys has been conferred on the Church, while in the second he only speaks of Peter. Even in the *Repertorium juris* drawn up long after the Council, the reader is startled by the statement that the Pope may render himself guilty of simony. Antonio Roselli, nick-named *Monarcha Juris*, who in 1443 in his capacity of a consistorial advocate had composed the fighting Bull *Deus novit* directed against Basle, upheld in his *Monarchia* the unlimited monarchical authority of the Pope over the bishops and the whole Church. Yet the same man endeavoured to preserve the decree of Constance on the Council's supremacy as an emergency measure. At the same time, true to the Ghibelline tradition of his native city, Arezzo, he defended Dante's notion of the Emperor's universal dominion, with the result that he, an officer of the Curia, shared the poet's fate of getting his name into the index of forbidden books.[3]

These examples show that opinion was still fluid, and that a number

[1] The Dominicans are: Cardinal Giovanni Casanova; Giuliano Tagliada, Bishop of Bosa in Sardinia; Giovanni di Montenero, provincial of Lombardy (on him, see G. Meerseman, *Giovanni di Montenero, difensore dei Mendicanti* (Rome 1938), and Hofmann, *Papato, conciliarismo, patriarcato*, pp. 38-54); and Juan de Torquemada. To the last-named, who is mentioned by Lorenzo of Arezzo, must be added Giovanni Leone de Urbe. He is the author of a treatise *De synodis et ecclesiastica potestate*, cf. G. Meerseman, in *A.F.P.*, IX (1939), pp. 76-85. On the subject as a whole see G. Meerseman, "Les Dominicains présents au concile de Ferrare-Florence jusqu'au décret d'union pour les Grecs", *ibid.*, IX (1939), pp. 62-75.

[2] Haller, *Piero da Monte*, pp. 25* ff., 61* ff., but in the light of R. Creytens's researches in *A.F.P.*, XIII (1943), pp. 108-37, the author of the treatise *De potentia papae et concilii generalis* is not Torquemada, under whose name it was indeed published at a later date, but Raphael de Pornaxio; see also Eckermann, *Studien*, pp. 128, 150 and *passim*.

[3] Eckermann, *Studien*, pp. 111 ff., 134 ff. As Haller has pointed out, Eckermann has failed to collate the two editions of the *Monarchia* (*Piero da Monte*, p. 31).

26

of problems had not been adequately worked out. For all that, the tendency to revert to the monarchical conception of the Church's constitution is unmistakable. However, a large-scale justification of it, one that would impose itself by the force of its logic, appeared only after the schism of Basle had been got out of the way. The Dominican Juan de Torquemada, a theologian of Salamanca like his opponent Juan of Segovia, and rewarded by Eugenius IV with a cardinal's hat in 1439, worked the basic ideas of the speeches and treatises on the Pope's authority, which he had composed during the conflict, into a *Summa de ecclesia* which from the time of its appearance—some time before 1453— became the arsenal of the defenders of papal primacy right up to the Council of Trent.[1] In four books Torquemada expounds the doctrine of the Church—papal primacy, the Councils, schism and heresy. Neither the Church, nor the Council as the advocates of the conciliar theory would have it, but the Pope as Peter's successor is the sole depositary of ecclesiastical authority. It is he who imparts authority both to the bishops and to the Council by the act of convocation, in appointing the president, and by confirming its decrees. The Council is not a representation of all the faithful or of all the various degrees of the hierarchy; it is essentially a gathering of the bishops under the authority of the Pope (III. 5). Hence the Council has no power to judge him unless he were to lapse into heresy. An appeal from the Pope to the Council is inadmissible (III. 47-9).

The well-known decrees of Constance and Basle cannot be alleged against this teaching. The decree *Sacrosancta* was not meant to be a definition of a truth universally binding for all time. Its sole purpose was to remedy an existing crisis when there was no unquestionably legitimate Pope. In point of fact that decree issued from the party of John XXIII and did not receive confirmation from the newly elected pontiff Martin V. In the Bull of Revocation, *Dudum sacrum*, which was extorted from Eugenius IV, as Torquemada learnt from the Pope's own lips, the pontiff sanctioned the continuation of the Council of Basle, but not the renewal of the decree concerning the superiority of the Council, which accordingly was no longer binding (II. 99-100).

[1] In the incunabulum (Hain, No. 15730) which I have used the title is: *Summa contra impugnatores potestatis summi pontificis ac Petri Apostolorum principis*. The folios are not numbered and I quote according to book and chapter. S. Lederer, *Der Spanische Kardinal Johann von Torquemada* (Freiburg 1879), is no longer adequate. A good preliminary study for an understanding of the MS is supplied by J. M. Garrastachú, "Los manoscritos del Card. Torquemada en la Biblioteca Vaticana", in *Ciencia Tomista*, XXII (1930), pp. 188-217, 291-322. For Torquemada's explanations at Nuremberg and Mainz see Hofmann, *Papato, conciliarismo, patriarcato*, pp. 9-30.

In this way Torquemada brushes aside the entire ecclesiastical theory of the Schism and the reform Councils. He unreservedly rejects the teaching of the new masters—*magistri novelli*—from Ockham to Gerson. Since he had taken part in both reform Councils, he was keenly aware of the dangers of ecclesiastical democracy: "God preserve the Church", he exclaims, "from mob domination or indirect domination by the secular princes, as a result of the extension to the lower orders of the hierarchy of the right to vote in Council. . . . With sorrow in my heart I have been an eye-witness of the shameful doings at the Council of Basle: there could be no greater danger for the faith and for peace and unity in the Church" (III. 14).

The Council a danger to the peace and unity of the Church! Such was the watchword Torquemada coined for use by the Popes of the period of the restoration, who were quite prepared to adopt his view that the decrees of Constance were no longer binding. Their theological advisers and defenders, such as Sánchez de Arevalo, Domenico de' Domenichi and Henricus Institoris, were to darken still further the shadow that fell from Torquemada's verdict not only upon the conciliar theory but upon the very idea of a Council. Although the *Summa* was not widely disseminated outside Italy, it was nevertheless the source from which the arguments of almost all those writers who, in the course of the following century, defended the Papacy against the supporters of the conciliar theory and against Gallicanism were drawn.[1] At the approach of the last period of the Council of Trent the work was re-printed, obviously for the purpose of the Council.[2]

However, it would be a mistake to see in Torquemada a blind absolutist and an opponent of the Council as such: for one thing he was too near to the agitated period of the Schism. He continues to

---

[1] Torquemada's influence on the writers of the period of the papal restoration could only be adequately assessed by writing their history. A few observations must suffice. It was natural that Dominicans like Prierias (*Summa summarii*, VOL. I, p. 7; VOL. II, p. 4) and Cajetan, *De comparatione papae et concilii*, chapters 8, 9, 12 and *passim*, would appeal to him, but even canonists of repute, e.g. Sangiorgio (*Lectura super 101 distinctionibus* (Rome 1493), distinctio xv, Nos. 12, 14) and Jacobazzi rely on him and quote him as "Cardinalis", a title by which Zabarella is usually designated. At the time of the Pisan attempt Pietro Quirini based on him the whole of his *Tractatus super concilium generale* (published by Mittarelli-Costadoni in *Annales Camald*, VOL. IX, Venice 1773, pp. 599-611) as did Bartolomeo Guidiccioni in 1535 in his treatise *De concilio* for Paul III; cf. my observations in *Rivista di storia della Chiesa in Italia*, II (1948), pp. 39 ff.

[2] In the preface addressed to Pius IV, Cardinal Vitellozzo writes: "Liber ipse multis abhinc annis semel impressus, aut nusquam aut raro invenitur." He was evidently not acquainted with Hain Nos. 15731 ff.

regard the Council as "the Church's last refuge in all her great needs", as the ultimate authority to which it belongs to issue decisions in disputed questions of faith, to reform the pastoral ministry, and to check the arbitrariness of certain Popes.[1] True, the decree *Frequens* did not bind the successors of Martin V. Even in the early centuries General Councils were of rare occurrence. On the other hand it was possible to escape the reproach that the fate of the Church was at the mercy of the arbitrary power of one man by convening papal Councils to which the bishops of several provinces, or even of only one, would be called (III. 16-18). Moreover the College of Cardinals, which in Torquemada's opinion is the successor of the Apostolic College and is by him traced back to Christ's own ordinance (I. 80-4), in its capacity of supreme senate of the Church, and as part, so to speak, of the Pope's very body—*pars corporis Papae*—has a share in the exercise of the supreme authority. Though the Pope is not bound by the decrees of the Councils, and may dispense with them, or even abolish them, honour—*honestas*—binds him to their observance (III. 51-7). Torquemada was evidently familiar with all the problems of supremacy.

There is one important gap in the *Summa de Ecclesia*: the question of reform is passed over in almost complete silence. The adherents of the conciliar theory had had for their object Church unity and Church reform by means of the Council. The former purpose had been attained, but not the latter. The decrees *Sacrosancta* and *Frequens*, which were meant to initiate and to ensure a reform of the Curia, remained a dead letter: the Popes reverted to the strict monarchical principle. By so doing they likewise assumed the task of reforming the Church. Was it not the duty, therefore, of the most distinguished exponent of the doctrine of papal authority to point out to those invested with it the heavy responsibility that was theirs?

There is no question at this day but that for his own person Torquemada exerted himself to the utmost, within his own circle, on behalf of reform.[2] For all that, one might have expected that like his fellow-

---

[1] *Summa*, VOL. III, p. 10. It is a significant fact that Torquemada should appeal to *Frequens* in connexion with the pastoral purpose of the Councils: "ad culturam agri dominici, ut canon concilii Constantiensis dicit *Frequens*".

[2] Ch. Gremper, "Des Kardinals Johannes de Turrecremata Kommentar zur Regel des hl. Benedikt", in *Studien und Mitteilungen aus dem Benediktiner und Zisterzienser Orden*, XLV (1927), pp. 223-83; Beltrán de Heredia, "Collección de documentos inéditos para illustrar la vida del Card. J. de Turrecremata", in *A.F.P.*, VII (1937), pp. 210-45, referring for the most part to San Benito de Valladolid. For Torquemada's views on the secular power see H. Jedin, "Johannes de Turrecremata und das Imperium Romanum", in *A.F.P.*, XII (1942), pp. 247-78.

Dominican, Antonino of Florence, he would have thrown his weight into the scales as a theologian and as a cardinal in favour of the reform which it was the duty of the Popes of the restoration to carry through. But of such an attempt there is no trace in the *Summa*.

Torquemada lived long enough to witness the wonderful ascendancy which the Papacy gained from the middle of the century onwards. It allied itself with the Renaissance, which made Rome the centre of the arts and culture; by a new organisation of the Papal States both its finances and its authority were laid on a sufficiently solid basis to secure its political independence. At the same time it developed its system of ecclesiastical officialdom beyond anything ever seen previous to the reform Councils. The series of pontiffs from Nicholas V to Leo X, even though distinguished by only one outstanding personality, is resplendent with the lustre which the word "Renaissance" sheds upon it.

It is the painful duty of Church history to point to the sombre, fateful shadows which are easily overlooked by writers whose sole concern is with the arts or even with political history. The conciliar theory was defeated, but its spirit was far from crushed. It survived side by side with the theology of papal primacy, which many brushed aside as a piece of fawning adulation. The demand for a great reform Council was not disposed of because a general reform of the Church, in spite of various starts, remained an unsatisfied aspiration. Actually the extension of curial officialdom, through the continual establishment of new categories of offices and posts that could be bought, and a fiscal policy which had become ever more exacting, especially since Sixtus IV, only increased the general dissatisfaction with the whole system of the Curia. Thus was born that anti-Roman feeling which was to play so incalculable a role in the break-up of Christian unity, and which made it difficult, even at Trent, to arrive at an understanding. The Popes' entanglement in Italian territorial politics hampered their spiritual action and created for them political opponents who were always ready with a threat of Council and reform. The abuses of nepotism and personal government impelled even the College of Cardinals to fight for a share in government by means of election capitulations. Canonists discussed the question how the Church and the States of the Church could be guarded against absolutism.

About the shortcomings of the Church there was substantial agreement, though not on the nature of the remedy. It almost seemed as if the disease would become chronic. At the turn of the century the tension became even more acute. The Church had to endure the pontificate of Alexander VI and to realise, as never before, the difference between theory and practice, between person and office; it also heard the preaching of Savonarola. The idea of the Council, as well as the conciliar theory, came once more to the surface and once again the hope of a comprehensive and thorough reform came to be associated with them. Neither the Gallican assembly of Pisa nor the fifth Council of the Lateran fulfilled these expectations. However, silently and out of man's sight, the Catholic reform was putting forth its shoots—nor were they the first, for at no time was the Church of the late Middle Ages unconscious of the fact that interior recollection, penance, a return to the ancient ideals of the priestly and the monastic life were the core of any reform. The shoots had not as yet come to light, and the Catholic reform had not yet sufficient strength to master both Church and Papacy, when the catastrophe supervened. It was the rupture of Christian unity that opened the way for the Tridentine renewal of the Church. The road thus opened it is now our business to tread.

CHAPTER II

Survival of Conciliar Theory

A MEMORIAL drawn up in the year 1442 by a partisan of Basle, and aimed at Eugenius IV, asserts that "nearly all Christians hold the Council of Constance's teaching concerning the authority of the Council as true and Catholic; this is above all the opinion of scholars within and without the universities".[1] The claim is undoubtedly an exaggeration. What is certain is that both the strict conciliar theory and its moderate episcopalist version continued to find exponents, and that the threat of the Council and the appeal to it were widely used as a means of bringing pressure to bear on the Popes. However, the real inner force of the idea of the Council lies neither in the conciliar theory nor in its misuse by the diplomatists, but in the widespread longing for a great Council invested with the requisite authority for carrying out a reform.

Gallican France was the real stronghold of the strict conciliar theory and the University of Paris its citadel. Ruthless treatment was meted out to any scholar who presumed to tamper with it. On the occasion of the graduation of a Cistercian, the Dominican John Munerii defended the thesis that the Apostles and the disciples had not received their powers immediately from Christ, but only mediately, through St Peter. He was at once called to order by the chancellor and the sub-dean of the theological faculty. On 17 August 1470 the latter compelled Munerii to make a recantation.[2] It goes without saying that the person

[1] *R.T.A.*, VOL. XVI, p. 581. In his *Germania* (1458) Piccolomini writes that in Germany all who are "paululum docti" are also adherents of the Council, *Opera*, p. 1037. The difficulties of the times made it impossible for me to examine such manuscripts and archives as are outside Rome, though they are indispensable for an exhaustive treatment of the subject. All I could do was to study the chief manifestations of the conciliar idea between the Councils of Basle and the Lateran—manifestations that are of the greatest consequence for the story of Trent—with the help of such printed and manuscript sources as were at my disposal. For this reason I must leave it to other pens to draw a complete picture of a period which has been described as "the most important, perhaps, in the history of conciliar thought" (J. Hashagen, *Staat und Kirche vor der Reformation* (Essen 1931), p. 98). I trust, however, that I have got beyond Hashagen's data, *op. cit.*, pp. 107-10, and in *Historische Vierteljahrsschrift*, XXIII (1926), pp. 330 ff., as well as Stoecklin's stimulating paper, "Das Ende der mittelalterlichen Konzilsbewegung", in *Zeitschrift für schweizerische Kirchengeschichte*, XXXVII (1943), pp. 8-30.

[2] Duplessis d'Argentré, *Coll. iud.*, VOL. I, ii (Paris 1724), pp. 256 ff.

the Faculty wished to hit was not merely the humble preaching friar but his great fellow-Dominican, the recently deceased Cardinal Torquemada. On 5 February 1483 the Faculty censured several statements made by John Angeli, a Friar Minor, in the course of a sermon preached at Tournai. It must be admitted that the friar's explanation of the Pope's fulness of power was couched in particularly provocative terms. Among other things he asserted that the Pope could abolish the entire Canon Law and replace it by a new one; anyone who opposed the Pope's will was a pagan and was *ipso facto* excommunicated; no one might find fault with the Pope unless he were to fall into heresy. The first assertion the Faculty characterised as "scandalous, blasphemous and definitely heretical", while the other two were described as "false, scandalous and suspect of heresy".[1] A year later the following theses were said to have been maintained by Maître Jean Laillier: "Peter has received no authority from Christ over the rest of the Apostles, nor has he been given the primacy; if you insist that I speak of the Pope, I shall pull down everything; the decrees and decretals of the Popes are a pure forgery." On this occasion the Faculty refrained from proceeding against the offender, probably because in the disputation in question, held on 30 July 1484, Laillier had not actually formulated his propositions in these terms. None of them were embodied in the nine theses for which Maître Jean was eventually condemned.[2] It is clear that the Faculty deemed it its duty not so much to safeguard the doctrine of the Pope's primacy as to make a stand against Torquemada's papalist theory.

On the other hand, it took up the defence of the notorious decrees of Constance and Basle. When, on 11 January 1497, the King put to it the question whether the decree *Frequens* was still valid, its answer was a decided affirmative.[3] On 15 March 1508 it proceeded against Maître Jacques Dumoulin, who, in his *Vesperiae*, had expounded Torquemada's opinion that the decree of Constance on the Council's superiority over the Pope was invalid on the ground that it had not been issued by an undoubted General Council. Dumoulin was compelled to subscribe to the following propositions which run counter to Torquemada's teaching: "The Council is the full and adequate representation of the Church and holds its authority from Christ; it has the power to depose the Pope not only for heresy, but for other reasons also. Everybody

---

[1] *Ibid.*, p. 305.
[2] *Ibid.*, p. 308.
[3] *Ibid.*, p. 335 f.

is bound to obey the Council in all that concerns faith and morals and reform, for the most holy and undoubted Council of Constance as well as the Council of Basle have defined that this is Catholic teaching." [1]

It was in keeping with these principles that in the autumn of 1511 the University sent representatives to the Gallican *conciliabulum* of Pisa; only at the beginning of 1513 when that rump Council, by then transferred to Lyons, had obviously to be written off as a failure scarcely deserving the name of a Council, did the dean and seventeen masters, against eighteen or nineteen opponents, prevail on the University to dissuade the King from further support of that venture.[2] With a view to avoiding an open conflict with the Pope, the Faculty, though requested to condemn the writings in which Cajetan, the General of the Dominicans, attacked the conciliar theory, put off compliance with the demand, although it had no intention of abandoning its principle. The Dominicans of Saint-Jacques and a handful of Spanish masters stood out for the dogma of the Roman primacy, but they were a minority while the two men who defended Pisa with their pens, Major and Almain, spoke for the bulk of the University.[3]

The German universities were less uniformly and consistently favourable to the conciliar theory than the University of Paris.[4] During the struggle for neutrality some of them had boldly sided with Basle, for instance Erfurt and Vienna [5]; others had at least accepted the principle of the Council's superiority, amongst them Cologne.[6] "Just as bread and water are necessary to maintain human life," Vienna wrote, "so does the welfare of the Church militant require the untrammelled authority of the Councils. How is the confusion that has arisen in the Church to be dealt with? Above all how are the encroachments of some Popes to be checked—if there is none higher than they

[1] A. Clerval, *Registre des procès-verbaux de la Faculté de Théologie de Paris*, VOL. I (Paris 1917), p. 38 f.

[2] *Ibid.*, p. 122 f.

[3] R. G. Villoslada, *La Universidad de Paris durante los estudios de Francisco de Vitoria 1507-1522* (Rome 1938), pp. 92, 156 f., 172 f.

[4] For what follows, see H. Bressler, *Die Stellung der deutschen Universitäten zum Basler Konzil, zum Schisma und zur deutschen Neutralität* (Leipzig 1885); G. Kaufmann, *Geschichte der deutschen Universitäten*, VOL. II (Stuttgart 1896), pp. 442-68. Both these works need to be supplemented by further research.

[5] *R.T.A.*, VOL. XV, pp. 434-47; VOL. XVI, pp. 289-92; Segovia, *Mon, conc. gen.*, VOL. III, p. 536, quotes only an extract from the Leipzig memorial.

[6] *R.T.A.*, VOL. XV, pp. 462-7. To this period belongs the conciliarist *Tractatus super neutralitate principum per quemdam fratrem ord. Carthusiensis apud Coloniam s. theologiae professorem compilatus a.d. 1440*, Vat. Lib., Reg. lat. 1020, fols. 199ᵛ-212ʳ.

on earth and if they acknowledge no judge—except by means of the Council?"[1]

Theologically soundest is the extensive memorial of the University of Cracow drawn up in March 1442.[2] "The decrees of Constance", we read in that document, "are a warning to the Church and must be regarded as such in time to come. They must be kept inviolably, even by the Pope." In view of its favourable attitude to the conciliar theory, Cracow was honoured by the University of Paris, under date of 16 March 1444, with a eulogy in which stress was laid on the struggle. If the Council of Basle were defeated, it said, little hope would remain that any Councils would be held in our days and perhaps in the future as well; their authority would be shaken, perhaps for ever, and what was won at Constance, Siena and Basle would be thrown away.[3]

The University of Heidelberg is the only one from which not a single expression in support of Basle has come down to us. Actually, one of its professors, Master Rudolph of Seeland, sharply criticised that assembly in a disputation—probably of the year 1442—and upheld the Pope's unqualified superiority over it.[4]

At Cologne also Eugenius IV was not without adherents. In 1435, Heimerich von Kampen, who had represented the University at the Council, went to Louvain, where he took his stand with the bishop of that city in support of Eugenius IV. In 1445 Godfrey Milter of Roermond, Dean of the Faculty of Arts, presented a treatise on the question of authority to Nicholas of Cusa, who had become a supporter of Eugenius IV. The Dominican Henry Kalteisen and the Franciscan Henry of Werl likewise went over to the party of Eugenius IV.[5]

The fact remains, however, that the old universities north of the Alps favoured the conciliar theory and continued to do so until the political collapse of 1448 compelled them to drop the cause of Basle. Cologne's action, which we know from the lively account of Sebastian de Viseto, is very significant.[6] The University insisted that, without

---

[1] R.T.A., VOL. XVI, p. 291.
[2] C. E. Bulaeus, *Historia Universitatis Parisiensis* (Paris 1665-73), VOL. V, pp. 479-517, especially pp. 500, 507.
[3] *Codex dipl. universitatis Cracoviensis*, VOL. II (Cracow 1873), p. 32 f.
[4] G. Ritter, *Die Heidelberger Universität*, VOL. I, pp. 308 ff., 314 ff.
[5] H. Keussen, "Die Stellung der Universität Köln im grossen Schisma und zu den Reformkonzilien", in *Annalen des Historischen Vereins für den Niederrhein*, CXV (1929), pp. 225-54.
[6] Kaufmann, *Geschichte der deutschen Universitäten*, VOL. II, pp. 89-92.

prejudice to its submission to Pope Eugenius IV, it regarded the decrees of Constance and Basle concerning the authority of the Councils as binding in law.[1] The University of Cracow identified itself with the opinions expressed by the Universities of Paris, Vienna, Leipzig, Erfurt and Cologne previous to its recognition, after prolonged hesitation, of Nicholas V, on 3 July 1449. Erfurt curtly stated that they had nothing to add to their previous declarations. Leipzig announced its submission, as did Cologne, in a rather subdued fashion, with the observation that there could be no question but that a legitimately convened General Council derived its authority directly from Christ and was accordingly entitled to demand submission even from the Pope, within the limits defined at Constance.[2] Vienna declined to commit itself, yet Thomas Ebendorfer, the outstanding figure of the University at that moment, found it very hard to induce his colleagues to take part in the reception of the papal legate Carvajal. Most of the professors only gave way after protesting that their participation must not in any way prejudice the authority of the Councils.[3] Presently—in 1452—the Viennese professors gave their support to the rebellious Austrians' appeal from the papal *Monitorium* to a Council; as a matter of fact Aeneas Silvius suspected them of being its instigators.[4] Ten years later the University supported a similar appeal by Duke Albrecht VI from the censures imposed on Frederick's opponent by Pius II.[5] On 23 October 1492 Master John Kaltenmarkter, after his absolution in Rome by Cardinal Oliviero Carafa and Cardinal George of Lisbon, was ordered to make the following declaration: "I disavow without any reservation whatsoever the following propositions, namely that the Council is above the Pope; that the Pope may not invalidate a decision of a General Council."[6] It should be noted that the University only moved in the matter at Rome's command and that the recantation refers only to an unqualified assertion of the above propositions, so that the door was left open for a qualified formulation of them. Indeed, even in 1508 one of the assistant clergy at the parish church of St Michael in

[1] Cologne to Cracow, 17 September 1448, F. J. Bianco, *Geschichte der alten Universität Köln*, VOL. I, ii (Cologne 1855), pp. 242 ff.; *Codex dipl. universitatis Cracoviensis*, VOL. II, pp. 86 ff.

[2] *Codex dipl. universitatis Cracoviensis*, VOL. II, p. 94.

[3] J. Aschbach, *Geschichte der Wiener Universität*, VOL. I (Vienna 1865), pp. 278 ff.; Bressler, *Die Stellung der deutschen Universitäten*, pp. 72 ff.

[4] *Historia rerum Friderici tertii imperatoris* (Strasbourg 1685), p. 101.

[5] Aschbach, *Geschichte der Wiener Universität*, VOL. I, p. 236 f.

[6] R. Kink, *Geschichte der kaiserlichen Universität Wien*, VOL. I, ii (Vienna 1854), p. 26.

Vienna was still voicing the opinions of Kaltenmarkter in the pulpit.[1]
When, in 1459, the Carthusian Vincent of Aggsbach observed that
Eugenius IV and his successors had persuaded almost all scholars to
abandon the conciliar theory and had succeeded in drawing them to their
side,[2] there was this much truth in the assertion that the theologians of the
German universities on the whole yielded to external pressure and in
course of time became increasingly favourable to the papal restoration.[3]
At the same time we must insist that the supporters of the conciliar
theory changed their attitude only by slow degrees. As a rule the
delicate question of authority was evaded, and even in the case of so
decided and at the same time so influential an advocate of the doctrine
of the primacy as Gabriel Biel we are aware of a certain reserve.

As early as the year 1462, this divine of the University of Tübingen
had championed the papal standpoint in the dispute over the See of
Mainz, and in his widely read *Explanation of the Canon of the Mass*,
written in 1488, he openly expounded the doctrine of the Roman
primacy.[4] "The Pope", he wrote, "is invested with supreme authority
and is the bishop of bishops. These derive their authority from him."
He refrains from discussing the authority of the Council. On the other
hand, he does not belong to Torquemada's retinue. We are sufficiently
cautioned against viewing him in that light by his assertion that the
Pope is *caput ministeriale* of the Church. Peter's dignity is not

---

[1] Th. Wiedemann, *Geschichte der Reformation und Gegenreformation im Lande
unter der Enns*, VOL. I (Prague 1879), pp. 1-4.

[2] Pez-Hueber, *Thesaurus anecd.*, VOL. V, iii (Augsburg 1729), p. 335.

[3] G. Ritter, "Romantische und revolutionäre Elemente in der deutschen Theologie
am Vorabend der Reformation", in *Deutsche Vierteljahrsschrift für Literaturwissen-
schaft und Geistesgeschichte*, v (1927), pp. 342-80. However, Ritter's assertion that
the papal hierarchy "found no more loyal defenders than the German scholastics of the
pre-reformation era" (p. 353), needs some qualification. Of the University of Louvain,
founded in 1432, H. de Jongh, *L'Ancienne Faculté de théologie de Louvain* (Louvain
1911), p. 89, says that there was in it "nulle trace de doctrines conciliaires". A. M.
Lanz, "L'autorità e l'infallibilità del Papa nella dottrina Lovaniese del secolo XVI",
in *Gregorianum*, XXIII (1942), pp. 348-74, sought to refute Baius's claim that his
opinion, that is, that the Pope is not "episcopus universalis" and that he only teaches
unerringly when he speaks in conjunction with the Council, or at least "col consiglio
di molti", had been taught at Louvain for a period of eighty years. To this end
Lanz draws on Driedo, Latomus, Pighius, Tapper and others, but the greatest difficulties arise precisely from the most important author of all, viz. Adrian VI; see also
below, p. 65, n. 3.

[4] *Expositio canonis missae* (Venice 1505) lect. 23, fols. 43ʳ-46ᵛ; cf. Haller, *Die
Anfänge der Universität Tübingen*, VOL. I (Stuttgart 1927), pp. 153-72; VOL. II (*ibid.*,
1929), pp. 54-64; as for the circulation, see *Gesamtkatalog der Wiegendrucke* (Leipzig
1925 f.), Nos. 4332-6; Panzer, *Annales typographici* (Nuremberg 1793-1803), VOL. X,
p. 173 (up to 1527 there were eleven editions).

exclusively based on the pre-eminence—*praelatio*—bestowed on him, it is also founded on his virtues. "What a difference between him", he observes, "and the manners and the ostentation of his successors!" So even this divine, who did so much to promote the doctrine of the primacy in Germany, may not be unreservedly reckoned among the men who led the papal theory to victory in the German universities of the pre-Reformation era. On the other hand, the last word on this point can only be spoken after a fuller examination of the manuscript material bearing on the subject.

In the summer of 1482 three professors of Basle drew up as many memorials on Zamometič's attempted Council. These documents, which were destined for the City Council, constitute an instructive cross-section of the views on the nature of the Council then prevailing in the German universities.[1]

While on the one hand John Siber, the professor of dogmatic theology, explained that there was no question but that the Pope was above the Council, had authority to call it, and was only subject to it in the event of his falling into heresy, the canonist Ulrich Surgant was no less emphatic in his support of the Council. Should the Pope neglect to summon a reform Council or should he himself be blame-worthy then, in Surgant's opinion, it may be convoked by the cardinals, by the Emperor, or even by a single individual bishop. In point of fact, the Pope may not hinder whatever is done for the good of the universal Church; hence he is subordinate to it.[2] The third of the trio, who remains anonymous, observes a cautious reserve, though his sympathies are with the Council. He may be regarded as the prototype of the opportunists, of whom there were many.

It is easy to account for Siber's and Surgant's attitude if we remember their respective spiritual homes. The former was a graduate of Heidelberg, a university devoted to the Papacy, so much so indeed that in 1462 it could boast of the support it had given to the Pope during the whole period of the Councils. At this time too it unreservedly condemned Zamometič's plan. Surgant, on the other hand, had studied in Paris. If we may believe a contemporary witness, Zamometič's theses on the authority of the Council, of which more will be said later, were approved not only by the University of Paris, but also by those of Louvain, Cologne, Erfurt, Cracow and Vienna.[3]

[1] J. Schlecht, *Zamometič*, pp. 118-24.
[2] St. Arch., Basle, Politisches Heft III, fol. 16 f.
[3] Schlecht, *Zamometič*, p. 65.

It may be true that the conciliar theory never struck deep roots in Italy during the period of the reform Councils, nor became as widespread as in France and Germany; yet even in that country it was not wholly inoperative. Its nurseries, however, were not the chairs of theology, which were almost exclusively occupied by mendicant friars, but those of canonists and jurists, more particularly at Padua and Pavia. This state of affairs was due to the prestige of men like Zabarella, Tudeschi, Pontano and other outstanding personalities of the period of the Schism. Even some of the officials of the Curia did not wholly escape its influence, as will be seen by an example we shall have to discuss later on. All this helps us to understand why the *conciliabulum* of Pisa in 1511 experienced but little difficulty in finding two Italian jurists ready to justify its conduct. They were Philip Decius and Jerome Boticellus. In his *Apologia*, Zaccaria Ferreri of Vicenza, a secretary of the Council, definitely adopted the standpoint of the conciliar theory.[1] At this time too Matthias Ugoni, Bishop of Famagusta and auxiliary to the Bishop of Brescia, a man who had studied at Padua, defended the decrees *Sacrosancta* and *Frequens* of Constance against Torquemada. The Councils, he maintained, are the nerves and sinews of ecclesiastical discipline.[2] In the person of the Bolognese jurist Giovanni Gozzadini the conciliar theory found its way into the very court of Julius II. In his work on the papal election, completed in 1511, in which Gerson's influence makes itself strongly felt, he preached the doctrine of the superiority of the Council and described the relevant decrees of Constance and Basle as so many articles of faith. In his opinion the decree *Frequens*, as it stands, is binding for all time and could only be altered by another Council. In view of the ignorance and worldliness of the bishops it would be necessary, when the reform Council came to be convened, to admit and to empower to vote, doctors, simple priests and suitable laymen, as was done at Constance and Basle. The first and most important duty of this Council would be a reform of the Church in head and members.[3]

Gozzadini's work is anything but an academic treatise. It is an impassioned appeal for a reform, a Cassandra's warning to the Popes of the Renaissance. "Scarcely ten bishops would be equal, at this day,

---

[1] The apologia is in Goldast, *Monarchia*, VOL. II, pp. 1653-65; Decius's memorial, *ibid.*, pp. 1667-76.

[2] M. Ugonius, *De conciliis* (*sine loco*, 1532), fols. 28 ff., 97 ff.

[3] For particulars see my paper: "Giovanni Gozzadini, ein Konziliarist am Hofe Julius II", in *R.Q.*, XLVII (1939), pp. 193-267.

to the demands of a General Council"; he writes, "unless we take thought and reform a just God will himself exact terrible vengeance, and that before long!" His faith in the triumph of the idea of the Council and of Church reform is unshaken: "Is it not written that the gates of hell shall not prevail against it, that is, against the Church?"

A little more than a decade earlier Savonarola had preached penance and conversion and prophesied imminent disaster. Was he too a partisan of the conciliar theory? No! Savonarola was a Thomist and a strict adherent of the doctrine of papal supremacy. For all that, in March 1498, even he entertained for a moment the idea of summoning a Council with the assistance of the Emperor and the Christian princes, for the purpose of calling Alexander VI to account.[1] He justified his plan for a Council by an appeal to the old, classical case which all papalists regarded as a valid reason for summoning a Council without the intervention of the Pope: "The Pope is no longer a Christian, he is an infidel, a heretic. As such he has ceased to be Pope." In these circumstances the Council's duty is to establish the fact and to initiate the election of a successor. Not a trace of the conciliar theory, yet a Council is planned!

Savonarola's famous letters to princes never got beyond the stage of mere projects. He never made a serious attempt to summon a Council in the hope of averting his own fate with its help. Nevertheless these rough drafts show that in the heat of the struggle for a reform even a Thomist wholly immune from the conciliar theory could fall back on a solution by means of a Council.[2]

In the late autumn of the same year 1498 two envoys of the King of Portugal arrived in Rome for the purpose of remonstrating with Alexander VI on his personal conduct, his nepotism, and the simoniacal practices that went on under his very eyes. They hinted that he ran the risk of being called to account before a Council.[3] The Catholic

---

[1] R. Ridolfi, *Le lettere di G. Savonarola* (Florence 1933), pp. 205-11; cf. Hurtaud, "Lettres de Savonarola aux princes chrétiens pour la réunion d'un concile", in *Revue thomiste*, VII (1899), pp. 631-74; J. Schnitzer, *Quellen und Forschungen zur Geschichte Savonarolas*, (Munich 1902 f.), VOL. II, pp. 735 ff.

[2] J. Schnitzer, "Die Flugschriftenliteratur für und wider Savonarola", in *Festgabe K. Th. von Heigel* (Munich 1903), pp. 196-235, especially p. 208. Conciliarist views appear for the first time in one of Savonarola's apologists—the Minorite Paolo da Fucecchio.

[3] Ascanio Sforza to the Duke of Milan, 3 December 1498, in *Bolletino storico della Svizzera italiana*, VII (1885), pp. 202 ff. Summary of the same despatch, wrongly dated 3 September 1499, in *Notizenblatt zum Archiv für österreichische Geschichte*, VII (1857), p. 54 f.

Kings also threatened to convene a Council.[1] Was the Iberian peninsula also infected with the spirit of the conciliar theory?

By no means. As far as we know, at the turn of the fifteenth century
it found scarcely any adherents in the peninsula, and the most resolute
defenders of the papal theory at the Curia—men like Torquemada and
Arevalo—were of Spanish origin. But even in Spain the question of
reform included the idea of a Council. However, as soon as it was
taken up, the question which had been discussed during the reform
Councils [2] arose anew: By what means could the decrees of the future
reform Council be insured against abolition by contrary papal decrees,
or against their being rendered inoperative by means of dispensations?

Peter of Osma's Gallican answer that the Pope had no power to
dispense from the decrees of the universal Church, in other words that
he was bound by them, was condemned by an assembly of theologians,
at Alcalá, on 24 May 1479.[3] The ecclesiastical-political advisers of
Ferdinand the Catholic sought and found another solution, one in which
we see the first symptoms of the proud episcopalism, deeply charged
with national feeling, of the men who later on were to represent Spain at
the Council of Trent. In view of the nearness of the forthcoming fifth
Lateran Council, they proposed that that assembly should ordain that
the ordinaries were empowered to examine the grounds of every papal
dispensation. If these did not correspond with facts, or if they were
unjust, the bishops should have authority to stay their execution. A
further decree should make it an obligation for the Pope to summon a
Council every five years; should he fail to do so, the cardinals must do
it in his stead. At his accession every Pope must be made to swear
observance of these two decrees.[4]

The Spaniards were not interested in the question of authority as
such. Their sole concern was the practical problem of making sure that
the reform Councils would be convened at frequent intervals and their
decrees carried into effect. What they thought and what they wanted
was thus summed up by a Spanish bishop: "If we do not make sure
that the decrees of the Council cannot be altered by the mere will of the

---

[1] Sanudo, *Diarii*, VOL. II, p. 279.

[2] For instance, the French proposals for a reform, at Siena, in 1423, *Mon. conc.
gen.*, VOL. I, pp. 32, 35; an Italian Benedictine abbot's memorial in 1432, *Conc. Bas.*,
VOL. VIII, pp. 34, 36. A solution in a strictly conciliarist sense by means of a *decretum
irritans* was opposed by the Bishop of Cadiz, *ibid.*, VOL. I, p. 111.

[3] Duplessis d'Argentré, *Coll. iud.*, VOL. I, ii, p. 298; F. Stegmüller in *R.Q.*, XLIII
(1935), p. 244.

[4] Protocol of session held at Burgos, 17 December 1511, in Döllinger, *Beiträge*,
VOL. III, pp. 200 ff.

Pope and the cardinals, the Council is useless and our time and money are wasted!"[1]

In the classic land of Catholic reform they wanted Councils to be held at even shorter intervals than those fixed by the decree *Frequens*. They also looked for means by which the Pope could be made to abide by the conciliar decrees, but without raising the question of authority. On the eve of the Council of Trent, Francisco de Vitoria studied the problem once more and passed on the result of his inquiries to those of his pupils who were to attend that assembly.

These Spanish discussions, and men like Savonarola and Gozzadini, make it abundantly clear that the strength of the idea of the Council did not lie in the conciliar theory which, by reason of its origin, was far too closely connected with the period of the Schism: it lay in the anxiety for reform. In their eagerness for a reform of the Church, even men charged with the cure of souls could be seen fighting for the validity of *Frequens* and the reform decrees of Basle. Naturally enough they also wanted the longed-for reform Council to be invested with the requisite authority to enable it to initiate a *reformatio capitis* and to ensure obedience to its decrees. It was no professional conceit, obstinately insisting on the observance of the decrees of Constance and Basle, that inspired them, but sincere solicitude for the welfare of the Church. Were it otherwise, it would be impossible to account for the opposition from this quarter to the reforming activities of Nicholas of Cusa in Germany. The opposition argued as follows: "The Cardinal's reform decrees are in part identical with those of Basle. If they are enforced and accepted as ordinances of the Legate, they are no longer conciliar decrees—the latter's authority is done away with. Moreover a particular reform of this kind injures the unity of the Church. A General Council alone is able to carry out a reform of head and members." [2]

Faith in the miraculous virtue of a General Council obviously blinded these men and prevented them from perceiving the advantages of a practical restoration. It is nevertheless highly significant that in spite of so many disappointments, such a belief endured, and that in circles which undoubtedly strove for what was best for the Church. These circles were the same as those in which Gerson's writings found most readers,[3] circles more interested in practical and mystical piety

[1] Döllinger, *Beiträge*, VOL. III, p. 203.

[2] Text in Walch, *Monimenta medii aevi*, VOL. I, pp. 103-10.

[3] Between 1483 and 1521 nine complete editions of Gerson's works, mostly in four volumes, were published at Cologne, Strasbourg, Basle and Paris; Schwab, *Johannes Gerson* (Würzburg 1858), pp. 786-94.

than in scholastic erudition or in the study of Canon Law. It is a remarkable thing that among them we find a number of men belonging to the strictest and most unworldly of all medieval Orders—the Carthusians.

During the Schism of Basle the Carthusian Bartholomew of Roermond (he died in 1446) gave his unqualified support to the Council.[1] The Venerable Denis Rickel (Denis the Carthusian) had attempted to harmonise the supremacy of the Council in matters of faith and reform with the doctrine of papal primacy.[2] When the question was finally decided, Vincent of Aggsbach, well known as the author of mystical treatises,[3] made an impassioned protest against the conduct of bishops and theologians whom he accused of disloyalty to the cause of the Council: "Can anyone imagine a greater confusion than the present, when so many bishops, masters and doctors from the secular and regular clergy, not only abandon a Catholic truth based on the Gospel, defined by two Councils and proclaimed to all the faithful, which moreover has satisfied the whole of Christendom for a long series of years, but obstinately cling to the opposite opinion and blindly persevere in their error?"[4] The opponents of the Council are made bishops, cardinals, and even Popes—these shafts are aimed at Nicholas of Cusa and at Pius II, the reigning Pope—and one of Eugenius IV's defenders has even been raised to the honours of the altar. Obedience should be denied to the Pope, as at the time of the Schism. In an emergency the bishops and the princes should summon a Council in spite of the Pope's opposition, for it is not right that the wickedness of a small party should be a hindrance to the general good of the Church. An experience of fifty years has taught us that the Roman Curia shrinks from the idea of a Council as from the plague, for it is afraid of being called to account. Hence it is necessary to act without it, and even against it; the ground must be systematically prepared; theologians and universities should have the affair of the Council at heart and begin by clarifying the basic

---

[1] Vat. Lib., Reg. lat. 1020, fols. 178^r-196^v; cf. Ritter, *Die Heidelberger Universität*, VOL. I, p. 315.

[2] Dionysius Carthusianus, *De auctoritate summi pontificis et generalis concilii* (*Opera omnia*, Tournai 1908, VOL. XXXVI, pp. 525-674); the decisive texts are in articles 26-9, pp. 565 ff.

[3] Vincent to Johann von Weilheim, previous to 26 June 1459, Pez-Hueber, *Thesaurus anecd.*, VOL. V, iii, pp. 332-41. For further literary activities see E. Vansteenberghe, "Un écrit de Vincent d'Aggsbach contre Gerson", in *Festgabe Cl. Bäumker* (Münster 1913), pp. 357-64; id., *Autour de la docte ignorance* (Münster 1915), pp. 24 ff., 58 ff., 189-218.

[4] Pez-Hueber, *Thesaurus anecd.*, VOL. V, iii, p. 333.

problem. If this is done, the idea of the Council will be revived and will triumph in the end. A General Council will cleanse, sanctify and reform the Church.[1]

There are passages which give the reader the impression that he is listening to Savonarola or to Luther, so impassioned and so revolutionary is the language of this Carthusian. He is completely under the influence of the conciliar theory. The papal restoration which, on the whole, only brought back the earlier conceptions which had been current before the Schism, appears to him as an error and as a shameful departure from a true conception of the nature of the Church. So much is clear: the great confusion occasioned by the Schism in this sphere was anything but clarified, the spirit of Basle was anything but dead. From the stillness of the Charterhouse there issued a loud call for a Council that would succeed where Constance and Basle had failed. "The reform Councils", wrote Jacob of Jüterbog,[2] "have made it abundantly clear that the doctrine of the Pope's supremacy is only a shield behind which the Italians and their party shelter from reform. Even if the Pope were a man of good will, the resistance which the people around him offer to reform is such that one may boldly affirm that a reform of the Church cannot be brought about by the Pope alone; it needs an effort by the whole Church gathered in Council. Everything must be done to ensure the execution of *Frequens*. By this means the wound inflicted on the Church by Eugenius IV may perhaps be healed."

So wrote Jacob of Jüterbog in 1449, the one-time partisan of Basle, under stress of the collapse of reform and in an apocalyptic mood. He also addressed to the newly elected Pope Nicholas V a memorial on reform. Like Vincent of Aggsbach he felt convinced that the Church was in grievous peril, hence his desire to help and to warn. For his own person he had already found a solution when he resigned his professor's chair at Cracow in 1441 in order to serve God in the stillness of a Carthusian's cell. In point of fact it was in the Charterhouse that the sacred flame of Christian piety and unselfish sacrifice was tended, and it was there too that, before long, it was to leap into a brilliant flame in the Catholic reform.

This apocalyptic frame of mind was greatly strengthened by the

---

[1] *Ibid.*, p. 336 f.

[2] *De septem statibus ecclesiae in Apocalypsi descriptis et de auctoritate ecclesiae et de eius reformatione*, Goldast, *Monarchia*, VOL. II, pp. 1567-75, especially pp. 1571 ff.; cf. J. Fijalek, *Mistrz Jacob z. Paradyza*, VOL. II (Cracow 1900), pp. 250 ff.

advance of the Turks in the Balkans and by the fall of Constantinople. Both events were widely regarded as a punishment for the sins of the Church. To the existing motives for a Council a new one was now added—the crusade. Urban II's call to Christendom to reconquer the Holy Places, at the Synods of Clermont and Piacenza, came to people's minds. Why should not a Council unite all the forces of Christendom under the banner of the Cross and so defeat the Crescent? Only through a Council, so we read in a tract written at the time of the Christian Congress (*Christentag*) of Ratisbon in 1471,[1] only in a Council can a great expedition against the Turks be got under way; above all only a Council can obtain from the various nations the tenth with which to finance the enterprise; only by this means can peace and confidence be re-established among the Christian princes; failure to bring this to pass would render an undertaking of this kind impossible.[2]

In the next chapter we shall see with what concern the Curia watched the growth of these ideas, and how it sought to refute or to deflect them. The author of the above-mentioned tract also takes it for granted that the Pope and the cardinals do not want a Council [3]; he accordingly seeks to show that the Pope is bound to call a Council both by the election capitulation which he has sworn to observe and by the decree *Frequens*; should he fail to do his duty he would run the risk of meeting with the fate of the last Pope of the period of the Schism. The writer, however, protests that he utters no threat. He is anxious to win over the Pope to his view; he insists that it was in his own best interest to convoke a Council, for by such an act he would silence the rumour that he was afraid of a reform. Then the Curia and the clergy would be reformed, the Pragmatic Sanctions would be done away with, the Church would recover her freedom and the Bohemian problem got out of the way. Meanwhile no one would prevent the Pope from carrying out the necessary reforms of his Curia even before the Council met. By so doing he would take the *reformatio capitis* out of the hands of the Council.

The anonymous writer of Kremsmünster is no supporter of the conciliar theory, nor is he in any way an opponent of the papal restoration;

---

[1] *Considerationes de concilium (sic!) generalis congregandi utilitate et necessitate,* Abbey Library, Kremsmünster, consid. 4, fols. 115ʳ-120ᵛ; cf. H. Schmid, *Catalogus codicum manuscriptorum in bibliotheca Cremifanensis* (Ebenhoesch: Lentii 1877), I, p. 66.

[2] *Considerationes de concilium generalis,* consid. 1-8, fols. 115ʳ-116ᵛ.

[3] "Inolevit enim fama quod papa et domini cardinales timeant, odiant, ymmo abhorreant concilia generalia, tamquam non possint facere quod velint si concilium sit congregandum vel de proximo congregandum, et tamquam reformident reformari per ipsa" (fol. 118ʳ).

his only aim is to remove Rome's misgivings about the Council. Unlike Vincent of Aggsbach he does not despair of the Pope's willingness to convoke a Council; on the contrary he hopes to persuade him to do so. But should the Pope turn a deaf ear to the demand for a Council there remained yet another possibility. All good bishops and priests are at one in their desire for a Council; but if they see that those whose duty it is to act are not interested, they will look to the Emperor in the hope that help may come from that quarter.

Was it likely that this appeal to the Emperor would be understood? Did the desire for a Council get any support from the Emperor Frederick III, as it had, two generations before, from King Sigismund? Were the higher clergy of the Empire prepared to use their influence in Church and State in favour of Council and reform?

With these questions we have left the world of the lecture-room, the study, and the monk's cell for that of state chancelleries and the political arena. If the idea of the Council was a live one we shall surely meet with it here too.

The appeal to the Emperor was in vain. In point of fact Frederick III had made a substantial contribution both to the Pope's triumph over the Council of Basle and to the termination of the Schism. By this action he had put Eugenius IV and Nicholas V under obligation to him, while on the other hand the Papacy was an exceedingly useful support for a politically helpless ruler. For this reason the Emperor sedulously refrained from lending effective support to the demands for a Council, which he knew to be distasteful to Nicholas V and his successors. When, some time before Frederick's coronation in 1452, Aeneas Silvius Piccolomini prayed in his name for a Council to be held in Germany, Rome was well aware that no serious danger threatened from that quarter. Moreover, Piccolomini added that if the Council did come about it would have to abstain from discussing the question of authority, and that, for his part, the Emperor stood by the doctrine of the Pope's universal jurisdiction. The request for a Council in Germany suited the Curia extremely well just then, for it made it possible to decline a simultaneous but far more dangerous demand for a Council in France.[1]

In the course of his second sojourn in Rome, at Christmas 1468,[2] Frederick laid before the Pope a plan for a meeting of princes to be held

[1] Freher-Struve, *Germ. rerum script.*, VOL. II (Strasbourg 1717), pp. 34-8; *Orationes politicae et ecclesiasticae*, ed. J. Mansi (1755), VOL. I, pp. 140-9.

[2] *Commentarii* BK VII, in *Pii II commentarii* (Frankfurt 1614), pp. 440 ff.; see Raynald, *Annales*, a. 1468, No. 46 f.

at Constance for the purpose of dealing with the Turkish problem. In the entourage of the Pope, Cardinal Ammanati relates, they racked their brains to know what could have induced the Emperor to make such a proposal. Were the Venetians behind it? Or was it solely in order to pacify public opinion in Germany? Paul II was annoyed. He expatiated on the futility of such gatherings, and only yielded after the Emperor, with characteristic obstinacy, had renewed and pressed his request at a second consistory. However, the convention was to be held not at Constance but in Rome. More the Pope would not concede and the Emperor was satisfied.

During the pontificate of Sixtus IV, Frederick III indulged for a while in conciliar intrigues with Louis XI of France.[1] His envoy, the versatile George Hessler, even managed, by using the threat of a Council, to induce the Pope to yield in the dispute over the See of Constance.[2] But the papal diplomatic counterstroke was immediate. Sixtus IV was well aware that a conciliar intrigue of Louis XI was a very different thing from a proposal for a Council by the Emperor alone. Such an intrigue might become dangerous if the imperial prestige were thrown in the scales by a real power. By himself, Frederick was too weak; he was also too shrewd to upset his relations with the Pope by a serious agitation for a reform Council. That is why Zamometič, his former favourite, was to experience a bitter disappointment when, perhaps on the strength of some casual remark of his master, he expected Frederick's support for his attempt to call a Council. The Habsburger, unenterprising though he was, nevertheless entertained strong monarchical and dynastic sentiments. Large assemblies such as imperial and provincial diets—hence Councils also—were odious to him. How could such a man, in the face of so many obstacles, bring about on his own initiative a convention of the whole of Christendom such as the Council of Constance had been and a future reform Council promised to become?

It was not the Emperor, but the Estates of the Empire—above all the territorial princes, who constituted the politically active elements,

---

[1] Our only knowledge of this project is through the counterplan unfolded in Corvinus's intercepted letter to Charles the Bold; see K. Rausch, *Die Burgundische Heirat Maximilians I* (Vienna 1880), pp. 148 ff.; A. P. Segesser, *Die Beziehungen der Schweitzer zu Mathias Corvinus 1476-1490* (Lucerne 1860), pp. 72 ff.; A. Bachmann, *Deutsche Reichsgeschichte im Zeitalter Friedrichs III und Maximilians I*, VOL. II (Leipzig 1894), p. 532 f.

[2] *Basler Chroniken*, VOL. III, p. 37. I am unable to accept W. Hollweg's interpretation as given in his book, *Dr. Georg Hessler* (Leipzig 1907), p. 45.

that conducted the ecclesiastical-political struggles of the period. But even in these struggles the idea of a Council only began to play a definite role about the middle of the century. It was then that the *gravamina* in which clergy and laity felt themselves oppressed by the Curia came into the foreground. In the end, personal interests became preponderant. Then there was question only of ecclesiastical tenths, benefices, and episcopal sees; the wider outlook, concern for the world-wide tasks of the Church, was completely lacking.

The demand for a "third Council" which would decide the conflict between Eugenius IV and the assembly of Basle [1]—a demand that had come from various quarters during the Schism—ended in a request for a new Council as soon as peace had been concluded. A German tract of 1451 which voiced a number of complaints, urged a national as well as an œcumenical council for the purpose of a reform of Church and Empire.[2] A memorial written in the following year—and entitled *Agreement between ecclesiastical Princes* [3]—urged the Emperor to follow the precedent set by Sigismund, to press the Pope to give effect to the decree *Frequens*, and above all to fix an early date for the next Council. What we are to think of this suggestion may be gathered from the further observation that by this means the Pope could be made more "amenable and ready" to grant concessions in the ecclesiastical sphere. Such "concessions" were the only concern of these great lords.[4]

When after the fall of Constantinople Calixtus III and Pius II summoned Christendom to war against the Turks and levied a tenth for that purpose, a recrudescence of the demand for a Council might have been expected. But it was otherwise. Inspired by the jurists Gregory Heimburg and Martin Mayr, the Electors' Diet of Frankfurt, in 1456, formulated the *gravamina* of the German nation and pressed for a "pragmatic" which would secure for the Church in Germany the same measure of independence from Rome as that enjoyed by the Church in France. Execution of the decrees of Constance and Basle was one of the measures with which it was intended to counter the papal policy in the sphere of prebends and finances.[5]

[1] Voigt, *Enea Silvio Piccolomini*, VOL. I, p. 392; Haller, in *H.Z.*, CIII (1909), p. 44 f.; *Collecta per D. Sancti Syxti super petitione D. Regis Franciae ut aliud tertium concilium universale celebretur*, in Vat. lat. 4039, fols. 13ʳ-16ᵛ.

[2] Walch, *Monimenta medii aevi*, VOL. I, pp. 103 ff.

[3] Ranke, *Deutsche Geschichte im Zeitalter der Reformation* (Berlin 1839 ff.), VOL. VI, pp. 13 ff.; *id.* VOL. I, p. 38; B. Gebhardt, *Gravamina*, p. 11.

[4] Gebhardt, *Gravamina*, pp. 142 ff.; cf. also pp. 15 ff.

[5] Werminghoff, *Nationalkirchliche Bestrebungen*, pp. 113 ff.; Hefele-Hergenröther, *Conziliengeschichte*, VOL. VIII, p. 90 f.

Cardinal Bessarion's appearance as legate in 1460 further intensified anti-Roman feeling. The papal taxes for the crusade and the annates, the Curia's policy in the bestowal of benefices, together with the other grievances, to which must be added Pius II's proceedings against Sigismund of Tirol and Diether von Isenburg, did much to strengthen the existing opposition. The great anti-papal union of princes which the Archbishop of Mainz succeeded in forming at Nuremberg in 1461 seemed at one moment to make of that union's conflict with the Curia a national concern. They complained that the decrees of Constance and Basle were being set aside and demanded a new General Council.[1] However, two able nuncios, Rudolf of Rüdesheim and Francis of Toledo, succeeded in exploding the princes' scheme and by the same stroke they also quashed the project for a Council. Actually the Council played but a very small part in the political schemes of the instigators and spokesmen of the anti-Roman movement of the time, Heimburg and Mayr. Gregory Heimburg, at that time the most bitter enemy of the Papacy on German soil, was in theory a strict upholder of the conciliar theory,[2] yet he did not advocate a conciliar solution. In his case especially the appeals to the Council by Sigismund of Tirol[3] and Diether von Isenburg,[4] which he had inspired, were only moves on the political chess-board, not the expression of a genuine desire for a Council. In the spring of 1461 Mayr went so far as to suggest to George Podiebrad that he should get the Pope to appoint him Regent of the Empire and commander of the army that was to fight the Turks. In the event of the Pope refusing he was to threaten him with a Council.[5]

---

[1] K. Menzel, *Diether von Isenburg* (Erlangen 1868), pp. 103-27; Gebhardt, *Gravamina*, p. 48.

[2] Confirmation in Heimburg's appeal against the brief of 18 October 1460, Goldast, *Monarchia*, VOL. II, pp. 1592-5; Freher-Struve, *Germ. rerum script.*, VOL. II, pp. 211 ff.; for German text, P. Joachimsohn, *G. Heimburg* (Bamberg 1891), pp. 197-204, but especially in the apologia against Teodoro de' Lelli, printed in Goldast, *Monarchia*, VOL. II, pp. 1604-23; Freher-Struve, *Germ. rerum script.*, VOL. II, pp. 228-55.

[3] Goldast, *Monarchia*, VOL. II, pp. 1587 ff. The appeal is dated 13 October 1460; on it, and on the earlier appeal of 14 July 1460, see A. Jäger, *Der Streit des Cardinals Nikolaus von Cusa mit dem Herzoge Sigmund von Österreich*, VOL. II (Innsbruck 1861), pp. 77 ff., 94 ff. Text of the appeal of 16 March in Goldast, *Monarchia*, VOL. II, pp. 1576 ff.; Freher-Struve, *Germ. rerum script.*, VOL. II, pp. 193 ff.

[4] Menzel, *Diether von Isenburg*, pp. 105 ff., 116 f.; text of first appeal in H. Ch. Senckenberg, *Selecta iuris et historiarum*, VOL. IV (Frankfurt 1738), pp. 392-9, with corrections in Menzel, p. 29 f. The text of the second appeal in Senckenberg, VOL. IV, pp. 369-80; cf. U. Paul, *Studien zur Geschichte des deutschen Nationalbewusstseins im Zeitalter des Humanismus und der Reformation* (Berlin 1936), p. 67.

[5] H. Markgraf, "Über Georgs von Podiebrad Projekt eines christlichen Fürstenbundes", in *H.Z.*, XXI (1869), pp. 245-304, particularly p. 263.

Thus was the Council degraded to a mere instrument of naked and unblushing extortion. It would have been strange if Podiebrad of Bohemia, the most active of all politicians of the Empire, had not taken advantage of a political chance arising out of the ideology of the period. At the beginning of December 1460, when he cherished hopes of becoming King of the Romans, Podiebrad entered into a pact with Diether von Isenburg which included a provision for a Council in some Rhineland city for the purpose of reiterating and executing the decrees of Basle.[1] As we have seen already, events took a different turn at the Diet of Nuremberg, and even more so later on. Two years later Podiebrad allied himself with the adventurer Antonio Marini. The latter's fantastic project for a league of the princes and peoples of Europe had not only an anti-papal bias (inasmuch as it aimed at thwarting Pius II's plan for a crusade)—it was also undoubtedly influenced by the conciliar theory and was conceived as a secular counterpart of the reform Councils. The league was to be directed by a committee presided over by one of the princes and its organisation was to be modelled on the conciliar "nations" of Constance. It was to meet at Basle in 1464, and at intervals of five years the seat of the executive was to be transferred to France or Italy, as the case might be. Marini's secular counter-council was a pure phantom; like a will-o'-the-wisp it fluttered about for a year until it vanished, like its creator, without leaving a trace.

Podiebrad took up his plan for a Council a second time in 1467.[2] In the meantime, he had been excommunicated and deposed by Paul II on the ground of heresy; however, a sentence of this kind, he argued, could only be pronounced by a General Council. He forgot that the teaching of Hus had been condemned at Constance. The new Council to which his affairs were to be submitted was to be organised according to nations, as at Constance. To Louis XI he represented it as an act of self-defence of the secular princes against the universal monarchy which was the Pope's aim. However, both arguments were in vain. The French King, who just then did not wish to be embroiled with the Curia, gave an evasive answer. Paul II upheld his sentence and Podiebrad was forced to have recourse to arms against the coalition

---

[1] For text see G. Freiherr von Hasselholdt-Stockheim, *Herzog Albrecht IV von Bayern* (Leipzig 1865), pp. 274-86; cf. Menzel, *Diether von Isenburg*, p. 88; Gebhardt, *Gravamina*, p. 41.

[2] J. Pazout, "Georg von Böhmen und die Konzilsfrage im Jahre 1467", in *Archiv für österreichische Geschichte*, XL (1867), pp. 323-71, especially pp. 364, 368.

formed against him. Soon afterwards death removed him from the scene of strife.

Apart from Podiebrad's final struggle for a Council, the ecclesiastical-political opposition in Germany presents substantially the same picture: the Council was on its lips but its heart was far from it. It affected solicitude for the authority of the decrees of Constance and Basle, especially for *Frequens*, but in reality the problems of the universal Church left it cold. In spite of the prohibition issued in the mean-time, it appealed to the Council, but only when it saw that its cause at the Curia was lost. When it spoke of a reform of the head, it meant, at best, only the removal of the *gravamina*. More often it aimed at purely personal advantages; about a reform of the members, which concerned everybody and would entail sacrifices, it chose to be silent. Even the ecclesiastical-national aspirations of the age lacked decision and steadi-ness; a miserly yet defiant selfishness dominated the thought both of society at large and of individual nations. Thus we can understand why the idea of a Council played only a modest role in the projects for imperial reform at the close of the fifteenth century.

Hans of Hermannsgrün refers to the Council in a memorial drawn up in the year 1494 in the literary dress of a dream. In this document he calls to account both the Pope and the French King for the wrong done by them to the Emperor.[1] Berthold von Henneberg, Archbishop of Mainz, and the very soul of a movement for a reform of the Empire, kept aloof from such vagaries. There is good reason to assume that he, as an upholder of "the old order", a zealous reformer within his ecclesiastical province and a man of inflexible integrity, conceived the reform of the Church in terms of the decrees of Constance and Basle and that he looked to the Council for the removal of the *gravamina*. We have no detailed information about the nature of the advice he gave to his friend Pius III when the latter was raised to the chair of St Peter. At any rate it does not appear that his ideas ever took concrete shape.[2] The same is true of those secular princes who were favourable to Church reform. In his funeral oration on Count Eberhard of Württemberg,

---

[1] H. Ulmann, "Der Traum des Hans von Hermannsgrün. Eine politische Denkschrift aus dem Jahre 1494", in *Forschungen zur deutschen Geschichte*, XX (1880), pp. 67-92, especially p. 87; Döllinger also gives the text, *Beiträge*, VOL. III, pp. 91-104.

[2] F. Hartung, "Berthold von Henneberg, Kurfürst von Mainz", in *H.Z.* CIII (1909), pp. 527-51; K. Bauermeister, "Berthold von Henneberg, Kurfürst und Erzbischof von Mainz", in *H.J.*, XXXIX (1918-19), pp. 731-40; E. Ziehen, *Mittelrhein und Reich im Zeitalter der Reichsreform*, VOL. I (Frankfurt 1934), pp. 166 ff., and *passim*. For the memorial to Pius III, see J. Schlecht, *Pius III und die deutsche Nation* (Kempten 1914), p. 19.

Konrad Summenhart relates that one of the dead man's most ardent wishes had been to live long enough to witness a great reform Council and the renewal of the Church in head and members.[1] Duke George of Saxony was convinced that the Council was the only remedy for the ailments of the Church; her history shows that at no time did she recover her health by mere human efforts, but solely with the help of God through the sacred Councils. To their neglect he ascribed the fact that at this time the face of the Bride of Christ was disfigured like the face of a corpse.[2]

These reflexions were embodied in the letter by which the zealous Duke accredited his representative, Nicholas von Schönberg, to the fifth Council of the Lateran. They might equally well have come from the pen of any one of the men who at that time promoted reform by their writings. They are characteristic of the ecclesiastical-political atmosphere of Germany, but for the time being they remained without effect. What applies to the princes is even more applicable to the contemporary head of the Empire.

The Emperor Maximilian I, whose soaring aspirations may well have been stimulated by the example of the Emperor Sigismund, toyed in various ways with a plan for a Council, but he gave it no more effective support than his father had done. The desire to forward simultaneously the war against the Turks and the reform of the Church may have induced him to sanction Charles VIII's Italian expedition.[3] Towards the end of 1500 he made overtures to Louis XII, Charles's successor, with a view to a Council for the good of Christendom and for a plan of campaign against the Turks.[4] They yielded no better results than the national-ecclesiastical views of his adviser, Matthew Lang, which proved to be the germ of the famous "consultation" addressed to Jakob Wimpfeling in 1510.[5] For a while Maximilian

[1] Haller, Anfänge der Universität Tübingen, VOL. II, p. 67.

[2] Credentials issued by Duke George to Nikolaus von Schönberg, 29 March 1513, Th. Kolde in Z.K.G., III (1879), pp. 604 ff.

[3] H. Ulmann, Kaiser Maximilian I, VOL. I (Stuttgart 1884), p. 270.

[4] Instructions of 11 December 1500 in V. von Kraus, Das Nürnberger Reichsregiment (Innsbruck 1883), pp. 200-05; the passage is on p. 204; further details of a plan for a Council are on pp. 206 ff. In point of fact in Rome they expected Maximilian's envoys with proposals of this kind as early as January 1499, at a time when Spain held out the threat of a Council, Sanudo, Diarii, VOL. II, p. 343.

[5] J. Knepper, Jakob Wimpfeling (Freiburg 1902), pp. 253 ff.; ibid. p. 365 f. (Spies's instructions dated 18 September 1510). On Lang's spiritual paternity of them, a circumstance to which P. Kalkoff was the first to draw attention in his Forschungen zu Luthers römischen Prozess (Rome 1905), p. 102 f., see Werminghoff, Nationalkirchliche Bestrebungen, pp. 121-32. Further documents based on the edition of 1520, in J. A. Riegger, Amoenitates literariae Friburgenses (Ulm 1715), pp. 479-515.

supported the Council of Pisa against Julius II, but he failed in his efforts to induce the German bishops to attend that gathering; he himself soon dropped the whole thing. His attitude towards the question of the Council was like his entire policy—desultory and unsteady—so that in his day also both Emperor and Empire failed to promote the cause of Council and reform. The great reform Council advocated by Vincent of Aggsbach and his sympathisers survived in the same way as Heimburg's heritage, the *gravamina*—in literature and in wishful dreams and aspirations. Practical results there were none. The writings of the Alsatian patriot Wimpfeling faithfully mirror the situation. He battles against the *gravamina* and on occasion speaks in sharp terms of the behaviour of the Roman "courtiers". He gleefully hails the fifth Council of the Lateran, from which he hopes for a return of Bohemia to the obedience of Peter, a great crusade for the reconquest of Constantinople, a comprehensive reform of the Church and a restoration of the majesty of the sacred Councils in which the whole Church is represented.[1] All this was fine and excellent, but it was only literature.

Conditions in the Western national states differed vastly from those prevailing in Germany. The Church in England had long enjoyed an extensive measure of independence of Rome. Here there was no need, for ecclesiastical-national reasons, to look for a reform Council. The Crown continued to maintain its customary good relations with the Popes, all the more willingly as at the time it was greatly preoccupied with domestic struggles.

The peoples of the Iberian peninsula were engaged in a holy war for their liberation from Moorish domination. Princes and clergy joined in the fight for what was both a national and an ecclesiastical aim. The intervention of the Kings of Aragon, Castile and Portugal in the affairs of the Church in their respective territories was already considerable in the later Middle Ages.[2] In 1467 the rebellious grandees of Castile appealed to a Council after the papal nuncio had excommunicated them,[3] but the appeal had no further consequences. As soon as the union of their territories was realised, the Catholic Kings began to develop royal patronage. In the Inquisition they forged an effective

---

[1] In addition to Werminghoff's observations referred to in the preceding note, see J. Knepper, *J. Wimpfeling*, pp. 67, 272 ff.
[2] J. Vincke, "Kirche und Staat in Spanien während des Spätmittelalters", in *R.Q.*, XLIII (1935), pp. 35-53, and his observations on Hashagen, relating for the most part to Spain, in *A.K.R.*, CXI (1931), pp. 685 ff.
[3] Raynald, *Annales, a.* 1467, No. 20.

instrument for their twofold power, while they favoured various reforms in the Church. But they were up in arms whenever papal provisions became inconvenient. Even the pious Isabella did not shrink from threatening Sixtus IV with a Council when instead of granting the See of Cuenca to her confessor, Alfonso of Burgos, the Pope bestowed it on his own nephew, Raffaele Riario, without previously sounding her.[1] Apart from this, the threat of a Council scarcely played any role at all in Spain's fifteenth-century ecclesiastical policy. It was only under Alexander VI that Ferdinand the Catholic sought to thwart the Pope's alliance with France, as well as the plans of Caesar Borgia, by accusing the Pope of simony and by threatening to call him to account before a Council.[2] It is obvious that Ferdinand merely exploited the enormous advantage which the Borgia Pope's conduct gave him. Viewed as a whole, Spanish policy, no less than Spanish theological speculation, kept off the idea of the Council.

France alone seemed destined to give practical significance to the idea of the Council, seeing that the doctrine of the Council's superiority over the Pope constituted a strong element in Gallicanism. In reality, however, there was no reason why the French clergy, by urging a new Council, should undermine the Pragmatic Sanction, which, as a matter of fact, had never been recognised by the Popes. The Sanction was law for Church and State and as long as the King upheld and observed it the clergy enjoyed a far-reaching administrative and financial autonomy. Only when he violated it, as happened very often, or when, in furtherance of his Italian policy, he even seemed prepared to yield to the Pope's pressure and to replace it by a concordat, was it to the advantage of ecclesiastical circles to stress the authority of the conciliar decrees embodied in the Sanction. Thus, in the year 1452, when the Pragmatic Sanction seemed in danger, Archbishop Jouvenel des Ursins of Rheims formulated the following question: "Is the King of France, and are the French bishops, entitled to alter or suppress the decrees of a General Council?" The answer was in the negative.[3] On the strength of this answer the Archbishop and, at his instigation, the Assembly of the clergy of Bourges demanded a new Council to be held on French territory.[4] After the attempt to attract the Papacy once more to France had proved a failure, the appeal to the Council served

[1] Pastor, VOL. II, p. 623; Eng. edn., VOL. III, p. 100.
[2] Sanudo, *Diarii*, VOL. II, p. 279; cf. p. 41, *n.* 1.
[3] Valois, *Sanction Pragmatique*, p. 208.
[4] *Ibid.*, pp. 226 ff.; also p. clxxxii of the introduction.

the French clergy chiefly as an emergency port to which one could turn for shelter whenever there was danger of the abolition of the Pragmatic Sanction. When at a later date, in the reign of Louis XI, the clergy claimed it once more as a right, it did so not on its own initiative but under pressure from the Crown.

In the same way, the French Crown's concern for a reform Council was not without certain reservations. Under the régime of Louis XI it increased its real power over the Church in France. Its aim, which was complete domination over the bishops and the disposal of Church property, was more likely to be attained by means of a concordat with the Pope than by a Council. Moreover, beyond an understanding of this kind there beckoned the prospect of a great gain for the King's foreign policy, namely the possibility of acquiring Naples. The abolition of the Pragmatic Sanction accordingly became a counter with which the King hoped to bargain with the Pope with a view to these great gains. But in the hands of Louis XI the demand for a Council became a common means of political pressure with the help of which the King sought to make the Pope amenable to his Italian policy. This was the lowest degradation as well as the most dangerous misuse of a basically sound idea and one that held the promise of much good.

Charles VII in his day had been an adept in wielding the threat of a Council,[1] but it was Louis XI who became a past master in the use of the new weapon. For him, in the words of a French historian, the Council was the bugbear with which the Popes could be threatened whenever he wished to extort some concession from them.[2] In the hope of making Pius II subservient to his Italian policy he abolished the Pragmatic Sanction,[3] but when he realised that he had made a miscalculation he threatened the Pope with a Council. In the meantime he furthered the anti-papal project of the adventurer Marini mentioned above.[4] A few years later the King told the Milanese envoys that he would force a Council on Paul II, so that the Pope "would rue his

---

[1] In the spring of 1453 Charles VII sounded Ladislaus of Hungary on the subject of a Council; Piccolomini to Nicholas V, 10 April 1453, *Correspondence*, ed. Wolkan, VOL. III, pp. 132, 134 f.; K. Pleyer, *Die Politik Nikolaus' V* (Stuttgart 1927), p. 16.

[2] J. Combet, *Louis XI et le Saint Siège* (Paris 1903), p. 69.

[3] The impact of the French Kings' Neapolitan policy on their attitude to the Curia has been described by Haller and his followers in a number of publications, e.g. Ch. Lucius, *Pius II und Ludwig XI von Frankreich* (Heidelberg 1913), pp. 75 ff. Pius II's fears of Louis XI's intrigues in connexion with the Council are mentioned in Carretto's report of 12 March 1462, L. Pastor, *Ungedr. Akten*, VOL. I, pp. 154 ff.

[4] Report of the Milanese envoy Malletta, dated 26 May 1464, Pastor, *Ungedr. Akten*, VOL. I, pp. 291 ff.; cf. p. 285.

having created so many difficulties for me".[1] For the time being this remained but a vague threat; it assumed a definite shape in the winter of 1469-70. By that time the King had thrown his former favourite Cardinal Balue into gaol. He was also incensed by Paul II's leaning towards the league between Burgundy and Venice, which was hostile to him. Guillaume Fichet, the Rector of the University of Paris, was accordingly commissioned to secure the support of the Duke of Milan— and through him that of Florence and Naples—for an anti-papal Council.[2] England, Spain and the Emperor were also to be informed of the plan. Once again the whole thing was no more than a political manœuvre. Galeazzo Sforza made his adherence to the plan dependent on that of his allies, but these held aloof. Louis accordingly dropped the scheme.

In 1476 the King went a step further. With a view to deterring Sixtus IV from favouring Charles the Bold, he announced, on 8 January 1476, on the basis of the decree *Frequens*, the imminent convocation of a General Council at Lyons.[3] The agenda included the following items: The question of the Turks, the Schism (viz. the heresy of Hus), and the reform of the Church. The Dean of Lyons informed Rome of the demand for a Council.[4] At a full consistory, the Pope gave an evasive reply but Cardinal Orsini, as spokesman of the Sacred College, was more definite: "This was not the time for the most Christian King arbitrarily to press for a Council; his proper task was to fight the Turks!" Both Pope and Cardinal knew what they were to think of Louis's plan for a Council: it was no more than a threat. Louis himself dropped it a few months later when, with the assistance of Cardinal Giuliano della Rovere, who had come to Lyons, he had obtained from the Pope all the concessions he wanted. The threat of the Council

---

[1] Sforza de Bettinis to the Duke of Milan, 6 April 1469, *Lettres de Louis XI*, ed. J. Vaesen (Paris 1883), VOL. IV, p. 337.

[2] Louis XI to Galeazzo Sforza, 3 November 1469, *Lettres de Louis XI*, VOL. IV, pp. 46 ff. Moufflet, *Etudes sur une négociation diplomatique de Louis XI* (Marseilles 1884) assigns these events to the previous year, but P. Ghinzoni establishes the right date in his paper "Galeazzo Maria Sforza e Luigi XI", in *Arch. storico lombardo*, XII (1885), pp. 17-32; see Combet, *Louis XI*, pp. 78-91, for the whole subject.

[3] Pithou, *Preuves des libertés de l'Eglise Gallicane*, ed. Dupuy (Rouen 1639), VOL. II, pp. 1284 ff. In favour of such an action a claim is put forward that the Council of Constance had granted the French king the right to demand a Council at intervals of five years. Needless to say this is incorrect. For what follows see also P. Ourliac, "Le Concordat de 1472; Etude sur les rapports de Louis XI et de Sixte IV", in *Revue historique de droit français et étranger*, Série IV, XXI (1942), pp. 174-223; XXII (1943), pp. 117-54.

[4] Combet, *Louis XI*, pp. 145 ff.

vanished from the agenda of the discussions—but only for a short while. It raised its head again in 1478. The conspiracy of the Pazzi provided Louis XI with a pretext for renewed political action in Italy. In the summer of 1478 two envoys, Clermont and Vives, went to Rome to inform the Pope that a Council was about to meet in France. The Pope refused to receive them.[1] Meanwhile the King mobilised the Gallican clergy. At its assembly at Orleans, between 13 September and 19 October 1478, the clergy, for its part, demanded a Council on the basis of the decrees of Pisa, Constance and Basle.[2] It declared that the King's action was legitimate, since it was part of the duties of the King of France to bring about the meeting of a Council whenever the Pope failed to do so. A fresh royal embassy took the manifesto of the assembly with its demand for a Council, to Rome.[3] "Contrary to the decree *Frequens*," so we read in that document, "no Council has been held for a period of forty years." There follows a formal summons to the Pope to call a Council; it must meet in a safe and suitable place, and the Pope must appear at it either in person or through legates. The chief matters on the agenda of the assembly were to be the reform of the Church in head and members and the creation of a defensive league against the Turks. The envoys had been instructed to suggest Lyons once more as an appropriate locality for the conciliar assembly.[4]

This time it looked as if the King meant business. The envoys reached Rome at the end of 1479. The Pope remained firm. He told the messengers that he was sole judge whether or not a Council should be convoked, and in an affair of this kind not only the King of France,

---

[1] Raynald, *Annales, a.* 1478, No. 16 f.

[2] The royal letter of convocation in *Lettres de Louis XI*, VOL. VII, p. 146 f.; for the programme, see E. Frantz, *Sixtus IV und die Republik Florenz* (Regensburg 1880), p. 285; on the course of the Assembly, Combet, *Louis XI*, pp. 159 ff. In the circular letter (Combet, pp. 256-63) we read: "Regi Christianissimo iure hereditario post S. tem V. spectat et pertinet concilium generale convocari facere" (p. 261).

[3] The envoys' credentials, dated 20 November 1478, in Pithou, *Preuves des libertés de l'Eglise Gallicane*, VOL. I, pp. 512 ff. In the event of the Pope's rejection of their demand they were instructed to appeal to a better informed Pope and to the future Council. They were also told "eidem summo pontifici supplicandum quatenus insequendo decreta generalium conciliorum Pisani, Constantiensis et Basiliensis, quae inter alia decreverunt quod de decennio in decennium ad minus concilium generale in ecclesia sancta Dei celebraretur, nullumque fuerit quadraginta anni sunt effluxi celebratum concilium generale, dignetur mandare, convocari et teneri facere generale concilium universalis ecclesiae in aliquo loco tuto, decenti et convenienti, prout per dicta decreta ordinatum exstitit . . ." (p. 514).

[4] A. Desjardins, *Négociations diplomatiques de la France avec la Toscane*, VOL. I (Paris 1859), pp. 175-84. Further documents of the embassy in *Lettres de Louis XI*, VOL. VII, pp. 201 ff. There is a résumé in Latin in Raynald, *Annales, a.* 1478, Nos. 18 ff.; Combet, *Louis XI*, pp. 165 ff.

but the Emperor and the other Christian princes must also be heard. Not content with justifying his refusal, the Pope passed to the offensive, or, more accurately, to a counter-threat. He was not afraid of the Council, he declared, for he felt convinced that the bishops and clergy gathered in Council would stand by him in his dispute with Florence and defend the freedom of the Church which had been violated.[1]

Negotiations dragged on into the summer; but Sixtus IV gained sufficient time to enable him to make sure that the Emperor and the King of Spain were with him.[2] This time too, as the Milanese ambassador at the French court had foretold as early as December 1478,[3] Louis did not press his threat of a Council. Meanwhile the argument between the Pope and Florence was transferred to the field of battle. The final issue was the submission of the Medici.

The pernicious example of Louis XI was not lost on his successors. Charles VIII threatened Alexander VI with a Council in the event of his recognising Alfonso II as King of Naples,[4] and during the whole of his Italian expedition he kept the Damocles-sword of the Council hanging over the Pope's head.[5] In the manifesto addressed to the whole of Christendom from Florence, on 22 November 1494, he made an unmistakable allusion to such a possibility, and he managed to link it up most skilfully with the idea of a crusade.[6] These plans for a Council—if they can be so described at all—were given no more effect than those of Louis XI. It was reserved to Louis XII to take a step from which his predecessors had always shrunk in the end. The *conciliabulum* of Pisa, convened by the cardinals who opposed Julius II, was in the last instance a French political manœuvre: it was also

[1] The Pope's reply in Combet, *Louis XI*, pp. 280-5, but earlier and better in Raynald, *Annales, a.* 1478, Nos. 20-8; Frantz, *Sixtus IV und die Republik Florenz*, pp. 283 ff. Raphael da Volterra thus describes the effect (Raynald, *Annales, a.* 1478, No. 29): "Quapropter quem illi metu expugnare sperabant, ab eodem perterrefacti discesserunt".

[2] The instructions for the protonotary de Agnellis and the auditor de Grassis who were being despatched to the imperial court, in Combet, *Louis XI*, pp. 267-74. Those for the Spanish nuncio Boil (*ibid.*, pp. 275-80) stress the risk of an armed enterprise by France against Naples and contain an assurance that the Pope's allies had bound themselves to protect the pontiff from agression "in spiritualibus et temporalibus".

[3] Report of the agent Cagnola to the Duchess of Milan, 30 December 1478, Kervyn de Lettenhove, *Lettres et négociations de Philippe de Commines*, VOL. I (Brussels 1867), p. 283.

[4] Pastor, VOL. III, i, pp. 382 ff.; Eng. edn., VOL. V, pp. 423 ff.

[5] According to a report of the Florentine envoys Vespucci and Capponi, of 6 June 1494, from Lyons, Cardinal Giuliano della Rovere was the heart and soul of the project, Desjardins, *Négociations diplomatiques de la France avec la Toscane*, VOL. I, p. 399.

[6] Burchard of Strasbourg, ed. Celani, VOL. I, p. 542; ed. Thuasne, VOL. II, p. 198.

the last link of a long chain of conciliar plans and threats by the French Kings. We shall treat the subject more fully in the fifth chapter.

Since the policy of the Most Christian Kings had included a skilful and unscrupulous manipulation of the bogey of the Council, was it likely that the potentates of Italy, those experts in political craft, would let such a device escape them? Better than anyone else they knew how averse the Renaissance Popes were to a Council. At bottom they too shared this aversion. No one stood to gain more by the papal restoration than the Italians. The College of Cardinals and the Curia became increasingly italianised. The Italian clergy, its humanists and canonists, saw no reason why a Council should jeopardise the material benefits that offered themselves. In the long run the states of the peninsula, Milan, Florence, Naples, and even that great power, Venice, were far too dependent on co-operation with the Papacy and the States of the Church and far too concerned for the maintenance of what they had gained through their restoration, to compromise them of their own accord by fostering an agitation for a Council. If they temporarily allied themselves with the conciliar projects of others, they were exclusively guided by considerations of foreign policy dictated by the grouping of the nations, which changed from month to month, or they took advantage of the exceedingly questionable means of an appeal to a Council in order to strengthen their position in their ecclesiastical-political conflicts with the Popes. Thus Venice appealed to a future Council on two occasions: the first time on 3 March 1483—this appeal was repeated on 15 June 1483, and again on 1 May 1509.[1] The aim of both appeals was to render nugatory, even if only in appearance, the censures threatened or already pronounced by Sixtus IV and Julius II. On both occasions the Republic appealed to the decree *Frequens*, while at the same time taking good care not to take a single serious step in preparation for such an assembly.[2]

The same is true of the hotly controverted, purely fictitious synod of Florence of 1478, and its demand for a Council against Sixtus IV. This synod never took place at all. The probability is that we have to

[1] G. Dalla Santa, "Le appellazioni della Reppublica di Venezia dalle scommuniche di Giulio II", in *Nuovo Archivo Veneto*, XVII (1899), pp. 216-42; *id.* "Il vero testo dell'appellazione di Venezia dalla scommunica di Giulio II", *ibid.*, XIX (1900), pp. 349-61.

[2] The transmission of the appeal of 1509 to Cardinal Bakócz, patriarch of Constantinople, need not be regarded as a serious step in this direction, Sanudo, *Diarii*, VOL. VIII, pp. 170, 187.

deal with a pamphlet by Gentile Becchi, Bishop of Arezzo, which gives particulars of the conspiracy of the Pazzi, holds the Pope responsible for the assassination of Giuliano de' Medici and reviles him in the crudest terms. It ends in a rhetorical appeal to the Emperor, the King of France and the Christian princes and peoples to rid the Church of the present Pope by means of a Council. The pamphlet circulated in print, so as to counter the Pope's Bull of Excommunication, which was also in print, on equal terms from the point of view of publicity. The only remarkable thing is that this libel should have appeared dressed up as a synodal decision.[1]

It was one of Zamometič's many delusions that he imagined he could count on the support of the anti-papal league between Milan, Florence and Naples for his attempt to convene a Council at Basle in 1482, of which more will be said later.[2] Lorenzo the Magnificent and Giangaleazzo Sforza sent observers to Basle, but no envoys with full powers, and in particular no bishops. Bishop Gatto of Cefalù, whom King Ferrante intended to send to the Council, was not to be found at the moment when he should have set out, and the ship with its cargo of Neapolitan bishops bound for the Council, of which (not without a tinge of irony) the Florentine Ugolino held out a prospect, never raised anchor.

However, Ferrante took the question of the Council of Basle more seriously than his allies. This may have been due to the influence of Luca da Tozio, a Roman emigrant. A few years later he too did not hesitate to brandish that trusty weapon, the threat of a Council. In the course of his dispute with Innocent VIII, which originated in the King's refusal to pay certain taxes, he appealed to a future Council; on 11 September 1489 he insisted on its convocation. His son-in-law, Matthias Corvinus, seconded him in this action.[3] The Pope, completely isolated and intimidated as he was, took the threat so seriously that he had a memorial drawn up by the canonist Felinus Sandaeus which

---

[1] Text in A. Fabroni, *Laurentii Medicis Magnifici vita*, VOL. II (Pisa 1784), p. 164 f. The original printed edition which Morelli, librarian of St Mark, saw in 1771, consisted of ten small folio sheets. Frantz's arguments (*Sixtus IV und die Republik Florenz*, pp. 237 ff.) for the historicity of the synod do not carry conviction.

[2] A. Stoecklin, *Der Basler Konzilsversuch des Andrea Zamometič* (Basle 1938), pp. 29 ff., 62-78. Of this more will be said in Ch. V.

[3] Infessura (*Diario della città di Roma*, ed. Tommasini, 1892, p. 250) merely says: "Appellavit ad concilium futurum et petiit dari sibi iudices"; for details see Pastor, VOL. II, i, pp. 227, 240, 248; Eng. edn., VOL. V, pp. 254, 269, 278. Alfonso I had actually appealed to the Council in 1457 when Calixtus III refused to bestow a canonry on one of his nephews (probably on account of illegitimacy), Pastor, VOL. I, p. 858.

demonstrated the illegality of Ferrante's demand and urged the Pope not to yield.[1] Ferrante's demand also had no sequel.

The appeals of the Italian powers to the Council, or their threats of such an assembly, complete the picture we have attempted to draw of the survival of the idea of the Council in the era of the papal restoration. Two things stand out prominently in this picture. The first is that the strict conciliar theory was visibly losing ground though it had not yet vanished altogether. It was officially recognised at the University of Paris, and occasionally found defenders elsewhere too. However, it is not here that we must look for the strength of the idea, but rather in the combination of the demand for a Council with the actual need of reform which was no less keenly felt by the solitaries of the Charter-houses than by the ecclesiastical-political advisers of Ferdinand the Catholic. The struggle was not about *Sacrosancta* but about *Frequens*: in other words, the great concern was not so much the question of the supremacy of the Council as the holding of a Council there and then. The pontificate of Sixtus IV and above all that of Alexander VI, added strength to the general conviction that a Council was indispensable if order was to be restored in the Church. On this point there was agreement between the advocates of the conciliar theory such as Gozzadini, and the faithful adherents of the Papacy like Giustiniani and Quirini. In the second place it was fatal for the idea of the Council when it was dragged into the politics of the day and when the threat of such an assembly came to be used as a means of bringing pressure to bear on the Popes. Such an abuse was bound to intensify their aversion for a new Council. This reaction of the Popes now demands our attention.

---

[1] Vat. lat. 5607, fols. 116ʳ-122ʳ. *Conclusio* 6 runs thus "Nullus potest monere papam ut congreget concilium". The reply drawn up at the time by Felinus is in Baluze-Mansi, *Miscellanea*, VOL. I, pp. 518 ff.

CHAPTER III

The Papal Reaction

THE political misuse of the idea of a Council gives us the measure of its strength, but even more of the aversion and the actual fear which it inspired in the Curia. For the Popes of the restoration period the convocation of a Council was a matter for grave and justifiable misgivings. They had good reason to fear that if a Council were convened, the long-standing and as yet undecided question of authority would come to life once more. There was also the possibility of the assembly becoming a handy tool for powerful princes, or a battleground for circles hostile to the Curia. Thus the spectre of a fresh conflict between Pope and Council, perhaps even that of a schism, could be seen rising on the horizon. Martin V, in his time, had been put on his guard against the Council, but he had thought that there was no escaping it. "Who knows", the Cardinal of Saluzzo wrote at that time, "whether the opportunity of deposing the Pope will not be seized, seeing that there are those who regard it as certain that he is only the administrator of the Church, not her master?"[1] The fears of the Cardinal were well founded, and after the termination of the Schism of Basle his misgivings received further confirmation. A Council was a dangerous venture both for the Popes and for the peace and the unity of the Church, and it was questionable whether the hoped-for benefits would balance the dangers there was reason to fear. The adherents of the idea of a Council demanded such an assembly with a view to the reform of the Church, the war against the Turks and the suppression of heresy. But all these problems, it was pointed out in Rome, could be solved by the Pope alone, and that much better than by a Council, for the Pope is the judge appointed by Jesus Christ in matters of faith. If the need arises he may call for the assistance of the secular arm against heretics. In virtue of his supreme authority it is for him to establish peace between Christian princes and to organise a joint crusade against the Turks, whereas a Council, from its very nature, is not able to initiate a political

---

[1] *Conc. Bas.*, VOL. I, p. 245 f.; see p. 117 f. In this, and in the next chapter, I comply with the wish expressed by R. Scholtz (in *Z.Sav.R.G.K.A.*, XXIII (1934), p. 419) that I should "outline the papal reactionary movement and the new attempts at reform, up to the Council of Trent".

and military undertaking of such dimensions. As for Church reform, the need for which no one denies, the Pope is able to carry it out as well as a Council since he alone is in a position to reconcile the often divergent aspirations of the various nations and of particular ecclesiastical groups, such as bishops, religious orders, universities and cathedral chapters.

These were some of the considerations by which the Popes of the restoration justified their negative attitude to the idea of the Council. To them were added personal motives which varied with each pontiff. Together these factors inspired their political tactics.

At his accession Nicholas V had confirmed Eugenius IV's Bull of 5 February 1447. This Bull, which was connected with the concordats with the princes, contained a promise that the Pope would do everything in his power to persuade the princes to send their deputies to a Council to be held on German soil, either at Constance, Strasbourg, Mainz, Worms or Trier. The Council was to be called within a period of eighteen months.[1] This promise was not expressly repeated in the Concordat of Vienna; its validity was taken for granted.[2] A further promise, which Nicholas V was alleged to have made in presence of the French envoy in the course of the discussions for the ending of the Schism, to the effect that he would convene a Council in some French town, lacks documentary confirmation.[3] When, therefore, Charles VII's envoys in the jubilee year 1450 demanded that a Council be convened at Toulouse, while Aeneas Silvius Piccolomini at the Emperor's bidding insisted on the choice of a German town,[4] it was not difficult for the Pope, in view of the contradictory demands in

[1] The Bull of 5 February 1447 in Mercati, *Raccolta*, p. 168; earlier publications of it: Raynald, *Annales*, a. 1447, No. 5; Koch, *Sanctio pragmatica Germanorum* (Strasbourg 1789), pp. 181 ff. For what follows see Pastor, VOL. I, pp. 403, 460; Eng. edn., VOL. II, pp. 38, 105.

[2] The proof is in the oft-repeated allusion to the "concilium futurum", especially the clause that all Eugenius's concessions to the Germans should remain in force "usque ad tempus futuri generalis concilii". Mercati, *Raccolta*, p. 180.

[3] Valois, *Le Pape*, VOL. II, p. 361. The events of the year 1450 show that the condition mentioned by Piccolomini (*Orationes politicae et ecclesiasticae*, VOL. I, p. 233) was actually laid down.

[4] Freher-Struve, *Germ. rerum script.*, VOL. II, i, pp. 34-8; *Aeneae Silvii Picc. Orationes politicae et ecclesiasticae*, VOL. I, pp. 140-9 (see above, p. 46, *n*. 1). With Voigt, *Enea Silvio Piccolomini*, VOL. II, pp. 19 ff., I am of opinion that this address (not the one that follows in the edition) was actually delivered in agreement with the Pope, and with the purpose of countering the French demand for a Council. Piccolomini's commentaries hint at this when they say: "Concilium quod Galli petebant, dissuasit", *Commentarii rerum memorabilium* (Frankfurt 1614), p. 17. But there is no proof that he acted on his own authority.

respect of the venue of the Council, to adopt a dilatory attitude to the whole question. This policy was the easier as everybody was weary of strife and longed for peace.

However, the policy of delay pursued by Nicholas V, and that of ignoring the general demand to which his successor Calixtus III resorted, could not yield a final solution. Weariness of the subject did not last. Old necessities and new events continued to whip up the demand for a Council. If Rome was unresponsive, some other means must be devised.

To counter the conciliar theory as such a very simple means was ready to hand, namely the abrogation of the decree *Sacrosancta* and its reiteration at Basle, or a declaration that it was not universally binding. Simple as this radical solution appeared, it was open to serious objections. For one thing, it would have encountered sharp opposition in France and would have conjured up the danger of a fresh schism. Moreover, the deposition of the three Popes of the Schism and the validity of the election of Martin V—hence also the legitimacy of his successors—rested on the authority of the Council of Constance. Another road must be found. The Piccolomini Pope was the first to tread it.

Pius II was acquainted with the conciliar theory; in fact he had been an adherent of it and had supported Basle against Eugenius IV. During his prolonged stay north of the Alps he had been in a position to become acquainted with the danger of the theory as well as with the weakness of its partisans. He seceded from the party and formally renounced it in his letter of retractation addressed to the Rector of the University of Cologne, and on becoming Pope he did so in the famous Bull of Retractation.[1] These retractations only concerned his own person, but the Congress of Mantua enabled him to take official action against the theory. Constantinople had fallen on 29 May 1453. To conjure the peril, the full gravity of which was evident to everyone, it was not enough to grant an indulgence to all who joined in a crusade—a league of Christian nations was imperative.[2] Two centuries earlier a Council would have been considered the proper place for bringing such a league

---

[1] The "Epistula retractationis" of 13 August 1447, last printed in the *Epistolario*, ed. Wolkan, VOL. II, pp. 54-65; the Bull of Retractation *In minoribus* of 26 April 1463, in *Bull. Rom.*, VOL. V, pp. 172-80. Exactly one century after its appearance and while Trent was discussing the relations between papal and episcopal authority, a new edition was printed at Brescia. On the question of sources, see Th. Buyken, *Enea Silvio Piccolomini, sein Leben und Werden bis zum Episkopat* (Bonn 1931).

[2] Raynald, *Annales, a.* 1453, Nos. 9-11.

to birth and for organising the financial and military mobilisation for a great crusade. The Popes of the restoration eschewed such means.

In the autumn of the same year Nicholas V summoned a congress of the Italian powers to Rome for the purpose of pacifying at least the peninsula, but at first his appeal fell on deaf ears. It was only in 1455 that an Italian league of peace came into being.[1] However, its structure was not harmonious and firm enough to enable it to initiate an undertaking of such magnitude as a crusade: the co-operation of the great powers was indispensable. Full of his plan for a new crusade, Pius II convoked the powers to a congress at Mantua.[2] As head of Christendom he wished to plan and to act with its political leaders; ecclesiastical opposition was to be eliminated.

In his various pronouncements the Pope carefully avoided describing the congress as a Council, though not a few of its features recalled a medieval Council; at any rate some of the methods of procedure were certainly borrowed from those assemblies. The solemn opening with the Mass of the Holy Ghost on 26 September 1459, as well as the concluding function on 14 January 1460, took place in the Cathedral. During the congress the Pope would have no plenary session; he negotiated separately with the princes and the envoys, dividing them according to nationality, as Martin V had done at Constance. At the audience of the French envoys he condemned the conciliar theory in sharp terms.

These wearisome negotiations yielded but meagre results. Venice and France adopted a frankly negative attitude, while that of most of the others was non-committal. The Pope, however, went on with his plan. To raise the necessary funds for the crusade he imposed a tax of a tenth on the income of the clergy and of a thirtieth on that of the laity.[3] According to Gallican teaching, an impost of this kind required the assent of those who were hit by it. This assent was lacking. It was for this reason that several ecclesiastical bodies in France had protested against the crusade-tenth imposed by Calixtus III and had

---

[1] Besides Pastor VOL. I, pp. 634 f. (Eng. edn., VOL. II, p. 299), see Pleyer, *Politik Nikolaus' V*, pp. 76 ff.; G. Nebbia, "La lega italica del 1455, sue vicende e sua rinovazione nel 1470", in *Arch. storico lombardo*, NS IV (1939), pp. 115-35.

[2] Acts in Mansi, VOL. XXXII, pp. 203 ff.; VOL. XXXV, pp. 105 ff.; cf. Pastor, VOL. II, pp. 49-81 (Eng. edn., VOL. III, p. 59), *id., Ungedr. Akten*, VOL. I, pp. 102-19. A. Silvestri, "Gli ultimi anni di Pio II", in *Atti e Memorie della Soc. Tiburtina di storia e d'arte*, XX, XXI (1940), pp. 88-246, produces nothing new for my purpose.

[3] The Bull of 14 January 1460, on the thirtieth in Italy, in Raynald, *Annales*, *a.* 1460, Nos. 7-9; the others, not as yet printed, are noted by Pastor, VOL. II, p. 78, n. 3 (Eng. edn., VOL. III, p. 243, *n.*5).

appealed to a future Council.[1] If the new tenth was to yield the desired revenue it was necessary to cut away the legal basis of the protests and the appeals that were to be expected. Moreover, certain incidents of the last few years had shown what a trusty tool the appeal to a Council could be in the hands of people who were anxious to evade papal censures and judgments.[2]

The Pope was resolved to eliminate this "deadly poison" from the Church's organism. On 18 January 1460, four days after the conclusion of the congress, he accordingly struck the great blow which was likewise meant, at least indirectly, to inflict a mortal wound on the conciliar theory.[3] By a decree published in consistory he forbade any future appeal from the Pope to a Council and declared such an act null and void in law. Offenders were threatened with excommunication reserved to the Pope, as abettors of heresy while corporations and localities were threatened with interdict. The decree was published, with obvious haste, on the following day, the day on which the Curia took its departure from Mantua, but the corresponding Bull (*Execrabilis*) was only completed and registered at a later date. With the Bull *Execrabilis* the restoration Papacy dealt the conciliar theory its first heavy blow. The result did not come up to expectations. In France and Germany it met with vigorous opposition and outside Rome it was

---

[1] The appeal of the University of Paris and the clergy of the ecclesiastical province of Rouen, in Raynald, *Annales*, a. 1457, No. 56 f., was condemned by Calixtus III on 28 June 1457; see Pastor, *Ungedr. Akten*, VOL. I, pp. 66 ff.; Card. Rolin, Bishop of Autun, *ibid.*, *n*.58. I cannot find the appeal of the University of Toulouse at the place in Raynald., *Annales*—x, 121 (=*a*. 1457, No. 56 f.)—to which Valois refers, *Sanction Pragmatique*, p. clxxxv. As regards the appeal of the Chapter of Verona mentioned by Pastor, VOL. I, p. 756, *n*.3 (not found in Eng. edn.), I am not sure whether it was to the Council; the brief of 13 April 1457 to the Spanish collector, Vat. Arch., Arm. 39, t. 7, fol. 86ᵛ, only speaks of an "Appellatio frivola a capitulo Gerundensi interposita".

[2] Thus in 1456 the Province of Turonia of the Franciscans-Observant appealed against a Bull of Calixtus III which subjected them to the Conventuals, on the ground that the decree issued by the Council of Constance for the protection of the Observants could not be abolished by the Pope, "Chronica Fr. Nicolai Glassberger", in *Analecta Franciscana*, II (1887), pp. 358-63.

[3] This state of affairs was clarified by G. Picotti, "La publicazione e i primi effetti della 'Execrabilis' di Pio II", in *Arch. della Soc. Romana di storia patria*, XXXVII (1914), pp. 5-56. Sixtus IV indeed, in the Bull *Qui monitis*, leaves publication to the Congress of Mantua. Sánchez de Arevalo asserts that it had been accepted by a number of envoys and prelates ("per plurimorum regum et principum aliorumque populorum et provinciarum legatos atque praelatos laudatum et receptum est", Barb. lat. 1487, fol. 79ᵛ). Both statements are unproven, as is the alleged promise of the Italian princes not to appeal to a Council. To this promise Innocent VIII appealed in 1487, against Ferrante of Naples, if the report of the envoy of Ferrara is correct; see A. Cappelli, "Lettere di Lorenzo de' Medici", in *Atti e memorie modenesi e parmensi*, I (1864), p. 296.

not generally accepted. In spite of repeated prohibitions of appeals to a Council by Pius II in the Bull *Infructuosos palmites* of 2 November 1460,[1] by Sixtus IV in the Bull *Qui monitis* of 15 July 1483,[2] and by Julius II in the Bull *Suscepti regiminis* of 1 July 1509,[3] secular princes as well as ecclesiastical bodies continued to use an appeal as a legitimate legal device.[4] How is this fact, so perplexing for modern Catholics, to be accounted for?

The arguments by which the appellants were wont to justify their action may be gathered from the above-mentioned work of the canonist Gozzadini.[5] Gozzadini contests the validity and the binding force of the prohibition on the ground that it deprives the accused of a right which rests on natural law. The Bulls of Pius II and Julius II—he is apparently unacquainted with that of Sixtus IV—were without force in law. If it was objected that the appeal was addressed to a tribunal which did not in fact exist, the answer was that the authority of the Church, which is greater than that of the Pope, endures even if no Council is actually sitting. Moreover, the decree *Frequens* provides for a Council every ten years and thereby creates, at stated intervals, a representation of the Church to which appeal can be made. If until now the Popes have not executed the decree *Frequens*, the blame is

---

[1] Text in Picotti (see previous note), pp. 50-6, against Sigismund of Tirol; see Jäger, *Der Streit des Card. Nikolaus von Cusa*, VOL. II, pp. 146 ff.

[2] Raynald, *Annales, a.* 1483, Nos. 18 ff.; J. Ch. Lünig, *Cod. Italiae dipl.*, VOL. IV (Frankfurt 1736), pp. 1819-24, directed against Venice.

[3] *Bull. Rom.*, VOL. V, pp. 479-81; for the original, Picotti, p. 49, *n.*1, also directed against Venice.

[4] Picotti's list (pp. 33 ff.) of appeals to the Council after, and in spite of *Execrabilis*, may be greatly lengthened. As already stated, the Castilian grandees appealed in 1467, Raynald, *Annales, a.* 1467, No. 20; the University of Paris on 23 September 1491, Bulaeus, *Historia universitatis Paris.*, VOL. V, pp. 795-804, and again on 18 December 1500. A. Renaudet, *Préréforme et Humanisme à Paris* (Paris 1916), pp. 398 ff.; Giovanni Bentivoglio 1506, Sigismondo de' Conti, *Le Storie de' suoi tempi*, edd. Zanelli and Calabro (Rome 1883), VOL. II, p. 350. As a matter of fact, Picotti does not adequately distinguish between the appeal to the Council as a legal procedure and the demand for a Council and its convocation. Although Sixtus IV did not base himself on *Execrabilis* in dealing with Zamometič, his silence was no proof that he was unacquainted with the Bull, for Zamometič had not appealed to the Council. *Execrabilis* did not hit the appeal to a better-informed Pope such as that which was at least discussed by the provincial council of Mainz in 1487 (L. A. Veit in *H.J.*, XXXI (1910), pp. 524, 536), and which the Chapter of Constance actually lodged against the provision of Dietrich von Freiberg. Göller nevertheless observes that in the two legal memorials published at the time "there breathes the atmosphere of the Council of Basle": *Freiburger Diözesenarchiv*, VOL. LII (1924), p. 20; *Reg. episcopatus Constant.*, Nos. 14239, 14361. It was against this kind of appeal that Sánchez de Arevalo wrote his *Tractatus de appellatione a sententia Romani pontificis non informati ad seipsum bene informandum*, Barb. lat. 1487, fols. 79ʳ-88ᵛ; also Vat. lat. 4167, fols. 177 ff.

[5] Proofs in *R.Q.*, XLVII (1939), pp. 222 ff.

theirs but the right remains unaltered. Gozzadini describes the Council's superiority over the Pope as an article of faith—as if there had been no Council of Florence, no Bull *Execrabilis*, no papal restoration.

Matthias Ugonius, a contemporary of Gozzadini, speaks at first very cautiously of the Bull *Execrabilis*. It may be urged against it that it had never been accepted by the faithful and was therefore invalid. But his conclusion leaves us in no doubt that he shared Gozzadini's views. He writes: "Pius II's Bull is no obstacle to an appeal to a Council, since it is at variance with natural law." [1]

We need not stop to show the untenability of these arguments: they dash themselves in vain against the rock of the papal supremacy by divine right. There is one thing, however, which these facts and discussions make quite clear, namely that a good deal of confusion about the conception of Church, Council and Papacy still prevailed. The Popes had to reckon with this fact as often as they were faced with a demand for a Council, hence they would urge the difficulties that stood in the way, take evasive action or make counter-proposals for which Pius II had actually left directions. The Congress of Mantua was the prototype of a whole series of plans and proposals which dragged through the remaining years of the fifteenth century.

In the preceding chapter reference was made to the fact that on the occasion of Frederick III's second visit to Rome the Emperor had submitted a plan for an œcumenical congress to be held at Constance for the purpose of a general peace and a crusade against the Turks. Although he entertained no high expectations from such a meeting the Pope ended by suggesting a congress of princes to be held not at Constance but in Rome. [2] Three months before his death he discussed very fully with Duke Borso of Ferrara a plan for a diet in the city of that name. "It is better", the Pope's nephew, Cardinal Zeno, said to Francesco Gonzaga, "that we should forestall our opponents and that the meeting should be held in a place of our own choice in Italy, rather

---

[1] M. Ugonius, *De conciliis*, fols. 42ʳ-45ᵛ: "Merito . . . concludendum et dicendum videtur secundum Panormitanum ubi supra, quod quocumque casu papa contra justitiam divinam et naturalem aliquem de facto vel aliter indebite gravat, ad concilium, sive congregatum sive non, intrepide appellari, querelari, reclamari denunciarique poterit, dicta Pii II constitutione non obstante" (fol. 45ʳ).

[2] Ammanati's report in the *Commentarii*, BK VII, in the Frankfurt edition of Pius II's *Commentarii*, pp. 440 ff.; in part also in Raynald, *Annales, a.* 1468, Nos. 46 ff.; see above, p. 46, *n.* 2.

than have one forced upon us elsewhere." [1] At the beginning of his pontificate Sixtus IV, Paul II's successor, thought of holding a princes' congress at the Lateran, at Mantua or at Ancona.[2] He took up the plan once more in 1479, at the time of the French agitation for a Council,[3] but it was only given effect when, after the fall of Otranto, the Turkish peril became acute in Italy. An ambassadors' conference in Rome, from March until May 1481, agreed on the imposition of a tenth for the Turkish war but failed to draw up a programme for joint action because the death of Mohammed II, news of which reached Rome on 5 May, removed the most pressing anxiety while at the same time it lessened the conference's enthusiasm for the crusade.[4] The ambassadors' conference convened in Rome by Innocent VIII in 1490 started from a plan to use the pretender to the Turkish throne, Djem, who had fallen into the Pope's power, for a great enterprise against the Ottomans. However, the grandiose three years' programme drawn up by the ambassadors turned out to be little more than a literary exercise, for none of them was empowered to enter into a binding agreement.[5] The failure of the princes' convention summoned by Alexander VI for 1 March 1500 in Rome [6] finally demonstrated the fact that these papal crusade-congresses—held, or planned to be held, at intervals of about ten years—were as unlikely to yield concrete results as were the

[1] Pastor, VOL. II, pp. 775 f.; Eng. edn., VOL. IV, p. 188: this report of Cardinal Gonzaga clearly shows the current confusion between plans for a Council and plans for a congress.

[2] Platina, *Liber de vita Christi ac omnium pontificum*, ed. Gaida (Città di Castella 1913), p. 404; Raynald, *Annales, a.* 1471, No. 76, speaks of a "concilium" though we learn from the envoy's letters (Pastor, VOL. II, p. 466; Eng. edn., VOL. IV, p. 217) that there was only question of a congress. For a locality Cardinal Orsini proposed Florence; others suggested Pisa, Pavia or Piacenza, while the Emperor proposed Udine. From the instructions of Cardinal Marco Barbo of 20 May 1472 (*Mon. medii aevi res gestas Poloniae illustrantia*, Lemberg (Lvov) 1874-1902. VOL. II, p. 260) we gather that the plan for a general congress ("universalis diaeta") had not been entirely dropped even after the despatch of the crusade legates.

[3] The proposal is only known through Frederick's reply to the legate Auxias de Podio, J. Chmel, *Mon. Hapsburgica*, VOL. I, i (Vienna 1854), pp. 380-3; see Bachmann, *Reichsgeschichte*, VOL. II, p. 669.

[4] E. Piva, "L'opposizione diplomatica di Venezia alle mire di Sixto IV su Pesaro e ai tentativi di una crociata contro il Turco" in *Nuovo Arch. Veneto*, NS V (1903), pp. 49-101, 402-66; VI (1903), pp. 132-72, esp. pp. 139 ff.; Pastor, VOL. II, pp. 564 ff. (Eng. edn., VOL. III, pp. 320 ff.). The arrival of the English envoys is mentioned by Gherardi, *Diarium Romanum*, ed. Carusi (Città di Castella 1904), p. 46.

[5] Pastor, VOL. III, pp. 269 ff. (Eng. edn., VOL. V, pp. 304 ff.).

[6] Pastor, VOL. III, p. 549 f. (Eng. edn., VOL. VI, p. 88 f.). To the literature there quoted must be added the undated invitation to the Grand Duke of Lithuania, *Mon. Poloniae*, VOL. II, p. 266 f. I have not been able to consult A. Suryal Atiya, *The Crusade in the later Middle Ages* (London 1938).

crusade-Councils. The cause of the failure of all these measures lay much deeper. The very notion of a crusade was as good as dead. Rulers and peoples of the West no longer viewed the fight against the Turks as the joint concern of Christendom, but rather as a political and military problem for the countries immediately threatened, such as Hungary, Venice, Naples and the hereditary states of the Habsburgs. Help against the Turks was viewed as a political concession to those directly threatened, and in this transaction the Pope no longer figured as the head of Christendom but solely as one contracting party among others. This was one more proof of the fact that since the reform Councils the idea of the *Respublica christiana*—the Christian commonwealth, as conceived by the early Middle Ages, with the Papacy at its head—was no longer a working reality.

Another proposal with which Pius II and his successors repeatedly countered the requests for a Council also harked back to the mentality of the Middle Ages. This was the assembly of a Papal Council in Rome. The instigator of the idea was none other than Torquemada. Since the Council derives its authority from the Pope, he argues in his *Summa* (III, 16), he need not call the bishops of the whole world for the purpose of taking counsel with them on the affairs of the Church. It is enough if he summons suitable bishops from various provinces of the Church, or in case of necessity only from one. Rome is the appropriate place for a Papal Council of this kind, and its prototypes are the Roman Councils of antiquity under Cornelius, Sylvester, Celestine I, as well as the Lateran Councils of the Middle Ages. In Torquemada's opinion such Councils, composed in accordance with the Pope's judgment and convened in Rome, fulfil all the conditions of a General Council and enjoy the same authority.

The solution was startling in its simplicity. Should the Pope adopt it, he could at any time tell the advocates of a Council that he too wanted one, only he insisted that it should conform to the conditions of the ancient Roman Councils. In this way he escaped the odium of a blunt refusal. A Council of the kind Torquemada had in mind was quite harmless. Exclusively attended by bishops, to the exclusion of other members of the clergy, and convened in Rome, or even in Bologna, it precluded the preponderence of the numerically superior non-Italians, while politically it was in the hands of the Pope: another Basle was impossible.

Pius II was the first Pope to propose a Roman Council with a view to neutralising the agitation for a Council which broke out in France

and Germany after the Mantuan Congress.[1] However, he did not
pursue his plan as he had successfully disarmed his opponents by a
counter-proposal. At the Diet of Nuremberg his nuncio [2] announced
that the Pope was willing, in principle, to agree to a Council; he would
not, however, entrust the execution of the reform decrees to the bishops,
but to the secular princes. This was hitting the nail on the head! "Be
sure of this," Peter Knorr, the Elector of Brandenburg's envoy, wrote
to his master, "we clerics do not accept such a Council."

Pius II knew as well as his successors that the proposal to hold a
Papal Council in Rome, or in some city within the papal dominions,
would not satisfy anyone north of the Alps; that it was, in fact, no
more than an expedient to ward off the tiresome demands for a Council,
demands which, for the most part, were not even seriously meant.
When he was informed of France's appeal to a Council in 1468, Paul II
announced that he would summon a Council to Rome in the course of
the same year.[3] However, there was no uncertainty about the Pope's
real intention. Eugenius IV's nephew, who had fought by the Pope's
side against the Council of Basle, did not want a Council at all. Nothing
in Platina's impudent protest against the abolition of the College of
Abbreviators so roused the Pope's nephew as the threat of an agitation
with foreign princes for a Council. It was this point that Teodoro de'
Lelli particularly stressed in Platina's interrogation. It was taken up
again when the latter was put on the rack for his share in the conspiracy
of the Roman Academy.[4] Up to his last days Paul II lived in terror
lest the legitimacy of his election should be contested at the forthcoming
Diet of Ratisbon (*Christentag*). According to the report of Sigismondo
de' Conti,[5] who was certainly not hostile to him, it was due to Francesco
Piccolomini, his legate at Ratisbon, that the Pope finally shook off his
fears. At the beginning of 1470 Sánchez de Arevalo, a former champion

---

[1] In March 1461 Pius II announced in consistory that he intended to convene a
Council in Rome, Picotti (see above, p. 66, *n*. 3), p. 38; but the matter must have
been mentioned even before this date, for the proposal had already been declined in
Dauvet's protest of 10 November 1460, Valois, *Sanction Pragmatique*, p. clxxxviii.

[2] Peter Knorr's report, ed. K. Höfler in *Archiv für österreichische Geschichte*, XII
(1854), p. 351; Gebhardt, *Gravamina*, p. 50, proves that it does not date from 1451
but from 1461.

[3] Pastor, VOL. II, p. 373 (Eng. edn., VOL. IV, p. 103).

[4] Platina, *Liber de vita Christi ac omnium pontificum*, ed. Gaida, pp. 369 ff.;
Zabughin, *Pomponio Leto*, VOL. I (Rome 1909), pp. 84, 89, 306.

[5] Sigismondo de' Conti, *Storie*, VOL. II, pp. 291 ff. Ammanati, who was ill-
disposed towards Paul II, regards the early death of the Pope as a punishment for his
failure to keep the promise of an early convocation of a Council which he had made
in the election capitulation; Pius II, *Commentarii*, Ep. 421, p. 751.

of Eugenius IV and now a confidant of his nephew, published a thesis in which he sought to show that a Council was unnecessary and even harmful. "Away with Councils," he exclaims, "in these days they are nothing but a revolt against the monarchical principle of the Church and against her monarch, the Pope. All the problems submitted to a Council can be solved far more easily by the Pope than by a large assembly. If for any reason a Council is necessary, it must not be convened in France or Germany: Rome is the proper place for it, Rome, the home of all Christians." [1]

In the course of his discussions with Louis XI in 1476, Sixtus IV explained that from the first days of his pontificate he had cherished an ardent desire to hold a Council.[2] He repeated this declaration three years later, adding that to him, as a trained theologian, nothing seemed more desirable than a Council; and it would bring him renown. If he had not called one as yet, it was on account of political difficulties and the opposition of his advisers.[3] "Fair, sweet words," was the caustic comment of Arrivabene, the Mantuan agent. That they do not adequately represent the Rovere Pope's attitude to the question of the Council is evident from his threats against Louis XI and the Medici which accompanied a second pronouncement of his. In this statement the Pope reminded his opponents that the Council is an ecclesiastical assembly presided over by the Pope. Should a Council actually be convened, it would soon become apparent who it was who stood in need of reform: none other, in fact, than the French King, whose own conduct and methods of government were only too well known. If the case of Florence, that is the Medici's proceedings against Cardinal Riario, the Pope's nephew, and against the Archbishop of Pisa, were laid before the tribunal of the Council there could be no doubt that the assembly would make a stand for the independence of the Church which had been violated. The Pope's purpose was clear. Instead of allowing himself to be intimidated, he went over to the offensive and threatened a reform of the princes and action against those who violated the independence of the Church. The Pope's opponents knew very well that on such a topic he would get a sympathetic hearing from the members of a Council!

---

[1] *De septem quaestionibus*, art. 6, Vat. lib., Barb. lat. 1487, fol. 102ʳ; the basic explanation in *De remediis afflictae ecclesiae*, cons. 10 f., *ibid.*, fols. 120ᵛ-122ʳ.

[2] Arrivabene to the Margrave of Mantua, 2 May 1476; Combet, *Louis XI*, p. 255. For what follows see also Schlecht, *Zamometič*, pp. 75 ff., 104 ff.

[3] Combet, *Louis XI*, pp. 280-5; Raynald, *Annales*, a. 1478, Nos. 17-27; table of contents in Frantz, *Sixtus IV und die Republik Florenz*, pp. 86 ff.

Like his predecessors, Sixtus IV also was anxious not to have a Council forced upon him. He was afraid that it would seek to curtail the papal authority.[1] His nuncio, Luca de Tollentis, whom he despatched to Trier in 1473, knew what was in the Rovere Pope's mind. In a note which he forwarded together with his official report and which he meant to be destroyed, the nuncio sought to allay the pontiff's anxiety concerning a Council which the Emperor and Charles the Bold were said to be planning.[2] However, he did not succeed in removing the Pope's misgivings. When Cardinal Marco Barbo was about to leave for Germany the Pope insisted on his attending the Diet in order to prevent that assembly from broaching the question of a Council.[3] It was enough for the Venetian envoy merely to mention a Council at the time of the conflict with Florence to earn him a sharp rebuke. Faithful to the tactics which he adopted in other instances, Sixtus IV made an immediate counter-attack. Let the Venetians beware of a Council! With its help he would compel them to give up all the places of the States of the Church which they had unjustly appropriated.[4]

Fear of the spectre of a Council haunted the Rovere Pope during the whole of his pontificate. In the end he encountered it when Zamometič unfurled once more the banner of Basle.[5] Of this, the first

[1] Numerous proofs in the documents printed by Combet and in the Bull against Venice (see above, p. 67, *n.* 2). Significant for Sixtus IV's personal attitude to the idea of the Council are the marginal notes to the Acts of the Council of Constance in his own hand, in Vat. lat. 1335, to which Finke has drawn attention, *Acta conc. Const.*, VOL. II, p. 9 f. Thus fol. 1ᵛ (choice of Constance for the assembly of the Council): "Papa habet determinare locum et tempus et solus habet congregare concilium, imo petitur ab eo"; fol. 2ʳ (general invitation to co-operate with a view to a reform): "Bonum fuit, sed non deponere papam, quem solus Dominus habet judicare"; the gloss relating to the rules to be observed by the members of the Council shows how strongly he disapproved of the deposition of John XXIII, fol. 2ʳ: "Bonum, si fecissent, sed oppositum fecerunt, clamantes contra caput et omnes infamias adducentes, quae non fuerunt facta in conciliis sanctorum patrum."

[2] Appendix to the report of 13 October 1473 from Trier: S. Ljubič, *Dispacci di Luca de Tollentis, Vescovo di Sebenico, e di Lionello Chieregato, Vescovo di Trau, nunzi apostolici in Borgogna e nella Fiandre 1472-88* (Agram 1876), p. 45. The following passage also seems to refer to the Council: "Non est opus, Pater Sancte, capere labores. Instruxi Maguntinum et Treverensem. Res, spero, est in tuto."

[3] Chieregato to Card. Barbo after 24 February 1474, P. Paschini, *Leonello Chieregato* (Rome 1935), p. 36.

[4] Pandolfini to the Ten, 31 May 1479, B. Buser, *Die Beziehungen der Medizeer zu Frankreich 1434-94* (Leipzig 1879), p. 487.

[5] In his *Epistula contra quendam conciliistam* Henricus Institoris, the author of *The Witches' Hammer*, defended the Pope against the accusation that he was an enemy both of Council and reform. Thereupon the secretary of the pseudo-council, Peter Numagen, thrust at him the rhetorical question: "Is there a man who will not say that you are a cursed liar?" J. H. Hottinger, *Historia ecclesiastica Novi Testamenti*, VOL. IV (Zürich 1657), pp. 412 ff., 517.

serious attempt since the Council of Basle to convene another Council, we shall have more to say presently.

In his fight against the threat of a Council Sixtus IV operated from the first with the counter-proposal of a Papal Council at Rome or elsewhere. This was in perfect keeping with what he, a Franciscan and a theologian, conceived to be the essence of a Council. In his view it was like a meeting of a king's counsellors, who remain subject to their master in every respect and are bound to comply with his directions.[1] However, he only had recourse to the proposal for a Roman Council when he could think of no other means to arrest the demand for a General Council. Such a situation apparently arose during the crisis of 1476, when he explained his counter-plan to his confederates Matthias Corvinus, Ferrante of Naples and Charles the Bold. This was a Council to be held at the Lateran, or at Bologna, Ferrara, Mantua or, if need be, at Geneva, "for", he observed, "it is better for one to take action than to allow oneself to be forestalled by others".[2] In the course of the great conflict with France and Florence, 1478-9, the Pope instructed his nuncios with the Emperor to put out feelers, cautiously and without binding themselves, for the purpose of ascertaining what would be Frederick III's reaction to a Council at the Lateran.[3] This non-committal sounding, and above all the fact that the envoy who was being despatched to Spain at the same time was given no corresponding instructions,[4] sufficiently show that Sixtus IV was in no hurry to resort to a Council at the Lateran: the project was for him no more than a last means of escape from an impasse. Consequently, in the instructions for the cardinal-legate Auxias de Podio, who was despatched to the imperial court a little later, the Council had already become a congress of princes to be held at the Lateran. But even in this form the proposal was summarily rejected by the Emperor. "It is unlikely that a sizable number of princes would attend a meeting of this kind," he told the legate.[5]

It may be asked why Sixtus IV did not revert to his original proposal

---

[1] Autograph marginal note of the Pope to the Acts of the Council of Constance, Vat. lat. 1335, fol. 2ʳ: "Nota quod papa statuit et concilium approbat, imo papa est supra concilium, quemadmodum rex est super consilium suum, quod facta per regem approbat."

[2] Rausch, *Die burgundische Heirat Maximilians I*, VOL. I, pp. 146 ff.

[3] Instruction of 1 December 1478, Combet, *Louis XI*, pp. 267-74, the quotation is on p. 274.

[4] Instructions (undated) for Bernard Boil, Combet, *Louis XI*, pp. 275-80.

[5] See above, p. 69, *n.* 3. The Pope's second reply to the French envoys was worded accordingly; see Frantz, *Sixtus IV und die Republik Florenz*, p. 303.

of a Council at the Lateran at the time of Zamometič's attempt. The answer is obvious: there was no need for the Pope to play his last trump against that improvised undertaking. It collapsed before the active co-operation of some of the great powers and the participation of an appreciable number of bishops had had time to render it dangerous. The quixotic attempt was stifled by diplomatic counter-action.

Innocent VIII did not have to contend with any serious demand for a Council. The threats of Ferrante of Naples had no repercussions and remained mere episodes. The demand only revived under Alexander VI, not only because the election, the conduct and the government of the Borgia Pope provided a pretext, but because he did not even pretend to favour a Council. This explains why the first thing Sigismondo de' Conti hoped for from his successor, Pius III, was a Council, a Lateran Council.[1] The programme which the newly elected pontiff unfolded in consistory was in keeping with these expectations: it held out the prospect of a reform of the Curia, a Council, and war against the Turks.[2] The second Piccolomini Pope was undoubtedly animated by the best will in the world, but like Marcellus II fifty years later, he died before his plans had taken shape. It was the pressure of simultaneous attack from two quarters that wrested from the redoubtable Julius II the Council which his uncle, Sixtus IV, had always managed to avoid and with which he himself, while yet a cardinal, had threatened his opponent, Alexander VI. Demands and threats of a Council did not always come from outside; they arose in the Pope's own house. For this reason, before we turn our attention to the attempt of Pisa and the fifth Council of the Lateran, we must cast a glance at the tensions within the restored Papacy.

---

[1] Sigismondo de' Conti, *Storie*, VOL. II, p. 291.
[2] All three points are mentioned by Raphael da Volterra, Raynald, *Annales, a.* 1503, No. 15; they were also in the report of the Spanish envoy, Francisco de Royas, as appears from the reply of the Catholic King printed by R. Villa in *Buletín de la Real Academia de la Historia*, XXVIII (1896), p. 365 f. The Venetian envoy, Antonio Giustiniani, only speaks of reform and peace, *Dispacci*, ed. P. Villari (Florence 1876), VOL. II, p. 208. Pius III's lively interest in the question of the Council while he was as yet a cardinal may be gathered from the extract from Juan of Segovia, which Patrizzi prepared for him in 1480: Vat. lat. 4193, fols. 1-201; see *Conc. Bas.*, VOL. I, p. 18.

CHAPTER IV

Tensions within the Restored Papacy

UNIVERSITIES, reformers and politicians were not the only advocates of a Council with whom the restored Papacy had to contend. These three groups constituted as it were an external front, the pressure of which the Popes countered by forbidding appeals to a Council, by a policy of procrastination, by creating a diversion in the form of crusade-congresses, or by the offer of a Roman Council. However, they were simultaneously faced by an internal front that had taken shape in their own house. The College of Cardinals seized upon the demand for a Council and embodied it in the election capitulations by means of which it hoped to gain influence in the government of the Church and to counteract the absolutism of the Renaissance Popes. The demand for a Council thus became a weapon in the cardinals' silent but stubborn fight for the security of their position in the new distribution of power. The Popes could not afford to underestimate these attempts, all the more so as they found support in the teaching of some canonists both ancient and contemporary. Canonists had not as yet shaken themselves completely free of the conciliar theory, especially with respect to the question of the convocation of the Council; they granted that in certain circumstances this right devolved from the Pope on the cardinals.

A glance at the internal evolution of the College of Cardinals at this period opens yet another perspective. If, on the one hand, we would understand the attitude of the Popes to the question of Council and reform at the beginning of the break-up of religious unity, and to the difficulties with which they had to reckon, and if on the other hand we wish to appreciate the significance of the change for which Paul III paved the way by a reform of the Sacred College, it is imperative that we should be acquainted with the spirit which prevailed both in the College of Cardinals and among the officials of the Curia. Although the restoration had strengthened the Popes' authority, weal and woe of the Church did not lie exclusively in their hands; they were subject to the pressure of their entourage and a tradition several centuries old.

The College of Cardinals' struggle for power was older than the conciliar movement. The College owed its character of a closed corporation to its exclusive right to elect the Pope, of which it had been in undisputed possession ever since the publication of Alexander III's Bull *Licet de vitanda*. Moreover, thanks to the struggle between Papacy and Empire in the period of the Salians and the Hohenstaufen, as well as to the political activity of individual members as negotiators and legates, it had secured for itself an ever-increasing share in the government of the Church, a share, however, which rested mainly on the Popes' custom of discussing weighty decisions in consistory.[1] In this way the cardinalate rose by slow degrees above the episcopate and became the highest rank of the hierarchy. Of the utmost significance for the cardinals' autonomy was the act of Nicholas IV by which he assigned to them a considerable portion of the papal revenue.[2] The fact that Boniface VIII annulled several episcopal nominations of his predecessor on the ground that they had been made without previous consultation with the cardinals, while Clement V on his part annulled a constitution of Boniface VIII for the March of Ancona for the same reason, led the canonist John the Monk, a member of the College, to lay down in his commentary on the *Liber sextus* the principle that when weighty matters have to be decided the Pope is bound, by prescription, to take counsel with the cardinals in the same way as a bishop is obliged to consult his chapter: if he omits such consultation he acts illegally.[3] This opinion rests on the canonical conception of a corporation: "The Pope is the head of the Roman Church, the cardinals are its members; together they 'represent' the Apostolic See." Nor was he at a loss to discover Biblical justification for such a conception of the relationship between Pope and cardinals. In their day, John VIII and Innocent III

---

[1] For what follows, see J. B. Sägmüller, *Die Tätigkeit und Stellung der Kardinäle bis Papst Bonifaz VIII* (Freiburg 1896), pp. 170 ff., 215 ff.; also the observations of K. Wenck, in *Göttinger Gelehrten Anzeigen*, CLXII, II (1900), pp. 139-75; for the earlier period H. W. Klewitz, "Die Entstehung des Kardinalkollegiums", in *Z.Sav.R.G.K.A.*, XXV (1936), pp. 115-221. M. Souchon, *Die Papstwahlen von Bonifaz VIII bis Urban VI* (Braunschweig 1888); *id.*, *Die Papstwahlen in der Zeit des grossen Schismas*, 2 Vols. (Braunschweig 1892); J. Lulvès, "Die Machtbestrebungen des Kardinalats bis zur Aufstellung der ersten päpstlichen Wahlkapitulationen. Ein Beitrag zur Entwicklungsgeschichte des Kardinalats", in *Q.F.*, XII (1909), pp. 212-35; *id.*, "Die Machtbestrebungen des Kardinalkollegiums gegenüber dem Papsttum", in *M.Ö.I.G.*, XXXV (1914), pp. 445-83—up to the time of Martin V.

[2] The Bull *Coelestis altitudo* of 18 July 1289, *Bull. Rom.*, VOL. IV, pp. 88 ff., Potthast, *Regesta pontificum romanorum* (Berlin 1873-5), No. 23010; J. P. Kirsch, *Die Finanzverwaltung des Kardinalkollegiums im XIII. und XIV. Jahrhundert* (Münster 1895), pp. 5 ff.

[3] On cap. *Super eo*, in *Sexto de haeres*, v, ii, fol. 319ʳ, in the Venice edition of 1585. The *additiones* by Philip of Bourges there printed give a good survey of the pertinent literature.

had compared the cardinals to the seventy elders with whom Moses was wont to take counsel. It was at this time that the opponents of the Pope and, at a later date, the defenders of papal supremacy, such as Aegidius Romanus and Augustinus Triumphus, formulated the thesis: "The cardinals are the successors of the Apostles in the same way as the bishops. If the latter succeed them in the office of preaching, the former succeed them in the office of assistance, which, previous to its dispersion, the Apostolic College had tendered first to Christ and later to Peter." [1]

Aegidius was not out to argue in favour of a limitation of papal authority. In the sequel, the teaching of John the Monk also met with opposition on the part of John Andreae and other canonists. During the Avignon period, when most of the cardinals were Frenchmen, the Sacred College took good care not to put its authority to the test even though it could have looked to the French Kings for outside support such as it never commanded either before or since. The election capitulation of 1352 remained an isolated incident. It had been provoked by the extravagance and autocratic bearing of Clement VI. Everyone realised that the Sacred College could only maintain its position through and with the Pope. The Great Schism revealed the closeness of this common destiny. Born of the numerical superiority of cardinals hostile to Urban VI, it undermined the prestige of both. The Schism was not terminated by the assembly of Pisa organised by the cardinals, but by the Council of Constance convened at the instigation of the Emperor. Constance was a victory for the conciliar idea over the oligarchy of the cardinals.

At Constance it also became apparent that the conciliar theory in no way favoured the cardinals' struggle for an increase of power.[2] They were regarded there as the authors of the unhappy schism and as the men who benefited by the hateful abuses of the curial system. Although their number included such outstanding men as D'Ailly, Zabarella and Fillastre—all of them protagonists of the idea of the Council—they only gradually gained a decisive influence in the course of the negotiations together with the right to participate in the election of Martin V. They also succeeded in obtaining a delay of the reform of the Curia. The reform of the Sacred College, which was agreed upon

---

[1] Sägmüller, *Kardinäle*, pp. 211 ff.

[2] For pamphlets hostile to the cardinals, see H. Finke, *Forschungen und Quellen zur Geschichte des Konstanzer Konzils* (Paderborn 1889), pp. 86 ff.; Souchon, *Papstwahlen in der Zeit des grossen Schismas*, VOL. II, pp. 145-72.

in concert with the conciliar "nations", was in substantial conformity with the papal proposals.[1]

The reform fixed the number of cardinals at twenty-four; it made various stipulations in regard to their qualifications and their income; all nations were to be considered, but there was not the slightest reference to their co-operation in the government of the Church. The only time the Pope was to be bound to consult the College as such was before the creation of new cardinals. Constance wished to prevent papal absolutism and a new schism, not by means of the constitutional rights of the cardinals, but by the decrees *Sacrosancta* and *Frequens*.

It was left to the Council of Basle, in the course of its second conflict with Eugenius IV, to make the most of the opening it saw in the demand for constitutional rights previously made by the College of Cardinals. Basle went far beyond Constance, for in its twenty-third session it decreed that the Pope was bound to seek the advice of the Sacred College in certain specified cases; it also assigned to each of its three orders the right to supervise some specified department of the administration, and to all three together the right to admonish the Pope.[2] The purpose of the decree was to erect the Sacred College—international in its composition—into a constitutional corporation next to, or rather parallel with, the Council.

The defeat of Basle sealed the fate of the conciliar theory and that of the attempts described above. The latter too came to an end, though not completely, for they enjoyed a literary survival, under various disguises, until the day when the Sacred College itself used them as weapons in its fight against the absolutism of the Renaissance Popes and in furtherance of its own interests.

The literary movement began with D'Ailly's *De potestate ecclesiastica* written in 1416, during the Council of Constance.[3] In this work, D'Ailly developed the above-mentioned opinion of the divine right of

---

[1] The papal proposal in Hübler, *Constanzer Reformation*, pp. 128 ff.; also the reform tracts and the "Avisamenta" in *Acta Conc. Const.*, VOL. II, pp. 585 ff., 635 ff., 680; VOL. IV, pp. 559 ff.; today I should have to add a good deal to my observations on the various proposals and drafts for a reform of the cardinalate which I made in *R.Q.*, XLIII (1935), pp. 87-128.

[2] Mansi, VOL. XXIX, pp. 116 ff.; *Mon. conc. gen.*, VOL. II, pp. 852 ff.; Hefele, *Conciliengeschichte*, VOL. VII, pp. 631 ff.; for the antecedents, *Conc. Bas.*, VOL. I, pp. 196 ff., 207 f., 216 ff.; VOL. VIII, p. 111 f.; R. Zwölfer in *Basler Zeitschrift*, XXIX (1930), pp. 32 ff.

[3] Dupin, VOL. II, pp. 925-60; see Tschackert, *P. Ailly* (Gotha 1877), pp. 247-56, 354 f.; L. Salembier, *Le Card. Pierre d'Ailly* (Cambrai 1932).

the College of Cardinals according to which they are the successors of
the Apostolic College in the first and second phase of its activity, that
is in the assistance it gave to Christ up to the Ascension, and after that
to Peter.[1] From this notion D'Ailly deduced not only the superiority
of the cardinals over the bishops, but their right also, as members of
the Roman Church, to take a share in the government of the universal
Church and in the event of the Pope's incapacity to intervene actively
like St Paul of old, if need be by convoking a Council.[2] D'Ailly is a
vigorous defender of the Roman Church. In his opinion the Pope
enjoys full jurisdiction over every particular church, yet his authority
is not unlimited; it is co-extensive with its usefulness to the churches.
For the attainment of this purpose he introduces two constitutional
factors besides the Pope, namely the College of Cardinals and the
Council. The Council is superior to the cardinals, for it represents the
whole Church and thereby constitutes the last and supreme court of
appeal for the whole ecclesiastical body.[3] As regards the constitutional
rights of the cardinals, he appeals, inter alia, to the so-called Professio
fidei of Boniface VIII.[4]

Unlike the conciliar theory, these ideas were not the signal for a
heresy-hunt in Rome. The conflict between Pope and Council was
not yet at an end when a Frenchman, Bernard de Rousergue, subsequently Archbishop of Toulouse, renewed it with a book which he
dedicated and indeed actually presented [5] to the Sacred College.
Basing himself on the doctrine of the jus divinum of the cardinalate, and

[1] Dupin, VOL. II, p. 934; see also p. 929.

[2] "Ubi necessitas aut utilitas imminet, pro conservanda fide vel bono regimine
ecclesiae ad papam vel in ejus defectu ad cardinales pertinet generale concilium
convocare, et hoc eis convenit non tam humana quam divina institutione vice et
nomine universalis ecclesiae." Dupin, VOL. II, p. 935.

[3] Dupin, VOL. II, pp. 949 ff.

[4] Dupin, VOL. II, pp. 929 ff. The "Professio fidei" of Boniface VIII says: "Cum
quorum (scil. cardinalium) consilio, consensu, directione et rememoratione minis-
terium meum geram et peragam." Baluze-Mansi, Miscellanea, VOL. III, p. 418.

[5] Liber de statu, auctoritate et potestate R. morum . . . S.R.E. cardinalium et de
eorum collegio sacrosancto, Vat. lat. 4680; 100 leaves—a bad copy dating from the
sixteenth century. According to some remarks at the beginning and at the end, the
work originated in the sixteenth year of the pontificate of Pope Eugenius IV, viz. in
the year of the Incarnation 1446, that is between 11 March 1446 and 15 February
1447, on which day the author was made Bishop of Bazas, Eubel, Hierarchia catholica,
VOL. II, p. 263. It is directed against those "qui temere in publico locuti sunt et in
scriptis tradere praesumpserunt tantum et talem statum ierarchicum . . . fuisse et esse
in ecclesia militanti superfluum". For Bernard de Rousergue (de Rosergio, Rosergis,
du Rosier), auditor of Cardinal Foix until 1427, and after that successively Bishop of
Bazas, Montauban and Toulouse, and who died in 1475, see above all F. Ehrle in
Archiv für Literatur und Kirchengeschichte des Mittelalters, VII (1900), pp. 429 ff., 496 ff.

applying the principle of a corporation to the Roman Church, he allots to the cardinals a large share in the government of the Church, especially in the appointment of bishops and abbots, the granting of exemptions, the promotion and deprivation of cardinals, the despatch of legates and the alienation of Church property. All this he concedes, though not—and the point is important—as a strict right, but for motives of convenience.[1] In de Rousergue's view the cardinals' right to elect the Pope is theirs because they are the representatives not only of the Roman but of the universal Church. In that capacity they may take action, and are bound to do so, whenever the Pope is prevented from governing the Church or fails to do his duty, or is a cause of scandal.[2] In the event of a schism, or when the Pope neglects or delays to call a Council when there is a pressing need for such an assembly, it belongs to them to convoke it.[3]

Two Italian jurists, Martin of Lodi and Andrew Barbatia, followed in de Rousergue's track in the treatises on the College of Cardinals published by them shortly after the Frenchman's book. The former, who subsequently lectured at Ferrara,[4] replied to the question whether the Pope may take important decisions without consulting the cardinals, with a distinction: *de potestate absoluta* he can do so, but *de potestate condecenti ordinaria et utiliori reipublicae* he must take their advice in accordance with the teaching of John the Monk.[5] As regards the *jus divinum*, Barbatia was more cautious than the rest. He thought that

---

[1] Details in Vat. lat. 4680, fols. 33^v-40^v ("decet, convenit", its omission "non expedit").

[2] Vat. lat. 4860, fols, 72^v-79^v; on the latter page we read: "Ad DD. SRE. cardinales pertinet ex potestatis plenitudine providere et rationabiliter obviare quotiens D. papam viderint facto suo universalem ecclesiam Dei notorie et proterve scandalizare."

[3] "Non solum in casu schismatis, sed etiam in casu cuiuscumque magnae urgentis et evidentis necessitatis Romanae ecclesiae vel apostolicae sanctae sedi seu universali ecclesiae militanti imminentis (MS *eminentis*), cum D. papa nequiret vel nollet aut diferret remediare, DD. SRE. cardinales omnes et singuli possunt, debent et tenentur iure suo se intromittere et apponere remedia opportuna." Vat. lat. 4680, fol. 94^r. That the "remedia" included the convocation of a Council is proved by the explanation on fol. 83^r.

[4] Martin's two treatises De cardinalibus are in the *Tract. ill. iuriscons.*, VOL. XIII, ii, fols. 59^r-63^r. The second, since it is dedicated to Cardinal Agnesi, was drawn up between 20 December 1448 and 10 October 1451; it was printed in 1512, at Pavia, during the conciliar attempt of Pisa. The collection of *quaestiones de concilio* by the same author and dedicated to the future Cardinal Theodore of Montferrat, in Vat. lat. 4129, fols. 171^r-173^v, was put together by one of his pupils, since the latter died while the work was being written. According to G. Secco Sardo, "Lo studio di Ferrara a tutto il seculo XV" in *Atti della deput. ferrarese di storia patria*, VI (1894), he was already laid low by sickness on 3 March 1453.

[5] *Tract. alter de card.*, 945, *Tract. ill. iuriscons.*, VOL. XIII, ii, fol. 61^v.

his opinion was "more tenable" than its contrary.[1] As for the question whether the Pope may take weighty decisions without consulting the cardinals, his answer was in the negative.[2]

Torquemada's adoption in his *Summa* of D'Ailly's teaching on the three "states" of the Apostles and the cardinalate's *jus divinum* based on it, became later a factor of the greatest consequence in the cardinals' struggle for power.[3] Torquemada, it is true, did not draw any conclusions as to the cardinals' constitutional activity in the Church, but these forced themselves on the mind and it only needed an occasion for the effective use of arguments so ready to hand. The occasion arose during the pontificate of Calixtus III. The fight began over a matter of immediate concern for the Sacred College, viz. the creation of new cardinals. When the Pope announced his intention, the Sacred College was up in arms at once. Calixtus III waited until the latter part of the summer when a considerable number of cardinals were out of Rome. On 17 September 1456 he proclaimed three cardinals, two of them nephews of his. In Advent there followed another promotion, this time of six cardinals, all of them members of Latin nations.[4] The three cardinals of the first promotion helped to overcome the opposition of the rest.

The first of the Borgia Popes had had his way, and, like him, his successors had theirs, whenever their choice of new cardinals was opposed by the Sacred College. They had the power, and they took advantage of it; nevertheless, they did their utmost to obtain the assent of the College of Cardinals. The Sacred College was invariably defeated whenever it offered resistance, but this did not discourage it from pursuing the same tactics on the next occasion. These peculiar proceedings need an explanation. In our search for one we enter once more into the sphere of the controversies concerning the distribution of authority in the Church.

[1] *De praestantia cardinalium; Tract. ill. iuriscons.*, VOL. XIII, ii, fols. 63ʳ-85ᵛ, dedicated to Cardinal Bessarion in his capacity as legate at Bologna, hence shortly after 1450. The statements about the "ius divinum" and the distinction of the three "status apostolorum" are on fol. 65ᵛ.

[2] *De praestant. card.*, q. 2; *ibid.*, fol. 69ʳ.

[3] Torquemada, *Summa*, VOL. I, pp. 80 ff.; for the arguments of the opponents "qui illum (scil. statum cardinalium) non a Christo, sed humana inventione asserunt introductum" and their refutation, see c. 82 f.

[4] The account in the printed edition of the *Commentarii* of Pius II, pp. 25 ff., is completed by the pieces printed by J. Cugnoni, *Aeneae Silvii Piccolomini opera inedita*, pp. 498 ff., which are missing in that edition. A few days before the death of Calixtus III, 2 August 1458, Sforza's Roman agent, Antonio da Pistoia, reports that the Pope had intended to create four or five cardinals, among them two Catalans, but that Estouteville, Orsini, Barbo and Mella had opposed him; Pastor, *Ungedr. Akten.* VOL. I, pp. 84 ff.

In the course of the discussions between Calixtus III and the cardinals, the latter had evidently raised the question whether cardinals created in opposition to the advice and the wishes of a majority of the Sacred College enjoyed all the rights of cardinals, particularly the right to elect the Pope. When the Bishop of Torcelli, Domenico Domenichi, who resided at the Curia, was asked his opinion, he replied that personally he felt inclined to answer in the affirmative; on the other hand the arguments for the opposite view appeared to him so weighty that in no circumstances could the Pope brush them aside and thereby expose the Church to the risk of a papal election that might be impeached.[1] Almost more interesting than this conclusion is the line of thought that led up to it, for Domenichi brushes aside all the customary arguments from John the Monk, Boniface VIII's *Professio fidei*, the *jus divinum* of the cardinalate, and the superiority decrees of Constance and Basle. He follows an entirely different track. In his opinion the College of Cardinals derives its right of election (of the Pope) from the universal Church; but the Church's commission is linked to the conditions for the creation of new cardinals laid down by the Council of Constance; hence the Pope is bound to take these conditions into account. That is, he may only create new cardinals *cum consensu cardinalium collegialiter*.[2]

One scarcely trusts one's own eyes! The papalist Domenichi, famous in the opinion of some, notorious in that of others, walks happily in the footsteps of D'Ailly and the adherents of the conciliar theory. If the cardinals' right to elect the Pope really derives from the Church, then the Church in Council assembled may lay down rules for their appointment. The Pope is consequently bound by the corresponding conciliar decree, so that the conciliar theory, which had been driven off, re-enters by the back door. However, there was a weak spot in the

[1] The MSS and the date of the *Tractus de cardinalium creatione* printed by M. A. de Dominis, *De re publica christiana*, VOL. I (London 1617), pp. 767-73, are fully discussed in my as yet unpublished work on Domenichi. The text of prop. XII, which is important in the present context, reads thus in Vat. lat. 5869, fol. 24ʳ: "Qui aliter sunt creati, scil. sine consilio cardinalium et assensu majoris partis eorum, in eos non consentit ecclesia, ut sint papae electores pro ea." And more precisely: "Resistentia istorum tamquam principalium membrorum ecclesiae, donec iterum concilium ipsam repraesentans congregetur, significat, quod ecclesia in illos sic pronuntiatos non consentit . . . ergo non sunt veri cardinales" (fol. 24ᵛ). The note in Domenichi's own handwriting on his agreement with D'Ailly, which he only noticed later, is in Vat. lat. 4120, fol. 70ᵛ.

[2] "Ideo quaestionem de 'potest' concludo per 'debet', scil. quod papa nullo modo debet sine consensu maioris partis alios creare, ne dubitationes insurgant circa hoc, et non existente alia necessitate exponat periculo factum suum et materiam scandali in ecclesia praebeat." Vat. lat. 5869, fol. 26ᵛ.

structure of the argument. Domenichi assumed the existence of a decree of the Council of Constance on the reform of the Cardinals' College which made the nomination of new members dependent on the latter's consent. This assumption was not altogether correct because the reform of the cardinals decreed by Constance was part of the concordats. When Domenichi eventually realised his mistake he dropped the argument but he could not prevent the doubts concerning the electoral rights of the cardinals created without the consent of the Sacred College from being revived at a later period.

In 1461, this time by command of Pius II, Domenichi drew up yet another memorial on the question in dispute; but by then the problem had entered a new phase. At the death of Calixtus III the cardinals had drawn up an election capitulation with the object of preventing a repetition, under the new Pope, of certain features of the pontificate of the first Borgia Pope, such as his blatant nepotism and the intolerable arbitrariness of his management of the States of the Church. In conformity with Domenichi's first memorial the Pope-elect swore, among other things, that he would only appoint new cardinals with the counsel and consent of the consistory and with due regard for the decrees of Constance in respect of the qualities required of a cardinal.[1] Pius II evidently felt bound by this oath. On 5 March 1460 he proceeded to his first creation, but only after consultation with the consistory. Thanks to his intellectual eminence and diplomatic skill he obtained its approval for all his candidates,[2] almost all of them men of great merit. They were the younger Capranica, Eroli, Fortiguerra, Alessandro of Sassoferrato, general of the Augustinians, Weissbriach, Archbishop of Salzburg and, lastly, his own nephew Francesco Piccolomini. Two years later, for ecclesiastical-political reasons, Pius II contemplated a second promotion, but this time he met with obstinate resistance. He accordingly weighed the possibility of carrying his point in spite of the cardinals' opposition—hence against the election capitulation. In his second memorial Domenichi assured the Pope that he was not bound in conscience either by his oath, or by the two conciliar decrees.[3] Was this because Domenichi had capitulated to the

[1] Raynald, *Annales*, a. 1453, No. 5; Mansi, VOL. XXXV, p. 128; there is a good fifteenth-century copy in Vat. lib., Ottob. lat. 3078, fol. 158.

[2] The famous scene with Ludovico, the Camerlengo, in Cugnoni, *Aeneae Silvii Piccolomini Opera inedita*, pp. 515 ff.; P. Paschini, *Ludovico card. Camerlengo* (Rome 1939), p. 194; W. Schürmeyer, *Das Kardinalskollegium unter Pius II* (Berlin 1914), pp. 61 ff.

[3] *Consilium in materia creationis cardinalium Mag. Dominici ep. Torcellani ad petitionem S. D. Pii papae II* 1461, Vat. lib., Barb. lat. 1201, fols. 32ᵛ-55ʳ; for the other MSS see p. 83, *n. 1*.

wishes of the Pope, with whom he had close personal ties? Be that as it may, the fact is that he saw the weakness of an argument which he had formerly regarded as decisive: he accordingly dropped it. However, in practice, the contrast between the second and the first memorial is not so great as might appear at first sight. He continued to press the pontiff to seek the consent of the Consistory as tradition required. Pius II followed the Venetian's advice. He did so most diplomatically. Before communicating the names of his six candidates to the Consistory, he made sure of the assent of a majority by negotiating with each cardinal separately.[1] Once Estouteville, Carvajal, Bessarion, Colonna and the influential Camerlengo had been won over, the opposition of Orsini, Cusa, and the two cardinals created by Calixtus III, Mila and Tebaldi, could no longer be dangerous. The Consistory accepted every one of the Pope's candidates, the first of whom was Jouffroy, Louis XI's favourite. In his disappointment at the subservience of his colleagues Tebaldi exclaimed [2]: "In God's name, then, let there be an end to this dignity! I shall offer no opposition, even if the Pope decides to create three hundred new cardinals." Nicholas of Cusa alone reminded the Pope of his oath to observe the election capitulation. He was sharply called to order: Nothing was farther from him, the Pope exclaimed, than to break his oath!

A change came with Paul II. Always a stickler for external correctness, no sooner was his coronation over than he altered the election capitulation, wresting his signature from each cardinal individually. Carvajal alone had the strength of character to refuse.[3] Ammanati's assertion that the Pope had covered the writing with his hand may be an exaggeration; what is certain is that by such proceedings nothing was saved except appearances. What Paul himself thought—or at least, what he wanted to hear—may be gathered from a treatise by his closest collaborator, Teodoro de' Lelli.[4] This document roundly rejects the pretensions of the Sacred College and contests the arguments on

[1] The account in Pius II, *Commentarii*, BK IV, should be supplemented by Cugnoni, *Opera inedita*, pp. 530-4; Schürmeyer, p. 67, is very one-sided.

[2] Cugnoni, *Opera inedita*, p. 534.

[3] Ammanati in Pius II, *Commentarii*, pp. 371 ff.; Ep. 181 to Paul II, undated, *ibid.*, pp. 603 ff.

[4] J. B. Sägmüller, *Ein Traktat des Bischofs von Feltre und Treviso, Teodoro de' Lelli, über das Verhältnis von Primat und Kardinalat* (Rome 1893). The editor thinks the work was composed in the autumn of 1464, but the fact that the magnificent MS, Vat. lat. 4923, from the library of Cardinal Sirleto, is dedicated to Pius II, points to an earlier date. This MS was unknown to Sägmüller. It can hardly be identical with the "impudens consilium" mentioned by Ammanati (Ep. 423) of which Paul II took cognisance previous to the alteration of the election capitulation.

which they rested, from John the Monk's right of prescription to Torquemada's *jus divinum*. The high water mark of the monarchical reaction was reached in Sánchez de Arevalo's rejection of the idea of the Council and in Lelli's condemnation of the pretensions of the cardinals. It was these two collaborators of Paul II—not Torquemada —who were the keenest champions of papal absolutism in the era of the restoration. They were presently joined by Barbatia. In a *consilium* addressed to Borso d'Este, but presumably intended for the Pope, the latter asserted that the election capitulation was null in law. John the Monk's appeal to prescription he refuted by pointing to the contrary practice of the last Popes.[1]

The attitude of Paul II, and that of his successors, to the election capitulations as well as to the claims of the Cardinals' College which they embodied, was inspired by these considerations. Without exception the Popes rejected every restriction of papal power. They refused to acknowledge the validity of the restraints of a spiritual kind that had been laid on them, such as oaths, pledges, threats of excommunication, and that of external means of control imposed by the election capitulations since 1464, such as the monthly reading of the capitulations in Consistory, the inquiry twice a year by a commission of cardinals into their execution, the admonition to be administered to the Pope should it be ascertained that he had infringed them.[2] All this was dropped: it had to be dropped if the Papacy was to preserve its true character.

However the nomination of new Cardinals was the one point of the line where the cardinals continued to venture forth. The election capitulation of 1464 no longer appealed to the Council of Constance but embodied the relevant stipulations of the concordats.[3] Only in the

---

[1] Andreas Barbatia, *Consilia sive responsa*, VOL. I (Venice 1581), fols. 2ʳ-15ʳ, composed sixteen years after the above-mentioned treatise *De praestantia card.*, that is about 1466-7 and previous to the creation of 18 September 1467. There (fol. 13ʳ) we read: "Quod papa non tenetur in arduis requirere consilium cardinalium . . . est opinio communis et ita videmus de facto observari", both by Calixtus III, who decided "multa ardua" without the cardinals, and by Pius II—"ita communiter audivi dici."

[2] The internal conditions are the theme of a tract by Felinus Sandaeus: *De modis et formis quibus futurus pontifex ad observantiam promissorum possit adstringi*, published by Mansi, VOL. XXXV, pp. 119-22. The tract was probably written towards the end of the century. Among these conditions are the following: 1. A vow to God and to the Apostles Peter and Paul; 2. an oath; 3. a contract between Pope and cardinals in the form of a legal instrument of which a duly authenticated copy is given to everyone concerned; 4. admission of only such conditions as the Pope is bound to submit to "ex obligatione naturalis charitatis"; 5. subjection to the Council in the event of non-observance; 6. anathema.

[3] According to Ammanati in Pius II, *Commentarii*, p. 371.

fourth year of his pontificate did Paul II succeed in overcoming the resistance of the Sacred College, when he created eight new cardinals and two more in the following year.[1] Among them were his nephews Barbo, Zeno and Michiel, in point of fact all three worthy men; also Oliviero Carafa, who became the strongest pillar of the College and the moving spirit in every reform within that body; the excellent Agnifilo, and Francesco della Rovere, the future Pope. It is evident that both in regard to the number as well as to the selection of the candidates Paul II proceeded with circumspection. He refused to be tied by the election capitulation but kept within self-imposed bounds.

Under Sixtus IV even these collapsed. Although the capitulation of 1471 contained the rigid clause that cardinals whose creation had not conformed to its stipulations would not be regarded as cardinals once the Pope was dead and would have neither active nor passive vote at the election,[2] he created in the course of his pontificate of thirteen years no fewer than thirty-four cardinals—including six nephews, and what nephews! Even now opposition was not wanting on the part of the College. On 16 December 1473, after a debate lasting three hours, the Consistory refused to give the Pope a blank cheque for the nomination of new cardinals.[3] Three years went by before he took steps for another creation. The promotion of George Hessler, the favourite of Frederick III, a man born out of wedlock, met with sharp opposition.[4] The letters of Cardinal Ammanati give a lively picture of the contests and intrigues within the Sacred College and of the failure of every effort to arrest so calamitous a development: "There is no purpose in fighting", he wrote in a dispirited mood to Cardinal Gonzaga towards the end of 1476, "and I have no mind to do so. Often enough I have been left in the lurch in the thick of the battle. I no longer have any desire to get involved in a hopeless struggle and, old as I am, to waste my strength; either I fall in with the views of those who speak before me, or I leave the decision to the Pope."[5] There were only too many reasons for Ammanati's mood of resignation. The pontificate of the Rovere Pope marked the opening of an outwardly brilliant period in the history of the Sacred College, an epoch destined to contribute

[1] See Pastor, VOL. II, pp. 387 ff. (Eng. edn., VOL. IV, pp. 120 ff.).
[2] Vat. lat. 12192, fol. 205ᵛ.
[3] Ammanati, Ep. 540 (to Fortiguerra, 16 December 1473); from Ep. 538 we gather that Estouteville, Orsini, Giuliano della Rovere and Calandrini were regarded as the sharpest opponents of a new promotion.
[4] Ammanati, Ep. 514f., 623.
[5] Ammanati, Ep. 657.

greatly to the development of the arts,[1] but also one that was to be disastrous for the Church. The great cardinals of the Basle period had died one after another: Domenico Capranica in 1458, Nicholas of Cusa in 1464, Ludovico, the Chamberlain, in 1465, Torquemada in 1468, Carvajal in 1469, Bessarion and Fortiguerra in 1473. Thus it came about that the favourites of Louis XI and, later on, those of Charles VIII—men like Balue, Briçonnet, Amboise; the sons of Italian princes of the houses of Aragon, Gonzaga, Este, Medici, Sforza; Roman barons bearing the ancient names of Colonna, Orsini, Savelli, obtained a preponderance over those members of the Sacred College whose character was that of true churchmen.

The forty-three creations by Alexander VI raised the number of cardinals to almost double the twenty-four that had been stipulated for at Constance. There were forty-five in 1503. With insignificant exceptions all of them belonged to the Latin nations. The creations of the Borgia Pope included seventeen Spaniards, among them five members of his own family; as many Italians; six Frenchmen, one Englishman, one Hungarian and one Pole. To this was added an even more disturbing circumstance. The papal master of ceremonies, Burchard of Strasbourg, was in a position to state the exact sum with which those nominated on 28 September 1500 had bought their dignity.[2] The highest dignity of the hierarchy had apparently become marketable, as had the offices of the Curia.

This latest development in the situation was not passively accepted by the Sacred College. Eleven cardinals absented themselves from Alexander's first large-scale promotion on 20 September 1493, by way of protest, and ten others withheld their consent even in the next Consistory. They maintained that the men created in these circumstances were not cardinals at all and they declined their visits. Thereupon the Pope threatened to create yet more cardinals to spite the opponents. This silenced the opposition.[3] The Venetian ambassador, Capello, was of course right when, in 1500, he wrote to the Signoria: "Without the Pope the cardinals are helpless."[4] Alexander VI merely laughed whenever the aged cardinal of Portugal contradicted him in Consistory.

[1] As against the brilliant description in E. Steinmann, *Die Sixtinische Kapelle*, VOL. I (Munich 1901), pp. 27-48, the religious aspect, in my opinion, should be more strongly emphasised than was done by Pastor, VOL. II, pp. 479 f., 633 ff. (Eng. edn., VOL. IV, pp. 197, 432 ff.).

[2] Celani, VOL. II, pp. 242 ff.

[3] Despatches of the Mantuan agent in Rome, G. Lucido Cattanei, of 18, 20 and 23 September 1493, published by A. Luzio in *Arch. storico lombardo*, XLII (1915), pp. 416 ff.   [4] Albèri, *Relazioni*, VOL. II, pp. 3, 5.

A situation like this could not fail to provoke a reaction. The election capitulation drawn up after Alexander VI's death sought to recover for the cardinals at least a limited share in the government of the Church and her States.[1] In view of the new creations which were bound to take place they hit on a novel remedy. Henceforth there were to be two degrees in the cardinalate. The old members would enjoy all the privileges of the Sacred College, without any restriction, but the right to vote of those newly created would be suspended for a time, that is, until the number of the old cardinals should have fallen to twenty. The new cardinals would not be allowed to vote at all in three circumstances, viz. in the creation of new cardinals, in the alienation or the collation of property of the Roman Church, and whenever the observance of the election capitulation was under discussion. Subsequently they were to swear observance of the capitulation.[2] The cardinals' purpose is obvious. They were anxious to have a say in the filling up of their ranks and to prevent a repetition of Caesar Borgia's attempt to secularise the States of the Church. It is equally evident that their plan could not be carried through. In point of fact, things took a very different turn. That masterful personality, Julius II, restored the States of the Church single-handed, and he was less inclined than any of his predecessors to allow the Sacred College to meddle with his schemes. All the cardinals' protests were in vain. In the winter of 1504, when Julius announced his intention to add others to the four cardinals he had created the year before, the election capitulation was read out and thus recalled to memory in the Consistories of 4, 8 and 11 November 1504, thanks to the efforts of Carafa. At this time the cardinals were spoiling for a fight; they refused to be treated "like youngsters (*ragazzi*)"; they insisted on being dealt with as brethren. Carafa hinted that, should the need arise, Christian princes would defend the freedom of the Church.[3] However, Julius II was not the man to be intimidated by such threats; he even found a canonist prepared to justify his conduct. Cardinal Sangiorgio took over the role at one time played by Domenichi and Lelli: he assured the Pope that he was not bound by the election capitulation. So all that could be

[1] Vat. lat. 12343, fol. 58ᵛ. The Pope undertakes not to grant to a lay person any kind of jurisdiction in important matters, whether of a spiritual or a secular nature (in view of Lucrezia Borgia's temporary position); not to expedite any consistorial business without the assent of a majority of the Consistory and to demand an oath of loyalty to the Sacred College from the captains of all the castles of the Papal States.

[2] Vat. lat. 12343, fol. 58ᵛ, also in Julius II's election capitulation, Raynald, *Annales*, a. 1503, Nos. 2-9; Thuasne, VOL. III, pp. 295-98.

[3] Giustiniani, *Dispacci*, ed. Villari, VOL. III, pp. 285 ff., 289 ff.

obtained was a postponement of the promotion. A year later, on 1 and 12 December 1505, nine candidates were raised to the purple, including two of the Pope's nephews.

In the period of the restoration the Sacred College did its utmost to retain, and even to enlarge, the all but constitutional authority which it had acquired during the Schism; but these efforts were in vain. The election capitulations were rearguard actions, not offensive strokes. They were backed by the theories of the Roman Church current in the late Middle Ages and in the era of the Councils and were only over-come by slow degrees. While a truly princely, hitherto unknown splendour surrounded the wearers of the purple and their familiars were numbered by the hundred, and one magnificent cardinal's palace after another rose out of the soil of Rome, the influence on the fortunes of the Church of the corporation as such was on the decline. This decline was inevitable, for it was due both to the fact that an ever-growing number of its members was no longer prepared to strive for the common good, and to the weakening of those Christian principles by which every institution in the Church justifies its existence.

The *capitula privata* which had been included in every election capitulation since the conclave of Sixtus IV were the outcome of the narrow, short-sighted egoism that was now abroad in the Sacred College. By means of these *capitula* the cardinals pressed their personal demands on the pontiff, sought financial advantages and courted honours and distinctions. It almost seemed as if they could only think of their own private interests. However, this would be a wrong judgment. In their fight for their ecclesiastical and political influence the interests of the Church were also at stake. The nepotism and the obsession with purely political considerations which are characteristic of most of the Renaissance Popes jeopardised these interests. The *capitula publica* of the election capitulations embodied a goodly part of the legitimate criticism which the conduct of the Popes called forth on the part of public opinion in the *Respublica christiana*. On the very eve of the Council of Trent Bartolomeo Guidiccioni, himself a convinced up-holder of the Curia, openly admitted that the Church would have been preserved from a great deal of harm if the Popes had acted in accordance with them.[1] Not to mention the nepotism which provided the families

---

[1] "Capitula in conclavi fieri solita magna laude observabis." Vat. lib., Barb. lat. 1165, fol. 137ʳ. Lulvès, too, says that certain recurring chapters of the election capitulations constitute "the permanent element in this development as against the variations due to the character of individual Popes": *Q.F.*, XII (1910), p. 233.

of the Rovere, Gibò, Farnese, with principalities carved out of the States of the Church, and led the Medici back to Florence, how greatly would the Church have benefited by a curtailment of the concessions made to secular princes from political motives—such as the right of nomination or proposal for bishoprics and abbeys, or requests for the removal of inconvenient prelates! [1] These concessions gradually drove the clergy into the arms of the state and prepared the ground for regalism in one country, for Protestantism in another. The cardinals' demand for a guarantee of their personal freedom in the interests of a free expression of opinion was by no means superfluous when they had to deal with men like Alexander VI and Julius II.[2] The demand that the Consistory should be heard in the nomination of bishops held out no guarantee that the best men would be appointed; it could, however, prevent many a mistake; moreover, it pointed in the direction which ecclesiastical legislation was eventually to take when it evolved the procedure known as the informative process.

It cannot be denied that more than once, when they stressed the papal supremacy in order to counter the remonstrances of the cardinals, the Popes merely sought to cover up their unblushing nepotism or their excessive personal arbitrariness. A more effective intervention by the Sacred College—without prejudice to the supremacy—would have had beneficial results. The cardinals were the mouthpiece of public opinion in the fullest sense of the word when, by means of capitulations, they demanded a Council, reform and war against the Turks. From the middle of the century these three articles headed every capitulation and they practically never changed, except for a few extraordinarily revealing variations. The election capitulation of 1458 obliged the Pope to undertake a crusade and a reform of the Curia, in so far as this lay within his power; there was no mention as yet of a Council.[3] Only after the death of Pius II, who did not favour the idea, did Article IV make it the Pope's duty to summon a Council within a period of three years. In Chapter I the revenues of the recently discovered alum mines at Tolfa were set apart for the war against the Turks.[4] One effect of Paul II's pontificate was that his successor was allowed only the short period of three months, to be reckoned from his coronation, for a

---

[1] Vat. lat. 12192, fols. 206^v-207^r (c. 7-9).
[2] *Ibid.*, fol. 207^r (c. 10).
[3] Raynald, *Annales, a.* 1458, No. 5; Mansi, VOL. XXXV, p. 128; a good copy in Vat. lib., Ottob. lat. 3078, fol. 158.
[4] Ammanati, in Pius II, *Commentarii*, p. 371; Raynald, *Annales, a.* 1464, No. 52.

beginning of a reform of the Curia, to be carried out in conjunction with the College of Cardinals.[1] Within three years, and likewise in consultation with the cardinals, a Council must be convened. This assembly must be modelled on the ancient Councils, not on those of the reform period. Its task would be to organise a crusade and to promote a reform of the whole Church in matters of faith and morals, in every estate including the secular princes.[2]

While the injunction relative to the reform of the Curia was embodied in all subsequent capitulations without any variation, so that it became a stereotyped formula, the ever-recurring threats of a Council by foreign powers caused the article concerning the Council to be recast in 1484. With a view to putting spokes in the wheels of the future Pope's opponents,[3] the clause about the time-limit of the Council was omitted and replaced by a non-committal "as soon as possible". A contrary tendency made its appearance after the pontificate of Alexander VI. Their experiences during the Borgia Pope's reign convinced the cardinals of the necessity of an early convocation of a Council. It should meet within two years of the election, at a place decided by a two-thirds majority of the Sacred College. The same majority would be required to establish the existence of an obstacle that would dispense from the obligation of summoning the assembly.[4] Its task would be the restoration of peace, the reform of the Church, the preservation of ecclesiastical immunity and a crusade.

It is evident that by means of this article the Sacred College attempted to make the Council its own affair. It judged the convocation

[1] Vat. lat. 12192, fol. 205ʳ.

[2] "Item quod intra triennium concilium generale celebrabit seu celebrari faciet solemniter secundum formam antiquorum conciliorum in loco tuto et commodo, prout ei visum videbitur, et consultum fuerit per maiorem partem DD. cardinalium, ad concitandum principes et populos ad defensionem fidei et generalem contra infideles expeditionem, ac ad reformandam universalem ecclesiam circa fidem, vitam et mores, tam respectu clericorum saecularium et regularium quam religiosorum etiam militarium (MS etc. *militarunt*), et tam respectu principum temporalium quam communitatum in et super eo, quod pertinebit ad iudicium et provisionem ecclesiae." Vat. lat. 12192, fol. 205ʳ⁻ᵛ.

[3] Celani, VOL. I, p. 40.

[4] "Item quia ad pacem christianorum et ecclesiae reformationem ac reductionem multarum exactionum, expeditionem quoque contra infideles plurimum convenit concilium generale celerius congregari, promittet, iurabit et vovebit intra biennium a creatione sua illud indicere et cum effectu incipere in Italia in loco libero et tuto, determinando per eum et duas partes R.morum DD. cardinalium, nisi evidentissimum impedimentum obstiterit, quod a duabus partibus DD. cardinalium per suffragia balotarum iudicetur." Vat. lat. 12343, fols. 58ᵛ-59ʳ. In Julius II's capitulation the words "in Italia" are missing, Raynald, *Annales, a.* 1503, No. 6.

of a Council to be necessary and wanted to have a say in the final decision. It may be that it even considered the possibility, should the occasion present itself, of playing it off against the Pope. The fact is that the pontificate of Alexander VI drove the cardinals into the ranks of those who appealed to a Council.

In this way the demand for a Council entered a new stage. According to the teaching of reputable canonists the College of Cardinals ranks first among the bodies concerned in an emergency convocation of a Council. If a Council could ever be convoked without the Pope, it was best done with the help of the cardinals. Before we discuss this opinion of the canonists one point must be made clear. Although the canonists grant the possibility of the convocation of a Council without the Pope, and in certain emergencies even in spite of him, it does not follow that they are in opposition to him on the question of authority. They do not abandon their own principle that the Pope is above the Council and that its convocation regularly belongs to him. For them the convocation of a Council without the concurrence of the head remains an emergency measure. Its subsequent authorisation by the Pope is by no means excluded and in no hypothesis do they claim for the Council any juridical power over the Pope.[1] Their chief concern is to provide some kind of security against imminent disaster.

The idea of the Council as an ecclesiastical emergency measure originated, of course, in the period of the Schism and the reform Councils. The early Middle Ages knew of only one circumstance in which the Pope forfeited the right of convocation together with all other rights: namely if he fell into heresy and obstinately persisted in it.[2] In such an eventuality he ceased to be Pope, since his heresy placed him without the Church and his authority devolved upon the Church. It then became the Council's duty formally to establish the fact that such was the case and to provide for a substitute. However, the gloss

---

[1] Jacobazzi has singled out this point: "Posito quod non possit concilium privare papam propter crimen scandalizans ecclesiam universalem, tamen non sequitur quod non sit causa sufficiens ad congregandum concilium." In his motivation he says: "Posset contingere quod (papa) convictus viso scandalo corrigeretur, vel saltem eum ecclesia toleraret cum maiori patientia." *De concilio*, lib. IV, art. 2, in the first edition (Rome 1538), pp. 195, 197.

[2] Sägmüller, *Kardinäle*, pp. 233 ff.; Martin, *Gallicanisme*, VOL. II, pp. 12 ff. What follows is from Augustinus Triumphus, *Summa de ecclesiastica potestate*, q. 5, art. 6. In arts. 3 and 4 Augustinus expressly rejects simony or some "crimen" as a reason for deposition, pp. 49 ff. in the edition used by me (Rome 1585), p. 49.

attached to the decree had already raised the question [1]: "Why may not the Pope be accused of other offences, if, in spite of admonitions, he does not amend and continues to give scandal to the Church?" Obstinacy identical with heresy! At that time, that is in the thirteenth century, the road thus hinted at had not been pursued any further; it was only in the period of the Schism that other analogous instances were added to this extreme one. Starting from the notion that the Pope's power exists for the sake of the Church, the Church must surely be in a position to take action, through the Council, in the event of his being no longer able to exercise his authority, for instance, if he becomes mentally deranged, or if he misuses it and thereby imperils the peace and harmony of the Church. The leaders of Gallicanism at Constance, D'Ailly and Gerson, were familiar with these notions,[2] but the canonists of the restoration were less impressed by them than they were by the teaching of the great Italian jurists of the conciliar period.

Zabarella maintained that in the event of a schism the right to summon a Council devolved either on the Emperor or on the cardinals. In conjunction with the gloss of the conciliar decree he laid down the following thesis [3]: "The Pope may be impeached for any notorious crime, should he prove incorrigible and give scandal to the Church: in such circumstances he must be regarded as a heretic." Ludovicus Romanus professed similar opinions. To the question whether a Pope guilty of public crimes and incorrigible may be deposed by the Council, he unhesitatingly replied in the affirmative.[4] Weightier even than the authority of these two canonists is that of Panormitanus. In his opinion, appeal from the Pope to the Council is lawful not only when the pontiff falls into heresy, but also when he gives scandal, or by mandate or juridical sentence alters the status of the universal Church

---

[1] The gloss to c. *Si papa* D. 40 reads as follows in the Lyons edition of 1543, fol. 44ʳ: "Quod intelligit Hugo, cum papa non vult corrigi. Si enim paratus esset corrigi, non posset accusari . . . Sed quare non potest accusari de alio crimine? Ponamus quod notorium sit crimen eius vel per confessionem vel per facti evidentiam, quare non accusatur vel de crimine simoniae vel adulterii, etiam cum admonetur, incorrigibilis est et scandalizatur ecclesia per factum eius? Certe credo, quod si notorium est crimen eius quodcumque et inde scandalizatur ecclesia, et incorrigibilis sit, quod inde possit accusari."

[2] Gerson, *De pot. eccl. consid.*, VIII and IX, Dupin, VOL. II, p. 243; D'Ailly, *De pot. eccl.*, PT i, ch. 3, and PT iii, ch. 1; Dupin, VOL. II, pp. 935, 949; see Fincke, *Forschungen und Quellen zur Geschichte des Konstanzer Konzils*, pp. 93 ff., 124 ff.; Tschackert, *D'Ailly*, pp. 247 ff., 354 f.

[3] F. Zabarella, *De schismate*, in *Repertorium*, on ch. "Licet X de elect." i, 6 (Lyons 1558), fol. 100ʳ. G. Zonta, *F. Zabarella* (Padua 1915), pp. 123 ff., is inadequate.

[4] L. Romanus, *Consilia sive responsa* (Venice 1568), fols. 385ʳ-387ʳ (*cons.* 523).

and thereby endangers her good order.[1] The latter case was the most elastic of all, for it meant that a state of emergency, which could only be remedied by a Council, might be brought about not only by a *crimen* of the Pope, or by a schism in the Church, but by any grave danger to the good order of the Church in consequence of some measure taken by her supreme head. These ideas were all born of the Schism and the conflict between Pope and Council. But they offered wide possibilities of application apart from such a situation. The Council was a recognised safety-valve, but the concept of a state of emergency in the Church had been widened to a most alarming extent. The authority of such luminaries of the science of Canon Law as Zabarella and Tudeschi did not fail to impress even canonists hostile to the conciliar theory.

Already Piero da Monte, in his very first work, had hinted at the possibility of a Council not called by the Pope being subsequently legitimised by him. In his opinion the right to convoke a Council in a state of emergency belongs to the Emperor in the event of a schism, or to the cardinals if the public good requires it. But before acting both parties must request the Pope to make the convocation.[2] "The public good"—what an elastic notion!

Even Torquemada makes an observation which points in the same direction. "If the Christian faith or the welfare of the whole Church are in danger, and the Pope obstinately refuses to convene a Council, he renders himself suspect of heresy." This sentence enunciates the classical exception to the rule which reserves convocation of the Council to the Pope: this right is then said to devolve on the cardinals.[3] "The welfare of the whole Church in danger!" This too is very vague. However, Torquemada was more careful than Piero da Monte to safeguard the papalist principle. The Pope's refusal to convoke a Council

[1] Abbas Panormitanus, *Consilia, tractatus, quaestiones* (Venice 1578), fols. 186ʳ-188ʳ (q. 1 dubium 2).

[2] Piero da Monte, *De potestate Rom. pontificis et gen. concilii*, PT i, q. 2, used by me according to the text of Vat. lat. 5607, fol. 132ʳ. The reprint of 1512 at Lyons, under Gallican influence, has a significant title-page: it shows the Pope standing before the chair of a jurist.

[3] Torquemada, *Summa de ecclesia*, BK III, 8 ad 3. The Sienese jurist Galgano Borghese, in his work *De potestate summi pontificis*, dedicated to Pius II and written, it would seem, in the year 1458, states that the meeting of a Council is necessary in the following five cases: 1. If a definition of a point of faith is required; 2. if the Pope is a heretic; 3. si papa sit criminosus incorrigibilis, ita ut ecclesia scandalizetur; 4. si papa constituerit aliqua contra concilia, quod deturparet seu decoloraret statum universalis ecclesiae; 5. si faceret aliquod statutum quod esset scandalosum. Vat. lat. 4129, fols. 8ᵛ-9ʳ.

in a serious crisis renders him suspect of heresy—the classical exception —but in practice, he opined, a situation of this kind is not likely to arise.

Such optimism was not shared by the leading canonists of the next generation. The possibility of a Pope misusing his authority and neglecting to deal with pressing ecclesiastical affairs caused the contemporaries of Sixtus IV and Alexander VI a great deal of anxiety. A careful study of the earlier literature, such as had not previously been undertaken, was facilitated by the diffusion of printed books, and had acquainted them with the thoughts of the jurists of the period of the Councils on this subject. Felinus Sandaeus indeed observes some restraint in his commentary on the decretals, but an examination of his sources [1] shows that he was as familiar with Tudeschi and Ludovicus Romanus as with Piero da Monte and St Antonino of Florence. "The canonists", he writes, somewhat impersonally, "assign to the Council authority over the Pope if he deserves to be deposed." [2] In the memorial already mentioned, which he drew up for Innocent VIII,[3] he grants, as does Torquemada, that when some grievous peril threatens the Church, and the Pope refuses to convoke a Council, such an assembly may be convened against his will if the danger requires it; by his refusal the Pope renders himself suspect of heresy.

Between 1486 and 1502 Felinus was an auditor of the Rota and from the seventh year of the pontificate of Innocent VIII also a referendary of the Segnatura. He died in 1503 as Bishop of Lucca.[4] His no less distinguished contemporary Sangiorgio, sometime Professor of Canon and Civil Law at Pavia, rose to the dignity of the cardinalate under Alexander VI.[5] He too is a thorough-going papalist. In his commentary on the first part of the *Decretum*,[6] written while he was still in Pavia, he adopts in the main Torquemada's teaching on the relation between the two powers, but whereas the latter deems it impossible in practice that a Pope should refuse to summon a Council even though imminent peril threatened the Church, Sangiorgio boldly faces

[1] Felinus Sandaeus, *Com. in V libros decretalium* (Basle 1565), p. 770, on c. "Nonnulii X de rescript.", BK I, iii.

[2] *Ibid.*, p. 652, on c. "Super litteris X de rescript.", BK I, iii. Felinus quotes Dominic of San Gimignano for the opinion that "in casu necessitatis possunt praelati congregare concilium irrequisito papa".

[3] Vat. lat. 5607, fol. 121ᵛ, in connexion with a controversy with Panormitanus.

[4] N. Hilling, "Felinus Sandaeus, Auditor der Rota" in *A.K.R.*, LXXXIV (1904), pp. 94-106.

[5] Schulte, *Die Geschichte der Quellen*, VOL. II, pp. 348 ff.; Cerchiari, *Sacra Romana Rota* (Rome 1920-1), VOL. II, pp. 69 ff.; Katterbach, *Referendarii*, p. 44.

[6] J. A. de S. Georgio, *Lectura super 101 distinctionibus* (Rome 1493), fols. 88 and 102 ff., on dist. 15 and 17.

such a possibility. He even supposes the other, more deplorable eventuality—that the Pope may do grievous harm to the Church by his conduct and scandalise Christian people. If this happens, it is the duty of the cardinals to admonish him and to resist unjust and harmful measures; when all other remedies have proved unavailing they must convoke a Council. However, it is not the Council's business to judge the Pope, as the conciliar theory taught. Its duty is to admonish him, to pray for him, and to take practical steps so as to prevent further harm. To this end it should invoke the secular arm, above all the Emperor's. In the first case, when the College of Cardinals, acting as the "Chapter of the universal Church", and after a previous but fruitless admonition of the Pope, decides to convoke a Council in order to meet a grave danger, it must once more request the pontiff to take part in the assembly or at least to sanction it. Should he refuse even that much he is suspect of heresy and must be deposed.

Domenico Jacobazzi discusses even more fully than either Felinus or Sangiorgio the convocation of a Council in an ecclesiastical emergency. He too had served the Popes for a whole lifetime, as an auditor and as Dean of the Rota, as a referendary under Julius II and Leo X, as a canon of St Peter's and Vicar of Rome, when in 1517 he received a cardinal's hat. His book on the Council was long regarded as a classic and was included in Mansi's collection of the Councils.[1] Its interest for us is all the greater for its having been written as late as the

---

[1] Domenico, son of Cristoforo Jacobazzi, born in Rome in 1458, or perhaps a little earlier, began his career as auditor with the papal governor of Bologna. By 1489 he was a consistorial advocate (Celani, VOL. I, p. 256). On 7 January 1493 he was admitted as an auditor of the Rota (Celani, VOL. I, p. 391; the interrogation of witnesses on 11 December 1492 in Cerchiari, *Sacra Romana Rota*, VOL. II, p. 76). He became dean of that tribunal on 14 February 1506. Previously to this, perhaps in view of his services during the vacancy of the Holy See (Celani, VOL. II, pp. 367 ff.) he had been made a canon of St Peter's and referendary of the Segnatura on 16 October 1503 (Katterbach, *Referendarii*, pp. 68, 77; W. von Hofmann, *Forschungen*, VOL. II, 1914, p. 137). On 8 November 1511 he became Bishop of Nocera dei Pagani and Vicarius Urbis (*R.Q.*, VIII (1894), p. 499). On his elevation to the cardinalate in 1517 he resigned his bishopric in favour of his brother Andrew, but resumed it in 1524 and retained it until his death in 1528 (Eubel, *Hierarchia catholica*, VOL. III, p. 247). As appears from a number of allusions, the book *De concilio* was written during the fifth Lateran Council, though additions were made to it at a later period, as e.g. in BK VII, art. 6 (p. 497), a quotation from Pope Adrian VI's commentary on the Sentences. After the death of its author his nephew, the future Cardinal Cristoforo, had it printed by Bladus in 1538. It was reprinted in the introduction to Mansi's *Councils* (Paris 1903), pp. 1-580. For convenience sake I quote book and article, the pages being within brackets. For the subject as a whole, see J. Klotzner, *Kardinal Dom. Jacobazzi und sein Konzilswerk* (Rome 1948), where the memorials mentioned below, p. 108, *n.* 2, and p. 109, *n.* 1, are also to be found.

conciliar attempt of Pisa and the fifth Council of the Lateran, at a time, therefore, when the theological reaction to the teaching of the canonists was beginning to make itself felt in the writings of Cajetan.

In several places Jacobazzi states, with all the clarity one could wish for, that a Council may be convoked without papal authorisation whenever a state of emergency exists, no matter whether the Pope is to blame or not, or in the event of the pontiff refusing to comply with the summons to convene it. Such a refusal renders him suspect of heresy.[1] An emergency exists when, for instance, the Church is in great danger, either by reason of some grave scandal on the part of the Pope, such as adultery, simony,[2] the elevation of unworthy relatives to the cardinalate,[3] a threat from external enemies, the refusal or the delay of urgently needed reforms.[4] But the devolution of the right of convocation to the cardinals or to the Emperor, in all these eventualities, presupposes that the Pope has been first formally requested to convene a Council and has refused to do so.

By comparison with those who wrote before him, Jacobazzi widens the notion of the state of emergency while presenting it more concretely. He is not blind to the fundamental and practical objections to which his teaching was bound to give rise. He even parts company with those canonists who, on the basis of the famous chapter *Si papa*, construe any notorious offence of the Pope into an emergency.[5] Above all, he forswears Zabarella's notion of the Pope's subordination to a Council and its decrees.[6] He likewise rejects the opinion of the

---

[1] "Quando ratione alicuius scandali adest necessitas et papa requisitus differt", and "quando concilium non esset directe congregandum contra papam, sed ex notione et denegatione vel detractione congregandi papa faceret se suspectum et urgeret maxima necessitas tenendi concilii, videl. quod facta prius requisitione concilium posset per alios, ad quos devolvitur potestas, vel a seipso congregari." *De concilio*, BK III, art. 1 (p. 137 f.). So also BK III, art. 2 (p. 160), BK IV, art. 2 (pp. 193 ff.); devolution to the princes in BK VII, art. 7 (p. 509).

[2] "Si monitus non desistat a venalitate istorum spiritualium et beneficiorum, erit sufficiens causa congregandi concilium." *De concilio*, BK IV, art. 4 (p. 239); see also BK IV, art. 3 (p. 218).

[3] "Credo tamen quod quando papa sola carnalitate ductus promoveret plures qui essent incapaces et Ro. ecclesiae inutiles, propter periculum quod immineret universali ecclesiae ex malis promotionibus, quod esset sufficiens causa petendi congregari concilium, et quod si detrectaret (the printed text has 'detractaret'), posset per seipsum congregari, quia tunc videretur facere se alienum et suspectum de fide." *De concilio*, BK VII, art. 6 (pp. 497 ff.).

[4] "Unde quantumcumque papa bene vivat, si negligit corrigere ecclesiam indigentem reformatione requisitus, vel fingit vel detrectat, et propterea requisitus quod congreget concilium, contemnit, alii congregabunt." *De concilio*, BK IV, art. 4 (p. 258).

[5] *De concilio*, BK III, art. 1 (p. 140).

[6] "Credo quod non bene dicat . . ." *De concilio*, BK IV, art. 2 (p. 203).

"Gadditanus", that the reform of the Church is a sufficient motive for a convocation, even though no fault could be found with the Pope.[1] He is well aware of the terrible nature of the weapon which such opinions put in the hands of the Pope's enemies. He warns the politicians not to be for ever on the lookout for the splinters in the Pope's eye, or to fall back upon the threat of a Council on every trifling occasion, that is as often as a political difference with him arises.[2] However, none of these restrictions alter his basic principle that besides the regular procedure which assigns to the Pope the right to convoke the Council, emergencies may arise when, by a devolution of rights, a Council may be called without the Pope, as when, for instance, he is guilty of simony, raises unworthy nephews to the cardinalate, or obstinately refuses to convoke a reform Council. Jacobazzi describes the hasty proceedings of the men of Pisa, who had acted without previously approaching the Pope, as foolish,[3] but makes no secret of his longing for a great reform Council: "I will say no more on this subject," he writes. "God knows if such a Council is needed in these days!" [4] He thinks that the ten-year time-limit fixed by the decree *Frequens* has been invalidated by custom; but this does not mean that no Council need be held.[5]

The development of the canonists' teaching on the convocation of the Council reflects the whole problem of the Renaissance Popes.

The first generation of canonists treats the possibility of devolution very scantily—it only hints at it, so to speak, for the idea was still in an early stage of evolution. The next generation gives it its full attention. At the turn of the century even the most determined defenders of the papal supremacy regard the safety-valve of the Council as indispensable. In this respect their views did not greatly differ from those of such

---

[1] "Ep. Gaditanus videtur fateri quod concilium, etiam cessante incorrigibilitate papae possit congregari pro reformatione in capite et membris." *De concilio*, BK IV, art. 2 (pp. 198 ff.). Under "the Bishop of Cadiz," Gundisalvus Villadiego (1442-72) must be considered in the first instance, though his treatise *De origine et dignitate et potestate SRE cardinalium* is silent on the point, at least the abridgment printed in *Tract. ill. iuriscons.*, VOL. XIII, ii, fols. 57^v-59^v is so. But since Gundisalvus lived at the Curia and was an auditor of the Rota, Jacobazzi may very well have had another work of his in view, one with which I am not acquainted.

[2] *De concilio*, BK III, art. 1 (p. 139).

[3] *De concilio*, BK III, art. 1 (p. 142); a detailed justification in BK VII.

[4] "An autem hodie (cum nihil boni videmus et ad superos Astraea recessit) indigeremus concilio pro reformatione, nihil dico: Deus scit." *De concilio*, BK IV, art. 4 (p. 258).

[5] "Licet respectu temporis celebrandi concilii . . . possit dici abiisse in desuetudinem, vel quod non fuerit recepta, tamen ratione actus agendi, idest concilium celebrandi, non videtur sublata nec circa alia." *De concilio*, BK IV, art. 1 (p. 189).

partisans of the conciliar theory as Ugoni and Gozzadini. All that was wanting was to carry their teaching into effect, and to say: "The present Pope's conduct causes grave scandal," or "The Pope refuses to undertake the necessary reform and to convoke a Council; the College of Cardinals therefore has the right, and even the duty, to convoke a Council, to act, and to take the convocation into its own hands"—for the dreaded spectre of a conciliar assembly without the Pope to become a reality. The only question was in what circumstances would the Sacred College decide on so dangerous and weighty a step, and whether it would ally itself with the demands for a council which came from beyond the Alps.

The story of the conciliar attempt of Pisa provides the answer to these questions. The course of that assembly can only be understood if one bears in mind the history of the idea of the Council since the days of Basle as sketched in the foregoing pages, and by studying, for the sake of comparison, Zamometič's belated attempt to convene a Council.

POPE SIXTUS IV

After the painting by Titian in the Uffizi Gallery, Florence

CHAPTER V

Failure of the Conciliar Attempts of Basle (1482) and Pisa (1511)

ON 25 March 1482, in the cathedral church of Basle, the Dominican Andrew Zamometič, Archbishop of Krania in Thessaly, called for a continuation of the Council of Basle.[1] Neither the cardinals nor the bishops, neither the University of Paris nor the King of France, had dared to take the revolutionary step of which there had been so much talk. It had an interesting personal background.

Zamometič came from the Balkans. He was undoubtedly a man of exceptional gifts and an adept in the diplomatic craft. He had studied and subsequently taught at Padua at the same time as Francesco della Rovere, at that time a Friar Minor. When the latter became Pope, Zamometič received from him, in 1476, the archbishopric of Krania, by then a mere titular see. He also made himself useful to the Emperor Frederick III in several diplomatic missions. One of these terminated abruptly, for in consequence of an incident that has never been fully explained he was unexpectedly summoned to Rome in 1479. In the autumn of 1481, during a stay in Rome as imperial envoy, he so far forgot himself as to indulge in unsparing criticism of the conduct of his former fellow-student Sixtus IV, his nephew Girolamo, and the papal court. Thereupon he was unceremoniously thrown into the Castle of Sant' Angelo. Through the intervention of Cardinal Michiel he was set at liberty. He left Rome burning with a desire to revenge himself on the Pope, now the object of his bitter hatred. The Basle proclamation of the Council was the answer to the humiliation of Sant' Angelo.

In a manifesto of 11 April 1482, antedated to 25 March, which was disseminated both in manuscript and in print, Zamometič called upon the Christian princes to prevent the ruination of the Church by the reigning Pope, on whose head he heaped a whole series of grave accusations. He accused him of heresy, simony and shameful vices, of wasting the possessions of the Church, of instigating the conspiracy of

---

[1] For what follows I use, unless otherwise indicated, J. Schlecht, *Zamometič*, and A. Stoecklin, *Der Basler Konzilsversuch des Andrea Zamometič*.

the Pazzi, and of concluding a secret understanding with the Sultan. He ended by summoning him to appear at the bar of the Council.[1] The summons in due legal form followed on 14 May.[2] How could Zamometič justify such unheard-of proceedings? Where did he look for support?

His legal arguments were exceedingly weak. In nine theses, published in April at the earliest, he merely repeated the old arguments of Basle against Eugenius IV and the translation to Ferrara.[3] He started from the fiction that the Council of Basle was not yet concluded hence he was acting as the spokesman of the *Sacrosancta Generalis Synodus in Spiritu Sancto Basileae legitime congregata, ecclesiam universalem repraesentans.* In point of fact the Council of Basle had dissolved itself at Lausanne; not a trace of it was left at Basle. Zamometič's manifesto was therefore the convocation of a new Council. Whence came his authority to summon it?

There can be no doubt that he was acting on the opinion that in presence of an obvious emergency, if the Pope were a heretic, or if his conduct led to the ruin of the Church, a single bishop, nay, a simple cleric or layman, was entitled to summon a Council.[4] However, he overlooked the fact that even in the conciliar theory this right supposes that the highest authorities, that is, the College of Cardinals, the Emperor and the rest of the Christian princes, together with the episcopate, neglected their duty, that is, refused to convoke a Council when summoned to do so. Above all, the facts by which Zamometič sought to prove that a state of emergency actually existed were for the most part either irrelevant or exaggerated. In particular, the accusation of heresy against Sixtus IV was quite groundless. If it had been true, it would indeed have created a state of emergency according to the unanimous opinion of canonists, but the Pope's intervention against the veneration of the stigmata of St Catherine of Siena could not seriously be branded as heresy. Even from the standpoint of the conciliar theory

---

[1] Schlecht, *Zamometič*, pp. 36*-41*, also 78 ff., 96 ff.; Stoecklin, *Basler Konzils-versuch*, pp. 33 ff. Copies of the manifesto and the convocation, e.g. in St. Arch., Modena, Roma 110, cop.

[2] Schlecht, *Zamometič*, pp. 66* ff.; see Stoecklin, *Basler Konzilsversuch*, pp. 39 ff.

[3] Schlecht, *Zamometič*, pp. 65* ff. Conciliar theory finds a particularly rigid expression in "Reply" drawn up by Peter Numagen's secretary to the Council, to Henricus Institoris's "Epistola" presently to be mentioned; it is printed by J. H. Hottinger in *Historia ecclesiastica Novi Testamenti*, VOL. IV, pp. 422-555, under the title of : *Tertia editio invectiva responsialis sub nomine archiepiscopi Craynensis per Petrum Trevirensem contra Henricum Institoris formata.*

[4] See above, Chapter IV.

juridical proceedings against an unquestionably legitimate Pope presupposed a Council actually sitting and accordingly entitled to claim that it represented the whole Church. But Zamometič was the only prelate at Basle. It remained to be seen whether his proclamation would find a hearing.

Zamometič undoubtedly imagined that he could count on the support of such ecclesiastical circles north of the Alps as favoured a Council, perhaps even on that of the Emperor who just then was nursing a grievance against the Pope. The anti-papal league between Milan, Florence and Naples seemed only to be waiting for a chance to embarrass its opponent in the ecclesiastical sphere, and as for the King of France, he was notoriously ready with the threat of a Council. Discontent was found even in the Sacred College on account of the Pope's nepotism.[1] Zamometič's hopes proved illusory. Encouragement came to him from many directions, but, as Jacob Burckhardt observes, "no one had the courage to stand openly by him". Though pressed by letters and envoys, the Emperor adopted a waiting policy while he put the awkward but quite pertinent question, by what authority did Zamometič act at all?[2] Louis XI stood on the brink of the grave. It was not to be expected that he would adhere to a council on German soil. Milan and Florence had their agents at Basle, but they sent no bishops. Ferrante of Naples only prepared to mobilise the numerous bishops of his realm in the autumn of 1482. By then it was too late. Once again it became evident that the Christian princes' demand for a Council was not seriously meant. If the attempt to call a Council had proved a success, they would have been willing to take advantage of it, but it never entered their minds to back a venture. As for the cardinals of the opposition, they were even less disposed to run risks since for them so much more was at stake.

In point of fact, Zamometič's venture only got a footing and maintained itself for a while because the city of Basle, mindful of the golden era of the great Council, granted him a safe-conduct and freedom of action, and before long, even active support. "We should be glad if the Council were to take place here," the city fathers declared, "if it can be suitably done." However, not even neighbouring Berne, whose influential provost, Stör, undoubtedly favoured the conciliar theory,

---

[1] In his letter of 13 July to the Emperor Zamometič appeals to the alleged agreement of the "Rev.mi praelati ecclesiae Rom." Hottinger, *Historia ecclesiastica*, vol. IV, p. 560.

[2] The letter itself has not been preserved; that it contained the above question appears from Zamometič's reply mentioned in the preceding note.

allowed itself to be won over. The fact that not a single prelate obeyed the summons proved decisive. Even the neighbouring bishops stayed away.[1] No cathedral chapter, no university sent a representative—in fact, on the motion of Wimpfeling, its rector, Heidelberg openly sided with the opposition. The Bishop of Würzburg made haste to despatch a copy of the manifesto to Rome. Zamometič was being punished for his neglect of diplomatic preparation as well as legal justification for his action.

It was only in the course of the summer that he sought to repair this omission. In two pamphlets, respectively entitled *Expositio*, of 20 July,[2] and *Appellatio*,[3] of 21 July, he appealed to the decree *Frequens* and quoted the theses published on the eve of the Council of Basle, on the duty of all Christians towards the Council and on the right of the Council to enter upon its deliberations even without papal authorisation. It was too late now. It hardly needed the rejoinder entitled: *Epistola contra quemdam conciliaristam*,[4] of the Dominican Henricus Institoris, who placed himself unconditionally by the Pope's side, to prejudice public opinion against Zamometič and to bring about the collapse of his undertaking.

Meanwhile the Pope had displayed a lively diplomatic activity in every direction with a view to stamping out the fire before it flared up.[5] On 6 August Basle was laid under an interdict. On 3 October the

---

[1] This applies especially to the Bishops of Basle and Constance. Kleinbasel, where Zamometič resided, was within the jurisdiction of the Bishop of Constance.

[2] Hottinger, *Historia ecclesiastica*, VOL. IV, pp. 360-7; see Stoecklin, *Basler Konzilsversuch*, p. 44 f. The text of the Basle conciliar theses in Hottinger differs in several places from that of John of Segovia, *Mon. conc. gen.*, VOL. II, p. 4.

[3] Hottinger, *Historia ecclesiastica*, VOL. IV, pp. 368-94; Stoecklin, *Basler Konzilsversuch*, pp. 46 ff. The most succinct summary of Zamometič's point of view is found in his letter to the Bishop of Basle (Hottinger, *Historia ecclesiastica*, VOL. IV, p. 600), where he says: "I am authorised to convoke a Council as a Christian, as a bishop and a successor of the Apostles, as a continuator of the Council of Basle and on the basis of *Frequens*."

[4] Hottinger, *Historia ecclesiastica*, VOL. IV, pp. 395-421. On the printed editions, see J. Hansen, *Quellen und Untersuchungen zur Geschichte des Hexenwahns im Mittelalter* (Bonn 1901), p. 383. For a biography of the author, see H. Wibel in *M.Ö.I.G.*, XXXIV (1913), pp. 121-5. As was to be expected, Institoris put his finger at once upon his opponent's weak spot: Sixtus IV was no heretic, and even if he were one, the Council had no power to judge him, but he would be deposed *ipso facto*. This is the strictly hierocratic point of view with which we are familiar. In Institoris's opinion the Pope is not even subject to fraternal correction.

[5] It is not necessary for our purpose to recount the Pope's embassies, described with so much detail by Schlecht and Stoecklin, first to Basle (Ockel, Hohenlandenberg, and later Gerardini and Carsetta), and then to the Emperor (Orsini and Gratiadei), nor the missions of Anthony de Rupe, the Minorite Emmerich von Kemel, Peter von Kettenheim, etc.

Franciscan Gratiadei, who had been despatched to the imperial court, persuaded Frederick III to send an extradition order to the city. Alarmed by the prospect of the injury to its economy which would result from an interdict, Basle was forced to yield. On 21 December 1482 the Archbishop was put in chains. He was no weakling. He played the man up to his dreadful end by suicide on 13 November 1484. The miserable failure of Zamometič's conciliar attempt was due to the fact that it was plain open revolution without a shadow of legitimacy, and one for which no preparation had been made either by means of diplomacy or literary propaganda. It was a desperate *coup de main*, not a carefully prepared campaign entered upon with adequate forces. It failed to rouse public opinion, which actually favoured the idea of a Council, and collapsed before it became a serious danger for the Papacy. The Pope made haste to have his triumph artistically perpetuated in the recently completed Sixtine Chapel, on the walls of which the master-hand of Botticelli depicted him—supported by Arevalo and Institoris—in the act of executing God's judgment against Corah and his band who rebelled against Moses.[1] The artist was right: the Vicar of Christ and successor of Peter had triumphed over a rebel. But the student of history who contemplates the picture cannot but feel that the victory was won far too easily. Not all Zamometič's accusations against his former fellow-student were groundless. A Council would have administered a wholesome shock, leading to reflexion and self-examination. Such a shock had not been given, and after so easy a triumph an exaggerated sense of security settled on the home of the Roman Renaissance.

Zamometič was defeated, in fact his defeat was inescapable, not only because his attempt had been an improvisation, but because he himself lacked that self-forgetting devotion to the cause of God, that indefinable mixture of courage and humility which alone achieves great things in the Church. The apostrophes to the Pope in the manuscript edition of his manifesto betray the fierce passion of a mortally offended man; they are not inspired by selfless zeal for God's house. Zamometič was not the man of destiny called to renew the Church.

The issue of the conciliar attempt of Basle throws light on two factors which proved equally decisive for the fate of a similar attempt that was to follow, namely the willing acceptance by Christendom of the papal primacy on the one hand and the insincerity of the politically

---

[1] E. Steinmann, *Die Sixtinische Kapelle*, VOL. I, pp. 262-73; see also the description on pp. 496-512, as well as my own article in *H.J.*, LXII (1942), pp. 161 ff.

conditioned demand for a Council on the other. In spite of the convulsions occasioned by schism and the conciliar theory, the restored Papacy—the undoubtedly legitimate Pope—continued to retain its extraordinary power over souls and over the social structure of the *Respublica christiana*. Even the city council of Basle, though it favoured Zamometič's attempt, addressed its seven appeals not to the General Council but to the Pope.[1] Contrariwise the negative attitude of the Emperor and the lukewarm interest of the powers of the Italian League were a warning to all ecclesiastical adherents of the Council not to rest their hopes on the quicksands of political combinations. The organisers of the next conciliar attempt did not heed the warning—to their own cost.

The *conciliabulum* of Pisa of 1511 owed its convocation to an alliance of the cardinals of the opposition with the external enemies of Julius II after the break-up of the League of Cambrai.[2] In the summer of 1510 that masterful pontiff, until recently an ally of Louis XII and Maximilian I against Venice, suddenly reversed his policy in the hope of driving the "barbarians" out of his beloved Italy, with the help of Venice. His chief enemy was France. Her two-hundred-year-old ambition to dominate the peninsula seemed to be on the eve of realisation. Louis XII's answer to the Pope's change of front was twofold. It took the form of a plan for a great political and military action, as well as an attack on Julius II on his own ground—the ecclesiastical one. On 30 July 1510 the King summoned an assembly of prelates to Orleans;

[1] *Urkundenbuch der Stadt Basel*, VOL. VIII (Basle 1901), pp. 488 ff.

[2] Chief sources: *Promotiones et progressus sacrosancti concilii Pisani Moderni* (*sine loco* 1512); the parchment copy, authenticated by the notary Chalmot, in Vat. Library, Membr. II, 23; printed (exclusive of sess. IX and X) Paris 1612. The schedule of convocation and the Pope's first Monitorium in Mansi, VOL. XXXII, pp. 563-74, in part also in Mansi's Supplement to Labbé, *Sanctorum conciliorum collectio nova*, 1728, VOL. V, pp. 349 ff. Decius's *Consilium* and Ferreri's *Apologia* were reprinted in Goldast, *Monarchia*, VOL. II, pp. 1653-76. The Acts for the diplomatic history are in A. Renaudet, *Le Concile gallican de Pise-Milan* (Paris 1922); J. M. Doussinague, *Fernando el Católico y el cisma de Pisa* (Madrid 1946); some of Bibbiena's *Letters* n the Carte Strozziane are published by G. Grimaldi, "Un episodio del pontificato di Giulio II", in *Archivium della Soc. Rom. di storia patria*, XXIII (1900), pp. 563-71. The earlier accounts by L. Sandret, "Le concile de Pise, 1511", in *R.Q.H.*, XXXIV (1883), pp. 415-56, and by P. Lehmann, *Das Pisaner Konzil 1511*, (Dissertation, Breslau 1874), are superseded by Pastor, VOL. III, pp. 774 ff. (Eng. edn., VOL. VI, pp. 353 ff.) and Doussinague's work, but Hefele-Hergenröther, *Conziliengeschichte*, VOL. VIII, pp. 431-97, remains indispensable. For a judgment the following should be consulted: Imbart de la Tour, *Origines*, VOL. II, pp. 127-78; C. Stange, *Erasmus und Julius II*, (Berlin 1937), pp. 179 ff. The same, "Luther und das Konzil von Pisa 1511", in *Zeitschrift für systematische Theologie*, X (1933), pp. 681-710; E. Guglia, "Zur Geschichte des 2. Conciliums von Pisa", in *M.Ö.I.G.*, XXXI (1910), p. 593, has a good survey of the sources.

they met in September, but at Tours. At the King's request the meeting decided to warn the Pope off his enterprise; they also proclaimed anew the Gallican principles. At the same time Louis won over some of the cardinals of the opposition for the attack in the ecclesiastical sphere which he planned. In October five of them, viz. two Frenchmen, two Spaniards and one Italian, went over to his side. By 15 February 1511 an anti-papal Council was finally decided upon. The King appointed three procurators to organise its convocation in conjunction with the opposition cardinals. In April a second assembly of prelates at Lyons went so far as to summon the Pope to appear before the future Council.[1]

On 16 May 1511 the die was cast. On that day, from Milan, Cardinals Carvajal, Sanseverino, Borgia, De Prie and Briçonnet, acting apparently in collusion with four other members of the Sacred College,[2] convoked a General Council for 1 September 1511, at Pisa, the city in which a century before the cardinals had vainly sought to put an end to the Great Schism. The Emperor Maximilian I and King Louis XII announced their adhesion and the Pope was summoned to appear before the assembly.[3]

This time the situation was serious. Action was being taken by two authorities which in the opinion of many canonists were entitled to convoke a Council without the Pope: they were the cardinals—not indeed the College as a whole but a small section—and the two most powerful rulers of Christendom, the Emperor and the most Christian King. The juridical arguments by which the minority cardinals justified their action were much better than those on which Zamometič had relied. By his non-compliance with the decree *Frequens*, they explained, and by infringing the election capitulation by which he was bound to call a Council within two years, as well as in several other ways, the Pope was giving scandal to the Church. Therefore a state of emergency existed, which "according to the statutes of the Holy Fathers

---

[1] Renaudet, *Le Concile gallican de Pise-Milan*, p. 28.

[2] The assertion in the Cedula that a "sufficiens mandatum" had been issued by all the absentees is demonstrably false; but this does not mean that they were not in sympathy with the convocation. It is certain that Este and Philip of Luxemburg expressed their agreement either in writing or at least by word of mouth, and in the case of Corneto and Carretto it is very probable that they also did so, and no subsequent declarations in an opposite sense make any difference. Only the five people mentioned above took part in the *conciliabulum*; Cardinal d'Albret was the sixth; Borgia died as early as 4 November.

[3] Mansi, VOL. XXXII, pp. 563 ff.; *id., Sanctorum conciliorum collectio nova,*VOL. V (1728), pp. 349 ff.

and the Council of Constance", authorises the cardinals to convoke a Council. Although those who issued the summons formed only a minority of the Sacred College, they were none the less entitled to act as its representatives, inasmuch as the majority at the Curia, in addition to its loss of freedom, was likewise suspect. The convoking cardinals prayed and admonished the Pope to appear at the Council in person or through a legate. As for the two secular rulers, they justified their share in the proceedings by the solicitude for the *Respublica christiana* incumbent on them.

The arguments adduced in the letter of convocation mainly rest on Louis XII's *procuratorium*, in which Gallican ideas blend with juridical considerations; it is evident that the cardinals preferred the latter. They were fully explained in a memorial drawn up previous to the convocation by the jurist Filippo Decio.[1] Basing himself on the chapter *Si papa*, Decio asserts that in the *communis opinio* of canonists, it is a duty to resist a Pope whose life is notoriously scandalous or who misuses his authority. Steps must be taken to remedy such a situation. He then justifies in detail the minority cardinals' action against the Pope. He takes the precaution of adding that even if many of those convoked should fail to put in an appearance, the full authority of a General Council would rest with those present. In support of this opinion he invokes the authority of Piero da Monte, to whom, together with Sangiorgio and Felinus, appeal is also made in an anonymous memorial drawn up for one of the opposition cardinals.[2] The aim of this paper was to prove that even a minority of the Sacred College is entitled to summon a Council without the intervention of the Pope,

[1] The *Consilium* is printed in the appendix to the *Promotiones et progressus sacrosancti concilii Pisani Moderni*, pp. 69-107; I use Goldast, *Monarchia*, VOL. II, pp. 1667-76. Though inspired by the French government and written before 16 May, its aim was to dispose of the cardinals' objections. As a former auditor of the Rota, Decius based himself upon the canonists' teaching explained above. That Decius continued to be esteemed as a canonist even after Pisa is shown by the fact that in 1530 he was requested to draw up a memorial on the question of Henry VIII's divorce; see S. Ehses, *Römische Dokumente zur Geschichte der Ehescheidung Heinrichs VIII von England* (Paderborn 1893), pp. 181 ff.; ambassador Mai's biting remark about his venality in *Cal. of St. Pap., Spain*, VOL. IV, i, p. 739 (No. 446).

[2] Vat. lib. Barb. lat. 843, fols. 234ʳ-240ᵛ—a contemporary but faulty copy without title. The destination appears from the *Incipit*: "Revme Pater. Quamvis impositi oneris magnitudo . . ." The memorial is an answer to five queries: 1. "Quando possit congregari conc. gen"; 2. "Quis possit . . ."; 3. "Quis modus sit servandus . . ."; 4. "Qui et quot intervenire debent . . ."; 5. "Quis cognoscat an causa examinanda sit digna concilio quod convocari possit." The author remains anonymous and does not betray his identity in the course of the document, but one may make a guess at Jerome Boticellus, a professor of Pavia who, together with Decius, was regarded as a pillar of the *conciliabulum*; see Renaudet, *Le Concile gallican de Pise-Milan*, p. 451.

provided there is clear proof that he has fallen into heresy or has become guilty of some notorious crime. Should he deny the need of a Council, while a subordinate authority, one entitled to call a Council, as for instance the Emperor, judges that such a need exists, the Council must be convened in order to resolve the conflict—otherwise the Pope might conceivably prevent the holding of a Council for all time.

Both Decio and the author of the anonymous memorial wrote, previous to the convocation of the Council, for the express purpose of demonstrating that the cardinals were within their rights. They assumed that the Pope was opposed to a Council; their assumption was stultified by the convocation of the Lateran Council by Julius II. So the arguments of the conciliar theory must needs be brought forward. A second anonymous memorial, probably by the same hand as the first,[1] defends Pisa with an appeal to the decree *Frequens* and Gerson's theory of devolution. At about the same time Ferreri, a secretary to the Council, published an *Apologia sacri Pisani concilii*,[2] in which he defends the Popeless, or rather the anti-papal Council by invoking the decrees *Sacrosancta* and *Frequens*, but without altogether dispensing with canonical arguments. This step was inevitable.

The weakness of the canonistic arguments lay not so much in the *quaestio juris* as in the *quaestio facti*. From the standpoint of canonistic teaching one might grant, in the abstract, the cardinals' right to convoke a Council in certain emergencies while contesting the lawfulness of the summons to Pisa and especially the continuation of that venture after the convocation of the Lateran Council by the Pope. Cardinal Sangiorgio, with whose teaching on emergencies we have become acquainted in the preceding chapter, stood by Julius II. Jacobazzi also, in spite of the opinions he had held at one time, turned unhesitatingly against Pisa. The Pope, he declared, was not guilty of criminal neglect, such as might have justified the devolution of his right

---

[1] *Quid de moderno sacro concilio Pisano tenendum sit, Vat. lib.*, Barb. lat. 843, fols. 244ʳ-246ʳ—a contemporary but faulty copy and without name of author. Among others Ludovicus Romanus, Felinus and Corsetus are appealed to about the cardinals' right to convoke a Council; fol. 244ᵛ says that the Pope is subject to the decree *Frequens*. The fact that fol. 245ʳ quotes a passage from the Bull *Sacrosanctae* proves that it was composed after 18 July.

[2] *Promotiones et progressus sacrosancti concilii Pisani Moderni*, appendix 1-51; Goldast, *Monarchia*, VOL. II, pp. 1635-65, dated Borgo San Donnino, 27 September 1511. For the author see especially B. Morsolin, "L'Abbate di Monte Subasio e il Concilio di Pisa" (Venice 1893), extract from the *Atti del R. Instituto Veneto*, Ser. VII, VOL. IV (1892-3), pp. 1689-1735; p. 10 mentions the printing of the Acts of the Councils of Constance and Basle by Ferreri at Milan in 1511—a further proof of dependence on the ideas of the reform Councils.

of convocation.[1] Nor could there be question of a state of emergency so long as the College of Cardinals—or at least a majority of its members —had not established the fact that such a situation was actually in being. The alleged notorious scandal was nothing else, at bottom, than the Pope's war against the French! Until now the cardinals had raised no protest against his non-compliance with the election capitulation and the decree *Frequens* had been in abeyance since the Council of Basle. If these omissions were made a reproach against Julius II, then all the Popes since the assembly of Basle were equally to blame. But the legal basis for these accusations, the decree *Frequens*, was, to say the least, extremely questionable.[2] To these errors of fact must be added a grave error of form. Even Ugoni, champion though he was of the conciliar theory, felt compelled to declare that the conduct of the Pisan cardinals was canonically indefensible since they had failed to admonish the Pope in due canonical form of his duty to summon a Council.[3] But their chief guilt, in Jacobazzi's opinion, lay in the fact that they went on with the conciliar attempt of Pisa after the convocation by the Pope of the Lateran Council. It was this, and their further collaboration with the French, that made them rebels and schismatics.[4]

With these explanations we have run far ahead of events, for before the actual assembling of the council of Pisa, in October 1511, its organisers had sought once more to negotiate with the Pope, Spain acting as mediator. It was only after these attempts had come to naught that the assembly opened at Pisa on 1 November. The first session was held on 5 November. Those present were nearly all Frenchmen: they were two archbishops, fourteen bishops, several abbots and the proctors of the Universities of Paris, Toulouse and Poitiers.[5] The composition of the assembly accounts for the turn it took. In its third session, on 12 November, it proclaimed anew the superiority decree of

---

[1] *De concilio*, BK VII (pp. 403-14).

[2] Memorial of the licentiate Illescas for Ferdinand the Catholic, dated 28 August 1511, in Doussinague, *Fernando el Católico y el cisma de Pisa*, pp. 477-85.

[3] "Per quae omnia . . . liquido patet quod venerandi illi patres, qui alias conciliabulum Pisanum novissimis temporibus indixerunt contra S. D. N. D. Julium II modernum pont. max. . . . , illi doctores, qui concilium congregari posse sine consensu pont. maximi, quando contra ipsum agendum est, non servata forma de qua supra, consuluerunt, longe a recta declinaverunt via, et propterea eorum desiderio frustrati fuere." Ugoni, *De conciliis*, fol. 39ʳ.

[4] Jacobazzi, *De concilio*, BK VII, art. 1 ad 3 (p. 421). Before this (p. 420) Jacobazzi says that in his opinion, in view of the Pope's previous threats, the cardinals' flight did not amount to a refusal of obedience.

[5] According to the Florentine Ridolfi, writing on 2 November, there were present about twelve bishops, eight abbots and twelve doctors.

Constance. By this act it definitely committed itself to the conciliar theory. Soon afterwards, in view of the hostile attitude of the population and the uncertain attitude of the government of Florence, the Council decided on a transfer to Milan, which lay within the sphere of power of the French army. In its sixth session, on 24 March 1512, an order of procedure on the model of that of Basle was agreed upon. The assembly ended by burning its last bridges when, in its eighth session, it pronounced a sentence of suspension against the Pope. Once again radicalism was triumphant.

The number of bishops present gradually rose to thirty; the French were in an overwhelming majority. The Italian and the German hierarchy refused participation; as for the English, Spanish, Hungarian and Polish prelates, their co-operation was not to be thought of, were it only because of the attitude of their rulers. In view of the composition and the radicalism of the Milanese gathering, Julius II's opponents in the Sacred College and in the Curia were afraid to identify themselves with the definitely Franco-Gallican aims of the assembly. Some of the cardinals who had been favourably disposed at first, and whose names had appeared in the letter of convocation, publicly disavowed the Council. Giovanni Gozzadini, who in his great work on the papal election had only recently accepted all the Pisans' arguments against the Pope, not only remained on his side but even positively championed his cause.

Before long even the two political props of Pisa turned out to be rotten. The Emperor did not even send a representative to Milan. His envoy at the French court was known to be a decided opponent of the conciliar project. His political adviser, Matthew Lang, was far more interested in the national autonomy of the German Church under a primate with legatine powers. Even in the *entourage* of Louis XII opinion was divided. Robertet, whose influence was considerable, had described it from the beginning as a political manœuvre. He was sceptical about its prospects [1]; as for the King, the Council was without a doubt no more than a weapon in his struggle with the Pope. As early as 3 July 1511 the experienced Venetian Girolamo Porzia foretold that the whole undertaking would come to nothing.[2] The event justified his prophecy. Not even the great French victory of Ravenna on 11 April 1512 was able to avert its fate, because in the critical summer of 1511 Julius II had shown that in political acumen and strength of will he

---

[1] Renaudet, *Le Concile gallican de Pise-Milan*, p. 44.
[2] Sanudo, *Diarii*, VOL. XII, p. 267.

was far superior to his opponents. By the Bull *Sacrosanctae romanae ecclesiae* of 18 July 1511 he convoked a General Council for 19 April 1512 at the Lateran.[1] With this bold step he took the wind out of the sails of the schismatical Council by a single stroke. From that moment the question was no longer: "Council or no Council?" but only "which Council?" There could only be one answer. By an overwhelming majority Christendom not only decided for the papal Council but hailed it with enthusiasm. At last the long desired Council was a fact!

Simultaneously with the convocation of the Lateran Council measures were taken against the leaders of the opposition in the Sacred College. In the Consistory of 24 October Carvajal, Briçonnet, Borgia and De Prie were degraded.[2] On 10 March 1512, after some heated discussions with the Sacred College, eight new cardinals were named in their place. Decio and Ferreri, the literary champions of Pisa, were suspended, while the seats of the assembly, the cities of Pisa and Milan, were laid under an interdict which was strictly observed. On 16 November 1511, at Burgos, Ferdinand the Catholic announced his adhesion to the Papal Council and named his delegates to it. The fortune of arms also changed in the Pope's favour. In spite of their victory at Ravenna the French were forced to evacuate almost the whole of Upper Italy under pressure from the combined Swiss, Venetian and papal forces. Towards the end of 1512 the Emperor made peace, and Louis XII also ended by taking no further interest in the assembly, the futility of which he realised. The *conciliabulum* thereupon transferred its seat to Asti, and from there to Lyons, where, after its tenth session, it gradually dissolved itself. The last anti-papal Council in the history of the Church thus ended in a miserable failure.

Since this book is only concerned with ideas, our main concern is to

---

[1] Mansi, VOL. XXXII, pp. 681-91; *Bull. Rom.*, VOL. V, pp. 499-509, several times reprinted.

[2] According to Bibbiena (ed. Grimaldi, in *Archivium della Soc. Rom. de storia patria*, XXIII (1900), pp. 567 ff.), at the consistory of 22 October Sangiorgio had pleaded for an extension of the time-limit but had eventually yielded to the Pope's decision. Del Monte and Accolti were believed to favour stern measures. Further information on the feelings of the majority cardinals may be gathered from the votes published by Guglia in *M.Ö.I.G.*, XXXI (1910), p. 597, from Vat. lat. 12146, fols. 25^r-61^r. Votes III-V refer to the consistory of 22 October 1511, while I judge II and VII, as does Guglia, to refer to Sanseverino's deprivation. Votes I and VI, which are also part of the discussions which preceded the deposition of the four, urge that consideration should be had for the hesitant (pp. 598, 602). Eubel, *Hierarchia Catholica*, VOL. III, n.4, mistakenly names Sanseverino as one of those deposed on 24 October instead of Borgia. The former was only deprived on 30 January 1512; Ferdinand's adhesion in Doussinague, *Fernando el Católico y el cisma de Pisa*, pp. 504-8.

ascertain the causes of such an issue. They lie on the surface and are easily perceived. Once again the insincerity and inner weakness of the threat of a Council as a political weapon were fully revealed. For Louis XII the *conciliabulum* was merely part of a political scheme— neither more nor less. It was at his command that the French bishops repaired to Pisa and Milan. There the gathering worked under the protection of his arms. The use of a purely ecclesiastical institution for a heterogeneous purpose was doomed to failure from the beginning. Gallicanism obediently gave its assistance and by so doing lost what power of attraction it may have possessed. To that extent the expression "Gallican Council" is accurate enough, though it does not cover the whole ground. The peculiarity of the conciliar attempt of Pisa lies in the participation, at least in the beginning, of the cardinals of the opposition and in the exploitation by them of the canonists' teaching on the state of emergency. A man like Carvajal was not likely to throw himself blindly into the arms of the French King or to fail to weigh the consequences of such an act. He knew that there was no prospect of success for the Council if its scope was identical with French policy. After their flight the renegade cardinals had allowed a whole year—a decisive year—to elapse before the opening of the *conciliabulum*. That year was spent in efforts to broaden the basis of the undertaking as well as to legitimise it, for they were anxious that theirs should be a canonical, not a revolutionary procedure. It was in the very nature of things that from opposition they should be driven into schism. As the date fixed for the opening drew near, it was clear that all their efforts to give the assembly the character of a General Council had been in vain: it was a French affair, and that character it retained to the end. Hence their last-hour efforts—futile ones—for a *rapprochement*. As late as 8 November 1511 the Florentine Ridolfi wrote to the Signoria of his city: "If he could do so, Carvajal would throw himself at the Pope's feet this very day." [1] After what had happened the offer of a neutral seat for the Council could not be other than unacceptable to the Pope: for the others it came too late.

The fate of the assembly of Pisa was sealed when the Pope convoked the Lateran Council and thus gave satisfaction to the desire for a Council which had been growing ever stronger and more general since the turn

---

[1] Renaudet, *Le Concile gallican de Pise-Milan*, p. 492. That the cardinals of the opposition were most anxious to avoid a rupture is shown by their letter of 11 September 1511, to the representative of the majority cardinals, Alessandro Guasco, Bishop of Alessandria; *Promotiones et progressus sacrosancti concilii Pisani Moderni*, pp. 67-74.

of the century. Instead of any hesitations and misgivings with which such a Council might have been regarded—not without good reason—[1] its announcement was hailed with enthusiasm as the dawn of a new and better age, as the beginning of the reform of the Church. It was easy for a Council convoked by the lawful successor of Peter to triumph over a venture of doubtful legitimacy,[2] one moreover discredited as a political manœuvre of a single nation.

The main stroke was succeeded by yet another, this time against the theory on which Pisa had relied. On 12 October 1511, Thomas de Vio, the Dominican and future cardinal Cajetan, completed his work entitled *De comparatione auctoritatis papae et concilii*.[3] In this book the author, not content to refute the conciliar theory, also deals with the arguments with which Decio and the other juridical advisers of the minority cardinals had attempted to justify their action, namely the canonists' teaching on the convocation of a Council without the Pope in an emergency, as well as with the background of that theory that is, Gerson's attribution to the Church and to the Council of the right to control the Pope's government.[4] It was a momentous event when, in the person of Cajetan, a theologian—perhaps the greatest theologian of his time—intervened in the debate and pushed the canonists aside. From that day the question became an integral part of dogmatic theology. The reply of Jacques Almain,[5] a young theologian of Paris, could no longer influence the course of events, nor was Cajetan's answer long delayed.[6] Among the other writers who entered the lists on behalf of Julius II,[7] the only one of some importance is Gianfrancesco, the

---

[1] It is significant that in his memorial (see above, p. 110, *n.* 2) Illescas recommends some place other than Rome for the assembly of the council, Doussinague, *Fernando el Católico y el cisma de Pisa*, p. 484.

[2] This idea is developed in Pietro Delfino's letter of 7 March 1512 to Vinc. Quirini; see *P. Delphini Epistolae* (Venice 1524), X, p. 60.

[3] New edition, together with the *Apologia* still to be mentioned, by V. J. Pollet, Rome 1936. The printing of the Roman edition was completed on 19 November 1511 .

[4] Especially in c. 27, Pollet, p. 127.

[5] Printed among the works of Gerson, Dupin, VOL. II, pp. 976-1002; Villoslada, *La Universidad de Paris durante los estudios de Francisco de Vitoria*, pp. 175 ff. I had no access to the treatise of the Paris canonist Pierre Cordier, mentioned by Pastor, VOL. III, p. 829 (Eng. edn., VOL. VI, p. 385), the MS of which is at Leyden. John Maior's tract *De auctoritate concilii supra Pont. Rom.* is in Dupin, VOL. II, pp. 1131-43; for the author see Villoslada, *La Universidad de Paris*, pp. 127-64.

[6] *Apologia de comparata auctoritate papae et concilii*, completed on 26 November 1512, in Pollet, pp. 201-320.

[7] Summed up in Hefele-Hergenröther, *Conziliengeschichte*, VOL. VIII, pp. 470-9; Pastor, VOL. III, pp. 829 ff. (Eng. edn., VOL. VI, p. 385); also Cyprianus Benetus, *De prima orbis sede, de concilio et ecclesiastica potestate ac de S. D. N. papae supremo insuperabilique dominio opus* (Rome 1512). The printing was completed on

son of the humanist Poggio, because in addition to the usual arguments of the conciliar theory he also notes those of the cardinals of the opposition.[1]

Thus the second attempt at an anti-papal Council in the restoration period proved a failure in spite of the fact that it had been more carefully prepared than the first and stronger arguments had been advanced in its favour; not to mention the support of a powerful ruler and a great nation. For all that, it could not be said that the latent anti-curial opposition, born of the conciliar theory, had been finally overcome, were it only because the Lateran Council failed to come up to the high expectations that had been set on it. Soon after Julius II's death—20 February 1513—a lampoon entitled *Julius exclusus* [2] gave vent to the prevailing discontent. The identity of the author has not been established with certainty, but he was familiar with conditions at the Curia, and most probably was not an Italian. Every just and unjust allegation against the worldly conduct of the masterful pontiff—in fact against the Renaissance Popes in general—is here served up in terms of the bitterest satire. The dead Pope is described as standing at the gate of heaven, praying for admission. However, instead of expressing regret for his wars and his financial transactions, he boasts of them before Peter and

---

13 December 1512, but the book was only published under Leo X. For the author, a Dominican then teaching at the Sapienza, see *Scriptores ordinis praedicatorum recensiti*, edd. J. Quétif and J. Echard, VOL. II (Paris 1721), pp. 49 ff.; Villoslada, *La Universidad de Paris durante los estudios de Francisco de Vitoria*, p. 329. On the motion of Cardinal Antonio del Monte, Benetus added an explanation of the two corollaries to *Concl. IV*, on the problem of simony by the Pope. His teaching on the council is based on that of Torquemada. Torquemada is also followed by P. Quirini, "Tractatus super concilium generale", in *Annales Camaldulenses*, VOL. IX (Venice 1773), pp. 599-611, composed after 22 February 1512, the day on which Quirini was given the name of Peter in religion; see J. Schnitzer, *Peter Delfin* (Munich 1926), pp. 149 ff. On the tract of the Dominican Alberto Pasquali, *De potestate papae super concilium*, see P. Paschini in *Memorie stor. Forogiuliesi*, XXXVIII (1942), pp. 42 ff.

[1] J. Poggius, *De potestate papae et concilii*, probably published in Rome (leaves not numbered). Important for our purpose are arguments 14 (Church and Council as a regulating authority), 19 ("the salt of the earth that has lost its savour"), 23 ("papa incorrigibilis"), 44 (the council without the Pope).

[2] *Julius exclusus e coelis*, last printed in *Erasmi opuscula*, ed. W. K. Ferguson (The Hague 1933), pp. 65-124; the passage on the Council, pp. 89-102; also C. Stange, *Erasmus und Julius II*, pp. 166-97. The earlier editor, Boecking, ascribed the authorship either to the Italian Faustus Andrelinus Foroliviensis who lived in Paris or to his friend Balbi; Allen and Ferguson thought of Erasmus and P. Paschini of Girolamo Rorario (see *Memorie stor. Forogiuliesi*, XXX (1934) pp. 169-216; *Atti dell' Accademia degli Arcadi*, XVIII (1934-5) pp. 85-98). C. Stange, "G. Rorario und Julius II" in *Zeitschrift für Systematische Theologie* (1941), pp. 535-88, is of a contrary opinion. There is a translation of the *Julius exclusus* in Froude's *Life and Letters of Erasmus* (London 1894).

when accused takes cover behind the papal supremacy. For us it is interesting to note what he has to say about his attitude to the Council. "It can do me no harm", he declares, "for I summon it and am above it; even in the famous exceptional case of *crimen haereseos*, there is a way out." He then relates with cynical frankness by what means he had managed to undo the Pisan gathering. First he had turned both the Emperor Maximilian and a number of opposition cardinals against it. After that he himself had convoked a Council in Rome, for he knew that none of his enemies would come there. He put off the opening and meanwhile saw to it that only a few foreign bishops would put in an appearance. In this way the composition of the Council was as he wished—and the result was what it was! But it does not matter: better three hundred schisms than to be called to account and to have to submit to a reform!

For the author of *Julius exclusus*, the policy of the Rovere Pope was but a network of cunningly devised ruses for the sole purpose of enabling him, under cover of the primacy, to act as he pleased and to avoid both Council and reform. When confronted with this unjust and spiteful interpretation of the Pope's policy in regard to the Council, an interpretation that denies to the greatest of the Renaissance Popes all sense of responsibility and every inclination to reform, we have to ask ourselves: "What have the Popes of the Renaissance period done to heal the injuries of ecclesiastical life of the existence of which they were well aware?" They entertained grave misgivings about a reform by means of a Council; but what did they do on their own initiative for a solution of the most pressing problem of their time?

POPE JULIUS II
After the painting by Raphael in the Uffizi Gallery, Florence

CHAPTER VI

The Papacy and Church Reform:
The Fifth Council of the Lateran

CHRISTENDOM's longing for a reform of the Church was the spring from which the idea of a Council was for ever drawing new strength. The question of the Council and the problem of reform had become so closely interwoven that we cannot discuss them separately in this story. No one could deny the need of reform, the only controversy was as to how to go about it.

North of the Alps, where the memory of the reform Councils was still alive, it was thought that the reform of the Church in her head and her members was the duty of a General Council. This strong faith in the healing virtue of such an assembly seemed all the greater for the lack of clarity and unanimity with regard to the programme for reform, and the prevailing unwillingness to begin reform with oneself.[1] The one thing on which there was general agreement was the reform of the head, that is the Roman Curia, so much so, indeed, that it was the proper thing for a writer to win his literary spurs with an exposure of the shortcomings of the Papacy which, in point of fact, were obvious enough.[2] A Council was particularly required for the reform of the Curia, people argued, because only the joint action of the nations would successfully overcome the resistance of those whose interest it was that abuses should continue [3]; only the decrees of a Council would ensure

---

[1] In his *Advisamenta*, presently to be mentioned, Capranica says: "Tanta enim adversus nos surrexit infamia ut ex omni parte obloquentes et conquerentes audiamus. Quorum plurimos ex hoc novam et impiam assertionem de auctoritate concilii supra papam amplecti videmus, dicentes oportere ut ecclesia his manum apponat". Vat. lat. 4039, fol. 17ᵛ. Forty years after the Council of Basle Peter Numagen gave it as his opinion that if Christendom were left without a Council for another forty years, there would only be left a small remnant. Hottinger, *Historia Ecclesiastica*, VOL. IV, p. 522.

[2] H. Finke, *Das ausgehende Mittelalter* (Munich 1900), p. 20.

[3] For these reasons Vincent of Aggsbach goes so far as to advocate a refusal of obedience and a demand for a schismatical Council, Pez-Hueber, *Thesaurus anecd.*, VOL. V, iii, p. 337.

the permanence of reform once it was begun, since the Pope would be bound by it.[1]

There is both truth and error in this statement. The truth is that strong external pressure was needed to break the chain of abuses; the error lies in the notion of the Pope's subordination to a Council. However, there is strength even in error if it obtains credence, most of all when it is based on experience, as in the present instance. Belief in the need and in the reforming virtue of the Council became one of the most powerful factors to which the Council of Trent owed its convocation. As late as the fifteen-thirties certain Spanish theologians, according to Ortwin Gratius, maintained that the root of all evils was the fact that the Popes would not obey a General Council.[2]

The Popes of the restoration declined to tread the path of conciliar theory. Whenever they and their advisers took up the problem of Church reform, they conceived it almost exclusively not as reform brought about by a Council, but as an effect of papal power operating through legislative acts, such as papal Bulls, or through the decrees of papal legates and visitors *in partibus*.[3] This procedure at once shut the door against the pretensions of the patrons of the conciliar theory, who sought to tie the Pope's hands by means of conciliar decrees and thus to subject him to the reform. It was also a practical solution of the controverted question of authority, besides other advantages that it brought in its train. Obvious abuses in the Pope's own house and in the Curia, in the sphere of benefices and finances and in the concession of dispensations, could be remedied without foregoing a single prerogative. A papal reform always remained under the control of the Pope as an instrument which it was possible to modify, to blunt or to render powerless. Arevalo, the Curia's best-informed spokesman in this matter, urged yet another argument in favour of a papal reform. The Pope alone, he explained, is in a position to reconcile the conflicting interests of the nations and to give due consideration to their individual requirements; the surest guarantee of the execution of reform decrees

---

[1] When Institoris says: "Autumnant conciliistae papam subiacere statutis concilii universalis" (Hottinger, *Historia Ecclesiastica*, VOL. IV, p. 414), it must be remembered that views of this kind were by no means exclusively held by strict conciliarists. We shall find them in Francisco de Vitoria and at the Council of Trent as the background for many a fight for reform.

[2] *Fasciculus rerum expetendarum seu fugiendarum* (Cologne 1535), fol. 240ᵛ.

[3] The alternative appears already in the memorial for Nicholas of Cusa (Walch, *Monimenta medii aevi*, VOL. I, p. 110): "Certe si dominus apostolicus et sua curia se reformaret vel per concilium generale fieret reformatio generalis, facile membrum ecclesiae unumquodque in suo statu reformaretur."

is the appointment of papal visitors.[1] On the reform of the Curia he
has next to nothing to say, while Institoris leaves it to divine omni-
potence, which would find ways and means to attain its ends.[2] The
election capitulations occupy an intermediary standpoint in so far as
they invariably leave the reform of the Curia to the Pope and the
general reform of the Church to a Council. However, they failed to
influence the Pope's line of action.

Which of the two ways was the right one? What is certain is that
the Popes of the restoration chose the latter. As often as they deemed it
necessary to lend ear to the demand for a Council and to cut the ground
from under the conciliar theory, they themselves initiated reforms and
thereby entered on the path of a papal reform of the Church. At
Constance, Martin V had bound himself to call a new Council within
five years. On the eve of the new Council, which was to meet at Pavia,
he requested Cardinals Orsini, Adimari and Carillo to submit a scheme
for a reform along these lines. Their work, the *Advisamenta*,[3] is still
influenced by the grievances voiced at Constance. There could be no
doubt that they would be renewed at the forthcoming Council by the
people north of the Alps. The book urges observance of the concordats
of Constance in respect of the election of bishops and abbots and warns
against too great a readiness to listen to princely recommendations. In
the appointment to reserved benefices there should be equal consideration for officials of the Curia and for outsiders. This can be done by
means of carefully drawn-up lists of candidates. Pallium fees should
be abolished altogether. The cardinals saw quite clearly that a number
of abuses which had crept into the appointment to offices and the
concession of privileges during the period of the Schism were due to
the Pope's financial straits. They accordingly press for a reorganisation of the revenues of the States of the Church and a guaranteed
income for the cardinals in accordance with the suggestions made at
Constance.

In 1430, on the eve of the Council of Basle, the *Advisamenta* were
revised and enlarged by a commission of cardinals consisting of John
de Rupescissa, Antonio Cavini, Alonso de Carillo and Ardicinus de
Porta. Among other items they added a section on the bishops' duty
of residence, and the Council's future president, Cesarini, inserted a

---

[1] Proofs in *H.J.*, LXII (1942), pp. 172, 174 ff.
[2] "Ecclesiam per concilium reformare non poterit omnis humana facultas, sed
alium modum Altissimus procurabit, nobis quidem pro nunc incognitum." Hottinger,
Historia ecclesiastica, VOL. IV, pp. 313 ff.
[3] *Conc. Bas.*, VOL. I, pp. 163-83; see J. Haller's treatment, pp. 108 ff.

section, *Extra curiam*, which dealt with conditions in England and Germany.

The *Advisamenta* were mere proposals; the Pope alone could give them binding force. This step Martin V did not take, either before the Council of Siena or before that of Basle; but even if he had taken it, it is very doubtful whether he would have forestalled the impending revolution. As a matter of fact no notice was taken of the *Advisamenta* at Basle.

At the termination of the great struggle between Pope and Council, in which the Pope was victorious, the problem of Church reform re-appeared. Now it would be seen whether the Popes were willing and able to solve it spontaneously and with their own resources. Nicholas V despatched Nicholas of Cusa to Germany as his legate for the purpose of reform. Cusa's fruitful activity is well known [1]; so are the serious objections of a fundamental character that his reforming acti-vities encountered. "The loss of a thousand talents caused by the neglect of the Council is to be made good with a gratuity of three-pence," was the bitter comment of the Carthusian of Aggsbach.[2] Another bluntly asked the legate: "What about the reform of the head? The reform of the members will be an easy thing once the Pope and the Curia reform themselves." [3]

These were no doubt the objections Cardinal Capranica had in mind when he drew up his *Advisamenta super reformatione papae et romanae curiae*, probably at the beginning of the pontificate of Nicholas V.[4] We are unfortunately ignorant of the circumstances that prompted the document, but its authority is very great, because in its pages we hear one of the outstanding personalities of the period of the papal restoration. Capranica is fully conscious of the responsibility that rests on the Pope as head of the whole Church. If all Christians are bound to obey him—if they wish to save their souls—then the Pope is bound to see to it that the Saviour's grace is made available for all men. If he neglects this duty, the souls that perish will be required at his hands.

---

[1] Pastor, VOL. I, pp. 467-93 (Eng. edn., VOL. II, pp. 104 ff.). The extraordinarily extensive literature on Cusa which has appeared since that time (1925) is due to the publication of his works by the Academy of Heidelberg, though the editors mostly ignore his ecclesiastical activities. For his legatine journey to Germany, see J. Koch, "Nikolaus von Cues und seine Umwelt", in *Sonderband der Heidelberger Akademie phil.-hist. Klasse*, II (1944-8) (Heidelberg 1948), pp. 45-78.

[2] Pez-Hueber, *Thesaurus anecd.*, VOL. V, iii, pp. 337 ff.

[3] See above, p. 118, *n.* 3.

[4] Vat. lat. 4039, fols. 16ᵛ-18ʳ, contemporary copy; see Pastor, VOL. I, pp. 414 ff.

Hence Capranica's greatest concern is the choice of good bishops and good parish priests. There must be an end to the practice of indiscriminately admitting to orders the more crafty among the benefice-hunters simply "because they run fastest", as well as known and unknown candidates. Previous to the nomination of a bishop papal commissaries must inquire on the spot into the state of the diocese and the personal character of the candidate. Here we have the germ of the informative process of a later post-Tridentine period. In connexion with the grant of foreign benefices, permanent executors must be appointed whose duty it will be to take care of the interests of the pastoral ministry. To this end they must be empowered to act on their own authority. This was to become the function of the nuncios in the period of the Catholic reformation and counter-reformation. The appointment of inspectors—*speculatores*—would cleanse the offices of the Curia from simony and other abuses.[1] Moral scandals will vanish from Rome if the Pope's court is made a pattern for others. In point of fact reform requires no new laws; if the Pope enforces the observance of the existing ones, and thereby shows that he is in earnest with regard to reform, his voice will be listened to throughout Christendom.

Capranica's memorial reads like a complete programme of the Catholic reformation. A century later it was actually carried out, but after what catastrophes! The Cardinal had a premonition of the approach of "scourges" and "straits"—partly divine punishment, partly simple consequences of neglect. One may wonder how things would have worked themselves out if, instead of Piccolomini, Capranica had obtained the triple crown in 1458.[2]

Pius II—singularly gifted as he was—did not lack a proper appreciation of what was required in the sphere of Church reform. At

---

[1] Capranica's remarks (fol. 17ᵛ) on the meddling by strangers with the business of the Segnatura, on the "expeditio per cameram", and on the payment of dues for the expedition of Bulls should be noted. From the remark about the Grand-Penitentiary ("deputandus videtur supra illos vir doctus, habens zelum Dei et salutis animarum") it follows that at this time Capranica did not as yet hold that office, hence the *Advisamenta* must have been written previous to 29 January 1449 (see Göller, *Pönitentiarie*, VOL. II, pp. 1, 9).

[2] For what follows see L. Célier, "L'Idée de réforme à la cour pontificale du concile de Bâle au concile du Latran", in *R.Q.H.*, LXXXVI (1909), pp. 418-35; Pastor, VOL. II, pp. 184-9 (Pius II) (Eng. edn., VOL. III, pp. 269 ff.); pp. 632 ff. (Sixtus IV) (Eng. edn., VOL. IV, pp. 405 ff.); VOL. III, i, pp. 458-62 (Alexander VI) (Eng. edn., VOL. V, pp. 513 ff.); on the reform of the officials of the Curia, see W. von Hofmann, *Forschungen*, VOL. I, pp. 304-21; VOL. II, pp. 227-40; on the reform of the cardinals see my account in *R.Q.*, XLIII (1935), pp. 87-128.

the very beginning of his pontificate he consulted with a number of cardinals, bishops and theologians. We still possess two memorials drawn up at that time, one by the shrewd Venetian Domenico Domenichi, the other by Nicholas of Cusa. However much they may differ on this point or that, on one subject both men are of one mind, namely the gravity of the situation and the need of a reform—hence they also agree with Capranica. "Obedience to the Holy See", Domenichi bluntly states,[1] "will only be restored on the day when the prelates of the Church, headed by the Pope and the cardinals, begin to seek the kingdom of God instead of their personal advantage." For him too the promotion to influential posts of men of merit is of the very essence of the reform, whereas papal nepotism, which quite recently, under Calixtus III, had yielded such ominous fruits, is its exact opposite. It is inevitable that a Pope addicted to nepotism should be regarded as a man clinging to flesh and blood instead of following in the steps of Christ. A good deal of space in Domenichi's memorial is taken up with the reform of the cardinals and their courts and of the prelates of the Curia, for he knew what kind of impression the doings at the Curia made on many pilgrims to Rome. A committee of cardinals should be appointed to see to it that the existing constitutions, more particularly the regulations relating to taxes, are observed in the offices of the Curia. He makes the remarkable recommendation that a fixed salary should be paid to certain categories of officials of the Chancery and the Rota so as to prevent irregularities in the levying of taxes. Nor does he hesitate to examine the problem of the reform Councils. The decrees of Constance and Basle may not be ignored as if they did not exist at all, as has been the case until now. Such conduct undermines in advance the authority of every future Council. The Pope should make a choice from among these decrees and publish them together with the reform decrees of his immediate predecessors, and give them effect, not because he is subject to the superiority decree, but because they are papal laws. Here we have the same procedure as that contemplated by Julius III after the second meeting of the Council of Trent. It actually came near realisation in the unpublished Bull *Supernae dispositionis arbitrio*. A scheme for reform drawn up in the

---

[1] *Tractatus de reformationibus Romanae curie* (Brescia 1495); Hain, No. 6321, a very rare print; MS Vat. lat. 5869, fols. 1^r-18^r; Barb. lat. 1201, fols. 1^r-20^r; Barb. lat. 1487, fols. 288^r-295^v (from the library of Cardinal Marco Barbo). *Considerationes* 18, 20-2, printed in Hofmann, *Forschungen*, VOL. II, pp. 227 ff.; *consid.* 6 in Steinmann, *Die Sixtinische Kapelle*, VOL. I, pp. 650 ff.

autumn of 1458 took up the suggestion; for the rest it bore a close resemblance to Martin V's reform plans, of which we have spoken above.[1]

Nicholas of Cusa [2] goes deeper and looks further back than either Capranica or Domenichi. For him the reform is a return to the *forma Christi*; its aim is to transform all Christians, beginning with the Pope, into the likeness of Christ. Such an aim determines the means. These are: a reform of the members through three visitors whose action is determined by fourteen rules, the quintessence of which consists in the restoration in all ecclesiastical corporations of the primitive mode of life; a reform of the head, the Pope giving a solemn undertaking that he will comply with the obligations assumed by him in the election capitulation and spontaneously submit to the correction of the visitors. The same undertaking must be given by the cardinals and the entire Curia. Nothing is said about a change in the officialdom of the Curia; what Cusa does stress is the creation of a College of Cardinals independent of external influences and morally irreproachable, whose duty it is to offer counsel to the Pope and, since they represent the Church, to co-operate with him when matters of importance have to be decided. These are familiar notions—Nicholas of Cusa does not allow us to forget that he was once an adherent of the conciliar theory. The institution of visitors and the extensive participation of the College of Cardinals in the government of the Church are intended to remove the lack of confidence in a voluntary reform of the Curia which prevailed abroad: they are a substitute for the controls created by the conciliar theory in the decree *Frequens*.

There can be no doubt that Pius II appreciated these suggestions. The reform Bull *Pastor aeternus*,[3] which appears to have been written by himself, or at least under his inspiration and supervision, during the last months of his pontificate, embodies more than one thought of Cusa's, as when the Cardinal prays the Pope to make a profession of

---

[1] Vat. lat. 3884, fols. 27ʳ-49ᵛ, quoted with press-mark V₁, in *Conc. Bas.*, VOL. I, pp. 163 ff.; the section on the Chancery in Tangl, *Kanzleiordnungen*, pp. 361 ff.

[2] Düx, *Nikolaus von Cusa*, VOL. II (Ratisbon 1847), pp. 451-66; better in Ehses, "Der Reformentwurf des Kardinals Nikolaus Cusanus", in *H.J.*, XXXII (1911), pp. 274-97. Unlike Domenichi's, Cusa's proposals were not drawn up at the beginning of the pontificate but at a somewhat later date.

[3] Vat. lat. 12192, fols. 7ʳ-42ᵛ (formerly Vat. Arch., Misc., XI, 134); Barb. lat. 1500, fols. 1ʳ-53ʳ; table of contents in Pastor, VOL. II, pp. 747 ff. (Eng. edn., VOL. III, pp. 397); the section on the Chancery in Tangl, *Kanzleiordnungen*, pp. 372-9; supplementary notes in Hofmann, *Forschungen*, VOL. II, pp. 229 ff.; on the Sistine Chapel, Steinmann, *Die Sixtinische Kapelle*, VOL. I, p. 652.

faith, to submit to fraternal correction and in important decisions to abide by the opinion of the cardinals. On the other hand, the Bull reduces the role of Cusa's visitors to a purely moral supervision—something like the *censura* of ancient Rome; Cusa's visitors would have wielded too much authority! The reform of the various offices of the Curia takes up far more space in the Bull than in the Cardinal's draft. The Cardinal was not very familiar with these things. A full century before Paul IV, the Bull foreshadows those public audiences by the Pope to which anyone who had a request to make would be admitted.

The unique feature of Pius II's reform Bull, and one never repeated, was that the Pope solemnly bound himself to abide by certain principles in the government of the Church. Aeneas Silvius Piccolomini had been personally present at Basle. He knew what was thought and said about the Curia's willingness to reform and how difficult it would be to overcome this distrust. His successors no longer possessed this insight into the mentality of the opposition beyond the Alps. Each succeeding decade increased the divergence. True, the Bull *Pastor aeternus* had one shortcoming in common with the later ones—it never became law; Pius II died when only the draft was ready.

As far as we know, Paul II made no attempt whatever to reform the Curia. His collaborator, Sánchez de Arevalo, so often mentioned, hardly refers to it in his reform tract *De remediis afflictae ecclesiae*, written in 1469.[1] He confines himself to generalities and to the reform of individuals; he is more concerned with other people's reform than with his own. He bluntly rejects the arguments of conciliar theory and looks for salvation from a spiritual and moral conversion of the members of the Church and from their submission to the Pope. If the faith of the Christian people grows stronger; if the clergy reform themselves; if the bishops fulfil the obligations of their state and use their authority with moderation; if the Christian princes shake themselves free of their disorderly passions—then the pressing needs of the Church will be met and a general peace, the crusade against the infidels and the preservation of the freedom of the Church will come of themselves.

All this was quite true. But the question was precisely how and by what means the Church, and above all the Pope, could forward the realisation of these conditions. The writer enumerates some of these means—and they are good ones, such as the appointment of worthy bishops, the despatch of visitors to the various countries, and considera-

[1] Particulars on the MSS and the contents in *H.J.*, LXII (1942), pp. 168 ff.

tion of the claims of scholars and universities in the distribution of benefices. However, even here he loses himself in generalities and remains silent about the one thing that a responsible counsellor should have put before a Pope of the period, namely that the world expected him to start the reform in his own person. In his strictly monarchical system the pyramid was placed on its apex.

The reform plans devised during the first pontificates of the Renaissance, which we have examined in the foregoing pages, continue to make concessions to the spirit of the reform Councils. Even in Arevalo's blunt intransigence some traces of the universalism of the period of the Councils still survive. The aims of the later reform schemes, which were drawn up in Rome, are more sharply defined. Their primary object is the reform of the Curia. Of Sixtus IV's attempts in this direction we know very little; even their date is uncertain, and only one of the reform Bulls drawn up at that time, but never published, dates from the opening days of 1481.[1] Its contents are kept in general terms. Another undated Bull [2] goes into greater detail. It treats first of the reform of the papal household, the cardinals and the Curia in general; it then passes on to the various departments—the Chancery, the Rota, the Segnatura, the Penitenzieria. When the scheme was once more taken up under Julius II, the reform of the Dataria was also passed over, yet it was precisely the Dataria that had undergone a most ominous development under the first Rovere Pope in consequence of the extension of compositions. No directions were laid down to ensure the reforms. We only hear a faint echo of the decree *Frequens*: instead of the Councils there prescribed, papal visitors were to be despatched to the various countries at intervals of ten years.

Pietro Barozzi, the reforming Bishop of Padua, blames the cardinals for the failure of Sixtus IV's reform. However, even if the accusation were justified, it must ultimately fall on the Pope, for it was precisely his pontificate that witnessed the greatest increase in the Sacred College's worldliness. His liberality in granting privileges, indulgences and favours of every kind, his weakness for his nephews, his underhand

---

[1] *Supernae dispositionis arbitrio*, Vat. lat. 3883, fols. 168 and 170, dated XI kal. Martii 1480 (1481) as calculated from the Incarnation.

[2] *Quoniam regnantium*, Vat. lat. 3883, fols. 14ʳ-24ᵛ; another copy, revised, Vat. lat. 3884, fols. 118ʳ-132ᵛ, also with additions from the time of Alexander VI, both undated. The corresponding parts are printed in Tangl, *Kanzleiordnungen*, pp. 379-85; Hofmann, *Forschungen*, VOL. II, p. 231; Steinmann, *Die Sixtinische Kapelle*, VOL. I, p. 653; ordinances against luxury in *Archiv. Soc. Rom. di Storia Patria*, I (1878), pp. 479 ff.

Italian policy, the increase of fiscal charges in consequence of his end-less financial straits, made the reign of this papal patron of the arts one of the most disastrous of the whole period. It was no accident that he should have had to contend so often with the demand for a Council. The government of this personally devout and good-natured pontiff gave his enemies too many openings for attack. He knew how to evade them, but not how to disarm them. Only an iron determination to reform could have achieved this: Sixtus IV lacked such will-power.

It goes without saying that no such determination could be looked for from Alexander VI. Yet it is a fact that the reform initiated by him in the summer of 1497, when he was badly shaken by the assassination of his favourite son, was seriously meant at first.[1] That it was so is guaranteed by the personal character of the cardinals to whom he en-trusted the preliminary work. They were the energetic Oliviero Carafa, the aged Portuguese Costa, the blameless Francesco Piccolomini. These men were assisted by the most famous canonists of the time, Sangiorgio and Felinus Sandaeus. The numerous drafts that have come down to us show that these men were not wanting in insight: they saw the core of the problem quite clearly: "The first thing is that our hearts be cleansed within us," Carafa wrote in his memorial. Whatever was required could be summed up in one word of St Bernard of Clairvaux: "Let the Pope realise that he is the successor of Peter, not of the Emperor Constantine, and that Peter was commissioned by our Lord to feed his sheep. The most grievous danger for any Pope lies in the fact that, encompassed as he is by flatterers, he never hears the truth about his own person and ends by not wishing to hear it." The psychological problem of supreme power is plainly stated in these words. These men were well aware that the rising flood of worldliness and corruption could only be arrested by stringent measures of control and punishment, and that the worst defect of the previous projects had been the lack of sanctions. It must have been the canonists of the reform commission who hit on the idea of guarding the prospective reform against arbitrary rule and ensuring its continuance by means of

[1] L. Célier, "Alexandre VI et la réforme de l'Eglise", in *Mélanges d'archéologie et d'histoire*, XXVII (1907), pp. 65-124, on the basis of material gathered in Vat. lat. 3883 and 3884. Célier prints the memorial of F. Piccolomini, pp. 100-3, that of Costa, p. 104, and an anonymous French one on pp. 105-8; Carafa's, Vat. lat. 3884, fols. 110^r-114^v, is not printed. The corresponding parts are printed in Tangl, *Kanzleiord-nungen*, pp. 386-421; Hofmann, *Forschungen*, VOL. II, pp. 232-40; Göller, *Pöniten-tiarie*, VOL. II, ii, pp. 101-32; Steinmann, *Die Sixtinische Kapelle*, VOL. I, pp. 654-6; for the Datary, see L. Célier, *Les Dataires du XV siècle* (Paris 1910), pp. 143-6.

a new collection of papal decretals under the title of *Constitutiones Alexandrinae.*

Were the authors of the project alarmed by their own boldness? Or did the Pope himself clip their wings through his confidants, the two secretaries Podocataro and Flores? The fact is that the final text of the reform proposals, that is, the Bull *In apostolicae sedis specula*, bears not the remotest resemblance to the excellent intentions of which the first drafts had given proof. The Bull by-passes precisely those issues which were the heart of the matter, viz. the personal reform of the Pope, while the question of guarantees is ignored. For the rest, it is more comprehensive than the previous Bulls, at least as regards the reform of the officials. From Pius II's draft it borrows the office of the censors of the Curia. It condemns the worldliness of the College of Cardinals in sterner terms than Sixtus IV's. Above all, the Bull criticises the College's growing tendency to become a political body. The chapters dealing with the nomination of bishops, their duty of residence and the routine of the Segnatura touch on topics of vital importance for the reform of the members. However, even this reform programme, the most comprehensive of the whole period between the Council of Basle and that of the Lateran, was only a straw fire. It went out at the same time as the Pope's grief over the tragic death of his son was assuaged. The reform Bull never became law.

Julius II took a first step towards a reform of the Curia by the appointment for this purpose of a committee of eight cardinals.[1] When he took this decision, on 10 March 1512, he was actuated by the same motive as Martin V in his day. The committee was charged to prepare a programme of reform in view of the forthcoming Lateran Council, which was convened for 1 May. The result of these labours was not long delayed. It took the form of a Bull published on 30 March 1512, by which the taxes were brought back to the level at which they had stood at about the middle of the fifteenth century. The Bull confined itself to the most crying abuses but did not go sufficiently into particulars and left gaps in its penal stipulations. It may be questioned whether it ever yielded any practical result. As early as the following year the Lateran Council busied itself with the same problem.

---

[1] Brief to Cardinal Medici in Desjardins, *Négociations*, VOL. II, pp. 574 ff.; the names of the cardinals are not known. Paris de Grassis (Döllinger, *Beiträge*, VOL. III, p. 416) speaks of ten "deputati super rebus concilii" whereas Sanudo, *Diarii*, VOL. XIV, pp. 48 f., 75 f., is silent on the subject. For the Bull on taxes, 30 March 1512, partly based on the reform plans of Pius II, Sixtus IV and Alexander VI, see Hofmann, *Forschungen*, VOL. I, pp. 273 ff., 313 ff., VOL. II, p. 54.

The fifth Lateran Council [1] was the last attempt at a papal reform of the Church before the break-up of Christian unity. It met in Rome under the eyes of the Pope, and was almost exclusively attended by Italian bishops. Thus it conformed perfectly to the conception of a papal General Council which had taken shape in the course of the restoration period. The Pope himself settled the order of procedure and named the officials of the Council at its first session, 10 May 1512. His influence was decisive in determining the composition of the committees formed on 3 May 1513 and further expanded on 26 October 1516.[2] The decrees were published in the form of papal Bulls.

The first period of the Council under Julius II (Sessions 1-5, from 3 May 1512 to 16 February 1513) was almost exclusively occupied with the fight against Pisa and the struggle for its own recognition by the various states. It was only after the danger of a schism had been averted, under Leo X, that the reform of the Church, which had been described as the Council's chief task in the opening discourse of Egidio of Viterbo, the General of the Augustinians, came up for discussion. At that time not a few people hoped that the thirty-seven-year-old Pope would bring about the finest thing of all—a renewal of the Church. Two Venetians, Tommaso Giustiniani and Vincenzo Quirini, who had recently entered the Order of Camaldoli, presented to the Pope a voluminous memorial which was both the widest and the boldest of all the many reform programmes drawn up since the conciliar era.[3]

[1] The conciliar acts printed in 1521 by Cardinal Antonio del Monte, uncle of the future Pope Julius III, in Labbé-Cossart, Sacrosancta concilia, VOL. XIV, pp. 1-343; Mansi, VOL. XXXII, pp. 649-1002; see Hefele, Conziliengeschichte, VOL. VIII, pp. 497-538, 558-735. For the remaining sources, few in number, see the Diarium of Paris de Grassis, the reports of Cardinal Lang and those of the Bishop of Vich; also E. Guglia, "Studien zur Gesch. des V. Laterankonzils", in Sitzungsberichte der Wiener Akad. phil.-hist. Klasse, CXL (1899), p. 10, and CLII (1906), p. 3; to which must be added a number of data in Books X and XI of Pietro Delfino's correspondence: P. Delphini Epistolae; the more recent literature in Pastor, VOL. III, ii, p. 846 (Eng. edn., VOL. VI, p. 406); VOL. IV, i, pp. 559 ff. (Eng. edn., VOL. VIII, pp. 384 ff.); Imbart de la Tour, Origines, VOL. II, pp. 515 ff. The controversy about the meaning of the definition of the immortality of the soul (in the eighth session) between C. Stange, in Zeitschrift für systematische Theologie, VI (1928), pp. 338-444; X (1932), pp. 301-67, and A. Deneffe, in Scholastik, V (1930), pp. 380-7; VIII (1933), pp. 359-79, does not touch on the question of reform which alone concerns us.

[2] Guglia observes (Wiener Sonderb., CXL, p. 33) very justly that neither these commissions nor the very rare general congregations played any marked role, but that the centre of gravity of all conciliar activity lay in the consistory and in the Pope's entourage.

[3] "Libellus ad Leonem X", J. B. Mittarelli-A. Costadini, in Annales Camaldulenses, VOL. IX (Venice 1773), pp. 612-719; discussed by J. Schnitzer, Peter Delfin (Munich 1926), pp. 227-47; see also the remarks of S. Merkle in Deutsche Literaturzeitung, XLIX (1928),

The grandeur of their plan chiefly lies in the fact that they do not waste words in laments over existing abuses and in suggesting punishments and prohibitions. Instead of spending their energies over the purely negative side of the problem they suggest to the head of the Church positive aims and tasks. Pride of place is assigned to the missions in the recently discovered continent of America and to union with the Eastern Christians, whose numbers, however, they overestimate considerably. They ruthlessly expose the internal injuries of the Church: the ignorance of the clergy and religious, of whom only two per cent. are said to understand the Latin of the liturgical books; ignorance among the laity, who should be instructed on the fundamental truths of the faith at least on all Sundays; superstition, which had infiltrated into every sphere of public and private life. Entangled as they are themselves in these and other miseries, the clergy have forgotten that it is their duty to act as leaders. Responsibility for all this lies largely with the Popes, who have surrounded themselves with benefice-hunting flatterers and allowed Rome to become a shameful *lupanar*!

The frankness with which Giustiniani and Quirini exposed the Church's infirmities calls to mind a later reform memorial which became widely known under the title of *Consilium de emendanda ecclesia*. The connexion is not a purely fanciful one, for one of the authors of the *Consilium* was Gasparo Contarini who had been connected from his youth with the two Camaldolese monks both by ties of close friendship and by a community of ideas. Although a whole fateful quarter of a century intervened between the publication of these two memorials, they are at one in their condemnation of the Renaissance Popes' absorption in politics and their bureaucratic centralisation. In its place the Papacy should promote a renewal of spiritual inwardness and concord within the Church. This new spirit which was to replace the old system is already stamped with all the essential characteristics of the Papacy of the Catholic reformation. Its outstanding feature is the principle that the Pope is responsible for the functioning of all the members of the ecclesiastical hierarchy. His immediate assistants, the cardinals, must assume no other obligations, with the sole exception of the administration of their titular churches. For their income they should depend on pensions. Every three years bishops must give an

pp. 1347 ff. H. Jedin, "V. Quirini und P. Bembo", in *Miscellanea Giovanni Mercati*, VOL. IV, pp. 407-24; *id.* "Ein Vorschlag für die Amerikamission aus dem Jahre 1513", in *Neue Zeitschrift für Missionswissenschaft*, 1946, pp. 81-4.

account of their administration to them, and this must be periodically verified on the spot by papal legates. Great care must be taken that only morally suitable and adequately trained candidates are admitted to holy orders. No one may be admitted to the higher orders who has not read the whole Bible through at least once. For the benefit of the laity the Bible must be translated into the vernacular. The religious orders must be reorganised and unified. Some of the lesser ones may be suppressed altogether. The houses that follow the Rule of St Benedict should be grouped together. The mendicant orders should be reduced to two, one following the Rule of St Francis, the other that of St Augustine, while their conventual offshoots should be allowed to die out by forbidding them to receive new subjects. A thorough revision of the *Corpus juris canonici*, omitting obsolete canons, will facilitate a comprehensive view of Church law. Uniformity in the liturgy must be achieved by the introduction of an identical Missal, Breviary and Calendar of Feasts throughout the Church. A selection of the decrees of some of the earlier Councils should be published. One indispensable means for ensuring the execution of these reforms is the frequent holding of chapters for the religious orders and of diocesan and provincial synods—the latter under the presidency of papal legates—as well as the convocation of a General Council every five years. Without making the slightest concession to the conciliar theory,[1] Giustiniani and Quirini view the Council as the regulator of the whole life of the Church. Let the Lateran Council make a start. It should be made a great Council of reform and unity to which the Eastern Christians should be invited. It would be a good thing to look thus early for men capable of carrying through the reforms which the Council would decide upon.

It is no exaggeration to say that the reform programme of the two Camaldolese monks preoccupied the Church for more than a century. The Council of Trent, the liturgical reforms of Pius V, the Bible of Sixtus V, the foundation of Propaganda, are all in line with these plans. But the vision which the trained and prophetic eye of the high-minded Venetians beheld was too lofty both for the Pope to whom they addressed themselves and for the Council assembled before their eyes. Pope and Council disappointed the hopes that had been set on them.

---

[1] Quirini's "Tractatus super concilio generali", printed in *Annales Camaldulenses*, VOL. IX, pp. 599-611, is an extract from Torquemada's *Summa de ecclesia*. Quirini's lively interest in the proceedings at Pisa appears from his letter of 21 January 1512, *ibid.*, VOL. IX, p. 538.

In the session of 25 April 1513, Leo X formed indeed a reform committee consisting of eight cardinals, ten bishops and two generals of religious orders. On 26 October of the same year this committee split up into five sub-committees, each consisting of two cardinals and two bishops, for the purpose of working out a reform of the Camera, the Chancery, the Rota, the Secretariat and the Penitenzieria.[1] However, each of these sub-committees had assigned to it, in the capacity of advisor, a representative of the category of officials concerned. This application of the brake effectively prevented any radical steps being taken.[2] Its evil consequences showed themselves as soon as the overdue regulation of the system of taxation came up for discussion. The Bull *Pastoralis officii* of 13 December 1513,[3] contrasting in this respect with the Bull of Julius II, enforced a firm system of taxation but also yielded to the demands of officials to such an extent that the result proved a step backwards rather than forwards. It is significant that in the eighth session, 19 December 1513, this taxation Bull was not presented but only a Bull of sanctions and threats of punishments which called forth protests from four Italian bishops.[4]

The great reform Bull which was submitted and accepted in the following session, the ninth, 5 May 1514,[5] imposed a reform of the Curia which conformed to the earlier schemes. Thus rules were laid down for the process of information about candidates for the episcopate; the cardinals were given directions for the administration of their titular churches and other benefices; they were enjoined to show moderation in providing for their relatives and in their household expenses. Stress was likewise laid on the observance of the professional secret. Further salutary ordinances were concerned with religious instruction in schools; with simony and the usurpation of Church property by laymen. But

[1] The composition of the sub-committees in Hefele, *Conziliengeschichte*, VOL. VIII, pp. 810 ff.

[2] Hofmann, *Forschungen*, VOL. I, p. 306, lays the blame for the blocking of the reform of offices mainly on the Datary Lorenzo Pucci, who was a member of the fourth sub-committee, which also included the General of the Camaldolese Delfino, a man wholly devoted to the Medici; the letters in *P. Delphini Epistolae*, VOL. XI, pp. 7 ff., refer to his share in its work.

[3] *Bull. Rom.*, VOL. V, pp. 571-601; Hofmann, *Forschungen*, VOL. I, p. 274; VOL. II, p. 55 (No. 242).

[4] The Bull *In apostolici culminis* in Labbé-Cossart, *Sacrosancta concilia*, VOL. XIV, pp. 219-30; Mansi, VOL. XXXII, pp. 845-85; Hofmann, *Forschungen*, VOL. II, p. 55 (No. 243).

[5] The Bull *Supernae dispositionis arbitrio*, Labbé-Cossart, *Sacrosancta concilia*, VOL. XIV, pp. 219-30; Mansi, VOL. XXXII, pp. 874-85; Hefele, *Conziliengeschichte*, VOL. VIII, pp. 602-10.

one misses the strong hand which alone could have coped with fundamental evils in the sphere of benefices and finances. What was the
good of forbidding the giving of monasteries *in commendam* if an
exception was made for the cardinals? And was it enough to restrict
to four the number of benefices that might be held by one individual?

Besides this reform Bull, a number of most timely decrees, such as
those on pawnshops (*Montes pietatis*) and the censoring of books, were
published in the tenth session, 4 May 1515, and a decree on preaching
in the eleventh session, 19 December 1516.[1] However, these and all
the other well-meant measures lost much of their value on account of
the lack of earnestness and determination of the leading personalities,
beginning with the Pope himself. Leo X's registers are all too
revealing on this subject. We see him dealing out with both hands, as
a man might scatter pennies, both benefices with the cure of souls
attached to them and dispensations. Of a sense of responsibility for
the souls whose salvation was at stake there is hardly a trace. Actually
there is no difference of opinion among experts about the fact that this
final attempt by a Pope at a reform, dressed up though it was as a
Council, was of little value. At Trent its formal recognition was
vehemently resisted by several Spanish bishops on the ground that
some of its decrees had increased rather than lessened the prevailing
disorder—*deformatio*—in the Church.[2] Of the other great aims which
Giustiniani and Quirini had proposed to the Council, only one was
realised, viz. union with the Maronites. As for the Turkish war, the
assembly never got beyond mere talk.[3]

As was to be expected, the Council followed the line which the
Curia had always taken against the conciliar theory, in fact it went even
further. The Bull *Pastor aeternus*, which condemned and suppressed
the Pragmatic Sanction of Bourges, contained a statement to the effect

---

[1] See e.g. Imbart de la Tour, *Origines*, VOL. II, pp. 531 ff.; Pastor, VOL. IV, pp. 576 f.
(Eng. edn., VOL. VIII, p. 409 f.). The general result is not altered in any way by the
reforms which were initiated in some instances under pressure of episcopal opposition
("instante gravissimo concilii periculo"); see Jedin, *Seripando*, VOL. I, pp. 159 ff.
(Eng. edn., p. 135).

[2] *C.T.*, VOL. I, pp. 127, 132. According to nuncio Verallo's report of 17 March
1547, the Emperor's confessor D. Soto regarded the Council of the Lateran as formally
unfree; *N.B.*, VOL. I, ix, p. 519.

[3] Guglia, "Die Türkenfrage auf dem Laterankonzil", in *M.Ö.I.G.*, XXI (1900),
pp. 679-91. E. Pelliccia, *La preparazione ed ammissione dei chierici ai santi ordini nella
Roma del seculo XVI* (Rome 1946), pp. 85 ff., also grants that the attempts of Julius II
and Leo X to make better provision for the conferring of holy orders suffered from two
defects—as did those of the fifth Lateran Council—viz. they were purely repressive
and the most important element was wanting, namely "effettiva e costante esecuzione".

that the Pope's authority extends over all Councils, hence he has full power to convoke, transfer and dissolve them.[1] To the papal prohibition of appeal to a Council the assembly now added a condemnation of the theory itself. On the other hand it is clear that the Curia did not feel equal to a formal declaration of the nullity of the superiority decree of Constance and Basle, as was suggested in Ferdinand the Catholic's instructions to his envoys to the Council. That declaration was not made, for in spite of what we have said about the composition, the progress and the spirit of the fifth Lateran Council, it was in this assembly that the vital tensions within the Church became apparent and the impending crisis cast its shadow before.

The alarm was first sounded in Spain. Soon after Ferdinand the Catholic had announced his adhesion to the Council he called a committee of six bishops, three diplomats and six theologians and canonists, for the purpose of briefing the delegates to the Council. The committee met at Burgos on 17 December 1511. Several other prelates were invited to submit memorials. It was on the basis of this material that the King had instructions drawn up for the Spanish envoys to the Council.[2] The reform programme there outlined betrays so profound a dissatisfaction on the part of the Church and the Crown of Spain with the Curia's policy in the sphere of benefices and dispensations that it ranks with the Pragmatic Sanction of Bourges and the *gravamina* of the German nation, although it is superior to the Sanction in that it makes no concession to the conciliar theory, and to the *gravamina* in that it is not so narrowly inspired by financial considerations. Above all, its positive and constructive elements raise it above both these documents and make of it a forerunner of the Tridentine reform programme.[3]

[1] Mansi, VOL. XXXII, p. 967; Hefele, *Conziliengeschichte*, VOL. VIII, pp. 710 ff.

[2] The Spanish preparations for the Council, of which until now only the two pieces published by Döllinger (*Beiträge*, VOL. III, pp. 200-8) were known, namely the protocol of Burgos and an episcopal "votum", have had light thrown upon them through the researches of Doussinague, *Fernando el Católico y el cisma de Pisa*, pp. 230-44, and the documents printed in the appendix, pp. 521-43. The most important piece is the "votum" of the Bishop of Burgos (No. 48), which is identical with the anonymous "votum" printed by Döllinger, the "votum" of the Archbishop of Seville (No. 49) and the instructions for the envoys to the Council (No. 50). All three documents probably date from the beginning of the year 1512.

[3] The positive side of the Spanish reform programme will be discussed later; for the moment it may suffice to point out that the Spanish bishops demanded the restoration of their episcopal rights, for the sake of their pastoral duties. Other particulars were: the effective establishment of two teaching-prebends in cathedral and collegiate churches, which was adopted at Trent, *sess. V de ref. c.* 1; the grant of parishes on the basis of a competition on the model of what was done at Palencia; adopted at Trent, *sess. XXIV de ref. c.* 18.

The Spaniards urge a *reformatio capitis*, for "judgment must begin in the house of the Lord", but by this they do not mean any petty restrictions of the papal household, but a reform of the College of Cardinals in the sense of the decree of Basle, which, though formally invalid, was yet, as regards its contents, "just and holy". They demand that the business of the Curia should be transacted in accordance with common law and in the interests of the pastoral ministry. They insist above all on the preservation of Spain's interests in the ecclesiastical sphere. The instructions demand that no Spanish benefices be granted to foreigners; that Spanish houses of Dominicans and Franciscans be placed under Spanish superiors in place of French ones, and that the dignity of Grand Master of the three Spanish orders of knighthood be for ever vested in the Crown. In accordance with the decree of Constance, the Curia's right to *spolia* must be completely given up, while annates must be abolished by a new conciliar decree on the lines of that of Basle, which, though formally invalid, is nevertheless materially right and just. Bishoprics and other benefices under royal patronage may not be considered as reserved, even if they become vacant in Rome; no expectatives may be granted for benefices subject to patronage in Castile.

This is the language of the modern state, anxious to use the authority of the Church for its own ends and to get the right of nomination to offices and positions into its own hands to the farthest possible limits. The memorials of the Bishops of Seville and Burgos are indeed silent about annates, but they complain all the more loudly of interference with the ecclesiastical order by curial dispositions, such as the appointment of apostolic judges on the proposal of a party, the indiscriminate granting of faculties to titular bishops, dispensations for the ordination of clerics who have been turned down in their own diocese, dispensations from fasting granted to layfolk, so much so that almost every *caballero* eats meat during Lent. They lament the neglect of the duty of residence by the pastoral clergy on the plea of apostolic indults, of exemptions which undermine discipline, of the commendams which are the ruin of monasteries. Every disorder and every kind of evil, in the opinion of the Archbishop of Seville, is due to the fact that the Curia is too ready with dispensations from common law and from the canons of the Councils.[1] The Bishop of Burgos, for his part, declares that "unless

---

[1] "Premieramente se deuria ynsystir que la disposiçion de los sacros canones y orden del derecho comun e las constituçiones de los conçilios generales que fueron ordenadas por bien universal de la yglesia y con tanta deliberaçion, no seo quebrantado tan continua-e ordinariamente como se haze, e que se reduga la orden de la yglesia e

care is taken that the general reform decrees of the forthcoming Council are not arbitrarily altered by the Pope and the cardinals, we shall waste both time and money".[1] In order to hit the nerve-centre of the curial bureaucracy he suggests that the thesis that the Pope is incapable of committing simony should be branded as heresy. King Ferdinand himself, though the Pope's ally, advocates, with his demand for a guarantee that a General Council should be held every ten or fifteen years,[2] a new *Frequens* in the same breath in which he supports the declaration of nullity of the superiority decree of Constance.

Thus it came about that the Catholic King and the representatives of the Spanish Church—the very factors from which the Catholic reform might expect lasting support, proclaimed that a change in the conditions at the centre of authority was inescapable. So great was their mistrust that they felt they could not dispense with the control which the regular holding of Councils would provide.

Leo X's fear that a strong representation of nations beyond the Alps—Spain, France, Germany—at the Council, would bode ill for the Papacy was not altogether groundless.[3] If the Spaniards came forward with reform plans such as these, the French with the decrees of Basle, and the Germans with their *gravamina*, the Curia would be hard pressed, and it was not yet certain whether it could rely upon the unconditional support of the Italian bishops. Actually, in spite of the fact that the personnel of the Lateran Council was made up almost exclusively of Italian bishops, a sharp opposition to the privileges of the mendicant orders arose from it and, parallel with it, a demand for the

de todos los negoçios eclesiasticos al derecho comun porque de aqui proçeden todos los ynconvenientes e desorden que ay en las cosas eclesiasticas." Doussinague, *Fernando el Católico y el cisma de Pisa*, p. 532.

[1] "El santo concilio suplique al Papa que la autoridad de este concilio y lo en el determinado quede perpetuo de manera que por sola la boluntad de santo padre ni de los Cardenales se puedan mudar las cosas en este concilio determinadas especialmente en lo que toca a la elettion del Papa e comun reformaçion de la yglesia. . . . Si esto no se hace por demas es expender tiempo y dinero en esto negocio." Doussinague, *Fernando el Católico y el cisma de Pisa*, p. 530; Döllinger, *Beiträge*, VOL. III, p. 203.

[2] "Yten porque vemos por la experiençia quanto provecho trahe a toda la yglesia catholica la congregaçion del conçilio universal y quanto daño de no se celebrar, proporneys que se guarde la constitucion 'frequens' del Concilio de Constançia en la session XXXIX la qual manda que le diez años aya conçilio general y se haga otra de nuevo que disponga lo mismo y si este paresçiere breve tiempo que sea de quinze en quinze años por manera que todavia se çelebre conçilio." Doussinague, *Fernando el Católico y el cisma de Pisa*, p. 539.

[3] In his conversation with Bembo and Quirini, on 15 April 1514, the Pope expressed a fear that "si riducesse l'autorità nostra e di nostri successori ad autorità solo spirituale". Their despatch was published by V. Cian in *Archivio Veneto*, xxx (1855), pp. 394 ff.

restitution of episcopal rights.[1] The bishops were loud in their complaints. Exempt religious, they say, administer the sacraments, preach and even build churches without their authorisation; in fact, they openly resist the bishops and, in contradiction with their rules, acquire property and possessions, not infrequently through legacy-hunting. They also encroach upon the claims of the secular clergy to the tenth and to burial fees. The bishops insist on the right of visitation at least of such religious as were engaged in the pastoral ministry, and in the withdrawal of all papal privileges which conflict with the rights of bishops and parish priests. In short, they complain that the extravagantly extended privileges of the exempt had robbed them of their authority as bishops.

There was nothing substantially new in these demands of the bishops. For the most part they were as old as the mendicant orders themselves and the inevitable consequence of their pastoral activity, which rested on papal authorisation. The problem had been the subject of heated discussion at Basle.[2] Up to this time the mendicants had always succeeded in warding off all attacks, and now also, under the inspiration of the General of the Dominicans, Cajetan, and the General of the Augustinians, Egidio of Viterbo, they put up an effective defence with the result that although the Bull *Regimini universalis ecclesiae* of 4 May 1515 [3] limited the circle of exempt secular clerics and subjected secular chapters and convents of nuns to episcopal visitation and correction and met the bishops in other ways also, for instance with regard to appeals, it nevertheless avoided trenching on the privileges of exempt orders of men. Even those demands which the ordinaries pressed with the utmost determination, such as the right of visitation of religious with the cure of souls and the approbation of confessors and preachers who were members of religious orders, were indeed granted by the Bull *Dum intra mentis arcana* of 19 December 1516, but only with important restrictive clauses.[4]

---

[1] The memorial of the bishops, unfortunately without date, in Hefele, *Conziliengeschichte*, VOL. VIII, pp. 813 ff.; *ibid.*, pp. 814-31, the very clever counter-proposals of the religious. In default of other sources it is impossible to reconstruct the chronological development of the dispute.

[2] For a good survey of the development of the controversy up to the Council of Basle, see G. Meersseman, *Giovanni di Montenero O.P., difensore dei Mendicanti* (Rome 1938), pp. 16 ff.

[3] Labbé-Cossart, *Sacrosancta concilia*, VOL. XIV, pp. 252-6; Mansi, VOL. XXXII, pp. 907-12.

[4] Labbé-Cossart, *Sacrosancta concilia*, VOL. XIV, pp. 315-19; Mansi, VOL. XXXII, pp. 970-4. From a letter of Egidio of Viterbo to the provincial of Aragon, dated 12 February 1517, we learn that he was entirely satisfied with the result; see Jedin, *Seripando*, VOL. I, p. 160.

What was new and unexpected in this agitation was the circumstance that this time opposition did not include any German or Spanish bishops or French doctors; on the contrary it came from Italian prelates whose sympathies with the Curia were unquestionable, and what is more, on the sole ground that they felt the privileges of the religious cramped their episcopal authority to an intolerable degree. Just as the College of Cardinals—though their position in the Church was of the Pope's making—sought to circumscribe the pontiff's freedom of action by means of election capitulations and continued to demand a reform and a Council, so did the bishops bring forward their much older demands. The most distinguished members of the hierarchy knew from personal experience that the balance of power in the ecclesiastical organism was somehow upset. It was not within their competence to restore it, were it only because by its policy of concordats and its other concessions to the states, the Papacy had had its spiritual authority recognised and had increased its political influence, the natural basis of which lay in the restored States of the Church.[1] Its alliance with the states had enabled the Papacy to triumph over the reform Councils. And now the French concordat of 1516 was to demonstrate before the whole world that even the most powerful European state—after the collapse of the ecclesiastical opposition of Pisa which it had engineered—chose to come to terms with the Pope, and that directly, without the intervention of a Council.

What a difference there is between Leo X's standing at the time of the Lateran Council and that of the fugitive Eugenius IV at the time of the Council of Basle! Surrounded as he was by the most brilliant court in Europe, in the Rome of the high Renaissance, which Bramante, Michelangelo and Raphael were busy adorning with their masterpieces, exalted to the sky by the humanists who enjoyed his favour, Leo X might well have persuaded himself that schism and Council were but a bad dream, the anti-Roman opposition of those beyond the Alps and the cry for a reform of the Curia no more than a protest of late-comers, malcontents and everlasting fault-finders. His was a dreadful mistake. The fire of a religious revolution broke out in the house before its

---

[1] In this matter I am in complete agreement with W. Bertram, *Der neuzeitliche Staatsgedanke und die Konkordate des ausgehenden Mittelalters* (Rome 1942), pp. 171 ff., except for the statement that at the beginning of the sixteenth century the idea of the Council had lost its force (pp. 175 ff.). It is a commonplace with the writers of the period of the restoration that the democratic ideas of the epoch of the Councils were a danger for the monarchy as an institution, but this did not prevent the political misuse of the idea of the Council by the princes, nor the aspirations for a Council in those ecclesiastical circles which desired a reform.

inmates were aware of it. Those who had watched the approach of the calamity and had endeavoured to arrest its progress were no more, while those who sought to put out the conflagration lacked the necessary strength. For more than a century and a half men had devised plans for a reform of the Curia and the Church. It had been discussed and written about, but never had a liberating step been taken by which the Papacy would have placed itself at the head of a movement for the Church's renewal. A grand opportunity had been missed.

CHAPTER VII

The Spontaneous Reform of the Members

WAS there no other means of reforming the Church except by way of the Council and the Pope? While the Council of Basle was sitting, the Dominican Johann Nider wrote [1]: "I have not the slightest hope of a general reform of the Church either at present or in the near future, for subjects lack good will and in the prelates the reform meets with ill will. Perhaps it is just as well, for the elect are refined by the persecutions of the wicked. On the other hand a partial reform is possible in many countries and localities. We see it gaining ground day by day in monasteries and convents, though God knows amid what difficulties!"

Nider demanded partial reforms, a reform by the members themselves, a reform, that is, which began with personal sanctification but got hold of others through example, through works of charity and apostolic activity and thereby created cells of living Christianity. A reform such as this must needs start from the lower ranks of the ecclesiastical hierarchy, progress from monastery to monastery, from parish to parish, must grip one country after another, until by an organic increase it attains the centre and the head. It was a wearisome and arduous way, because it sent the chosen ones to the school of self-denial and sacrifice and led them to perfection through misunderstandings and failures: it was the way of the saints. This is the way by which Christ led His Church. By comparison with the two others it was a roundabout way. We must now endeavour to trace it out and understand it.

From the end of the fourteenth century cells of personal reform had sprung up in the religious orders—in the old monastic orders as well as in the mendicant ones. It could hardly have been otherwise. It was precisely in these communities, vowed as they were to strive after perfection through the observance of the evangelical counsels, that the contrast between the ideal and the real was most marked in consequence

---

[1] Johann Nider, *Formicarius*, VOL. I, p. 7 (I make use of the Douai edition of 1602). See K. Schieler, *Mag. Johannes Nider* (Mainz 1885), pp. 174 ff.; for his activities as a reformer of his order see G. Löhr, *Die Teutonia im 15. Jahrhundert* (Leipzig 1924), p. 74 and *passim*.

of the worldliness of many of their members.[1] That is why every monastic reform of the late Middle Ages began with a renewed sense of the ideal of perfection peculiar to each order. This applies to the Congregations of Saint Justina, Valladolid and Chézal-Benoît, and the somewhat looser unions of Melk and Bursfeld, within the Order of St Benedict; to the Canons of Windesheim and the observant Congregations of the mendicant orders. Personal sanctification by a return to the primitive strictness of the rule is always the first step. In the orders devoted to the priestly ministry this step is invariably followed by another, viz. apostolic activity. The first of these two elements is most marked in the Zoccolanti of Foligno, the Hermits of St Augustine of Lecceto and the Servites of Monte Senario; but it is not wanting in the Carmelite monastery of Mantua, in the founders of the Teutonia and the Lombard Congregation of the Dominicans, in Raymond of Capua and John Dominici. None of them presumes to reform the whole Church; they begin with themselves and with their own religious family. Instead of drawing up grandiose reform plans they set to work in good earnest.

Their next step was invariably the re-establishment of an ordered common life, in accordance with the constitutions of each particular order. Common life was imperilled, and that not only in the monastic orders but among the mendicants as well, by the infiltration of private ownership in the shape of money, furniture, books and sometimes even real estate, while the property of the community was often enough very badly managed. For this reason the reformed statutes inculcate the strict observance of the vow of personal poverty while at the same time

[1] For what follows, in addition to Heimbucher, the reader is referred to my paper: "Zur Vorgeschichte der Regularenreform Trid. Sess. XXIV", in R.Q., XLIV (1936), pp. 231-81. For the orders there only briefly referred to, I have sought information in the works of U. Berlière on Melk in Revue Bén., XII (1895), pp. 204 ff., 289 ff., Chézal-Benoît, ibid., XVII (1900), pp. 29 ff., 113 ff., 252 ff., 337 ff.; XVIII (1901), 1 ff., and Bursfeld, ibid., XVI (1899), pp. 360 ff.; for the last named also in J. Linneborn, in Studien und Mitteilungen aus dem Benediktiner und Zisterzienser-Orden, XX (1899), pp. 266 ff., 531 ff.; XXI (1900), pp. 53 ff., 315 ff., 554 ff.; XXII (1901), pp. 48 ff., 396 ff., and P. Volk, Die Generalkapitel der Bursvelder Benediktinerkongregation (Münster 1928); also a number of documents on Valladolid in E. Pacheco y de Leva, La Política española en Italia. Correspondencia de Don Fernando Marín, abad de Najera, con Carlos I, VOL. I (Madrid 1919); in addition to this there has also been published lately: Statuta capitulorum gen. Ord. Cisterciensis VI (Louvain 1938). Cz. Bogdalski, Bernardyniw Polsce 1453-1530, 2 vols. (Cracow 1933), only came to my knowledge through a review in Jahrbücher für Kultur und Geschichte der Slaven, XI (1935), pp. 129 ff; A. Barthelmé, La Réforme dominicaine au XV siècle en Alsace et dans l'ensemble de la province de Teutonie (Strasbourg 1931); A. de Meyer, La Congrégation de Hollande ou la réforme dominicaine en territoire bourguignon 1465-1515 (Liège 1945).

they lay down rules for the administration and disposal of the community's property, prescribe a common table and enjoin that every member of the community, especially the sick, should be provided with whatever was required. The monastic enclosure, infraction of which might easily lead to transgressions of the vow of chastity, was re-established. Rules for the novitiate provided for the training of aspirants and the education of the younger brethren. It was in the nature of things that the personal question would be the decisive one, that is, the removal of the reform-shy and the appointment of able local and provincial superiors.[1]

In 1471 the Vicar General of the Dutch Dominicans of the Observance, Jan Uytenhove, wrote: "Partly through the intervention of the Apostolic See, partly at the instigation of princes and other secular lords, and with the concurrence of well-disposed religious the orders have begun to reform in divers parts, nay in every part of Christendom."[2] Begun they had indeed, but the final result was modest enough. Not a single order was completely reformed. Sometimes the new spirit died out with one generation. Endless friction between observants and conventuals hindered the progress of reform. Support by ecclesiastical and secular authorities was spasmodic. Abbeys continued to be granted to cardinals and other great personages and were thereby ruined. The laxity of the Segnatura and the Penitenzieria in granting dispensations undermined discipline in the mendicant orders. The truth was that it was simply not possible to restore any one individual member to full health while the disease-germs were running through the whole organism. The impulse which the fifth Lateran Council gave to the reform of the orders produced no substantial and lasting improvement.

The limited success of the conventual reforms in the late Middle Ages should not lead us to underestimate their internal result. They contributed effectively to the preservation of the Christian spirit in the Church, both within and without the cloister, for the reform of the orders was not without effect upon the outer world. From the monastic

---

[1] For documents and particulars on the Augustinians, see my book *Seripando*, VOL. I, pp. 157 ff. (Eng. edn., pp. 126 ff.); on the Dominicans, see Löhr, *Die Teutonia im 15. Jahrhundert*, pp. 2 ff., and the lively description of the struggle for a reform of the convents of Ypres and Bergues by G. Meerseman in *A.F.P.*, VII (1937), pp. 191-209; on the Franciscans, see Doelle, *Die Observanzbewegung in der sächsischen Franziskanerprovinz* (Münster 1918), pp. 59 ff.

[2] *Analecta Ordinis fr. Praedicatorum*, XVI (1923-4), pp. 290. Uytenhove's reform tract was intended for Charles the Bold.

cell it penetrated into the pulpit and occupied the chairs of bishops. Thus the Italy of the fifteenth century can point to popular preachers such as Bernardine of Siena, John of Capestrano, Bernardino of Feltre, Giacomo della Marca, all of them Franciscans; to Leonard of Udine, a Dominican; to bishops such as Antonino of Florence and Antonio Bertini of Foligno, a Jesuate; to cardinals such as the Carthusian Niccolò Albergati, the Hermit of St Augustine, Alessandro of Sasso-ferrato, the Camaldolese Maffeo Gerardi. Many more names might be added to this list.

In the person of Savonarola the reform of the orders sailed into political waters and foundered in them. Nevertheless we know what a rich harvest the deep spirituality and the stern asceticism of the Florentine prophet yielded among the Spanish Dominicans and thereby prepared the ground for the flowering of the classical Dominican theology of the sixteenth century.[1]

In the person of Ximenes, an observant, the Franciscan Order produced a great reformer of the Spanish Church, a man in whom ascetic rigour was matched with a profound understanding of what was required for a renewal of the Church. His foundation, the University of Alcalá, became a centre of modern humanistic and ecclesiastical studies and was only eclipsed by the great theologians of Salamanca. By the side of Ximenes, the large-scale organiser, stands that apostolic man Talavera, the first Archbishop of Granada, a Hieronymite and sometime confessor to Queen Isabella. When already an archbishop he took up the study of Arabic to enable him to convert the Moors of his diocese.[2]

Germany does not exhibit personalities of the stature of either Ximenes or Talavera. The Church of the Empire admitted no religious into the ranks of its prince-bishops. But in Germany also members of the orders were busy as preachers and writers of religious books. Thus the Minorite Dietrich Coelde made a splendid contribution to the religious formation of the people by his *Christenspiegel* (*Mirror of the Christian*) which went through thirty-four editions. His sermons were for north-west Germany what those of his fellow Franciscan Capestrano were for the north-east.[3] Thomas Murner's activity in the region of the

---

[1] V. Beltrán de Heredia, *Historia de la reforma de la provincia de España 1450-1550* (Rome 1939), pp. 78 ff., brings out the negative side; *id.*, *Las corrientes de espiritualidad entre los Dominicos de Castilla durante la prima mitad del siglo XVI* (Salamanca 1941), pp. 6 ff., in which he elaborates the positive aspect of this influence.

[2] M. Bataillon, *Erasme en Espagne*, pp. 62 ff., 366.

[3] *H.J.*, XII (1891), p. 59.

Upper Rhine falls partly in the period of the religious disruption.[1] How widespread was the preaching activity of the Dominican Nigri may be gathered from his itinerary for the years 1508-11.[2] Of the works of edification and instruction of Johann Nider, a leading figure of the Dominican Order, we have no less than seventy-five *incunabula*: seventeen of them being editions of his explanation of the Creed.[3] Members of religious orders were usually chosen to deliver the inaugural sermon at synods and they acted as confessors and spiritual advisers to princes. Gabriel Biel, the counsellor of Eberhard, Duke of Württemberg, and one of the most highly esteemed German theologians of the end of the fifteenth century, was a Brother of the Common Life. Frederick the Wise of Saxony had for a counsellor Johann Staupitz, Vicar General of the German province of the Augustinians.

In France, the vitality of the Church asserted itself with fresh vigour as soon as the Hundred Years' War came to an end. This renewal was greatly furthered by the activities of that powerful preacher of penance Olivier Maillard, a Minorite, and by those of Francis of Paula, founder of the Friars Minim whom the aging King Louis XI had invited to France. The old monastic orders also took their share in the efforts for the reform of the Church in France which had been initiated at the beginning of the reign of Charles VIII. At the assembly of the clergy which the King convened at Tours in 1493, the Abbots of Marmoutiers and Cîteaux and the Augustinian Hacqueville played an outstanding role. But the most influential of them all was the Fleming Standonck, of the Congregation of Windesheim, who reformed a number of monasteries of canons, among them the ancient and celebrated one of Saint-Victor. At one time there was question of his being made Archbishop of Rheims. The *Rosetum*, a work of his assistant Jean Mombaer, was to influence Cisneros at a later date.[4]

Only one order could boast of having always remained true to its ideal: *Carthusia nunquam reformata, quia nunquam deformata*. By its very remoteness from the world the Charterhouse seemed to attract the world all the more powerfully. Thus, during his term of office as Prior of Gaming in Lower Austria, from 1451 to 1458, Nicholas Kempf of

---

[1] F. Landmann, "Thomas Murner als Prediger", in *Archiv für elsässische Kirchengeschichte*, x (1935), pp. 295-368.

[2] P. Landmann, *Das Predigtwesen in Westfalen* (Münster 1900), pp. 22 ff.

[3] Hain, Nos. 11780-854.

[4] Imbart de la Tour, *Origines*, VOL. II, pp. 486 ff.; A. Renaudet, *Préréforme et Humanisme à Paris* (Paris 1916), pp. 208 ff.; P. Debongnie, *Jean Mombaer de Bruxelles, Abbé de Ligny, et ses réformes* (Louvain 1928), pp. 87 ff., 292 ff.

Strasbourg, sometime professor of philosophy at Vienna, admitted no less than five masters and seven bachelors to the habit of St Bruno.[1] The prayers of Ludolph of Saxony were probably used by more people in the fifteenth century than was *The Imitation of Christ*, and his *Vita Christi* stood on the shelves of a knight bearing the name of Iñigo de Loyola.[2] Adolph of Essen (d. 1439) and Dominic of Prussia (d. 1460), both of them priors of the Charterhouse of Trier, introduced the Meditation of the Passion into the traditional "Psalter of Our Lady". Jacob of Jüterbog (d. 1465), a prolific writer, won for himself a distinguished place in the literature of reform. However, from the point of view of productivity, Denis Rickel surpasses them all with his numerous moral and ascetic treatises.

Even the Carthusian Order was involved to some extent in the transition from contemplation to the apostolate which is characteristic of the new epoch in the history of the Church.[3] In the person of John Rode it provided a leader for the monastic reform in south-west Germany. Gregory Reisch of Freiburg and John Heynlin of Basle knew how to combine the austerity of the Charterhouse with a sympathetic understanding for the new learning, so much so that in 1523 Johann Eck pressed the Pope to attach the former to the legate who was about to be appointed for Germany, in the capacity of adviser on matters connected with reform.[4] Under Prior Peter Blommeveen (1509-36), and through the mystical writings of John Justus Landsberg (d. 1539), the Charterhouse of Cologne became a nursery of piety for the entire region of the Lower Rhine.[5] Blommeveen had been through the spiritual school of the Minorite Herp, who had been Superior of the Brethren of Delft before he joined the Franciscans. In this way the Carthusian Order recovered what it had bestowed on the *devotio moderna*. Henry of Kalkar, Prior of the Charterhouse of Cologne, had a share in the conversion of Geert Groote. Of this devout man, who never became a priest, Thomas à Kempis writes: "*Docuit sancte vivendo.*" After many years of tireless activity as a mission preacher, his bishop enjoined silence on him. He obeyed the command to the day of his death in

[1] N. Paulus in *Archiv für elsässische Kirchengeschichte*, III (1928), p. 26. The alleged influence on Ignatius is denied by P. Leturia, *El gentilhombre Iñigo de Loyola en sua patria y en su siglo* (Montevideo 1938), p. 191.

[2] N. Paulus, "Der Strassburger Kartäuser Ludolf von Sachsen", in *Archiv für elsässische Kirchengeschichte*, II (1927), pp. 207-22.

[3] Lortz, *Die Reformation in Deutschland* (Freiburg i.B. 1941), VOL. II, p. 133.

[4] *Beiträge zur bayrischen Kirchengeschichte*, II (1896), p. 238.

[5] J. Greven, *Die Kölner Kartause und die Anfänge der Kath. Reform in Deutschland* (Münster 1935), pp. 7 ff., 12 ff.

1384.[1] By his simple spirituality Geert Groote started a movement of such depth and strength that Johann Busch likened it to the marvels of primitive Christianity.[2] He drew up no reform programme and founded no order, but the two religious societies which claimed him as their originator, viz. the Canons of St Augustine of Windesheim and the Brethren of the Common Life, kept his spirit alive. *The Imitation of Christ* is the most exquisite fruit of that spirit.

The *devotio moderna* meant personal reform through a return to Christian inwardness. As a free movement it was not limited, as were the monastic reforms, to a corporation already in existence and regulated by law, nor was it burdened by any traditions; hence it was able to develop in every direction; but it cannot be said that it exhibited any novel features [3]: the only new thing about it was the earnestness with which it strove for the unchanging goal—the following of Christ. It would be a serious error of judgment to see in this world-forsaking piety a symptom of weariness, or to interpret its abandonment of technical theology as undogmatic Christianity.[4] It was a pause for breath in preparation for further exertions. Like all genuine religious movements it issued in active work. Groote himself had been a missionary. Throughout north and west Germany, by their writings and by their schools, the Brethren of Deventer and Zwolle were engaged in the apostolate of the spoken and the printed word, and, best of all, that of example. There was a pronounced "lay" touch in the "devout" movement. By a remarkable coincidence similar symptoms appeared also in the southern half of Europe. The laity began to reform itself.

---

[1] The best summing up in R. Post, *De moderne devotie* (Amsterdam 1940); also F. v. d. Borne, "Geert Groote en de moderne devotie in de geschiedenis van het middeleeuwsche ordewezen", in *Studia catholica*, XVI (1940), pp. 397-414; XVII (1941), pp. 120-33, 197-209; XVIII (1942), pp. 19-40, 203-24; the dissertation of I. G. I. Tiecke, *De werken van G. Groote* (Nijmegen 1941), and M. H. Mulders, *G. Groote en het Huwelijk* (Nijmegen 1941); H. Nottarp, "Die Brüder vom gemeinsamen Leben", in *Z.Sav.R.G.K.A.*, XXXII (1943), pp. 384-418; H. Radermacher, *Mystik und Humanismus der Devotio moderna in den Predigten und Traktaten des Joh. Veghe* (Hiltrup 1935); D. Kalverkamp, *Die Vollkommenheitslehre des Franziskaners H. Herp* (Werl 1940).

[2] *Des Augustinerpropstes Joh. Busch Chronicon Windeshemense* (Halle 1886), p. 245.

[3] Post, *De moderne devotie*, p. 136 ff.

[4] Thus R. Stadelmann, *Vom Geist des ausgehenden Mittelalters* (Halle 1929). The attempt of the Dominican Matthew Grabow to prove that the observance of the evangelical counsels as practised by the Brethren of the Common Life was sinful because it was practised outside any of the approved orders, ended with the condemnation of seventeen propositions of his pamphlet (26 May 1419); see S. Wachter, *Festschrift zum 50 jährigen Bestandsjubiläum des Missionshauses St Gabriel* (Wien-Mödling 1939), pp. 289-376.

Two groups, whose origin dates from the fourteenth century, consolidated themselves into religious orders; they were the Hieronymites in Spain and Colombini's Jesuates in Italy. A third group, which only took definite shape at the turn of the fifteenth century, was content to remain a confraternity: this was the Oratory of Divine Love. It became the most famous of them all, and its rise is usually regarded as the beginning of the Catholic reformation.

The Oratory's fundamental principle is that personal sanctification must be achieved by means of good works on behalf of others. Its aim is not so much activity born of holiness as the formation of saints through charitable activity. The charitable confraternities established in various parts of Italy were both a preparation for and a concomitant symptom of the Oratory: such was the Oratory of St Jerome, founded in 1494 at Vicenza by Bernardino of Feltre. Its object was the practice of piety and the care of the poor. Its members, seventy at most, belonged for the most part to the upper classes.[1] Shortly before the year 1500, Ettore Vernazza, a layman, inspired by the Genoese mystic St Catherine founded the first Oratory of Divine Love in his native city.[2] Its aim was personal sanctification and the practice of charity; only a restricted number of priests were admitted. At a date which it is not possible to ascertain, Vernazza transferred his institution to Rome. Before long it counted among its members several high officials of the Curia. The aims of the confraternity remained the same as at Genoa.

The Oratory gave birth to the Order of the Theatines. Its founder, Cajetan of Thiene, had at first followed a diplomatic career in the Curia. At a later date he devoted himself to the service of the sick at Vicenza and Verona. Only in his riper years did he understand that his real vocation was the foundation of a community of priests who would be a pattern of the priestly life and activity. The society received papal approbation in 1524.[3]

The influence of the Oratory and that of the Theatines upon the

[1] P. Paschini, *La beneficenza in Italia e le Compagnie del divino amore nei primi decenni del Cinquecento* (Rome 1925), pp. 6 ff.; a reprint in *Tre ricerche sulla storia della Chiese nel Cinquecento* (Rome 1945), pp. 3-88.

[2] In addition to Paschini, see A. Bianconi, *L'opera delle Compagnie del Divino amore nella riforma cattolica* (Città di Castello 1914), pp. 33 ff.; the Genoa statutes in P. Tacchi Venturi, *Storia della Compagnia di Gesù in Italia* (Rome 1910), VOL. I, pp. 423 ff. The recently published list of the members of the Roman Oratory (1517-24) by A. Cistellini, *Figure della riforma pretridentina* (Brescia 1948), p. 288, confirms my opinion. Giberti and Sadoleto are not mentioned in the list.

[3] P. Paschini, *S. Gaetano Thiene, G. P. Carafa e le origine dei Chierici Regolari Theatini* (Rome 1926). E. Lovatelli's *S. Gaetano e gli inizi della riforma cattolica* (Milan 1941) is a popular compilation of no special value.

rise of the Catholic reformation has been undoubtedly exaggerated in recent years. These institutions were only like a rivulet which eventually becomes a stream through the affluents that bring it their tribute. Soon after the turn of the century, at Venice, Thomas Giustiniani gathered around him a number of like-minded young men of the best families of the city, men of excellent intellectual formation and all of them resolved to take Christianity seriously. For a time they lived communally on the island of Murano, but they never coagulated into a confraternity or a new order. Giustiniani, Sebastiano Giorgi and the highly gifted Quirini, who had served the Republic as an able ambassador, joined the Camaldolese and started a reform of an order which had become still more worldly during the generalate of Pietro Delfino. Their friends Niccolò Tiepolo and Gaspar Contarini remained in the world; we shall meet the former at the Diet of Augsburg of 1530; the latter was raised to the purple and became Paul III's right-hand man in the reform of the Church. All the members of the circle were laymen with the exception of the humanist Egnazio, and none of them held a benefice. Their conduct was a silent protest against the worldliness of the hierarchy, but their loyalty to the Church remained unshaken.[1]

Also of lay origin was the establishment of the Somaschi whose founder, Jerome Emiliani, was a soldier who became an apostle of charity, and that of the Barnabites, whose activity consisted in preaching popular missions. Of their three founders, one (Antonio Maria Zaccaria) had been a physician, another (Ferrari) a lawyer, and the third (Morigia) an elegant courtier.[2] The origin of these orders falls in a later period, but they are the ripe fruit of tendencies which had long been at work—viz. the impetus of the laity towards personal sanctification and apostolic activity. In view of these endeavours for a spiritual renewal in the regular clergy and the laity, the question arises whether similar essays of personal reform took place in the ranks of the secular clergy, in the dioceses and the parishes?

It must be stated emphatically: such attempts were made, but they do not catch the eye as do the reform of the orders or the foundation of new ones, and there are many gaps in their history, the study of which has been very much neglected. But even in the present state of our

[1] Part of the correspondence in J. B. Mittarelli-A. Costadini, *Annales Camaldulenses*, VOL. IX (Venice 1773), pp. 446-559. I intend to publish Contarini's letters in *Archivio per la storia della pietà*.

[2] O. Premoli, *Storia dei Barnabiti nel Cinquecento* (Rome 1913), pp. 2 ff.; *id.*, *Le lettere e lo spirito religioso di S. Antonio M. Zaccaria* (Rome 1909), but only starting in the year 1530.

information, this much may be said: in every country bishops and priests were found who, by means of visitations and synods, by the spoken and the written word, but above all by their personal example, did their utmost to improve conditions in their respective spheres. Among the Italian bishops of the fifteenth century who are justly renowned for their pastoral zeal and their visitations and synods, mention must be made of Lorenzo Giustiniani, Patriarch of Venice, Archbishop Antonino of Florence, and Antonio Bertini, Bishop of Foligno. A worthy contemporary of theirs was Pietro Barozzi, a balanced character, who reformed his dioceses of Belluno and Padua by means of excellent statutes and who personally preached the word of God; such was his whole conduct that to so keen an observer as Contarini he appeared as a pattern of all that a good bishop should be.[1] Other personalities will come forward when, ultimately, the acts of visitations,[2] and the synodal decrees [3] and other documents relating to diocesan administration and the organisation of the parochial system, now buried in the archives, have been thoroughly explored. It is evident that an orderly cure of souls cannot have been entirely neglected; else popular piety would have become so anaemic that the revival which began in the fifteen-thirties would have been unthinkable.[4]

Similar considerations impose themselves with regard to the Church in France. In the diocese of Paris it might happen that if the absentee parish priest failed to provide a substitute the people of the village would get one for themselves and provide for his support out of the proceeds of the tithe.[5] This was self-help indeed, canonically indefensible, but perfectly natural when a religious people was determined

---

[1] A biography of Barozzi, which is greatly needed, is still wanting; particulars for an appreciation of his personality are supplied by J. Schnitzer, *Peter Delfin* (Munich 1926), pp. 33 ff., 329 ff.; for his Paduan Constitutions, see F. Scipione, *Dissertazione IX sopra l'Historia ecclesiastica di Padova* (Padua 1817), pp. 119-30.

[2] On this task which remains yet to be performed see my study: "Ciò che la storia del Concilio si attende dalla storia ecclesiastica italiana", in *Il Concilio di Trento*, II (1943), pp. 163-75; a sample of ancient Visitation Acts in P. de Angelis, "Un frammento di Sacra visita della diocesi Spoletana", in *Archivio per la storia ecclesiastica dell' Umbria*, III (1916), pp. 446-539.

[3] One instance may be quoted, viz. Carafa's Constitutions for Chieti, published by E. Carusi in "Convegno storico abruzzese-molisano 1931", in *Atti e Memorie*, III (Casalbordino 1940), pp. 917-34.

[4] To the pertinent passages in Pastor and Tacchi Venturi must be added P. Paschini, *Noterelle eucaristiche per la vita religiosa italiana nel primo Rinascimento* (Rome 1936); F. Chabod, *Per la storia religiosa dello Stato di Milano durante il dominio di Carlo V* (Bologna 1938), pp. 44 ff.

[5] J. M. Alliot, *Visites archidiaconales de Josas* (Paris 1902); Ch. Petit Dutaillis, "Un nouveau document sur l'Eglise de France", in *R.H.*, LXXXVIII (1905), pp. 296-315.

to remain so and the ecclesiastical authorities failed to do their duty. With greater enthusiasm than ever, after the termination of the Hundred Years' War, the French nation resumed the construction of its cathedrals. the adornment of its parish churches and the erection of new ones.[1] The clergy grew in numbers; thus in the period between 1445 and 1514 the diocese of Séez quadrupled the number of its clergy. The provincial synod of Sens of 1485 led to the revival of diocesan synods at Chartres, Langres, Nantes and Troyes. A number of bishops concerned themselves personally with the reform of the monasteries as, for instance, Poncher of Paris.[2] François d'Estraing, Bishop of Rodez (1504-29), saw to the instruction of the people and the formation of his clergy, reformed his chapter and carried out the visitation of his diocese. During the epidemics that ravaged it he gave an example of the most admirable charity.[3] At the Convention of Tours in 1493, Standonck unfolded a comprehensive scheme for the reform of the secular clergy. He sought to remedy the worst abuses in the choice of bishops, the granting of benefices with the cure of souls attached to them, the administration of the sacraments and the ministry of preaching, and promised himself great results from the revival of provincial and diocesan synods.[4] However, after the year 1500 these efforts began to languish. Cardinal d'Amboise, papal legate in France, brought the reform into discredit by the use of physical coercion and its progress was arrested. Flowers do not bloom in the shadow of ecclesiastical dictatorship.

A similar phenomenon is observable in England a little later. It was inevitable that the Church should suffer from the effects of the Wars of the Roses. Nevertheless, the visitations in the diocese of Norwich in 1492 and 1514 brought to light no gross disorders in most of the parishes and religious houses.[5] Churchwardens' accounts and other sources present a favourable picture of the people's attitude towards religion. They contributed gladly and liberally to the construction and embellishment of their churches. In many parishes the church

[1] Imbart de la Tour, *Origines*, VOL. II, pp. 535 ff.; Renaudet, *Préréforme et humanisme à Paris*, pp. 160 ff.
[2] Renaudet, *Préréforme et humanisme à Paris*, p. 353.
[3] C. Belmont, *Le bienheureux François d'Estraing, évêque de Rodez* (Rodez 1924).
[4] M. Godet, "Consultations de Tours sur la réforme de l'Eglise de France", in *R.H.E.*, II (1911), pp. 175 ff., 333 ff.; Renaudet, *Préréforme et humanisme à Paris*, pp. 178 ff.
[5] A. Jessop, *Visitations of the diocese of Norwich 1492-1532* (London 1888): conditions in Southwell Minster are less satisfactory; *Visitations and Memorials of Southwell Minster*, ed. A. F. Leach (London 1891).

building was the focus of parochial life. The small parish of St Dunstan at Canterbury numbered no more than four hundred souls, yet it boasted a library of fifty volumes. From the people's attachment to the Church we may infer that neither the bishops nor the parochial clergy failed entirely in their duty.[1] On the other hand no perceptible impetus seems to have been given by the synods.[2] In the same way the collection of the provincial statutes of York ordered by Cardinal Wolsey made no appreciable impression.[3] The ecclesiastical dictatorship which that masterful personality exercised over the Church in England after his appointment as papal legate in 1518 did as little for a reform in England as that of d'Amboise in France.

It was in the German hierarchy, more than in any other, that the personal reform encountered the greatest psychological obstacles. The princely rank of the bishops of the Empire tended to divert them from their spiritual duties while the mediatised prelates were far too prone to regard themselves solely as territorial lords. For all that, the fifteenth century produced in Germany particularly a remarkable number of excellent bishops. At the time of the Council of Basle, Nider knew of only three bishops who gave the lie to the universal complaint about the worldliness of the hierarchy, viz. Frederick of Bamberg, Erhard (or Eckhard) of Worms, and Sebastian of Trent.[4] We are now in a position to add many more names to this list: for instance, that of the learned Bishop of Brandenburg, Stephen Bodeker, who promulgated an ordinance for his diocese at the synod of 1435, revised the Breviary and fostered the religious instruction of the people by means of solid treatises on the Creed, the Decalogue and the Lord's Prayer.[5] To him we may add Baldwin, Archbishop of Bremen, who declined the assistance of an auxiliary because he wished to carry out in person all episcopal functions.

These reforming bishops were followed by others in the second half of the fifteenth century. Of the Bishop of Constance, Heinrich von

---

[1] F. A. Gasquet, *The Eve of the Reformation* (London 1900), pp. 323 ff.

[2] We know of the following provincial synods: Canterbury 1487, York 1489 and 1497, St Andrews 1487. Hefele-Hergenröther, *Conziliengeschichte*, VOL. VIII, pp. 285 ff., 369.

[3] Wilkins, *Concilia Magnae Britanniae et Hiberniae*, VOL. III (London 1737), pp. 662 ff.

[4] *Formicarius*, VOL. I, p. 6. To guard against any misunderstanding, I wish to state that it is not the purpose of the following observations to sum up the oft-discussed problem of the "causes of the Reformation", or the religious situation in Germany on the eve of the Reformation; hence I do not mention the surveys of W. Andreas and K. Eder and still less the immense literature on the subject.

[5] K. H. Schäfer, *Märkisches Bildungswesen vor der Reformation* (Berlin 1928), pp. 29 ff.

Hewen (1436-62), it has been said that "inspired by an exemplary priestly zeal he strove with unswerving perseverance for the one object —the reform of his diocese in its head and its members".[1] Heinrich was even surpassed by his successor, Burkhard von Randegg, a man of a truly apostolic character. A contemporary of these two prelates, Matthias Ramung, Bishop of Speyer (1463-78), is regarded as the "regenerator of his cathedral chapter". He was the first German bishop to instruct parish priests to draw up a register of their parishioners.[2] Bishop Wedego of Havelberg's (1460-78) directions for the examination of candidates for holy orders are inspired by the same principles as those that prompted the subsequent Tridentine legislation.[3] Frederick von Zollern, Bishop of Augsburg (1486-1505), a pupil of the celebrated popular preacher Geiler von Kaisersberg, was as conscious of a bishop's duty to preach the word of God as any prelate of the Tridentine epoch. He revised the liturgical books of his diocese and invited the first printers to Augsburg.[4] The synodal allocution of his next successor but one, Christoph von Stadion (1517-43), is filled with the spirit of the *devotio moderna*. His diocesan visitation in 1518, and two further diocesan synods held by him in 1520 and 1536, belong to the period of the religious disruption. Of the Bishop of Würzburg, Schenk von Limburg (1443-55), a scholar of our own days says that he opened every door to reform.[5] His second successor, Rudolph von Scherenberg (1466-95), completed the reform which was "the ultimate aim of every measure taken by him". Bishop John of Meissen (1487-1518) is regarded as "one of the most active and conscientious bishops" of this Saxon diocese.[6]

These examples must suffice. The frequency of synodal assemblies in Germany more than in other parts of Christendom is surely a good symptom. Nearly all the above-named bishops held synods. For

[1] A. Braun, *Der Klerus des Bistums Konstanz im Ausgang des Mittelalters* (Münster 1938), pp. 172, 174.

[2] *Collectio processuum synodalium et constitutionum ecclesiasticarum dioecesis Spirensis*, VOL. I (1786), p. 117.

[3] A. F. Riedel, *Codex dipl. Brandenburgensis* (Berlin 1838-58), A III, pp. 254 ff.

[4] P. Braun, *Geschichte des Bistums Augsburg*, VOL. III (Augsburg 1814), pp. 89-151; for Stadion, *ibid.*, pp. 178-357. Th. Dreher, *Das Tagebuch über Friedrich von Hohenzollern, Bischof von Augsburg 1486-1505* (Sigmaringen 1888), pp. 80 ff. (Synod of 1486), pp. 155, 162; (Visitations), pp. 191 ff., 209 ff. More will be said about Stadion in Book II.

[5] See Freiherr von Pölnitz, *Die bischöfliche Reformarbeit im Hochstift Würzburg während des 15. Jahrhunderts* (Würzburg 1941), p. 121.

[6] E. Machatschek, *Die Geschichte der Bischöfe des Hochstifts Meissen* (Dresden 1884), p. 610.

Cologne alone we have evidence of no less than fifteen diocesan synods during the rule of Hermann von Hessen and Philip von Oberstein (1480-1515); it would even seem that two such assemblies were held every year.[1] The provincial synod of Salzburg in 1512 formally adopted the principle of self-reform.[2] There can be no doubt that more reforming went on in Germany than anywhere else. That things eventually took a very different turn was not due to the fact that the pastoral ministry was more neglected, the clergy worse behaved, or the people more ignorant of their religion, or more indifferent to it, than in other countries. It was due to the fact that the laity, the urban burghers and the intellectuals who were beginning to constitute an estate by themselves, expected more from their priests and were more keenly sensitive to the contrast between the ideal and the real in their lives. They were determined to make a radical clearance of abuses—real or imaginary ones—on their own initiative, instead of resigning themselves, with a shrug of the shoulder, to prevailing conditions as something that could not be altered. Most of the tensions within the German Church, between the higher and the lower clergy, between seculars and regulars, between clergy and laity, between the secular and the spiritual authority —tensions which, in point of fact, were in part caused by social conditions—were also felt in other countries, in a greater or less degree, but only in Germany, after 1520, did people imagine they could endure them no longer; in this way the reform became a revolution. A circumstance of another kind proved a decisive factor in the course of the revolution. This was that the bishops' initiative for a reform was paralleled by one publicly advocated by the secular princes.[3] The German territorial princes promoted a reform of the Church in sundry ways. In itself it was gratifying that the Margrave Frederick II of Brandenburg should assist the monastic reformer Johann Busch and should be ready to lend a hand whenever there was question of putting an end to some of the worst abuses,[4] or that the Counts Palatine on the

[1] F. Gescher, "Die Kölner Diözesansynoden am Vorabend der Reformation", in Z.Sav.R.G.K.A., XXI (1932), pp. 190-288, especially p. 220.
[2] Concilia Salisburgensia, ed. Dalham (Augsburg 1788), pp. 279 ff.: "Primum in se ipsis ea emendantes quae sacris canonibus obviare noscuntur."
[3] J. Hashagen, Staat und Kirche vor der Reformation (Essen 1931), and the reviews by H. Finke in H.J., LI (1931), pp. 219 ff., and that of J. Fincke in A.K.R., XI (1931), pp. 685 ff. A good survey of the literature in W. Dersch, "Territorium, Stadt und Kirche im ausgehenden Mittelalter", in Korrespondenzblatt des Gesamtvereins der deutschen Geschichts- und Altertumsvereine, LXXX (1932) pp. 31-51.
[4] F. Priebatsch, "Staat und Kirche in der Mark Brandenburg am Ende des Mittelalters", in Z.K.G., XIX (1899), pp. 397-430.

Rhine should set great store by a regular discharge of their duties by the pastoral clergy.[1] Often enough the secular arm alone was in a position to break the resistance of depraved elements. For all that, the reforming activities of the secular authorities could not but inspire serious misgivings. The secular princes' concern for the reform of the monasteries within their territories was not invariably prompted by zeal for discipline and piety. All too often the inspiration came from a fiscal interest in the taxability of monastic property. At times the real need of a reform of the secular clergy provided a welcome pretext for the extension of the princes' influence upon the Church, from the nomination of bishops down to the appointment of parish priests. Their example was followed by the big towns, which sought to arrogate to themselves the patronage of their parish churches and other minor benefices, as well as the administration of schools and charitable bequests.[2] As a rule, from a purely formal standpoint everything was in order. In 1485 the Saxon Dukes Ernest and Albrecht had been empowered to reform the monasteries by Innocent VIII,[3] and in 1491 the Cardinal-legate Peraudi authorised the Margrave John of Brandenburg to have the monasteries of his territory visited by its three bishops. However, the participation of counsellors appointed by the princes in the visitation of the monasteries of the Duchies of Cleves and Saxony, their interference with the inner life of many monasteries—to the extent of ordering the divine office—and the supervision by lay officials of the beneficed clergy of the Palatinate in respect of the duty of residence, may have been well meant; nevertheless, these actions were extremely questionable inasmuch as they made the ecclesiastical life far too dependent on the state, entailed endless disputes with the bishops over questions of jurisdiction, and thus paved the way for that subjection of the Church to temporal sovereigns which was to come in with Protestantism. People got used to the notion that Church reform was the business of the temporal sovereign.

What the territorial princes of Germany did on a small scale was carried out in the grand manner by the western national states. We

[1] R. Lossen, *Staat und Kirche in der Pfalz im Ausgang des Mittelalters* (Munich 1907), pp. 125 ff. Of the Dominican Province of Saxony G. Löhr says that progress was only reported in those places where the secular or the ecclesiastical princes intervened; *A.F.P.*, VIII (1938), p. 215.

[2] The following are basic works: A. Schultz, *Staatsgemeinde und Kirche im Mittelalter* (Munich-Leipzig 1914); K. Fröhlich, "Kirche und Städtisches Verfassungsleben im Mittelalter" in *Z.Sav.R.G.K.A.*, XXII (1933), pp. 188-287.

[3] F. Gess, *Akten und Briefe zur Kirchenpolitik Herzog Georgs von Sachsen*, VOL. I (Leipzig 1905), p. xxxvii.

have already mentioned Charles VIII's attempts to promote a reform within the Church, and we know that Louis XI favoured the Observants.[1] Yet on the whole it cannot be said that the French Kings used the great influence on the Church which they enjoyed *de facto* by the terms of the Pragmatic Sanction and still more by those of the concordat of 1516, to further Church reform. Nor had the Church anything to gain from the pretensions of the *parlements*, particularly that of Paris, to decide disputes over benefices, to confirm monastic reforms and synodal statutes and in other ways also to supervise ecclesiastical affairs.[2]

The Spanish Kings alone made a large-scale and successful contribution to the reform of the Church within their domains. In this task they were assisted by the circumstance that as a result of the century-old crusade for the peninsula's deliverance from the yoke of Islam religious and national ideals had become closely interwoven in the popular consciousness. Moreover, in the fifteenth century and at the beginning of the sixteenth, Spain produced a number of able monastic reformers and prudent and energetic bishops; men like Pablo and his son Alfonso of Burgos, of Jewish descent,[3] Pedro González de Mendoza, "the Great Cardinal", as he has been surnamed, whose predecessor at Toledo was Alonso de Carillo, while at Seville he was succeeded by Diego Hurtado de Mendoza and the Grand Inquisitor Deza, both of whom have left provincial statutes.[4] Over all these towers the figure of Ximenes de Cisneros of Toledo.[5] The acts of the national council of Seville in 1478 make it perfectly clear that the bishops did not look on themselves as the slaves of the Crown.[6] Crown and hierarchy were indeed agreed upon certain fundamental lines of reform, such as the strengthening of episcopal authority against exempt clergy, opposition

[1] See above, p. 149, *n.* 4. P. Gratien, "Un épisode de la réforme catholique avant Luther", in *Etudes Franciscaines*, XXVII (1912), pp. 605-21; XXVIII, pp. 272-90, 504-16.

[2] Imbart de la Tour, *Origines*, VOL. II, pp. 84 ff., 213 ff.; E. Maugis, *Histoire du Parlement de Paris*, VOL. I (Paris 1913), pp. 704 ff.

[3] L. Serrano, *Los conversos Don Pablo de Santa Maria y Don Alfonso de Cartagena, obispos de Burgos* (Madrid 1942). The history of the ecclesiastical movement of reform in Spain which P. Leturia demanded long ago (see *Estudios ecclesiásticos*, VIII (1929), pp. 97-114) is not yet written; it probably still needs a good deal of preparatory work.

[4] Mansi, VOL. XXXII, pp. 571-650. For Toledo, see C. Sánchez Aliseda, "Precedentes Toledanos de la Reforma Tridentina", in *Revista Española de Derecho Canónico*, 1948, separately printed.

[5] L. F. de Retana, *Cisneros y su siglo*, VOL. I (Madrid 1929), pp. 174 ff., 265 ff., 560 ff.

[6] F. Fita, "Concilios españoles inéditos", in *Buletino de la Real Academia de Historia*, XXII (1893), pp. 209-57; text of the acts, pp. 215-50.

to the nomination of foreigners to Spanish benefices, the duty of residence—but all the while the bishops fought valiantly for the freedom of the Church and would not hear of any interference with the rights of papal supremacy. The Church retained the initiative while the State assisted her and lent its arm whenever the need arose. The State secured for itself the right of nomination to episcopal sees and, consequently, a decisive influence on the hierarchy's policy, and it established the ecclesiastical Inquisition for its own security. At the time of the Lateran Council, the State saw to it that the national aspirations for reform were formulated at a conference so that they could be submitted collectively.[1] There can be no doubt that it was due to this collaboration of King and clergy that a generation later the Spanish Church was able to take the lead in the restoration movement.

From the turn of the century ecclesiastical reform had been caught in a spiritual current whose origin was not in the religious sphere but in the cultural one: we know it under the name of humanism.

A religious reform in the spirit of a baptised Plato, or, to speak more accurately, in the spirit of the Neoplatonic philosophy, had already been the dream of Marsilio Ficino. His "universalism" bore an apologetic character.[2] The Neoplatonic teaching about God and the soul, and the syncretistic theology of the late pre-Christian period, were pressed by him into the defence of Christianity against the new Averroism that was being taught in the chairs of Padua and Bologna. Ficino actually imagined that his Platonic theology would do for the formation of the clergy what later scholasticism had failed to achieve. In letters to Pope Sixtus IV and his nephew, Raffaele Riario, he urged them in glowing terms to initiate a reform. His friend the youthful, greatly admired Giovanni Pico became an adherent of Savonarola.[3]

---

[1] Döllinger, *Beiträge*, VOL. III, pp. 200 ff.; Hefele-Hergenröther, *Conziliengeschichte*, VOL. VIII, pp. 463 ff.

[2] This tendency of Ficino has been stressed (as against Saita, who sees in him an immanentist) by G. Anichini, *L'Umanesimo e il problema della salvezza in Marsilio Ficino* (Milan 1937); see also R. Montano, "Ficiniana", in *La Rinascita*, III (1940), pp. 71-104; this has not escaped W. Dress, *Die Mystik des Marsilio Ficino* (Berlin-Leipzig 1929), pp. 13 ff.; see my observations in *R.Q.*, XXXIX (1931), pp. 281-7. Ficino's letters to Sixtus IV and Riario are in the *Opera*, VOL. I (Basle 1576), pp. 795 ff., 808 ff.

[3] E. Garin, *Giovanni Pico della Mirandola* (Florence 1937), accounts for Savonarola's sympathy for Pico by "la sempre maggiore austerità di costumi, la profonda aderenza al valore eterno del cristianesimo". On Garin's book see the contemporary work of E. Anagnine, *Giovanni Pico della Mirandola, Sincretismo religioso-filosofico* (Bari 1937), and the editions of Pico's writings by B. Cicognani (1941) and E. Garin (1942). See also the reviews by P. Marucchi in *La Rinascita*, I, iii (1938), pp. 147-60; VI (1943), pp. 137-44.

For the real reform of the Church these rare aristocratic spirits were of small significance.[1] It was only when Colet came to study St Paul, and Pico's nephew Gianfrancesco realised the superiority of the Fathers over Plato and Cicero and Seripando renounced Platonism for St Augustine—in other words, when the Bible and Christian antiquity became the centre of interest for the humanists—that new perspectives opened out before the Church. The beginnings of humanism's interest in the Bible and the Fathers must be traced back to Ambrogio Traversari's work of translation and Lorenzo Valla's critique.[2] The influence of the Fathers is already perceptible in the treatment by the humanists of the fifteenth century of such a theme as human dignity.[3] But it was Erasmus of Rotterdam who pioneered the movement and with him it attained its full momentum.

Until quite recently both the person of Erasmus and the spiritual temper of which he is the prototype have been most diversely interpreted and at times severely condemned.[4] An unfavourable verdict is inevitable if we base our judgment mainly on his attitude towards the religious revolution and if from his many activities we single out those which have had destructive and disastrous results in the religious sphere. His personality and its impact on his time are so complex that they cannot be compressed into a single formula.[5] I myself must forgo a general appreciation of the man; my task is to consider what contribution he and those who shared his views made to the reform of the Church,

---

[1] I must make this reservation as against A. Corsano's statements, *Il pensiero religioso italiano dall' Umanesimo al Giurisdizionalismo* (Bari 1937), pp. 5-64. The influence of Florentine Platonism in the sphere of philosophy and literature, which was recently stressed by J. Festugière, E. Garin and P. O. Kristeller, the excellent editor of the *Supplementum Ficinianum*, is not affected thereby; see especially the latter's book *The Philosophy of Marsilio Ficino* (New York 1943).

[2] Traversari's letters to Francesco Barbaro and Leonardo Giustiniani in *Epistolae* (Florence 1759), pp. 283 ff., 311 ff.

[3] Garin, "La 'dignitas hominis' e la letteratura patristica", in *La Rinascita*, i, iii (1938), pp. 102-46.

[4] In German Catholic literature the line starts with J. Kerber (*T.Q.*, XLI (1859), pp. 531-66) and through Janssen goes on to Lortz, *Reformation in Deutschland*, VOL. I, pp. 127 ff. Godet in *D.Th.C.*, VOL. V, pp. 388-97, is somewhat less critical, though on the whole his judgment is unfavourable. The Italian studies of V. Zabughin, *Il Cristianesimo durante il Rinascimento* (Milan 1924), and L. Borghi, *Umanesimo e concezione religiosa in Erasmo di Rotterdam* (Florence 1935), scarcely touch the ecclesiastical-political problem of Erasmus. K. Holl and G. Ritter go further in their rejection of Erasmus than any other Protestant writers.

[5] This is the chief merit, in my opinion, of J. Huizinga's biography, *Erasmus* (London and New York 1924). A quite objective appreciation of Erasmus is likewise found in K. A. Meissinger, *Erasmus von Rotterdam* (Zürich 1942, 2nd edn. Berlin 1948). See also R. Newald, *Erasmus Roterodamus* (Freiburg i.B. 1947).

without allowing myself to be swayed by the opinions of critics, whether old or new.

Erasmus belongs to the era of the *devotio moderna*, but he himself never was a *"devotus"*. By instinct a scholar and philologist, his one interest was culture, and culture for him was the culture of antiquity, crowned and perfected by Christianity.[1] Hence he does not stop at the writers of classical antiquity, but goes further. Work on the original text of Holy Scripture and on the works of ancient commentators—men still instinct with the ancient culture—opened for him the road to his ideal of culture, *eruditio* and *pietas*. The great sin is "barbarism": religious culture produces the upright man. This culture is to be found in the "old and genuine theology", in the Bible and the Fathers.[2] To open up these "sources" of Christianity by means of critical editions was Erasmus's mission in life. His most important contribution to Biblical studies is his first edition of the Greek New Testament in 1516. "Meticulous work on the sacred text", he wrote in his preface, "is justified by reverence for Him who is the eternal Word of the Father; its purpose is to lead the way back to the original source of God's word instead of drawing it from conduits of stale water."[3] In spite of numerous mistakes and imperfections, the work proved an enormous success: "I would not give my copy for two hundred florins", wrote Gregory Reisch.[4] Valla's *Annotations to the New Testament* and Lefèvre's *Quintuplex psalterium* (1509), and his commentary on St Paul's epistles (1512), had appeared before Erasmus's work. The Complutensian Polyglot Bible (1514-17) coincided with it. The highest ambition of the intellectual élite of the time was to be able to read the Scriptures in the original Greek and Hebrew. For this purpose Vincenzo Quirini, while still a layman, had learnt both languages. From this time the *Collegium trinlingue* of Alcalá, and that of Louvain, provided splendid facilities for those whose ambition it was to become experts in Biblical studies. The new translations published by Lefèvre and Erasmus opened the contest round the Vulgate. As

---

[1] R. Pfeiffer, *Humanitas Erasmiana* (Leipzig 1931), pp. 9 ff., and O. Schottenloher's views in *Erasmus im Ringen um die humanistische Bildungsform* (Münster 1933), pp. 14, 18 ff., directed against P. Mestwerdt. As a matter of fact the whole problem of Erasmus is summed up in his own phrase "Not Martyrs but Doctors" discussed *ibid.*, p. 92.

[2] *Opus Epistolarum Des. Erasmi Roterodami*, ed. P. S. Allen, VOL. I (Oxford 1906), p. 247. Erasmus to Colet, October 1499.

[3] Erasmus, *Epist.*, VOL. II, pp. 164-72, 244, 257; A. Bludau, *Die beiden ersten Erasmusausgaben des NT und ihre Gegner* (Freiburg 1902), pp. 21 ff.

[4] Erasmus, *Epist.*, VOL. II, p. 14.

early as 1514 Martin Dorpius had laid down for its defence the principles which were subsequently sanctioned by the Church in the Tridentine decrees on the Vulgate. The controversy about the Magdalen was a prelude to the higher criticism of the Bible. But the most important thing was the realisation that not only professional theologians but priests in the ministry equally needed to know the Scriptures. Giustiniani and Quirini proposed that no one should be ordained who had not read the whole Bible at least once.[1] The time was at hand when the greatest theologian of the period, Cardinal Cajetan, would apply himself, to begin with, to the writing of handy commentaries on the New Testament, because lectures on the Bible were being given not only at the universities, on the model of Colet's Oxford lectures on St Paul, but even before a wider public.

From his youth Erasmus had been an enthusiastic admirer of St Jerome in whom he saw the embodiment of his ideal of the cultured man—erudition combined with piety. St Jerome was the first Church Father whom he was determined to "recall to life" by a complete edition of his works. He worked at this edition at the same time as he was preparing his New Testament. In this field—patrology—others had gone before him.[2] Johann Amerbach, a printer of Basle, undertook to bring out a complete critical edition of the four great Western Fathers. In Johann Froben he found a congenial associate and an eventual successor. In 1506 the two men published the works of St Augustine in nine volumes. In the same year Johann Petri brought out the works of St Ambrose in three volumes. Paris vied with Basle with editions of Lactantius (1509), Cyprian (1512) and Gregory of Tours (1512). By slow degrees the Greek Fathers also began to appear, though at first mostly in Latin translations. Chrysostom appeared at Basle in 1504; Origen and John Damascene were published in Paris in 1512. With the editions of Ignatius and Polycarp prepared by Lefèvre and Clichtove and printed by Estienne (Stephanus)—to which pseudo-Dionysius was added in 1515—the sub-apostolic era was opened up.

To bring out a complete edition of the Fathers is a far greater undertaking than the haphazard printing of some isolated work of theirs.[3]

[1] *Annales Camaldulenses*, VOL. IX, p. 679. Cajetan's exegetical writings start with a translation of the Psalms in 1527, and were followed by the commentaries of the N.T. in 1529 and those on the O.T., as far as *Isaias*, in 1534.

[2] The following data are based on Panzer, *Annales typographici*, VOLS. VI-VIII.

[3] Up to the year 1500 one hundred and eighty-seven separate printed editions of isolated writings of St Augustine had been published, more than half of them spurious, but not one complete edition had appeared: *Gesamtkatalog der Wiegendrücte*, Nos. 2862-3048.

For the execution of such a task an editor must make himself thoroughly acquainted with the whole of the particular Father's literary output; he must eschew what is spurious and appraise his individual character and place in history. To Erasmus, the theology of the Fathers, so deeply inspired by Scripture and so relevant, seemed so far superior to the scholastic theology of the later period that he could not understand how anyone could lay aside Origen or Arnobius for the writings of Ockham, Durandus or Lyra.[1] True, to read the Fathers one must master both classical languages: "No man may claim the title of theologian", he wrote in 1515 to Martin Dorpius, "who has not passed through this door." [2] He questioned the value of the scholastic systems so laboriously built up in the course of the centuries. He was repelled by the "barbarous" language of the schools. Thus it came about that the opposition which his Biblical and patristic studies met with, on the part of certain scholastics, led him astray and caused him to indulge in extravagant exaggerations of the notorious weaknesses of the scholastic system. The question: "What has Christ to do with Aristotle?" implied in the last analysis not only the rejection of the Aristotelian teaching of the Middle Ages, but of scholastic theology itself. The Sorbonne very properly defended itself against such an aberration. The University could not allow its systematic investigation of the truths of the faith to be disposed of with the remark that it was no more than "a drawing of stale water" or even "a splashing in muddy puddles".[3]

There can be no progress without criticism of what has been achieved —not even in theology. However, the partisans of Biblical and patristic theology were not merely fighting for the life of their particular discipline—they were actually endangering the continuity of the theological tradition. The Middle Ages were not a period of deterioration for the Church, as Johannes Caesarius imagined [4]—on the contrary, they were an authentic stage in her growth and one that could not be skipped with impunity. So superficial a work as Cortese's Sentences did not deserve the encomiums with which Peutinger hailed the German edition. To use such a book as a university text-book, as Beatus Rhenanus proposed, would have been a retrograde step.[5] Nor was

---

[1] Erasmus, *Epist.*, vol. II, p. 213. I was unable to consult Ch. Dolfer, *Die Stellung des Erasmus von Rotterdam zur scholastichen Methode*, Dissertation, Münster 1936.

[2] Erasmus, *Epist.*, vol. II, p. 106.

[3] Duplessis d'Argentré, *Coll. iud.*, vol. II, p. 72.

[4] Erasmus, *Epist.*, vol. II, p. 173.

[5] A. Horawitz-K. Hartfelder, *Briefwechsel des Beatus Rhenanus* (Leipzig 1886), pp. 57, 61.

Erasmus's *Methodus* an adequate substitute for serious scholastic studies. His shyness of technical terms, such as "hypostasis" and "transubstantiation", which was ultimately due to a dislike of authoritative definitions and a scholar's fondness for question marks, led to his being suspected of indifference or scepticism in respect of dogmas defined by the Church. But far more dangerous than this shyness and wrong-headedness about Aristotle and the scholastics was the subtle, but for that very reason all the more deadly irony in which he indulged in his *Praise of Folly* and the *Colloquies*, at the expense of the higher and lower clergy, monks and theologians, the ceremonies of the Church and the manifestations of popular devotion. In spite of his loud protests that he only meant to hit unworthy members of those states and only the abuses in the life of the Church,[1] the fact remained that he had exposed to ridicule persons and institutions which up till then had been held in reverence. The circumstance that the *Praise of Folly* was written while he was staying at the house of a canonised Saint does not alter that fact. In vain did he deny responsibility for the mischievous and foul satire of the *Letters of Obscure Men*—it somehow stuck to him.[2] From such a spirit no genuine reform could proceed. When a preacher of reform like Geiler von Kaisersberg castigated abuses in the Church, his words vibrated with the awful earnestness of an accuser. Behind Erasmus's satire one seems to detect the grin of a sceptic. This, and not the alleged three hundred or more mistakes with which Stunica and Lee credit the editor and the translator of the New Testament, is the ultimate reason why the leaders of the Catholic reform, headed by St Ignatius of Loyola, declined to accept Erasmus as an educator.[3]

The *Enchiridion*, in which Erasmus advocated his "Philosophy of Christ", bears traces of the Platonist Giovanni Pico's influence.[4] It has been described as the most Christian of all his writings and an eminent patrologist declares that he would not hesitate to ascribe it to

---

[1] Particularly in the letter to Dorpius of the end of May 1515, Erasmus, *Epist.*, VOL. II, pp. 95 ff.

[2] "Quod istorum sint familia, quos Moria tam gnaviter pridem celebraverit," Wolfgang Angst writes on 19 October 1515 to Erasmus. Erasmus, *Epist.*, VOL. II, p. 153.

[3] Erasmus to Jonas, 19 October 1518: "Ex meis libellis pestem hauriri pietatis," his opponents assert. Erasmus, *Epist.*, VOL. III, p. 414. R. G. Villoslada, "San Ignacio de Loyola y Erasmo de Rotterdam", in *Estudios eclesiásticos*, XVI (1942), pp. 235-64, 399-426; XVII (1943), pp. 75-103. See G. Schnürer, "Warum wurde Erasmus nicht ein Führer der kirchlichen Erneuerung?" in *H.J.*, LV (1935), pp. 332-49.

[4] I. Pusino, "Der Einfluss Picos auf Erasmus", in *Z.K.G.*, XLVI (1928), pp. 75-96.

one of the Church Fathers.[1] Christoph von Utenheim, one of the best bishops of the period, always kept it by him, and Erasmus saw with his own eyes the numerous marginal notes in the prelate's own hand.[2] Even at the Council of Trent someone suggested in all seriousness that the book should be placed in the hands of all future priests.[3] However, there can be no question but that this lay theology is as deficient in clear-cut definitions as is Ficino's Platonic theology; yet even men like Colet and Lefèvre were taken in by it. But while Renaissance Platonism was wrecked on the rocks of gnosis and the cabbala, the "Philosophy of Christ" glided all too lightly over the deeps of the Christian mysteries. Neither work could inspire a genuine renewal. *Mediocritatem suadeo*, Francesco Pico wrote to Leo X in support of his proposals for a reform.[4] Here it was precisely that their weakness lay. Not by the easy road of mediocrity, but by the steep path of holiness alone would the Church rise again.

About the year 1515 not only many humanists, but statesmen like Thomas More and Duke George of Saxony, bishops such as Warham of Canterbury and Utenheim of Basle, were under the impression that a reform as planned by Erasmus would renew the Church. Leo X spoke of him in the most flattering terms.[5] Their expectations remained unfulfilled. Schism supervened, and the extent to which Lutheran criticism of scholasticism and the pious practices of the Church tallied with that of Erasmus suggested the conclusion drawn by Carpi and other ecclesiastics of the sixteenth century,[6] namely that the chief result of Erasmus's activity had been to pave the way for Luther. This conclusion is wrong, for in spite of some dangerous tendencies—

---

[1] S. Merkle told me of this saying of F. X. Funk, but unfortunately I have no printed authority for it.

[2] Erasmus, *Epist.*, VOL. II, pp. 242 ff.

[3] *C.T.*, VOL. V, p. 117.

[4] J. F. Pico, *Opera omnia*, VOL. II (Basle 1601), p. 888.

[5] The briefs of 10 July 1515 in Erasmus, *Epist.*, VOL. II, pp. 114 ff. On 15 July 1519 Justus Jonas wrote to Joh. Lang: "Erasmus vel uno triennio ecclesiam Christi atque adeo orbem novavit." G. Kawerau, *Briefwechsel des J. Jonas*, VOL. I (Halle 1884), p. 28.

[6] *Albertus Pius Carporum comes, ad Erasmi Roterodami expostulationem responsio* (Paris 1529), fols. 7 ff.; see F. Lauchert, *Die ital. literarischen Gegner Luthers* (Freiburg 1912), pp. 283 ff. It is greatly to be desired that the attitude of ecclesiastical authorities to Erasmus and the literary campaign against him should be examined by a Catholic theologian. If I am not mistaken, the turning-point in their opposition was the condemnation of certain of his propositions by the Sorbonne in 1526, Duplessis d'Argentré, *Coll. iud.*, VOL. II, pp. 47-77. Bataillon, *Erasme en Espagne*, pp. 467 ff., is the best authority on the point but of course without adequate theological appreciation.

tendencies which, in fact, we only know to have been such because we view them in retrospect and in the light of subsequent events— humanism made an important and positive contribution to the Catholic movement of reform and renewal.

The Bible and the Fathers, the philological study of ancient texts, historical criticism and tradition won for themselves a strong position in theology—one they maintained even after Luther's attacks on the Vulgate and the canon of the Bible, the Papacy and the sacraments had rendered suspect every form of critical study based on historical arguments. On the other hand, one result of the controversies then raging was to demonstrate the fact that scholasticism was indispensable for the defence of the faith. Pius II's open-mindedness with regard to the Donation of Constantine was well known to his intimates. Wimpfeling, on his part, dared to attack the legend which ascribed the foundation of the Augustinians to the great Bishop of Hippo. All this underwent a change as soon as the innovators began to deny the fact of St Peter's residence in Rome and to describe the Epistle of St James as "an epistle of straw". The Sorbonne would not hear of Erasmus's proposal that the Bible should be translated into the vernacular, or of his assertion that the author of the works of St Dionysius was not identical with the Areopagite of Acts. But this reaction, of which more will be said later, did not prevent the study of the original text of the Bible nor the popularity of the great editions of the Fathers prepared by Erasmus in conjunction with Beatus Rhenanus and Oecolampadius. Francisco de Vitoria's and Melchior Cano's work would have been as impossible without the achievements of humanism as would Sirleto's patristic studies in preparation for the Council of Trent. The scholarly defenders of the dogmas and institutions of the Church leaned on the shoulders of Erasmus, so that when Paul IV prohibited his editions of the Bible and the Fathers together with those published by the Protestants, Rome itself was greatly embarrassed. In the preface to his edition of Gratian's *Decretum* in 1512, Beatus Rhenanus formulated the motto: "Back to the Fathers and to the ancient papal Decretals by way of Gratian." [1] Such a challenge could not be disregarded at Trent. Positive theology was on the march, and with it flowed the ideals of the ancient Church like a broad tributary into the stream of reform.

The University of Alcalá was wont to observe the feast of the four great Western Doctors of the Church with special solemnity. There was high purpose in the practice, none other in fact than the renovation

---

[1] Horawitz-Hartfelder, *Briefwechsel des Beatus Rhenanus*, p. 51.

of the contemporary Church on the model of the ancient one. The study of the Fathers conjured up a lively picture of the ancient Church. It became the standard by which existing conditions were assessed. But unlike the medieval "spirituals" who believed in a universal corruption, those thus engaged cherished no apocalyptic expectations of a new Jerusalem, nor were they out for criticism of their neighbour; their aim was to regulate their own conduct in accordance with their ideal. Wimpfeling and Clichtove preached the purity and the dignity of the priestly life.[1] A collection of homilies of the Fathers was intended to open new paths for preachers.[2] One abbot was singled out for praise because he walked in the footsteps of the fathers of monachism, St Hilarion and St Jerome.[3] Bishops were urged to model their conduct on the rules laid down in the Pastoral Epistles and on the pastoral work of the Fathers as revealed in their homilies and their correspondence.[4] A bishop who spent his energy in ostentatious display and in the administration of his temporal possessions was described as a survival of a barbarous age; the conduct of the typical benefice-hunter was countered by that of the devout and learned priest engaged in pastoral work. Together with St Gregory's *Regula pastoralis*, a popular work throughout the Middle Ages, and St Ambrose's *De Officiis*, St John Chrysostom's work on the priesthood and St Gregory Nazianzen's *Apologia* were put before the clergy as so many mirrors of the virtues of their state. In 1516, the year of publication of Erasmus's New Testament and his St Jerome, a layman, Contarini, wrote a book for bishops for which that reforming prelate, Pietro Barozzi, served as model. But the book was likewise inspired by the ideals of the era of the Fathers. Thus through the interaction of life and letters a new ideal of a bishop arose. It took shape on the eve of the Council of Trent in the person of Giberti, Bishop of Verona, received its classical form at the height of that gathering in the *Stimulus pastorum* of Bartolomeo de' Martiri, and its historical living embodiment in St Charles Borromeo.

Almost every page of the history of the early Church tells of a synod; the whole discipline of the ancient Church rested on synodal

[1] J. Wimpfeling, *De integritate* (1505); see Knepper, *J. Wimpfeling*, pp. 183-91; J. Clichtoveus, *De vita et moribus sacerdotum* (1519). The author draws upon Chrysostom more than on any other Father.

[2] For the editions of the *Omeliarius doctorum de tempore* ("ex quattuor orthodoxis et aliis sanctis doctoribus"), see Panzer, *Annales typographici*; Basle 1505, 1506, 1516; Lyons 1516, 1520, and one edition *sine loco et anno*.

[3] Erasmus, *Epist.*, VOL. II, p. 155.

[4] For what follows I draw on my essay: *Das Bischofsideal der kath. Reformation: Sacramentum Ordinis* (Breslau 1942), pp. 200-56.

canons. People accordingly asked whether the prevailing state of affairs was not due to the neglect in recent times of such a means of reform. Though Erasmus himself entertained no high expectations from them, the revival of provincial and diocesan synods became one of the items in the programme of many advocates of reform. For a knowledge of the ancient canons a collection of the acts and decrees of the Councils was needed. The need of such a work had been realised before; even the Middle Ages were aware that the *Decretum* of Gratian was not enough.[1] Quirini and Giustiniani voiced the need anew.[2] It was given satisfaction in the editions of Merle and Crabbe.[3]

In the meantime the problem of Church reform had entered a new stage. Personal reform had left the territory of the Church and had become a revolution. Up to the rise of Luther countless members of the Church had striven for self-reform and had entered on the path traced out by Johann Nider after the Council of Basle. Much had been done for a reform of the secular clergy and the orders; neither the laity nor the secular authorities had lagged behind, while the *devotio moderna* and humanism had pointed to new ideals. But what did it lead to?

The fact is that not one of these efforts had been completely successful, even in some restricted sphere such as a religious order or a particular country, much less therefore in the whole Church. A general reform was only possible if it reached the top and laid hold of the Papacy. It never got so far. True, the Popes of the Restoration and the Renaissance encouraged self-reform of the members,[4] but they rarely took a personal initiative in this direction and did but little to remove the obstacles that hampered the progress of the new movement. It was left to the post-Tridentine pontiffs to show what could be done in this sphere.

One preliminary condition for an effective movement towards reform, one that would affect the whole Church, was the presence of a new spirit not only at the centre but also at the periphery of the Church.

[1] In connexion with the reform of the University Durandus had suggested "quod concilia generalia hactenus celebrata in singulis studiis et insuper in omnibus cathedralibus et collegiatis ecclesiis haberentur, ut qui vellent possent habere copiam de iisdem". *Tract. ill. iuriscons.*, VOL. XIII, i, 180ᵛ.

[2] *Annales Camaldulenses*, VOL. IX, p. 680.

[3] H. Quentin, *J. D. Mansi et les grandes collections conciliaires* (Paris 1900), pp. 7 ff.

[4] For a number of particular regulations, especially such as were intended to promote the reform of the orders, see Pastor, VOL. II, p. 632 (Sixtus IV), (Eng. edn., VOL. IV, p. 389); VOL. III, p. 315 f. (Innocent VIII), (Eng. edn., VOL. V, p. 340); VOL. III, pp. 106 ff. (Alexander VI), (Eng. edn. VOL. VI, pp. 142 ff.); VOL. III, pp. 888 ff. (Julius II), (Eng. edn., VOL. VI, pp. 444); VOL. IV, i, p. 605 (Leo X), (Eng. edn., VOL. VIII, pp. 455 ff.); VOL. IV, ii, pp. 579 ff. (Clement VII), (Eng. edn., VOL. X, p. 454).

Regulations and administrative measures can only lead to a reform if they are consistently upheld by superiors and if subjects are willing to comply with them. Ideas and ideals demand internal assent and assimilation by those who are prepared to uphold them at their personal cost and at the price of some sacrifice. There was little enough of this spirit in the ranks of the hierarchy or any other estate of the Church. If there was no real improvement in the condition of the Church in spite of numerous schemes and attempts at a reform, responsibility for the failure must be shared by all.

The notion that before the Schism the Church was sunk in worldliness, superstition and abuses, which used to prevail in Protestant circles, has long been known to be untenable. On the other hand, we should refrain from viewing Catholic attempts at reform in the period of the Middle Ages as a mighty stream which, by its own momentum, would have led to a general reform even if there had been no schism. The latter event did more than merely tamper with its course or divert it. The Protestant Reformation owed its success to the fact that the attempts at reform which sprouted from the soil of the Church did not come to maturity. They nevertheless constituted the preliminaries and even the beginning of that regeneration of the Church in the last years of the sixteenth century which is usually referred to as the Catholic Reformation. The reform decrees of the Council of Trent are the most notable fruits of this transformation. The Schism did much more than provide the occasion for the Council of Trent. Not only were its dogmatic definitions called for by the errors of the Reformers, but even its reform decrees might not have been promulgated but for the Schism. This is the lesson of the story of the conciliar idea and reform from the days of Basle which we have followed up thus far. It has provided plentiful material to enable us to answer the grave and, for a Catholic, depressing question: "Why was the Council so long delayed?"

Book Two

CHAPTER I

Luther's " Reform " and Council

WHEN the Wittenberg professor Martin Luther, of the German Congregation of the Augustinians-Observant, was appointed by his Superior Staupitz to the chair of Holy Scripture at the newly founded state university of the Electorate of Saxony, he no more thought of setting up as a reformer of the whole Church than any of the other leaders of the movement for personal reform. He was fully occupied with the preparation of his lectures, but even more so with the doubts that tortured his soul.[1] Before his mind there rose the awful thought of God's justice, inexorable in its condemnation of sin. A conviction forced itself on him that his life, his prayers, his works and sacrifices did not measure up to God's exigencies in regard to purity of intention and perfection of execution. What was he to think of himself, as he contemplated the state of his soul in the light of the assertion of nominalist theologians that man was able, by his own power, to love God above all things? Inexorably sincere as he was where his own person was concerned, he collapsed at the sight of the abyss between what he felt himself to be in his innermost self and the demands of God. He was conscious of the power of sin, but not of the quickening virtue of grace and sacraments. Hence even confession brought him no peace. Evil desires kept rising in him after absolution as they had arisen previous to it. Worse still, he was aware that a self-complacent satisfaction at the good he had done poisoned his soul, as frost nips

---

[1] It is obviously impossible to substantiate in detail the assessment of Luther's evolution as compressed in the above propositions. This judgment is based upon a prolonged study of the sources, extending in part over a period of more than twenty years, and upon an exchange of views with authoritative Catholic biographers of Luther —Denifle, Grisar, Lortz—as well as with the Protestants Scheel and Holl. During my sojourn in Rome my access to the literature of recent years was limited, but the following works seem to me to deserve notice: E. Vogelsang, *Die Anfänge von Luthers Christologie* (Berlin-Leipzig 1929) and his *Unbekannte Fragmente aus Luthers zweiter Psalmenvorlesung* (Berlin 1940); also E. Seeberg, "Die Anfänge der Theologie Luthers", in *Z.K.G.*, LIII (1934), pp. 229-41. For the dating and the significance of Luther's first sermons, Vogelsang in *Z.K.G.*, L (1931), pp. 112-45 and H. S. Bluhm in *Harvard Theological Review*, XXXVII (1944), pp. 175-84.

flowers in the bud. There were times when he felt as if on the brink of hell and on the verge of despair. The counsel of understanding brethren was of no avail in the long run. Then there came a day when he fancied he had found a solution: his notion of God had been all wrong! The study of the epistle to the Romans convinced him that the justice of God before which he trembled is not exacting, does not condemn, but is wholly beneficent—that it is a justice that justifies the sinner in the eyes of God in virtue of Christ's redemption. His experience in the convent tower, which probably falls in the year 1512, opened the gates of paradise for his terrified spirit.

Almost at this very time, in far-away Venice, young Contarini found a solution for an interior conflict and for the problem of his vocation through trust in Christ and by means of his Easter confession.[1] On the other hand in the small university town of Wittenberg on the banks of the Elbe, Luther, Contarini's contemporary, laboriously reached a conviction which is a prerequisite, as well as the very heart, of a live Christianity, and therefore, cannot be at variance with Catholic dogma.

After his Easter experience the layman Contarini entered upon his career in the world. Often tempted and tortured by doubts, he sought counsel from his spiritual advisers whereas Luther the priest put a theological construction on his experience in the monastery tower and on this crucial incident built up for himself a new theology and a new conception of Christianity. In his opinion scholastic theology had been corrupted by Aristotelianism and had gone utterly astray, yet up to a point he remained faithful to it, though not as a follower of St Thomas and the scholastics, but in the wake of Ockham with whose "modern" system he had become acquainted at Erfurt.[2] Just as he imagined that his "tower experience" had taught him to shake off a theory of grace which he wrongly thought to be that of the Catholic Church—for it was not—so now he fought a scholasticism which had forsaken its best traditions. In Augustine and Tauler he sought and found confirmation for his "Pauline" doctrine of justification which ultimately had its

---

[1] The letter of 24 April 1511 to Giustiniani in which Contarini relates his spiritual experience was published for the first time in my paper "Contarini e Camaldoli", in *Archivio per la storia della pietà*.

[2] The influence of nominalism on Luther's teaching on sin and justification has been proved by Denifle, *Luther und Luthertum* (Mainz 1904), VOL. I, pp. 569 ff., though not without some exaggeration. It has been further examined by C. Feckes, *Die Rechtfertigungslehre des Gabriel Biel* (Münster 1925), pp. 140 ff., and by O. Müller, *Die Rechtfertigungslehre nominalistischer Reformationsgegner* (Breslau 1940), especially pp. 164 ff. The critique of the latter work by V. Heynick in *Franziskanische Studien*, XXVIII (1941), pp. 129-51, though noteworthy, does not alter the result on this point.

roots in his own inner self. His lectures on the Psalms hint at it; in those on Romans and Galatians it is fully worked out. Its two pivots are the doctrine of concupiscence as a sin which remains after baptism, and that of the acceptance by God of the sinner, in view of the merits of Christ, without any objective justification through sanctifying grace. The first point appeared to Luther as a fact of experience confirmed by St Paul and St Augustine, for experience proves the survival of sinful tendencies after baptism and penance; the second was linked with Ockham's opinion that absolutely speaking—*de potentia absoluta* and leaving revelation on one side—God can take a sinner—*quâ* sinner—into his favour, that is, justify him. Christ's justice fills up the chasm that yawns between God and the sinner, provided the sinner appropriates that justice by faith. Thus we get the paradox that the believer may be at one and the same time justified yet remain a sinner. Luther does not deny altogether the need of sanctification, but he conceives it as an ethical process, not as an objective transformation. Without objective sanctification there is no possibility of merit. In Luther's view faith renders external works of piety superfluous and reduces the sacraments to mere symbols. Though Luther demands works of charity from the justified, these works have nothing to do with justification itself, and he coins the fateful formula: "Faith alone without works." To the erroneous teaching of the nominalist school, that unaided nature is able to love God above all things, Luther opposes the thesis of its utter corruption, so that justification is exclusively God's work. He fails to see that God's primary activity in the supernatural sphere by no means excludes the possibility of fallen man's co-operation. The conclusion of his doctrine of salvation is "the theology of the cross".

Thus Luther makes of his extremely personal experience the centre of a new theory of salvation which is no longer in harmony with the faith taught by the Church. In the course of the next few years, under pressure of external circumstances as well as from an internal necessity, this theory gave birth to a novel conception of the Church—the second of the two essential elements of Luther's theology. In Luther's mind, the Church is no longer Christ's own creation as the instrument of grace and salvation: she is the community of the predestined. All that the eye can see of the Church is a number of communities whose organisation is based not on divine law but on a purely positive (human) one. This does away with the doctrine of the divine institution of papal supremacy and the authority of the hierarchy, a fundamentally distinct priesthood and the sacrifice of the Mass. From Holy Scripture, his only source of theological information, Luther attempts to prove that under the leadership of the Popes the Church has gone astray for centuries.

In 1517 Luther had not yet drawn all these conclusions, but his theory of salvation was completely worked out. Thus the process against which Egidio of Viterbo, the General of the Augustinians, had warned the Fathers of the Council of the Lateran, was an accomplished fact—that is, the lowering of the supernatural to man's level instead of the transformation of man by the informing energy of the supernatural; the centre of gravity had shifted to the individual. By this time Luther was no longer within the Church, though he knew it not. He only realised the bearing of his theological opinions and drew the conclusions which led to his conception of the Church when the controversy over indulgences suddenly made him the centre of public interest and the leader of a powerful movement.

Tetzel, a Dominican, had been preaching in the neighbourhood of Wittenberg the indulgence granted in connexion with the building of the new St Peter's. Certain exaggerations and abuses moved Luther to take up the fight against indulgences. His first step was to put up ninety-five propositions at the door of the castle church of the small university town. Among other statements he asserts that indulgences are exclusively limited to canonical penalties and are of no effect in another world, so that they cannot relieve souls in Purgatory. He denies the existence of an ecclesiastical treasury—*thesaurus ecclesiae*—constituted by the merits of Christ and the Saints and subject to the power of the keys. By stripping the sacraments of their virtue as against faith, Luther attacked the Church in her role of a mediator of grace, and by denying the value of indulgences he denied her authority in the sphere of conscience, an authority that extends beyond the ordinances of Canon Law. In attacking indulgences Luther's theory of salvation trenched on a sphere of the Church's life in which undeniable exaggerations and abuses had occurred: theology became reform.

It is unlikely that when he nailed up his theses on 31 October 1517 Luther had any presentiment of the storm he was unleashing. He was a professor and looked for an academic discussion. However, the theses were printed and soon passed from hand to hand. The preachers of the indulgence were held up as impostors before all the world; the consequence was that the yield of the proclamation diminished rapidly. The injured party defended itself. Tetzel and Wimpina, a professor of

Frankfurt, countered Luther's theses with theses of their own [1]: Johann Eck, a professor of Ingolstadt, published a vigorous refutation of Luther's errors. The controversy thus engaged could not, from its very nature, remain a purely academic question. Before long the highest authority took cognisance of it. The Roman process against Luther began.[2] As early as 13 December 1517, Archbishop Albrecht of Mainz, who was charged with the proclamation of the indulgence in Germany and thus was personally interested in the revenue derived from it, had informed the Pope of Luther's novel teaching. Moreover, together with the ninety-five theses, he had also forwarded some further printed writings of the Augustinian friar, among them his theses against scholastic theology. A denunciation for heresy by the Dominicans (who were attacked in the person of Tetzel) probably occurred in February 1518. A first attempt through the machinery of his Order to persuade Luther to withdraw his theses proved a failure. The formal process was opened in June. On the motion of the fiscal procurator Marius de Perusco, the Pope instructed an auditor of the Apostolic Camera, Jerome Ghinucci, to cite Luther to Rome, while at the same time he requested the Master of the Sacred Palace, Sylvester Prierias, to draw up a theological memorial on Luther's teaching. The citation, together with the memorial known as the *Dialogus*, which was at once set up in print, was despatched to Wittenberg by the Dominican General Thomas de Vio of Gaeta, better known under the name of Cajetan, who later on was to attend the Diet of Augsburg as papal legate. The documents arrived at Wittenberg on 7 August 1518.

Meanwhile, on the strength of the material at hand the Roman authorities had come to the conclusion that Luther was a notorious

---

[1] The sources for what follows are most conveniently put together by W. Köhler, *Dokumente zum Ablassstreit* (Tübingen 1902), and in the same author's *Luthers 95 Theses samt seinen Resolutionen, etc.* (Leipzig 1903).

[2] The course of the proceedings against Luther was first established by K. Müller, "Luthers römischer Prozess", in *Z.K.G.*, xxxiv (1903), pp. 46-85. His account is further supplemented by A. Schulte, "Die römischen Verhandlungen über Luther", in *Q.F.*, vi (1904), pp. 34 ff., 174 ff., 374 ff., with extracts from the consistorial acts. P. Kalkoff has thrown further light upon it in several large volumes for which he drew on all the available sources: *Forschungen zu Luthers römischem Prozess* (Rome 1905), and for its second phase in a series of articles in *Z.K.G.*, xxv (1904), pp. 90-147, 273-90, 399-459, 503-603; finally, on the first phase (1518) and on the influence of the Dominicans, in *Z.K.G.*, xxxi (1910), pp. 48-65, 368-414; xxxii (1911), pp. 1-67, 199-258, 408-56; xxxiii (1912), pp. 1-72, was also published separately. Of these works, and of those to be quoted later, I can only say that his knowledge of people and events in the first years of the Reformation is unequalled but he tends to put his own construction on them and more than once he fails to restrain his dislike for everything Catholic.

heretic so that there was no need of a regular inquiry to establish the fact. Moreover, the Emperor Maximilian I offered to proceed against him in accordance with the laws of the Empire, so that there was every prospect of a speedy conclusion of the process. On 23 August the Pope instructed the legate to cite the accused to appear at Augsburg,[1] to examine him and, if he recanted, to absolve him. Should he refuse to recant, he was to be arrested and extradited to Rome. If he refused to put in an appearance, the legate was to excommunicate him as an obstinate heretic. At the same time an order for Luther's extradition was sent to his territorial sovereign, Frederick the Wise, and an order for his arrest to Hecker, the Provincial of the Order. These orders crossed a request made by Luther and supported by Frederick the Wise to the effect that the affair should be dealt with in Germany and, if possible, submitted to the arbitration of scholars. The latter proposal rested on a view which was no longer valid, viz. that the controversy over the theses was no more than a quarrel of scholars, which should accordingly go before an academic tribunal.

These misunderstandings on both sides led to the examination of Augsburg (12-15 October 1518).[2] Cajetan was the greatest theologian of his time. So sure was he of his mastery of the subject that he imagined he would have no difficulty in convincing the young professor of the error of his opinions. Although the available material was still scanty enough, Cajetan's wonderful acumen had enabled him to isolate Luther's two main errors, viz. his teaching on the nature of indulgences and on the efficacy of faith. The experienced friar hoped to attain his object—recantation—by fatherly exhortations. His touching patience went unrewarded. Luther denied the validity of Clement VI's decretals on the indulgence with which the cardinal countered him. His conscience, he declared, would not let him recant so long as he was not convinced of the error of his teaching by proofs from Holy Scripture. The written justification which he handed to the legate satisfied the

---

[1] Kalkoff assumes that the briefs of 23 August arrived at Augsburg on the thirtieth. This is possible if couriers were employed, but it is not certain. I am of opinion that the *colloquium* between Cajetan and Frederick the Wise took place in the first days of September, though before the fifth. It should be noted that the brief to Cajetan which Kalkoff assigns to 11 September does not in any way modify the instructions he had received on 23 August.

[2] The *Acta Augustana*, *L.W.*, vol. II, pp. 6-26, in part in Le Plat, vol. II, pp. 16 ff., 26 ff. For the bibliography I refer to Schottenloher, Nos. 27917a-22. Here I may observe that I have made a much greater use of Schottenloher's wealth of bibliographical information than appears from my quotations. In the same way I only mention the current theological works of reference such as *L.Th.K.*, *D.Th.C.* and *R.E.* when I had no complete biography at my disposal.

latter no more than the offer to submit to arbitration by the Universities of Basle, Freiburg, Louvain and Paris.

Had the negotiations merely reached a deadlock, or were they already wrecked? Neither party knew, and both adopted a waiting policy. In order to protect himself Luther made a formal statement before a notary and witnesses by which he refused to acknowledge the competence of the judges who had conducted the inquiry up to that time, namely Ghinucci, Prierias and Cajetan, on the plea that they were biased; he further asserted that he was not bound by the citation to Rome and ended by appealing to a better-informed Pope. This was done on 16 October at the convent of the Carmelites. On the following day he wrote to the cardinal to express regret for his violent outburst against the Pope; he also assured him of his willingness to stop writing on the indulgence and his readiness to listen to the Church. But of a recantation he breathed not a word although at their last interview the cardinal had told him that if he refused to recant he did not want to see him again. As nothing happened until 20 October Luther's silence became suspect; the fact was that he had fled from Augsburg.

Cajetan had been thwarted of his purpose. He had neither succeeded in persuading Luther to recant nor had he been able to execute the order for his arrest owing to the guarantees previously given. He accordingly addressed an extradition demand to the Elector; at the same time he informed the Elector that the process would forthwith take its course in Rome. This information reached Wittenberg on 19 November. On 28 November Luther lodged his first appeal— *in cautionem*—from a misinformed Pope to the next General Council. This appeal has been regarded by some as marking the start of the conciliar movement,[1] but this is incorrect. In the strictly legal sections of his appeal Luther leans on the conciliar appeal of the University of Paris of 27 March 1518 against the French concordat.[2] His purpose was none other than to substitute for the obviously useless appeal of Augsburg a more effective legal device which would make it possible

---

[1] *L.W.*, VOL. II, pp. 36-40; Le Plat, VOL. II, pp. 37-42. For the dates of the correspondence between Cajetan and Frederick the Wise (25 October and 18—not 8— December 1518), see Kalkoff in *Z.K.G.*, XXVII (1906), pp. 323 ff. On the subject as a whole: S. Ehses, "Luthers Appellation an ein allgemeines Konzil", in *H.J.*, XXXIX (1918-19), pp. 740-8. The *Antwort Jo. Cochlaei auff Martin Luthers freveliche Apellation anno 1520 von bapst auff ein zukünftig Concilium* (1524), Spahn, *Johannes Cochlaeus*, bibliography No. 20, came of course too late.

[2] Comparison of the parallels in J. Thomas, *Le Concordat de 1516*, VOL. III (Paris 1910), pp. 73 ff.; complete text of the appeal on pp. 429-37. It should be noted that only the juridical formulas agreed, not the "narratio".

to arrest the civil effects of the ecclesiastical penalties that were bound to ensue. It was not at first intended to disseminate the appeal by means of the press. Luther had but recently printed the *Acta Augustana*. He would wait for the arrival of the excommunication before circulating his appeal among the people; its immediate publication was due to the printer Grunenberg, who acted on his own authority.[1] Thus the appeal became public. In itself it was no more than a legal manœuvre, suggested by the jurists of Wittenberg, in the hope of intimidating the Curia. It could not in any way affect the canonical process since it was invalid in consequence of the prohibitions of Pius II and Julius II.

As a matter of fact it did not affect the further course of the process. The fact that no immediate progress was made, as Cajetan had announced, was due to a consideration of high policy. The Curia was anxious to spare Luther's sovereign and patron, Frederick the Wise, and to take advantage of his prestige throughout the Empire in order to prevent, if possible, the election as emperor of the youthful prince of Habsburg, Charles of Spain, by means of the election either of Frederick himself or of Francis I of France. Charles's election was thought to constitute a threat to the territorial independence of the Pope on account of his sovereignty over Naples. More than that—by means of small attentions and the bestowal of the Golden Rose—the Curia hoped to win over Frederick for this great plan. A secondary commission of the bearer of the Golden Rose, Karl von Miltiz, was to persuade the Elector to consent to Luther's extradition, but it had not been the Pope's original intention that he should engage in a great policy of mediation during his stay in the castle of Altenberg from 4 to 6 January 1519. The conceited junker was allowed to swagger because a semblance of a conciliatory disposition in the affair of Luther would forward the main political business—the imperial election. The plan devised by Miltiz, which was that the Archbishop of Trier should decide Luther's affair in Germany itself, was not authorised by the Curia. Luther also rejected it, for he regarded it as a trap.[2] Setting on one side the mixture of good-natured, sly and at bottom unsuspecting *bonhomie* with which Miltiz, as a fellow Saxon, sought to settle Luther's affair, the idea of entrusting the inquiry to a German bishop had much to recommend

[1] Luther to Spalatin, 20 December 1518, *L.W.*, *Briefwechsel*, VOL. I, p. 280 f.
[2] The acts of the election in *R.T.A.*, VOL. I, pp. 143-876. Kalkoff's attempt, "Die Kaiserwahl Friedrichs des Weisen", in *A.R.G.*, XXI (1924), pp. 134-40; *id.*, *Die Kaiserwahl Friedrichs IV und Karls V* (Weimar 1925), to prove a valid election of Frederick the Wise as Emperor is a failure.

itself and would not have been without precedent. At any rate it took
into account the fact that the controversy over the theses had long ago
come to the knowledge of the masses in Germany. This was better
than the suggestion to stick to the fiction that the dispute was of a purely
academic character and should be submitted to the arbitration of a
university.

As was to be expected, the disputation between Eck and the two
Wittenbergers, Karlstadt and Luther, which took place at Leipzig at
the request of Duke George of Saxony and against the wishes of the
University, led to no agreement and only served to underline the
differences, while the publicity connected with it added fuel to the
excitement. As for the Universities of Paris and Erfurt, which were to
arbitrate, they withheld their decision in view of the canonical
ordinances to the contrary.[1]

In any case a precious year had been wasted when on 28 June 1519
Charles V's election as German Emperor stultified the Curia's plans
for Frederick the Wise. The Roman process was resumed, but though
the Curia was anxious to bring it to a speedy conclusion it did not in
any way depart from its traditional caution in dealing with matters of
faith. At a consistory on 11 January 1520, after Cardinal Bibbiena's
return from his French legation, an Italian speaker not otherwise known
insisted on stern measures being taken against Luther and his protector.[2]
A committee of theologians formed at the beginning of February and
presided over by Cardinals Accolti and Cajetan, and in which every
mendicant order was represented by its General or its Procurator-
General, subjected several of Luther's theses to a searching examination,
and at least the last-named handed in their verdict in writing.[3] There
was general agreement that the propositions must be condemned; the
only difference of opinion bore on the question whether they were to
be condemned *seriatim* as erroneous, scandalous and heretical. After
Johann Eck's arrival in Rome the two cardinals set to work on the draft

[1] Contract for the disputation in Gess, *Akten und Briefe*, VOL. I, pp. 91 ff.
[2] Our only source of information is Melchior von Watt's account, in *Q.F.*, VI
(1905), pp. 174 ff. Kalkoff's dating of the consistory on 9 January instead of 11 is
open to doubt, *Z.K.G.*, XXV (1904), p. 95.
[3] Sanudo, *Diarii*, VOL. XXVIII, pp. 246, 256 ff. Kalkoff's assumption of a first
commission exclusively composed of Franciscans Observant, on the basis of the report
of 11 February (*ibid.*, p. 260), seems to me extremely doubtful. "Quella congre-
gazione" is surely that of 4 February already mentioned, at which the Observants of
all the orders were represented. Why should the Franciscans alone have been
summoned to a commission of this kind? Either the words "di S. Francesco" are a
mistake of Sanudo's or information on the other orders is lacking. Gabriele della
Volta made no reference to such a commission on 16 March (*ibid.*, p. 376).

of the Bull of Condemnation. It was discussed in four consistories between 21 May and 1 June.[1] When the question of the mode of condemnation cropped up again, the theologians were called in once more on 23 May. Eck's proposal that all the propositions submitted should be condemned *in globo* as erroneous, scandalous and heretical prevailed over the contrary opinion held by most members of the theological commission—probably also by Cajetan—which was that each proposition should be given its individual note.[2] The opposition was met to some extent by the decision not to condemn Luther at once but to give him a time-limit of sixty days in which to make his submission. On 15 June the Bull *Exsurge* was published in Rome.[3]

Most of the forty-one propositions of Luther condemned in the Bull (arts. 1-20, 37-40) were taken from the verdict of the University of Louvain of 7 November 1519. They bore on Luther's teaching on indulgences and the efficacy of the sacraments. Eck was responsible for the inclusion of the articles on the primacy (25-30) on which Louvain had expressed no opinion; art. 28 included a condemnation of the conciliar theory. The Bull expressly rejected Luther's appeal to a Council on the basis of Pius II's and Julius II's prohibitions. No less a man than Eck himself admitted at a later date that this compilation of Luther's errors in the Bull of Condemnation was far from adequate and was, in point of fact, already obsolete at the time of publication. It stuck too much to the principle of the enumeration of erroneous

---

[1] The very concise consistorial acts are in *Q.F.*, VI (1905), pp. 33 ff., those for 21 May in Sanudo, *Diarii*, VOL. XXVIII, p. 549.

[2] Cajetan's observation reported by Martin Bucer on 30 July 1519: "Sint errores non haereses", and his warning against drawing exaggerated conclusions: "Non nimium oportet emergere", Horawitz-Hartfelder, *Briefwechsel des B. Rhenanus*, p. 166, is wholly in keeping with Cajetan's memorial of the year 1531 to be mentioned later. He reveals his greatness as a theologian by the moderation of his judgments. The assertion in *Acta Academiae Lovaniensis* (*Erasmi opuscula*, ed. Ferguson, p. 322) that Carvajal had offered strong opposition in the consistory ("vehementer obsistente Cardinale S. Crucis") may be correct. In that case there would be question of thesis 28 the condemnation of which the old adherent of the conciliar theory would have opposed. That he had not abandoned his conciliarist standpoint even after the failure of the abortive Council of Pisa appears from his remark on the occasion of the reconciliation recorded by Christoph Scheurl (*Briefbuch*, VOL. II, p. 72): "Testatus est, etsi crederet se non errasse, tamen si secutus esset scandalum, agnosceret errorem." On the other hand the testimony of the *Acta Acad. Lovan.* does not seem to me sufficiently strong to justify the far-reaching conclusions drawn by Kalkoff in *Z.K.G.*, XXV (1904), pp. 120 ff.

[3] *Bull. Rom.*, VOL. V, pp. 748-57; Le Plat, VOL. II, pp. 60-72; also Kalkoff's observations in *Z.K.G.*, XXV (1904), pp. 104 ff., and in *Forschungen zu Luthers röm. Prozess*, pp. 188 ff. On the German translation of the Bull see *Z.K.G.*, XLV (1927), pp. 382-99. There is evidence that the Bull went through nineteen printed editions. Further bibliography in Schottenloher, Nos. 12043-56.

propositions, whereas the fundamental points of the system were not given sufficient prominence. However, we must bear in mind that it was only in the writings in which he unfolded his programme between 1520 and 1521 that a number of Luther's opinions—with their consequences —were fully worked out and defined.

Eck personally took the Bull to North and Central Germany. Towards the end of September he published it in the diocese of Brandenburg in which Wittenberg was situated, as well as in the adjoining Saxon dioceses. Even before the expiration of the sixty days' time-limit on 17 November 1520 Luther appealed a second time from the Pope to a future Council at which he could appear without risk, either in person or through a representative.[1] In this conciliar appeal the motive of legal insurance as well as propaganda is even more apparent than in the first, that of 28 November 1518. The Elector had privately advised Luther to write to the princes of the Empire in order to make sure of their protection when the Bull came to be executed. Luther declined to follow this advice and elected to appeal to a Council in spite of the fact that in the meantime his attitude to a Council as such had undergone a complete change. Rome was actually in possession of a declaration, duly attested by a notary, made by him in the course of the disputation of Leipzig on 6 and 7 July 1519, when he had stated that even Councils could err and had actually erred.[2] With such a declaration he himself cut the doctrinal ground from under his conciliar appeal. He appealed to a tribunal whose competence he denied and thereby branded his action as a mere manœuvre; he was building on the conciliarist sentiments of a number of princes of the Empire.[3]

[1] *L.W.*, VOL. VII, pp. 75-82; German text, *ibid.*, pp. 85-90; Le Plat, VOL. II, pp. 77 ff. For Karlstadt's appeal of 19 October 1520 cf. H. Barge, *Andreas Bodenstein von Karlstadt*, VOL. I (Leipzig 1905), pp. 229 ff. Cochlaeus's "Reply" (Spahn, *Cochlaeus,* bibliography No. 20), as I have already observed, came much too late.

[2] *L.W.*, VOL. II, pp. 288, 303. In the second passage Luther admits the authority of a Council in matters of faith: "Consentio cum D. Doctore quod conciliorum statuta in iis quae sunt fidei sunt omnino complectenda; hoc solum mihi reservo, quod et reservandum est, concilium aliquando errasse et aliquando posse errare, praesertim in iis quae non sunt fidei nec habet concilium auctoritatem novorum articulorum condendorum in fide, alioquin tot tandem habebimus articulos quot hominum opiniones." More clearly still, in his letter to the Elector, 18 August 1519 (*L.W.*, *Briefwechsel*, VOL. II, pp. 479 ff.), he says: "Mir ist genug dass Concilia nit Jus divinum machen", and further on "ein Concilium mag irren . . . und hat etlich Mal geirrt, wie die Historien beweisen und das letzt römisch anzeigt wider das Costnitzer und Basler."

[3] Luther to Spalatin, 4 November 1520: "Non scribam privatim ad principes, sed publica schedula appellationem innovabo, invocaturus ad adhaesionem quoslibet Germaniae magnos et parvos et rei indignitatem expositurus" (*L.W.*, *Briefwechsel*, VOL. II, p. 211). He had announced this intention soon after the arrival of the Bull,

The appeal could neither prevent nor delay the ecclesiastical penalties. The Bull *Decet Romanum pontificem* of 3 January 1521 pronounced sentence of excommunication against Luther and his abettors.[1]

Roma locuta est, causa finita est! should have been the last word on the subject. It was not to be. The Pope's condemnation of Luther and his teaching did not put a stop to the spread of that teaching. A variety of circumstances combined to rob the papal sentence of its effectiveness. The most important are these three. 1. The reserve of the authoritative ecclesiastical-political circles in Germany, above all that of the bishops, partly from opportunist considerations, but partly also on account of objections inspired by motives which must ultimately be traced back to the survival of conciliar theory. 2. The reaction of public opinion, which rebelled against the condemnation of a man in whom the people saw the mouthpiece of its aspirations for ecclesiastical and national reform. 3. The widespread self-delusion which led people to imagine that Luther and his adherents were not definitely cut off from the Church as long as a Council had not pronounced judgment. Behind the personal guilt of those concerned we can see, as through a glass, the deeper causes, such as the obscuring of the notion of primacy by conciliar theory and the failure of extra-conciliar attempts at reform up to that time. These were the reasons why so many of Luther's adherents fell into the fatal error that they were not following a heretic and were, therefore, not cut off from the Church. They caused even loyal sons of the Church to imagine that the last word on Luther's teaching could only be spoken by a General Council and that order could only be restored in the Church by means of conciliar reform. It is these views, not Luther's appeals, that started the demand for a Council which received satisfaction at Trent.

Difficulties began with the very publication of the Bull *Exsurge*.[2]

11 October, *ibid.*, p. 195; cf. also pp. 217 ff. It may have been at the Elector's suggestion that he called upon the town of Wittenberg to give its adhesion to the appeal in order to counter the threat of an interdict. The memorial submitted by the Wittenberg jurists Goede, Schurff and Baer in the spring of that year has not been preserved.

[1] *Bull. Rom.*, VOL. V, pp. 761-4; Le Plat, VOL. II, pp. 79-83.

[2] The correspondence of Bishop Philip of Freising with Eichstätt, Salzburg and Augsburg has been published by A. von Druffel, *Sitzungsberichte der Münchner Akademie, phil.-hist. Klasse*, 1880, pp. 571-97. Eck's correspondence with Bishop Christoph of Augsburg was published by J. Greving, in *R.S.T.*, XXI, XXII (Münster 1912), pp. 196, 221. In what follows, unless otherwise stated, I follow Kalkoff, "Die Bulle *Exsurge*", in *Z.K.G.*, XXXV (1914), pp. 166-203; XXXVII (1917-18), pp. 89-174. For the execution of the Bull *Exsurge* in the diocese of Würzburg in particular see *Z.K.G.*, XXXIX (1921), pp. 1-14. Much information also in Th. Wiedemann, *Dr Johann Eck* (Ratisbon 1865), pp. 153 ff.

Although Eck managed to publish in due legal form original copies of the Bull in the cathedrals of Brandenburg, Merseburg and Meissen, all of which were mentioned by name in the document itself as well as in the brief of 18 July which commissioned him, the publication of printed copies, even though duly authenticated, and above all the Bull's execution, which included the surrender and burning of Luther's writings, met with strong opposition. The University of Wittenberg brushed the Bull aside as one of Eck's knavish tricks, and even the ordinary, Bishop Schulz of Brandenburg, did not dare to publish it. At Leipzig, students' riots forced the executor to flee from the town, and at Erfurt the document was thrown into the river. The University of Vienna, in spite of the opposition of the theological faculty, refused to act in the matter until the hierarchy and the University of Paris should have spoken. On 30 December an imperial decree ordered it to submit.[1]

Much more serious was the hesitation of the bishops. Only a handful of them, among them the Bishops of Trier and Liège, saw from the first the danger that threatened both the Church and themselves and acted accordingly. On the other hand the Bishops of Salzburg and Passau indulged for a while in passive resistance. The jurists at the episcopal courts of Augsburg, Freising, Eichstätt, Würzburg and Naumburg, most of whom had read law in Italy,[2] refused to stigmatise Luther's teaching unreservedly as heretical in conformity with the Roman decision, and in their mandates, in some cases delayed for months, they omitted precisely that decisive term. There was question of a conference of all the bishops of the province of Salzburg. The jurists of Naumburg went so far as to justify their attitude on the ground that Luther had appealed to a Council. In many places it was impossible to find a printer prepared to print the Bull together with the relevant episcopal mandates, so that for the dioceses of Augsburg, Eichstätt and Ratisbon Eck was obliged to get it done clandestinely by Lutz of Ingolstadt,[3] although Ulrich von Hutten had long before

---

[1] Balan, *Monumenta*, 11-15 (11 December 1520); *ibid.*, Aleander's draft for the reply, pp. 16 ff.; the final text in Kink, *Geschichte der kaiserlichen Universität Wien*, VOL. I, ii, pp. 124 ff.; on p. 120 extracts from the protocols of the faculty of theology.

[2] In view of the proofs adduced in Book I, Chapters II and V, of the conciliarist opinions of some Italian canonists, it would be expedient to examine, on the basis of the registers of Padua, Pavia, Bologna, etc., which bishops and jurists of the Reformation period had studied law in Italy and under which professors.

[3] K. Schottenloher, "Magister Andreas Lutz in Ingolstadt, der Druck der Bulle *Exsurge Domine*", in *Zentralblatt für Bibliothekswesen*, XXXII (1915), pp. 249-66.

published it in pamphlet form with sundry ironical glosses of his own.[1] Thus it came about that such a decisive utterance by the supreme doctrinal authority as the Bull *Exsurge* was only tardily and inadequately published in Germany, while the public burning of Luther's writings, which were permeated with errors, was not carried out at all [2] except in the Rhineland and in the Low Countries, where the nuncio Aleander was able to enforce it with the help of the Emperor.

This conduct of a number of German bishops, which bordered on sabotage, was not just opportunism; in the case of some of them at least it was prompted by considerations based on principle. Let us try to visualise the situation. Eck, Luther's opponent in the dispute about indulgences, and hence a partisan, presents the sentence pronounced against his opponent. It is a condemnation for heresy, hence a matter of life and death. An insignificant university lecturer, acting as apostolic nuncio, demands the obedience of bishops who are also princes and profoundly conscious of that fact. From the point of view of formalities, everything was in order, but those prelates resented Eck's manner, and from the Reuchlin controversy there still lingered an impression that these condemnations of doctrines and books were not irrevocable. However, they overlooked the fact that in the present instance the highest authority had pronounced sentence in a matter of faith. Ecclesiastical politics were conducted not by the theologians, who for the most part saw clear, but by the jurists,[3] and in the case of not a few of these, such as Jung, the Vicar General of Freising, and Gabriel, Bishop of Eichstätt, one senses the after-effects of their schooling by canonists like Decius and Gozzadini. Bishop Gabriel gave it as his opinion that the public burning of Luther's writings would only widen and deepen the disagreement, which could not be the

---

[1] Böcking, *Ulrich Hutteni Opera*, VOL. V, pp. 303-31.

[2] According to the above-mentioned works of Kalkoff and Schottenloher the episcopal mandates for the publication of the Bull bear the following dates: Eichstätt, 24 October 1520; Augsburg, 8 November 1520; Ratisbon, 4 January 1521; Würzburg, 31 January 1521; Vienna, 17 February 1521; Naumburg, 10 March 1521.

[3] In its memorial for Archbishop Albrecht dated 17 December 1517, the theological faculty of Mainz declined to pass judgment on Luther's theses on the ground that they trenched on the authority of the Pope; *Z.K.G.*, XXIII (1902), p. 266 f. The hesitation of the Leipzig faculty with regard to the Disputation (Gess, *Akten und Briefe*, VOL. I, pp. 40 ff.) may be explained at least in part in like manner. The counter-theses of the Frankfurt professor Wimpina are included in Köhler's edition of the 95 theses (see above, p. 170, *n.* 4). The judgments of the Universities of Cologne, Louvain and Paris will be discussed later.

intention of the Pope. He also pleaded for a final effort to keep the dispute within the boundaries of the scholastic world.[1]

In point of fact it is difficult to deny that it was a mistake to exclude the German episcopate altogether from the proceedings against Luther. That Eck himself felt this appears from the circumstance that he suggested to the Roman authorities that it would add to the solemnity of the Bull of Condemnation if the signatures of the cardinals and bishops actually at Rome were appended to it.[2] In that case it would be received more readily in Germany. However, by the time the Bishop of Eichstätt and the University of Vienna suggested the con-currence of the episcopate the road was already blocked, for Rome her-self had spoken. The proposal of the theological faculty of Leipzig to submit the controversy on indulgences to a provincial synod was sent to the wrong address and had not been considered.[3] However, even if a synod of this kind had been convened, Archbishop Albrecht of Mainz was not the man to steer into the right channel a problem which, in addition to its intrinsic theological complexity, also raised questions of politics. For ever in financial straits by reason of his expensive tastes, and consumed with the ambition to win for himself in the ecclesiastical sphere of Germany a position such as Cardinal d'Amboise had occupied in France and Cardinal Wolsey was still enjoying in England, the Arch-bishop swayed between anger at the loss of revenue from the indulgence owing to Luther's activities and resentment against the Curia on account of its reserve in respect of his appointment as legate for Germany. He accordingly lent a willing ear to his adviser, Capito, a man of decided Lutheran sympathies. The Archbishop assumed a heavy responsibility when he refused to take a single step against Luther during the whole of 1518. In the sequel also his greatest anxiety was to avoid rousing public resentment by proceeding against him.[4]

Thus we encounter once more the second obstacle to the execution of the Bull *Exsurge*—public opinion. In the public places of the cities resistance to the Roman sentence was no less strong than in the offices

---

[1] On 8 November 1520 Gabriel von Eyb writes (*Münchner Sonderblatt*, 1880, p. 584): "Denn uns getreulich laid ist, das durch Luther und Ecken dies sachen so weit gewachsen, und ganz dafür haben, das unsers heiligen Vaters des bapsts so hoch fürnehmen nit sei."

[2] Eck to an unknown correspondent, 3 May 1520, Böcking, *Hutteni Opera*, VOL. V, p. 342 f.

[3] Gess, *Akten und Briefe*, VOL. I, pp. 49 ff.

[4] P. Kalkoff, "Die Beziehungen der Hohenzollern zur Kurie unter dem Einfluss der lutherischen Frage", in *Q.F.*, IX (1906), pp. 88-139; *Aleander gegen Luther* (Leipzig-New York 1908), p. 114 and *passim*.

of bishops and princes. Luther's German writings had stirred the heart of the people. His book *Freiheit des Christenmenschen* alone went through twenty-three editions. From the very day on which he nailed up his theses the nation had come to look upon him as its champion in the fight against the abuses of both the Curia and the native clergy; and now that man was condemned and banned! Against such an injustice, as they saw it, the more progressive section of the people protested with unprecedented vehemence. Luther's pamphlet *Wider die Bulle des Endchrists*, in which he gives full vent to his hatred of the Papacy, gave a lead to a whole line of pamphleteers.[1] The literary creation of *Karsthans* was the typical figure of the German citizen—honourable, homely, but dull—whose affection for his very own Luther was not to be shaken even by the most striking arguments of a divine like Murner.[2] No! he would stick to his man! At the same time as Luther, in his book on *The Church's Babylonish Captivity* did away with five of the seven sacraments, proclaimed the universal priesthood of the laity in his pamphlet on private Masses, and in his *Assertio* reiterated the condemned propositions in even bolder terms, thereby opening the eyes of trained theologians to the real character of his teaching,[3] that section of the nation which was intellectually most alive hailed him as the great reformer.[4] In his *Appeal to the nobility*, written

[1] For guidance in the pamphlets collected by O. Schade, *Satiren und Pasquille der Reformationszeit*, VOLS. I-III (Hanover 1856-8), O. Clemen, *Flugschriften aus den ersten Jahren der Reformation*, VOLS. I-IV (Leipzig 1907-11), and in the reprints of German works of the sixteenth and seventeenth centuries (begun in 1877), see also besides Goedeke's *Grundriss zur Geschichte der deutschen Dichtung* (2nd edn. Dresden 1881), VOL. II, pp. 213 ff., W. Lücke in *Deutsche Geschichtsblätter*, IX (1908), pp. 183-205. A selection of texts is found in A. E. Berger, *Die Sturmtruppen der Reformation* (Leipzig 1931.)

[2] *Karsthans* was composed at the close of 1520 and printed at the beginning of 1521; text in Clemen, *Flugschriften*, VOL. IV, pp. 1-133; its attribution to Joachim Vadian is not free from uncertainty. Aleander's opinion "tota Germania infecta est ex odio potius Romanae curiae et ordinis ecclesiastici quam quod Luthero consentiant" (Kalkoff, *Aleander gegen Luther*, p. 137) is correct, but it must be borne in mind that Luther embodies both these tendencies so that it was possible for Chieregati to get the impression at the beginning of 1523 "che la sola cosa di Luther ha tanti radici qui che mile homeni non bastaria ad sradicarla non che io che sono solo"; letter to Isabella Gonzaga, 10 January 1523, in Morsolin, *F. Chiericati* (Vicenza 1873), pp. 111 ff.

[3] Glapion, the Emperor's confessor, confided to the Saxon chancellor Brück that when he read the *Captivitas* he felt as if he had been whipped from head to foot; *R.T.A.*, VOL. II, p. 478; cf. the corresponding observation of Quiñónez to Pellican; *H.J.*, XVII (1896), p. 52.

[4] The pamphlet *Von dem Pfründenmarkt der Curtisanen und Tempelknechte* written in September 1521, states that for the last two hundred years the clergy had opposed a reform. Schade, *Satiren*, VOL. III, pp. 59 ff.

in the summer of 1520 while still under the influence of his recent condemnation, Luther outlined a programme of Church reform with which he put himself at the head of the anti-Roman [1] and anticlerical [2] movement in Germany. The appeal was also intended as a programme for a Council.[3]

For anyone acquainted with the reform literature of the late Middle Ages this small work scarcely provides anything really new,[4] apart from the nationalistic strain which runs through it. On the other hand the doctrinal errors on which many of its proposals rest are carefully masked. With regard to the reform of the Pope—that most sensitive point of all previous reform programmes—Luther's chief concern is that he should be unpolitical. The Pope should give up the portion of the States of the Church north of the Appenines lest these territories involve him in high politics, as Julius II had been involved. Let him renounce the *Monarchia sicula* as well as all claims based on Constantine's Donation, for the latter document is so clumsy a forgery that a drunken peasant could lie more cleverly. In Luther's opinion the *translatio imperii* was bought at too high a price. In any case the Pope's right to crown the Emperor does not imply that he is the Emperor's overlord.

As for the officials of the Curia, Luther's opinion is that ninety-nine per cent of them might disappear without loss to the Church. A staff of officials with a fixed salary would suffice to deal with all the ecclesiastical affairs which may remain within the Pope's competence. The College of Cardinals must be reduced to twelve members. The payment

---

[1] The strongest in this sense is Hutten's *Vadiscus*; Böcking, *Hutteni Opera*, VOL. IV, pp. 145-261, composed during the course of the process in 1520.

[2] Here too one example must suffice. The *Schöne Dialogus* was probably written by Martin Bucer in 1521 and disseminated in thirteen editions; cf. A. Götze, "Martin Butzers Erstlingsschrift", in *A.R.G.*, IV (1906), pp. 1-64.

[3] *L.W.*, VOL. VI, pp. 404-69. The first edition of 4000 copies was sold out in five days (18-23 August 1520). E. Kohlmeyer's opinion, *Z.K.G.*, XLIV (1925), pp. 582-94, that in the second part of the work (pp. 427 ff.) Luther places the secular authorities in the foreground as being the executants of reform seems to me preferable to that of W. Köhler, *Z.Sav.R.G.K.A.*, XIV (1925), pp. 1-38, who holds that all the proposals for a reform in this section are also intended for the Council. Kohlmeyer's further hypothesis that there are two drafts of the work seems to me superfluous. It was perfectly natural that on hearing of his condemnation while at work on the book Luther should have adopted an increasingly "radical" tone towards the Papacy.

[4] Many tracts of the reform period demanded a reduction of the number of the cardinals to 12, 18 or 24. The latter number had also been demanded by the Council of Basle in its twenty-third session. The annual income of 1000 florins which Luther described as adequate had already been suggested by D'Ailly. Cf. *R.Q.*, XLIII (1935), pp. 87 ff.; *ibid.*, XLIV (1936), pp. 249 ff., on the proposals for a reduction of the religious orders.

of annates must cease; so must the reservation of benefices, particularly the *reservatio pectoralis*, as well as the exemptions, together with the cumulation of benefices and the legal quibbles by which these abuses are made possible, likewise all regresses, unions and incorporations. The right of nomination to benefices must be restored to the bishops and their ordinary authority recognised so that they should not continue to be mere helpless figure-heads (*Ölgötzen*). Their relations with the Holy See are to be considerably eased. In future they must seek confirmation from the metropolitan and no longer take the oath of obedience prescribed by Canon Law. Secular disputes, and even ecclesiastical ones of minor importance, must no longer be called to Rome, but disputes between archbishops are reserved to the Pope in view of his supreme authority (*Ubirkeit*). The primate of Germany is to be assisted by a supreme tribunal which will deal with problems connected with benefices.

The number of orders must be restricted. Those monasteries which are allowed to remain must be reformed in the spirit of their founders. All religious must refrain from begging. Papal dispensations, especially dispensations from marriage impediments in the third and fourth degrees and spiritual relationship, are abolished. Excommunication is only operative in the spiritual sphere; interdicts and other censures must not be used at all. Saints' feasts are transferred to Sundays. Pilgrimages to Rome must be controlled and certain pilgrimages at home, such as that to the "Beautiful Madonna" of Ratisbon, must be suppressed. The number of foundation Masses is to be limited. Each community chooses its own parish priest. In order to put an end to certain moral abuses the Council must leave priests free to marry.

The reform of the laity must go hand in hand with that of the clergy. Luther is anxious to remedy the abuses of an early capitalist system which injure and irritate the small man, such as the luxuriant growth of commercialism, the trading companies, loans at high interest, extravagance in dress and the artificial creation of new necessities. These proposals for a reform are seasoned with many a sally against the luxury of Pope and cardinals, the trade in benefices in the "warehouse" of the Dataria and the Fuggers' connexion with it, as well as with exaggerated assertions, or such as could only be proved with difficulty, for instance that the Pope's total revenue from the curial benefices amounted to a million ducats a year; that from Germany alone three hundred thousand ducats annually flowed to

Rome.[1] All this was accompanied with a robust invitation to self-help.
The people were invited to throw the emissaries of the Roman court
unceremoniously into the nearest stream together with their letters of
appointment to benefices in Germany.

The most grievous accusation of all was that covetousness had
betrayed the Popes into breaking their own laws and that a similar
motive stood in the way of a reform. This accusation was but an echo
of the radical writings of the advocates of the conciliar theory in the
period of reform.

The positive proposals for reform are addressed to a future Council,
but at the same time Luther urges the German nobility, that is the
princes, to take their execution into their own hands, in other words to
see to it that a *recht frei Concilium*, a really free Council, was convened.
The practice of antiquity shows that the Emperor is entitled to convoke
a Council. The doctrine that the Pope alone can do so is one of the
three walls that bar the road to a true reformation. If the Pope gives
scandal and opposes the convocation of a Council with a view to
preventing the "amendment" of the Church, no notice need be taken
of him for "there is no authority in the Church except for its better
estate".

The circle is thus complete. While Luther's revolutionary errors,
such as the denial of primacy, the doctrine of universal priesthood and
the principle of the Bible as the only basis of faith, are skilfully kept in
the background so that only the initiated are aware of their presence,
the book proclaims the old principle of the conciliar theory and accepts
its teaching on the convocation of a Council in an emergency. The
new revolutionary ideas mingle with the old familiar ones and hide
their true nature beneath them. This "restorer" of the religious and
ecclesiastical life, this German "reformer", was the object of the
enthusiasm of the people in the decisive years between 1520 and 1522.
It was a plunge into the unknown, a break-up of the order on which

---

[1] Even when one bears in mind the difficulty, not to say the impossibility, of
ascertaining the revenues accruing from spiritual sources, and leaving those from the
Papal States on one side, these sums are fantastic. The Venetian envoy Gradenigo,
basing himself on observations made under Leo X, estimated the total income of the
Pope at fully 500,000 scudi, of which 200,000 came from the Dataria and other
ecclesiastical dues. Albèri, *Relazioni*, VOL. II, iii, p. 72; Hofmann, *Forschungen*,
VOL. I, p. 98, reckons the income of the Dataria alone at 144,000 scudi for the year
1525. However, it must be remembered that a large part of the money that flowed to
Rome went to the officials in the form of taxes, and to that extent these sums
did not appear in the papal balance-sheets. More will be said on this subject in
Ch. IX.

the world had rested until then. However, the fixed star of the Council still shone in the sky.

Did Luther seriously look to that luminary? How can the two conciliar manifestos of 1520—the pamphlet on reform addressed to the nobility and the appeal to a Council—be reconciled with his standpoint at the Leipzig disputation in the previous year? What is certain is that in the summer of 1518 Luther still regarded a Council as the supreme and infallible authority in matters of faith. "As long as a Council does not condemn my view of the efficacy of indulgences", he wrote in his reply to Prierias,[1] "I am not a heretic and am entitled to defend my opinion as a theologian quite as much as the Dominicans are entitled to defend their doctrine of the preservation of the Blessed Virgin from original sin, though by maintaining it they are at variance with the Council of Basle." In the "Resolutions" written at this time and added to the ninety-five theses, he defines his standpoint even more clearly: "A Council alone, not the Pope, defines what must be believed. In the hypothesis of the Pope maintaining a specific doctrine with the approval of a part of the Church—hence not the whole Church as represented in the Council—it is no heresy to teach the opposite as long as a General Council has not issued a decision." [2]

This assertion is undiluted conciliar theory: it is condemned in article 28 of the Bull *Exsurge*. At the Augsburg interrogation Luther therefore quite logically sided with the "Gersonites" and the University of Paris against Cajetan.[3] In his first appeal he accordingly stated that in matters of faith a Council was above the Pope. Up to this moment Luther continued to regard a Council as the highest visible teaching authority in the Church. But this conviction vanished when, in his sermon on excommunication, he unfolded for the first time his new conception of the Church, of which universal priesthood and the principle of the Scriptures were the corner-stones, and abandoned the notion of the Church as an institution founded by Christ for man's

---

[1] *L.W.*, VOL. I, pp. 655 ff. For what follows see Th. Kolde, *Luthers Stellung zu Konzil und Kirche bis zum Wormser Reichstag* (Gütersloh 1876). I have not been able to consult W. Köhler, *Luther und die Kirchengeschichte*, VOL. I (Erlangen 1900), and O. Starck, *Luthers Stellung zur Institution des Papsttums von 1520-46 unter besonderer Berücksichtigung des ius humanum* (Dissertation, Münster 1930).

[2] *L.W.*, VOL. I, p. 568 (concl. 20) and p. 582 (concl. 26).

[3] Preface to the *Acta Augustana*, *L.W.*, VOL. II, p. 8. He also observes that Cajetan's teaching on the primacy was "nova in auribus meis". The passage in the first appeal reads: "Cum satis sit in professo (hence a universally held doctrine!) sacrosanctum concilium in Spiritu Sancto legitime congregatum s. ecclesiam catholicam repraesentans, sit in causis fidem concernentibus supra papam."

salvation and endowed with authority over the human conscience and guided by a hierarchy culminating in the Papacy.[1] No room was now left in his system for a General Council invested with supreme authority as conceived by the conciliar theory. Just as the Papacy merely discharged certain regulating functions in the visible community of the faithful, and that solely on the basis of a human ordinance confirmed by tradition, so may the Council continue to regulate Church discipline, but it cannot decide authoritatively what the faithful must believe. From now onwards Luther's supreme canon in matters of faith is Holy Scripture; only in so far as the decisions of a Council are founded on it, or, more accurately, in so far as they agree with his interpretation of Scripture, is he prepared to accept them. In other words, he does away with the infallibility of a Council in matters of faith.[2] But this does not yet imply a rejection of the whole idea of a Council. For the time being he may have thought that a reform Council would take more than one measure in accordance with his demands for reform. It was only two decades later, at a time when the Lutheran opposition Churches had attained their full development, that he found it necessary to circumscribe even this sphere of a Council's activity. But even then he stuck to the old principle of conciliar theory that the Pope must be subject to a Council if there is to be reform at all.[3]

In 1520, therefore, the rejection of the Catholic conception of the Church did not as yet prevent Luther from appealing to a reform Council. In his view such a Council was a gathering of Christendom, summoned by the Emperor, at which clergy and laity would co-operate for the purpose of putting an end to the abuses in the Church, especially those prevailing in the bitterly hated Roman Curia. The co-operation of the Emperor and the secular authorities in the reform of the Church,

[1] Out of the vast literature on Luther's conception of the Church I mention K. Holl, *Die Enstehung von Luthers Kirchenbegriff: Gesammelte Aufsätze zur Kirchengeschichte*, VOL. I (Tübingen 1927), pp. 288-325, because he has collected all the material pertaining to the first period. As always with Holl, the interpretation is shrewd but over-simplified.

[2] This opinion finds its clearest expression in the *Disputatio de potestate concilii* held in 1536; *L.W.*, VOL. XXXIX, i, pp. 184-97. In theses 3, 5, 12 and 16 Luther rejects the assistance of the Holy Ghost and the formula describing the Council as "in Spiritu Sancto legitime congregatum" together with the idea that the Council is a "representation" of the whole Church. It is one of Luther's many inconsequences that in 1539, in his *Von den Konziliis und Kirchen*, *L.W.*, VOL. L, pp. 549 ff., 606, he assigns to the Council, "as to the supreme judge and greatest bishop", the duty of defending the ancient faith and repressing heresies, though it may not lay down new articles of faith.

[3] *L.W.*, VOL. L, pp. 619 ff. Above all the Council may not order any new "good works", e.g. new feast and fast days. The ordering of Church discipline must be left to the parochial clergy! *L.W.*, VOL. L, p. 609.

above all the convocation of a Council by them, was connected with certain canonistic views and carried a step further certain political-ecclesiastical tendencies with which we are already acquainted. The only new thing was the extent of the competence assigned to the laity and its justification by the new conception of the Church. It was precisely this circumstance that escaped the notice of people unacquainted with theology and with Luther's Latin writings. These people had the impression that Luther was pressing for the long-desired great reform Council which had been clamoured for throughout a whole century. On this point they were in full sympathy with him: the word "reform" masked the heresy and the nascent schism.

We are thus in presence of a fact of fundamental importance both for the further course of the Reformation and for the history of the idea of a Council. Luther's, and his adherents', assertion that they wanted to reform the Church and that the papal sentence against them was dictated by fear of such a reform, found credence with a great number of Catholics, particularly among the laity, because they entertained the erroneous notion that the last word on Luther's teaching had not been spoken as long as a General Council had not pronounced upon it. As a result of this widespread error on the bearing of the papal condemnation, decades went by before it was generally realised that the Lutheran movement would lead to a permanent split in the Church.

Before all else it is necessary to rid ourselves of the notion of a sharply defined cleavage between Catholics and Protestants from the very first years of the movement.[1] At the Diets of Worms and Nuremberg the party of Duke Ernest were Luther's only patrons; all the other princes were convinced Catholics and the papal nuncio Aleander judged them solely according to their tractability in ecclesiastical-political questions.[2] Measures taken at the time by this or that prince which seemed to favour Luther were no evidence of disloyalty to the Catholic Church.[3] The war of the peasants opened the princes' eyes far more effectively than the Bull *Exsurge*. There were excellent laymen at the

[1] H. Holmquist, *Die schwedische Reformation* (Leipzig 1925), p. 18, justly observes: "It is easy for us to trace back the division between Catholicism and Lutheranism to the very beginning when it only existed in the intrinsic consequences of ideas but not in actual fact".

[2] The *Libellus de personarum conditione* was published and discussed by P. Kalkoff, *Aleander gegen Luther*, pp. 111-40; on Count Palatine Louis V, see p. 128.

[3] Cf. e.g. G. Kattermann, *Die Kirchenpolitik Markgraf Philips von Baden 1515-33* (Lahr 1936). Up till 1525 Philip favoured Lutheranism and hoped for a Council; at a later date he reverted to Catholic principles.

time, such as the jurists Scheurl [1] and Zasius,[2] who had been temporarily won over to Luther's side by some of his writings and who only turned from him when the study of his later writings and their personal observation of their practical result convinced them that here there was question of heresy and revolution. On the other hand, even Protestants readily grant [3] that the authors of the numerous pamphlets which so greatly fostered the progress of the Lutheran movement adopted with enthusiasm the ideas of reform as laid down in the appeal to the nobility while they showed but little understanding for the theological considerations on which they were based. Though these writers took up Luther's cause, they were by no means "evangelicals" in the later sense of the term. As late as 1524 so convinced a Lutheran as Lazarus Spengler sought to keep up the fiction that the controversy about Luther was no more than a contest of divines, a dispute about particular opinions which, given good-will on the part of the Church, could be tolerated in the same way as the opinions of Albertus Magnus and Thomas Aquinas, Scotus and Ockham had been tolerated.[4] In the eyes of many of their contemporaries Luther's Catholic opponents who endeavoured to show his errors, men like Eck, Emser, Fabri, Cochlaeus, were just quarrelsome, hair-splitting defenders not of Catholic truth, but of a bad cause.[5]

[1] On 18 February 1519 Scheurl wrote to Eck that with Luther the problem was the reform of theological teaching and the rediscovery of St Paul, *Briefbuch*, VOL. II, p. 83. On the appearance of the Bull of Excommunication he wrote to his friend Beckmann, at that time a professor at Wittenberg: "Ego spectator horum", and added with emphasis, as against Eck "omnes nos unius tantum Christi factionis", *Briefbuch*, VOL. II, pp. 114 f., 117. On the evolution of Pirkheimer and Dürer, see Grisar, *Luther* (Freiburg i.B. 1911-12), VOL. I, pp. 360 ff. Eng. edn. London 1913-17.

[2] Most revealing are the letters to Zwingli dated 13 November 1519 and 16 February 1520, *Corp. Ref.*, VOL. XCLV, pp. 218 ff., 265 ff.

[3] G. Blochwitz, "Die antirömischen deutschen Flugschriften der frühen Reformationszeit in ihrer religiös-sittlichen Eigenart", in *A.R.G.*, XXVII (1930), pp. 145, 254, is of opinion that even writers like Heinrich von Kettenbach, Hartmut von Kronberg and Martin Bucer continued to hold many truths of the Catholic faith. With most writers the accent is on the fight against Rome and the clergy.

[4] *Verantwortung und Auflösung etlicher vermeintlicher Argumente*, Clemen, *Flugschriften*, VOL. II, p. 355. Even after the Bull *Exsurge* had become public Spengler continued to deny the Pope's right of passing final judgment on Luther's teaching; this could only be done by a "rechts ordentliches Konzil"; cf. H. von Schubert, *Lazarus Spengler und die Reformation in Nürnberg* (Leipzig 1934), pp. 219, 250 ff. In his final volume Schubert—against Kalkoff—corrects the erroneous attribution of several anonymous pamphlets to Spengler. *Die Reformation in der Reichsstadt Nürnberg nach den Flugschriften ihres Ratsschreibers Lazarus Spengler* (Halle 1926).

[5] Examples: *Ein schöner Dialogus* (1521), Schade, *Satiren*, VOL. II, pp. 119-27; *Die lutherische Strebkatz* (1524-5), Schade, *Satiren*, VOL. III, pp. 112-35; to say nothing of *Eckius desolatus* and the filthy satires in Gussmann, *Quellen und Forsch.*, VOL. II, pp. 199 ff.

Luther's adherents emphatically denied any intention to break with the Church nor would they admit that they were actually cut off from her. As late as 1530 Melanchthon stated his conviction that he did not diverge from the Catholic Church on a single dogma. To the end of his life he claimed to be a Catholic and he was wont to issue to the ordinands of Wittenberg a certificate that they believed the teaching of the Catholic Church.[1] The princes and the town councillors in particular looked on the religious changes introduced by Luther as a restoration of true primitive Christianity, hence as a reform of the one true Church. At the Diet of Augsburg the Elector John of Saxony indignantly rejected the accusation that the Protestants had separated themselves from the Church.[2] When invited to attend the council of Mantua, the Estates of Schmalkalden affirmed their loyalty to the true Catholic Church from whose unity they would not be parted.[3] No less a man than Cardinal Campeggio clearly diagnosed the danger implicit in the Protestant claim, and it was precisely because of this danger that he opposed every concession and every form of toleration, lest Catholicism and Lutheranism should come to be regarded as parallel representations of the Church (*come due fedi*).[4]

Erasmus's humanism contributed not a little, at least in the beginning, to obscure the divergences. A pamphlet of the year 1521 entitled *Lamentationes Petri*, and inspired by him, still regards Luther as the restorer of the Church in the spirit of Holy Scripture and the Fathers and as the continuator of Erasmus's own work.[5] For a while

[1] *Corp. Ref.*, VOL. II, pp. 170, 431; VOL. VIII, p. 664; cf. also Pastor, *Reunionsbestrebungen*, p. 13. In October 1530 Oecolampadius wrote to the Waldensians that their confession was "plane catholica et a nobis quoque recepta", E. Stählin, *Briefe und Akten zur Geschichte Ökolampads*, VOL. II (Leipzig 1934), p. 511. At the "colloquium" of Ratisbon Bucer went so far as to contest the Catholics' right to describe themselves by this name because they—the Protestants—were the real "catholics", "Tagebuch des Grafen Wolrad zu Waldeck", in *A.R.G.*, VIII (1910), p. 183. Further details on the use of the term "Catholic" by Luther, Melanchthon and Calvin are supplied by F. Heiler, *Urkirche und Ostkirche* (Munich 1937), pp. 8-13.

[2] Bucholtz, *Ferdinand I*, VOL. III, p. 481. W. Köhler's observation in his *Luther und Luthertum in ihrer weltgeschichtlichen Auswirkung* (Leipzig 1933), p. 65, is parcularly true of the laity: "on the Protestant side no one thought of a separation from the Catholic Church; they meant to remain on the terrain of a common Christian society as during the Middle Ages; all they wanted was a reform".

[3] *C.T.*, VOL. IV, p. 78. This is not to deny that a political tendency was connected with the claim; it was even more marked in the Austrian Estates in 1562, when they described their religion as the true Catholic Church cleansed from abuses. K. Eder, *Glaubensspaltung und Landstände in Österreich ob der Enns* (Linz 1936), p. 103.

[4] Lämmer, *Mon. Vat.*, p. 124 f.

[5] O. Clemen, "Die Lamentationes Petri", in *Z.K.G.*, XIX (1899), pp. 431-48. Similar ideas are found in the dialogue *Die göttliche Mühle*, written in Switzerland in 1521. Schade, *Satiren*, VOL. I, pp. 19-26.

Erasmus sought to prove that the Bull *Exsurge* was surreptitious and invalid.[1] In the *Acta Academiae Lovaniensis* he maintained that Luther's teaching went back to Augustine, Bernard of Clairvaux, Gerson and Nicholas of Cusa; hence he brushed aside his first literary opponents, men like Prierias, Radinus, Cajetan and Alveld on the plea that they were little more than base flatterers of the Pope. The representatives of the new culture were warned of impending danger, "when fanatics like Hochstraten, the inquisitor of Cologne, are at liberty to condemn any one they please, without obligation to furnish evidence!"

Long after Erasmus had definitely broken with Luther, many of his followers, though they too would have nothing to do with the innovator, nevertheless failed to appreciate the greatness of the divergence. Thus in 1540 the above-mentioned Christoph Scheurl, a member of the city council of Nuremberg and a friend of Eck and Witzel, admitted that many Catholic practices had been suppressed in his home-town, to the detriment of religious life, but comforted himself with the thought that baptism, the Eucharist and whatever is necessary for salvation had been retained.[2] We shall see later on that it was this mental attitude that gave birth to the policy of the "religious colloquies".

The broad mass of the people in town and country was not fully aware that they had been torn from the Catholic Church by Luther's action. His shrewdly calculated conservatism with regard to the outward forms of the Catholic liturgy deceived many church-goers about the dogmatic bearing of the changes that had been introduced, so much so that even as late as 1535 the nuncio Vergerio observed, on the occasion of his visit to Wittenberg, that Catholic vestments were still in use there.[3] In the parish church of Wittenberg the elevation of the Host at the consecration—a ceremony at variance with Lutheran theology—continued until 1542.[4] Many Lutheran directories retained the use of

---

[1] P. Kalkoff, "Die Vermittlungspolitik des Erasmus und sein Anteil an den Flugschriften der ersten Reformationszeit", in *A.R.G.*, I, (1903), pp. 1-83; *ibid.*, German translation of the *Acta Acad. Lovan.*; a new edition by Ferguson, *Erasmi opuscula*, pp. 316-28.

[2] Scheurl to an unknown correspondent, 4 December 1540, *Briefbuch*, VOL. II, p. 246.

[3] *N.B.*, VOL. I, i, p. 545.

[4] Grisar, *Luther*, VOL. II, p. 536 (Eng. edn., VOL. IV, p. 195, *n.*4). At Breslau the elevation of the Host was still in use in 1557, Sehling, *Die evangelische Kirchenanordnungen*, VOL. III, p. 404. A Lutheran calendar of feasts of a remarkably Catholic character is that of Teschen in 1584, *ibid.*, VOL. III, p. 461. Further instances in L. Fendt, *Der lutherische Gottesdienst des 16. Jahrhunderts* (Munich 1923), pp. 114 ff., 140 ff., 166 ff., 186 ff. In Silesia Moiban's Canon, which eliminated the sacrificial

Latin for parts of the Mass, as well as a whole series of feasts of the Blessed Virgin Mary and the Saints. In country districts in particular the people, on the whole, remained loyal to the parish priests and from the acts of visitation we learn how difficult it was, even about the middle of the century, to ascertain with complete certainty whether or no these priests were in sympathy with Lutheranism. Even in the case of those who had dropped certain Catholic practices and introduced Lutheran ones, such as Communion in both kinds, it was often doubtful whether they were convinced Lutherans, especially when one remembers how inadequate their theological training had been in most cases.[1]

However paradoxical it may sound, it is a fact that nothing furthered the schism more effectively than the delusion about its actual existence. This delusion was a dangerous fact which must be taken into account, an error that must be reckoned with, though not excused, if we would understand what actually happened. The German schism was a gradual drifting apart rather than a conscious process. To explain how a self-deception of this kind was possible is perhaps the most difficult problem in the history of the Reformation.

For the Catholic of today, firmly set as he is on the standpoint of the Vatican Council, the situation is perfectly clear: the Pope condemns Luther's preaching as heretical; the latter refuses to submit and is excommunicated; thereupon he and his adherents are cut off from the Church; what they describe as reform is the beginning of an opposition Church—a schism. For a large section of Luther's contemporaries the situation was not so simple. It was one of the fatal relics of the conciliar era that many people were not sufficiently clear in their own minds about the infallibility of the dogmatic definitions of the Pope. The Florentine Bull of Union which affirms the universal episcopal authority of the Bishop of Rome encountered some resistance even at Trent, both in regard to its authoritativeness and its interpretation. Theologians whose teaching on the primacy was in agreement with the Bull, from Torquemada to Cajetan, as well as the controversialists Prierias, Alveld,

character of the Mass, was distributed to the clergy of the parishes in the greatest secrecy; cf. A. Sabisch, "Der Messkanon des Breslauer Pfarrers Dr. Ambrosius Moiban", in *Archiv für schlesische Kirchengeschichte*, III (1938), pp. 98-126.

[1] Only one example! Konrad Stuffler, parish priest of Wissing, in the diocese of Eichstätt, accepted the ecclesiastical order of the Palatinate but celebrated the Catholic Mass in the neighbouring locality of Luppurg, heard confessions and gave Communion under both kinds. He was unmarried; *Archiv für Kulturgeschichte*, XII (1916) p. 385. At Würzburg the Lutheran parochial clergy continued to take part in rural conferences as late as 1582; cf. G. Freiherr von Pölnitz, *Julius Echter von Mespelbrunn* (Munich 1934), p. 336.

Eck, Murner and Catharinus,[1] were regarded by many, particularly by the jurists, as defenders of a scholastic opinion, not as witnesses to an acknowledged doctrine of the Church. Thus it came about that the Bull *Exsurge* did not lead to a definite parting of the ways, and although Luther's teaching evolved still further and became more clearly defined after its publication, the Bull remained the sole authoritative papal intervention in the Lutheran affair right up to the Council of Trent. On the other hand, as a result of the negligence and remissness of a whole century on the part of ecclesiastical authority, the catchwords "restoration", "reformation", had acquired an almost magical fascination which made possible the wide diffusion and rapid progress of the Lutheran movement.

In the decisive years of the period of the reformation, between 1521 and 1525, there was only one means, humanly speaking, of arresting the movement of secession, viz. a Council—a Council that would lay down with unquestionable authority the rule of faith for the benefit of the undecided, that would condemn those who had fallen away and strengthen those who remained faithful, a Council that would not only prescribe reform but would find ways and means to carry it through. Why did not the Popes have recourse to such an expedient? There were not wanting men who, in these first years of the reformation, fully appreciated the value of such a remedy. Even in the days of Leo X, Johann Faber, Prior of the Dominicans of Augsburg, urged in his *Ratschlag* that, without prejudice to the Pope's authority in matters of faith, Luther's affair should be entrusted either to a court of arbitration appointed by the Emperor and the Kings of England and Hungary, or to a General Council which should also be a reform council.[2] The Dutchman Aurelius of Gouda and the Spanish humanist Luis Vives besought Adrian VI to seek a solution by means of a Council. At the beginning of 1524 the Bishop of Breslau, Jacob von Salza, in a memorial addressed to Clement VII placed at the head of his list of measures against the innovators the early convocation of a Council, though he

---

[1] Scheurl says of Catharinus that his being a Dominican explained everything, *Briefbuch*, VOL. II, p. 126, while Hummelberger calls him a stubborn Thomist, *Z.K.G.*, XXXII (1911), p. 49. More will be said in Ch. VIII.

[2] N. Paulus, "Der Dominikaner Johann Faber und sein Gutachten über Luther", in *H.J.*, XVII (1896), pp. 39-60. The passage in question is on p. 57. Cf. also the same author's *Dominikaner*, pp. 292-313. Five Latin and four German printed editions are known to exist. Faber advocates practically the same ideas in the *Consilium* composed for Frederick the Wise during the Diet of Worms; *R.T.A.*, VOL. II, p. 484, n.2. On Erasmus's influence cf. Erasmus, *Epist.*, VOL. IV, pp. 357 ff., and Kalkoff in *A.R.G.*, I (1903), pp. 6-23.

deemed it necessary even thus early to justify its postponement.[1] That most selfless and most loyal adherent of the Holy See of all German princes as well as the most earnest advocate of a reform, Duke George of Saxony, never wearied of insisting on the double need of a reform of the Church and of a Council.[2]

All the same it would be a great mistake to infer from these appeals that in the Catholic camp a solution by means of a Council was universally understood to be the right one. The truth is otherwise. The majority of the qualified and unqualified counsellors who submitted their views to the Pope advocated other remedies against a movement which was becoming more and more alarming. Their only motive was that they were aware of the internal resistance and the external obstacles which stood in the way of the seemingly simple solution of a Council. They placed themselves, for the most part, on the legal standpoint—in itself an unassailable one—that Luther's affair had been disposed of by the condemnation of his teaching and his personal excommunication— and endeavoured to persuade the undecided to fall in with this view by furnishing evidence that Luther's particular opinions had all been condemned by earlier Councils.[3] What was needed was to enlighten public opinion and by carrying out reforms to snatch away the shield which the catchword "reform" provided for opponents. In 1521 Cardinal Albrecht of Mainz suggested a German provincial Council.[4] In a memorial addressed to Adrian VI in 1523, Eck linked this proposal with a detailed plan for a reform of the Curia and a draft for a new and more comprehensive Bull against Luther.[5] The Minorite Antony

[1] On Salza's proposals and the covering letter of 2 April 1542, see *Zeitschrift für die Geschichte Schlesiens*, LXII (1928), pp. 91 ff. Ehses published it, without the covering letter, in *H.J.*, XIV (1893), p. 834. At the disputation with Zwingli at Zurich 28 January 1523, the Vicar General of Constance, Johann Fabri, declared that the question of faith could not be discussed at that meeting; it should be examined "unter einer gantzen christlichen versammlung aller nation oder vor einem concilio der bischoffen unnd anderer gelerten, so man findt uff den hohen schulen", *Corp. Ref.*, VOL. LXXXVIII, pp. 491 ff. On the proposals of Aurelius Goudanus and Luis Vives see Ch. IX.

[2] L. Cardauns, "Zur Kirchenpolitik Herzog Georgs von Sachsen", in *Q.F.*, X (1907), pp. 105 ff.

[3] This thesis was defended at Worms by Eck and Vehus (Balan, *Monumenta*, p. 187; *R.T.A.*, VOL. II, pp. 555, 614 ff.) and later on became the "caeterum censeo" of the Curia; *C.T.*, VOL. IV, p. xli; Lämmer, *Mon. Vat.*, p. 64, and of the Augsburg "confutatores"; Ficker, *Die Konfutation des Augsburger Bekenntnisses* (Leipzig 1891), p. xlix.

[4] Balan, *Monumenta*, pp. 267-71.

[5] W. Friedensburg, "Dr. Johann Ecks Denkschriften zur deutschen Kirchen-reformation", in *Beiträge zur bayrischen Kirchengeschichte*, II (1896), pp. 159-96, 222-53; the relevant passages are on pp. 189 ff.

Bomhauwer likewise advocates another Bull.[1] His memorial agrees
with that of Johann Haner, the cathedral preacher of Würzburg,[2] in
pleading that the grievances of the German nation against the Curia
be met with reforms. It also recommends a systematic literary campaign to counter the propaganda of the innovators. The zealous
Cochlaeus also looks for good results from such a counter-stroke. A
foolish overestimation of his own ability tempts him to suggest that a
private disputation with Luther would confound the widespread notion
that the heretic had never been decisively refuted.[3] Even so experienced
a politician as Cardinal Schiner makes no mention of a Council in his
memorial to Adrian VI,[4] and the Dominican Archbishop Nicholas von
Schönberg, who was held in high esteem by the Medici Popes and who
by reason of his Saxon origin and his connexion with the country could
be credited with expert knowledge, maintained even in the last years
of Clement VII that a Council would no more put an end to the conflict
than the use of force.[5]

We pass over the other Italian advisers of the Pope, to mention only
the three best informed, all three men who had had an opportunity of
studying the problems at close quarters in the course of their diplomatic
missions in Germany. None of them—neither Cajetan, nor Campeggio
nor Aleander—recommended a Council.[6] They only urged more or
less drastic reforms by the Pope as an indirect means of countering the
movement of secession. The imaginative, experienced Aleander would
exhaust all the resources of diplomacy before recourse was had to the
last remedy—force. Campeggio felt convinced from the very beginning
of his second legation in 1530 that only the latter means—that is, a war
of religion—would yield decisive results. All three knew that both
Leo X and Clement VII were opposed to a Council—particularly

---

[1] J. P. Kirsch, "Vorschläge eines Lektors der Minoriten zur Bekämpfung der Häresie Luthers", in *H.J.*, x (1889), pp. 807-12.
[2] Balan, *Monumenta*, pp. 316-20 (5 January 1524). It is a curious circumstance that Haner should have become estranged from the Church in Catholic Würzburg and that he should have found his way back in Protestant Nuremberg. For his subsequent attitude see the letters to Duke George and Witzel, Döllinger, *Beiträge*, VOL. III, p. 105.
[3] Cochlaeus to Leo X, 19 June 1521, *Z.K.G.*, xi (1897), pp. 116 ff.
[4] Pastor, VOL. IV, ii, pp. 722 ff. (Eng. edn., VOL. IX, p. 472).
[5] Pastor, VOL. IV, ii, p. 423, *n.*6 (Eng. edn., VOL. X, p. 151, *n.*2); Kalkoff, in *Z.K.G.*, XXXI (1910), pp. 390 ff.
[6] *C.T.*, VOL. XII, pp. 5-17 (Campeggio); *C.T.*, VOL. XII, pp. 32-9 (Cajetan); Döllinger, *Beiträge*, VOL. III, p. 253 (Aleander). It is worth noting that Zaccaria Ferreri, the former adherent of the Pisan assembly, makes no reference whatever to a Council in his *Suasoria* printed in 1523 (now *C.T.*, VOL. XII, pp. 21 ff.).

Clement VII. Their theological and legal training enabled them to see clearly the great danger for the unity of the Church from a Council at which all the nations would be represented. Their diplomatic experience had taught them how difficult it would be to harmonise the divergent interests of the powers so as to further the aims of the Church. They had lived long enough at the Curia to be aware of its deep-rooted aversion for a Council and for conciliar reforms. It cannot be denied that considerable sections of the College of Cardinals and of the officials of the Curia were afraid of a Council because they knew that the nations would make a combined onslaught on their traditional administration of benefices and their financial system, with a consequent loss of income and an end of the luxurious style in which they were wont to live. In these circles it was thought that the problem of Luther could be solved by the simple expedient of calling him a whore-monger and a drunkard.[1] These silent but tough opponents of reform and a Council wielded great power, far greater indeed than official documents would lead us to believe. Their influence is made particularly evident when one surveys a period of some duration and examines impartially both the internal and the external history of events. To pass these things over in silence would be no less wrong than the one-sidedness of Sleidan, Sarpi and others,[2] who lay the blame for all the evils of the schism upon the alleged ill will of the Roman Curia and who refuse to make allowance either for any just reasons these men may have had, or for the concurrence of other factors.

[1] Jakob Ziegler to Erasmus, 16 February 1522, Erasmus, *Epist.*, VOL. V, p. 22, previously published by Kalkoff in *A.R.G.*, III (1906), p. 79. In his despatches Aleander bestows on Luther the epithets of "ladro, assassino, monstro, dracone, cane, pazzo", Balan, *Monumenta*, pp. 153, 164, 197, 237.

[2] Sleidan, *Zwei Reden*, ed. Böhmer (Tübingen 1879), pp. 111-21; Sarpi, *Istoria*, VOL. I, pp. 1-6 (ed. Gambarin, VOL. I, pp. 3-171). For the period of Adrian VI and Clement VII the narratives based on very questionable sources—in VOL. I, p. 36 f. (Soderini), p. 61 (consistory of 13—actually 19—September 1526), p. 79 (the fictitious discourse of Clement VII at Bologna), are characteristic of the man. For the much wider and more solid documentary basis of the historical background in Pallavicino, *Istoria del Concilio di Trento* (Rome 1656), VOLS. I-V, cf. H. Jedin in, *Der Quellenapparat der Konzilsgeschichte Pallavicinos* (Rome 1940), pp. 27 ff., 36 ff. The best modern survey of the background up to 1537 is provided by Ehses, *C.T.*, VOL. IV, pp. cvi-cxli. It furnishes the main basis for what Pastor has to say about the Council in VOLS. IV, VII, and V (Eng. edn., VOLS. VII, VIII, XI and XII), as well as for the latest summary by R. Villoslada, "La Cristianidad pide un concilio", in *Razón y Fe*, CXXXL (1945), pp. 13-50. For L. Cristiani's account, *L'Eglise à l'époque du concile de Trente* (Paris 1948), see my review in *Rivista di storia della Chiesa in Italia*, II (1948), pp. 274-84. In the chapters of this book which now follow I have frequently been more concise than Ehses; on the other hand I have endeavoured to put in stronger relief not only the diplomatic negotiations, but likewise the internal religious and ecclesiastical evolution as well as public opinion as revealed in literature and private correspondence.

The fact remains that a Council did not come off betimes because Rome regarded it as a dangerous venture the issue of which was questionable; for that reason it refused to promote it energetically. Yet as things stood, only a Council could issue a decision on the controversy which all concerned would regard as undoubtedly binding in conscience. Moreover, a positive statement of the contents of the Catholic faith—which was no less urgently needed—if accompanied by an effective Catholic reform, would have cut the ground from under Luther's "reformation". Instead of a Council recourse was first had to the authority of the state. In the Edict of Worms the Emperor undertook to execute the Bull *Exsurge*; but he too was unable to enforce it because he became involved in a great war, and he did not reside in Germany. On their part, at the Diet of Nuremberg, the German Estates of the Empire demanded "a free, Christian council in a German land". The formula was calculated to act as a warning rather than as an invitation for, on the part of the Lutherans, it was but a thin disguise of conditions which were at variance with the hierarchical constitution of the Church. The Council was put off from year to year: Lutheranism spread on the wings of the spoken and the printed word; prince after prince, town after town "reformed" in the direction of the new teaching—the opposition Churches became organised bodies. Futile negotiations for a Council dragged on for years; the prospect of its convocation grew steadily dimmer. The first attempt of a new Pope to convoke it proved a failure; the Emperor's intervention led nowhere. With despair in their hearts those who remained loyal to the Church were forced to look on while a whole generation was growing up estranged from the Catholic faith and from Catholic piety and the seamless coat of Christ was being rent by an enduring schism.

CHAPTER II

"A Free Christian Council in German Lands"

AFTER Luther's condemnation and excommunication for heresy by the Bulls *Exsurge* and *Decet Romanum Pontificem* it was the duty of the secular arm, in accordance with the medieval conception of the State, to co-operate in the execution of the sentence. However, Luther's sovereign, the Elector Frederick the Wise of Saxony,[1] found means to evade the Church's demand. Frederick was held in general esteem as a conscientious and pious prince. In his younger days he had made a pilgrimage to the Holy Land and in the chapel of his castle at Wittenberg he had collected an amazing quantity of relics. For all that, he could not be shaken out of his conviction that Luther stood for the true Catholic faith. On the advice of his court-chaplain and secretary, Spalatin, and the jurists Brück, Schurff and Planitz, he sought, as an adept in every political shift, to create an impression that he was not interested in the Wittenberg Augustinian—actually he had always avoided a personal interview with Luther—and that he was prepared, in principle, to let the law take its course. When on 4 November 1520, at Cologne, the nuncio Aleander, who had been despatched to the Emperor on a special mission in connexion with Luther's affairs, demanded the extradition of the culprit, Frederick bluntly refused on the plea that Luther had not yet been convicted. He ended by

---

[1] Kalkoff's view as summed up in his study "Friedrich der Weise, der Beschützer Luthers und des Reformationswerk", in *A.R.G.*, XIV (1917), pp. 249-62, has been criticised by E. Wagner, "Luther und Friedrich der Weise auf dem Wormser Reichstag", in *Z.K.G.*, XLII (1923), pp. 331-90, and defended by A. Koch, "Die Kontroverse über die Stellung Friedrichs des Weisen zur Reformation", in *A.R.G.*, XXIII (1926), pp. 213-60. In my opinion Frederick the Wise was not merely a defender of his favourite creation, the University of Wittenberg, he was also a convinced adherent of Luther, though not a Protestant in the later sense of that word; on the contrary, he was under the delusion that he was righting an alleged wrong done to Luther and furthering a "reform" of the Church. His ideas were fundamentally orthodox and conservative. It is worth noting that Luther only married after Frederick was dead. For the wholly Catholic and medieval piety that prevailed at the court of the Elector of Saxony, see Kalkoff, *Ablass und Reliquienverehrung an der Schlosskirche zu Wittenberg unter Friedrich dem Weisen* (Gotha 1907). For the Elector's liberal support of religious activities as proved by his account books, see G. Buchwald, in *A.R.G.*, XXVII (1930), pp. 62-110. For a general impression, cf. P. Kirn, *Friedrich der Weise und die Kirche* (Leipzig 1926).

suggesting once more a court of arbitration presided over by the Arch-bishop of Trier. In point of fact, in view of the extent to which the Lutheran movement had spread in the meantime, the extradition of Luther's person would not have ended the matter. Aleander accord-ingly did all in his power to obtain from the Emperor the most comprehensive execution of the Bull *Exsurge*, in accordance with the law of the Empire.

In the person of Aleander [1] there enters upon the scene of reforma-tion and Council the most controversial figure after Eck and the best-hated champion of papal policy. This humanist was born at Motta, in the territory of Venice. After lecturing for a time in Paris he entered the service of Erhard von der Mark, Prince-Bishop of Liège, and thus became acquainted with conditions in the Empire. More clearly than most he realised the danger that threatened the Papacy from the Lutheran movement. From the first he advocated a policy of iron determination against its adherents. His uncommon gifts both as a speaker and a writer, his multiple sources of information—even questionable ones—his tenacity and energy in the pursuit of his goal, seemed to promise the most complete success. But when compared with Morone, who was to play a role in German policy at a later date, and above all by comparison with Contarini, he lacked something that these men possessed: namely an intimate personal sense of the religious nature of the questions that were being decided in Germany. He only saw the revolt against the traditional order, the greed for Church property, but was blind to the silver streak of genuine, though mis-guided piety which was also to be found in the Lutheran movement. Hence during the whole of the two decades in which he influenced papal policy towards Germany, he pursued an intransigent line of action. At his first appearance in Germany the humanist in him laboured under a strong feeling of jealousy of Erasmus, whom he did his best to represent as the forerunner and accomplice of Luther. Yet the only thing that mattered just then was to detach Erasmus's followers from their leader. Aleander's burning ambition led him to stress in his

[1] For Aleander, in addition to his *Diarium* (H. Omont, *Journal autobiographique du Cardinal Aleander 1480-1530*, Paris 1896) and Friedenburg's introduction to his legatine reports of 1538-9, *N.B.*, VOL. I, iii, pp. 28-41, cf. especially the works of J. Paquier, viz. his collection of the sources: *Aleander et la Principauté de Liège* (Paris 1896); *Lettres familières d'Aleander 1510-40* (Paris 1909), and his biography up to 1529: *J. Aléandre de sa naissance jusqu'à la fin de son séjour à Brindes* (Paris 1900), and a resumé in *D.Th.C.*, VOL. I, pp. 693 ff. Whereas Kalkoff is inspired by positive hatred for Aleander, Paquier does his utmost to minimise his defects of character which are perceptible even after 1527 (cf. Morone's judgment, *N.B.*, VOL. I, iv, p. 222).

reports, with pitiful self-complacency, the dangers he underwent in the execution of his mission and his personal sacrifices, and to exaggerate his successes. Seen from the point of view of the politics of the hour, they were indeed extraordinary, but they are not so in the perspective of history.

Soon after his arrival at the imperial court, at his instigation severe measures were taken in the Low Countries against Luther's adherents and against his writings. During the festivities of Charles V's coronation at Aachen at the end of October, he submitted a preliminary draft for an imperial edict against Luther. By the 29th it had been passed by the Privy Council. It looked as if he had got all he wanted, when the Elector of Saxony protested against the proceedings on the basis of a clause in the imperial election capitulation which forbade the infliction of the ban of empire on a German subject without previous examination and trial by the common judge.[1] Frederick the Wise was the most highly respected prince of the Empire; two years earlier the Pope himself had deemed him worthy of the imperial crown. The Emperor's counsellors thought it would be a serious matter to alienate such a man on the eve of the Diet, all the more so when one took into account the feelings of the masses in favour of Luther and the threatening attitude of the Imperial Knights whom Hutten was inciting to revolt. Moreover, the tension between the Empire and France was growing. Chièvres, who had been the Emperor's tutor and was now his Grand Chamberlain, and the Lord High Chancellor Gattinara, saw in the proceedings against Luther, which the Pope had so much at heart, a possibility for a bargain for which a high price could be asked.[2] The edict was accordingly withheld.

The great Diet of Worms opened on 27 January 1521. From the first day the religious problem became its supreme preoccupation.[3] In

---

[1] *R.T.A.*, vol. i, p. 871. The applicability of art. 17 was questionable for it only forbade the passing of sentence on German subjects outside the boundaries of the German Nation and by other than their ordinary judges.

[2] Aleander's report of 19 March 1521, Balan, *Monumenta*, p. 131. For the bibliography on Chièvres see Brandi, *Quellen*, pp. 76, 81.

[3] There are two editions of Aleander's despatches, for us the most important sources of information on the Diet of Worms: Th. Brieger, *Aleander und Luther* (Gotha 1884), and Balan, *Monumenta*, with the supplements of Kalkoff in *Z.K.G.*, xxviii (1907), pp. 201-34; Kalkoff, *Die Depeschen des Nuntius Aleander vom Wormser Reichstag 1521* (2nd edn. Halle 1897); *id., Briefe, Depeschen und Berichte über Luther vom Wormser Reichstag* (Halle 1898). The Acts proper in *R.T.A.*, vol. ii, pp. 449-743. Bibliography: P. Kalkoff, *Die Entstehung des Wormser Ediktes* (Leipzig 1913); *id., Der Grosse Wormser Reichstag von 1521* (Worms 1921); on the question of the Council at Worms, cf. K. Hofmann, *Die Konzilsfrage auf den deutschen Reichstagen von 1521-24* (Diss. theol., Heidelberg 1932), pp. 9-30.

the hope of inducing the Elector of Saxony to give up his opposition the Franciscan confessor of the Emperor, Glapion, suggested that they content themselves with an examination of Luther by a court committee and with a limited recantation. His aim was to prevent Luther's personal appearance at the Diet, but the attempt was frustrated.[1] Nor did Frederick the Wise allow himself to be persuaded by Aleander's moving and impressive discourse on 13 February to abandon his standpoint. Luther, he claimed, had not been refuted; he must be heard by the Diet, were it only to calm the people. The Elector of Brandenburg, Joachim I, opposed him sharply; a heated discussion ensued in which the two men came near drawing swords. The Saxon had his way. On 5 March a decree against Luther, drafted under Aleander's inspiration, was rejected by the Diet, which insisted on his being summoned to Worms.[2] Under pressure of the political considerations mentioned above, the Emperor gave way and granted Luther a safe-conduct, but at the same time he showed his real feelings by ordering the sequestration of his writings.[3]

Luther's summons to Worms was an undoubted defeat for Aleander, for though the Emperor had no intention whatever to take it on himself to check the papal decision, the citation of Luther for the purpose of questioning him on the authorship of the books circulating under his name and summoning him once more to recant nevertheless amounted to an inadmissible concession.[4] The citation was the first formal departure from the path of strict Canon Law. Aleander permitted it in order to prevent what he thought would be an even greater evil. "The whole world shouts 'Council, Council'." he reported to the vice-chancellor while the decisive negotiations were in progress,[5] and his

---

[1] The reports of the Saxon chancellor Brück who acted as intermediary, *R.T.A.*, VOL. II, pp. 477 ff. I see no reason to doubt Glapion's sincerity and I also regard his second attempt, at the beginning of April, to keep Luther away from Worms and to bring about a meeting with him at the Ebernburg, as sincerely meant, *R.T.A.*, VOL. II, pp. 537 ff.

[2] The drafts of 15 February and 2 March and the replies of the Estates, *R.T.A.*, VOL. II, pp. 507-26.

[3] *R.T.A.*, VOL. II, pp. 529-32.

[4] Thus quite accurately P. Rassow, *Die Kaiseridee Karls V* (Berlin 1932), pp. 32 ff., but in that case it is impossible to reduce the proceedings of Worms to a harmless "transference from the spiritual to the secular sphere while the accused is allowed to have the last word".

[5] "Ognuno domanda et crida (Brieger: 'strida'), concilio, et lo voleno in Germania"; and presently "El rumor di tutti in la dieta è di voler concilio, de disobedir Roma, de insurger contro il clero". Brieger, *Aleander und Luther*, pp. 48, 55; Balan, *Monumenta*, pp. 98, 103.

colleague Raffaele de' Medici added the observation: "Many among the great ones are of opinion that this affair must be investigated by a Council." [1] These "great ones" were not to be exclusively found on the princes' benches at the Diet. The Grand Chancellor Gattinara, whose influence at the Diet was still further increased when Chièvres died, never wearied of repeating: "Without a Council we shall not master the heresy." [2] The further ambiguous and pessimistic remark *Fata obstant*, from the lips of such a man was an only too significant warning for a sensitive diplomatist like Aleander. A memorial which has been preserved with the acts of the Diet [3] throws light on the views that had to be reckoned with on the part of the juristically trained councillors who crowded round the princes and bishops at the Diet: "A Council alone", we read, "is in a position to ascertain whether Dr. Martinus has written against the faith; he has appealed to a Council and thereby tied the Pope's hands. Pius II's and Julius II's prohibitions are invalid because they are at variance with natural and divine law, as well as with the decrees of Constance, and they have not been recognised by the University of Paris." Here we have another instance of undiluted conciliar theory! These were the very ideas with which the Papacy had had to contend ever since the Council of Basle. Hutten, a mortal enemy of Rome, sought to revive their popularity by publishing a new edition of a work dating from that period and of which he had found a copy in the Ebernburg. On the title page were blazoned the words: *Concilium, Concilium, Concilium!* [4]

These warnings of the impending storm were not lost on Aleander and he acted accordingly.

The circumstances of Luther's examination before the Emperor and the Diet on 17 and 18 April 1521 belong to history and are well known. On the first day he asked to be given time for reflexion. On the second he admitted he was the author of the incriminated books but refused to recant. The youthful Emperor was painfully impressed, so much so that on the following day he set down in writing the celebrated declaration that he was ready to stake his life and crown for the extirpation

---

[1] Balan, *Monumenta*, p. 53. The anonymous reporter is the nuncio Medici.
[2] Aleander's despatches of 28 February and 4 March, Brieger, *Aleander und Luther*, pp. 79, 87; Balan, *Monumenta*, pp. 78, 115. The next chapter will show that these statements of Gattinara were no feints as Hofmann imagines (*Konzilsfrage*, p. 22).
[3] *R.T.A.*, VOL. II, pp. 534 ff.
[4] Weller, *Repertorium typographicum* (Nördlingen 1864), No. 1792; Böcking, *Hutteni Opera*, VOL. I, pp. 76 ff., VOL. II, pp. 78 ff.

of heresy.[1] The statement was one of the first expressions of independent thinking by the young monarch and a programme for the whole of his reign. The way was open for the execution of the Bull in accordance with imperial law; all that was necessary was to give Luther time to get back to Wittenberg in accordance with the guarantee that had been given him. The Estates were dissatisfied with the issue. What would happen if the idol of the masses were burnt at the stake? Would it not be said that he had died without having been convicted?

The result of these considerations was that on 20 April the Estates decided that Luther should be examined once more by a committee, but without juridical formality and without arguing.

The Chancellor of Baden, Doctor Vehus, undertook this thankless task on 24 April.[2] There can be no doubt that when he endeavoured to get Luther to accept a common basis—viz. the authority of the Councils—he was acting in accordance with a previous arrangement with the committee which besides Joachim, the Elector of Brandenburg, and Duke George of Saxony, included the Bishops of Trier, Augsburg and Brandenburg. In his solemn address to the Diet Aleander had touched no less than four times on this cardinal point. He had also made a skilfully calculated reference to the Council of Constance which had lost none of its popularity in Germany. In the examination of 18 April the chancellor of Trier, Johann von der Ecken, had taken the same line: "what has been settled by the Councils needs no further discussion". Vehus strove to convince Luther that the diversity of conciliar decisions implied no contradiction between them: they were *diversa, non contraria*. All was in vain. Even after the deputies of Augsburg and Strasbourg, Peutinger and Bock, and finally on 25 April the Archbishop of Trier, Richard von Greiffenklau, had pressed Luther in a friendly manner to leave the decision of his affair to a Council, Luther stuck to his impossible pretensions that a Council could only judge his teaching on the basis of Holy Scripture and that the articles submitted to it must be previously approved by himself.[3]

---

[1] *R.T.A.*, VOL. II, pp. 594 ff.; a Latin translation was printed by Schöffer at Mainz, O. Clemen, *Unbekannte Drucke und Akten aus der Reformationszeit* (Leipzig 1942), pp. 91 ff. Brandi, *Kaiser Karl V*, p. 112 (Eng. edn., p. 130), describes the document as "the most weighty utterance of his youth".

[2] The fullest account is that of Chancellor Vehus, *R.T.A.*, VOL. II, pp. 611-24.

[3] The two conditions are only found in the *Acta et res gestae*, Lutheran in tendency, *R.T.A.*, VOL. II, p. 565, and in the equally Lutheran *Deutscher Bericht*, ibid., p. 609. Vehus makes no mention of the second condition; in its place he has another, namely that "die Haltung eins concilium nit lang verzogen wurde", ibid., p. 622. Vehus also reports that Luther had undertaken not to preach and not to write about the articles reserved to the Council.

Luther knew only too well that at this stage of the movement the condemnation of his teaching by a General Council would mean the loss of most of his adherents, hence a conciliar decision was the last thing he wanted. It was a tragedy that Aleander also was against a Council though for a very different reason. Luther was afraid of a Council that would deal with questions concerning the faith; Aleander feared the anti-Roman tendencies of a reform Council. The fact was that the heat of the battle around Luther was chiefly fanned by the anti-Roman and anticlerical feelings of the laity,[1] which also inflamed the debate on Church reform. But it was impossible to mention Church reform without broaching the question of a Council. Even before the opening of the Diet, on 21 January, the above-mentioned Dominican Johann Faber had urged the Estates in his sermon to lend help to the Emperor for his Italian expedition and to pave the way for a reform of the Church by means of a great Council on an episcopalist basis.[2] It almost looked as if the days of Charles VIII and Louis XII were about to return, for though it was a tradition for the Estates— princes and towns, clergy and laity—to disagree among themselves, they were all of one mind on one point, namely, that the hour for the reform of the Church had struck.

Duke George of Saxony submitted a list of fourteen proposals for reform in which he stated that a Council was the best means for the suppression of scandals among the clergy and for a "general reform".[3] Another set of complaints, probably also submitted to the Diet, suggested that in future papal reservations, pensions, dispensations enabling a man to hold incompatible benefices, exemptions from the normal course of justice, should only be recognised in so far as a future Council permitted them with the explicit assent of the German nation.[4] Another long list of complaints and grievances was also drawn up which sounds like a strong echo of Luther's appeal to the nobility. The whole of the first part (articles 1-28) is exclusively directed against the Curia's policy with regard to benefices and its fiscal system.[5] But, strangely

---

[1] "La rabbia di tutti i principi di Germania che cridano a Cesare contra di noi," says Aleander on 8 February. Brieger, *Aleander und Luther*, p. 49.

[2] Medici's report of 22 January, Balan, *Monumenta*, p. 42. Faber's episcopalist expressions in the report of the English envoy Tunstall, 29 January, in *R.T.A.*, VOL. II, p. 784. They were probably the reason why Aleander styled him "a second Luther"; Spinelli to Wolsey, 24 January, *Cal. of Letters*, VOL. III, ii, 1577.

[3] *R.T.A.*, VOL. II, p. 666; Gess, *Akten und Briefe*, VOL. I, p. 153.

[4] *R.T.A.*, VOL. II, p. 705, *n.*1.

[5] *R.T.A.*, VOL. II, pp. 700-04.

enough, a Council is not mentioned in this list of *gravamina*. What had happened? Only this, that Aleander had had recourse to the trusty tactics with which Sixtus IV in his day was wont to ward off inconvenient demands for a Council—he himself had threatened with a Council. The nuncio dropped a hint to the effect that he had in his possession a papal notification of a Council. For the benefit of princes and bishops—separately, of course—he drew a lively picture of what they might expect from a reform Council. The threat silenced them.[1] The bishops withdrew their adhesion to the *gravamina*, and though the secular princes still mentioned a Council in their "Supplica" to the Emperor, the text of which has not been preserved, no joint demand for a Council was made by the Estates as a whole: dogma and reform were kept apart.[2] Aleander might feel well content; his trick had succeeded, and it was his opponent, Luther, who had done his best to make such a success possible. Although the majority of the Estates present at Worms were convinced that a Council alone held any prospect of a satisfactory solution of both problems, the Diet took no steps to bring it about.

The Edict of Worms, which was finally drafted on 8 May, received the approval of a section of the Estates on the 25th, after the conclusion of the Diet, and was signed by the Emperor on the following day.[3] It was all that Aleander had wished for. It put Luther under the ban of the Empire, ordered his writings, without exception, to be burnt and forbade their publication and diffusion. At the same time a political alliance between Pope and Emperor was concluded in Rome. On 28 May Leo X wrote at the bottom of the document by which he bound

---

[1] There is no reason to doubt Aleander's subsequent report on the incident in his memorial to Clement VII, Döllinger, *Beiträge*, VOL. III, p. 255.

[2] According to Aleander's report of 27 February (Brieger, *Aleander und Luther* p. 72; Balan, *Monumenta*, p. 73), the Emperor had already replied by word of mouth, on 19 February to the "responsio" of the Estates. It was to the effect "che le querele di Roma lui non voleva che si mescalessino con la cosa di Luther che toccava la fede". The written reply of 2 March (*ibid.*, pp. 518 ff.) does not mention this desire but takes it for granted since it invites them to set down their grievances in writing.

[3] Text in *R.T.A.*, VOL. II, pp. 640-59; the Latin draft is by Aleander, the German text by the imperial secretaries Ziegler and Spiegel. A Roman edition of the Latin text of 6 May prepared by Jacob Mazochi, "Romanae Academiae bibliopola", in Vat. Lib., Racc. I, IV, 1680 int. 37, has been overlooked by Wrede. Bibliography: P. Kalkoff, *Die Enstehung des Wormser Ediktes* (Leipzig 1913), with the supplements in *A.R.G.*, XIII (1916), pp. 241-76. Kalkoff's assertion that the edict was surreptitious and illegal has been refuted by N. Paulus, in *H.J.*, XXXIX (1918-19), pp. 269 ff. The only thing that is accurate is that the claim made in the edict (p. 653, 16th line) that it was the result of the unanimous advice and will of the Estates does not correspond with the facts.

himself to lend armed assistance against Francis I of France, the words: "Thus we promise." [1]

Aleander was jubilant! "The victory is ours," he wrote, "nine tenths of Luther's adherents have deserted him; the imperial edict will put an end to this abomination." [2] He was grievously mistaken. Like the Bull *Exsurge*, the Edict of Worms was not carried into effect within the Empire. On his return journey from Worms Luther was kidnapped in an attack staged by his Saxon friends, who took him to a place of safety in the Wartburg and all the while his writings continued to woo the soul of the German people.[3] It is true that on 20 January 1522, at the instance of Duke George of Saxony, the commission of princes to whom the Emperor had entrusted the government of the Empire on his departure for Spain, and who directed the affairs of the state from Nuremberg, forbade all innovations in the Church until a Diet or a Council should have given directions to that effect,[4] but by reason of successive changes in its composition and the consequent influence of the Elector of Saxony, the commission's policy lacked consistency; above all it lacked the power to impose its decisions.[5]

At this point the death of Leo X and the election of the Netherlander Adrian of Utrecht, on 9 January 1522, opened up the most surprising possibilities.[6] As a trained theologian, Adrian VI had

[1] Brandi, *Kaiser Karl V*, pp. 128-32 (Eng. edn. pp. 149 ff.), has a masterly summing up of the political situation.

[2] Aleander's reports of 26 May and 27 June, Brieger, *Aleander und Luther*, pp. 224-41; Balan, *Monumenta*, pp. 251, 261. How grievously mistaken he was Aleander was to learn in July from Capito's reports of the disturbances at Erfurt and Magdeburg, *Z.K.G.*, XVI (1896), pp. 496 ff.

[3] K. Schottenloher estimates at 2000 the number of the printed editions of some of Luther's writings between 1517 and 1525 *R. E.*, VOL. XXIII, p. 272. The first edition of the September Bible, of 5000 copies published by the Wittenberg printer Michael Lotter on 22 September 1522, was sold out within three months in spite of the high price of one and a half ducats.

[4] Gess, *Akten und Briefe*, VOL. I, p. 252. Hofmann's observation (*Konzilsfrage*, p. 31) that thereafter the idea of the Council only proceeded from the religious problem is inaccurate—for Duke George it was always connected with Church reform.

[5] I was not able to consult P. Kalkoff, *Das Wormser Edikt und die Erlasse des Reichsregiments und einzelner Reichsfürsten* (Munich 1917). A. Grabner, *Zur Geschichte des zweiten Nürnberger Reichsregiments* (Berlin 1903), pp. 38 ff., is biased.

[6] The bibliography of Adrian VI has been increased, since Pastor VOL. IV, ii, pp. 1-157 (Eng. edn., VOL. IX, p. 22 ff.), by the popular but, on the whole, successful biography by E. Hock, *Der letzte deutsche Papst Adrian VI* (Freiburg 1939), and a number of special studies among which the following may be singled out: A. H. L. Hensen and G. J. Hoogewerff, on medals and portraits of Adrian VI, in *Mededeelingen*, III (1923), pp. 1-20; VII (1927), pp. 97-100; P. Kalkoff, "Kleine Beiträge zur Geschichte Hadrians VI", in *H.J.*, XXXIX (1918-19), pp. 31-72, on the Pope's collaborators; E. Göller, "Hadrian VI und der Ämterverkauf an der päpstlichen Kurie",

realised from the very beginning that Luther's teaching was untenable. He entirely concurred with the verdict which the theological faculty of Louvain, whose dean he had been at one time, pronounced upon it on 7 November 1519.[1] On the other hand he was fully aware that many of the complaints about the Curia and the clergy were justified,[2] and he was equally convinced of the urgent necessity of far-reaching reforms if the movement of secession was to be arrested. His own blameless life, his somewhat frigid but incorruptible honesty, his simple, genuine piety inspired by the *devotio moderna*, were in perfect harmony with this conviction. The simplicity and parsimony with which he ordered his life at the Vatican—his daily personal expenditure was one ducat—constituted the greatest contrast imaginable to the sumptuousness of his predecessor. "I could have sworn he was a *Frate*", wrote an eye-witness of the Pope's entry into Rome.[3] Now, if ever, there was a prospect of arresting the Lutheran movement by energetic counter-measures and an internal renewal of the Church.[4]

in *Festgabe Finke* (Freiburg 1925), pp. 375-407; A. Albareda, "Adrià VI i els conselles de Barcelona 1522", in *Analecta sacra Tarraconensia*, XI (1935), pp. 235-49; see also *n.* 2 below.

[1] When the faculty published its *Condemnatio*, 6 November 1519 (Le Plat, VOL. II, pp. 47-50; *Corpus Inquisitionis Neerlandicae*, ed. P. Fredericq (Ghent 1927), VOL. IV, pp. 14-16), it forwarded to Adrian VI extracts from Luther's writings (printed by Kalkoff, *Forschungen zu Luthers römischen Prozess*, pp. 194-203); in his reply of 4 December the cardinal described them as "rudes et palpabiles haereses" (Le Plat, VOL. II, pp. 50 ff.; *Corp. Inquis. Neerl.*, VOL. IV, pp. 17 ff.).

[2] The synodal sermon and the discourse to the clergy at Louvain on 13 May 1498, printed by E. H. J. Reussens, *Syntagma doctrinae theologicae Adriani VI P.M.* (Louvain 1862), pp. 215-32, are of fundamental importance. The *Quaestiones quodlibetales* (I quote from the Lyons edition of 1546) should also be taken into account; thus, for instance q. 6 shows that Adrian was profoundly aware of the problem "Jus divinum—Jus humanum"; q. 9 treats of simony. For Adrian's theology see also B. Kurtscheid, "De obligatione sigilli confessionis iuxta doctrinam Adriani VI", in *Antonianum*, I (1926), pp. 84-101; W. Lampen, "Paus Adriaan VI over de veelvondige communio", in *Katholiek*, CLXIV (1923), pp. 137-45.

[3] Sanudo, *Diarii*, VOL. XXXIII, pp. 432 ff. (5 September 1522). Gradenigo's reports to the Senate in Sanudo, *Diarii*, VOLS. XXXIII and XXXIV; those of Negri to Micheli in *Lettere di principi*, VOL. I (Venice 1564) fols. 87^r-100^v, as well as the entry in the catalogue of the Order of the Augustinians quoted by me (*Seripando*, VOL. II, p. 51: Eng. edn., p. 508) show that not all Italians judged Adrian as unjustly as does V. Albergati. For the rest the text given by E. Bacha, "Les Commentaires de V. Albergati", in *Comte-rendu de la Commission Royale d'histoire de la Belgique*, V, i (1891), pp. 102-66, is more odious in some passages than that of a subsequent revision of the commentaries, in Vat. Lib., Vat. lat. 4937.

[4] This expectation is given expression in the "Dialogue between a courtier, an abbot and the devil", in Clemen, *Flugschriften*, VOL. III, pp. 16-23. The editor, A. Richel, ascribes it to Pamphilus von Gengenbach. I think the author is a Catholic reformer, not a courtier expelled from Rome as claimed by J. F. M. Sterck, "Over Paus Adriaan VI", in *Mededeelingen*, X (1927), pp. 101 ff.

Long before the Schism Adrian had often proclaimed from his professorial chair at Louvain that a Council alone could bring peace to the nations and renewal to the Church.[1] As a cardinal he had expressed the opinion that on account of its importance the Reuchlin dispute should be dealt with by a Council.[2] On accepting his election to the Papacy he had sworn to promote the salutary project of a Council in so far as in the opinion of the cardinals its convocation would benefit the Church.[3] In these circumstances he could not but be powerfully impressed by the words of Cardinal Carvajal, the one-time leader of the opposition to Pisa and now the Dean of the Sacred College who, on welcoming the new Pope on his arrival in Rome on 28 August 1522 urged him to renew the Church on the basis of the sacred Councils and the prescriptions of Canon Law.[4]

One of the best representatives of the humanist culture, the Spaniard Luis Vives, pointed out to him, in the light of Church history, that the storm that had struck the Church could only be stilled by a Council which would decide Luther's affair impartially and in the spirit of Christ, for the good of the countless souls whose salvation was endangered. Such an assembly would also initiate a reform of the Church. "A number of Popes, in the remote and the recent past, had shunned such a gathering like poison, concerned, as they were, for their authority and their revenues. You yourself have no cause for anxiety; your conduct and your conscience are blameless; you need have no fear of being called to account." [5] Adrian's fellow-countryman Aurelius of Gouda already saw the great purpose nearing fulfilment and rejoiced in the present good fortune amid so many misfortunes, for "with the help of his imperial pupil, Adrian would make good the mistake of the Emperor Constantine, who to the Church's injury, bestowed wealth and power upon her".[6]

In spite of the Pope's sincere determination to do his duty by the

[1] "Suis ad populum concionibus creberrime affirmabat, neque rebus humanis pacem neque profectum ecclesiae unquam dari posse, nisi publica sacratisimae synodi editione provideretur"; thus Aurelius of Gouda in his *Apocalypsis*, C. Burmann, *Hadrianus VI* (Utrecht 1727), p. 269; an extract is to be found in *C.T.*, VOL. XII, p. xlvii.
[2] L. Geiger, *J. Reuchlin* (Leipzig 1871), pp. 311 ff.
[3] I use the *Professio fidei Adriani VI* in the bad copy in Vat. Lib., Vat. lat. 12193, fol. 5.
[4] Text of the address, edited by C. von Höfler in *Abhandlungen der Münchner Akad., historische Klasse*, IV, iii (1846), pp. 57-62; *C.T.*, VOL. XII, pp. 18-21.
[5] Burmann, *Hadrianus VI*, pp. 462 ff.; *C.T.*, VOL. XII, pp. xlviii ff.; cf. J. B. Gomis, "Vives pro Concilio", in *Verdad y vida*, III (1945), pp. 193-205.
[6] Burmann, *Hadrianus VI*, p. 313.

Church, he failed to fulfil the hopes of the advocates of a Council. There is not a trace in the record of the first months of his pontificate of a personal initiative in favour of a Council, and when the German Estates pressed him on the subject, he did nothing to meet their demand. So surprising a fact calls for an explanation. The events themselves supply it.

Adrian VI did nothing to forward the conciliar project. The whole of his pontificate is only a fragment. During the short year—reckoning from his arrival in Rome—which he had at his disposal, the tenacious but cautious and slow-moving pontiff had to contend with the countless difficulties that were bound to confront a stranger to the ways of the Curia and a foreigner into the bargain. These difficulties increased all the more as from the first day he made no secret of his determination to make a radical break with the method of government of his predecessor. He needed the assistance of able men who shared his views. He did not find them, at least not in sufficient numbers.[1] His fellow-countrymen Enckenvoirt and Heeze, and Bishop Teodoli of Cosenza, whose acquaintance he had made in Spain, enjoyed his confidence. They were conscientious workers but without experience of affairs and as slow-moving as their master. The experienced and energetic Cardinal Schiner, to whom the Pope assigned a residence in the Vatican, died in the month of December 1522.[2] Cajetan, as keen a reformer as he was a great theologian, was an "outsider" in Rome and in all probability even he was not quite clear in his own mind whether his proposals for reform [3]—some of them of a drastic kind—were capable of realisation. The jurist Campeggio was familiar with the methods of the Curia, but the Pope appears to have taken him only

[1] More thorough than Pastor, VOL. IV, ii, pp. 56 ff. (Eng. edn., VOL. IX, pp. 78 ff.), is Kalkoff's work in *H.J.*, XXXIX (1918-19), pp. 31-72, already referred to. The imperial envoy Sessa judged the collaborators exclusively by their attitude towards the Emperor; despatch of 17 October in *Cal. of St. Pap.*, *Spain*, VOL. II, pp. 493 ff.

[2] On 29 December 1522 Schiner informs Duke George of Saxony of the excellent dispositions of the Pope and promises his co-operation towards the attainment of their aim: "Nova facio omnia"; A. Büchi, *Korrespondenzen und Akten zur Geschichte des Kardinals M. Schiner*, VOL. II (Basle 1925), pp. 502 ff.; his memorial on the reform, 1 March (Pastor VOL. IV, ii, pp. 722 ff.; Eng. edn., VOL. IX, pp. 472 ff.), which has already been mentioned, is silent about the Council.

[3] It is impossible to imagine the repercussions upon the development of the Church's constitution if these proposals had been given effect; e.g. the proposal to make the election of bishops by the chapters the rule, or that of restricting the cardinals to the income they derived from the countries whose protectors they were (*C.T.*, VOL. XII, pp. 34, 37). More will be said about the suggestion, so rich of promise for the future, for the improved training of the future clergy.

gradually into his confidence.[1]   The two Neapolitans Gianpietro Carafa and Tommaso Gazzella,[2] whom Adrian had also known in Spain, have left no visible trace of their activities at the Vatican.   The Pope, in fact, did not succeed in getting in touch with those Italian circles which favoured reform.   They were still weak, it is true, but Adrian did not invite their co-operation.   But even if he had established contact with them, the fact remained that not one of the people who came to him with their proposals for reform could have been won over to the idea of a Council.[3]   They kept plodding along in the old track of the papal reform plans elaborated by the Popes of the previous generations which actually stood a chance of being carried out by the reigning pontiff: "You need no reform, the head is already reformed", Cardinal Cajetan joyfully exclaimed in the consistory of 1 September 1522.[4]

However, as often as Adrian made an attempt to reform the Curia, he discovered to his horror that every interference with the complicated system of the sale of offices and the collation of benefices threatened the financial basis of papal policy [5] and added fuel to the deep aversion and hatred of which he, as a foreigner, was the object.   His slowness in the transaction of business, of which the ambassadors complained bitterly,[6] held up ecclesiastical reforms no less than political decisions.

From conscientious motives Adrian hesitated to pursue the policy of his predecessor and to give effect to the alliance with the Emperor, to the intense annoyance of the imperial ambassador in Rome, the

---

[1] Campeggio's memorial is primarily concerned with the reform of the Curia and is remarkable for its grasp of actuality which leads him to strive for what is obtainable. It was probably inspired by Tommaso Campeggio; text in *C.T.*, VOL. XII, pp. 5-12.

[2] The invitation to the two Neapolitans is solidly attested by Carraciolo (Pastor, VOL. IV, ii, p. 31; Eng. edn., VOL. IX, p. 42), by Giovio (Burmann, *Hadrianus VI*, pp. 137 ff.) and by Seripando (Jedin, *Seripando*, VOL. II, p. 51; Eng. edn., p. 508).

[3] Severoli (Hofmann, *Forschungen*, VOL. II, p. 248; Pastor, VOL. IV, ii, pp. 69 ff.; Eng. edn., VOL. IX p. 84), confines himself to the reform of the offices; Zaccaria Ferreri (*C.T.*, VOL. XII, pp. 21-30) indulges in mere declamation; J. A. Flaminius (Vat. Lib., Vat. lat. 7754—dedication copy) is exclusively concerned with the Turkish war and Italian politics.   The small tract of Zacharias de Rhodigio (Vat. Lib., Vat. lat. 3588) is almost illegible.   To my knowledge the Minorite Thomas Illyricus alone counsels the holding of a General Council as well as provincial councils; cf. his *Clypeus status papalis* (Turin 1523), in *C.T.*, VOL. XII, p. xlix.

[4] *C.T.*, VOL. XII, p. 31.

[5] The most important result of the above-mentioned work by Göller (p. 205, *n.* 6) is to show that Adrian VI did not put a stop to the sale of offices and certain resignations, for fear of bankruptcy.   As a matter of fact the Venetian envoy also observed that the Pope was granting the regresses which he had refused at first.   Sanudo, *Diarii*, VOL. XXXIII, p. 481.

[6] Albèri, *Relazioni*, VOL. II, pp. 3, 112 f.; *Corpo diplomatico Portuguez* (Lisbon 1862-1910), VOL. II, p. 153; *Lettere di principi*, VOL. II, fol. 94ᵛ.

Duke of Sessa. He only overcame his scruples when he discovered that his political adviser, Cardinal Soderini, did not hesitate to betray him to the French. Thus the fond dream of the medieval idealists— the close alliance of Pope and Emperor for the good of Christendom— seemed about to become a reality. But it was too late, the pontificate of the last Pope of Germanic origin was drawing to its close.

In spite of its short duration Adrian's pontificate was not without an element of greatness. "Poor Christendom!" he sobbed, when told that Rhodes had fallen.[1] He thereupon set himself to organise military action against the Turks. In keeping with his thrifty character he began by saving every penny, with the result that in his lifetime he was decried as a miser, but when after his death the disappointed parasites entered his strictly guarded private room in the Torre Borgia, in the hope of treasure, all they found was some books and 2000 ducats in cash—all his other savings had been applied to purposes of public utility.[2]

Like all his undertakings, Adrian's action against the Lutheran movement was spasmodic. For him, as for every Christian whose judgment was not biased by the ideas of the conciliar theory, Luther was a heretic, hence the only charge laid on the nuncio Francesco Chieregati [3] on his departure for the Diet of Nuremberg [4] was to see to it that the Bull *Exsurge* and the Edict of Worms were obeyed. Chieregati was also the bearer of the celebrated instruction of 25 November 1522,[5] drawn up at least in substance by Adrian VI himself. In this document the Pope publicly admitted that the sins of the clergy and the Curia were largely responsible for the present troubles and announced his determination to grapple energetically with the disease. The action was without precedent and was never repeated.

---

[1] Sanudo, *Diarii*, VOL. XXXIV, p. 28.

[2] "Verum postea cognitum est Adrianum . . . multa aureorum millia praeter privatos sumptus publicis impensis reipublicae causa erogaverat." Albergati, Vat. Lib., Vat. lat. 4937, fol. 2ᵛ.

[3] Chieregati was at first in the service of Mantua and came to the future Pope's notice while the latter held the post of nuncio in Spain. Adrian raised him to the See of Teramo (1522-39). After the Pope's death Chieregati was left out in the cold. The *Diarium* referred to by Sarpi, VOL. I, p. 2 (ed. Gambarin, VOL. I, p. 38) could no longer be found in 1630, Jedin, *Der Quellenapparat der Konzilsgeschichte Pallavicinos*, pp. 60 ff. In any case Pallavicino had no access to part of the family papers which were in the possession of one Francesco Chieregati.

[4] Chieregati raised this demand already at the audience of 10 December 1522, *R.T.A.*, VOL. III, pp. 387 ff.; it is also found in the brief of 25 November (*ibid.*, pp. 399-404). For what follows see Hofmann's study, *Konzilsfrage*, pp. 34-66, on the Acts in *R.T.A.*, VOL. III, pp. 383-452.

[5] *R.T.A.*, VOL. III, pp. 390-9.

There can be no doubt that the Pope meant to defeat the revolution that had broken out by means of reforms and that he was firmly resolved to start at the top. But reforms had been promised too often and never implemented, so no one believed him.

The instruction was read at the Diet of Nuremberg on 3 January 1523, but it fell flat. Such were the princes' distrust and hatred of the Roman Curia that while they were gratified by the fact that the Pope shared their view of the religious problem—though this could not be said without reservation—they, on their part, were unable to emulate his magnanimity and breadth of outlook.[1] That which the Emperor had successfully prevented at Worms—viz. the linking of the examination of Luther's affairs with the reform of the Church—now became an actuality: the Estates demanded a Council. But they tied up their demand with conditions which bore no relation to the good-will and the magnanimity of which the Pope had given proof, so that it was difficult for him to accede to their request, justified though it was in itself. On 5 February they demanded that, with the consent of the Emperor, the Pope should convoke, if possible within a year, "a free Christian council in a city on the German border, such as Strasbourg, Mainz, Cologne or Metz".[2] It would be the Council's task to organise the war against the Turks and to take all necessary measures in the affair of Luther and on the question of reform. Meanwhile an attempt would be made, through Luther's sovereign, to persuade the heresiarch to refrain from publishing any new books, while preachers would be instructed to stick to Holy Scripture and the four Doctors of the Church.

"A free Christian council in German lands!" Such was the formula —repeated time and again—in which the German demand for a Council was presented to the Pope. It sounds unobjectionable enough, but its true significance and the pretensions it implied are only brought to light by a study of its historical background. In the memorial of the so-called "small committee",[3] the authors, the jurists Schwarzenberg,

---

[1] The remark of the Saxon councillor Planitz (Hofmann, *Konzilsfrage*, p. 45) is characteristic: "Ich halt lauter nichts davon." George of Saxony, on the other hand, felt differently for in the instructions to his representative he expressed the hope that this "teutsche babst" would bring about a Council with the help of the Emperor. *R.T.A.*, vol. III, p. 67; Gess, *Akten und Briefe*, vol. I, p. 300.

[2] *R.T.A.*, vol. III, pp. 435-43.

[3] *R.T.A.*, vol. III, pp. 417-29. On the composition of the committee see Hofmann, *Konzilsfrage*, pp. 45-54; in my opinion, however, Hofmann's view that the Council was not meant to be a general one is untenable for a far greater fight would have been put up for the addition "gemein=allgemein", and the word would not have been allowed to drop out so easily.

Zoch and Rotenhan—all of them men of Lutheran sympathies—
make it perfectly plain that for them "free" is equivalent to "independent of the Pope". The idea is that all the members of the Council
must be freed from all obligations to the Pope so that they might speak
without hindrance. For the authors of the memorial the Council is not
just a gathering of Catholic bishops under the presidency of the Pope,
the laity are also entitled to a place and a vote in it. It must be convoked
by the Pope, "with the Emperor's approval", so that "both Christian
heads" may be regarded as convening it. It must meet in a German
town. Yet in view of the ferment among the masses it would be
utterly unable to maintain its freedom and independence if it ventured
to proceed against Luther. The fact of the matter was that the intention
of the authors of the memorial was to tie the Pope's hands from the
moment of convocation, to eliminate his influence from the Council
itself, and to paralyse that of the clergy by the participation of the laity.

The memorial of the towns uses the formula in the same sense,[1] and
though the ecclesiastical princes secured a number of alterations in the
final text of the secular princes' statement,[2] none of them exclude the
original sense of the formula. Chieregati's suggestions for a revision
which would have removed at least the most objectionable features of
the document [3] were flatly rejected. The decree of 6 March brought
no elucidation of a kind that would have made the formula more
acceptable.[4]

The demand for a Council was closely linked with another equally
radical step in the affair of reform. By the terms of the above-
mentioned decree of the Diet, a list of "*gravamina* of the German
nation" was to be submitted to the Pope. The definitive formula of
this document as officially settled by the secular Estates [5] was not only
sharply anti-Roman and anticlerical, it also betrayed unmistakable

---

[1] *R.T.A.*, VOL. III, pp. 433 ff.

[2] From the memorial (*R.T.A.*, VOL. III, pp. 419-33) by a lay jurist it appears that
the ecclesiastical Estates, including Stadion of Augsburg who was being decried as a
friend of Luther, protested against the abolition of the episcopal oath and the equal
rights of the laity at the Council. They suggested Mantua for its assembly. I regard
the fact that the undoubtedly orthodox majority of the members of the Diet should
have been satisfied with a formula of this kind as one of the strongest proofs for the
view I have previously expounded on the spread of conciliarist ideas in Germany.

[3] *R.T.A.*, VOL. III, pp. 443-7. He does not refer to the equal rights of the laity
because they are taken for granted in the reply (*ibid.*, p. 449: "ecclesiastici vel laicalis
ordinis") though not explicitly stated.

[4] *R.T.A.*, VOL. III, pp. 745-8. I can find no evidence of "a falsification of the
original tendencies" by the Recess (Hofmann, *Konzilsfrage*, p. 66).

[5] *R.T.A.*, VOL. III, pp. 645-88.

traces of the Lutheran spirit.[1] The emphasis was on financial grievances while positive proposals for reform were kept in the background. This was an alarming reminder of the aims of the radicals of Basle during the conflict with Eugenius IV. To both tendencies Rome was bound to offer the most determined resistance.

We do not know what was Adrian VI's reaction to the demands of Nuremberg. Chieregati declared in general terms that the Pope would certainly not turn a deaf ear to the Estates' request for a General Council, but this does not entitle us to draw any far-reaching conclusions. Johann Eck, who went to Rome soon after the Diet on ecclesiastical business for his sovereign, dissuaded the Pope from calling a General Council; in its place he recommended a great papal reform Bull, supplemented for Germany by a new, exhaustive condemnation of Luther's teaching, as well as a special reform, to be directed from Rome.[2] On account of the gaps in our information we are not in a position to draw definite conclusions about Adrian's views and intentions, but the fact remains that during the six months, from the day when he learnt of the Nuremberg resolutions to that of his death, on 14 September 1523, he did not take a single step to meet the demand for a Council.[3]

The new Pope, Clement VII, despatched Cardinal Lorenzo Campeggio to Nuremberg as his legate.[4] In the whole College of Cardinals

---

[1] For example art. 1 on "human ordinances"; art. 4 on "Christian liberty".

[2] The piece here under consideration, *Pro Smo. D.N. Adriano VI*, is in *Beiträge zur bayrischen Kirchengeschichte*, II (1896), pp. 181-6. There we read (p. 183), "Non est alia commodior via et facilior emendandi mores corruptos et tollendi sectam Ludderanam quam per synodos provinciales, et multo efficacior quam per concilium generale quod cum difficultate potest congregari et in universali non bene applicatur medicina ad speciales morbos secundum varietatem personarum, regionum, etc." If the Council were really to meet, Eck adds (p. 189) "cavillarentur aliqui non esse liberum, aut si esset liberum, possent laici velle se immiscere". The memorial of the Bishop of Meissen, published by A. Postina in *R.Q.*, XIII (1899), pp. 337-46, takes only local problems into account.

[3] I do not deny that Adrian VI may not have thought of convoking a Council after the restoration of peace, as is asserted in the text quoted by Raynald, *Annales, a.* 1523, No. 115; such a plan would have been in keeping with his earlier views as described above. But the decisive fact is that, at least as far as we know, he did nothing to carry his intentions into effect.

[4] E. V. Cardinal, *Card. Lorenzo Campeggio* (Boston 1935), in the section about the Diet of Nuremberg (pp. 83 ff.), failed to draw on *R.T.A.*, that is, on the most important source of all. For the earlier bibliography cf. Hofmann, *Konzilsfrage*, pp. 66-94. Girolamo Rorario, who continued to assist Campeggio as nuncio to Archduke Ferdinand, does not appear to have played an important role in the matter of the Council; cf. P. Paschini, "Un Pordenonese nunzio papale nel secolo XVI, G. Rorario", in *Memorie storiche Forogiuliesi*, XXX (1934), pp. 169-216; also Gess, *Akten und Briefe*, VOL. II, pp. 57, 67, and *Monumenta Vatic. Hungariae*, II, i (Budapest 1884), pp. 94 and *passim*.

there was no one better qualified to act as his representative than this Bolognese jurist, a man with a humanistic training and, like his brother Tommaso, from whom he was inseparable, an advocate of a thorough reform of the Curia. In the course of his legation in England Campeggio had acquired sufficient political experience to enable him to appear successfully on the difficult stage of a German imperial diet. But his was an impossible task. It availed him nothing that, in accordance with his instructions, he refrained from broaching the question of a Council both at his first audience before the Diet, on 17 March 1524, and in the discussions with the Estates on the following day,[1] for the latter reiterated their demand. A "gemein concilium" (General Council) still seemed to most of them the best remedy, though they did not overlook the objections that could be raised against such a solution. Some were of opinion that a Council convoked by the Pope was not likely to meet the wishes of the Estates on account of its composition and procedure; "the holding of it would do no injury to the papal See of Rome", and it would get the Lutherans into a very dangerous situation [2]; others feared that the postponement of the Council, which was almost inevitable, would be to the advantage of the ever-spreading new religion. It was this last consideration, a justifiable one from the point of view of the Church, that led the Bavarian Dukes to propose "ain sinodum teutscher nacion"—a synod of the German nation.[3]

The idea of a provisional settlement of the religious problem by a national council had first emerged at a conference of the episcopal counsellors of the ecclesiastical province of Salzburg towards the end of 1523.[4] The Bavarians now took it up in their turn and caused it to prevail. On 5 April 1524, the Estates agreed to ask the papal legate for "ein gemain oder nacional Consilium"—a general or a national Council. Though they used less captious terms in dealing with him and were content to speak of a provincial or a general Council,[5] at bottom they meant the same thing.

Campeggio saw the danger at once: from Scylla he had drifted into

[1] *R.T.A.*, VOL. IV, pp. 471 ff., 483 ff.; cf. p. 197.
[2] Report of George von Klingenbeck, *R.T.A.*, VOL. IV, pp. 200 ff., and Lazarus Spengler's memorial, *ibid.*, pp. 484-95, esp. p. 492.
[3] *R.T.A.*, VOL. IV, p. 434.
[4] The Recess of 4 December 1523, in a German translation, published by W. Hauthaler in *Mitteilungen der Gesellschaft für Salzburger Landeskunde*, XXXVI (1896), pp. 356-63.
[5] *R.T.A.*, VOL. IV, pp. 165, 500. The towns demanded a "frei christlich Konzil oder ein anderes christliches Verhör" by honourable persons of the ecclesiastical and lay state at some suitable place in Germany, *ibid.*, p. 508.

Charybdis. He represented to the Estates [1] that a national Council composed of representatives of bishops, universities and secular princes would not be entitled even to discuss Luther's affair, much less to judge it; to permit the meeting of such an assembly would amount to allowing one nation to hold another faith than that of the universal Church and thus to conjure up a schism. There could be no question of admitting laymen to discussions on questions of faith, yet if they were excluded there was reason to fear that they would not submit to its decisions just as they had refused up till then to submit to the commands of the Pope and the Emperor. With regard to the *gravamina*, which would likewise come up for discussion at the prospective national Council, the legate denied that they had ever been officially submitted to the Pope. He left them free to send a delegation to Rome for the purpose of presenting them, but if there was only question of simple and particular reform measures, he himself was prepared to discuss them at once, since for the purpose of reform no new laws were required, it was enough to carry out the existing ones.

The demand for a national Council was emphatically rejected by the papal legate because it involved the danger of the apostasy of a whole nation; so there only remained the alternative of a General Council. He declared his readiness to press for its early convocation but added at once that there would be a delay of at least two or three years since the Pope would have to summon six different nations and he would also have to come to an understanding on the subject with the princes. Thus they were back at the point from which they had started, for it was precisely the prospect of the delay in summoning a General Council that had brought the idea of a national Council to maturity in the ranks of the Catholic-minded Estates. If things were to go on for another three years as they had up till now, Lutheranism would strike ever deeper roots in Germany in spite of *Exsurge* and the Edict of Worms. This explains why the legate's answer failed to persuade the Estates to drop their first proposal,[2] and why they persisted in their demand that a "gemein frei universal Concilium" (a free General Council) should be proclaimed while in the meantime an assembly of the German nation

---

[1] I combine the contents of the oral reply of 6 April (*R.T.A.*, VOL. IV, pp. 165 ff.) with those of the written one of 7 April (*ibid.*, pp. 167 ff.); Campeggio's duplicate (*R.T.A.*, VOL. IV, pp. 522 ff.) merely develops the arguments previously put forward. The College of Cardinals' letter to Campeggio, 8 April (publ. by E. Carusi, *In memoria di Giovanni Monticolo*, Venice 1914, pp. 141-5), exhorts the legate to remain firm and to render harmless "Lutherum serpentem, bestiam".

[2] *R.T.A.*, VOL. IV, p. 514.

which the Recess of 11 April convened for St Martin's Day, 11 November, was to be held at Speyer.[1]

There was genuine dismay in Rome when the Nuremberg decision became known. A discussion of Luther's affairs by a national Council at which secular princes would be present, amounted to a shelving both of the Bull *Exsurge* and of the Edict of Worms. It was a deliberate blow to the authority of Pope and Emperor alike. To link Luther's affair with the removal of the *gravamina*, perhaps to seek an interim solution until the Council met, would be to pave the way for Germany's permanent break with the Papacy. When consulted by the Pope the cardinals declared that the assembly of Speyer must be prevented by every means in their power.[2] In May 1524 the Pope instructed his nuncios at the imperial court, Giovanni Corsi and Bernardino Capellari, to do their utmost to prevent the Emperor from entrusting the negotiations to the Grand Chancellor Gattinara whom Rome regarded as unreliable, and to persuade him to despatch at once a special plenipotentiary to Germany with instructions to forbid the discussion of the religious problem by the assembly of Speyer.[3]

Such a step, which the Pope followed up with a letter of earnest exhortation,[4] was hardly necessary in the case of a man like Charles V, for the solution of the religious problem along ecclesiastical-national lines was contrary to his Catholic feelings as well as to his conception of the imperial authority. At this time the monarch did not yet venture to take it on himself to settle the religious question on the ground of an imperial protectorate over the Church. While Hannart, the Emperor's Nuremberg plenipotentiary, pressed him to despatch special envoys to Speyer, to name the Archduke Ferdinand his vicar, to

[1] *R.T.A.*, VOL. IV, p. 604. This solution agrees with the one proposed in the so-called Draft of Bamberg (*ibid.*, p. 500, *n.*3). The term "Nationalkonzil" was indeed avoided and even Hannart, the Emperor's representative, observed (*ibid.*, p. 777) that the convention of Speyer was not a national council. Hofmann (*Konzilsfrage*, pp. 94 ff.) has accordingly suggested that it should be described as a "national assembly", but such an appellation would obscure the ecclesiastical purpose of the gathering. I maintain the title of "national council" because the participation of the lay Estates was wholly in keeping with the ideas of the advocates of a Council. J. Weizsäcker, "Der Versuch eines Nationalkonzils in Speyer", in *H.Z.*, LXIV (1890), pp. 199-215, is among the more important works of an earlier period, as is H. Werminghoff's *Nationalkirchliche Bestrebungen im deutschen Mittelalter* (Stuttgart 1910), pp. 110 ff., for the antecedents of the idea.
[2] The memorials of Antonio del Monte and Cristoforo da Forli, publ. by W. Friedensburg, in *Q.F.*, III (1900), pp. 9, 14 ff.
[3] Balan, *Monumenta*, pp. 342 ff.
[4] Le Plat, VOL. II, pp. 223 ff. The text in Balan, *Monumenta*, pp. 335-9, appears to have been drafted by Aleander.

summon reliable theologians from Louvain and other Catholic universities with a view to strengthening the position of the Catholics,[1] and in general to act in close understanding with the Pope, Charles had recourse to a radical remedy—on 15 July he forbade the assembly.[2] "How dare one nation alter the Church's ordinances", he wrote to the Estates, "when not all the princes acting in concert with the Pope would be so bold as to attempt it?" The last of the universal monarchs was as strongly opposed to a national Council as the Pope himself.

The energetic intervention of the Emperor put an end to the plan for a national Council at Speyer. Although the Archduke Ferdinand and several princes had instructed their universities and their divines to make preparations for it,[3] they complied with the Emperor's stringent orders. For the moment the danger of a national Council as a means of solving the problem of the Church was averted, though not finally, for in the next decades the idea emerged repeatedly not only in Germany but in other threatened countries as well, such as France and Poland and competed with the idea of a General Council.

Even before the text of the imperial prohibition reached Germany, the cardinal legate had taken an important step in the matter of the reform. On 24 June the Catholic Estates of Upper Germany met at Ratisbon under his presidency, for the purpose of an agreed policy for the suppression of certain abuses among the clergy. The first part of the Formula Reformationis (cap. 1-20)[4] submitted by Campeggio was based on the Mühldorf mandate, which the delegates of the ecclesiastical province of Salzburg had agreed upon on 31 May 1522.[5] It was supplemented by a number of additional decrees, such as a decree for the reduction of holy days (c. 21) and another authorising the secular power to proceed against apostate priests (c. 26). It was easy to see

---

[1] The decisive passages in Gilles' instructions of 26 April 1524 in K. Lanz, Korrespondenz des Kaisers Karl V, VOL. I (Leipzig 1944), pp. 127 ff.

[2] C. E. Förstemann, Neues Urkundenbuch zur Geschichte der evangelischen Kirchenreformation, VOL. I (Hamburg 1842), pp. 204 ff.; Latin text in Raynald, Annales, a. 1524, Nos. 12-22; extract in Le Plat, VOL. II, pp. 237 ff. For its motivation, P. Rassow, Kaiseridee, p. 50.

[3] List of memorials of universities and theologians of the period in Hofmann, Konzilsfrage, pp. 95 ff.

[4] Le Plat, VOL. II, pp. 227-37. On the origin cf. W. Friedensburg, "Der Regensburger Convent 1524", in Historische Aufsätze Georg Waitz (Hannover 1886), pp. 502-39; supplemented by W. Hauthaler in Mitteilungen der Gesellschaft für Salzburger Landeskunde, XXXVI (1896), pp. 386 ff. This was overlooked by Hofmann, Konzilsfrage, pp. 107 ff. Further literature in Schottenloher, Nos. 41253-7.

[5] Concilia Salisburgensia, ed. Dalham (Augsburg 1788), pp. 281-7, and Hauthaler in Mitteilungen der Gesellschaft für Salzburger Landeskunde, XXXV (1895), pp. 177 ff.

that the secular princes, above all the Dukes of Bavaria, had had a hand in the drafting of the formula. The principles laid down for admission to holy orders (c. 14), for control by the ordinaries of substitutes for absentee parish priests, and for the administration of incorporated parishes (c. 10-13) as well as for the determining of an appropriate indemnification for this large category of the pastoral clergy, foreshadow the line which the Council of Trent was to adopt at a later date.

The barren criticism of the Curia which formed the main constituent of the *gravamina* was left on one side; in its place the Estates took steps to raise the standard of the pastoral ministry at home. If the Ratisbon formula had been given effect throughout Germany, as had been planned, the term "reformation" would no longer have stood for something exclusively Lutheran and a national Council would have been superfluous. It must be borne in mind that if a plan for a national Council emerged at all, the cause was the delay of a general one: the former was conceived as a substitute for the latter, or as an interim solution. By forbidding it the Emperor assumed the obligation to speed the convocation of a General Council. Hannart had come away from Nuremberg with the conviction that it could not be avoided. On his advice Charles V instructed his Roman ambassador to press the Pope to proclaim a General Council, if possible in the course of the summer and to fix the date of its assembly in the spring of the following year. For the first time Trent was mentioned as the meeting-place, on the ground that it was regarded as a German town, that is as being within the Empire though it was actually situated in Italy.[1]

A Council of Trent, convoked in the year 1524, in spite of all misgivings, in answer to the demand of the Estates of the Empire for a "free Christian council in German lands", before the new teaching and piety had struck deep roots, at the moment too when the social revolution—the war of the peasants—was provoking a great reaction on the part of all responsible people—what a perspective! It is enough to say that the Emperor's proposal fell on deaf ears; nor did he himself seriously press it. He hinted in Rome that he would not oppose the translation of the Council into the interior of Italy and to Rome itself, even before it actually met. By this action he let it be seen how anxious he was to avoid annoying the Pope and thereby driving him into the camp of his opponent Francis I of France. He accepted the fact of

---

[1] Balan, *Monumenta*, p. 351 f.

Clement VII's notorious aversion from a Council and was not inclined to try to overcome it at the cost of political disadvantages. At this time he was involved in a political conflict of world-wide significance, the issue of which would decide the fate of Europe for a hundred years: war, not a Council, was his concern at the moment.

CHAPTER III

War—No Council

THREE men settled the fate of the Council at this time: Pope Clement VII, the Emperor Charles V and King Francis I of France.

The election of the Vice-Chancellor, Giulio de' Medici, as Pope was hailed with enthusiasm in Italy. Bembo prophesied that he would be the most highly honoured and revered, the greatest and wisest of all the Popes that had ruled the Church for centuries.[1] Events failed to justify these expectations. As a cardinal, Medici had been a decided partisan of the Emperor and he owed his election to the cardinals who favoured the Emperor. It was generally expected that his policy would show a decidedly imperial orientation. These speculations proved illusory. As early as 1522 he had made secret overtures to France through his secretary Giberti. When he became Pope he regarded it as his duty—as his predecessors had done—to extricate the States of the Church from encirclement by the empire of the Habsburgs, who were masters of Naples in the South and of Milan in the North, so as to secure the independence of the Holy See. This aim, so it seemed to him, could only be attained by means of an entente with France. True, an even higher aim beckoned, one that Julius II had worked for, namely the expulsion of the "barbarians" from his beloved Italy. But even if this aim was unattainable, it was enough for the re-establishment of political equilibrium in the peninsula and for the continuation of the domination of the Medici family at Florence if France was mistress of Milan.

Clement VII failed to see that his forces and those of Italy, disunited as they were, were not adequate to the pursuit of an independent policy, for only on this presupposition would an alliance with the weaker of the two rival powers make sense. But even then such an alliance would have to be accompanied by a pooling of all available resources and carried through with determination. In this respect Clement VII was found wanting. However we may judge the French policy of this Pope, there can be no question but that its unhappy issue, with all its fatal consequences for the Church, must be laid to the pontiff's charge.

[1] Bembo to Accolti, 11 December 1523, *Opera*, VOL. III (Venice 1729), p. 54.

If it is ever right to affirm that character, not talent, decides the success or failure of a man's life, it is so in the present instance. The new Pope was intellectually wide-awake, earnest and free from moral taint.[1] His conscientiousness and thriftiness constituted a pleasing contrast to the frivolity and prodigality of his cousin Leo X, though he did not entirely disown the literary and artistic traditions of the Medici family. When he spoke he did so readily and prudently, but he was also willing to listen to others. On the other hand, he had two fatal characteristics. Standing as he was in the very centre of an epoch of momentous decisions in the spiritual sphere, he became wholly tied up in politics: his thoughts were almost exclusively determined by the categories of Italian dynastic politics. To this were added a dreadful indecision, vacillation and timidity, so that amid endless negotiations and half-measures he let slip his best opportunites and ended by earning for himself from friend and foe alike a reputation for unreliability.[2]

[1] Since Pastor, VOL. IV, ii, pp. 176-643 (1907), Eng. edn., VOL. IX, pp. 243, F. X. Seppelt alone in *Das Papsttum im Spätmittelalter und in der Zeit der Renaissance* (Leipzig 1941) has provided a general survey based on personal studies. The works of G. Constant, *La Réforme en Angleterre*, VOL. I (Paris 1930), English translation, *The Reformation in England*, London 1934-41, and P. Grabites, *Clement VII and Henry VIII* (London 1936), on the English schism, and those of A. Lodolini, *L'assedio di Firenze, 1529-31* (Florence 1930), and F. Gilbert in *Archivio storico italiano*, XCIII (1935), pp. 3-24, on Clement VII's domestic policy, touch on our subject only indirectly. W. Rolf, "Klemens VII und Carnesecchi", in *Repertorium für Kunstwissenschaft*, XLV (1925), pp. 117-40, discusses the portrait of the years 1530-2 by Sebastiano del Piombo; E. Constantini in *Atti della deput. storica delle Marche*, 1928, pp. 119-34, comments on a satire on the Pope composed after his death. For a character-study of Clement VII the Venetian Albèri, *Relazioni*, VOL. II, iii, pp. 126 f., 277 ff., Giovio, *Historia sui temporis*, XXXII (I use the Venice edn. of 1553), and especially Guicciardini, *Storia d'Italia* (ed. Panigada, Bari 1929, VOL. IV, pp. 327 ff.), remain indispensable. The collection of political briefs begun by P. Arendt, which should supplement the very incomplete accounts of the nunciatures (cf. A. Pieper, *Zur Entstehungsgeschichte der ständigen Nuntiaturen*, Freiburg 1894, pp. 65-93), is unfortunately not yet in print. Ordinary nuncio at the imperial court between 1524 and 1529 was Baldassare Castiglione, whose letters were published by P. A. Serassi, *Lettere del Conte B. Castiglione*, VOL. I, Padua 1769; VOL. II, Parma 1771. There is a good deal of information on the imperial court in *Cal. of St. Pap., Spain*, VOLS. II-IV, and in the reports of the Polish envoy Dantiscus, *Acta Tomiciana*, VOLS. VII-XII. Parallel with Castiglione's nunciature were the legations of Cardinal Giovanni Salviati and several extraordinary nunciatures. Under Clement VII the latter were often more important than the ordinary ones. Aleander was the first ordinary nuncio to France, cf. J. Paquier, "Nonciature d'Aléandre auprès de François I", in *Annales de St Louis des Français*, I (1896), pp. 271-326; *id., J. Aléandre* (Paris 1900), pp. 303-36; Acciajuoli was nuncio from 1525 to 1527 (E. L. Fraikin, *Nonciatures de Clement VII*, VOL. I, Paris 1906). The introduction to the unpublished continuation of this work appears in *Mélanges d'archéologie et d'histoire*, XXVI (1906), pp. 513-63.

[2] "Discorre bene ma risolve male", says Soriano, Albèri, *Relazioni*, VOL. II, iii, p. 285.

This is not to say that Clement VII was personally lacking in religious sense or concern for the Church.[1] A provincial Council in 1517, while he was still Archbishop of Florence, proves that he was well aware of the need of reform in the Church. Soon after his elevation to the Chair of St Peter he appointed a commission of cardinals for the purpose of giving effect to the decrees of the Lateran Council. He saw to it that the justly acquired rights of third parties were not infringed by the Segnatura. He refrained from simony and crass nepotism and here and there encouraged attempts at personal reform. For all that, after six years of his pontificate Contarini had to admit that "though the Pope desires the suppression of abuses in holy Church he never carries his desires into effect and takes no step to that end".[2] Reform was co-ordinated with, not to say subordinated to, other undertakings. The safeguarding of his political position was the Pope's chief concern. With all the resources of a tortuous and positively cunning diplomacy, this inscrutable, scheming exponent of the politician's craft[3] worked for one grand objective, viz. the preservation of his personal prestige and the securing for the Medici of a leading position in Italy. Instead of choosing *one* political adviser, whose clear-sightedness and determination would have made up for the qualities he lacked himself, Clement had *two*, and these were engaged in an unending political tug of war. They were the Dominican Nicholas von Schönberg, Archbishop of Capua[4] and the Datary, Gian Matteo Giberti, Bishop of Verona.[5] All the latter's sympathies were with France. From the first he contrived to get his imperial rival out of Rome, for months at a time, on diplomatic missions to the Western powers, so as to secure a preponderant influence for himself. His collaborators were two Italians in the service of France—Alberto Pio of Carpi and Ludovico di Canossa, Bishop of

---

[1] Pastor, VOL. IV, ii, pp. 577 ff.; Eng. edn., VOL. X, pp. 378 ff. An authenticated copy of the Bull *Meditatio cordis* of 21 November 1524 is in Vat. Lib., Raccolta I, p. iv, 1680.

[2] Albèri, *Relazioni*, VOL. II, iii, p. 265.

[3] Thus Cardinal Loaysa; G. Heine, *Briefe an Karl V geschrieben von seinem Beichtvater Loaysa in den Jahren 1530-32* (Berlin 1848), pp. 86, 195, 401; in what follows I quote from the extremely important letters of Loaysa sometimes from the second edition in *Collección de documentos inéditos*, VOL. XIV (Madrid 1849).

[4] Cf. P. Kalkoff, in *Z.K.G.*, XXXI (1910), pp. 382 ff.; XXXII (1911), pp. 60 ff.; M. A. Walz, "Zur Lebensgeschichte des Kardinals N. von Schönberg", in *Mélanges Mandonnet*, VOL. II (Paris 1930), pp. 371-87.

[5] Most important for Giberti's political activity is T. Pandolfi's "G. M. Giberti e l'ultima difesa della libertà d'Italia negli anni 1521-25", in *Archivio della Soc. Rom. di storia patria*, XXXIV (1911), pp. 231-7. The biography of Pighius (2nd edn., Verona 1934), is inadequate in this respect.

Bayeux. The imperial party could not cope with these men, were it only that Charles V's diplomatists, the Duke of Sessa and later on Miguel Mai, had none of the skill that his military leaders displayed in their respective sphere. Jacopo Salviati, a brother-in-law of Leo X and closely connected with the Pope, was powerless, even with the assistance of his son Cardinal Giovanni Salviati, to neutralise these naturally opposed influences. However, the Emperor's military successes were not lost on the Pope, with the result that his policy pursued a zigzag course towards an uncertain goal. His neutrality, which he observed with great outward show, was not inspired by a sense of his spiritual authority as head of the whole Church but solely by an Italian dynast's fluctuations between two great powers.

All the contemporary students of Clement VII's character are agreed that he was exceedingly timorous.[1] This trait of his character affected his attitude to the question of a Council.[2] Since the days of Basle the convocation of a General Council was very properly regarded as a grave venture; but now that a great movement of apostasy had started north of the Alps the risk was immeasurably increased. How could a Pope who was generally thought to have been born out of wedlock, whose election was suspect on the ground of simony, whose domestic policy was open to so much criticism, face with equanimity an assembly of this kind?

The election capitulation which he had sworn to observe did not

[1] G. Contarini: "La natura del papa è supra modum timida e vile", in Dittrich, *Regesten*, p. 60; Foscari: "molto timido"; Soriano: "di non ordinaria timidità", Albèri, *Relazioni*, VOL. II, iii, pp. 126, 278; Guicciardini also speaks of "timidità d'animo", xx, xii.

[2] The fact of Clement VII's fear of a Council is beyond doubt. When Loaysa wrote on 8 October 1530 (*Coll. doc. inéd.*, VOL. XIV, p. 90): "Este nombre de concilio aborresce el papa come si le mentasen al diablo", he is in agreement with such well-informed and trained observers as Guicciardini (xx, iii, ed. Panigada, VOL. V, p. 300), Antonio Soriano (Albèri, *Relazioni*, VOL. II, iii, pp. 297 ff.) and Gattinara ("Historia vite", ed. C. Bornate, in *Miscellanea di storia italiana*, XLVII (1915), p. 235). It is worth noting that the Venetian diplomatists only hint at this *arcanum* but at no time speak of it openly, e.g. Tiepolo (Albèri, *Relazioni*, VOL. I, i, p. 69), during the lifetime of the pontiff. Against this cloud of contemporary witnesses to the Pope's fear of the Council his own words, even when embodied in official documents, are unable to prevail because they are confuted by events. In my opinion discussion can only be about the motives of this fear, that is, whether material or personal ones predominated, for there can be no doubt that both were at work. As for the birth of the Pope, I must point out that the Bull of Legitimisation of 20 September 1513 (Balan, *Monumenta*, pp. 470 ff.) failed to remove the widely held opinion that Floreta had been the mistress, not the clandestine wife, of Giuliano de' Medici, were it only that before his investiture with benefices Giulio had not hesitated to pray for a dispensation from the "defectus natalium".

bind him in any way.[1] When approached with a request for a Council he promptly took evasive action. Both he and his legate Campeggio followed Aleander's advice [2]: "Never offer a Council, never refuse it directly; on the contrary, show a readiness to comply with the request but at the same time stress the difficulties that stand in the way; by this means you will be able to ward it off." On this principle Clement VII acted throughout his pontificate. When challenged with a demand for a Council, he never answered with a blunt negative; as a matter of fact, he answered in the affirmative on more than one occasion, but his assent was qualified by a number of clauses and by the hope that events would prevent the fulfilment of his promise. In his heart of hearts the Pope feared and abhorred a Council.[3]

The longer a Council was delayed, the more emphatically did Charles V become the driving power in the matter.[4] Charles was the son of easy-going Philip of Burgundy and unhappy Joanna of Castile. Under the supervision of his aunt Margaret he had been given a strict religious upbringing. But he had also been trained in the ways and manners of the Burgundian court. All his life, in spite of a gradual assimilation to a Spaniard's appearance, he retained his Burgundian nature. His love for knightly exercises and the solemn pomp that had obtained at the court of Philip the Good [5] he owed to his lay tutor

---

[1] P. Berti, "Alcuni documenti che servono ad illustrare il pontificato e la vita di Clemente VII", in *Giornale storico degli archivi Toscani*, II (1858), pp. 102-28; text of the election capitulation, pp. 107-16.

[2] Döllinger, *Beiträge*, VOL. III, p. 254.

[3] Thus also Rassow, *Kaiseridee*, p. 34; for the Pope the Council was the heaviest blow that could have been dealt him.

[4] It will be enough to single out here the monograph by K. Brandi, *Kaiser Karl V*, a remarkable work on account of the author's mastery of his material. In a second volume, *Quellen und Erörterungen*, the pertinent literature is presented not in the form of a dead bibliography but in that of a lively discussion. The vast collection of sources about which he and his collaborators were wont to keep us informed in *Nachrichten der Göttinger Akademie* is not likely to be published in present circumstances. The Spanish conception developed by R. Menéndez Pidal, *La idea imperial de Carlos V* (Madrid 1940), is also held by F. Cereceda, "Origen español de la idea imperial en Carlos V", in *Razón y Fe*, CXXVI (1942), pp. 239-47. For Charles's attitude to the Council see Rassow, *Kaiseridee*, which is still a useful source of information. I was unfortunately unable to consult O. Lehnoff's *Die Beichtväter Karls V* (Dissertation, Göttingen 1932). Utterly foreign to Charles's mind was the "romgelöste deutsche Kaiseridee" of some German humanists and dreamers of whom W. Köhler speaks in his essay "Die Deutsche Kaiseridee zum Anfang des 16. Jahrhunderts", in *H.Z.*, CXLIX (1934), pp. 35-56.

[5] For Burgundian culture see the colourful descriptions of J. Huizinga, *Herbst des Mittelalters*, 2nd edn. Munich 1928 (Eng. edn., *The Waning of the Middle Ages*, London 1924); "L'Etat Bourguignon, ses rapports avec la France et les origines d'une nationalité néerlandaise", in *Le Moyen Age*, XL (1940), pp. 171-93; XLI (1931),

Chièvres, while for his deep, solid and enlightened piety and his devotion to the Holy See he had to thank his ecclesiastical teacher, Adrian of Utrecht, the future Pope. In 1516 he came of age and so entered first into the inheritance of one grandfather in Spain, and on his election as Emperor into that of the other in the Empire. Chièvres, who leaned towards France, remained at the head of affairs until 1521 when the Piedmontese Gattinara, who had succeeded Sauvage as Grand Chancellor, took over from him. Gattinara's position by the side of the young prince differed from that of a Grand-Chamberlain. He was not a guardian; his task was to educate the prince for independent action. Under his wise guidance Charles grew up amid the problems, big with consequences, with which this third decade of the century faced him, as the autocrat of the first world-wide empire known to Western history since the fall of the Roman Empire.

Gasparo Contarini, who had watched the young monarch over a period of several years, draws a masterly portrait of him.[1] He describes him as "well-proportioned in body—including even his prominent chin—second to none in his entourage in the use of arms; sincerely devout, a lover of justice, without a flaw in his character and with no taste for the amusements which young men usually delight in. The chase is his only recreation; the affairs of state constitute his real pleasure. The greater part of the day is spent in attending the sessions of the Council of State, where he gives proof of great powers of endurance. He speaks little and is less affable than his brother Ferdinand, stingy rather than liberal, and for that reason unpopular with the Spaniards and the Aragonese. His conduct remains unchanged in good and in bad fortune, but since his is a melancholy temperament he is more inclined to gloom than to cheerfulness. He is slow to forget injuries; he does not lust after territorial acquisitions, his ambition is to preserve what he has inherited and nothing would please him more than a great crusade and to fight in a big battle. The Spaniards have no real love for him because he continues to favour the Flemings among whom he grew up; they prefer his brother for whom, on the other hand, the Germans have no love because of his adoption of Spanish ways."

pp. 11-35, 83-96; "Burgund", in *H.Z.*, CXLVIII (1933), pp. 1-28, also in *Im Bann der Geschichte* (Basle 1943), pp. 303-39; *ibid.*, the fine character-study of Philip the Good as sketched in contemporary literature, pp. 340-76. On Charles's aunt, cf. C. de Wiart, *Marguerite d'Autriche* (Paris 1935), and Brandi, *Quellen*, pp. 62 ff., 73 ff.

[1] Albèri, *Relazioni*, VOL. I, ii, pp. 60 ff.; for later characteristics, Gachard, *Relations des ambassadeurs vénitiens sur Charles V et Philippe II* (Brussels 1855).

Later observers have added further traits to the Emperor's portrait in the period of his maturity and his triumphs, but the internal motive power of his rule remained unchanged, namely, a strong dynastic consciousness and a medieval conception of the imperial dignity. Both these dispositions were firmly anchored in a strong, living profession of Catholic Christianity. These sentiments are revealed in the above-mentioned protestation written with his own hand at the time of the Diet of Worms, in which the twenty-one-year-old monarch defined his attitude to Luther [1]: "I am a descendant of the Christian Emperors of the noble German nation and of the Catholic Kings of Spain, the Archdukes of Austria and the Dukes of Burgundy, all of whom were loyal sons of the Roman Church until death. I am ready at all times to defend the Catholic faith, the sacred ceremonies, decrees, ordinances and sacred traditions of the Church, for the glory of God, the spread of the faith and the salvation of souls. It would be an everlasting shame for myself, for you and for the noble German nation, who by a special privilege are called to defend and protect the Catholic faith, if in our time, I do not say heresy, but the mere suspicion of heresy, or any other injury to the Christian religion, were to gain ground through any fault of ours. . . ." The young monarch is conscious that it is his duty before God and before history to preserve the inheritance that came to him through his birth—his crown, lands, and peoples and the Christian way of life. He sees the vast territories he has inherited and the power they represent as a gift from God, calling for gratitude on his part. This he is resolved to show by his services to Christendom, of which his elevation to the Empire has made him the secular head. To serve Christendom is to make war against the infidels, to extirpate heresy, to cleanse the Church from abuses.[2] When, on the eve of the battle of Pavia, fear seized him that he might die without a single great achievement to his credit, there arose before his eyes the tempting vision of an expedition to Italy, the imperial crown, and the example of Charlemagne.[3] The coronation at Bologna was the realisation of this dream, even if only a partial one, as well as the symbol of the wonderfully complete philosophy of life of this, the last medieval Emperor.

[1] *R.T.A.*, VOL. II, p. 595; Charles spoke in the same terms at Augsburg in 1530, Rassow, *Kaiseridee*, p. 402 f.

[2] On the eve of the Diet of Augsburg, 14 June 1530, Loaysa reminded the monarch of an earlier protestation: "Que deseaba emplear su vida en defension de la fé, porque con otra cosa no os parecía poder recompensar las mercedes que de Dios habiades recibidos." *Coll. doc. inéd.*, VOL. XIV, p. 26, Rassow, *Kaiseridee*, p. 30.

[3] Brandi, *Berichte*, x, p. 258 f.; see below, p. 227, *n.* 2.

To a ruler inspired by such ideals the thought of a Council for the solution of pending ecclesiastical problems was bound to occur spontaneously; as a matter of fact the convocation of such an assembly had been one of his youthful dreams. "Even as a boy", he told Niccolò Tiepolo in 1530,[1] "I thought of making arrangements for a Council." As a mature man he became the most energetic and most persistent champion of the idea of a Council. The influence of his political tutor, Gattinara, had something to do with these dispositions.

Gattinara too was an adherent of the idea of a Council; in fact it was a substantial ingredient of his political philosophy.[2] Moved by Ghibelline ideals—which recall the memory of Dante—he never wearied of drawing Charles's attention to the fact that Italy was the key to his political predominance in Europe, and to press on him his own notions of empire and universal monarchy. In a memorial of the year 1523 [3] he told the Emperor: "Your affairs are the affairs of the whole of Christendom and in a sense those of the whole world." Two years later he wrote that if the Emperor, in his role of advocate and defender of the Church, wished to turn all his strength against the enemies of the holy faith, to suppress the errors of Luther, to reform Christendom and to drive off the Turks, he must see to it that a Council was convened. We have already heard the High Chancellor's remark to Aleander at the Diet of Worms, that Luther's business could only be disposed of by a Council. That he viewed such a gathering as a reform Council we learn from his autobiography, in which he states that he had declined Leo X's offer of a cardinal's hat because he foresaw a great persecution of the clergy and felt that he could promote the reform of the Church

---

[1] J. von Walter, *Die Depeschen des Venezianischen Gesandten N. Tiepolo* (Berlin 1928), p. 66.

[2] K. Brandi, *Berichte*, IX, "Eigenhändige Aufzeichnungen Karls V aus dem Jahre 1525"; "Der Kaiser und sein Kanzler", in *Nachrichten der Göttinger Gesellschaft der Wissenschaften, phil.-hist. Klasse 1933* (Berlin 1933), pp. 240 ff. The chief source for the life of Gattinara is C. Bornate "Historia vite et gestorum per d. magnum cancellarium", in *Miscellanea di storia italiana*, XLVII (1915), pp. 231-585; the earlier bibliography by H. Van der Linden, "Le Chancelier Gattinara et la politique mediteranéenne de Charles Quint", in *Acad. Royale de Belgique, Bulletin des lettres*, CI (1936), pp. 361-72. It would be delightful, from the point of view of the history of ideas, to look for the sources of Gattinara's notion of the Council. The Pavia law school may be ruled out for he was self-taught on the whole and I am rather thinking of such authors as Roselli and Ludovicus Romanus. It may be that during his stay in Franche-Comté he became acquainted with parliamentary Gallicanism. The influence of his idea of a Council upon Charles V is not disproved by the otherwise very remarkable explanations given by Menéndez Pidal, *La idea imperial de Carlos V*, pp. 17 ff.

[3] Brandi, *Berichte*, IX, p. 243 f.; Balan, *Monumenta*, pp. 78 ff.

more effectively as a layman.[1] For all that, Gattinara realised full well what a formidable political weapon the demand for a Council might prove when used against a Pope such as Clement VII. The threat of a Council in 1526 was his work. Contrariwise, as often as he felt the need of securing the Pope's support for the Emperor's cause, he took good care not to put him out by talk about conciliar plans since this would have driven the pontiff into the arms of France. But as soon as he felt stronger he took them up once more. Thus, after the victory of Pavia, he advised the Emperor to proceed to Italy in order to restore peace to Christendom in conjunction with the Pope, to concert measures for war against the Turks and the suppression of Lutheranism and to make arrangements for a reform Council. But, he added, this last point should not be mentioned as yet because there was nothing the Pope was more afraid of than such a Council. On the other hand he would never convoke it of his own accord, hence the plan must be kept back until a suitable time.[2] It is clear that for Gattinara a Council was not just an ecclesiastical postulate, it was also an instrument of imperial power-politics and one of the requirements of *raison d'Etat*. His keenness for a Council subsided with the rise of political misgivings; he only took action when the Emperor removed the question of the Council from the sphere of diplomacy to transfer it to that of conscience. Charles V himself confirms the fact in his memoirs, when he says that from the year 1529 he had steadily worked for a Council.[3] Up to that time Gattinara had always restrained him whenever he took a step in that direction.

The Venetian envoy, Giustiniano Capello, reports that Francis I of France was wont to say that the Emperor went out of his way to do always the opposite of what he himself was doing.[4] As a matter of fact the "roi chevalier", whose passion for tournaments and the chase was only equalled by his passion for women, formed in many respects a complete contrast to the Habsburg ruler.[5] His imposing appearance and regal dignity, joined with great affability, won for him the love of his people; his wit and his ability to speak with ease on every possible

[1] Bornate, "Historia vite", in *Miscellanea di storia italiana*, XLVII (1915), p. 277 f.
[2] Bornate, "Historia vite", *ibid.*, p. 463.
[3] A. Morel-Fatio, *Historiographie de Charles-Quint*, VOL. I (Paris 1913), p. 254 f.
[4] Albèri, *Relazioni*, VOL. I, i, p. 204.
[5] Among modern character-sketches I mention the following: Ranke, *Französische Geschichte* (Stuttgart and Tübingen 1852), VOL. I, pp. 84-115; Lavisse-Lemonnier, *Histoire de France*, VOL. V, i (Paris 1911), pp. 187-95; F. Hackett, *Francis the First* (New York 1936), "colourful but pure journalism" in Brandi's opinion (*Quellen*, p. 81). Ch. Terrasse, *François I, le Roi et le Règne* (Paris 1943), up to the Peace of Madrid.

AETHERNA IPSE SVAE MENTIS SIMVLACHRA LVTHERVS
EXPRIMIT·AT VVLTVS CÉRA LVCAE OCCIDVOS
·M·D·X·X·

MARTIN LUTHER AS A MONK

*After the engraving by Cranach in the British Museum,
dated 1520*

subject fascinated ambassadors while his patronage of literature and the arts attracted humanists and artists to France. Although he never missed an opportunity to boast of his Catholicism and his devotion to the Holy See and suppressed the French followers of Luther, he lacked any deep personal piety. While Charles V devoted every hour of the day to the discharge of his duties, Francis, to the despair of the papal nuncio Acciajuoli,[1] would spend whole days in frivolous amusements or in the chase and so let slip important political opportunities. Spoilt from his childhood by his mother and sister, he remained all his life an egoist of disarming naivety, with a gift of dazzling people, not without noble and generous feelings but lacking that loyalty and reliability which presuppose a solid moral foundation. There were times when he felt the urge to do great things but indolence rendered him irresolute in the affairs of state and he was for ever dependent on an all-powerful minister, whether it was Louise of Savoy or Montmorency. He was always ready with promises which were never followed by deeds; skilful in looking after his own interests, he knew no scruples in the choice of means—in a word, Francis was a prince after Macchiavelli's own heart and poles apart from the ideals that inspired the soul of Charles V.

As the ruler of the most populous and most powerful single state in Europe, Francis I was not prepared to surrender the hegemony of the continent to the Habsburg monarch, his superior by reason of the number and extent of his widely distributed states, though not their homogeneous strength. Francis's whole life was accordingly one long fight—a political and military duel—with his slow-moving, cautious but tenacious opponent. The chief prizes of the contest were, firstly, the Duchy of Milan, the possession of which would secure for Francis the mastery of Italy and deprive his adversary's two great territorial masses of their connecting link, and, secondly, that pearl of the Burgundian dominions—the Netherlands. It was an advantage for him that he had behind him a willing, united country whose aristocracy fought his battles, whose clergy provided him with diplomats and money, whose people paid high taxes and endured the hardships of his many campaigns. Uninhibited by religious considerations, the Most Christian King joined hands with Charles's enemies—the Turks and the German Protestants—and allied himself with them in order to weaken the power of the Habsburg world-empire. The Emperor was never able to understand why this open treason to the cause of

[1] Fraikin, *Nonciatures de Clement VII*, VOL. I, p. 213 f.

Christendom did not immediately cause the Pope and other Christian princes to swing round to his side. But the Emperor's thoughts were still running in the categories of medieval universalism, whereas his opponent pursued the policy of a European equilibrium to which, in his opinion, infidels and heretics alike should make their contribution.

In the eyes of Francis I a Council was no longer a representative assembly of Christendom, as it had been viewed in the early and late Middle Ages. For him it was only a move on the chess-board of European politics by which the Emperor sought to defeat political and religious opposition within the Empire, to obtain help against the Turks and to extend his personal power. It was precisely this that Francis wished to prevent. Thus it came about that the French King became the most powerful opponent of a Council. During two whole decades he thwarted every attempt to secure Luther's condemnation and the solution of the problem of reform by means of a Council. The historic opposition between the house of Habsburg and the house of Valois[1] became the chief political obstacle to a Council. France, that citadel of conciliar theory, did more to prevent the Council of Trent than any other country.

If we would understand the course of the mighty struggle between the two monarchs we must retrace our steps somewhat and recapitulate what has been said already. The prelude to the first campaign, which lasted seven years, was Robert von der Mark's irruption into the Low Countries in the spring of 1521 and the attack of the French against Navarre. At this time, that is on 28 May 1521, Charles V was concluding the alliance with Leo X which protected his flank in Italy. On his part the Emperor undertook to reinstate the Sforzas in the Duchy of Milan, to restore Parma and Piacenza to the States of the Church and to guarantee the sovereignty of the Medici at Florence. The negotiations for a compromise over which Cardinal Wolsey presided

---

[1] The earlier German, Italian and French specialised works on the course of the war (especially Grethen, Hellwig, Balan, Professione) are listed by Pastor, VOL. IV, ii (Eng. edn., VOL. VIII). His views agree with those of Ehses in "Die Politik Clemens' VII bis zur Schlacht von Pavia", in *H.J.*, VI (1885), pp. 557-603, VII (1886), pp. 553-593. G. de Leva's presentation, *Storia documentata di Carlo V in correlazione all' Italia*, VOL. II (Venice 1864), remains indispensable by reason of its documentation. E. Pacheco y de Leva, *La Política española en Italia. Correspondencia de Don Fernando Marín, Abad de Nájera con Carlos V*, VOL. I (Madrid 1919), embraces only the years 1521-3. K. Brandi, "Der Weltreichsgedanke Karls V", in *Ibero-amerikanisches Archiv*, XIII (1939), pp. 259 ff., makes the acute observation that the opposition between Charles and Francis was but the continuation of the opposition between the houses of Burgundy and Valois.

at Calais and Bruges came to nothing. Gattinara gave it as his opinion that war was inevitable. On 19 November 1521 Charles V's generals Colonna and Pescara entered Milan and their victory at Bicocca, on 27 April 1522, overthrew the French domination in Lombardy. Gattinara's first objective had been attained; another beckoned from near by. The elevation of Adrian of Utrecht to the Papacy opened the prospect of a much closer and firmer understanding between the two heads of Christendom than had been possible under Leo X. However, the one-time teacher now disappointed his pupil. Adrian refused to lend the Emperor any active assistance; on the other hand he carefully refrained from the least symptom of partiality towards France, and all the time he urged the need of warlike action against the Turks. This attitude of the Pope hit Charles V all the more painfully as in the meantime his military situation had deteriorated and he experienced the greatest difficulty in extricating himself from his financial straits; hence he felt greatly relieved when, after the fall of the traitor Cardinal Soderini on 30 April 1523, the Pope proclaimed a three years' truce. However, the swing-round came too late: four months later Adrian was dead.

It looked as if his successor would at the very least turn to Leo X's policy; but Clement VII also proved a disappointment for the Emperor. While Schönberg's two missions to the courts of France, Spain and England were little more than a peace gesture which the Pope owed it to his office to make, other symptoms showed that the Pope was bent on pursuing an Italian, and above all a Medician policy. In this political scheme Milan dependent on France would constitute a natural counterpoise to Naples controlled by the Habsburgs. The Pope accordingly refused openly to renew the convention of 1521. He continued to pay his subsidies, but did so in secret, and ended by sending to the theatre of war in Upper Italy an ardent Italian patriot, Gian Giberti, who was nevertheless heart and soul with the French. In northern Italy the situation had changed in favour of the latter. The defection of the Connétable Charles de Bourbon and his throwing in his lot with the Emperor did not produce the results that had been expected. While an imperial army vainly besieged Marseilles, Francis I invaded Lombardy at the head of a powerful army and occupied Milan on 26 October 1524. Was Charles VIII's victorious progress about to be repeated?

Clement VII had not forgotten the fate of his house on that occasion. Though he could not shut his eyes to the dangers to which another march of the French upon Naples exposed the Papacy and the States of the Church, he thought the safest course was to support what looked like the winning side. He accordingly concluded a treaty with Francis I on 12 December 1524, by the terms of which he granted the French troops a passage through the Papal States. However, all his calculations were shattered by the crushing defeat of the French at Pavia on 24 February 1525. This victory made the Emperor the unchallenged master of Italy, not to say of Europe. To the French King, now his prisoner, he dictated the Peace of Madrid (14 January 1526), the conditions of which could not possibly be fulfilled. The Pope deemed it expedient to attempt a *rapprochement* with Charles. But at this moment fear of the hegemony of the house of Habsburg once more brought together all its enemies and won new ones for it. England, until now the Emperor's ally, concluded an advantageous separate peace with France. In Italy, the Emperor's enemies sought to win over to their side Pescara, the commander of Charles's armies, with a promise of the crown of Naples. With his help they hoped to shake off the Spanish yoke and to restore her liberty to Italy. Pescara was not to be tempted. The Emperor had the chief instigator of the plot, the Milanese Chancellor Girolamo Morone, thrown into prison and took the duchy under his immediate control. This was precisely what both Clement VII and Giberti had been most afraid of. Thereupon the Pope openly took the part of Francis I, who had been set at liberty in the meantime and now refused to implement the terms of the Peace of Madrid. On 22 May 1526 the Pope concluded with him the League of Cognac.

We pass over the confused negotiations that ensued: they culminated in the horror of the "Sack of Rome". On 6 May 1527, a mutinous imperial army composed of Germans, Spaniards and Italians and led by the Connétable seized Rome and sacked it ruthlessly. The Pope was besieged in the Castle of Sant' Angelo. On 5 June he was forced to capitulate; he remained a prisoner in the castle and was only set at liberty six months later. Thus a Medici was forced to look on while the Rome of the Renaissance was being battered by barbarians who executed with sacrilegious fury the judgment foretold by Savonarola. There was only one thing for him to do—he must come to terms with the Emperor. On 29 June 1529 the Pope concluded the Peace of Barcelona with Charles V and on 3 August of the same year Francis I followed suit with the conclusion of the "Ladies' Peace" of Cambrai.

It was necessary to describe this medley of negotiations, alliances and battles so as to make it perfectly clear that a truly oecumenical Council—one that could deal with questions of faith and reform— could not be thought of during those years. Not one of those in a position of authority—they all belonged to the Latin world—fully appreciated the import of the religious movement in Germany. All three treated the question of a Council more or less as a political opportunity, as in the days of Louis XI, not as a requirement of the Church. Prisoners as they were of the old way of seeing things, they kept to the track laid down in those days. Not one of them really wanted a Council. As star shells momentarily light up a nocturnal battlefield only to go out after a brief while, so did the idea of a Council arise in the course of the negotiations only to fade out before a single step had been taken to bring it about. The initiative lay with the imperial court. We have already mentioned in the previous chapter that in the summer of 1524, when the Emperor forbade the projected national council of Speyer, he instructed his Roman ambassador to press the Pope to convoke a General Council. With a view to calming the Pope's fears he assured him that he would protect him in every way; he even let it transpire that he would put no obstacle to the translation of the Council from Trent, which he had proposed for the gathering, to some town in Italy and even to Rome itself. Yet the Duke of Sessa did not dare to carry out his commission [1] lest the mere mention of the word Council should definitely throw the Pope into the arms of the French King. The imperial proposal for a Council was not delivered. Clement VII, however, had seen it coming and had long ago taken his counter-measures: they came out of the political-ecclesiastical arsenal of the Renaissance Popes. A Roman reform convention, reinforced by representatives of foreign nations, would render a General Council superfluous. A plan of this kind undoubtedly existed, but owing to the fragmentary nature of the account that has come down to us our reconstruction of it must of necessity be incomplete.

It would seem that the preparations for this Roman reform convention dated from the first months of Clement's pontificate. They were not prompted by the decisions of Nuremberg. In a letter to the Emperor, dated 31 July 1524,[2] Clement wrote: "Soon after the beginning of our pontificate we summoned prelates and bishops from

---

[1] Instruction of 24 July 1524, Heine, *Briefe*, p. 518 f.; without date in Balan, *Monumenta*, p. 351 f.; *Cal. of St. Pap., Spain*, VOL. II, p. 660 (24 August 1524).

[2] Balan, *Monumenta saec. XVI*, pp. 24 ff.; corresponding answer to the chancellor of Gnesen, Miszkowski, *Acta Tomiciana*, VOL. VII, pp. 285 ff.

almost every nation, so that we might have the benefit of their counsel and their co-operation in the task of the reform of the Church." One of those summoned at that time we know: he was Bishop Bobadilla of Salamanca. The fate of his summons was also the fate of the reform convention. Just as Bobadilla was about to obey the call he received two imperial orders enforcing the duty of residence and threatening him with the sequestration of his revenues in case of non-compliance. Bobadilla bowed to the injunction. There was no doubt about it, the Emperor was determined to do his utmost to prevent the convention. However, the Pope stuck to his plan. In the autumn of 1524, made wise, perhaps, by his experience with Spain, he requested King Sigismund of Poland to despatch some Polish prelates to Rome for the purpose of discussing the question of Church reform. However, at this very time the King had taken the field. The Pope's letter was put on one side. The King only answered it on 1 May 1525. In principle, he wrote, he was willing to comply with the Pope's request; but he feared that the proposed measures were inadequate; what was needed was a General Council. This reply was as good as a refusal, all the more so as the Archbishop of Gnesen, John Laski, who had inspired it, was at this very time making a formal proposal, through Chancellor Miszkowski, for the convocation of a General Council [1] and at this very moment was successfully engaged in persuading Hungary to make a similar demand.[2]

A memorial on the projected convention which Clement VII submitted to the Grand Chancellor Gattinara, probably through Cardinal Salviati, in the spring of 1525,[3] also failed to elicit a favourable reply. The Pope saw clearly that his project could not be carried into effect. In a letter to King Sigismund, dated 2 June 1525,[4] he admits in a tone of resignation that not a single foreign prelate had complied with his invitation; hence the projected convention must be postponed until less troublous times. The attempt to forestall the demand for a Council by means of a Roman reform convention had not only proved a pitiable failure, it had actually provoked a fresh proposal for a Council. In point of fact, no one could believe that such a project had any chance of success unless his mind continued to stick to the obsolete track of

[1] Theiner, *Mon. Pol.*, VOL. II, p. 427 f.; *Acta Tomiciana*, VOL. VII, pp. 282 ff.
[2] The Polish envoy Tarnowski was assured by the Archbishop of Gran "velle se hoc ipsum facere et committere suo oratori", *Acta Tomiciana*, VOL. VII, p. 306 (23 July 1525).
[3] Rome, Biblioteca Corsiniana, codex 677, fols. 492-495.
[4] *C.T.*, VOL. IV, p. xxl.

Renaissance politics and thus completely misjudged the situation created by the rise of Lutheranism.

After the Emperor's overwhelming victory at Pavia there was no longer any reason for him to hold back the demand for a Council which he had allowed to drop in the summer of 1524. In view of Gattinara's political creed Clement VII had cause to fear that the Emperor himself would come to Italy to reopen the question of a Council.[1] He sought the cardinals' opinion about the attitude which Cardinal Salviati, who had been accredited to the imperial court, should adopt towards such a plan. His fears were premature, for in the course of the summer the Emperor's position had deteriorated to such a degree that prudence obliged him to avoid irritating the Pope by inconsiderate talk about a Council; in fact he expressly warned his brother Ferdinand to commit no such folly.[2] With a view to calming the Pope, a plan for a princes' convention on the model of the one held at Mantua under Pius II was elaborated. Its aim would be to unite the forces of Christendom for a common objective, that is the fight against the Turks and against heresy.[3] By the terms of the Peace of Madrid the two contracting parties bound themselves to propose to the Pope a convention of this kind.[4] Thus Gattinara returned to the Papacy the ball which the Renaissance Popes had first thrown into the field in the hope of thereby saving themselves from a demand for a Council.

The imperial court adopted a very different tone as soon as the Pope joined the hostile League of Cognac; in fact, Charles V went so far as to threaten an opposition Council, a Council hostile to the Pope. When the papal nuncio Baldassare Castiglione presented the brief dated 23 June 1526 [5] in which the Pope justified his latest change of policy the Emperor became greatly agitated. He described the reproaches levelled at him in the papal brief as so many lies and for the first time let fall the word "Council".[6] At the next audience, on 17 August, he told the nuncio that in view of accusations of such gravity he felt bound to justify his conduct before the whole world; this could only be done

---

[1] Marco Foscari, Sanudo, *Diarii*, VOL. XXXIX, pp. 101, 115.

[2] Bucholtz, *Ferdinand I*, VOL. II, p. 306 (31 October 1525).

[3] Charles V to Clement VII, 21 July 1525, Balan, *Mon. saec. XVI*, p. 350.

[4] *C.T.*, VOL. IV, p. xxiii.

[5] Le Plat, VOL. II, pp. 240-6; Balan, *Mon. saec. XVI*, pp. 364-71.

[6] What follows is based on Castiglione's letters to Jacopo Salviati and Schönberg, 8 September 1526, Serassi, *Lettere del Castiglione*, VOL. II, pp. 64-85. For a character-sketch of Castiglione, cf. "Graf Castiglione und die Renaissance", in *Archiv für Kulturgeschichte*, X (1913), pp. 245-71. The biography by E. Bianchi di San Secondo, B, *Castiglione nella vita e negli scritti* (Verona 1941) is a popular work.

before a Council. Castiglione—the author of *Il Cortegiano*—did not lose his self-control, though he was very much perturbed by the rumours that circulated at the imperial court. On the following day, in an address of some length, he represented to the Emperor the grave dangers which his threat would conjure up. The Pope would have to have recourse to his spiritual weapons which, as everybody knew, inflicted far greater injury than weapons of steel, and every possibility of an understanding would be finally cut off. However, the Emperor refused to give up his plan. What other remedy was left to him, he asked? By his command a reply to the accusations of the brief destined for the general public was drawn up. The asperity of its tone was without precedent in imperial policy. Its author was the imperial secretary, Alfonso Valdés, a follower of Erasmus. The imperial council approved the document, though after some pruning, which removed the sharpest passages.[1] Its object was to forestall whatever legal steps the Pope might take with a view to the Emperor's deposition: it was a formal admonition to the Pope to speed a Council—neither more nor less.[2] The Emperor, it said, was at all times prepared to co-operate with the Pope, that other luminary of Christendom, but if he spurned his peaceful proposals the responsibility for the evils that would ensue for Christendom must be the Pope's. He himself had always been willing to justify his conduct before a General Council representing the whole of Christendom, and to be judged by such an assembly. The warning concludes in these terms: "We pray and exhort your Holiness to convoke the holy General Council in virtue of your pastoral office, for the greater good of the flock entrusted to your care. Let the Council be summoned to a suitable and safe place and within a fixed time-limit. The good order of the Church and the Christian religion no less than our own interests and those of Christendom are endangered, as appears from the reasons here given and from others. We accordingly deem it necessary to pray for a holy General Council."

This was the language of a canonical admonition. If the Pope took no notice, the right of convocation, in the opinion of the imperial

---

[1] From Dantiscus's report (*Acta Tomiciana*, VOL. VIII, p. 356) we learn how the brief of 23 June was received by Gattinara's entourage. For that entourage see M. Bataillon, *Erasme en Espagne*, pp. 395.

[2] Le Plat, VOL. II, pp. 247-88. As late as 17 September the Emperor had handed to the nuncio a much more disarming text (Serassi, *Lettere del Castiglione*, VOL. II, pp. 88 ff. On the contemporary polemical Dialogues of Alfonso Valdés, *Diálogo de las cosas occurridas en Roma*, and *Diálogo de Mercurio y Carón*, newly published by J. F. Montesinos in Clásicos Castellanos (Madrid 1928-9), cf. Bataillon, *Erasme en Espagne*, pp. 399 ff., 410.

canonists, devolved to the College of Cardinals. Small wonder, then, that the Emperor should have warned that body on 6 October 1526, to act, "as in law bound", should the Pope refuse to convoke a Council or inordinately delay it.[1]

The presentation of the reply was made in strict conformity with legal formalities. It was merely read to the nuncio; by the Emperor's formal command the Roman ambassador Pérez was to hand it to the Pope in a secret consistory, in presence of a notary and witnesses so that the document thus formally authenticated might be produced in evidence at any time.[2] On a lawyer such proceedings must have had the effect of a thunderclap.

The Pope was so put out by the Emperor's agent that at the next audience he completely ignored him. But he was greatly intimidated. None of the cardinals saw the original of the Emperor's reply; they asked Pérez for a copy; it was in vain, for he had none.[3] However, they somehow got knowledge of its contents. This was another cause of complaint by the Pope. What was the reason for all this secretiveness? The answer is not difficult. The fact was that the Pope did not feel sure of the cardinals; he was afraid of opposition on their part, perhaps even of a repetition of the schism of 1511. His anxiety was not altogether groundless. When the monarch's letter to the cardinals was read and discussed in the consistory of 21 December, there ensued a heated discussion on the Emperor's right to convoke a Council.[4] Behind these discussions which, in the main, were purely theoretical, there was nevertheless an actual opposition which came out into the open when at the consistory of 29 December the Pope published the text of the imperial reply and appointed a commission of nine members for the purpose of studying it. One group of cardinals opposed the rejection of the Emperor's demand for a Council and insisted that it should be allowed and the time and place for the Council determined.[5] The discussion dragged on for over a month. The commission examined both the

---

[1] Le Plat, VOL. II, pp. 290-4.

[2] Notary's instrument in Le Plat, VOL. II, p. 294 f. On this incident and the narrative that follows, cf. Pérez's reports of 15 and 24 December 1526 and 10 and 26 January 1527, Cal. of St. Pap., Spain, VOL. III, i, Nos. 633, 642; III, ii, Nos. 3 and 9.

[3] Cal. of St. Pap., Spain, VOL. III, i, p. 1056 f. (No. 642).

[4] With the editor, Gayangos (Cal. of St. Pap., Spain, VOL. III, i, p. 1056), I connect Pérez's remark that "the Emperor's letter" had been read on 21 December, with the letter of 6 October to the cardinals because the Pope's second letter of 18 September, which one might think of, would scarcely have occasioned the dispute mentioned by Pérez. The difficulty remains that the Emperor's letter to the cardinals was also read on 28 December, together with the monitorium, C.T., VOL. IV, p. xxiv.

[5] Cal. of St. Pap., Spain, VOL. III, ii, p. 8 (No. 3).

quaestio facti, that is, whether a Council should be held, and the *quaestio juris*, that is, whether the Emperor had any right at all to demand a Council.[1] No decision was reached, for while in the course of the negotiations with the Emperor's *chargés d'affaires*, de Lannoy, Quiñónez and Fieramosca, the whole problem seemed to be taking a more friendly turn, the approach of the imperial army put an abrupt end to further discussions. It had nevertheless become apparent that in the matter of the Council the Pope did not have all the cardinals with him. One of them even dared at this very time to lodge an appeal to a Council. His action had no immediate connexion with the Emperor's admonition; it was only the epilogue of a tragedy of the darkest years of the Middle Ages, namely the armed attack of the Colonna on the Vatican and the Borgo on 20 September 1526. On 7 November the Pope had summoned the instigator of the opposition, Pompeo Colonna, to appear before him, but like his ancestors Giacomo and Pietro Colonna in the days of Boniface VIII, Pompeo refused to account for his conduct. On 8 November, from Naples, he lodged an appeal to a future Council whose task it would be to examine the legality of the Pope's election. A Council alone, he alleged, not the Pope, had the right to degrade a cardinal.[2] On 13 November he reiterated his appeal and at the same time proclaimed—all by himself—a General Council which was to meet at Speyer on 14 January 1527.[3]

Cardinal Pompeo Colonna's conciliar appeal was but an incident, but it might have gained some importance if anything had come of the Emperor's threat of a Council. When one reads the documents exchanged between Pope and Emperor, one gets the impression that a grim struggle over principles was preparing between the two heads. Actually no conflict of the kind ever broke out and the above impression vanishes entirely as one studies a series of contemporary documents and pronouncements by the persons concerned. Swords were drawn, but

[1] *Cal. of St. Pap., Spain*, VOL. III, ii, p. 39 (No. 9).

[2] I have not been able to see the text of the *Convocatio concilii generalis super privatione Clementis VII per Pompeium Card. Columnam*, Leyden, University Library, cod. 41, quoted by Pastor, but in the State Archives of Modena (Roma 110) I was able to consult a copy of the two appeals and the proclamation of the Council printed at Naples on 28 November 1526; cf. also Sanudo, *Diarii*, VOL. XLIII, p. 448.

[3] The author of the *Consultatio de concilio generali*, Petrus Albinianus Tretius (37 leaves, dedication copy), which is preserved in Cod. Vat. lat. 3664, was evidently not cognisant of the text of the appeal. Tretius writes that it is reported (dicitur . . . emanasse, fol. lv) that it was "sacratissimi Romanorum regis ac imperatoris consensu". The aim of the hasty and superficial work is to prove that both appeal and citation are invalid. The chief authorities invoked are Panormitanus, Felinus and San Giorgio.

there was never any danger of their being crossed: one hand threatened, the other stroked.

In the course of his negotiations with Castiglione the Emperor repeatedly assured the nuncio that his filial devotion towards the Pope remained unaltered; that he did not feel hurt and had no wish to hurt. Provided he was properly treated, he would be subject to the Pope like a good son to his father. "If I tell you lies," he exclaimed, "you may regard me as a good-for-nothing."

The sincerity of the Emperor's declarations is not in doubt; they were actually put down in writing. Charles had no intention of pushing things too far; he went on hoping that the Pope would alter his policy. He was actually playing a double game—but so was Clement VII. The Pope followed up his first brief, one full of reproaches, with another couched in milder terms and instructed his nuncio to keep the former back.[1] However, both the instructions and the second brief came too late. When Castiglione subsequently produced them the Emperor's reply was short but conciliatory in tone.[2] The same monarch who on 17 September had approved the admonition now sent the Pope a soothing letter on 26 September: he was far from arrogating to himself the right to convoke a Council, he wrote; he would never take a single step in that direction without the Pope's consent.[3] He wrote in the same strain to the General of the Franciscans Quiñónez who, as already stated, had been engaged all that autumn and winter, in conjunction with de Lannoy and Schönberg, in working for an accommodation.[4] He came very near succeeding. If during those months the Pope betrayed more than once symptoms of discouragement and timidity, declaring that he would prefer to lead a *vita da prete*,[5] his depression must not be exclusively ascribed to the threat of a Council for he was equally harassed by lack of money, the failure of French assistance and the danger to which the city of Rome was exposed. If he had been in earnest we should have heard of counter-measures. He knew that the Emperor's sole object was to detach him from the League of Cognac.

The catastrophe of the "Sack of Rome" created an entirely new situation. To all appearances, the Pope was at the mercy of the Emperor and incapable of resisting a demand for a Council should he decide to make it. Charles V was urged to take advantage of the

---

[1] Le Plat, VOL. II, p. 246 f.; Balan, *Mon. saec. XVI*, p. 233 f. (25 June).
[2] Le Plat, VOL. II, p. 289 f. (19 September).
[3] Serassi, *Lettere del Castiglione*, VOL. II, p. 92 f.
[4] Bucholtz, *Ferdinand I*, VOL. III, p. 49.
[5] Sanudo, *Diarii*, VOL. XLIII, p. 670.

situation. On 30 May his brother Ferdinand wrote to him [1]: "Now you have the Pope in your hands; now the Catholic faith may be restored and a successful Council held." In a memorial dated 7 June, Gattinara who had gone to his estate in Piedmont advised his master to address a circular to kings and princes, declining all responsibility for the outrages committed in Rome and at the same time proposing the convocation of a Council for the purpose of restoring peace, extirpating heresy and reforming the Church.[2] The Grand Chancellor went so far as to suggest that, whether convened with or without the Pope, the future Council should call him to account for his government and enforce his deposition or at least his resignation; in any case it should destroy him morally.[3] A second Sutri would frustrate the enemies' plan to form an ecclesiastical opposition government on the plea that the Pope was a prisoner.[4] If at all feasible the convocation should come from the Pope himself. The Emperor's instructions for Pierre de Veyre who was despatched to de Lannoy, the viceroy who was about to negotiate with Clement VII, expressed the hope that the catastrophe might open the way to peace and a Council and that the reform of the Church decreed by that assembly might also solve the Lutheran problem.[5] So confident was Charles that he had the Pope in his hand, that he deemed it superfluous to put him under further pressure, and in his letters to the College of Cardinals and the Kings of Portugal and Poland he carefully avoided all mention of a Council.[6] If Alfonso Valdés canvassed the Polish envoy Dantiscus for the conciliar project, he did so clandestinely and without betraying his hostility towards the Pope.[7] He succeeded so well that King Sigismund formally requested the Emperor to press the Pope for a Council since his own efforts both with Leo X and the present pontiff had been of no avail.[8] This was

---

[1] Brandi, *Quellen*, p. 184.

[2] Brandi, *Berichte*, IX, p. 252 f.

[3] According to the autobiography Gattinara represented to the Emperor that the "Sack of Rome" could be justified "tanquam in pseudopontificem scandalosum, incorrigibilem ac universum christianae religionis statum perturbantem, universaleque concilium sepius imploratum detractantem". Bornate, "Hist. vite", in *Miscellanea di storia italiana*, XLVII, p. 348. This was the kind of argument the canonists were in the habit of urging as valid reasons for the deposition of a Pope.

[4] Pastor, VOL. IV, ii, p. 303 (Eng. edn., VOL. IX, p. 446).

[5] Bucholtz, *Ferdinand I*, VOL. III, p. 96 (29 July 1527).

[6] *Cal. of St. Pap.*, *Spain*, VOL. III, ii, Nos. 124, 135-8, 142 f. The letter to Sigismund of Poland dated 31 July (*Acta Tomiciana*, VOL. IX, p. 240 f.) urges the King "publicam nobiscum causam complecti", by which is meant the Council.

[7] Dantiscus to King Sigismund, 17 August 1527, *Acta Tomiciana*, VOL. IX, p. 257.

[8] *Acta Tomiciana*, VOL. X, p. 356 f.

in the month of August 1528. Meanwhile the whole situation had undergone a complete change.

The Pope is never so strong as when in chains. From every quarter hands were stretched out to loosen his bonds. In August 1527 Cardinal Wolsey brought about an agreement between the Kings of France and England by which they bound themselves to resist by every means in their power the convocation of a Council by the Emperor alone, or by the Emperor with the consent of the Pope, or by the latter alone, and only to assent to such an assembly by mutual agreement.[1] In this way any conciliar attempt during the Pope's imprisonment was blocked and the weapon of a Council blunted since the liberation of the Pope was a preliminary condition for any further step in the matter. Gattinara himself came round to this view. He represented to the Council of State [2] that it was a mistake to imprison the Pope as one might imprison a secular potentate. No action could be taken against him unless he were guilty of simony.[3] The only thing to do was to set him at liberty, subject to certain guarantees, and induce him to call a Council. The best thing would be if the Emperor were to proceed to Rome in person, at the earliest date possible, to have himself crowned and to make arrangements for a Council in conjunction with the Pope.

The Pope was set at liberty on 6 December 1527 and thus recovered his freedom of action. This meant that the imperial policy was confronted with the same problem as previous to the victory of Pavia— that of persuading the Pope of the need of a Council. In view of other questions then pending recourse was had to the old tactics, namely to keep the delicate question in the background lest the partner in the negotiations should prove intractable, seeing that the chief aim was the conclusion of a separate peace with him. Now that the defeat of the French in Lombardy and before Naples had put an end to all expectations of his ally's victory, Clement VII was ready for peace.

The imperial negotiators deemed it nevertheless inadvisable to hamper the peace negotiations by prematurely dragging in the question of a Council. This accounts for the complete silence about plans for Council and reform in the Emperor's letters and instructions in the

---

[1] Le Plat, VOL. II, pp. 296 ff. (18 August 1527).

[2] Brandi, *Kaiser Karl V*, pp. 227 (Eng. edn., p. 262).

[3] A commentary on the Bull *Cum tam divino* by Petrus Andreas Gammarus was published in Rome in 1528 in connexion with plans for proceedings against Clement VII on account of alleged simoniacal practices at his election. This action would have proceeded on the basis of the Bull of Julius II. The object of the work is to counter the danger of a schism which that "perniciosum decretum" rendered more acute. There is a copy in the Vat. Lib., Vat. lat. 3914, fols. 61^r-109^v.

autumn of 1528.[1] Similar precautions were apparently observed in the deliberations with Quiñónez whom the Pope had despatched to the imperial court for the purpose of discussing peace and Council.[2] Only before the Castilian Estates, and in the words of the Spaniard Antonio Guevara, did the Emperor openly declare that the purpose of his journey to Rome was to urge the convocation of a Council, the reform of the Church and the extirpation of heresy.[3] However, in spite of the reticence of the imperial diplomatists, the Pope was aware of the Emperor's plans and the knowledge was enough to decide him to adopt a policy of extreme reserve. He only agreed to the conclusion of a separate peace after the imperial envoy, Miguel Mai, and Ferdinand's envoy, Andrea da Burgo, had given formal assurances in respect of these intentions. The episode is so characteristic of Clement's attitude to a Council that it may not be passed over.

At the audience of 24 April 1529, Burgo assured the Pope that his fear of a Council was groundless. The aim of the two Habsburg brothers was peace and tranquillity in the world and in Italy. They did not want the fresh complications which it was easy to foresee a Council would lead to. Luther's business could be settled without a Council on condition that it was submitted to a committee of specialists, one half of whom would be named by the Emperor and the German Estates while the Pope would appoint the other half. All this was nothing but a camouflaged version of Erasmus's proposal of an arbitration court of scholars, but it sufficed to provoke a complete reversal of feelings in the Pope. As if a load had been taken off his shoulders he jumped out of his chair exclaiming: "Yes, you speak a true word! in that case one might even grant the Lutherans more than one concession."[4]

The project for a Council was accordingly adjourned. The papal nuncio's promise of such an assembly made on 13 April at the Diet of Speyer had become obsolete before the ink on the document was dry, and though Jacopo Salviati, in a communication of 30 May, continued

[1] Weiss, *Papiers*, VOL. I, pp. 247 ff. (instructions for Balançon, September 1528); letter to Clement VII, Lanz, *Correspondenz*, VOL. I, pp. 296 ff.; Rassow, *Kaiseridee*, p. 17, places it in the autumn of 1528, however it dates from the spring of 1529.

[2] Lanz, *Correspondenz*, VOL. I, pp. 257; for his oral instructions we only have Gattinara's remark to Dantiscus, *Acta Tomiciana*, VOL. x, p. 398.

[3] On the attribution of authorship to Gattinara see Brandi, *Berichte*, IX, pp. 229 ff. Rassow, *Kaiseridee*, pp. 16 ff. regards the discourse as the Emperor's own work.

[4] Mai's report of 11 May 1529 in H. Baumgarten, *Geschichte Karls V*, VOL. II (Stuttgart 1888), pp. 715 ff.; the chief passage also in Brandi, *Quellen*, p. 198. As for Ehses's comment in *C.T.*, VOL. IV, p. xxvii, I will only say that I do not regard Burgo's soothing message as the only reason for the Pope's willingness to conclude peace.

to uphold the fiction, his only aim was to avoid offending the Estates of the Empire.[1] On 26 April Giberti, who had hastened to Rome in order to prevent the Pope from signing a separate peace, returned to his episcopal city of Verona.[2] The game was definitely up. The peace of Barcelona was signed: there was not a word in it about a Council.

However, the Emperor had not dropped his plan for such a gathering. He was resolved to proceed to Italy. Gattinara, who had suggested the expedition, felt confident that the Emperor would succeed in wresting the proclamation of a Council from the Pope. On 12 August 1529 Charles landed at Genoa; on 5 November he and the Pope met at Bologna.[3] For a period of over four months the two heads of Christendom lived under the same roof in the Palazzo Publico. There can be no doubt that Charles exerted himself to the utmost for an early convocation of a Council. Contrary to an account of the negotiations drawn up after the Emperor's death, in which Melanchthon asserts that the negotiations were conducted in presence of a large gathering of clergy and laity,[4] they were entirely private, hence our information about their progress and result is extremely scanty. Charles V personally recorded the general impression in a letter of 11 January 1530 addressed to his brother.[5] It was to the effect that the Pope

[1] *Lettere di principi*, VOL. I, fol. 121ᵛ, where we read that after the conclusion of peace everybody would see what were the Pope's intentions with regard to a Council: no one could desire it more than he did.

[2] Dittrich, *Regesten*, p. 52 f. How reluctantly the Pope came to terms with the Emperor may be gathered from Contarini's despatches of 7 June and 31 July 1529, *ibid.*, pp. 54 f., 60.

[3] Pastor, VOL. IV, ii, pp. 377-89 (Eng. edn., VOL. X, pp. 68 ff.). This should be supplemented by the wholly unpolitical report of the Fleming de Lannoy published by Gh. de Boom, "Voyage et couronnement de Charles V à Bologne", in *Bulletin de la Comm. Royale de Belgique d'hist*, CI (1936), pp. 55-106.

[4] *Corp. Ref.*, VOL. XII, pp. 307-17; the German text, which is probably earlier, is in *Corp. Ref.*, VOL. IX, pp. 710-17. Ehses, *C.T.*, VOL. IV, pp. xxix ff., has shown that it is inadmissible. According to A. Hasenclever, "Kritische Bemerkungen zu Melanchthons *Oratio de congressu bononiensi*, etc.", in *Z.K.G.*, XXIX (1908), pp. 154-73, the writing was occasioned not only by the Emperor's death but even more by the political climate of 1559. By recalling the meekness of the deceased monarch Melanchthon sought to warn his successor against the use of stern measures.

[5] Lanz, *Correspondenz*, VOL. I, p. 371. On 10 January Danticus writes from Bologna: "Caesar etiam instat multis rationibus ut concilium fiat, sed adhuc surdis haec fabula canitur", *Acta Tomiciana*, VOL. XII, p. 15. Melanchthon's note (*Corp. Ref.*, VOL. II, p. 219) that as regards the Council Gattinara had "den Kaiser vermahnet er soll nicht davon lassen" is as devoid of foundation, as is Sarpi's assertion to the contrary, *Istoria*, VOL. I, p. 3 (ed. Gambarin, VOL. I, p. 82). Bornate ("Hist. vite", in *Miscellanea di storia italiana*, XLVII, p. 396) had already described the latter assertion as incredible. On the other hand it must be remembered that shortly afterwards Gattinara thought of obtaining from Erasmus suggestions for an agreement without a Council.

would always view a Council as a tiresome affair, though he would no doubt agree to its convocation once peace was assured; however, both the convocation and the actual assembly demanded time. The Emperor evidently regarded the Pope's reluctance as insurmountable; he nevertheless continued to hope for at least a qualified acceptance, and such an acceptance he actually secured. From a letter of the Emperor to the Pope dated 14 July, of which more will be said further on, and from the Pope's reply of 31 July 1530,[1] we learn that Clement promised to convoke a Council if the Emperor judged that the situation in Germany made it necessary, but only on condition that peace was restored and the danger of politically inspired schisms removed. In a word the Pope gave his assent but reserved the final decision to himself. He also did his best to influence the Emperor's judgment in his own sense. To this end Cardinal Campeggio was ordered to accompany the Emperor to Germany in the capacity of papal legate. From the Emperor's memoirs it appears that he treated the Pope's reply as a straightforward affirmation,[2] which it was not. Its conditional nature did not escape Guicciardini.[3]

Events soon proved that he was right. Crowned as Roman Emperor on 24 February—his lucky day, for it was the anniversary of the victory of Pavia and his birthday—Charles V journeyed north to attend the Diet convened at Augsburg. Everything had gone as he wished: Soliman's attack on Vienna had collapsed; Italy was pacified; Sforza was reinstated as Duke of Milan; imperial troops had subdued Florence for the benefit of the Medici after the city had put up a heroic defence of its liberty—only a Council eluded his efforts. That problem would be solved at Augsburg.

[1] Heine, *Briefe*, p. 524. Italian translation in *Archivio storico ital.*, VIII (1891), p. 132. The Pope's reply is in *Lettere di principi*, VOL. III, fols. 109^v-111^r.

[2] Morel-Fatio, *Historiographie de Charles-Quint*, p. 202 f.

[3] *Storia d'Italia*, xx, 1 (ed. Panigada, VOL. V, p. 293).

FREDERICK THE WISE, ELECTOR OF SAXONY

After a drawing by Dürer in the Ecole Nationale des Beaux Arts,
Paris

CHAPTER IV

Augsburg and the Emperor's Proposal for a Council (1530)

DURING the six years that had elapsed since the Diet of Nuremberg the religious question in Germany had undergone a significant change. With the collapse of the social revolution Lutheranism ceased to be a popular movement as at the time of the Diet of Worms. The territorial authorities, princes and towns now controlled it and by means of church visitations and various regulations had reduced the hastily introduced innovations to a system. Electoral Saxony, Hesse and the great cities of the Empire set the pace. What they called "reformation" was not merely the appointment of Lutheran preachers and the ordering of divine service in the spirit of Luther, it also meant a more or less violent suppression of what remained of Catholic forms of worship and of the monastic houses, the application of Church property thus acquired to educational purposes, provision for the poor and other needs. The innovators appealed to their "Christian conscience" but could not prevent their opponents from observing that this kind of reform seemed exceedingly profitable to themselves while it greatly strengthened their internal and external position. As a matter of fact they were fully aware of this themselves. Pope and Emperor were no longer faced by a popular movement, powerful and impassioned but devoid of organisation. What they had to deal with now was a group of compact ecclesiastical-political bodies led by men with a clearly defined purpose, held together at first by the idea of the gospel as understood by Luther but before long, under pressure of events, by a common faith and an increasingly powerful political confederation.

As yet the Empire was not finally split into two great religious parties. The definitely Lutheran Estates still constituted only a small group, comprising the Elector John Frederick of Saxony who had succeeded Frederick the Wise, the young, energetic Landgrave Philip of Hesse, the Franconian Hohenzollern princes Casimir and George of Brandenburg, a few smaller territorial lords of Northern Germany and among the great imperial cities Augsburg, Nuremberg, Ulm, Frankfurt and Strasbourg. On the side of strict orthodoxy there were the Elector

Joachim I of Brandenburg, Duke George of Saxony, the Bavarian dukes and the majority of the ecclesiastical princes. But the number of the undecided was considerable. It included the Wittelsbachs of the Palatinate. Although the schism had actually been in progress for a long time, as a result of the establishment of Lutheran ecclesiastical communities, the adherents of the new faith were emphatic in disclaiming any schismatic intention. They maintained that now as before they stood on the ground of the medieval commonwealth of nations, the *Respublica christiana*, and that like the orthodox they regarded a General Council as its representative. However, a General Council as understood by them was the "free, Christian Council in German lands" which was undoubtedly irreconcilable with the Church's constitution. Though Luther himself had long ceased to expect anything from a Council his adherents persisted in their demand for such an assembly for they knew only too well what heavy obstacles lay in its way and how remote its convocation was—time was on their side. In this way there arose the remarkable situation that in Germany Lutherans, Catholics eager for reform, and the mass of the undecided—all favoured a Council. For the Lutherans the demand for a Council provided cover under which they pursued their work without hindrance. For the Catholics it was an objective for which they strove desperately for it was bound to bring the longed-for renewal of the Church which would cut off the ground on which Lutheranism grew. For the undecided it was the unerring scales in which the new belief and the new piety would be weighed. Thus it came about that even during the great war between France and the Empire the idea of the Council never vanished from the political order of the day.

One year after the Recess of Nuremberg, in August 1525, the Count Palatine Frederick and the Margrave Casimir of Brandenburg, having previously sounded the Elector of Saxony, jointly proposed to the Emperor the convocation of a General Council, or at least a national one "so that they might decide on a common interpretation and understanding of God's word".[1] Duke George of Saxony on his part instructed his counsellor, Pack, to press the Diet which had been convened at Augsburg, to request the Pope and the Emperor to consent to the summoning of a Council for the reform of both Estates, the ecclesiastical and the secular.[2] The above-mentioned Diet of Augsburg never materialised because the princes stayed away while the powers

---

[1] Janssen, *Geschichte des deutschen Volkes*, VOL. III, p. 29 (Eng. edn., VOL. V, p. 38).
[2] Gess, *Akten und Briefe*, VOL. II, pp. 461-71 (26 December 1525).

of the envoys who did attend were inadequate. The Recess of 9 January 1526 saw no better way out of the impasse than to request the Emperor once more to promote the affair of the Council because, so it said, "unless they achieved unity and harmony in a common Christian faith peace could not be restored in the Empire".[1]

How dangerous it was thus to play with the question of the Council became apparent at the Diet of Speyer in 1526.[2] The imperial "Proposition" of 26 June forbade any alteration in the existing legal status in respect of religious affairs and left it to the Estates to take the necessary measures for safeguarding traditional customs and ceremonies of the Church as well as for preventing the introduction of novelties, until a Council should meet.[3] That these half-measures were but little calculated to arrest further developments appears from the Estates' reply. True, the majority agreed that Christian belief and the Christian order should remain unchanged until a Council met,[4] but they disagreed on the question as to what these things actually stood for. Whereas the spiritual Estates were of opinion that even the suppression of ecclesiastical abuses should be reserved to a Council, the representatives of the towns, who were imbued with Lutheran sentiments,[5] claimed that certain institutions which were at variance with the Christian faith and the word of God could not on conscientious grounds be tolerated till a Council met. At the same time they submitted a memorial enumerating their proposals for reform; they were of such a nature as to leave no room for uncertainty about their aims. They were— freedom to preach Lutheran doctrine, abolition of the Mass, confiscation of monastic property, the marriage of priests. In their "Answer" to the Emperor's "Proposition" they stated that since there could be no question of a Council on account of the war, a German national Council should carry out the necessary reforms and formally suspend the execution of the Edict of Worms.

These proposals meant neither more nor less than complete freedom

[1] Lünig, *Reichsarchiv* (Leipzig 1710-22), VOL. II, pp. 457 ff.: Janssen, *Geschichte*, VOL. III, p. 32 (Eng. edn., VOL. V, p. 43).

[2] *R.T.A.* are not yet published, hence W. Friedensburg's *Der Reichstag zu Speyer 1526 im Zusammenhang der politischen und kirchlichen Entwicklung im Reformationszeitalter* (Berlin 1887) remains authoritative. Further literature on the subject in Schottenloher, Nos. 27960b-74.

[3] Friedensburg, *Der Reichstag zu Speyer*, pp. 523-34.

[4] Friedensburg, *Der Reichstag zu Speyer*, pp. 634-8; Pack's report, Gess, *Akten und Briefe*, VOL. II (Leipzig), pp. 565-9.

[5] The memorial of the towns, 30 June, in J. E. Kapp, *Kleine Nachlese einiger . . . Urkunden*, VOL. II (Leipzig 1727); also Duke George's observations in Gess, *Akten und Briefe*, VOL. II, pp. 599 ff.

for the new teaching, in defiance of the laws of Church and State. The Catholic majority sought to check the progress of the new religion by suggestions of their own which, while they went some way to meet their opponents, were not altogether irreconcilable with the Catholic standpoint. Two committees appointed by the Diet, a small one of eight members and a large one of twenty-one members, suggested [1] that the wishes of the secular Estates could be met by means of annual visitations and a reduction of feasts and fasts, indulgences and annates. As eventual concessions to their opponents they mentioned the marriage of priests and Communion in both kinds. It was all in vain. The Lutheran Estates rejected every compromise which guaranteed the continuation of the existing Catholic situation. On the other hand an imperial message forbade all discussion of the religious question and of reform at the Diet, or any change in the existing situation until a Council met. The divergences could not be bridged.

However, the Emperor's lieutenant, Archduke Ferdinand, sorely needed the help of the Estates against the Turks. In the hope of securing it he hit upon a flexible formula which did not bridge the differences but merely disguised them. The Diet's Recess of 27 August 1526 [2] demanded the convocation within a year and a half either of a General or a National Council, forbade all further innovations and guaranteed all lawfully acquired rights and revenues. On their part the Estates declared that their attitude to the Edict of Worms would be such as they felt able to answer for before God and before the Emperor's majesty. Thus the attitude of each of the Estates of the Empire during the interval before the Council was left to the individual conscience as informed by the law of God and that of the Empire. The decision did not create a new law justifying the establishment of Lutheran territorial churches, but it proved the starting-point of a development which ended in the formation of a territorial ecclesiastical system and the management of ecclesiastical affairs by the imperial cities mentioned at the beginning of this chapter.

When, at the end of three eventful years, a new Diet opened at Speyer on 15 March 1529 strong resentment prevailed among the

---

[1] The memorial of the princes' committee of eight, 23 July, with the memorials on the *gravamina*, edited by J. Ney in *Z.K.G.*, IX (1888), pp. 140-81; XII (1891), pp. 338-60; the advice of the great committee, 18 August, in Ranke, *Deutsche Geschichte*, VOL. VI, pp. 41-61 (Eng. edn., VOL. III, BK VI, Ch. i).

[2] Lünig, *Reichsarchiv*, VOL. II, pp. 460 ff.; Janssen, VOL. III, pp. 54 ff. (Eng. edn., VOL. V, p. 74 ff.). Friedensburg defends his interpretation against Brieger in *A.R.G.*, VIII (1910), pp. 93 ff.

Catholic Estates on account of the conduct of the Lutherans.[1] The Emperor's victories and his impending return to Germany breathed fresh courage into them, but the attitude of the adherents of the new faith also stiffened. The main object of the Diet was to obtain subsidies for the Turkish war—Soliman stood at the gates of Vienna. As for the religious problem, there was only question of *interim* ordinances, pending the convocation of a Council. The imperial "Proposition" held out a prospect of its assembly at an early date and in the meantime forbade every form of coercion as well as the introduction of new sects. Although the Estates' memorial of 15 April [2] limited this prohibition to the introduction of the new, that is the Zwinglian, teaching on the Eucharist, Anabaptism and the suppression of the Mass, while it expressly tolerated other innovations until the Council should materialise, it met with opposition from the towns that had embraced the new faith. The delegate of Strasbourg, Jacob Sturm, declared [3] that the innovations introduced by them were dictated by their conscience and that their cancellation would provoke a riot; however, they were prepared to submit to a Council. Sturm was sure he could rely on the Lutheran princes and he felt confident of the support of the Swiss. Neither he nor his sympathisers were impressed when the papal nuncio, Giovanni Tommaso Pico della Mirandola, in a speech delivered on 13 April [4] held out a prospect of the convocation of a Council as soon as the restoration of peace would make such a step practicable. The further promise that the Pope would promote the plan by means of a personal visit to Charles V and Francis I also left them cold. Unwillingness to give credence to such a promise was general, all the more so as it was conditional, whereas all the time the Emperor was doing his utmost to create an impression that a final decision had already been arrived at. The Lutheran estates maintained their standpoint and flatly rejected even the modified Recess of the Diet which demanded from them no more than toleration of Catholics and Catholic worship. On 19 and 20 April the Elector of Saxony, the Dukes of Hesse and

---

[1] *R.T.A.*, VOL. VII, pp. 478-880, and the account by the editor, J. Kühn, *Die Geschichte des Speyrer Reichstags 1529* (Leipzig 1929); for the Strasbourg reports see *Politische Korrespondenz*, VOL. I, pp. 319-59, and for the earlier literature Schottenloher, Nos. 27975-8010.

[2] *R.T.A.*, VOL. VII, pp. 1133 ff.; corresponding reports pp. 550 ff.

[3] *R.T.A.*, VOL. VII, pp. 649, 703; *Politische Korrespondenz*, VOL. I, p. 324. The memorials of the theologians and jurists of Nuremberg, which had been drawn up in the month of March, in *R.T.A.*, VOL. VII, pp. 1187-93. The jurists advocated another appeal to a future, free, Christian Council.

[4] *R.T.A.*, VOL. VII, pp. 725, 734 f.; text of the discourse pp. 1244 ff.

Brandenburg-Kulmbach and three other princes, together with Jacob Sturm as representing the towns, lodged the protest which thereafter gave its name to their group.[1]

The majority Recess [2] prayed the Emperor to propose to the Pope a "frei general concilium in teutscher nacion" (a free General Council within the German nation)—to be proclaimed within a year and to be convened within two years. Metz, Cologne, Mainz and Strasbourg were proposed as possible meeting-places. If no General Council was held, a general assembly of the Estates of the Empire and other interested bodies should be convened, in other words, some sort of national Council should be held. It is evident that the idea of a national assembly to deal with the religious problem continued side by side with the now stereotyped demand for a Council even though more and more people began to despair of the demand ever being complied with.

The arrival of the Emperor in Germany opened the flood-gates of controversy at one stroke. Charles V still refused to despair of the Protestants' return to the Church, for the simple reason that he did not fully realise the extent of the dogmatic cleavage. Such a state of mind, after the Diet of Worms, is surprising. To appreciate it we must remember that in Charles's view of the situation the Protestant Estates, not the person of Luther, were his opponents. Friends of Erasmus had led him to think that even now their belief could be reconciled with the fundamental dogmas of the Church as formulated in the Apostles' Creed and that the prevailing divergences were solely concerned with theological opinions and ecclesiastical traditions. A broad-minded approach to them on the part of the Church and greater respect for authority on the part of the Protestants might yet pave the way to reunion, especially if he himself were to intervene with all the weight of the imperial dignity and power.

This conception shows through the paragraph of the promulgation of the Diet in which the Protestants were summoned to justify their conduct in writing.[3] Their defence would form the basis of the

---

[1] Both formulas of the protest in *R.T.A.*, VOL. VII, pp. 1260 ff., 1273 ff.; J. Boehmer, "'Protestari' und 'protestatio' protestierende Obrigkeiten und protestantische Christen", in *A.R.G.*, XXXI (1934), pp. 1-22.

[2] *R.T.A.*, VOL. VII, p. 1299, with p. 1142; the main lines had already been laid down at the sitting of 19 March, *ibid.*, p. 573.

[3] German text in Lünig, *Reichsarchiv*, VOL. II, pp. 496 ff. (20 January 1530); extract in Le Plat, VOL. II, p. 321. I discuss the Diet of Augsburg more fully because up to the Diet of Ratisbon 1541 this was the only serious attempt to render a Council superfluous by means of a direct understanding with the Protestants. *R.T.A.* are unfortunately not yet available. C. E. Förstemann, *Urkundenbuch zur Geschichte des*

forthcoming discussion. Powerful influences in the Emperor's entourage pressed for a compromise at any price. From the Emperor's secretary, Cornelius Schepper,[1] we learn that Gattinara was thinking of, inviting Erasmus to Augsburg, where his opposite number would have been Melanchthon, who was there in the capacity of theological adviser to the Elector of Saxony. Erasmus and Melanchthon at Augsburg— what a prospect for reunion! and what a confusion of ideas!

Gattinara's death at Innsbruck on 4 May 1530 prevented the execution of the plan, but there were left a number of people who favoured a reconciliation on Erasmian terms, as for instance, the two secretaries Valdés and Schepper, Charles's sister, Mary of Hungary, who kept a preacher of Protestant leanings, Bishop Christoph von Stadion and, to some extent, even Cardinal Cles of Trent.[2] As a matter of fact, at one critical moment, when faced by the League of Cognac, even Charles seems to have thought of winning allies for the impending struggle by means of an amnesty for the transgressors of the Edict of Worms and concessions in the ecclesiastical sphere.

A Council remained a very definite item in the Emperor's plans.[3]

Reichstags zu Augsburg 1530, 2 Vols., Halle 1833-5, is supplemented, for the first days of July, by Th. Brieger, "Beiträge", in *Z.K.G.*, XII (1891), pp. 126-36. Melanchthon's correspondence with Luther and the reports of the envoys of Nuremberg in *Corp. Ref.*, VOL. II, pp. 34 ff.; cf. also Aurifaber's collections of the acts in *Briefe und Akten zur Geschichte des Religionsgesprächs zu Marburg 1529 und des Reichstags zu Augsburg 1530*, ed. F. W. Schirrmacher, Gütersloh 1876, and those of Veit Dietrich in *Acta comitiorum Augustae ex litteris Philippi, Jonae et aliorum ad M[artinum] L[utherum]*, ed. G. Berbig, Halle 1907. Authoritative for the question of the Council are Campeggio's reports published, in part, by Laemmer, *Mon. Vat.*, pp. 64 ff., completed and revised by St. Ehses, "Kardinal L. Campeggio auf dem Reichstag von Augsburg 1530", in *R.Q.*, XVII (1903), pp. 383-406; XVIII (1904), pp. 358-84; XIX (1905) *Gesch.*, pp. 129-52; XX (1906) *Gesch.*, pp. 54-80; also three letters of Campeggio to Henry VIII, Jedin, *Quellenapparat*, pp. 99-104; likewise the despatches of the Venetian envoy Niccolò Tiepolo, who was in close touch with Campeggio, cf. J. von Walter, "Die Depeschen des venezianischen Gesandten N. Tiepolo über die Religionsfrage auf dem Augsburger Reichstag 1530", in *Abhandlungen der Göttinger Gesellschaft der Wissenschaften, phil.-hist. Klasse N.F.*, XXIII (1928), No. 1 (Berlin 1928). Information about events in Rome is furnished by the letters of Cardinal Loaysa mentioned above (Ch. x) and the despatches of the Roman envoy Mai, *Cal. of St. Pap., Spain*, VOL. IV, i, Nos. 381 ff. The following works in the special literature are important for the question of the Council: Schottenloher, Nos. 28011-67; E. W. Mayer, "Forschungen zur Politik Karls V während des Augsburger Reichstages von 1530", in *A.R.G.*, XIII (1916), pp. 40-73, 124-46; Rassow, *Kaiseridee*, pp. 26-87.

[1] Erasmus, *Epist.*, VOL. VIII, pp. 462 ff.; Rassow, *Kaiseridee*, pp. 35 ff.; Melanchthon's letter to Baumgartner, 21 May, *Corp. Ref.*, VOL. II, p. 58.

[2] Erasmus's correspondence with the above-named (except Mary of Hungary), and with Melanchthon, Pistorius, Campeggio and Bonfio in Erasmus, *Epist.*, VOL. VIII, pp. 446 ff.; VOL. IX, pp. 1 ff.

[3] Brandi, *Berichte*, IX, pp. 247 ff.; Bauer, *Korrespondenz Ferdinands I*, VOL. I (1912), pp. 407 ff. Marco Foscari also heard of it, Albèri, *Relazioni*, VOL. II, iii, p. 133.

Before all else he saw in it a means of reforming the Church. If he brought about such a reform he would be discharging a debt of gratitude he owed Almighty God for the victorious conclusion of the war. The promise of a Council, he imagined, would facilitate the return of the dissidents. On the other hand, should they refuse to submit to its decisions, he would have moral support for the use of force. As a matter of fact he was even then considering the latter remedy. It is as inaccurate to visualise the Emperor merely as a benign arbitrator as it is to picture him as a raging, warlike tyrant speeding to Germany in order to make the rebels feel the weight of his authority.

The course of events could not but be considerably influenced by the bearing of the cardinal-legate. Campeggio was resolved not to swerve from the basic line to which the Curia had strictly adhered until this time. This meant, for one thing, that he would uphold the Bull *Exsurge* and the Edict of Worms. Although he regarded the attempt to win over the Protestant princes by means of concessions and to intimidate the towns by threats as not altogether hopeless, he was convinced that should these tactics fail there only remained the use of force. This programme he submitted to the Emperor while they were still on the way.[1] It was undoubtedly consistent, but it suffered from two weaknesses; on the one hand it failed to take into account the Protestants' unwillingness to yield on the question of belief, and on the other it left unsolved the problem of conducting simultaneously a war of religion and a campaign against the Turks. It also by-passed the solution by means of a Council; in fact, during the journey from Innsbruck to Augsburg, the legate did his best to persuade Duke George of Saxony and the Dukes of Bavaria not to insist upon such a solution.

Once again it was the Protestants who carried the idea of a Council into the discussion and it was an ominous sign that those responsible were precisely the most radical of their number, namely Philip of Hesse and the representatives of Strasbourg. The latter were in sympathy with the Swiss. Philip successfully urged that the preamble to the profession of faith, which they presented to the Emperor on 25 June, should contain a reminder of the Estates' previous demand for a Council as well as of the Emperor's promises to that effect at the last two Diets of Speyer. The Protestants promised in advance to submit

---

[1] The text of this undated Italian memorial is given by W. Maurenbrecher, *Karl V und die deutschen Protestanten* (Düsseldorf 1865), appendix 3-14. On 19 June Melanchthon wrote to Luther, "Campegius tantum est auctor ut vi opprimamur. Neque quidquam in aula mitior est Caesare". *Acta comitiorum*, p. 6.

while at the same time they appealed to it.[1] Campeggio hit the nail on the head when he roundly declared that their offer was insincere,[2] that its authors did not believe that a Council would materialise and that their only desire was to gain time. The legate accordingly did all in his power to dissuade the Emperor from seeking a solution by means of a Council. In a memorandum of 4 July [3] he pointed out that if the Protestants refused to bow to the Emperor's decision there remained no other remedy except to proceed against them with severity—that is, the use of force. It would be both useless and dangerous to throw out hints of a Council—useless, because they would not submit to it; dangerous, because they would take advantage of the interval to disseminate their errors still further.

Objections of this kind had been foreseen by the Emperor. Hence, if he promised a Council he would attach a condition to his offer. This was that until its assembly the Protestants should comply with the Edict of Worms and take up once more Catholic practice. This condition was meant to humour the Pope and to remove his objections to a Council but it had one weakness—there was not the slightest prospect of the Protestants accepting it, were it only that they would suspect—not altogether without reason—that it was no more than a feint for the purpose of deceiving them. Once they should have returned to the practice of Catholicism there would be no hurry to assemble the Council. Hence, notwithstanding this condition, Campeggio would not agree to the promise of a Council. The only step he was prepared to take was to renew the offer made at Nuremberg, namely that the nation's wishes for reform would be laid before the Roman authorities by a special deputation. However, the Emperor stuck to his point of view. The "Programme" which he laid before the Catholic Estates on

---

[1] Die Bekenntnisschriften der evangelisch-lutherischen Kirche, published by the "Deutscher Evangelischer Kirchenausschuss" (Göttingen 1930), p. 47 f. The copious literature on the "Confessio Augustana" in Schottenloher, Nos. 34504-635, of which the following works are of special importance: E. von Schubert, Bekenntnisbilder und Religionspolitik (Gotha 1910), and W. Gussmann, Quellen und Forschungen zur Geschichte des Augsburger Glaubensbekenntnisses, VOL. I (Leipzig 1911), VOL. II (Kassel 1930); a survey of the literature of the Luther jubilee by H. Bornkamm in Z.K.G., L (1931), pp. 207-18. On Landgrave Philip's "complete victory with regard to the question of the Council", see W. E. Nagel, Festgabe Johannes Ficker (Leipzig 1931), pp. 107-23.

[2] Memorials drawn up in the last days of June in Lanz, Staatspapiere, p. 48; also Gussmann, Quellen und Forsch., VOL. I, i, p. 56; Corp. Ref., VOL. II, pp. 98, 101.

[3] C.T., VOL. IV, p. xxxvii f.; R.Q., XVIII (1904), p. 359: "A bocca ragionando seco molto detestai la cosa del concilio con le ragioni efficacissime altre volte dette."

5 July[1] contained this alternative: either the Protestants submit to the imperial decision in respect of their profession of faith, or to a future Council; if they refuse there only remain "sharpness and severity".

The Estates' desire for a mutual understanding was keener, their dread of the horrors of a war of religion deeper, than the Emperor's. They declared their readiness to do all they could in the hope of persuading the "confessionists" to yield. If no agreement was reached —but not until then—the promise of a Council would be in order. They promised to draw up a list of ecclesiastical *gravamina* to serve as a basis for the negotiations with the Curia, as Campeggio had suggested.

The Emperor acted on these lines during the weeks that followed. First of all he had a refutation of the *Confessio Augustana* drawn up. Its tone was mild and the matter clearly stated, but when it came to be submitted to the Protestants, they rejected it. Thereupon the Emperor sought to reach an understanding by means of direct negotiations. Only when these failed did he take up once more the idea of a solution by means of a Council. In order to be prepared for any eventuality he took steps betimes in Rome so as to prepare the authorities for the offer he intended to make. In a letter of 14 July he drew this picture of the situation for the benefit of the Pope: "The Protestants are more unyielding and more obstinate than ever—while the Catholics are generally lukewarm and but little inclined to lend a hand in the forcible conversion of those who have fallen away." It was his opinion as well as that of the Estates that the offer of a Council could not be avoided, not only in order that errors might be finally exposed and their further dissemination arrested, but also for the purpose of regulating the ecclesiastical situation, encouraging the Catholics and preventing the rise of further heresies. The Protestants' intention was to let the time that would necessarily elapse before the Council work in their favour. But this aim would be thwarted by the condition attached to the promise of a Council, namely that they return to the practice of the Catholic religion. Should the Council fail to materialise there was reason to fear that all the evils that must surely ensue would be laid to the Pope's and the Emperor's charge. The abscess must be lanced, lest the poison infect the whole body. "That which we spoke of at Bologna has come true; the welfare of Christendom peremptorily

[1] The "Bedencken" of 5 July and the reply of the Estates of 7(13) July published by Th. Brieger in *Z.K.G.*, XII (1891), pp. 128 ff.

requires a Council. Up till now the war has stood in the way, but that is now at an end. Should peace be disturbed from any quarter, the blame would lie wholly with the author of the disturbance." The letter ended with a request that the Pope would indicate the date and place of the Council so that the Emperor might be in a position to make concrete proposals to the Estates. Charles concluded with a declaration that he submitted in advance to the decision of the Vicar of Christ.[1]

Even before the arrival of the Emperor's letter Rome had learnt the nature of its contents from a report of Campeggio and the imperial ambassador Mai.[2] On 18 July it was submitted to the committee of cardinals for German affairs and shortly afterwards to the consistory. The Pope and the majority of the cardinals were agreed that the Emperor's request for a Council could not be openly declined. The monarch's proposal of a Council was not by any means the same thing as a Council. In any case the well-known condition, that is the Protestants' previous resumption of the practice of the Catholic religion, robbed it of its sting. For, as Campeggio wrote,[3] in this affair of the Council they might imitate Solon of old, who made the Athenians promise to keep the laws he had given them until his return. Having got the promise, Solon departed, never to return. Moreover, Granvella had given an assurance in Charles's name that he would defend the person and the privileges of the Pope like his own at the Council. There was therefore no doubt about the Emperor's good-will. Clement VII accordingly decided to accede to the monarch's wish. On 31 July he pledged himself to convoke a Council as soon as the Protestants should declare their intention to fulfil the well-known condition. As a meeting-place he proposed, in the first instance, Rome; then Bologna, Mantua or Piacenza.[4]

It was a promise, and again it was not a promise. Every line of the document betrays the reluctance with which the Pope gave his assent, an assent qualified by a number of stipulations. So great in fact was his reluctance that just then he would have been more willing to put up with a national Council than with a general one. He was even prepared for far-reaching concessions if by this means he could escape

---

[1] Heine, *Briefe*, pp. 522 ff. Italian text in *Archivio storico ital.*, VOL. VIII (1891), pp. 129-34.
[2] *Cal. of St. Pap.*, Spain, VOL. IV, i, p. 644 f. (18 July 1530); Campeggio's report of 5 July in *R.Q.*, XVIII (1904), pp. 358 ff. For what follows cf. also Loaysa's letters of 18 and 31 July, Heine, *Briefe*, pp. 18 ff.; *Coll. doc. inéd.*, VOL. XIV, pp. 43 ff., 52 ff.
[3] *R.Q.*, XVIII (1904), p. 363.
[4] Last printed in *C.T.*, VOL. IV, pp. xli ff.

a Council.[1] At the Curia feeling in regard to such an assembly was more hostile than ever. The dangers which a Council was sure to conjure up in both the ecclesiastical and the political spheres were painted in lurid colours. Not only the Germans but other nations also would endeavour to wrest concessions from the assembly by threats of a schism in the event of a refusal, while the presence of Francis I and other princes would revive the differences between the great powers which had been composed so very recently. As for Henry VIII, he would make his participation depend on a favourable decision in his matrimonial affair. The French party in Rome, of which Cardinal Grammont was the heart and inspiration, did its best to exacerbate the general aversion for the Council, so much so indeed that even Charles's own ambassador, Mai, as well as Cardinal Loaysa, the nominee of the Spanish crown, did not remain unscathed. The latter, at any rate, who had been at one time Charles's confessor, was convinced in his heart of hearts that fire and sword were the only effective weapons against heresy. If these could not be brought into action, an understanding with the Protestants and a tacit toleration of their errors would always be preferable to a conciliar solution.

The Pope's letter of 31 July arrived at Augsburg on 9 August. By that time the first phase of the negotiations was at an end. The imperial *Confutatio* had been read to the Protestant Estates on 3 August. It was bluntly rejected by their divines; Melanchthon described it as perfectly childish.[2] Neither the personal intervention of the Emperor nor the threats of Joachim, the Elector of Brandenburg, made the slightest impression on the Protestants. The Landgrave Philip of Hesse's flight on the evening of 6 August still further increased the confusion and mutual distrust. The Protestants persisted in taking cover behind their appeal to, and offer of, a Council.[3] They were not to be put off by the Elector Joachim's pointed query how their show of readiness for a Council was to be reconciled with Luther's rejection of it at Worms.[4]

---

[1] *Cal. of St. Pap., Spain*, VOL. IV, i, p. 645; *Coll. doc. inéd.*, VOL. XIV, pp. 52 ff. That the Emperor was well aware of the Pope's sentiments appears from Tiepolo's despatch of 12 August, cf. Walter, *Die Depeschen des venezianischen Gesandten N. Tiepolo*, p. 66 and an anonymous memorial in *A.R.G.*, XIII (1916), p. 63 f.

[2] "Valde pueriliter scriptum," *Acta comitiorum*, p. 35. The origin of the "Confutatio" is fully described in J. Ficker, *Die Konfutation des Augsburger Bekenntnisses* (Leipzig 1891); see also A. Paetzold, *Die Konfutation des Vierstädtebekenntnisses* (Leipzig 1900).

[3] Schirrmacher, *Briefe und Akten*, p. 118.

[4] Schirrmacher, *Briefe und Akten*, p. 200; cf. Förstemann, *Neues Urkundenbuch zur Geschichte der evangelischen Kirchenreformation*, VOL. II, p. 205. On 30 July Melanchthon wrote to Luther: "Quidam significant appellationem ad synodum non

They knew only too well that here was the weak spot in the Emperor's position. Nothing could throw a clearer light on the monarch's embarrassment than the recent papal letter. Both he and the Catholic Estates shrank from the use of force at this stage, while the Protestants greatly feared such a step. So negotiations were resumed in an attempt to reach an agreement on particular points. This was Melanchthon's hour.

For Luther's outstanding collaborator secession from the universal Church was as unthinkable as armed resistance to the Emperor, whose love of peace and religion he could not sufficiently extol.[1] With a view to creating a favourable impression in the monarch's mind Melanchthon had put in the foreground of the *Confessio Augustana* those things which the Protestants held in common with the Catholics, while throwing a veil over those that separated them or even leaving them out altogether, as, for instance, the doctrine of the papal primacy, Purgatory and indulgences. As early as June he made contact with Valdés and Schepper, both of them adherents of Erasmus, and on 5 July he paid his first visit to Campeggio. This visit was followed by two others, on 8 and 28 July, at which he also submitted some written explanations. Firmly convinced as he was that there was no "Span und Irrung" (mote and error) [2] in the teaching of the Protestants, he imagined he would be able to bring about their return to the Church provided they were granted certain concessions of a practical kind, such as Communion in both kinds, the marriage of priests, such alterations in the Canon of the Mass as harmonised with the Protestant teaching on the Lord's Supper, the abolition of private Masses and certain mitigations in the sphere of the *Jus humanum*.[3] He ended by declaring that he would be satisfied with only the first two of these concessions.

Campeggio interpreted Melanchthon's growing readiness to meet the Catholics as a sign of weakness. His remark on the possibility of

---

obfuturam nobis", *Acta comitiorum*, p. 34; cf. K. H. Hammer, "Kurfürst Joachim I von Brandenburg auf dem Reichstag zu Augsburg 1530", in *Wichmann-Jahrbuch*, 1 (1930), pp. 116-33.

[1] For what follows, see H. Virk, "Melanchthons politische Stellung auf dem Reichstag zu Augsburg 1530", in *Z.K.G.*, IX (1888), pp. 67-104, 293-340.

[2] Schirrmacher, *Briefe und Akten*, p. 97; *Corp. Ref.*, VOL. II, p. 170.

[3] For what follows, in addition to Melanchthon's letters (to those printed in *Corp. Ref.* must be added that of 3 June to Albrecht of Mainz in *A.R.G.*, XVII (1920), p. 67), see also the memorials in *Corp. Ref.*, VOL. II, pp. 246, 268 ff., 280 ff.; VOL. III, pp. 168 ff., and Campeggio's reports, Lämmer, *Mon. Vat.*, pp. 48, 52; *R.Q.*, XVII (1903), p. 401; XVIII (1904), p. 360.

concessions at the beginning of July sounded a good deal more encouraging than the reply which Campeggio's secretary Bonfio delivered in the name of the legate, who had been taken ill, to Melanchthon who was also laid low by sickness.[1] It is difficult to ascertain how far his action agreed with the Pope's views at this time. On the whole, Campeggio saw quite clearly that the trench which divided the Protestants from the Church was much deeper than Melanchthon was willing to admit, nor did it escape him that the one man who really mattered, viz. Luther, as well as the other authoritative political leaders could not be persuaded to come to terms at any price. For these reasons Campeggio was opposed to the negotiations for a compromise which opened in mid-August. They were organised by the Emperor though it is unlikely that he still believed that complete agreement on all points in dispute was attainable. The Protestants' rejection of the *Confutatio* had taught him that their obstinacy was greater and the existing divergences more fundamental than he had at first imagined. He was nevertheless in a position to claim that his policy of accommodation would be an immense gain if, as a result of a *rapprochement* to the Church on the part of the Protestants, even if it had to be bought at the price of concessions in the disciplinary sphere, the movement of secession were arrested and the Catholic position secured until a Council should speak the last word on all the questions in dispute. The repeated reference to a future Council in the course of these discussions is sufficient proof that on a number of points the negotiators themselves regarded their work as purely provisional.

Apart from the inherent difficulties of the discussions the prospects of an accommodation were further jeopardised by the very composition of the negotiating committee. It consisted of seven princes, jurists and theologians for each of the two parties to the controversy. Thus Melanchthon, who was prepared to come to an understanding, was faced by Johann Eck as the leading theologian of the opposite party. It was hardly to be expected that Bishop Stadion of Augsburg, a friend of Erasmus, and the Chancellor of Baden, Vehus, known for his previous attempts at mediation, would be able to hold their own against a man like Eck, especially after the replacement of Duke Henry of Brunswick by Duke George of Saxony. It was equally evident that John Frederick of Saxony, the Saxon Chancellor Brück, and Philip of Hesse's theologian

---

[1] Salviati on 10 August, *R.Q.*, XVIII (1904), p. 383; Mai's reports of 18 and 26 July already mentioned in part, *Cal. of St. Pap., Spain*, VOL. IV, i, pp. 644 f., 660 f.

Schnepf, had been instructed to restrain their theological spokesman Melanchthon from making over-generous concessions. The committee of fourteen entered upon its task on 16 August. The negotiations turned not so much on the actual dogmas of the faith as on those manifestations of the religious life of the Church which embodied most clearly the differences between Catholics and Protestants,[1] such as Communion in both kinds, the marriage of priests, the sacrifice of the Mass, the fate of the monasteries and lastly, and this was the heart of the matter, recognition of episcopal jurisdiction. The Protestants' return to obedience at least for the limited period before a Council was regarded by the Catholics as the touchstone of their sincerity while the former feared that in that case the bishops would forcibly suppress all the innovations that had crept in up to then and restore the previous order of things. In the end they were very glad that this concession, to which Melanchthon had consented in principle on 21 August, was never put into effect, for as the negotiations progressed they became increasingly convinced that Melanchthon was going too far in his readiness to meet their opponents. The aggressive tendency of the Hessians was visibly gaining ground,[2] with the result that when, on 24 August, Melanchthon joined the discussions of a smaller committee composed of only three learned representatives of each party, he was instructed to refrain from further concessions.[3] In vain Eck besought his opponent on 27 August to moderate his demands and to leave all difficulties to the Council. On 29 August the Protestants broke off negotiations with a *non possumus* while maintaining their appeal to the Council.[4]

The Catholics on their part also asked themselves, and with good reason, whether they had not gone too far when they agreed to tolerate certain Protestant practices, such as the Lutheran Mass, to the injury

[1] Account of the course of the negotiations in "Acta septem deputatorum", *R.Q.*, XIX (1905) *Gesch.*, pp. 138-43; Schirrmacher, *Briefe und Akten*, pp. 217 ff., 229 ff.

[2] Philip's letter to the councillors who had remained at Augsburg, *Corp. Ref.*, VOL. II, pp. 323 ff.

[3] Schirrmacher, *Briefe und Akten*, p. 242 f. Melanchthon nevertheless continued his efforts for a tolerable compromise for the Protestants, as is proved by his memorial on the Catholic proposals in the committee of six, 24 August, published by Schornbaum in *Z.K.G.*, XXVI (1905), pp. 144 ff.

[4] The "Non possumus" of the *Responsio exhibita cancellario Leodiensi* in the first days of September, *Corp. Ref.*, VOL. II, pp. 345 ff. The Protestants were well aware that behind the three articles on which they declared themselves unable to yield, viz. Communion in both kinds, the marriage of priests, the Canon of the Mass, there were other divergences of profound dogmatic significance, Schirrmacher, *Briefe und Akten*, p. 252; *Acta comitiorum*, p. 42 f.

of the very substance of Catholicism.[1] The Cardinal of Liège, who was still working for a compromise at the beginning of September, became hesitant and Campeggio deemed it advisable to warn the Emperor against concessions of too far-reaching a nature.[2] The warning was scarcely needed. When even his personal intervention on 7 September proved ineffective[3] Charles understood that they had come to the parting of the ways. The question was whether a policy of accommodation, together with the promise of a Council, would serve any good purpose, or whether a war of religion was the only remedy left. It had become necessary to face even that possibility. The Emperor had come to Germany without an army; if he was to wage a war of religion he must perforce rely on the help of the Catholic Estates and the Pope. When he broached the subject to the committee of princes, throwing out hints rather than unfolding a definite plan,[4] they refused to listen. They shrank from the sacrifices such a war would demand. In their embarrassment they suggested legal action against the Protestants, but as the Emperor would not desist they could think of no better way out of the impasse than fresh negotiations and a firm announcement of a Council, at the very latest at Christmas, as if the Emperor had not long ago done his utmost to get Rome to fix a date.

So yet another attempt at a compromise was made, though this time its scope was strictly limited. The proposals submitted to the Protestants on 12 September by William Truchsess, the father of the future Cardinal Otto of Augsburg, and by Dr Vehus[5] no longer aimed at a permanent reunion to be approved and completed by a Council; all that was aimed at was a temporary *modus vivendi* which would guarantee the tranquillity of the Empire; not an "ecclesiastical peace", but merely a "political" one. The articles on which agreement had been arrived at in August, as well as those which were still in dispute, were to be submitted to a Council. The Protestants were to pledge themselves not to introduce any further novelties in the meantime; not

---

[1] *Corp. Ref.*, VOL. II, pp. 341 ff.

[2] Walter, *Die Depeschen des venezianischen Gesandten N. Tiepolo*, p. 73.

[3] Schirrmacher, *Briefe und Akten*, pp. 257 ff.

[4] The "Proposition" of 8 September to the Estates, in the original French, in Rassow, *Kaiseridee*, pp. 401-5; the Latin translation, which differs on many points, in Raynald, *Annales, a.* 1530, Nos. 100-5; Le Plat, VOL. II, pp. 469 ff.; further correspondence in *R.Q.*, XX (1906) *Gesch.*, pp. 54-9.

[5] The eight articles, drawn up on 8 September, in *R.Q.*, XIX (1905) *Gesch.*, pp. 149 ff.; Le Plat, VOL. II, pp. 467 ff.; two different German formulas in Schirrmacher, *Briefe und Akten*, pp. 294-9. The idea of a temporary solution, one limited to externals, until the Council should meet, occurs already in the Protestants' reply to the chancellor of Liège; Schirrmacher, p. 251.

to give asylum to subjects of other princes; to retain the Mass and its Canon, while with regard to Communion in both kinds and the marriage of priests they would have to act in such a way as to be able to account for their conduct to the Emperor and the Council. The monasteries still in existence were to remain; the property of those already suppressed was to be administered by imperial trustees and the revenues derived from it devoted to the support of their banished inmates until the Council met.

These proposals went a long way to meet the Protestants. Of the original condition, their resumption of the practice of the Catholic religion, there practically remained not a trace except the restoration of the Canon of the Mass and the sequestration of the confiscated monastic property: the recognition of episcopal jurisdiction had been dropped. All the other innovations were tolerated, only the introduction of fresh ones was barred. But it was precisely to this attempt to halt them that the Protestants refused to submit. It prevented their progress and even jeopardised their very existence. "If we tolerate the monasteries that still remain," Justus Jonas wrote in a memorial of 13 September,[1] "above all, if we suffer the expelled religious to return, it will not take long before the private Mass and all other Catholic ceremonies are brought back." The fact is that it is of the very essence of a religious revolution that it cannot stop half way. Toleration is against its very nature: it must pull down and build anew if it wants to maintain itself. On 21 September the Protestant Estates accordingly rejected Truchsess's proposed *Provisorium*. In the collective memorial of their theologians [2] there is a remark to the effect that they did not regard the *Confessio Augustana* as a complete statement of Protestant doctrine. This then was the result of three months' negotiations for a compromise! The differences were more sharply accentuated than ever: Luther had triumphed over Melanchthon.[3]

In view of this issue the Protestants were bound to reject the Recess which the Emperor submitted to them on 22 September.[4] Once again they were granted time for reflexion until 15 April 1531, when they would have to submit a written explanation of their attitude to the

---

[1] *Corp. Ref.*, VOL. II, pp. 368 ff.
[2] *Corp. Ref.*, VOL. II, pp. 373 ff.
[3] *Corp. Ref.*, VOL. II, pp. 377 ff.
[4] Goldast, *Collectio constitutorum imperialium* (Frankfurt 1713), VOL. III, p. 513 f.; Le Plat, VOL. II, p. 472 f.; extract in *C.T.*, VOL. IV, p. xlv. Reports on the negotiations of 22 and 23 September in Lämmer, *Mon. Vat.*, p. 57 f.; *R.Q.*, xx (1906) *Gesch.*, pp. 60-4; Schirrmacher, *Briefe und Akten*, pp. 313-20.

articles on which no agreement had been arrived at. On the other hand, for the sake of public peace, the Emperor categorically ordered them to refrain from further propaganda and to tolerate the exercise of the Catholic religion wherever it was still practised. He also enjoined them to take strong measures against the Zwinglians and the Anabaptists. However, all the arguments, adjurations and threats of Joachim of Brandenburg, who again acted as spokesman for the Emperor and the Estates, failed to impress the Elector John of Saxony and his sympathisers. The Elector departed on 23 September; the rest followed his example.

The Emperor was greatly incensed by their obstinacy. He refused to accept Melanchthon's *Apologia*, a markedly polemical reply to the *Confutatio*. At a council of princes Charles dropped the remark, "Words and negotiations are useless—a strong fist alone avails!" [1] The rupture seemed an accomplished fact and forcible measures against the transgressors of the Edict of Worms the only solution. A point seemed to have been reached at which, fifteen years later, the Pope and the Emperor were to decide to declare war against the German Protestants.

If the war of religion did not break out there and then the reason was that the Emperor lacked the means to wage it. A great offensive alliance of the Catholic Estates, such as Joachim of Brandenburg and George of Saxony desired, was not to be thought of, and the ecclesiastical Electors of Cologne and Mainz were no less averse to it than the Count Palatine and the Bavarians. The Pope also was unhelpful. The imperial agent in Rome, Muscetula, sounded him, but to no effect. [2] The more clearly the Emperor realised that no help was forthcoming for a war of religion, the more anxious he was to keep the idea of a solution by means of a Council in the foreground. The Recess of the

---

[1] "Non verbis et consiliis, sed forti manu opus est," *R.Q.*, xx (1906) *Gesch.*, p. 63. "Wenig wort, aber ein starke faust" is the feeling of the men of Strasbourg, *Politische Correspondenz*, VOL. I, p. 501 f.; for the procedure, cf. the memorial published by Maurenbrecher, *Karl V und die deutschen Protestanten*, appendix, pp. 16*-21*.

[2] In the Emperor's letter of 23 September to Muscetula, in *A.R.G.*, XXIII (1906), pp. 68-71, the use for the war of religion of the 6000 mercenaries set free by the capitulation of Florence is only hinted at. In the letter of 4 October, which has not been preserved but the contents of which may be inferred from Loaysa's letter of 20 October (*Coll. doc. inéd.*, VOL. XIV, p. 92 f.), Muscetula was formally charged to ask the Pope for financial assistance. The latter, on his part, wrote to Lucca, Genoa, Venice, etc., *R.Q.*, XXI (1907), pp. 114 ff. As for public opinion, cf. Niño's report from Venice, 26 August and 27 October, *Cal. of St. Pap.*, *Spain*, VOL. IV, i, p. 619, and *A.R.G.*, XIII (1916-17), p. 72 f. Only at the beginning of December did the Pope offer 10,000 scudi a month, *R.Q.*, XXI (1907), p. 136.

Diet of 22 September accordingly contained a fresh promise of a Council. With the agreement of the Estates assembled at Augsburg the Emperor pledged himself to bring pressure to bear on the Pope and on Christian princes to the end that within six months of the conclusion of the Diet a General Council should be proclaimed and assembled within a year of its convocation. He described a Council as "the only remedy". In his mouth this was no mere commonplace. It was not his fault if once again he had to present himself before the Estates with a promise on his lips instead of with a papal Bull of Convocation in his hand.

The Pope's last word on the question of the Council was his letter of 31 July. During the month of August the imperial chancery had drawn up a reply in which the Emperor disposed of the Pope's objections. He pointed out that a Council was absolutely indispensable, were it only in order to refute the innovators' pretension that they, not the Roman Church, stood for genuine, original Christianity.[1] The document was not despatched because the Emperor wished to await the issue of the negotiations for reunion. Now that they had failed, and owing to the impossibility of a display of force, a Council no longer appeared to him as the crown and conclusion of a peaceful reunion. As such he had viewed it in the summer: now he saw it as an emergency escape from an almost hopeless embarrassment.[2] In an autograph letter of 30 October he explained the new complication to the Pope.[3] "No danger", he wrote, "that a Council might conjure up is commensurable with the terrible harm that its neglect would entail. It is even more urgently needed to ensure the very existence of Catholicism than for the disposal of the actual dispute." This was exactly the idea that was to prove decisive for the convocation of the Council of Trent. In order to leave the Lutherans no pretext for boycotting the assembly the Emperor named two cities still nominally subject to imperial overlordship, viz. Mantua and Milan, as suitable localities. On 15 November the bearer of the letter, Pedro de la Cueva, arrived in Rome,[4] where during the summer months, the rosiest hopes had been entertained.

---

[1] *A.R.G.*, XIII (1906), pp. 64-8; cf. p. 48 f.

[2] Charles V to Loaysa, 20 October 1530, *A.R.G.*, XIII (1916), p. 71 f.

[3] Heine, *Briefe*, pp. 530-3; before this the instructions for Cueva; information about the contents in *Cal. of St. Pap.*, *Spain*, VOL. IV, i, p. 787 f.; *C.T.*, VOL. IV, i, p. xlvi f.

[4] Salviati puts Cueva's arrival on 16 November for on the 18th he writes that Cueva arrived "the day before yesterday", *R.Q.*, XXI (1907), p. 133, but Cueva himself gives the date of 15 November, *Cal. of St. Pap.*, *Spain*, VOL. IV, i, p. 809.

The Corpus Christi procession through the streets of Augsburg, in which the Emperor and most of the princes had taken part,[1] as well as Melanchthon's conciliatory attitude, the obvious good-will and apparently unlimited authority of the head of the Empire, had combined to create the erroneous impression that the power of the Protestants was broken and that they were prepared to yield. The committee of cardinals were thunderstruck when on 29 September they listened to Campeggio's report of the 13th [2] in which he described the ineffectual negotiations for a compromise and foreshadowed an eventual rupture. The Pope was beside himself.[3] The spectre of a Council was now actually at his door, more menacing than ever. If he refused to convoke it he would be accused of hindering the settlement of the religious conflict in Germany. If he yielded he would be swept out into a sea of peril.

The policy he had hitherto pursued was based upon the opposition between the houses of Habsburg and Valois. But what if Francis I should decide to come to the Council at the same time as the Emperor— a prospect that looked likely enough? [4] In spite of all their protestations of loyalty it might well come about that one day he would be faced, all alone, by an overwhelming opposition. His own person would be dragged into the debate; gossip about his birth and his election would be revived, nay, as at Constance, they might even proceed to elect a new Pope.[5] Even the wishful dream of certain Venetians might come true, for there were those who hoped that a Council would partition the States of the Church, when Venice would come into possession of certain long-coveted territories in the Romagna.[6]

When Cueva presented the Emperor's letter on 16 November the Pope read it at once in presence of the envoy.[7] After reading the first

---

[1] Soriano's reports on impressions in Rome, July 1530, in Sanudo, *Diarii*, VOL. LIII, pp. 330, 368.

[2] Loaysa on 1 October, *Coll. doc. inéd.*, VOL. XIV, pp. 80 ff.; also Campeggio's report of 13 September, *R.Q.*, XIX (1905) *Gesch.*, pp. 145-9.

[3] Mai's report of 30 September, *Cal. of St. Pap.*, *Spain*, VOL. IV, i, p. 732.

[4] *Cal. of St. Pap.*, *Spain*, VOL. IV, i, p. 815; more in the next chapter.

[5] According to Mai's report of 10 October, *Cal. of St. Pap.*, VOL. IV, i, p. 748, Ghinucci "had sold" to Henry VIII two Bulls of Julius II on the election of a Pope, "for the purpose of seeing what harm the English can do with or without a council". Mai felt that if either of these two Bulls were to be submitted to the Council, the Emperor would find it difficult to save the Pope. The reference is undoubtedly to the Bull *Cum tam divino* of 14 January 1505 and the Bull of Approval of 16 February 1513; Pastor, VOL. IV, ii, p. 876 f.

[6] *Cal. of St. Pap.*, *Spain*, VOL. IV, i, p. 699; Niño's report of 26 August 1530.

[7] Cueva's and Mai's reports of 17 November, *Cal. of St. Pap.*, *Spain*, VOL. IV, ii, pp. 809 ff. Cueva simultaneously presented a letter of the Emperor on the affairs of Florence and on Ferdinand's election as King of the Romans.

half the pontiff heaved a deep sigh. When he had read to the end he groaned a second time. His whole bearing betrayed deep depression. No! he could not say; to say Yes! seemed to him like signing his own death-warrant. Of the Emperor's good intentions he had no doubt, but would not events prove too strong for him? "A handful of drunken Germans are out to upset the Council and the whole world!" Quiñónez heard him say in a bitter tone.[1] "Let them! I shall then flee into the mountains. The Council may elect a new Pope—a dozen Popes—for each nation will want its own particular Pope!"

Cueva failed to dispel the Pope's fears, his only reply was more groans.[2] The envoy had a strong impression that they wished him to the devil—him and his demand for a Council. There was a general conviction that the Pope would never consent to the meeting of a Council. On the other hand well-informed people like Muscetula, Quiñónez and Loaysa knew by the end of November that there was no danger of a flat refusal. On 18 November Clement VII acknowledged the Emperor's letter[3] and asked for time to take counsel with the cardinals. As in June the committee of cardinals discussed the question in the first instance on 21 and 25 November; the consistory did so on the 28th. Cardinal Cibo read a letter from the Emperor addressed to the Sacred College, the text of which has not been preserved. All the documents relating to the affair, including those in Loaysa's possession, were laid before the cardinals.

There were those in the Sacred College who saw clearly what was wanted and who accordingly pressed for an immediate convocation of a Council. Among the keenest Loaysa mentions the canonist Del Monte, who had purposely returned to Rome in order to urge his opinion. He was supported by the one-time General of the Augustinians, Egidio of Viterbo, and by Alessandro Farnese.[4] The opinion of these men had great weight, but they were too few. The majority of the cardinals were utterly averse to a Council. They did not say so openly, but disguised their real sentiments under cover of sundry more or less plausible counter-proposals. Some demanded that a decision

---

[1] Mai on 28 November, *Cal. of St. Pap.*, *Spain*, VOL. IV, i, p. 822 f. and No. 219, though this, like No. 215, is wrongly dated 1529.

[2] *Cal. of St. Pap.*, *Spain*, VOL. IV, i, p. 828 f.; Cueva's report of 29 November.

[3] *Cal. of St. Pap.*, *Spain*, VOL. IV, i, p. 812, and Salviati to Campeggio, *R.Q.*, XXI (1907), p. 133 f. The extracts from this papal letter and those of 6, 9 and 20 December, which were made at the imperial court are in *Coll. doc. inéd.*, VOL. IX, pp. 81 ff.

[4] Loaysa to Charles V, 30 November 1530; Heine, *Briefe*, pp. 68 ff.; *Coll. doc. inéd.*, VOL. XIV, pp. 104-11; description of the parties in Mai's report of 28 November, *Cal. of St. Pap.*, *Spain*, VOL. IV, i, p. 822; Schönberg's objections, *ibid.*, p. 826.

should be held over until the rest of the princes had been informed. Others advocated a congress on the model of that of Mantua. No uncertainty exists about the chief motive of their aversion to a Council: they were aware that a great reforming Council, such as the one Charles V had in mind, threatened the foundations on which their style of living had been based for a hundred years. They also felt that any danger that might arise for the Pope from the partisans of conciliar theory threatened them equally.[1] However, they did not venture to advise the Pope to reject the demand. When it came to voting, all the twenty-six cardinals present spoke in favour of an affirmative answer though, as Loaysa sarcastically observes, they did so like merchants who jettison their wares in order to save the ship and their own lives.

The most competent of all the Pope's advisers, Cardinal Campeggio, set down his views in a confidential letter.[2] He saw three possibilities: a sincere Yes! which must be followed up with appropriate measures; a clear No! which must be fully justified; a qualified Yes! which would make the convocation of the Council dependent on the rest of the powers. The next steps, if the latter course were adopted, would be the postponement of the opening of the assembly and its eventual translation to a safe place. Campeggio excused himself for so much as mentioning this third course since it was in keeping neither with the dignity of the Vicar of Christ nor with the importance of the question. However, he knew the Pope too well not to be aware that it was the one course that would commend itself to a vacillating, timorous nature such as Clement VII's. As a matter of fact this was the path the Pope decided to enter upon.

In this way an impression was created abroad that a decision in favour of the Emperor's demand for a Council had been arrived at. The Pope seized every opportunity to appeal to the Emperor's sense of responsibility. To Muscetula he observed, "I place my life and my

[1] On the whole subject, cf. Salviati to Campeggio, 26 November 1530, *R.Q.*, XXI (1907), pp. 134 ff., and Sanseverino's consistorial acts in *C.T.*, VOL. IV, p. xlviii. Campeggio's letter which, according to *Cal. of St. Pap., Spain*, VOL. IV, i, p. 814, was read in consistory cannot be the one of 31 October, nor that of 11 November, since there is no mention in either of any observations by the Emperor on the Council's duty to initiate a reform, hence the reference must be to the letter of 11 August, Lämmer, *Mon. Vat.*, pp. 49 ff.; see also Walter, *Die Depeschen des venezianischen Gesandten N. Tiepolo*, p. 66; in that case Cardinal Quiñónez's instructions to his agent are to be placed not in November but at the end of September. They are nevertheless important for an estimate of the attitude of the cardinals.

[2] Lämmer, *Mon. Vat.*, pp. 64 ff. It is immaterial that this letter, dated 13 November, only reached Rome on 10 January, *R.Q.*, XXI (1907), p. 132; in the circumstances it had no direct influence on the Pope.

dignity under the Emperor's protection." [1]   In all these discussions the personal intervention at the Council of both heads of Christendom was, of course, taken for granted.   Had Clement VII at last satisfied himself as to the necessity of a Council?   And was he in earnest about it as some eminent observers, even in the imperial camp, believed?

The first question may be answered in the affirmative, the second in the negative.   One of the Pope's confidants, his secretary Sanga, admitted at a later period that, at bottom, Clement VII had always been opposed to a Council and had only yielded for the Emperor's sake. He gave way, but reluctantly and with many misgivings.   He did not dare to refuse a Council, but he had no intention of bringing it about. He continued to tack according as the wind blew, and all the time at the back of his mind he cherished a hope that something would crop up which would put a stop to the whole affair.   Nevertheless, as far as we know, he did not deceive the Emperor nor indulge in any double-dealing.[2]   Nothing is known about a hint he is alleged to have given to France to sabotage the Council.   The Pope gave a half-hearted assent, kept putting off a final decision and hoped for some obstacle to stop the project.   And all the time he kept negotiating.

[1] *Cal. of St. Pap., Spain*, VOL. IV, i, p. 817.
[2] Even Loaysa excluded the idea of a deliberate deception.   *Coll. doc. inéd.*, VOL. XIV, p. 147.

CHAPTER V

Fruitless Negotiations (1531-1534)

IN the consistory of 28 November 1530 Cardinal Farnese reminded the cardinals that it was necessary to inform the other Christian princes of the prospective convocation of a Council. Briefs to this effect were despatched as early as 1 December to the Kings of France, England and Scotland and to the Italian potentates. To the Emperor the Pope addressed a short letter in his own hand, dated 6 December, in which he announced the arrival of a nuncio extraordinary.[1] Nicholas von Schönberg, who had been considered for the post, was prevented by illness,[2] so the choice fell on the Vice-Legate of Bologna, Uberto Gambara,[3] a scion of an ancient family of Brescia, who had acted as nuncio in England and whose family connexions would make him acceptable to the imperial party. He left Rome on 20 December, armed with instructions drawn up by Cardinal Cajetan and with oral directions from the Pope. The instructions raised a number of fundamental questions which, in reality, trenched on the sphere of theology. "Would the new Council have greater authority with the Protestants than the old ones? How is the discussion of their teaching, on which they insist, to be reconciled with the condemnation passed on it by earlier Councils? On what basis is it possible to discuss with them the nature of the Church and the sacraments since they claim to take their stand exclusively on the Bible and reject tradition as represented by the Fathers and the Councils?" In addition to these theological

---

[1] *Cal. of St. Pap., Spain*, VOL. IV, i, p. 817.

[2] According to a report of Cueva's, 29 November, *Cal. of St. Pap., Spain*, VOL. IV, i, p. 829, besides Muscetula, the nephew of Cardinal del Monte, the future Pope Julius III, had also been considered.

[3] On the future Cardinal Gambara (1539) who died in 1549, see Buonaccorsi, *Antichità ed eccellenza del Protonotariato* (Faenza 1751), pp. 295 ff.; P. Guerrini, *Cardinali e vescovi bresciani* (Brescia 1915), p. 7; there is much information about his English nunciature in *Cal. of St. Pap., Venice*, edd. Rawdon Brown and Bentinck (London 1864 f.), VOLS. III and IV, index. Four of Bembo's letters in the latter's *Opera*, VOL. III (Venice 1729), pp. 62 ff. Uberto's brother Francesco was a captain in the Emperor's service. The instructions of 19 December, *C.T.*, VOL. IV, pp. lii ff.; credentials of the Pope and the cardinals of the same date, Lanz, *Correspondenz*, VOL. I, p. 409 f.; the contemporary letters of Cueva, Muscetula and Loaysa in *Cal. of St. Pap., Spain*, VOL. IV, i, pp. 849 ff.

problems the instructions raised others of an ecclesiastical-political character. The Protestants' conduct at Augsburg had made it clear that their sole aim in demanding a Council was to gain time. But would not a Council enable them to contrive a schism even more dangerous than that of Basle? When one recalled the fruitless efforts then made by the Emperor Sigismund, one might well ask, "Will the Emperor's presence at a Council that may go on for years guarantee the safety of the Pope as well as public order and tranquillity? Will he be strong enough to assert himself at a Council which claims superiority over the Pope? A Council actually claiming supreme authority on earth, even over emperors and kings? Lastly, is not the Turkish menace against which the Council is bound to take measures too pressing for defence measures to be so long delayed?"

To sum up: far from being the bearer of an expression of assent, Gambara was burdened with a packet of objections and queries which were nothing else but the Pope's supreme attempt to restrain the Emperor from proposing a Council. Gambara began by delivering his message by word of mouth on 16 and 17 January at Liège, where the court was resting on its progress to the Netherlands after the coronation of Ferdinand as King of the Romans at Aachen. He subsequently submitted them also in writing,[1] and in case the Emperor should stick to his proposal he enumerated the conditions which the Pope had attached to the convocation of the Council. They were five in number: (1) The only subjects of discussion at the Council were to be the new heresy and the Turkish war; (2) the Emperor was to pledge himself to assist in person at the Council during its entire duration; should he withdraw the assembly would be regarded as dissolved; (3) the Council was to meet in Italy and at a place designated by the Pope; (4) only those persons would have a vote who were entitled to it by canon law; (5) the Lutherans were to make a formal demand for a Council and to send plenipotentiaries.[2]

These conditions amounted to a rejection of the Emperor's proposal since the reform of the Church, which was the chief reason why he wanted a Council, was excluded from the agenda. And how could the ruler of a world-wide empire bind himself to attend from start to finish a gathering the duration of which no man could foretell? The Protestants were required to make a fresh request for a Council. In view of their former appeals they would surely refuse to do so, and if the Council

[1] *C.T.*, vol. IV, p. liv f.
[2] *C.T.*, vol. IV, p. lvii.

were to meet in Italy they would allege that there was no guarantee for their personal safety.

Gambara's objections and conditions did not take the Emperor by surprise; the reports from Rome of Cueva and other diplomatists had left him but little hope of anything else. Cautious and conscientious as he was, he sought the advice of his brother and the German princes.[1] He refused to be discouraged but stuck to his plan for a Council with the utmost tenacity. If he gained nothing else he was at least determined that the blame for the delay, or the failure to convoke a Council, should not rest on his shoulders. Before all else it seemed necessary to ascertain clearly Francis I's attitude to the question of a Council.

While the Diet was still in progress he had instructed his agent Noircarmes, who was about to proceed to Paris, not to broach the subject, or to do so only if a suitable occasion presented itself.[2] On the other hand he himself sounded Queen Eleanor, his sister.[3] The information he elicited sounded reassuring, in fact it was surprisingly favourable. More than that—on 21 November the King openly declared himself in favour of the convocation of a Council! The only suspicious circumstance was that he urged the choice of a locality that would suit the various nations and prayed that the time-limit within which the Council was to meet should not be too precisely laid down.[4] But when Charles's new agent, Louis de Praët,[5] arrived at the French court on 1 February, the King kept him waiting for an answer for nearly two months. The information he then gave could only be regarded as a delaying manœuvre.[6] Francis proposed a convention of ambassadors in Rome whose task it would be to examine all particular questions connected with a Council. Whether or no a Council would meet would depend on the reply of the Lutherans. He made no comment on the Pope's conditions. This gave rise to a suspicion of the existence

---

[1] Lanz, *Correspondenz*, VOL. I, pp. 429 ff. (3 April 1531); on 27 April Ferdinand replied, "No . . . es razón de dexarlo caer," *ibid.*, p. 443.

[2] Weiss, *Papiers*, VOL. I, p. 478. Noircarmes was told to insist that Charles's desire for a Council was not prompted by personal considerations but by his concern for the general good of Christendom.

[3] *C.T.*, VOL. IV, p. xliv, *n.*1.

[4] *C.T.*, VOL. IV, p. l.

[5] Instructions of 1 February 1531 in Weiss, *Papiers*, VOL. I, p. 502 f. Here too Charles stresses once more the general good of Christendom ("au bien de nostre sainte foy et à la respublique crestienne"). He does not wish his envoy de Praët to enter into particulars about the convocation and eventual celebration of the Council.

[6] I have not the text at hand, but the Emperor's reply of 3 April 1531 (Weiss, *Papiers*, VOL. I, pp. 512 ff.) and his letter to Ferdinand of the same day already mentioned (Lanz, *Correspondenz*, VOL. I, pp. 429 ff.) enable us to infer its contents.

of a secret understanding between him and the Curia [1] for the purpose of putting off a Council indefinitely while laying the responsibility to the Emperor's charge.

This unwelcome but by no means unexpected information did not prevent the Emperor from assuring Gambara on 4 April at Ghent that the objections which had been laid before him did not shake his conviction of the absolute necessity of a Council, though it was for the Pope to take the appropriate steps for its realisation.[2] He explained his attitude to the five conditions in a note which his ministers Granvella and Cobos presented to the internuncio. He insisted that the agenda of the Council must not be restricted from the start to the heresy and the Turkish war. The convocation, therefore, must be couched in a general formula and without any restriction of the above kind. Nor would he hear of the procedure being exclusively governed by written Canon Law, the stipulations of which, as a matter of fact, were inadequate. He added yet another guiding rule—a highly questionable one—namely, the practice of earlier Councils. He held out the prospect of his personal attendance for as long as the business of the Council made it desirable and once again designated Milan or Mantua as the most convenient places of assembly. The last condition, that the Protestants should make a fresh demand for a Council, had been dropped by Gambara.[3] Before returning to Rome with this information the internuncio repaired once more to Brussels to put the Emperor on his guard against "the deadly medicine" which he was in the act of prescribing for ailing Christendom.[4] Unless the Council's range of business was restricted beforehand it would undoubtedly pounce at once upon the question of authority, proclaim itself superior to the Pope and devise an order of procedure on the model of Constance, with the result that ten or eleven Englishmen would count for as much as one or two hundred prelates of any other conciliar nation. From one piece of advice which Gambara gave to the Emperor, no doubt without

---

[1] Mai expresses this suspicion already on 10 January and gives it as his opinion that Francis I would exact payment for his support of the papal policy in some other way, *Cal. of St. Pap., Spain*, VOL. IV, ii, p. 11; Muscetula's view, *ibid.*, p. 18 f.

[2] In the "Respuesta" we read: "A él (S.S.dad) toca la determinación de lo que se debe y es necesario y conviene hacer," *Coll. doc. inéd.*, VOL. IX, p. 87.

[3] *C.T.*, VOL. IV, p. lx.

[4] Ehses has furnished convincing proof that Gambara, not Campeggio, is the author of the memorial in *C.T.*, VOL. IV, pp. lxi-lxiii. The text is unfortunately so corrupt in many places that the meaning is obscure. The manuscript which Gambara took with him to Rome from the imperial court is in the Vatican Archives, Lettere di principi, 11, fol. 232ʳ.

any formal commission by the Pope, though certainly in accordance with his intentions, we learn what was uppermost in his mind. It was that, come what may, the opening of the Council should be delayed for two years. Much might happen in two years. Like the King of France, Gambara also strove to gain time.

In Rome Francis I's reply to Praët gave great satisfaction to the opponents of the Council.[1] "It is all up with the plan for a council," they said, with a sigh of relief. At the same time rumours were circulating about a forthcoming meeting of the three heads, either at Bologna or at Nice. The Pope energetically disclaimed his having instigated the French intrigue.[2] In the opinion of the imperial diplomatists it was the work of the former French ambassador in Rome, Grammont, now a cardinal. The cardinal reasoned thus: "If we put the Pope under obligation by preventing a Council we may succeed in drawing him once more into the main stream of French policy; and this all the more surely if we offer him an advantageous family connexion such as the marriage of his niece Catherine with the King's second son, Duke Henry of Orleans." Events were to show that Grammont's calculations were correct; but it took time before the Pope got over his unpleasant experiences with his French allies during the war. Meanwhile he continued the policy on which he had agreed with the Emperor. His nuncio, Trivulzio, sought to win over Francis I for the convocation of a Council. Among the places suggested for its assembly, besides Mantua and Milan, were Bologna and Piacenza, both within the Papal States.[3]

However, neither the Pope's own action nor a fresh mission of de Praët to the French court helped in any way to forward the affair of the Council in that quarter. When Cardinal Grammont came to Rome in May 1531 to negotiate the marriage of Catherine de' Medici with Henry of Orleans, he bluntly announced that the King would only accept Turin as a meeting-place.[4] No further doubt remained: Francis I

---

[1] Mai's despatches of 28 March, 5 and 14 April, and Muscetula's of 13 April are in *Cal. of St. Pap., Spain*, VOL. IV, ii, pp. 105, 111, 118 ff.

[2] Thus Mai's above-mentioned report of 28 March. Loaysa felt the Pope's assurances could be relied upon because in the course of the audience the pontiff did not hesitate to read to him two despatches from the French nuncio which had only just been handed to him and which he had not yet seen himself, *Coll. doc. inéd.*, VOL. XIV, p. 147, and he stuck to this opinion even later on, *ibid.*, p. 188 f.

[3] The text of the Pope's letter to Francis I is not known; our only knowledge of the nature of its contents is derived from the letters of Loaysa and Salviati, Heine, *Briefe*, pp. 421, 541; cf. *C.T.*, VOL. IV, p. lxv.

[4] Extracts of the correspondence in *C.T.*, VOL. IV, p. lxvi f.

sought to prevent a Council. His chief motive was no less clear. A settlement of the religious discord in Germany by means of a Council would have meant an immense increase of power for the Emperor, while a further smouldering of the conflagration could only diminish it. The political alliance of the Protestant princes and towns—the so-called League of Schmalkalden, founded on 27 February 1531—constituted a natural ally for the French King against the head of the Empire. For reasons of state Francis favoured the division of the Empire into two religious parties and sought to frustrate every measure that could have led to a permanent understanding, among which a Council would have been by far the most effective.

The exchange of ideas on the question of a Council which Campeggio kept going throughout the summer of 1531 did not lead to an appreciable reconciliation of the two opposite points of view. The consistory of 10 August 1531 arrived at the unanimous conclusion that a Council could not be convoked before all obstacles had been removed and all Christian princes had given their assent.[1] These preliminary conditions were incapable of fulfilment. France's attitude, as well as that of England, her ally, made it evident that the Recess of Augsburg would not be executed. The Emperor accordingly decided to summon another Diet before returning to Spain. This Diet was all the more necessary as he needed more than ever the assistance of the Estates against the Turks. With a view to inducing the members of the League of Schmalkalden to supply him with auxiliaries he instructed Cardinal Albrecht of Mainz and the Count Palatine Frederick to enter into negotiations with them, first at Schweinfurt and later on at Nuremberg, in the hope of reaching an *Interim* which, while it sacrificed no dogmatic principle, would guarantee, in the name of the Emperor and the Empire, the continuation of the *status quo* until a Council should meet.

The Curia took good care to hold aloof from these negotiations so as to avoid anything that might be interpreted as a recognition of basic Protestant principles.[2] On the other hand the Pope was more willing

---

[1] Text of the consistorial acts in P. Kalkoff, *Forschungen zu Luthers römischen Prozess*, p. 93.

[2] If we may give credence to Aleander's later reports, there were people in Rome also who advocated an understanding with the Protestants, Lämmer, *Mon. Vat.*, pp. 114, 129, 134. The nuncio based one of his many warnings against any kind of participation of the Curia (to those printed in Lämmer must be added that of 26 March, Vat. Arch., Germania, 54, fol. 113ʳ) on this particular motive—that if an understanding were to be brought about, it could only be revoked by a Council "quod non solum est contra propositum nostrum, ma etiamdio tanto lungo da farse", Lämmer, *Mon. Vat.*, p. 118.

than ever to come to terms with the innovators on the basis of concessions in the sphere of discipline. For by this means he hoped to render a Council superfluous and to rid himself of the worry it was causing him. By his order Cardinal Cajetan drew up a memorial in which he marked off the boundary lines beyond which there could be no concessions.[1] For so great a theologian it was obvious that there could be no question, to give only one instance, of tampering with the sacrificial character of the Mass, by the elimination of the Canon, which had been discussed at Augsburg. On the other hand he recommended for Germany the concession of the marriage of priests, on the model of the Greek Church, as well as Communion in both kinds, subject to the stipulations laid down at Basle. But his most far-reaching proposal was the issue of a general decree, that is one that would be valid throughout the whole Church, to the effect that the commandments of the Church regarding the reception of the sacraments and the feast and fast days were not binding under grave sin. Such a decree would have removed a number of difficulties arising from the Protestants' attitude to the *jus humanum*. The concessions advocated by Cajetan appeared so extraordinary to his canonist colleague Accolti that he deemed it incumbent on him to warn the Pope against granting them, on the ground that he would run the risk of deposition by the Council as a disturber of ecclesiastical discipline. Cajetan even went a step further. He gave it as his opinion that reunion with the Protestants could be brought about provided they gave an assurance that they believed all that the universal Church believed; no need to demand a formal recantation from their theologians, or a formal profession of faith from

---

[1] Cajetan's and Accolti's memorials are published by W. Friedensburg in *Q.F.*, III (1900), pp. 16 ff.; cf. the letters of Loaysa and Mai, in Heine, *Briefe*, pp. 154 ff. also *Cal. of St. Pap.*, *Spain*, VOL. IV, ii, p. 660 f. If the date of the last-named letter is correct (26 July 1530), Cajetan's memorial would fall in the month of July 1530, that is during the sitting of the Diet of Augsburg. The discussion between Cajetan, L. Campeggio and Egidio of Viterbo, of which Sadoleto speaks in his commentary on *Romans* (*Opera*, ed. Ransilius, 1607, VOL. IV, p. 323 f. and p. 328) falls in the same period. The three cardinals were agreed that a papal declaration to the effect that the law of fasting did not bind under sin was desirable. Sadoleto, however, counselled the Pope to wait until a formal demand to that effect should be made. If we are to judge fairly the readiness of these circles for concessions, we must bear in mind that after Aleander had read the *Confessio Augustana* and the *Apologia* (May 1532), even he came to the conclusion that an understanding might have been reached at Augsburg. As for the *Apologia*, it was said in Rome itself that "esserli dentro molte cose buone", Lämmer, *Mon. Vat.*, pp. 114, 122. The Wittenberg divines put together the concessions which they found acceptable in the "*Consilium*" of 14 September 1531 cf. K. Graebert, "Konsilium für den 1531 zu Speyer angesetzten Reichstag", in *Z.K.G.*, XXVI (1905), pp. 150-8.

the Estates. It was impossible to go further in an endeavour to facilitate their return to the Church: the uttermost limit of what was possible had been reached, it may even have been crossed. Ten years earlier an offer such as this might have led to the return of a large part of the Lutherans, but by now their progress in the direction of a separate confessional community had advanced too far. Clement VII never made an offer of this kind to the German Protestants. How little he understood their mentality is glaringly illustrated by an incident which occurred about this time.[1] In the autumn of 1531 a Milanese of the name of Raffaele Palazzolo presented himself at the Vatican. The man claimed to have established contact with the court of the Elector of Saxony through a certain Master Jacob of Dresden. In this way he claimed to have ascertained that at that court there existed extraordinarily favourable conditions for reunion. He produced letters which seemed to confirm his assertions. With the Pope's approval Jacopo Salviati provided him with the means for another journey to Germany. At Augsburg Palazzolo got in touch with the local divines, especially with Urbanus Rhegius and Musculus, as well as with a Venetian Minorite of the name of Bartolomeo Fonzio, a fugitive from the Inquisition. From Augsburg he journeyed to Wittenberg by way of Nuremberg. The result of his negotiations was embodied in three documents, namely a statement by Luther on his attitude to reunion; a collective memorial of the divines of Augsburg, and, thirdly, a separate memorial by the Zwinglian Keller. These three documents stated that on certain specified conditions in the material as well as the personal spheres the theologians of Augsburg and Wittenberg were prepared to come to an agreement. Thus what had been vainly attempted at the Diets of Worms and Augsburg, with an enormous expenditure of human energy and material resources, appeared to have been achieved, or at least to have been brought within reach, by a single, skilful agent.

The pity of it was that the whole thing was a fraud. Luther's alleged statement is undoubtedly spurious, and if the two theological memorials are not a forgery, they were at least touched up by Palazzolo. A cheat had attempted to make a good thing out of a historic tension while Fonzio, his accomplice, hoped to rehabilitate himself by means

[1] J. Schlecht, "Ein abenteuerlicher Reunionsversuch", in R.Q., VII (1893), pp. 333-85; Th. Kolde "Über einen römischen Reunionsversuch", in Z.K.G., XVII (1897), pp. 258-69. Although Salviati wrote to the legate on 12 September 1531 that "S.B^ne non da intera fede a questa offerta" (Lämmer, Mon. Vat., pp. 78), it is nevertheless painful to see that so shady a "pratica" should have received any consideration at all.

of a trick. The Pope had been hoodwinked by a pair of rogues. Palazzolo's scheme for reunion, of which the papal diplomatists at the imperial court were duly informed—when too late—burst like the bubble that it was.

After all that had happened or, more accurately, had failed to happen, it was to be expected that during the forthcoming Diet the barometer would point to stormy weather. To conjure away the storm the Pope assigned to the Cardinal-Legate Campeggio, who was still at the imperial court but was often incapacitated by bouts of illness, a younger assistant in the person of Aleander, in the capacity of nuncio extraordinary. Thus, after an interval of ten years the creator of the Edict of Worms found himself once more on German soil.[1] It did not escape Aleander that in the meantime heads had cooled. At Mainz where he had barely escaped stoning, people vied with one another in doing him honour, and persons of position, who formerly avoided him, now sought him out. From the heights of religious and national enthusiasm people had come down into the lowlands of religious politics. In this field the resourceful Aleander saw many more opportunities than Campeggio, whose *caeterum censeo* was "only by force of arms can the Protestants be brought back to the obedience of the Emperor and the Roman Church".[2] In his reports Aleander unhesitatingly laid on the shoulders of the legate most of the blame for the failure of the Augsburg negotiations for a compromise and of the attempts to win back Melanchthon.[3] Opportunities had been allowed to slip; all they could do was to keep their eyes open for other chances. On the other hand even Aleander did not dare to make a stand for the solution which Quintana, the Emperor's confessor, represented as the only possible one.[4] "My whole frame trembles", he wrote to Salviati,[5]

[1] The chief sources for what follows are Aleander's register, Vat. Arch., Germania, 54, and Campeggio's despatches (original text) in Vat. Arch., Lettere de principi, 11, and Germania, 51. The extracts in Lämmer, *Mon. Vat.*, pp. 70-146, reproduce most of the passages relating to the Council but are not always complete: in what follows I fill in the gaps. A. Westermann's *Die Türkenhilfe und die politischkirchlichen Parteien auf dem Reichstag zu Regensburg 1532* (Heidelberg 1910) reached me too late.

[2] Lämmer, *Mon. Vat.*, pp. 73, 127.

[3] From Aleander's many sharp observations about the legate I cull only a few: Lämmer, *Mon. Vat.*, pp. 114, 120, 128 ("Dio perdoni a chi per negligentia o altri rispetti lo lassi perder"), p. 130 ("Il cuor mi creppa quando comprendo che si habbii persa una bella occasion di far bene"). The tension was further increased by the circumstance that both Aleander and Campeggio's brother Tommaso aspired to the Venetian nunciature.

[4] Aleander's report of 30 December 1531, Lämmer, *Mon. Vat.*, p. 93.

[5] Aleander's report of 25 November 1531, Vat. Arch., Germania, 54, fol. 55^v, Lämmer, *Mon. Vat.*, p. 90, but incomplete.

"whenever I have to make a report about the Council, for as soon as I open my mouth to utter a word I seem to feel the blows of those who accuse me of having thought of nothing but a Council during the whole of the last quarter of a century. Yet the reproach is without foundation. I have always felt that it would be better to reform the Church without a Council, that is, through the Pope alone; on the other hand a reform is inescapable."

If a nuncio had to reckon with sentiments of this kind in Rome, what are we to think of a brief which he presented at his first audience? In this document the Pope assured the Emperor once more that he was ready to hold a Council whose task it would be not only to recall the heretics but to reform the Church *in capite et membris*. In view of the fact that the Pope insisted at the same time that in no circumstances could it be convened without the assent of France and England, the whole thing remained problematic.[1]

As soon as the Diet opened at Ratisbon on 17 April 1532, the storm broke. The outbreak was not due to the League of Schmalkalden, whose members stayed away. Moreover, after protracted negotiations, the Emperor had concluded with them the Pacification of Nuremberg on 23 July.[2] This time trouble came from the Catholic Estates. "Each and all" Aleander wrote to Salviati,[3] "stubbornly demand that a Council be proclaimed within six months and convened within a year. Our best friends refuse to listen when we suggest a better remedy; they assure us that if we could only witness how passionately this affair is being discussed at the Diet we would not dare open our mouths."

The Estates' reply which was presented to the Emperor on 9 June,[4] was not restricted to this demand which would have been in accordance with the Recess of Augsburg—it went a good deal further. "If the Pope fails to call a Council," it said, "then our humble but pressing admonition and prayer is to the effect that your imperial majesty should yourself convoke and convene a General Council in your capacity as Roman Emperor." If the Emperor felt unable or unwilling to take

---

[1] Aleander's report of 19 November 1531, Lämmer, *Mon. Vat.*, p. 87 f.

[2] According to Granvella and Cobos both Campeggio and Aleander were kept informed of the negotiations. The most valuable appreciation of the situation is in Campeggio's memorial of 1 June, Vat. Arch., Lettere di principi, 11, fols. 180ʳ-182ᵛ, printed by Lämmer, *Mon. Vat.*, pp. 123-7. A. Engelhardt, "Der Nürnberger Religionsfriede" in *Mitteilungen des Vereins für Geschichte der Stadt Nürnberg*, xxxi (1933), pp. 17-123.

[3] Aleander to Sanga, 25 June 1532, Lämmer, *Mon. Vat.*, p. 138 f.

[4] *C.T.*, vol. iv, pp. lxxiii ff. The German text of the correspondence between the Emperor and the Estates is given by J. Ficker in *Z.K.G.*, xii (1891), pp. 583-618.

such a step there only remained the alternative of a national convention. Their suggestion, in other words, amounted to this, namely that the monarch should follow the example of Constantine and his successors in Christian antiquity and that of the Emperor Sigismund at the time of the Great Schism, by taking the convocation of a Council into his own hands. So embittered were the Catholic Estates by the dilatory tactics of the Curia and so great was their distrust of its intentions [1]— a distrust still further fomented from certain Italian quarters—that they encouraged the Emperor to make a schismatic conciliar proclamation and even reverted to the project of a national convention at Nuremberg so long ago condemned.

Charles V had no intention of allowing himself to be driven into so slippery a path. In his reply [2] he most loyally defended both his own and the Pope's conduct in the affair of the Council and requested the Estates to support his future endeavours which would take the form of an embassy to the Pope and eventually also to the King of France and other Christian princes. He was well aware that the man who in his blind hatred of the house of Habsburg was even then rousing the Catholic Estates against him, while seeking to push him on to the slippery slope of schism, namely the Bavarian chancellor Leonhard von Eck—had long ago entered into a secret agreement with the French and the men of Schmalkalden and was actually looking after the latter's interests.[3] The fact remained, however, that this time the Catholic Estates refused to be fobbed off with vague promises; they insisted on full compliance with the demands embodied in their first reply. They also drew attention to the fact that nothing had been done since the Diet of Augsburg in respect of the *gravamina*.[4]

One grave aspect of the Ratisbon demand for a Council was that

[1] The Duke of Ferrara claimed to have in his hands letters of the Pope in which the pontiff gave an assurance that for the time being he would issue no decision in the matter of Henry VIII's marriage "pur che per qualunque via si dimorasse il concilio", Lämmer, *Mon. Vat.*, pp. 77, 90 f.

[2] *C.T.*, VOL. IV, p. lxxvi f.; Granvella communicated the contents to Campeggio on 22 June, Vat. Arch., Lettere di principi, 11, fol. 139ᵛ.

[3] On Eck's intrigues, cf. Janssen, *Geschichte*, VOL. III, pp. 295 ff. (Eng. edn., VOL. V, pp. 367 ff.). It is a significant circumstance that both the plan for a national Council at Speyer in 1524 and the even more far-reaching proposals made to the Emperor originated in Bavaria.

[4] The "Replik" of 22 June is in *C.T.*, VOL. IV, pp. lxxvii ff. It was with difficulty that the Emperor succeeded in keeping out of the Recess of the Diet the proposal made to him that he himself should convoke a Council, Lämmer, *Mon. Vat.*, p. 143 f.; the Estates would not hear of the embassy which the Emperor wished to send to Rome in connexion with the affair of the Council and the *gravamina*; Z.K.G., XII (1891), p. 603, 27 June.

unlike a similar demand at Nuremberg nine years earlier it was not weighted with conciliarist and semi-Lutheran conditions. It came from the Catholic Estates exclusively and without any appendage of clauses that could never be fulfilled. The question of place and composition of the Council and the right to vote remained open and was left to the Pope's decision. It is evident that to some extent the ideas of the Catholic Estates had been clarified, a circumstance that would make it easier for the Pope to accede to their request for a Council. The Protestants, on the other hand, stuck to their idea of a Council as stated in the familiar Nuremberg formula.

By the terms of the Pacification of Nuremberg the Emperor was bound to work for the convocation of a "free Christian Council" within the agreed time-limit or to summon a new imperial Diet. An ambiguous situation was thus created which was bound to make it more difficult to accede to the demand for a Council.[1]

This embarrassing situation led to another meeting between Charles V and Clement VII at Bologna from 13 December 1532 to 28 February 1533.[2] During the three years since the first encounter of the two monarchs in the second city of the States of the Church the Council had not only not come one step nearer, but on the contrary, chiefly owing to the difficulties created by France and England, such an assembly had receded still further into the background. This time the Emperor came to Bologna firmly resolved to get the Pope to call a Council at once regardless, if necessary, of the two Western powers. It was to meet not in some German town, as the Protestants persisted in demanding, but in a city of Northern Italy, though not one situated in the States of the Church since in that case the Protestants would question the freedom of the assembly.[3] The Emperor failed in his resolve. Though voices were raised in the consistory of 16 December in favour of an immediate summons of a Council,[4] four days later the

---

[1] This equivocation did not escape the sharp eye of Aleander. On 21 June he notes that the Catholics "non contradicono che non si facci il concilio al modo antiquo di la Chiesa Catholica alcontrario di gli heretici li quali il demandono libero et in Germania", Lämmer, *Mon. Vat.*, p. 139, cf. p. 129.

[2] Its course is best described by Pastor, VOL. IV, ii, pp. 468 ff. (Eng. edn., VOL. X, pp. 216 ff.). However, it must be borne in mind that in this second encounter also most of the negotiations were conducted without witnesses and no record in writing was made.

[3] The chief witness is Guicciardini, who took a personal part in the negotiations, *Storia d'Italia*, xx, vi (ed. Panigada, VOL. V, p. 310 f.): (Cesare) "instava che il Papa *allora* lo intimasse". However even the attitude of the minority in the College of Cardinals, as shown on 16 December, presupposes a proposal of this kind by the Emperor.

[4] Report of the French ambassador François de Dinteville, Bishop of Auxerre, 24 December, Ranke, *Deutsche Geschichte*, VOL. III, p. 316.

majority of the cardinals swung round to the Pope's view that Francis I should be approached once more. The brief addressed to him on 2 January 1533 and briefs couched in almost identical terms destined for the Kings of England, Poland and Portugal had scarcely been despatched when on 3 January Cardinals Grammont and Tournon arrived at Bologna. It was generally believed that the only purpose for which the King had sent them was to prevent the proclamation of a Council.[1] The French reply, as was to be expected, was evasive, that is, in the circumstances negative.

The last uncertainty was thus disposed of: it was evident that for political considerations France was sabotaging a Council. If Clement VII nevertheless stuck to his condition that Francis I's assent to the convocation must be secured and if with the despatch of nuncios to France and Germany he took up once more the diplomatic game at the end of February, there is only one explanation for his conduct. He had given up every intention of convoking a Council and was merely pursuing a face-saving policy against the ceaseless pressure by the Emperor and the Catholic Estates.[2]

Three years earlier, at the Emperor's request, he had started negotiations, but had done so reluctantly. Now that France's attitude left no room for uncertainty he was unable to make up his mind to convoke a Council in virtue of his own apostolic authority, nor did he dare to break off negotiations with the Emperor before his political ties with France had been made more secure and the prospective family alliance between the houses of Valois and Medici brought about. The negotiations were no more than a façade which Clement VII actually needed, were it only because Charles V had promised the Estates that he would call a national convention in the event of the negotiations for a Council proving fruitless. Now a gathering of this kind was equally distasteful to the Pope and to the Emperor, as was shown by what happened in 1524. On the advice of Aleander, who had a seat in the mixed commission formed at the beginning of January,[3] soothing letters reporting

---

[1] "E opinion questi stà destinati per far cessar ogni pratica zerca il consilio," report of the Venetian envoys, 3 January, Sanudo, *Diarii*, VOL. LVII, p. 418.

[2] Sanudo, *Diarii*, VOL. LVII, p. 481 f. (28 January): "L'Imperator solicita al papa per il concilio"; also p. 499 (3 February): "Solicita li tre deputati per Sua Beatitudine a intimar il concilio"; cf. also pp. 515, 517.

[3] According to Aleander's account, whose observations in Cod. Vat. lat. 3914 are our main source of information on this point, the papal members of the commission included Farnese, Campeggio, Cesi, and Aleander, while the imperial side was represented by Merino, Cobos, Granvella and Mai. The Venetians also mention de Praët (Sanudo, *Diarii*, VOL. LVII, pp. 405, 452), whom Guicciardini (xx, vi) mentions

progress were despatched to King Ferdinand and to the Estates.[1]
When the nuncio was about to set out for Germany the Emperor
assigned to him a companion in the person of one of his counsellors,
Lambert de Briaerde, with secret instructions to keep a sharp eye on
his colleague lest he should sabotage the Council by some underhand
trick.[2] Charles V's distrust of the Pope's intentions was deep, but it
was not unjustified.

In the secret treaty [3] which the Pope and the Emperor concluded
at Bologna on 24 February, provision was made for a fresh attempt at
an understanding in the event of Germany, that is, the German
Protestants, rejecting a Council. The Pope undertook to do his utmost
to dissuade Francis I from putting any obstacles either to a Council
or to an understanding. No mention was made in the treaty of the
convocation of a Council even without France's assent. From this
fact we must infer that though the sixth and eighth paragraphs of the
instructions for the nuncio who was about to leave for Germany
contained a promise to ignore the opposition that might be expected
from one of the Christian potentates, and to convene within six months
—with the help of the *pars sanior* of the princes—a Council that would
deal with questions of faith and reform, the allusion was not to the
King of France but exclusively to the German Protestants.[4] In point
of fact it was they who constituted the second difficulty.

When Ugo Rangoni, Bishop of Reggio-Emilia [5] arrived in Germany

in connexion with the negotiations for an Italian alliance; in these some of the deputies
of the papal side also took part.
[1] The brief of 10 January to Ferdinand I in *C.T.*, VOL. IV, p. lxxxiv; the briefs to
the circles of the Empire and to the Electors in Raynald, *Annales, a.* 1533, No. 6; Le
Plat, VOL. II, p. 513 f. The Emperor's letters in Lünig, *Reichsarchiv*, VOL. II, p. 606 f.
(with the date of 8 January 1533).
[2] Lanz, *Staatspapiere*, p. 101. Lambert de Briaerde's commission to find out
what Ferdinand and the other princes thought of the possibility of satisfying Germany
in the event of the failure of the plan for a Council points in the same direction.
[3] Critical text by S. Ehses, in *R.Q.*, v (1891), pp. 299-307; the relevant passages
are on pp. 302 and 304.
[4] The instructions of 27 February 1533 which were approved by the mixed
commission and which are in complete agreement with Aleander's memorial (Lämmer,
Mantissa, pp. 139-43) are in *C.T.*, VOL. IV, p. lxxxvii f.
[5] Biographical details in Tiraboschi, *Biblioteca Modenese* (Modena 1781-6), VOL.
IV, p. 313; documents about his family in L. Rangoni Machiavelli, *Notizie sulla
famiglia Rangoni di Modena* (Rome 1909). According to Tiraboschi, *Biblioteca
Modenese*, VOL. IV, pp. 299 ff., Ugo's cousin Guido was a celebrated condottiere in the
service of the Emperor; Brown, *Cal. of St. Pap., Venice*, VOL. IV, p. 358. Ugo's
credentials for Ferdinand I, dated 20 February, in Raynald, *Annales, a.* 1533, No. 7;
those for Joachim I of Brandenburg in Lämmer, *Mantissa*, p. 141 f. S. Ehses, "Eine
Konzilsreise durch Deutschland im Jahre 1533", in *Pastor bonus*, XIV (1901-2), pp.
29-34.

in the capacity of nuncio he began by calling upon King Ferdinand in company with Briaerde. Afterwards he saw the Electors and the most influential members of the princely body. All of them hailed the announcement of the Council with enthusiasm and declared themselves satisfied with any of the prospective meeting-places—Mantua, Bologna, or Piacenza—even though two of them were within the boundaries of the Papal States. All of them protested their readiness to accept its decisions.[1] The Elector of Saxony, John Frederick, alone reserved his decision. He would only be in a position to give a definite answer after the convention of the League of Schmalkalden, which was fixed for the last days of June.[2] The League consulted the Wittenberg divines [3]; its answer eventually was what was to be expected in view of the theological principles on which it was based. The League roundly declined "a Council conducted according to the custom of the Church —*iuxta morem ecclesiae consuetum*"—because such an assembly would not be the "free Christian Council" they had been promised since there would be no guarantee that the controverted doctrines would be examined exclusively on the basis of Holy Writ. Moreover, the freedom of the assembly was already jeopardised by the fact that the princes had accepted its decisions in advance.[4]

[1] While Cardinal Albrecht of Mainz and his brother Joachim of Brandenburg expressly accepted not only any of the three localities proposed for the Council, but any place agreed upon by the two heads, Trier objected that the localities mentioned at previous Diets, viz. Metz, Cologne, Strasbourg and Mainz, could not be dropped without the agreement of the Estates. The Palatine Louis agreed for his own person but was of opinion that all the Estates of the Empire should be consulted.

[2] The *Articuli responsionis electoris Saxoniae* of 4 June in C.T., VOL. IV, p. xcii f.

[3] Melanchthon's opinion was "that they should be ready to attend" lest they put themselves in the wrong with other nations, but without engaging themselves to submit since the promise that the Council would be held according to ecclesiastical tradition was not unequivocal, Corp. Ref., VOL. II, p. 655. Jakob Ziegler's attack on Rangoni's conditions in K. Schottenloher, *Jacob Ziegler aus Landau* (Münster 1910), pp. 296 ff. The South German theologians did not agree altogether with the attitude of the Saxons; cf. "A. Blaurer to M. Bucer on 19 July 1533", in T. Schiess, *Brief-wechsel der Brüder A. und Th. Blaurer*, VOL. I (Freiburg 1908), p. 406. Martin Bucer published at this time his *Fürbereytung zum Concilio* (Strasbourg 1533).

[4] "Responsum electoris Saxoniae et conjunctorum principum, comitum ac civitatum datum Caes. M^tis oratori et Romani Pontificis nuntio", Schmalkalden, 30 June 1533, in C.T., VOL. IV, pp. xcvii-ci. Cochlaeus, who published the "Answer" together with other pieces in the following year (Dresden 1534, Spahn, *Cochlaeus*, bibliography No. 95) under the title of *De futuro concilio rite celebrando*, sarcastically observed in his preface that the *novus mos* according to which the Protestants wished to hold the Council would mean that the Pope was subject to the Emperor, that the cardinals and bishops were subordinate to the princes and the priests to the laity. The decisive significance of the principle of the Scriptures escaped him.

Thus for the first time the Protestants openly and formally refused "on principle" to recognise a Council proclaimed by the Pope. Up to this time they had joined the Catholics in the equivocal formula of a "free Christian Council". Now they parted company with them, unfolded before the papal envoy their own Lutheran conception of what a Council should be and rejected the Pope's offer of such a gathering. From this moment no more joint request for a Council was made by the German Estates.

However, the Protestants' rejection alone would not have prevented a Council had not France maintained her negative attitude. Ubaldini, the nuncio accredited to the Western powers, achieved even less than Rangoni. Francis I told him to begin by ascertaining Henry VIII's views. The latter sent him back to the French court. There he was finally told that the King would treat with the Pope personally at his forthcoming meeting with him. This meeting, for which Francis I had long been working, took place at Marseilles from 11 October to 12 November 1533.[1] The silence observed by both parties to the negotiations, which were exclusively conducted by word of mouth and without witnesses, wraps them in even greater mystery than the encounter of the Pope and the Emperor at Bologna. However, this much is certain, the question of a Council was discussed, but with the sole result that it was definitely shelved for the remaining years of Clement's pontificate.[2] According to information given by the Pope to Count Cifuentes, the imperial ambassador,[3] Francis I had declared that there could be no question of a Council because it could not possibly serve any useful purpose in the present state of tension between himself and the Emperor. It was a clear refusal which only thinly veiled the King's

[1] For what follows, see Pastor, VOL. IV, ii, pp. 477-82 (Eng. edn., VOL. X, p. 232).

[2] Antonio Soriano, the Venetian envoy who entered upon his duties immediately after the Pope's return from Marseilles, was in a position to base his judgment on what he learnt from the pontiff's most confidential advisers, viz. the Florentines Salviati, Pucci, Carnesecchi and Neri. He gave it as his opinion that Clement VII's journey to Marseilles had been chiefly inspired by his desire to rid himself of the incubus of the imperial demand for a Council, Albèri, *Relazioni*, VOL. II, iii, pp. 306 ff.

[3] Report of 14 October 1533 in *Cal. of St. Pap., Spain*, VOL. IV, ii, p. 825 f. This agrees with the Pope's letter of excuses to Ferdinand I and the circles of the Empire, 20 March 1534, Lämmer, *Mantissa*, p. 145; *C.T.*, VOL. IV, p. cvii. In the Pope's letter to the Emperor, 20 October 1533, published by Ehses, *Römische Dokumente zur Geschichte der Ehescheidung Heinrichs VIII von England* (Paderborn 1893), pp. 274 ff., the Council is not mentioned. Francis I's statements in his two letters of justification to the Estates of the Empire dated 1 and 25 February 1534 (publ. in *C.T.*, VOL. IV, pp. civ ff.) are tendentious and in part quite untrue.

aggressive designs on Milan.[1] We shall never know to what extent the Pope fell in with these designs, but that he had been gravitating towards France for some time appears from his renewed attempt to attract Giberti to Rome. The nomination at Marseilles of four French cardinals (at Bologna Charles V had with difficulty obtained the nomination of one) and the marriage on 28 October of Catherine de' Medici with Duke Henry of Orleans, at which the Pope himself officiated, filled the imperial diplomatists with profound distrust which even the soothing explanations of the Pope failed to dispel.[2]

Shortly before his departure from Marseilles the Pope was subjected to a painful humiliation. On 11 July 1533, after prolonged vacillation, he had declared Henry VIII's union with Anne Boleyn invalid. He had also fixed a time-limit—up to the end of September—within which Henry was to restore his lawful wife to her rightful position under pain of excommunication. On 7 November Dr Bonner, the King's agent, protested against the sentence in the presence of the Pope and, with the obvious purpose of intimidating him, appealed to a future Council. Since Pius II's prohibition no one had dared to do such a thing. When Bonner, as he read his document, came to the words *ad sacrosanctum concilium proxime jam futurum*, the Pope became exceedingly angry. How could it have been otherwise! Not many weeks before his nuncio had been unable to get an answer from Henry on the question of a Council, and now that same king appealed to a Council the convocation of which he had rendered impossible![3]

The result of the encounter of Marseilles, the postponement of a Council to an indefinite date, finally crushed the faith of the two Habsburg courts and that of the German Catholics in the Pope's intention to call such a gathering. Weak as that faith had been for a long time, Clement's attempt to exonerate himself and to lay the blame on Francis I only made matters worse.[4] Duke George of Saxony

[1] The draft of a treaty of seven points in Francis I's own hand foreshadows an offensive alliance for the conquest of Milan for the benefit of the Duke of Orleans as well as the cession of Parma and Piacenza; text in R. Reumont-A. Baschet, *La Jeunesse de Cathérine de Médicis* (Paris 1866), pp. 325 ff. Soriano too states that a delay of eighteen months before the outbreak of hostilities had been fixed, Albèri, *Relazioni*, VOL. II, iii, p. 309.

[2] *Cal. of St. Pap., Spain*, VOL. IV, ii, p. 846; so also, as against Soriano, Albèri, *Relazioni*, VOL. II, iii, p. 308.

[3] The chief source is Bonner's report of 13 November, *Cal. of Letters*, VOL. VI, pp. 566 ff.; also Cifuentes in *Cal. of St. Pap., Spain*, VOL. IV, ii, p. 852. The instructions of 1 November in P. Friedmann, *Anne Boleyn* (London 1884), p. 252 f.

[4] "La continentia dei brevi" (of 30 March), Vergerio wrote on 3 July 1534, "che io ho mandati in materia del concilio ha strannamente irritati tutti questi animi",

wrote bitterly: "While a hundred thousand souls perish, the appointed shepherd of souls makes common cause with our avowed enemy!" [1]

Dissatisfaction with the Pope's conciliar policy was general. The new nuncio at the court of Ferdinand I, Pier Paolo Vergerio, was faced with a difficult task. On top of everything, in the spring of 1534, Landgrave Philip of Hesse, an ally of France, by a swift, victorious campaign, conquered Württemberg for Duke Ulrich, hence for the new teaching. On the other hand when King Ferdinand appealed to the Pope for help his request was met with a cold refusal. This was too much even for a prince so sincerely devoted to the Pope, so much so that even he hinted at the possibility of a Popeless Council at which even France would not be able to protect him. In view of the conflict that he saw coming, Cardinal Cles withdrew from the court of Vienna.[2] But at this moment an unexpected event put an end to this most unpleasant chapter of the history of the Council. On 25 September 1534 Pope Clement VII died at the early age of fifty-six years.

De concilio verba et de reformatione: about a Council and reform, nothing but words! This is how so wise and right-minded a man as Seripando summed up this Pope's attitude to the two most pressing problems of the Church.[3] Only a few weeks before his death, in the consistory of 10 June 1534, the Pope had spoken of a Council, as he had so often done before,[4] though he never took one serious step to bring it about. Fear of a Council, it is true, was not the only obstacle. The conditions which the German Protestants laid down for such an assembly not only diminished the chances of a reunion which was still hoped for, they also inspired fears of grave complications. Even the question of the locality of the assembly was not easy to solve. Francis I's refusal to co-operate excluded the participation of one great nation, while England could not be counted upon at all. These were serious obstacles. In the circumstances the Pope should have regarded it as

---

N.B., VOL. I, i, p. 269. The briefs had been preceded by detailed instructions of the private secretary Carnesecchi to Vergerio on 14 February (*ibid.*, pp. 176-83). These were bound to miss the mark in the matter of the Council, were it only by reason of the argument that the German princes had not responded to Rangoni's campaign for a Council. This was quite inaccurate. At a later period both Carnesecchi and Vergerio came in conflict with the Church.

[1] Extract from George's letter of 14 June 1534, in *N.B.*, VOL. I, p. 266, *n.*1.

[2] *N.B.*, VOL. I, i, pp. 274 f., 277.

[3] Jedin, *Seripando*, VOL. II, p. 52 (Eng. edn., p. 509).

[4] Extracts from the consistorial acts, *C.T.*, VOL. IV, p. cx.

his duty, for the sake of men's souls, to do his utmost to overcome them. He lacked the will to do so.[1]

"The Pope does not want a Council; he quietly allows the plans for one to slide", we read in a German pamphlet of the early twenties of the century.[2] Crotus Rubeanus and Ulrich von Hutten sarcastically observed in their tirades: "Three things Rome does not wish to hear of, a Council, reform of the clergy and that the Germans are having their eyes opened."[3] Were they altogether wrong? Towards the close of Clement VII's pontificate, a German satirical pamphlet summed up his conciliar policy.[4] The pamphlet was cast in the form of a Bull of Convocation: "Since the Pope, acting in concert with the cardinals and the bishops, refuses to convoke the Council which the Emperor and the faithful long for, the Holy Ghost Himself is compelled to do so. He charges the Archangel Gabriel to prepare for distribution duly authenticated copies of the Bull of Convocation."

So spoke the Pope's enemies, while his friends were in despair. The Prior of the Charterhouse of Cologne, Peter Blommeveen, took heart and in an open letter to the Pope spoke out what others only thought [5]: "The postponement of a Council has become a terrible scandal for the faithful! Many Catholics are of opinion that the Pope shrinks from a Council in order to save himself from reform. He is unwilling to renounce the worldly pomp with which the Papacy has surrounded itself and takes no steps against the lawlessness of the clergy. The loss of so many souls leaves him cold. There is only one means to end this dreadful scandal—let a Council come together!"

Blomeveen's ideas were shared by the convert Witzel [6] and by that

[1] Here I find myself in agreement with Ehses's views, C.T., VOL. IV, p. cviii, and Pastor, VOL. IV, ii, p. 539 f. (Eng. edn., VOL. X, p. 385).

[2] Schade, Satiren, VOL. I, p. 37.

[3] Böcking, Hutteni Opera, VOL. IV, p. 262; also Z.K.G., XIX (1899), p. 446.

[4] "Convocatio concilii liberi christiani", L.W., VOL. XXXVIII, pp. 284-9, also published in German. Th. Kold shows that Luther is not the author, in his paper "Über die Echtheit des Luther zugeschriebenen Schriftchens 'Convocatio concilii liberi christiani'", in Z.K.G., XV (1895), pp. 94 ff.

[5] Undated dedicatory letter for the Opera minora of Denis the Carthusian, Cologne 1532, reprinted in his Opera omnia, VOL. XXXIII, pp. 9-12; also J. Greven, Die Kölner Kartause und die Anfänge der katholischen Reform in Deutschland (Münster 1935), p. 82 f.

[6] Letter to the Archbishop of Mainz (1532) in Goldast, Monarchia, VOL. I, pp. 653 ff., in which reference is also made to Frequens. Christoph Scheurl wrote to the same prelate on 26 March 1533: "The Italians say little and think even less about the Council," Ch. Scheurl, Briefbuch, VOL. II, p. 138.

old warrior, Eck.[1] A new national conciliar theory was in the making. Ortwin Gratius recalled the decree *Frequens* and declared that "if the reform decrees of Basle had been carried out there would be no Lutheranism".[2] Before all else the *gravamina* must be redressed. A future Council would decide the question of the superiority. By means of a collection of a number of documents coloured by the conciliar theory Gratius meant to pave the way for a Council.

This is how people thought and wrote in Germany where the consequences of the delay in calling such an assembly were plain for all to see. In Spain too, the great Francisco de Vitoria sadly noted that "ever since the Popes began to fear a Council, the Church has been without one and will remain without one, to the detriment and utter ruin of religion".[3]

This was the most disastrous of all the consequences of the delay in summoning a Council. To the obstacles which a Council encountered from various quarters, a fresh one came to be added: the world no longer believed that it would ever take place. The world had become sceptical and resigned. When the new Pope actually convoked a Council his summons evoked but a faint response.

[1] On 10 May 1535 Eck wrote to Paul III: "Alii enim pontifices, praedecessores Sanctitatis Tuae, saepe promiserunt concilii congregationem iam 20 lustris, sed ita profecto promiserunt ut facile omnes intelligerent eos nunquam concilium celebraturos; sic nuncios mittebant cum mandatis et articulis oneratos cum multis verborum involucris, punctis disputabilibus ac conditionibus intricatis, ut patenter procrastinationem negocii quaererent ac iam magnificae promissiones concilii apud Germanos in ludibrium abierint," *Z.K.G.*, XIX (1899), p. 220. Although Eck is speaking of the Popes of the last hundred years his description hits immediately Paul III's predecessor, Clement VII, whose conciliar policy could not have been more graphically pictured.
[2] "Si concilii illius pretracti decreta in hunc usque diem servata fuisent nunquam tam periculosis errorum fluctibus per universum immersi fuissemus," *Fasciculus rerum expetendarum ac fugiendarum* (Cologne 1535), fol. xxxiv f., with the other prefaces and the appendix, fol. ccxxxvi^r-ccxlii^r. For our purpose it is of small consequence that H. Cremans, *Annalen des historischen Vereins für den Niederrhein*, XXIII (1871), pp. 192-224, has brought forward some weighty objections to Gratius being the author. But I do not think that the author was a Protestant; the conciliarist character of the work was enough for it to be put on the Index (Reusch, *Index*, VOL. I, p. 247).
[3] *Relectio IV*, prop. 20: "Ab eo tempore quo propter novas opiniones doctorum pontifices inceperunt timere concilia, ecclesia manet sine conciliis et manebit cum magna calamitate et pernicie religionis," *Relectiones theologicae XII* (Lyons 1587), p.160.

CHAPTER VI

Paul III and the Convocation of a Council at Mantua

ON 13 October 1534 Cardinal Alessandro Farnese issued from an un-
usually short conclave of only two days as Pope Paul III. His election
meant a complete break with Clement VII's ecclesiastical and conciliar
policy.

Although he had been a cardinal since 1493 and Dean of the Sacred
College since 1524 Farnese had kept aloof from the disastrous policy
of the last of the Medici Popes and had carefully avoided all legatine
functions. During the vacancy of the Apostolic See he observed
repeatedly that he regarded a Council as absolutely necessary.[1] That
was why the two German cardinals, Lang and Cles, gave him their
votes. Shortly after his election, in the consistories of 17 October and
13 November, he announced his intention to convoke a Council. There
can be no longer any doubt that he was in earnest when he made that
announcement.[2]

This true Roman on the Papal throne,[3] whose robust vigour belied

---

[1] The statement in the Bull of Convocation, "Cum in minoribus essemus a nobis
maxime desideratum", *C.T.*, VOL. IV, p. 3, and in the instructions of 27 April 1536,
which take the French cardinals to witness, *C.T.*, VOL. IV, p. 109, is supported by
Soriano, Albèri, *Relazioni*, VOL. II, III, p. 313, by Aleander's notes of the year 1533, *C.T.*,
VOL. IV, pp. lxxxii and lxxxvii, and by Cardinal Loaysa, *Coll. doc. inéd.*, VOL. XIV,
p. 106. According to a report of the imperial ambassador Cifuentes, the Pope told
him soon after his election: "I was the first in the conclave to stress the need of a
Council," *Cal. of St. Pap.*, *Spain*, VOL. V, i, p. 287 (No. 100).

[2] Soriano's observation, which however dates from the year 1535 (Albèri, *Relazioni*,
VOL. II, iii, p. 314): "Sebbene divulga di volere il Concilio e di non lo temere, pure
le fuggierà volontieri, ne sarà mai per procurarlo effetualmente", is refuted by Ehses's
and Pastor's documentation. For the necessary qualifications see the conclusion of
the next chapter.

[3] Since the publication of Pastor's *History of the Popes*, VOL. V (1909) (Eng. edn.,
VOLS. XI and XII), the literature on Paul III has been enriched by C. Capasso's *Paolo
III*, in which the writer elaborates his previous study, *La politica di Paolo III e l'Italia*
(Camerino 1901), on the basis of considerable material from Italian sources. How-
ever, the value of the work is lessened by reason of the author's deep aversion for
Charles V and the Gonzagas and his consequent defence of Paul III in every respect.
Thus Capasso deems it "meschino" to blame the Pope's nepotism (VOL. II, p. 722).
L. Dorez, *La Cour du Pape Paul III*, 2 Vols. (Paris 1932), appraises the account-books
chiefly from the angle of culture and the arts. The biography by J. Edwards, *Paul
III oder die geistliche Gegenreformation* (Leipzig 1933), is rich in brilliant *aperçus*.
The author sees Paul III as the restorer of Roman Republican thought and Roman

288

his age—he was sixty-seven—and who laughed at the customary expectation of a new conclave at an early date,[1] was nevertheless at heart a child of the Renaissance. To its corruption he owed his cardinalate and to it he also had paid tribute in his early life. However, he was shrewd enough to perceive that Clement VII's policy of avoiding a Council at any price was leading to chaos and that his predecessor's unprincipled scheming for political combinations, dictated by purely opportunist considerations, had destroyed all trust in the diplomacy of the Curia. He was strongly convinced that the real strength of papal policy lay in a proper regard for the Church's own point of view and that a genuine renewal based on this principle was the only way to restore the prestige of the Holy See. Above all he was fully conscious that the nations' cry for serious ecclesiastical reform must be met at least to some extent and that after a century of talk the world must be shown positive deeds.

Paul III was a man of outstanding intelligence. He appreciated the situation aright, though it is unlikely that he had a clear idea of what should be done or to what extent current values needed to be adjusted. He imagined that it would suffice to jettison ballast, without further painful sacrifices. When these were nevertheless demanded of him he shrank back. The most grievous charge against his pontificate is his family policy, which was not limited to the enrichment of his children and grandchildren. What he aimed at was that they should marry into the great dynasties and thereby secure for the house of Farnese a strong position among the princely houses of Italy. In this he was successful, but at a heavy cost—none other than that he lives in the history of the Church merely as a far-sighted pontiff who prepared the way for the

skill in the art of government and as the man who put an end to the political character of the Renaissance Papacy. Although there is a grain of truth in both ideas, the book teems with errors; cf. my appreciation in H.J., LIV (1934), pp. 259-62. W. Friedensburg's *Kaiser Karl V und Papst Paul III* (Leipzig 1932), written in his old age, gives us the final result of the author's study of the reports of the German nunciatures, but it does so very summarily and not without confessional bias. For the present state of the question, cf. e.g. F. X. Seppelt, *Geschichte des Papsttums*, VOL. v (Leipzig 1936), pp. 7-55, 503 f. For an appreciation of the Pope's high politics the following three studies of L. Cardauns remain indispensable: "Paul III, Karl V und Franz I in den Jahren *1535-36*, in *Q.F.*, XI (1908), pp. 147-244, with the appendices in *Q.F.*, XII (1909), pp. 189-211, 321-67; *Zur Geschichte der kirchlichen Unions- und Reformsbestrebungen 1538-42* (Rome 1910) and *Von Nizza bis Crépy* (Rome 1923).

[1] In January 1535 Vergerio found the Pope looking well and full of life; he accordingly prophesied for him a long reign, all the more so as he took care of himself, granted but few audiences and frequently went out into the country. On the other hand the pontiff cherished exceedingly ambitious plans which it was to be feared he would not live to carry into effect, *N.B.*, VOL. I, i, p. 324 f.

Catholic reform but not as the man whose energy steered and executed it.

When the Augustinian Seripando came to pay his respects to him at the beginning of 1535 the Pope told him that his pontificate would be devoted to a threefold task, viz. a plan for a general pacification, a General Council and war against the infidels.[1] These three aims were closely connected. A general Council was impossible if the tension between the two rival powers, which had increased since the meeting at Marseilles, were to lead to a new war. It was equally impossible to mount a powerful offensive against the Turks, who were advancing simultaneously in Hungary and in the Mediterranean, as long as there existed an understanding between Francis I and the Grand Turk. If the Pope was really bent on a Council he must do his utmost for a settlement of the differences between Charles V and Francis I, and to this end it was essential that he should remain neutral.

It has been objected that Paul III's neutrality actually favoured France and that it was dictated by a deep, secret dislike of the Emperor.[2] True though it is that Charles V's power appeared to the Pope as something ominous and awe-inspiring, and that his own ambitious plans for the exaltation of the house of Farnese exasperated the Emperor, it would be a perversion of the facts to assign the Farnese Pope's undoubted personal dislike of the Emperor, which developed only at a later period, to the first period of his pontificate. It is a fact that the Pope feared the predominance of the Emperor and regarded France as a natural counterweight which he was unwilling to forgo, even though Francis I's connexions with his own and the Emperor's opponents, the Turks and the Protestants, made it extremely difficult for him to remain neutral. It is unprofitable to try to picture how much he might have accomplished in conjunction with the Emperor. The cost would have been too high: possibly an alliance between France, schismatic England and the League of Schmalkalden, perhaps even a Gallican schism.

In the spring of 1535 the Pope threw himself with youthful energy into the task of translating ideals into actuality. In view of the fact that he always conducted his policy in person or, as we would say today, he was his own "Secretary of State",[3] he felt the need of exhaustive

---

[1] *C.T.*, VOL. II, p. 402, line 15 ff.

[2] Cardauns, "Paul III", p. 140. Cardauns's view receives support from the circumstance that in his conversations with the nuncio Carpi, Francis I never failed to comment favourably on the Pope's policy of neutrality.

[3] Alessandro Farnese, who became Secretary of State after the fall of Ricalcati, was too young at the time to pursue a personal policy. Only in the last years of the

information on the central problem—Germany.[1] He accordingly summoned the nuncio at the court of King Ferdinand, Pier Paolo Vergerio, to Rome, to report; and in the quiet of the Roman Campagna, at the hunting lodge of Magliana on the way to Ostia, the two men discussed the situation of the Church in Germany. It was a truly alarming one.[2]

The whole of Germany, not only the Protestant part, was exasperated at the delay in summoning a Council and laid the blame for it on the Curia: no one believed any longer in its good faith in this respect. Protestantism was making rapid progress; one principality after another, one city after another, succumbed to it. Vergerio gave it as his opinion that if a Council were not summoned at once a German national Council would be unavoidable and it would be almost impossible to prevent the apostasy of the whole nation. On 18 December 1534 the nuncio had written [3] that it was not enough to discuss a Council in Rome; it was here, on the spot, that people must be able to see with their own eyes that the Pope was actually doing something about it. What was to be done? "Nothing at all!" was the answer of those who stood for the traditional policy. One of the cardinals to whom Vergerio explained the awful gravity of the situation laid all the blame on the princes' shoulders. "At the proper time", he said, "they did nothing to stem the flood: now they get what they want." To the nuncio's question: "And the loss of souls, is it nothing to you?" the answer was: "Everything must first collapse, then will reform come about".[4] With a catastrophic policy such as this Paul III would have nothing to do, but he had to reckon with the fact that a powerful opposition [5] to a Council in the College of Cardinals and in the Curia was doing its utmost to delay it indefinitely. As in Clement VII's days, the opposition favoured a convention of princes. Paul III was convinced that this would lead nowhere, hence as early as the first days of January he informed the imperial ambassador Cifuentes of his intention to obtain,

---

pontificate did he conduct an independent family policy. At the Congress of Nice the Venetians observed with surprise that the Pope conducted all the negotiations alone, without taking counsel even with the most trusted of the cardinals, Albèri, *Relazioni*, VOL. I, ii, p. 84.

[1] On 27 January Vergerio wrote: "Visa est mihi S.S^{tas} valde parum informata in quo statu sint res Germaniae et Hungariae," *N.B.*, VOL. I, i, p. 326.

[2] Cf. Vergerio's reports of November 1534, *N.B.*, VOL. I, i, pp. 313, 315.

[3] Vergerio on 18 December 1534, *N.B.*, VOL. I, i, p. 321 f.

[4] Vergerio on 27 January 1535, *N.B.*, VOL. I, i, p. 327.

[5] Sánchez, Ferdinand I's agent in Rome, on 20 January 1535: "Totum collegium cardinalium renititur," Pastor, VOL. V, p. 820 (Eng. edn., VOL. XI, p. 560).

through nuncios, the assent of the principal powers, above all that of France.[1] A month later the nuncios were despatched: Vergerio to Germany, Carpi to France, Guidiccioni to the Emperor, then in Spain. In accordance with a decision of the consistory of 15 January they were to inform the three courts of the Pope's firm resolve to convoke a Council and to ask their opinion about the locality where it should be held.[2] The first suggestion was Mantua, out of consideration for the Germans; then Turin, as a concession to the French, and finally two towns in the Papal States, the acceptance of which would have met the wishes of the Pope himself, namely Piacenza and Bologna.

One is tempted to ask whether it would not have been better to summon a Council without further delay to some frontier town, for instance Mantua, and to provide the nuncios with authentic copies of the Bull of Convocation. No doubt objections would have been raised in France and Germany, but they would have been neutralised by the advantages accruing from the fact that the sceptics would have had tangible proof that the Pope was in earnest about a Council. Paul III's policy of compromise was a concession to the opposition and left the road open for negotiations, but at the cost of much time.

The most difficult task of all, the proclamation of the Council in Germany, was allotted to Vergerio. The Habsburg diplomatists in Rome had strained every nerve in an effort to overcome the opposition to his return to Germany.[3] In point of fact this undoubtedly gifted man lacked the balanced character and sure judgment which were indispensable for an office such as his, and at a later date he was to justify his opponents when he, a Catholic bishop, but a disappointed and embittered man, apostatised from the Church.[4] But at this time his

[1] Cifuentes to the Emperor, 9 January 1535, Spanish text in E. Ferrandis-Bordonau *El Concilio de Trento*, VOL. I, pp. 20 ff.; English transl. in *Cal. of St. Pap., Spain*, VOL. V, i, pp. 372 ff. (No. 125).
[2] Up to this day these instructions have not been brought to light. On the question of the locality, cf. Vergerio's notes on his audience with Ferdinand I, *N.B.*, VOL. I, i, p. 342. Soriano mentions Mantua, Trent and Verona; the last-mentioned city was eventually dropped, Albèri, *Relazioni*, VOL. II, iii, p. 316.
[3] Sánchez to Cles, 12 and 24 February 1535, St. Arch., Trent, Cles, Mazzo 10.
[4] To the literature enumerated by me in *L.Th.K.*, VOL. X, p. 559, must be added P. Paschini, *Pier Paolo Vergerio il Giovane e la sua apostasia* (Rome 1925). The reports of the nunciatures contain rich material for a character-study of Vergerio. He draws attention to his labours and services on every possible occasion (e.g. VOL. I, i, pp. 509, 518); he even goes so far as to hand to Nausea the draft of a letter of appreciation of his services which the latter was to send to Rome (*ibid.*, p. 511). There can be no doubt that he hoped for promotion with the help of Ferdinand, who dropped him when Sánchez informed him of his intrigues in Rome.

positive qualities alone mattered. Soon after his arrival in Vienna towards the end of March 1535 he threw himself with burning zeal into the work of proclaiming the Council.

The monarch to whom he was accredited, Ferdinand I, King-elect of the Romans since 1530, was the person who created the fewest difficulties for him. It was only very gradually that the younger of the two Habsburg brothers assumed a certain independence of the Emperor, for whom he cherished the profoundest reverence.[1] As a result of the maladministration of the Habsburg patrimony his own power was not great and there was no end to his financial straits. The Venetian Giustiniani estimated his available revenues at no more than 30,000 gulden. Half of his time was spent in going from place to place for the purpose of soliciting money grants from the Estates of his Austrian and Bohemian lands; not only for the war against John Zapolya who contested his possession of Hungary, but against the latter's abettor, the Grand Turk. He had been brought up in Spain and was much more like a Spaniard than his brother. He fulfilled his religious duties most conscientiously; his marriage with Anne of Hungary had been blessed with many children; in fact, his married life could be described as exemplary and his devotion to the Papacy could hardly be surpassed. Homely and affable in his bearing, he loved to invite foreign envoys to his table and to the chase, to which he was passionately addicted. But it did not escape so acute an observer as Morone that although he worked hard as a ruler he was exceedingly slow and dependent on his counsellors, the shrewdest of whom, Johann Hoffmann, was regarded as an avowed Lutheran. The real prop of Catholicism at the court was Ferdinand's leading minister, Cardinal Cles. It was a cause of profound grief for the King that he was unable to stem the movement of secession in his hereditary lands and in the city of Vienna. And it was an even greater sorrow for him that Clement VII could look at the desperate fight of the German Catholics yet do practically nothing to assist them, so much so indeed that the Pope was even suspected of being in some

---

[1] F. B. Bucholtz's work, *Ferdinand I*, full of rich material but untidy, can only be replaced by a modern biography when the Vienna edition of the letters (2 Vols. up to now) is more advanced. For a character-study of Ferdinand I, I draw on Vergerio's reports (*N.B.*, VOL. I, i, pp. 85 f., 102, 186, 314 and *passim*), and on those of Morone (*N.B.*, VOL. I, ii, pp. 123 f., 181 ff.), as well as on the relations of the Venetians which enable us to follow clearly the growth of Ferdinand's political ability, viz., those of Carlo Contarini (1527), fragmentarily published by Fiedler, *Relationen venetianer Botschafter über Deutschland und Österreich im XVI. Jahrhundert* (Vienna 1870), pp. 1-4; those of Marino Giustiniani (1541), in Albèri, *Relazioni*, VOL. I, ii, pp. 120 ff.; and those of Lorenzo Contarini (1548), Albèri, *Relazioni*, VOL. I, i, pp. 448 ff.

way connected with the Protestant *coup de main* against Württemberg. His relations with Paul III were troubled by the fact that the Pope favoured John Zapolya.

Ferdinand was easily won over for the projected Council. No one was more convinced than he of the need for such a gathering. No one had pleaded for its early convocation with greater earnestness. For a locality he would have preferred Trent, which was also Cardinal Cles's choice, but he declared himself personally satisfied with Mantua. For the purpose of enabling him to counter the expected opposition of the Protestant Estates he judged it indispensable to obtain the Emperor's approval for this border-city before approaching the Protestants. While awaiting an answer from Spain, Vergerio decided to visit the Catholic Estates of the Bavarian, Swabian and Franconian circles. Accompanied by a numerous suite—he was escorted by fourteen mounted men—he set out on his errand about mid-April.[1]

His first impressions were favourable on the whole. Cardinal Lang of Salzburg did not betray his deep-seated scepticism of the papal announcement of the Council.[2] Before committing himself further he wished to have the Emperor's view about the place of assembly. The Wittelsbachs were much more forthcoming. On 30 April Duke William of Bavaria declared his own and his brother Louis' readiness to attend a Council not only at Mantua but in Rome itself. At the same time he put the nuncio on his guard against a convention of princes on the ground that it might easily degenerate into a national council. On hearing the announcement of the Council the Bishop of Freising, Count Palatine Philip, exclaimed, "Now I can die in peace!" The Bishop of Eichstätt, Gabriel von Eyb, pledged himself, in spite of his advanced age, to appear in person wherever the Council might be held. The Administrator of Ratisbon, also a Palatine Wittelsbach, alone hesitated and declared that he would wait for the decision of the Bavarian Diet. Vergerio was profoundly impressed by what he experienced at Ratisbon. That imperial city had gone almost wholly Lutheran and only a score of people attended the Sunday services at the cathedral. But when the nuncio announced the Council to the

---

[1] What follows is based on Vergerio's despatches, *N.B.*, VOL. I, i, pp. 362-555, with the written answers published by Ehses, *C.T.*, VOL. IV, pp. cxii ff. Pastor treats it very fully, VOL. V, pp. 39-51 (Eng. edn., VOL. XI, pp. 49).

[2] Sánchez saw the archbishop's letter in which he said: "He talks a great deal about the Pope's determination to call a Council but there is no sign of a concrete step towards its realisation," Sánchez to Cles, 1 July 1536, St. Arch., Trent, Cles, Mazzo 10.

senators they raised their hands to heaven, praising God and the Pope. The same spectacle was repeated at Augsburg, where the new teaching, in its Zwinglian mould, had been but recently introduced. Vergerio saw himself in the role of a herald of glad tidings. "The all-important thing is", he reported to Rome and Vienna, "that when I announce the Council I have not to begin by producing a sheet of paper, with sundry conditions as was the case under Clement VII, but am in a position to make the straightforward announcement—'The Pope is resolved to hold a Council'."

Vergerio's first doubts about the success of his mission arose at Dillingen. The aged and experienced Bishop Stadion of Augsburg, who in his capacity of lieutenant of the largely Protestant Swabian circle was well acquainted with the sentiments of the adherents of the new faith, personally regarded either Mantua or Trent as suitable localities for the Council but deprecated the choice of a German town lest the excited masses should endanger the freedom of the assembly. On the other hand he thought it would hardly be possible to get the Protestants to attend the Council unless the secular princes were admitted. He advocated several possible concessions to the former, such as Communion in both kinds, suppression of the law of fasting and a declaration that certain "human" traditions were optional.

Another and most unpleasant surprise awaited Vergerio on his return to Munich. By the terms of the original agreement with Duke William, the Diet of the Bavarian circle should have accepted Vergerio's announcement of the Council as a body. Instead of this Vergerio was told by the Bavarian Chancellor Leonhard Eck that his policy of negotiating about the Council with each Estate separately was a mistake. The right thing would have been to present them with a *fait accompli*, that is with an announcement that the Pope, in agreement with the Emperor, was about to convoke a Council at Mantua. Not only the League of Schmalkalden, but many princes still regarded as Catholic at heart but already won over to the new doctrine—among whom Eck was not ashamed to count George of Saxony—would refuse to attend a Council in Italy, no matter where. A refusal on their part would tie the hands of Pope and Emperor. Leonhard Eck evidently stood for a policy of the strong hand and the *fait accompli*. Actually there was a good deal to be said for such a policy. On the other hand there was little mystery about the motive that prompted the old intriguer. His sole object was to create difficulties for the bitterly hated Emperor; in any other circumstances Leonhard Eck would have been the very first

to protest against a policy which he would have decried as an interference with the princes' liberty. However, Duke William adopted the
view of his chancellor; the Diet of the Bavarian circle did not take
place. On 6 June 1535 Vergerio was back at Vienna, where in the
meantime a reply had been received from Spain, but one which did
not advance affairs by a single step. For fear of finding himself at
variance with earlier decisions of the Diet and thereby giving free play
to French intrigues, the Emperor declined to give a firm answer with
regard to Mantua and contented himself with a declaration that he
would approve of any place accepted by the Estates of the Empire. The
nuncio was now faced with the problem whether to leave the decision
to the latter. His refusal to do so was right, otherwise the whole
conciliar enterprise would have been compromised. There was very
little doubt that the League of Schmalkalden would decline Mantua
and in its place propose a Diet from which, in view of the anti-papal
feeling in Germany, little good was to be expected. If the Pope really
wished the Council to materialise he must not on any account take this
path. He should instruct the nuncio to inform the Estates that "the
Pope and the Emperor are agreed that the Council must be held at
Mantua". However, an announcement in these terms had been made
impossible by the message which had come from Barcelona.

King Ferdinand also realised this difficulty but took good care not
to cross his brother's plans by a definite pronouncement in favour of
Mantua. In the end he agreed with the nuncio on a tortuous declaration, basically non-committal, to the effect that the Emperor and the
King would not resist the Pope's will. Vergerio had to forgo an
imperial escort, such as had been assigned to the nuncio Rangoni in the
days of Clement VII. Nevertheless on 19 July he set out once more for
Germany, encouraged by the Pope's recognition of his untiring exertions
on behalf of the Council. King Ferdinand had also ended by accepting
the following formula which, like the first, committed him to nothing:
"I am convinced that the Emperor will accept Mantua." Once again
Vergerio appealed first to the Catholic princes in the hope of obtaining
a satisfactory declaration by the Emperor before he tackled the
confederation of Schmalkalden.

The Lutheran Margrave George of Brandenburg received Vergerio
at Ansbach with a friendliness that surprised the nuncio. That adroit
and cunning prince claimed that the religious innovations introduced
by him were only provisional and that he would submit to the decision
of a future Council. He was unwilling to agree unconditionally to

Mantua because he did not wish to find himself at variance with earlier decisions of the Diet, though personally he had no objection to that city. The Protestant council of Nuremberg replied that it would obey the Emperor's will in all things.

All the bishops of the Rhine and Main district gave their assent. Weigand von Redwitz, Bishop of Bamberg, concurred with whatever the Pope and the Emperor might arrange between them,[1] but Konrad von Thüngen, Bishop of Würzburg, instructed his chancellor, Konrad Braun, to inform the nuncio that he thought it would be dangerous formally to accept a locality outside Germany since this would be against the decisions of the Diet. However, for his own person, he was prepared to fall in with the Pope's arrangements. The Bishop of Liège, Cardinal Erhard von der Mark, viewed the Council with a good deal of anxiety but judged it absolutely necessary and Mantua seemed a suitable place. Even the Archbishop of Cologne, Hermann von Wied, whose leanings towards Protestantism were no secret even at this time, returned an affirmative answer though couched in general terms. When Vergerio met him at Paderborn on 22 October, Cardinal Albrecht of Mainz gave a similar reply.

Only two secular princes took up a negative attitude, namely the Elector Palatine Louis and Duke John of Cleves. The former declined to receive the nuncio. Through his councillors he informed Vergerio in brusque terms that without a corresponding decision by a new Diet he could not accept Mantua or any other town in Italy as a suitable locality for a Council. Though couched in more courteous terms, the answer of the Duke of Cleves, who was perceptibly under French influence, amounted to the same thing. He would make up his mind when the other Estates had made known their decision. The answer of Joachim II, who had but recently succeeded his father as Elector of Brandenburg, was less favourable than might have been expected. He agreed to Mantua provided Charles and Ferdinand approved of it. Joachim's inclination towards Protestantism was well known. For his sake alone there was need of the utmost speed, so Duke George of Saxony told the nuncio, otherwise he would succumb to the influence of his Lutheran mother. Duke George recalled with satisfaction that he himself had mentioned Mantua as a suitable locality for a Council as early as the year 1532.

---

[1] During Vergerio's stay at Bamberg the convert Johann Haner handed in his "Votum de concilio", C.T., VOL. XII, pp. 85-108, in which he spoke of the speedy convocation of a Council as an inescapable necessity.

The most difficult part of Vergerio's task still remained to be done, viz. the announcement of the Council to the confederates of Schmalkalden. One of the two heads of the League, the Landgrave Philip of Hesse, he had already met at Vienna in April. He had found him relatively well disposed though he raised objections to Mantua.[1] In order to visit the other head of the League, the Elector John Frederick of Saxony, in his own residence, Vergerio ventured to journey to Wittenberg in the month of November. While there, on 13 November, he had the memorable interview with Luther in the course of which the latter was reported to have declared himself ready to defend his teaching at a Council held either at Mantua or at Verona.[2] The Elector himself Vergerio did not see at Wittenberg; he only met him on his return to Prague. He introduced himself as the herald of a new Roman policy. Unlike his predecessor, Pope Paul III did not attach any conditions to his convocation of a Council. If the Elector nevertheless persisted in his refusal it would be seen that he did not want a Council at all, though a Council would take place all the same, and at Mantua. As was to be expected, the Elector appealed to the earlier resolutions of the Diet and insisted on positive written guarantees for the safety of the Protestant participants in the Council. But a final reply to the announcement of the Council could only be given by the forthcoming assembly of the League at Schmalkalden.[3] At the Elector's request, on 1 December, Vergerio drew up a memorandum for submission to that assembly.[4] He recalled the Prague discussions and pointed out that on account of its geographical situation between imperial Milan and neutral Venice, Mantua, as a fief of the Empire, would offer adequate security to the Protestants; moreover, both the Pope and the Emperor would give every requisite guarantee.

The Prague conversations had been courteously conducted. The Elector and the nuncio shook hands on parting. At their Diet the confederates of Schmalkalden put personal considerations on one side.

[1] N.B., vol. I, i, pp. 344 ff.

[2] Vergerio's account of his meeting with Luther, in N.B., vol. I, i, pp. 539-47, where the earlier editions by Lämmer and Cantù are noted. In his audience with the Elector John Frederick, Vergerio was silent about Luther's willingness to appear in person at the Council and only put the following declaration in the latter's mouth: "Ego existimo concilium generale, liberum, christianum quale Pontifex pollicetur omnibus modis utile ac necessarium fore," Corp. Ref., vol. III, p. 987.

[3] Spalatin's written record—he probably acted as interpreter—in Corp. Ref., vol. II, pp. 982-9, is only briefly alluded to in Vergerio's despatch of 9 December, N.B., vol. I, i, pp. 553 ff. G. Mentz, Johann Friedrich der Grossmütige, vol. II (Jena 1908), pp. 72 ff.

[4] Corp. Ref., vol. II, pp. 991-5 (No. 1367).

In their reply to the invitation to the Council, a document drawn up by Melanchthon,[1] they took their stand on the Nuremberg formula—as if nothing had happened in the meantime—and declared themselves most willing to participate in "a free, Christian council in German lands". Mantua as a place of assembly was contrary to earlier resolutions of the Diet; there was no guarantee either for the safety of the participants or for the freedom of the decisions so long as the Pope refused to submit from the start to the superior authority of the universal Church as represented by a Council and declined to admit the representatives of the secular authorities. In plain language this amounted to a demand that the Pope should be simply one of the parties at the Council and surrender his supremacy. The Pope's generous and wise abandonment of Clement VII's conditions was described as a ruse. Surely the accusation of impudence, which they threw in the face of the defenders of papal supremacy, recoiled upon themselves.

When this answer of the Schmalkaldic League reached Vergerio he was no longer in Germany. Passing through Rome he had journeyed to Naples in order to report personally to the Emperor on the state of the negotiations. That they had not been universally successful was in no small measure due to Charles's refusal to declare himself explicitly in favour of Mantua.

The nuncio had done all he could in the circumstances. In some instances the intimation of the Council had met with a brusque rejection; by many it had been accepted with some scepticism; and by a relatively small number with complete confidence and cheerful willingness. The nuncio was appalled as he realised how grievously Clement VII's conciliar policy had injured people's confidence in the Papacy.[2] However, all was not lost. If by prompt action the Germans could be convinced that the Pope was in earnest in his resolve to hold a Council, the participation of a great number of prelates, theologians and envoys from that country could be counted upon. The Schmalkaldic League still constituted only a relatively small minority. The majority of the German princes could be saved for the Church provided an end was put to the dangerous state of uncertainty. That this consummation was not reached was due to the Western powers' attitude to a Council.

[1] *C.T.*, VOL. IV, pp. cxvi-cxix (21 December 1535); also *Corp. Ref.*, VOL. II, pp. 1018-22 (No. 1379). The men of Schmalkalden's addition of the word "pio" to the Nuremberg formula adds nothing new to its significance.

[2] Numerous proofs in Vergerio's reports, *N.B.*, VOL. I, i, pp. 350, 355, 365 f., 375 f., 383, 387, 413 f.

Besides the announcement of the Council three further tasks had been assigned to Rodolfo Pio of Carpi,[1] who had been despatched to France as papal nuncio; namely to work against the English, to defend the Pope's policy of neutrality and, if possible, to obtain France's help, or at least her neutrality, for the Pope's joint action with the Emperor against the pirate Chaireddin Barbarossa. As the son of a minor prince whom the Emperor had ousted from his domain, Carpi was treated by Francis I with the utmost friendliness, not to say familiarity. After a very few days Carpi became aware of the French court's exceedingly hostile sentiments towards the Emperor. On 22 February 1535, four days after his first audience, he wrote: "The King's hatred has grown to such an extent that he makes it his business to provoke the Emperor."[2] Help for the expedition against Barbarossa was not to be thought of. Actually Francis openly treated with the corsair and Carpi had reason to congratulate himself that the assistance clandestinely given had not become open co-operation. The news of the Emperor's swift victory at Tunis and his safe crossing to Italy, which arrived early in August, came as a very disagreeable piece of news for the French court.[3] Montmorency, who was for a compromise with the Emperor, was out of favour with his king, while the Anglophile Grand-Admiral, the Cardinal of Lorraine and the two brothers du Bellay—all of them bitter enemies of Charles V—had the monarch's ear. The financial preparations for a new campaign for Milan were in full swing when Duke Francesco Sforza died on 1 November 1535. The King immediately issued orders for all military measures to be taken in view of imminent war. In February 1536 French troops invaded Savoy in order to secure it as a base for their advance on Milan. Thus war had become as good as inevitable. The Pope's efforts for peace succeeded in delaying it: they failed to prevent it.

Thus it came about that the announcement of the Council met with the same obstacles in France as in the days of Clement VII, except that

---

[1] The extracts published by Ehses are inadequate for a just appreciation of France's conciliar policy. I have therefore gone through Carpi's reports in the Vatican Archives, AA I-XVIII 6528 and 6529 (originals) and Lettere di principi, 10, and Nunziatura di Francia (copies). There is no recent study of Carpi, the nephew of the well-known humanist Alberto Pio, so that I must refer the reader to Pompeo Litta, *Famiglie celebri italiane*, 10 Vols. (Milan 1819-74), VOL. V, p. 580; Ciaconius, *Vitae et res gestae*, VOL. III, pp. 619-22. At a later date he joined the imperial party (d. 1564).

[2] Vat. Arch., AA I-XVIII 6528, fol. 100ʳ, official decoding; on 23 May Carpi writes, "Whatever the Emperor calls white is called black here," *ibid.*, fol. 173ᵛ.

[3] Vat. Arch., Lettere di principi, 10, fol. 270ʳ (7 August 1535).

the memory of the insincerity of the papal diplomacy of that period rendered people still more intractable. Carpi did his best to convince the French statesmen that times had changed; that the present Pope had abandoned the methods formerly in vogue and was sincere in his desire for a Council.[1] The reaction was all the stronger as Francis I viewed the Pope's plan for a Council first and foremost as an attempt on the part of the Emperor to master the Protestants' opposition in Germany by ecclesiastical means and to revenge himself on Henry VIII for his dismissal of Catherine. In his opinion the whole thing was but another milestone on his powerful opponent's road to universal monarchy. He intimated his readiness to accept the Council on condition that it was truly universal and was held at a place where its freedom was guaranteed, for instance at Turin.[2]

He emphatically deprecated an "imperial" Council, that is, one held within the Emperor's sphere of influence and chiefly attended by prelates from imperial territories. These conditions were utterly irreconcilable with the German demands, hence in practice they amounted to a rejection of the Council.

French policy did not stop at this passive, essentially negative attitude—it took positive steps to render a Council superfluous by means of a direct understanding with the German Protestants.[3] In a manifesto which he ordered to be widely distributed in Germany, Francis I defended himself against the accusations of which he was the object on account of his earlier attitude to the question of a Council. At the beginning of 1535 he sent Guillaume du Bellay, the brother of the future cardinal, to Germany for the purpose of entering into negotiations with the League of Schmalkalden and certain Catholic anti-Habsburg princes, but above all for the purpose of preventing acceptance of a Council. In the summer of that year Melanchthon received a formal invitation to Paris for the purpose of seeking an understanding with the theologians of the Sorbonne, if possible in presence of a papal commissary. Prospects seemed favourable; quite recently, in his

---

[1] Vat. Arch., Lettere de principi, 10, fol. 196ʳ (26 February 1535); so also on 1 March: "Che non si negotia al modo usato et che questo è un altro tempo", AA I-CVIII 6528, fol. 110ᵛ (decoded).

[2] C.T., VOL. IV, p. cxx f.

[3] Imbart de la Tour, Origines, VOL. III, pp. 497-568, and esp. pp. 599 ff., has a masterly description of the French "Rêve de l'unité", though the question of the Council is kept somewhat in the background. The memoirs of the brothers Martin and Guillaume du Bellay (ed. Petitot, Paris 1827) unfortunately ignore these negotiations altogether. I was not able to consult V. L. Bourilly, Guillaume du Bellay (Paris 1905).

"Ratschlag", Melanchthon had acknowledged the jurisdiction of the bishops and the Pope as their head (*ut Romanus Pontifex praesit omnibus episcopis*).[1] What a triumph for Francis I, were he to succed in putting the Pope under obligation by bringing about the reunion with the Protestants for which the Emperor had striven in vain! In that event a General Council would be superfluous. They could be content with a Roman reform convention at which the Protestants would be represented by their delegates.[2] French diplomacy was sufficiently familiar with the history of the idea of the Council during the last century to know what impression such a prospect would create in Rome.

However, the dream of reunion vanished even before it had taken shape. In view of Melanchthon's negotiations with King Ferdinand at this very time the Saxon Elector forbade his journey to Paris. Thereupon du Bellay tried his luck once more with Brück, the Saxon chancellor. In order to give the negotiations for reunion a start and thus prevent a Council all the more surely,[3] he endeavoured to create an impression that Francis I was coming round to the Protestant standpoint. The King, he alleged, approved the doctrine of justification and that of free will as propounded by Melanchthon; he regarded the Pope's primacy as of human institution, condemned the veneration of images and was willing to let the Protestants retain their Mass without the Canon.[4] It is hardly necessary to say that the representative of the Most Christian King went beyond the boundaries within which, previous to the Council of Trent, Catholics enjoyed freedom of opinion. But this time also success was denied him. The Elector John Frederick recoiled from a rupture with the Emperor and brought the rest of the Schmalkaldic confederates round to his point of view. On 22 December 1535 they gave du Bellay an evasive answer, to the effect that the envoys present at Schmalkalden were not authorised to initiate negotiations for reunion.[5] As in 1530 at Augsburg this time also Luther's intransigent standpoint prevailed over Melanchthon's and Bucer's tendency to compromise. It was this intransigence that wrecked France's attempt

[1] *Corp. Ref.*, VOL. II, pp. 741-75—two versions; *ibid.*, p. 739 f., the covering letter of 1 August 1535.
[2] Carpi to Ricalcati, 4 July 1537, Vat. Arch., Lettere di principi, 10, fol. 251ᵛ; the original is almost wholly in cypher (AA 1-XVIII 6528, fols. 221ʳ-226ʳ) without accompanying decoded copy.
[3] This intention is already foreshadowed in the discourse before John Frederick on 16 December, *Corp. Ref.*, VOL. II, pp. 1009 ff. (No. 1376).
[4] *Corp. Ref.*, VOL. II, pp. 1014-18 (No. 1378).
[5] *Corp. Ref.*, VOL. II, pp. 1022-7 (No. 1380).

to circumvent a Council by means of direct negotiations for reunion.

The Bishop of Paris, Jean du Bellay, had promised Carpi that he would not only bring back the German Protestants but that he would also "work wonders" with the King of England.[1] The second of these pledges was almost more tempting than the first. That both were no more than a feint for the purpose of crossing the Pope's conciliar policy the nuncio failed to perceive.[2] He became even more hopelessly entangled in the finely spun web of Anglo-French relations than in that of the Franco-imperial ones. Yet the focus of all anti-conciliar efforts was not the French but the English court.

Henry VIII's answer to Clement VII's final sentence of 23 March 1534, which upheld the validity of his marriage with Catherine, was the Act of Supremacy of 3 November 1534, which made it high treason to refuse to acknowledge the King as supreme head of the English Church. John Fisher, the valiant Bishop of Rochester, was beheaded on 22 June 1535,[3] and on 6 July the former Chancellor, Thomas More, followed him to death. These executions were an open declaration of war against the Papacy and were regarded as such. By 30 August the solemn Bull of Excommunication against Henry VIII was ready. However, it was not published because the Pope was anxious first to make sure of the co-operation of the two chief powers in its execution. If, at this moment, the Pope could have the sentence approved by a Council, and if he called on the Christian princes to execute it, the English crown might find itself faced, within a few months, by a united array of continental States against which it would not be able to stand indefinitely in spite of the vast financial resources it had acquired by the

---

[1] Carpi to Ricalcati, 12 April 1535, Vat. Arch., AA I-XVIII 6528, fol. 158^v.

[2] On 13 October 1535 Chapuis wrote to the Emperor in a very different strain: "The long speeches of the French ambassador and the Bishop of Winchester about the Council strengthen the suspicion that France and England are working hand in hand to prevent it," Cal. of Letters, VOL. IX, p. 197 (No. 594).

[3] For the purpose of orientation in the pertinent literature: G. Constant, La Réforme en Angleterre (Paris 1930), pp. 116-32, 474 f. (Eng. edn., VOL. I, pp. 200-3). The copious literature about the canonisation includes: Ph. Hughes, The earliest English Life of St John Fisher (London 1935); P. E. Hallett, The Defence of the Priesthood by John Fisher (London 1935); D. O'Connor, A spiritual Consolation and other Treatises of John Fisher (London 1935); H. O. Evennett, "John Fisher and Cambridge" in The Clergy Review, IX (1935), pp. 377-91. According to Carpi it was fatal for Fisher that in the brief informing him of his elevation to the cardinalate the Pope told him of his intention to make use of him at the Council. Henry was afraid that Fisher would maintain his attitude to the King's matrimonial affairs and the royal supremacy in that assembly, Carpi to Ricalcati, 21 June 1535, Vat. Arch., Lettere de principi, 10, fol. 243^r. For Francis I's attitude mentioned further on, cf. the despatches of 4 and 29 July 1535, AA I-XVIII 6528, fols. 313^r, 219^v, 284^r-289^r.

ruthless suppression of the monasteries.[1] However, as long as the two great opponents, Valois and Habsburg, remained unreconciled, neither a Council nor the great coalition would materialise. It accordingly became the aim of English diplomacy to keep them apart and to exacerbate their mutual hostility as well as to thwart a Council by every available means. This policy it pursued with iron determination. Henry VIII was playing for high stakes. France's aggressive plans and the League of Schmalkalden's fear of a Council were his natural allies. It must be granted that he exploited both in masterly fashion.

As long as the Pope's reaction to the two executions was not made clear, Henry put on a show of coyness and allowed himself to be wooed by the two men who were to be the enemies of the morrow—the Emperor who, though angered by Henry's treatment of Catherine of Aragon, did not wish to drive him into the arms of France, and Francis I who, in view of the forthcoming conflict, was anxious to retain his one and only ally. When, therefore, in mid-summer 1535 the danger of sanctions became acute, Henry made overtures to France, encouraged her to strike, and thus spoilt the papal peace plan. The game was his the moment swords were drawn. From that moment also the fear of a Council could be regarded as over, and England found herself in the enviable position of a courted neutral.

Up to the summer of 1535 Carpi reported with visible satisfaction that nothing like intimacy obtained between the French and English courts. Francis I let slip no opportunity of criticising Henry VIII's ecclesiastical policy. "One cannot be friends with such a man," he said, on hearing of John Fisher's execution, and on learning of the death of Thomas More he shed tears in presence of the nuncio. It was rumoured that it was due to the latter that the negotiations for an alliance with England broke down, chiefly because England demanded that France should defend Henry's marriage to Anne Boleyn at the Council. But the scene underwent an abrupt change as soon as Carpi urged the King to participate in the sanctions against England. The King coldly replied that the sentence against Henry had been pronounced by Clement VII at the instigation of the Emperor, otherwise it would probably never have been inflicted. Let the Emperor be the

---

[1] Carpi states repeatedly that it was for the sake of England in particular that the Pope desired a Council: "Per questi rispetti et per ogni altro S.S^{tà} pensava omninamente di voler il concilio," Vat. Arch., AA I-XVIII 6528, fol. 383^r; so also already on 19 September, *ibid.*, fol. 332^v. The chief defect of Ehses's account, in my opinion, is that he fails to appreciate the importance of England in the matter of the Council and stresses instead France's opposition somewhat one-sidedly.

first to apply sanctions and lay an embargo on England's trade with Flanders.[1] Chabot summed up the French case in these words: "We shall never support Henry against a papal sentence, but we shall defend him if he is attacked by the Emperor."[2] With the intention of rendering the King of England more amenable to an anti-imperial alliance, French diplomacy went so far as to press the Pope to take stern measures against him.[3] Its calculations proved correct. In the first days of December 1535 things had got so far that the English envoys, Gardiner and Wallop, were in a position to inform the dismayed nuncio that the relations between the two kings could not be closer.[4] For all that, Francis I still sought to save appearances in Rome. While he assured the nuncio that he was doing his best to convince Gardiner of the necessity of a Council,[5] he instructed his envoy in Germany, Guillaume du Bellay, to collaborate with Henry VIII's emissaries to the Diet of the Schmalkaldic League so as to make sure that that assembly declined a Council.[6]

Henry VIII and Francis I were both agreed that they must co-operate with the Schmalkaldic League, but whereas the latter's chief motive was to create difficulties for the Emperor in Germany with a view to weakening him, the danger of a Council was the main pre-occupation of the King of England. In the latter half of the summer of 1535, when the Bull of Excommunication could be expected any day, Henry despatched Bishop Fox of Hereford to Germany for the purpose of securing the Schmalkaldic League's concurrence in a joint action against a Council,[7] and above all for the purpose of preventing it from approving of Mantua as its place of assembly. The King's agent, Robert Barnes, a man of pronounced Protestant sympathies, had already smoothed the bishop's path with the Elector John Frederick; Fox was

[1] Carpi to Ricalcati, 21-22 August 1535, Vat. Arch., AA I-XVIII 6528, fols. 310^r-314^r.
[2] Id., 15 November 1535, ibid., fols. 405^r-409^r.
[3] Id., 21 November 1535, ibid., fol. 432^v. The game was so transparent that even Carpi saw through it and warned against precipitate steps against Henry, 8 December 1535, Vat. Arch., Lettere di principi, 10, fols. 315^v-320^r, the original ibid., fols. 473^r-480^v, without decoded text.
[4] Carpi to Ricalcati, 2 December 1535, Vat. Arch., Lettere di principi, 10, fols. 314^r-315^r.
[5] I use the despatch of 20 December 1535 on the King's and Chabot's explanations as given in Lettere di principi, 10, fols. 324^r-329^v, because the decoded copy joined to the duplicated original AA I-XVIII 6528, fols. 509^r-515^r, is very much damaged.
[6] Du Bellay revealed his intention to Mont, the English agent, at the meeting of Châlons, 5-7 September 1535, Cal. of Letters, VOL. IX, p. 101 (Nos. 281 and 298): "to prevent the Germans from consenting to a General Council".
[7] Cal. of Letters, VOL. IX, p. 69 f. (No. 213). For what follows, cf. F. Prüser, England und die Schmalkaldener 1535-40 (Leipzig 1929).

accordingly given an opportunity, on 24 December, to discharge his commission before the assembly of the confederates.[1] His real aim, which was to prevent the Council, was camouflaged with fair words: "England also", he said, "wants a free, Christian Council, at which controversies can be decided in accordance with God's word, but she declines every sort of Council that only ministers to the Pope's ambition."

The League had not yet quite forgotten that by his book against Luther Henry had earned for himself the title of *Fidei Defensor*. Although they declared that they would only accept a Council by mutual agreement they refrained from rejecting it unconditionally and fell back upon the answer given shortly before to Vergerio. Should the Pope actually open a Council they intended to lodge a joint protest.[2] But no agreement was reached on the doctrinal question which for the Protestants was a preliminary for joint action in the affair of the Council. The theological discussions held at Wittenberg between January and March 1536 led to a measure of agreement on some points, but they also brought to light the existence of irreconcilable divergences on essential questions.[3] The Wittenberg divines could not bring themselves to adopt Henry's standpoint with regard to his matrimonial problem while the latter refused to accept the *Confessio Augustana*.[4] The English attempt at reunion shared the fate of the French one; as a matter of fact Henry had lost interest in it for, since the beginning of 1536, he had had a series of successes.

The solemn Bull of Excommunication remained unpublished as long as its execution was not assured. The affair of the Council did not advance one inch on account of France's passive resistance. On 7 January there occurred an event which made it possible for Henry to make overtures to the Emperor—this was the death of the unfortunate Queen Catherine. Through Chapuis, his *chargé d'affaires* in London, Charles V let Henry VIII know that better treatment and the eventual legitimisation of Catherine's surviving daughter Mary might lead to an improvement in their mutual relations; he even went so far as to offer his services as a mediator in Rome. However, in all this the Emperor sacrificed none of his Catholic principles. He made it a first

---

[1] *Corp. Ref.*, VOL. II, pp. 1028-32 (No. 1382); index of contents, *Cal. of Letters*, VOL. IX, p. 344 f. (No. 1014).

[2] *Corp. Ref.*, VOL. II, pp. 1032-6 (No. 1383); index of contents, *Cal. of Letters*, VOL. IX, p. 345 f. (No. 1016).

[3] Prüser, *England und die Schmalkaldener*, pp. 38-66; the divines' memorial on the divorce in *Corp. Ref.*, VOL. II, pp. 527 ff.

[4] Henry's reply of 12 March 1536, *Corp. Ref.*, VOL. III, pp. 45-50 (No. 1407).

condition that Henry should acknowledge the Pope's supremacy over the Church in England and acknowledge the supreme authority of a General Council.[1] He declined the religious conference suggested by England but pledged himself to Pate, the British envoy, to work for a favourable issue of the Council should Henry accept it.[2]

Henry VIII had no intention of committing himself to a Council. One of the conditions stipulated by him was that the Council must be convoked by the Emperor. He was well aware that neither the Pope nor France would accept such a proposal.[3] In his simultaneous communication to the French he stated that the Council must be convened with the consent of all Christian princes.[4] As for Mantua, it was described as "a most objectionable place" for such a gathering. Henry was not particular about the choice of means so long as he prevented the assembly of the Council.

Thus a year after the despatch of the conciliar nuncios the situation that emerged was as follows: Henry VIII fought the Council everywhere and by every means for he saw it as the greatest danger to his crown and realm. In Germany the Protestants, and a number of the Catholic princes of the Empire, would not accept Mantua as a locality, while the majority was prepared to fall in with any arrangements made by the Pope and the Emperor. France secretly encouraged the opponents of the Council and was about to render its assembly impossible by a great war of aggression. And what was the Emperor doing in order to ensure the realisation of a demand so often made by him and now at last gratified?

The nuncio to the imperial court was Giovanni Guidiccioni,[5] a

[1] Chapuis' report on his conversation with Cromwell on 25 February 1536 in *Cal. of Letters*, VOL. X, pp. 131 ff. (No. 351); *ibid.*, the Emperor's instructions to Chapuis dated 29 February and 28 March, pp. 148 and 224 f. (Nos. 373 and 575). The imperial ambassador at the French court endeavoured at the same time to influence Gardiner and Wallop in this sense, *ibid.*, p. 151 f. (No. 375).

[2] Pate to Henry VIII, 14 April 1536, *Cal. of Letters*, VOL. X, p. 269 (No. 670).

[3] Chapuis to Granvella, 24 April 1536, *Cal. of Letters*, VOL. X, p. 303 (No. 720), cf. also No. 1069.

[4] Henry VIII to Gardiner and Wallop, 30 April 1536, *Cal. of Letters*, VOL. X, p. 320 (No. 760).

[5] The letters published in the *Opere di Giovanni Guidiccioni*, ed. C. Minutoli, VOL. II (Florence 1867), pp. 5-166, date for the most part from the years 1536 and 1537; others are in L. Berra, "Nuove lettere inedite di Mons. Giovanni Guidiccioni e nuove notizie sulla sua nunziatura di Spagna", in *Giornale storico della letteratura italiana*, LXXIX (1922), pp. 274-89; the acts of Guidiccioni's nunciature which Ehses quotes under Arm. VIII Ordo i, VOL. D, are now registered under AA I-XVIII 6524. Berra's verdict on Guidiccioni's diplomatic skill appears to me accurate enough, but it must be borne in mind that he was pushed aside by the collector Poggio. For the life of Guidiccioni see C. Dionisotti in the introduction to *Giovanni Guidiccioni, Orazione ai nobili di Lucca* (Rome 1944).

nephew of Bartolomeo Guidiccioni who for several decades had acted as the Pope's Vicar General in his diocese of Parma and was regarded as his trusted confidant. Giovanni was a poet and a humanist of some distinction, but as a diplomatist he was a match neither for the Emperor (now in his full maturity) nor for his collaborators, the Burgundian Granvella and the Spaniard Cobos. Charles V also saw the contest with France drawing near and was taking measures accordingly. Out of consideration for France he had refrained from pronouncing openly in favour of Mantua before the Estates of the Empire and from providing an escort for Vergerio as he had done for Rangoni. His adviser Croy went to Germany alone, for the purpose of neutralising du Bellay's intrigues. The Emperor's declaration that he had no intention to use force against the Protestants was inspired by the same motive.

The campaign against Barbarossa had claimed Charles V until mid-summer. After its swift and victorious termination, he crossed over to Italy, but with very few troops, so as not to provide more food for the rumours spread by the French that he was about to carry out a high-handed reform of the Curia, would secularise the States of the Church and reduce the Pope to the rank of an imperial chaplain.[1] Charles V's real purpose was to clear up, by means of a personal meeting with Paul III, all questions, both great and small, that were pending.

Causes of tension between the two monarchs were not wanting. The Pope took it amiss that the Emperor should prevent him from proceeding against the Duke of Urbino, who, although a vassal of the Holy See, had taken advantage of the vacancy of the Apostolic See to arrange a marriage between his son Guidobaldo and the heiress of Camerino,[2] and he was deeply hurt by Charles's refusal to allow the young Cardinal Farnese to take possession of the wealthy bishopric of Jaén. It was rumoured that the Emperor had observed that after the Pope's mistake of raising the young Farnese to the cardinalate, he was not going to add to the mischief by granting him a bishopric. In both cases the Pope was theoretically in the right. Both Urbino and Camerino were papal fiefs and as Jaén had become vacant by the death of Cardinal

---

[1] The chief agitator was Grand Admiral Chabot, cf. Carpi's reports of 19 March, 13 October and 3 November 1535, Vat. Arch., Lettere di principi, 10, fols. 213ʳ-217,ᵛ 288ʳ-289ʳ, 292ʳ-297ʳ.
[2] On these differences see Pastor, VOL. V, pp. 215 ff. (Eng. edn., VOL. XI, pp. 304 ff.) and Cardauns, "Paul III", p. 162 f.

Merino "in Curia" it was "reserved". But it was equally certain that warlike action by the Pope against Urbino would upset the tranquillity of Italy now so happily restored. It might easily lead to French intervention as well as jeopardise the Council. It was said, not without a show of reason, that the Pope's motive in this affair was his wish to bestow Camerino on a nephew of his. The bestowal of so important a see as Jaén on a boy of fifteen was in contradiction with the principles which had hitherto guided Charles V in all his nominations, to the great advantage of the Spanish Church.

Unsuccessful attempts to settle these differences, petty in themselves yet tiresome, had already been made at Palermo by Lunello, General of the Franciscans, and subsequently by the Pope's son, Pierluigi Farnese, who had been sent to meet the Emperor in southern Italy.[1] They were really of very small significance by comparison with the high aims the Emperor had set himself for his first encounter with the Pope. These he stated in the instructions of 9 December 1535, which Pier Luigi Farnese took back with him to Rome.[2] First on the list was the holding of a Council. "It is impossible", the monarch explained, "to master Lutheranism and the other sects unless their errors are condemned by a Council. The French negotiations for reunion are so many intrigues against a Council; they lead nowhere, as is shown by the attempts made at Augsburg and Ratisbon. All Christian princes, with the sole exception of Henry VIII and the League of Schmalkalden, are in favour of a Council; Francis I is the only one to make difficulties. The only way to stop him is for the Pope to announce that a Council will take place in spite of everything."

Another item of the instructions was a proposal of a political kind. It was that the Pope should join a defensive league for the protection of Italy. This would mean the abandonment of his neutrality. During his memorable stay in Rome between 5 and 18 April 1536, the Emperor moved heaven and earth to win over the Pope to his point of view. The dramatic climax of this fight for the Pope's political soul was the Emperor's great discourse on Easter Monday, in the Sala dei Paramenti, in the presence of the whole papal court and immediately before the

---

[1] The minutes of Ricalcati's letters to P. L. Farnese, dated 17 October and 19 November 1535, which Cardauns, "Paul III", pp. 162, 166, quotes after Lettere di principi, 10, are in Vat. Arch., AA I-XVIII 6537, fols. 72ʳ-76ᵛ. The attitude in the affair of Jaén is interesting: There is no question of yielding, "ne pensino d'haver ad far con papa Celestino" (fol. 73ʳ)—the reference is of course to Celestine V.

[2] Cardauns, "Paul III", pp. 205-10.

solemn High Mass of the day.[1] With all the repressed passion of his melancholic temperament Charles protested against the fact that the Pope, by persisting in his neutrality, put him on a level with the ally of the Turks and the secret patron of the Lutherans. He enumerated the long list of Francis I's sins, from the days of Leo X up to his recent invasion of Savoy, and ended by challenging the French King to settle the dispute over Milan by single combat. The passion with which the Emperor spoke rebounded ineffectively from the cool shrewdness of the Farnese Pope. Paul III had no thought of abandoning his neutrality.[2] He contented himself with initiating fresh negotiations, the futility of which it was easy to foresee in view of the aggressiveness of the French King and the tenacity with which his opponent asserted his will to power and domination. On 9 June the Pope despatched Cardinal Caracciolo to the Emperor and Cardinal Trivulzio to Francis I as legates, with a view to peace negotiations.[3] All was in vain; things had gone too far. Francis I declined the candidature of his third son, the Duke of Angoulême, for the Duchy of Milan which had been proposed to him, and refused to evacuate Savoy. The counter-proposal that Milan should be conferred on the Duke of Orleans was unacceptable to the Emperor, if only on account of the Duke's Italian wife, Catherine de' Medici. The truth was that he was unwilling to give up Milan.

The Pope's firm maintenance of neutrality brought him a great reward. France assented to the convocation of a Council. It required no small effort on the part of Carpi to wring this concession from the King, though its value was considerably lessened by the restrictive clause "on condition that the King shall be able to assist at it without danger to his person and in a manner agreeable to his dignity".[4] Although now as before France's participation remained doubtful, the decision to hold the Council at Mantua was nevertheless finally taken

---

[1] The best account of the Emperor's discourse of 17 April is in Rassow, *Kaiseridee*, pp. 379-92; cf. also pp. 421-30, where there is the full text of the report of the "Italian diplomatist B" of which Cardauns gives only extracts, *loc. cit.*, pp. 211-14. For an appreciation see, besides the literature listed in Pastor, VOL. v, pp. 174 ff. (Eng. edn., VOL. XI, p. 241), Rassow, *Kaiseridee*, pp. 173-268; Brandi, *Quellen*, pp. 258 ff. Francis I's reply of 11 May, which was also read in the *Sala dei paramenti* by the French ambassador on 25 May, as well as Charles V's reply of 16 May are published in *Q.F.*, XII (1909), pp. 324-43, but have no bearing on the question of the Council.

[2] To the joint declaration of neutrality by Granvella and Cobos on 14 April, published by Hefele-Hergenröther, *Conziliengeschichte*, VOL. IX, pp. 947-50, must be added Ricalcati's instructions to Carpi, 27 April, Cardauns, "Paul III", p. 231 f.

[3] Briefs of 14 June in *C.T.*, VOL. IV, pp. 7 ff.

[4] *C.T.*, VOL. IV, p. cxxviii.

during the Emperor's stay in Rome. In the consistory of 8 April seven cardinals were instructed to draw up the Bull of Convocation; they were the Cardinal-bishops Piccolomini and Campeggio, the Cardinal-priests Ghinucci, Simonetta and Contarini, and the Cardinal-deacons Cesi and Cesarini.[1] They were to be assisted by experts in the persons of the former German nuncios Aleander, Rangoni and Vergerio.

In the last days of April Aleander's draft was submitted to the Emperor's chief counsellors Granvella and Cobos, both of whom had remained in Rome. They suggested a number of alterations such as that the present convocation of a Council was the fulfilment of proposals frequently made to Clement VII by the Emperor and his brother, and that the King of France was in agreement with it. The object of the latter clause was, of course, to tie down Francis I by so public a statement. Thereupon the French envoy demanded that his master should also be mentioned in the Bull as having actively promoted a Council. Although no formal proposal by Francis I could be found in the acts, beyond the non-committal commonplaces about the usefulness of a Council with which we are familiar, the Pope insisted that mention should be made of the King's "exceedingly pious" letters to his predecessor. He was evidently anxious not to jeopardise the affair of the Council from the outset by further exacerbating Francis's jealousy.

When everything was ready Vergerio asked to be heard once more. In his opinion the announcement that the Council would be conducted "on the model of the earlier Councils" as well as the choice of Mantua for its location, was bound to incense the Protestants and induce them to stay away. In point of fact this very formula was one of Clement VII's conditions and had created much bad blood at the time. It was accordingly dropped but, as was natural enough, the Pope would have no further discussion of the decision concerning Mantua which it had been so difficult to arrive at.[2]

The draft of the Bull was read in the consistory of 5 May, accepted on the 15th, but the final text was only approved on 2 June. On Whit Sunday, 4 June, it was signed by twenty-six cardinals after which it was read in St Peter's and in the Lateran and posted up on the doors of these

---

[1] Consistorial acts in *C.T.*, VOL. IV, p. 1 f.; Sanchez's reports to Cles dated 8, 13, 16 and 27 May and 15 June, St. Arch., Trent, Cles, Mazzo 10; to Ferdinand I, 7 July, Bucholtz, *Ferdinand I*, VOL. IX, pp. 136 ff.; the imperial minister's and Vergerio's memorials in *N.B.*, VOL. I, i, pp. 583-8.

[2] From Cifuentes' report of 18 May we learn that Vergerio's objections were the main cause of the delay of the Bull of Convocation, *Cal. of St. Pap., Spain*, VOL. v, ii, p. 132 (No. 56).

THE COUNCIL OF TRENT

two basilicas as well as at the Cancellaria and in the Campo Fiore.[1] The peace-legates Caracciolo and Trivulzio presented authentic copies to the Emperor and to Francis I. For other princes and prelates printed copies were provided which were authenticated in each case by the nuncios and a notary.

The Bull *Ad dominici gregis curam* of 2 June 1536 summoned a General Council to Mantua on 23 May 1537, and called upon all bishops, abbots and other prelates of the whole world to appear there in person: the Emperor and other princes were requested to attend in person if possible, and if this was not feasible to send representatives. As for the purpose of the Council, the Bull specified the traditional tasks, namely the extirpation of errors and heresies, the reform of morals, the restoration of peace in Christendom and preparation for a great expedition against the infidels.

The Council was convoked. The great, long-expected step was taken. Yet the goal was further off than anyone would have imagined. The first step was to set in motion the machinery of ecclesiastical administration in order to make sure that the convocation of those who were legally bound to attend the Council was made with due formality, lest anyone should challenge it. There nevertheless followed a whole chain of difficulties both old and new, with the result that after three whole years of discussion this way and that, the hope of a Council faded out once more.

---

[1] The original text of the Bull of Convocation is lost, nor is there a registration of it. Ehses has accordingly used the new draft made in 1545 and kept in Vat. Arch., Concilio 90, for the text published by him in *C.T.*, VOL. IV, pp. 2-6. The Bull bears the signatures of only six cardinals, the remaining signatures are reproduced from the copies preserved in Concilio 1 and 116 and from a broadsheet; cf. Ehses, "Konzilsbullen vor Beginn des Trienter Konzils", in *R.Q.*, XII (1898), p. 224 f. The previous editions are all based on Raynald, *Annales*, a. 1536, No. 35.

CHAPTER VII

The Miscarriage of Mantua and Vicenza

THERE were no definite directions in the written code of the Church
with regard to the persons to be summoned to a General Council, but
canonists were agreed that all *praelati majores*, that is, bishops and others
enjoying episcopal jurisdiction, had to be summoned in due canonical
form.[1] Cardinal Jacobazzi [2] maintained that by right of prescription
abbots and generals of Orders, in fact all those who, on assuming office,
promised under oath to attend a Council, could be made to attend.
There was a consensus of opinion that though the laity were not
entitled to vote it was possible and even necessary for them to be represented for the defence of their interests. It was therefore in keeping
with practical requirements as well as with the still unbroken medieval
conception of the *corpus christianum* that princes, including "protesting"
ones, should be invited. The Mantuan convocation was inspired by
these principles. Briefs were despatched to all metropolitans [3] in which
the Pope ordered them to summon their suffragans, the abbots and
other prelates as well as the universities within their territories to attend
the Council, by means of authenticated copies of the Bull of Convocation. They were likewise charged to hand to the bishops the briefs
addressed to each of them individually. In southern Europe the
distribution of these documents was entrusted to the ordinary nuncios.
In the Spanish realm and in Naples the citation met with some difficulties. By mid-April 1537, acknowledgment of receipt had reached
Rome from 110 Neapolitan bishops and a considerable number of
Spanish prelates, among them the Archbishops of Toledo and Granada,

---

[1] D. Jacobazzi, *De concilio* (Rome 1538), Lib. II, arts. 2 and 3; M. Ugoni, *De
conciliis* (Venice 1532), fols. 61-70; F. Nausea, *Rerum conciliarium libri V* (Leipzig
1538), BK III, Ch. 11 f., has the formula: "Omnes quorum adesse interest".

[2] "Hodie tamen inolevit consuetudo, quod etiam abbates et generales ministri
ordinum religiosorum et omnes, qui, cum promoventur ad dignitatem, iurant venire
ad synodum, sunt vocandi ad generale concilium", Jacobazzi, *loc. cit.*, p. 80. He
even leaves open the possibility of inviting cathedral chapters (p. 82), but is silent
about the universities which, as we shall see, did get an invitation but, of course,
no right to a vote.

[3] The briefs to the Archbishops of Toledo and Mainz in *C.T.*, VOL. IV, pp. 28, 30.
For the bishops of the Kingdom of Naples—in view of their great number—the
nuncio had the Bull printed locally.

the Bishops of Segovia, Palencia, Osma, Córdoba and Concha, the cathedral chapter of Jaén, and a number of abbots and universities. The Bishop of Mexico, however, who had received the Bull of Convocation at the beginning of 1537 and who intended to obey the invitation together with the Bishops of Guatemala and Oaxaca, was prevented by the Spanish government from undertaking the journey to Europe, evidently because the government was afraid lest the participation of American bishops should provide an opportunity for outsiders to meddle with the internal affairs of the Spanish colonies. With a view to quieting the bishops' consciences, the Emperor charged Aguilar, his envoy in Rome, on 18 March 1538 and again on 21 February 1539 to request the Pope to grant them a dispensation.[1]

The Bull only reached Portugal, after many delays, in the spring of 1537 through the newly appointed nuncio Jerome Capodiferro.[2] The King made excuses for all his prelates and sought authority to appoint a Portuguese deputation to the Council made up of prelates and theologians. The Pope rejected the proposal and insisted on the principle that all prelates must appear in person.[3]

For the countries of northern and eastern Europe the Pope appointed nuncios extraordinary. They were the General of the Servites, Dionisio Loreri, for Scotland, Pamfilo Strassoldo of Friuli for Poland, and the Dutchman Peter van der Vorst for the Empire, the Netherlands and the Scandinavian States.

Loreri contented himself with a personal invitation to King James, who just then happened to be in France for his marriage to Madeleine, daughter of Francis I; the citation of the Scottish bishops was entrusted to the King's favourite, the future Cardinal Beaton.[4] The itinerary of the other two nuncios extraordinary had been laid down for them in Aleander's instructions.[5] The fact was that the Pope attached

---

[1] C.T., VOL. IV, p. 105 f. The lists preserved in Vat. lat. 3915, fols. 111ʳ-113ᵛ (93+34 names of places), contain the names of abbots also. The summary of the Spanish summonses is in Vat. lat. 3918, fols. 116ʳ-119ʳ. For the American bishops cf. P. Leturia, "Perchè la nascente Chiesa ispano-americana non fu rappresentata a Trento", in Il Concilio di Trento, I (1942), pp. 35-43.

[2] Brief of 24 December 1536, Corpo diplomatico Portuguez (Lisbon 1862-1910), VOL. III, p. 347 f., with the brief of 23 April announcing the postponement of the opening and John III's reply; also in J. de Castro, Portugal, VOL. I, pp. 449-56. I can find no proof for Ehses's assertion, C.T., VOL. IV, p. 127, n.1, that Capodiferro's predecessor Poggio had had any instructions to this effect.

[3] Brief of 30 August 1537, Corpo diplomatico Portuguez, VOL. III, p. 399 f.; de Castro, Portugal, VOL. I, p. 457 f.

[4] The as yet unpublished acknowledgment of receipt in Vat. lat. 3915, fol. 154ʳ (Paris 28 January 1537) cop., contains nothing of importance.

[5] C.T., VOL. IV, pp. 31-40 (10 September 1536).

great importance to the summons to the Council being carried out in a strictly juridical form in countries affected by the schism. He charged the nuncios always to use the same terms in their oral announcement and to have a notary at hand, so that a notarial instrument of the act could be drawn up at any time. From bishops they were to demand a formal receipt, from princes they were to pray for one. They were strictly forbidden to allow themselves to be drawn into any discussions, especially about the locality of the Council. All such attempts were to be cut short with a declaration that the Council was taking place in consequence of an agreement between Pope and Emperor, hence they alone were qualified to enter into negotiations.

With a view to easing van der Vorst's task, Strassoldo [1] had been commissioned to inform Cardinal Lang of Salzburg of the forthcoming Council, notwithstanding the fact that the nuncio accredited to the Empire would have to call on him in any case since the cardinal was the head of the Bavarian Circle. After discharging his mission at Salzburg, Strassoldo passed through Vienna on his way to Bishop Stanislaus Thurzo [2] of Olmütz. From there he went to Cracow, where on 7 December the Archbishop of Gnesen, Andrew Critius, communicated to him the King's affirmative answer.[3] The delivery of the documents intended for the Archbishop of Riga and his suffragans he entrusted to messengers.[4] As was to be expected, the bishops of the territory of the Teutonic Knights in Prussia, who had embraced Protestantism, only gave a conditional assent.[5] In December Strassoldo returned to Rome via Neisse, where on 20 December the Bishop of Breslau, Jacob von Salza, gave him an attestation of receipt of the Bull and the covering brief.[6]

[1] P. Paschini, "Un nobile Friulano ai servigi di Paolo III: Pamfilo Strassoldo", in *Memorie storiche Forogiuliesi*, XXIII (1927), pp. 109-14. Strassoldo was only made a protonotary on 9 September 1536; at a later date he became *governatore* of Fano, vice-legate of Viterbo, *governatore* of the Campagna Marittima and Archbishop of Ragusa in 1544. He died some time after 1 July 1545.

[2] For the order observed in the invitation to the bishop, the cathedral chapter and the Premonstratensian abbot Martin, cf. Vat. lat. 3915, fol. 144^r.

[3] Reports from Cracow, 28 November and 11 December 1536, *C.T.*, VOL. IV, pp. 50 ff.; the replies p. 52, *n.*1.

[4] The Archbishop of Riga's reply, 25 December 1536, in *C.T.*, VOL. IV, p. 52, *n.*1, that of the Bishop of Dorpat of 5 January, in Theiner, *Mon. Pol.*, VOL. II, p. 518.

[5] *C.T.*, VOL. IV, p. 80; Theiner, *Mon. Pol.*, VOL. II, p. 519; the records of the previous negotiations in P. Tschackert, *Urkundenbuch zur Reformationsgeschichte des Herzogtums Preussen*, VOL. II (Leipzig 1890), pp. 348-52.

[6] H. Jedin, "Die Beschickung des Konzils von Trient durch die Bischöfe von Breslau", in *Archiv für schlesische Kirchengeschichte*, I (1936), pp. 60-74; the Bishop's receipt is on p. 63.

THE COUNCIL OF TRENT

Van der Vorst's programme was far more extensive.[1] Accompanied by a numerous suite which included his own brother Jacob, the Provost of Lübeck, Jodocus Hoetfilter, and the secretary Cornelius Ettenius to whom we owe the description of the journey—a document of the greatest interest from a sociological point of view—he travelled via Trent and Brixen where he delivered the Bulls and briefs intended respectively for Cardinal Cles and for the Vicar of the Prince-Bishop, George of Austria, and so reached Vienna and the court of Ferdinand I. On 11 November, in presence of the privy council, he presented to Ferdinand I the conciliar Bull in a red folder adorned with the arms of the Pope and the King. Four days later Cardinal Cles returned an affirmative answer on all points. The written attestation of receipt of the Bull which was handed to van der Vorst on 18 November, stated that the convocation of the Council gave the King of the Romans extraordinary satisfaction—*singulare gaudium eximiamque laetitiam*.

The journey from Vienna to Passau, via Linz, took Brueghel's pleasure-loving countrymen ten days, for the great abbeys of Klosterneuburg, Melk and St Florian vied with one another in treating the Pope's messenger to sumptuous banquets. They, on their part, did ample justice to the good things offered to them and admired the magnificent organs and rich libraries of their hosts. They called on Cardinal Lang, as head of the Bavarian Circle, and visited Duke William of Bavaria in his hunting-lodge at Hechenkirchen. When William expressed some doubts about the Council really coming off, the nuncio told him emphatically that it would take place whatever happened. He then continued his tour at a leisurely pace, calling on the smaller Wittelsbach princes at Freiburg and in the Upper Palatinate and on Bishop

---

[1] For van der Vorst's nunciature the two papers by F. X. de Ram are still indispensable, viz. "Nonciature de Pierre van der Vorst d'Anvers, évêque d'Acqui, en Allemagne et dans les Pays-Bas 1536-37", in *Nouveaux mémoires de l'Academie royale de Bruxelles*, XII (1839), hereafter quoted as "Nonciature", supplemented by "Documents relatifs à la Nonciature de Pierre van der Vorst", in *Bulletin de la Commission Royale de Belgique*, third series, VOL. VI (1864), quoted as "Documents". Cornelius Ettenius's diary there quoted is important because—as bound by his instructions—he made an official record, in his capacity as a notary, of the notifications of the Council, together with an accurate record also of the witnesses. The Vatican records in the second of the above-mentioned writings are now available in a better edition by Ehses, *C.T.*, VOL. IV, pp. 42-141. Van der Vorst himself belonged to the circle of Adrian VI, after whose death he became one of the familiars of Cardinal Enckenvoirt, auditor of the Rota and in 1534 Bishop of Acqui. He moreover held a number of benefices on the Lower Rhine and in the Low Countries. There is no need, for our present purpose, to enumerate all the local sources for Vorst's journey, as for instance the account in J. Schlecht's *Kilian Leibs Briefwechsel und Diarien* (Münster 1909), p. 123, entitled "Weihnachten in Eichstätt".

Stadion at Dillingen. While at Augsburg he received a strong warning from the Pope to hurry. He had been on the way three months and had not yet seen a single Protestant prince.

In a somewhat accelerated tempo van der Vorst called on Margrave George of Brandenburg. Like Vergerio in the previous year he too met with a most gracious reception at the court of Ansbach, but like him with a similar refusal. When he attempted to justify the choice of Mantua on the ground that it met the wishes of the other nations, the Margrave put to him the disconcerting question: "But what if I can prove that a west German locality would be acceptable to the King of France?" "What we want", he added, "is not the promise of a free passage but a formal *salvus conductus* executed by the Emperor and guaranteeing the personal security of our envoys and our theologians." Van der Vorst had no such document. Moreover, on account of his inadequate acquaintance with the background of the conciliar question, particularly with the Nuremberg negotiations, he cut a somewhat helpless figure before the wily Margrave. However, this scene was only a prelude; worse was to follow.

While the nuncio continued in exceedingly leisurely fashion his round of visits to the Prince-Bishops of Bamberg and Würzburg, and while great honour was being paid him wherever he went,[1] news reached him that on 8 February 1537 the League of Schmalkalden was to hold a meeting in the city of its origin. Van der Vorst's request to see the Elector of Saxony before the gathering was not granted. He was told to repair to Schmalkalden, and though he and John Frederick met at Weimar while on their way to the assembly, the Elector refused to speak to him. At Schmalkalden itself the nuncio experienced the deepest humiliation ever inflicted upon a representative of the Pope in Germany. On 25 February he was at last received by John Frederick, to whom he handed both the conciliar Bull and the covering briefs. The Elector took the documents from the table on which the nuncio had laid them but left the room under some pretext without taking the papers.[2] The councillors who had remained in the room invited the nuncio to collect them. He refused to do so. They told him that they would give him an answer after consultation with their confederates, whereupon the nuncio asked how it was possible for them to give an

---

[1] Ettenius in de Ram, "Documents", pp. 150-6. The Bishop of Bamberg presented the nuncio with a precious sapphire and the Bishop of Würzburg went out to meet him with an escort of 100 mounted men.

[2] In addition to van der Vorst's report of 2 March, *C.T.*, VOL. IV, pp. 89-92, cf. the detailed account by Ettenius in de Ram, "Nonciatures", pp. 17-20.

answer to a letter which they had not read? In the end he left the room, leaving the documents on the table. The next day Landgrave Philip of Hesse and the Dukes of Pommerania, Württemberg and Lüneburg informed him that they shared the views of the Elector, hence there was no purpose in another interview. The nuncio waited for another four days without anything happening. At length, on 2 March, Brück, the Saxon chancellor, supported by four princely councillors, presented himself at the nuncio's lodgings to return both Bull and briefs. He also handed to the nuncio a copy of the League's reply to the imperial vice-chancellor, Matthias Held, who was also at Schmalkalden at this time, for it was with the latter not with van der Vorst that the League was prepared to negotiate on the affair of the Council. As a matter of fact van der Vorst's instructions forbade him to enter into any negotiations. All he was entitled to do was to have the conciliar citations legally attested, whereas Held was not only empowered but actually charged to negotiate in the name of the Emperor. The course of his mission is the best commentary on the unheard-of proceedings at Schmalkalden.

Held had been sent to Germany for the purpose of finding ways and means, after consultation with King Ferdinand, for a settlement of the religious dispute.[1] The Emperor's affairs were in a bad way. The great offensive in Provence had failed. If the Turks were to attack now he would be faced with a war on two fronts. Hence the monarch's most pressing concern was to heal the deepest wound in his world-wide empire—the religious cleavage. Held was charged, in the first instance, to ascertain the attitude of the Estates of the Empire to the Council of Mantua, and in the event of that assembly not taking place, that is if the Pope himself withdrew, to examine what further possibilities remained. Should a Popeless Council be held, perhaps with the co-operation of Portugal, Poland and the small Italian States? Or a German national assembly which might meet the Protestants' demands on such points as were not of the substance of the faith? Or should

[1] On Held's mission, 1536-9, and on the course of historical inquiry starting from Ranke and back to him, see Rassow, *Die Kaiseridee Karls V* (Berlin 1932), pp. 393-8, Brandi, *Quellen*, p. 276 f.; G. Heide's reconstruction of the text of the German instruction which is lost, in *Historisch-politische Blätter*, CII (1888), pp. 718 ff.; the French secret instructions in Lanz, *Correspondenz*, VOL. II, pp. 268-72. I too am of opinion that Held's action at Schmalkalden was at variance with the Emperor's real intentions, for the latter aimed at an *entente* with the Protestants. The possibilities mentioned in the instructions did not constitute formal directives. Held's further commissions—help for the Turkish war, French propaganda, a Catholic league—I deliberately leave on one side; cf. Cardauns in *Q.F.*, XII (1909), pp. 195-211. Biographical literature on Held in Schottenloher, Nos. 8138-43.

they be content with a political armistice on the model of the religious Pacification of Nuremberg?[1]

The perspectives which the Emperor himself thus opened betray profound distrust of the Pope's intentions, a disposition not justified by the pontiff's conduct in the affair of the Council but rather based on personal impressions and opinions. In his address to the members of the League at Schmalkalden on 15 February 1537, Held made no reference to these future possibilities.[2] On the contrary, the Emperor stated his firm determination to attend the Council in person if it was at all possible; in spite of the war he would do his utmost to bring it about and he urged the princes to accept it and to send their representatives to it.

Held's proposal and van der Vorst's mission did not take the confederates unawares. Already in the summer of 1536, that is as soon as he became cognisant of the text of the conciliar Bull, the Elector John Frederick of Saxony had sought the advice of his divines and jurists.[3] These strongly dissuaded him from a summary rejection of the Council, not only in the event of the Protestant princes being invited to attend like all other Christian princes, but even in the event of their being cited with the usual legal formalities, otherwise, as the advisers justly observed, they ran the risk of being declared contumacious, in which case they would be debarred by their own act from future opportunities.[4] When John Frederick, in agreement with the Landgrave of Hesse, went the length of proposing a Protestant opposition Council to be convened by Luther—to which the English and the French would be invited and which would assemble under the protection of an army of eighteen thousand men—these erudite advisers roundly dismissed so fantastic a scheme. They based their verdict on a consideration which reveals their consciousness of ecclesiastical unity—such a Council, they said, would raise the great, the terrible spectre of a possible schism.[5]

---

[1] The decisive passage in the French instructions is also given by Brandi, *Quellen*, p. 276.

[2] Intimation of the Council in French, Lanz, *Staatspapiere*, p. 238 f.; Latin translation in *C.T.*, VOL. IV, p. 71 f.

[3] The documents in *Corp. Ref.*, VOL. III, pp. 99-158 (Nos. 1449-65), have been put in their chronological order by H. Virck in *Z.K.G.*, XIII (1893), pp. 487-512; W. Gussmann has produced a better text of Nos. 1460, 1461 and 1521 in *A.R.G.*, XXIII (1926), pp. 269-86; for the whole subject see G. Mentz, *Johann Friedrich der Grossmütige*, VOL. II (Jena 1908), pp. 105 ff.

[4] The "first counsel" in *Corp. Ref.*, VOL. III, pp. 119-25 (No. 1456); Melanchthon is the author of this piece, and of No. 1459.

[5] The Elector's memorial, written in the first days of December, in which the project for a counter-council is unfolded, in *Corp. Ref.*, VOL. III, pp. 139-44 (No. 1462); *ibid.*, the "second counsel", pp. 126-31 (No. 1458).

At the request of the Elector Luther, assisted by Melanchthon and six other divines, drew up a list of the doctrines which divided Protestants and Catholics and which were therefore to be upheld at any price. These doctrines are the famous Schmalkaldic Articles.[1] Whereas the *Confessio Augustana* had been conciliatory, the articles draw a firm line of demarcation between Protestantism and Catholic dogma. However, in the end it was the politicians,[2] not the theologians,[3] who turned the scales at the Diet of the Confederation in favour of intransigence and a flat rejection of the Council.

The answer which they handed to Held on 24 February 1537 [4] recounted once more the long story of the question of the Council since Chieregati's appearance at Nuremberg. It came to this: "The Council convoked by Paul III was not the free, Christian Council in German lands demanded by the Estates and promised by the Emperor. The Bull of Convocation spoke of condemning recent heresies, hence it passed judgment on the teaching of the Lutherans even before the Council met. As for the announcement of the reform of the Church, its sole aim was to delude the Emperor. Though a party to the dispute, the Pope set himself up as a judge." In their arrogance the men of Schmalkalden took it on themselves to declare that the Pope stood for errors and abuses which were at variance with Holy Scripture, the Councils and the unanimous teaching of the Fathers. "We accuse him", they went on, "—him and his adherents—of simony, neglect of his pastoral office and of the worst kind of immorality. How could we feel safe at a Council held in Italy, where the Pope wields so much power and where our enemies are so many?"

The men of Schmalkalden thus arrogated to themselves a right to pass final judgment in matters of faith which they denied to the Pope. The accusation that the Pope was bent on deception was as incapable

---

[1] For the genesis of the articles, cf. H. Volz, *Luthers Schmalkaldische Artikel und Melanchthons "Tractatus de potestate papae"* (Gotha 1931).

[2] As late as 13 February Bugenhagen wrote to Justus Jonas: "Nos suademus non recusandum esse concilium", but continues "mire oderunt nostri principes et confederati Romanum Antichristum"; *Z.K.G.*, XXXI (1910), p. 91 f.

[3] As early as 3 August 1536 Brück had laid down the axiom: "Je gelinder die Leute (viz. the Pope) desto grösser die Gefahr dass Betrug dahinter steckt", *Corp. Ref.*, VOL. III, p. 151. The invitation was actually couched in mild terms, in the sense that it was not a formal citation. Even the 14 questions submitted to the League on 24 December and to which the members were to reply, still contemplated the possibility of their attending the Council. Text in *Forschungen zur deutschen Geschichte*, XXII (1882), pp. 633 ff.

[4] *C.T.*, VOL. IV, pp. 73-8; for the preliminaries, cf. *Politische Correspondenz*, VOL. II, pp. 414-29; Mentz, *Johann Friedrich der Grossmütige*, VOL. III, pp. 357 ff.

of proof as their other accusations against his person. The tone of their answer was as unprecedented as was their treatment of the nuncio. Held declared his solidarity with the latter in so far as he utterly rejected every attempt to drive a wedge between the Pope and the Emperor in the affair of the Council. The Emperor, he explained, had no intention of defending doctrines, institutions or abuses which were at variance with the word of God; he was determined to resist every kind of partiality and intrigue at the Council and to see to it that it was conducted in a free and Christian manner. On the other hand he did not feel qualified to lay down rules of procedure for the assembly as the men of Schmalkalden were attempting to do, though no one would prevent them from submitting to it their wishes in this respect. He ended by justifying the choice of Mantua on the ground that this was the wish of the other nations. The Duke of Mantua was the Emperor's vassal and he would give them every guarantee they might require for their personal safety. Let them reconsider their answer and accept the Council without reservation.[1]

These exhortations fell on deaf ears. In their reply of 28 February,[2] the confederates said: "We are unable to alter our view of the Pope's intentions and to accept the Council since acceptance would be the same as submitting in advance to the verdict which will surely be pronounced." "The freedom of the Council", they now stated with all the clarity that could be wished for, "does not consist in the possibility of a free expression of opinion but in the Pope being debarred from the presidency. By a Christian Council we mean one whose only standard is Holy Scripture. This was the meaning of the earlier decisions of the Diet and from these we will not depart. The Diet's demand for a German locality for the Council conforms to the practice of the ancient Church, when theological controversies were decided in the place of their origin.[3] Mantua is suspect by the mere fact that the Duke's brother is a Roman cardinal. We do not doubt the Emperor's good intentions, but he will be as powerless to give them effect as was the Emperor Sigismund at Constance. We are not going to walk into the Pope's trap; for us Mantua is unacceptable. If the Pope prevents the assembly of a free Christian Council in Germany, we protest

---

[1] *C.T.*, VOL. IV, pp. 78 ff.
[2] *Ibid.*, pp. 81-7.
[3] For this alleged practice Melanchthon appeals to canon 19 of the Council of Chalcedon (*Corp. Ref.*, VOL. III, p. 136), but the Greek text shows that his translation is wrong (Hefele, *Conziliengeschichte*, VOL. II, p. 522): the canon only prescribes provincial synods.

before God and the whole of Christendom that we are not responsible for the consequences and we reserve our complete freedom of action."

The kind of Council favoured by the League of Schmalkalden was neither a general Council as understood by Christian antiquity nor an assembly of Christendom like the General Councils of the early and late Middle Ages, but a plain Protestant lay assembly. Their suggestion was that the Pope should waive his supreme authority and that the teaching Church should accept the Lutheran principle of the Scriptures as the only authority in matters of faith. On such a basis no understanding was possible; if the Protestants insisted on it, there was no alternative except to hold the Council without them. The Protestants explained their standpoint to the general public in an official pamphlet published on 5 March, the first of a long series of Protestant writings in defence of their rejection of the Council.[1]

Van der Vorst left Schmalkalden on 3 March. After an exchange of views on the new situation at Halle with Cardinal Albrecht of Mainz and the imperial vice-chancellor he journeyed to Zeitz where, on the 13th, he presented the invitation to the Council to the Elector Joachim II of Brandenburg, to Duke George of Saxony and to Duke Henry of Brunswick.[2] All three accepted it and the Elector Joachim promised to send representatives, provided freedom of speech and freedom to make proposals was guaranteed to his envoys.

Time pressed: the Council should have been opened on 23 May. Crossing north Germany,[3] van der Vorst reached Verden, where he entrusted to the Archbishop of Bremen ten packets containing the Bulls and briefs for the Scandinavian Kings, the Archbishops of Lund, Drontheim and Upsala and the Hanseatic city of Lübeck. At the castle of Iburg he invited Francis von Waldeck, Bishop of Münster, Minden

---

[1] The copy sent to the Duke of Mantua together with a covering letter from John Frederick of Saxony and Philip of Hesse, dated 26 March 1537, in St. Arch., Mantua, Busta 3356; a new edition by Le Plat, VOL. II, pp. 657-83. In the archives of the *Gregoriana* in Rome (Cod. 621, fols. 39ʳ-44ᵛ) there is a pamphlet (without indication of place of printing) entitled: "Ratio, cur synodus illa, quam Paulus Ro. Pontifex eius nominis III Mantuae celebrandum parum candide indicit et se habiturum esse significat, neque aequa videri possit neque utilis ecclesiae, unde ab iis, qui sacrosanctum evangelium ineffabili Dei misericordia revelatum acceperunt atque ecclesiae Christi consultum esse volunt, optimo iure ut suspecta recusari debeat, regibus et monarchis praesertim exterarum nationum adeoque omnibus bonis viris exposita."

[2] Report of 23 March, *C.T.*, VOL. IV, pp. 95-8; *ibid.*, p. 93 f., George of Saxony's and Joachim II's declarations of assent.

[3] Report of 8 May, *C.T.*, VOL. IV, pp. 115-20; also de Ram, "Documents", pp. 172 ff.; "Nonciature", pp. 42 ff.

and Osnabrück, to the Council, after which he journeyed towards the Rhine, that life-artery of the west which on the whole still remained Catholic. Fresh surprises were in store for him there. The Duke of Cleves, of whom he had no high expectations, seeing that he was the father-in-law of John Frederick of Saxony, accepted the Council but asked many questions about a safe-conduct. The ecclesiastical Electors of Cologne and Trier, Hermann von Wied who was already wavering and was only kept in the Church by Gropper, and Johann von Metzenhausen, an otherwise well-disposed prelate, pleaded an earlier agreement of the Rhenish Electors and declared that they could only promise to put in an appearance at Mantua after they had consulted together. Count Palatine Louis repeated the more than curious game which he had played before at the expense of Vergerio; he refused to see van der Vorst as he passed hard by his residence and instructed his councillors to tell him at Heidelberg that they were ignorant of their master's whereabouts. The nuncio had to be satisfied with a document attesting receipt of the Bull and bearing the seal but not the signature of the Palatine.

The Bulls and briefs for the ecclesiastical province of Besançon had been despatched by van der Vorst during his stay at Mainz. During his first stay at Cologne he had invited the university and the senate of that imperial city to the Council. On his return to the Lower Rhine he received from them the strange reply that they would adopt exactly the same attitude to the Council of Mantua as the one they had adopted, at an earlier period, to Constance and Basle.[1] On reaching his native Netherlands the nuncio presented the convocation documents to the Duke of Geldern at Arnheim. The Bishops of Utrecht and Liège he only met at Brussels, where he arrived on 4 June.[2] With an invitation to the regent of the Netherlands, Queen Mary of Hungary, the nuncio provisionally terminated his mission on 12 June 1537. On his return journey to Italy he acted once again as conciliar nuncio to the Swiss Confederation.

It must be admitted that van der Vorst took advantage of his stay on the Lower Rhine to obtain possession of the provostships of Bonn and Emmerich which had been granted to him by the Pope. For this he was severely taken to task, not altogether without reason, by Giberti,

---

[1] De Ram, "Nonciature", p. 60. For this last part of the journey Ettenius is our only source since the report of 7 June is missing.

[2] Report of 16 June, *C.T.*, VOL. IV, p. 125; *ibid.*, p. 123, the receipt of reception of the Bishop of Utrecht, Georg von Egmont. Van der Vorst's address at Lucerne in *Eidgenössische Abschiede*, VOL. IV, 1(c), p. 909.

who happened to be in the Low Countries at the same time. For all that, it was a happy inspiration when the Pope chose for this mission—a mission more juridical than diplomatic—a jurist who spoke the language of the country and who had had experience of the ways of the Curia. It is certain that van der Vorst displayed both circumspection and endurance in the performance of the far too extensive task allotted to him. However, all his exertions were in vain. He was recalled to Rome while at Brussels; at the same time he received information that the Council had not been opened at the appointed date, that it could not be held at Mantua and that in fact it had been postponed until 1 November. What had happened?

The Council of Mantua did not fail to meet because of the brusque refusal of the League of Schmalkalden; nor can the blame be laid on schismatical England, where no invitation to the Council had even been attempted; the failure must be ascribed to the attitude of France. When the first reports of the Rome negotiations reached him, Francis I poured out a torrent of complaints against the Pope, but when the Cardinal of Lorraine explained the true state of affairs he expressed his entire satisfaction.[1] The convocation of Mantua had followed upon his assent, qualified though it was. The Pope firmly maintained a neutrality which greatly favoured France. One might therefore have expected that that country would refrain from further opposition to the plan for the Council. Yet the very opposite happened. As soon as the Pope's representatives, the peace-legate Trivulzio and the ordinary nuncio Carpi, attempted to give effect to the convocation, Francis I reverted to his old tactics, made fair speeches on the need and the usefulness of what he called a "good" Council and protested his devotion to the person of the Pope. But he refused to send envoys to the Council on the plea that neither he himself nor his bishops would be able to put in an appearance at Mantua while the war was on.[2] Yet even now, a full year after the failure of his attempt to get Melanchthon to come to Paris, he had the impudence to utter grandiloquent promises that he would bring about a reunion with the German Protestants and even with Henry VIII. Even the arrival of Cesare de' Nobili as nuncio

---

[1] Ehses, "Franz I von Frankreich und die Konzilsfrage in den Jahren 1536-39", in *R.Q.*, XII (1898), pp. 306-23; Cardauns, "Paul III", p. 198 f., and the same writer's account in *Q.F.*, XII (1909), p. 189 f.

[2] Extracts from Carpi's reports of 3 July and 5 September 1536, *C.T.*, VOL. IV, p. 109 f. In his despatch of 10 May he reports that the King boasted of his understanding with the German Electors and Henry VIII. In respect of the latter he displayed "un desiderio extremo di haver questo honore di ritornarlo alla obedienza di S.S.^tà ", Vat. Arch., Nunz. di Francia, 1 B, fol. 36^v.

extraordinary led to no change in the King's determination to boycott the Council. No copy of the Bull of Convocation came into the hands of a single French bishop. When Carpi, who had been raised to the cardinalate in December 1536, came to take leave of the King in the first days of May 1537, the monarch's last words were that for reasons of security Mantua was unacceptable both to himself and to his prelates. When Carpi invited the court-cardinals to the Council, their answer was significant enough; "they would discuss it with the King", they said.[1] Not one of them stirred.

To the complete failure of the convocation in France a further obstacle came to be added at the last moment in Mantua itself. Strange though it seems, no direct official approach had been made to Federigo, Duke of Mantua, either before or after publication of the Bull of Convocation, no doubt under an impression that his brother, Cardinal Ercole, who lived in Rome, would keep him fully informed. As a matter of fact Ercole had announced at once, though in general terms, that Mantua was at the Pope's disposal for the Council, but he had not breathed a word of the fact that as early as 1530, when Mantua was first mentioned as the place of assembly, his brother had made it a condition that none but himself should command the guard of the Council and in fact all armed forces on the spot, and that his expenses should be refunded to him.[2]

As early as the last days of December 1536 the nuncio to Vienna, Morone, had spoken of the pressing need of demonstrating the Pope's determination to hold the Council by some positive preparations at Mantua,[3] yet it was only in the spring of 1537, when the opening date was ominously near, that an attempt was made to settle material details.[4] By a brief dated 15 February the Pope requested the Duke to make arrangements for the reception and the security of the members of the Council.[5] Ercole had expressly warned his brother not to make conditions which he thought would provide the Pope with a welcome pretext

---

[1] Carpi's report of 3 May 1537, *ibid.*, fols. 98ʳ-103ᵛ.

[2] Letter of an anonymous writer to Francesco Gonzaga, 12 August 1530, St. Arch., Mantua, Busta 2194. The report that Mantua was being considered rested on a letter of the Mantuan agent Bagarotto, 1 August 1530, *ibid.* For Ercole's statement, cf. the letter of 2 August 1536 to Federigo, *C.T.*, VOL. IV, p. cxxxi.

[3] *N.B.*, VOL. I, PT ii, p. 93, cf. also p. 131.

[4] The most important documents are, in part, in *N.B.*, VOL. I, PT ii, pp. 425-35, and more fully in *C.T.*, VOL. IV, pp. 70 ff., 94 f., 98-104; supplementary matter in A. Casadei, "Trattative per l'apertura del Concilio a Mantova", in *Il Concilio di Trento*, II (1943), pp. 83-105.

[5] *C.T.*, VOL. IV, p. 70 f.

for abandoning the idea of the Council—an action that would annoy the Emperor.[1] In spite of this warning, Federigo's official reply of 24 February was not limited to a promise to provide accommodation and maintenance. While leaving it to the Pope to take the necessary measures for his personal security, the Duke charged his brother to inform the pontiff that in his opinion a guard of from five to six thousand men would be required.

For a moment Paul III thought there must be some misunderstanding. In the consistory he said that he had no thought of asking Federigo to defend the Council against external enemies. He would see to this himself by diplomatic means. When he spoke of security he only meant the maintenance of public order in the city. He wrote to Federigo in this sense on 21 March, announcing at the same time the arrival of a prelate for further negotiations.[2] However, there had been no misunderstanding. In a letter of 24 March addressed to his brother but actually meant for the Pope, Federigo explained with much detail why he demanded so disproportionate an armed force.[3] The city, he said, lacked a citadel which would have facilitated the preservation of internal order. The streets would have to be guarded continuously, but the burghers would not be able to undertake the armed protection of the assembly, as at Constance a century earlier. It was therefore for the Pope to provide a conciliar guard of the required strength.

Cardinal Ercole was so disconcerted by this letter that he kept it back for several days without showing it to the Pope. The letter contained the very thing against which he had warned his brother—a condition which it was hardly possible to fulfil. If the Pope were to maintain so strong a body of armed men, wholly or even partially at his own expense, the freedom of the Council as well as the legality of its decisions might be questioned. Such a condition could not be accepted on any account. When Ercole eventually submitted his brother's letter in the consistory of 9 April, that which he had feared happened. The Pope interpreted the condition as a refusal and declared that the raising of a papal guard for the Council, above all one of such strength, could not be thought of. To this decision he stuck even after Federigo informed him through his secretary Abbadino that he would be satisfied with a hundred

---

[1] *Ibid.*, p. cxxxiii, Ercole's letter to Federigo, 16 February 1537.

[2] *C.T.*, VOL. IV, p. 94 f.

[3] *Ibid.*, p. 98. There is no proof that Federigo was under the influence of Schmalkalden. I remarked above that the covering letter which went with the document of refusal is dated 26 March.

mounted men and fifteen hundred foot-soldiers; in fact he would be content to start with only a thousand, on condition that he should have the right, should the need arise, to reinforce these troops at his own expense.[1] In the consistory of 18 April it was decided to postpone the Pope's departure for Mantua. Two days later the foreign ambassadors were informed in the presence of the assembled consistory that "on account of difficulties created by the Duke of Mantua", the Council was postponed until 1 November.[2] The Bull *Decet Romanum Pontificem*, of the same date, justified the decision, a most unpleasant one for the Pope—*molestissimum*—by pleading the magnitude of the expenses and the incongruity of "an armed Council". In the Bull, as in the message to the powers,[3] all the blame was laid on the shoulders of Duke Federigo. But was he the real culprit? Or was he merely a scapegoat? Did he not provide the Pope with a convenient pretext for countermanding a Council which had become impossible in any case, and so enable him to exculpate himself before public opinion by laying the blame on another's shoulders?

There can be no doubt that if the Pope had agreed to maintain a guard of the strength suggested by the Duke, he would have provided not only Henry VIII but the League of Schmalkalden also with a pretext for questioning the freedom of the Council. Even some of the members of the Council, in their anxiety for their personal safety, might have entertained serious misgivings. By rejecting the Mantuan's demands the Pope acted in the best interests of the Church. But one may well ask whether the Council would have materialised even if Federigo had not laid down his condition. A number of cardinals doubted the success of the undertaking and warned the Pope against compromising his authority by journeying to Mantua; at the same time the Roman populace were loud in their laments about the impending desolation of the city.[4] Paul III had repeatedly allowed it to become known that he would open the Council even though the war went on and even if the Lutherans refused to attend. But, we may well ask,

[1] Abbadino's instructions of 12 April in *C.T.*, VOL. IV, pp. 102 ff. On the 16th he was in Rome; cf. also Ercole's letter of 17 April to Ferrante Gonzaga, Casadei, in *Il Concilio di Trento*, II (1943), p. 99 f.
[2] Consistorial acts and Bull in *C.T.*, VOL. IV, pp. 104-8, 111 f. One printed copy of the Bull (6 leaves without indication of place of printing) is in Munich, Hauptstaatsarchiv, Staatsverwaltung 2721, fol. 75ʳ.
[3] Identical briefs to the Emperor, the Kings of France, Poland, Portugal and Scotland, the Doge of Venice and the Dukes of Lorraine and Savoy, dated 23 April in *C.T.*, VOL. IV, p. 112 f.
[4] Sánchez to Cles, 8 April 1537, St. Arch., Trent, Cles, Mazzo 10.

could he dispense with the concurrence of the French?[1] At the very least it must be admitted that the Duke's condition proved very convenient; it enabled the Pope to circumvent, or at least to put off, a political decision fraught with such far-reaching consequences as was his attitude towards Francis I. On the other hand, the warnings of his closest advisers prevented him from shelving the plan for a Council altogether.

In their reports to Rome both van der Vorst and Morone, Vergerio's successor at the court of Ferdinand I, had repeatedly insisted that unless a General Council took place the collapse of the Catholic resistance in Germany as well as a national Council were inevitable.[2] Aleander also laid great stress on this point in the two memorials on the question of the prorogation which he submitted on 16 April. In the first, in which he supported the postponement to 1 November, he said that on no account must the Bull and the covering briefs allow the determination of the new place to depend on the assent of the princes for in the eyes of the world this would be a postponement, not *ad Calendas Novembris* but *ad Calendas Graecas*.[3] In the second memorial we find this statement: "However loudly we may blame the Duke of Mantua for the postponement, in the opinion of the world the real culprit is the Pope." [4] With a view to avoiding the fatal impression that the Pope sought to avoid a Council Aleander would have wished him to start on that journey which Morone had for so long pressed him to undertake [5] but which was only planned for the beginning of April.[6] The Pope could have awaited at Bologna the arrival of the bishops who were coming to the Council and opened the assembly in that city, after which he might have come to a decision about its eventual translation to some other town. There were strong objections to the opening of the Council in a city of the Papal States, but in the present instance it would have been the lesser evil.

The Pope did not fall in with the views of his adviser. On 29 April

[1] In the above-mentioned letter of 17 April (Casadei, in *Il Concilio di Trento*, II (1943), p. 99) to Ferrante, Ercole Gonzaga enumerates three obstacles, viz. the attitude of Schmalkalden, that of the French, and the impossibility for the members to arrive in time.

[2] Van der Vorst's reports from Zeitz, *C.T.*, VOL. IV, pp. 95 ff.; those of Morone of 17 December 1536, *N.B.*, VOL. I, PT ii, pp. 77-84; those of 16 March 1537, *ibid.*, pp. 127 ff.

[3] *N.B.*, VOL. I, PT ii, p. 438.

[4] *Ibid.*, p. 440.

[5] *Ibid.*, p. 93.

[6] *C.T.*, VOL. IV, p. 100, brief to Carpi, 3 April.

he despatched the Bishop of Segni to Trent for the purpose of stopping possible arrivals from Germany and informing them of the postponement of the Council.[1] However, the most urgent task of papal diplomacy was to convince the great powers, above all the Emperor, whose suspicions were sufficiently roused already, as well as the Emperor's brother Ferdinand, that the Pope was in earnest with his plan for a Council. The nuncios Guidiccioni and Morone [2] were instructed to protest emphatically that the Pope's decision to hold the Council remained unshaken and that he was resolved to bring it about at any cost (*ad ogni modo*). True, Mantua must be eliminated, not only on account of the above-mentioned condition of the Duke's, but likewise out of consideration for France, which for reasons of security declined both that town and Milan. Out of regard for France the Pope thereafter suggested none but neutral localities; either a city on the Venetian mainland, such as Verona or Padua, or if the Signoria would not hear of these, then papal Bologna or Piacenza, which would be subject to the authority of the Council for the whole period of its duration.

The Pope had evidently come round to Aleander's view that there was no longer any reason to take into account the views of the Protestants as to the choice of a locality; the Catholics alone need be considered. As a matter of fact the Pope was gradually drawing closer to the still more far-reaching view of his adviser, namely that the purpose of the Council was not the return of the Protestants but the preservation of the Catholics and the strengthening of the undecided.[3] The conception of a Council as realised at Trent was gradually gaining ground. Charles V, however, and his brother Ferdinand stuck to their notion of a Council of reunion in which the Protestants would participate: "even the presence of the Elector of Saxony is not out of the question", the Emperor observed in conversation with Guidiccioni. His refusal to bring his authority to bear upon the German Estates in favour of Mantua, a refusal that proved so fatal to the conciliar propaganda of 1535, was justified by him with the familiar argument that he

[1] *Ibid.*, p. 113.
[2] Instructions for Morone, 27 April 1537, *N.B.*, VOL. I, PT ii, pp. 152 ff.: those for Giovanni Guidiccioni, 30 April, *C.T.*, VOL. IV, p. 114 f.
[3] "La cosa resta solo da trattarsi da Cattolici," *C.T.*, VOL. IV, p. 114, and almost identical with *N.B.*, VOL. I, PT ii, p. 154, and *ibid.*, p. 440, in Aleander's second memorial: "conservandi saltem sunt et consolandi catholici et alii qui titubant confirmandi et stabiliendi". But Aleander overlooked the fact that a Council in German lands was not exclusively a demand of Schmalkalden—it was also a decision of the imperial Diet.

did not wish to drive the Protestants to extremities, that is to revolt and an alliance with France. Even at this stage he still refrained from mentioning a definite locality.

Ferdinand was less reserved.[1] Probably at Cles's suggestion he mentioned Trent as the most suitable place for the Council. He too held out hopes of the presence of the Protestants. "Once the Council is assembled", he told the nuncio, "it will be in a position to issue an invitation to them in the same way as the Council of Basle invited the Hussites. In that case, of course, Bologna and Piacenza are out of the question for they would never consent to set foot on Church territory." Ferdinand I showed that he appreciated the Pope's dilemma in consequence of Francis I's refusal. There was only one way out of the impasse: let the Pope come down on the Emperor's side! Ferdinand's programme was the same as that of his brother in his Roman Easter oration: first joint war against Francis I, then a Council and, if need be, the crushing of the Lutherans by force.

Such a solution, which the Habsburg brothers proposed again and again, viz. the solution of the problem of a Council by the abandonment of neutrality, was unacceptable to the Pope for a number of reasons, many of them inspired by considerations of ecclesiastical policy. Francis I had made no secret of what he would do in the event of the Pope's abandoning his neutrality. He would have gone the way of Henry VIII.[2] A papal alliance with the Emperor would have meant a French schism. So the only thing the Pope could do was to resume negotiations with Francis I for some other place of assembly for the Council. Once again the result was purely negative. The King adopted the standpoint that both the summoning and the postponement of the Council had been decided without his assent, hence he was under no obligation of any kind. Of all this only this much was true: the French envoys had not attended the consistory of 20 April 1537, they may even have been absent from the decisive one of 2 June 1536. Filiberto Ferreri,[3] who had succeeded Carpi as nuncio, very properly countered this argument by pointing out that the mere absence of the envoys for the purpose of showing their opposition was not enough; they should

---

[1] Morone's report of 16 May 1537, *N.B.*, vol. I, pt ii, pp. 165 ff.

[2] "Senza dubbio la farebbe all' Inglese," Carpi on 12 March 1535, Vat. Arch., Lettere di principi, 10, fol. 204ᵛ.

[3] Ferreri's reports in Vat. Arch., AA I-XVIII, 6530 orr., and Nunz. di Francia 1 A, copies; also Pieper, *Zur Enstehungsgeschichte*, p. 101. Ferreri, a nephew of Cardinal Bonifacio, was eighteen years old when he became administrator of the diocese of Ivrea on 17 May 1518; he was therefore born in 1500. In 1532 he was appointed nuncio to the court of the Duke of Savoy. He died on 14 August 1549.

have lodged a formal protest.[1] With regard to the question of locality, the King suddenly constituted himself the advocate of the Protestant claim that the Council must be held in Germany; he mentioned Basle or Constance and, as an alternative, Lyons. On the other hand he roundly rejected any Italian town, even a Venetian one, inasmuch as it would be beneath his dignity and that of the French prelates to attend a Council under the protection of an imperial safe-conduct. No notice was taken of the nuncio's request for permission to publish the Bull of Postponement. The nuncio extraordinary, Cesare de' Nobili, returned to Rome in the summer of 1537 without having achieved anything in the affair of the Council.[2] When Ferreri expressed his disappointment and commented on the annoyance the Pope was bound to experience,[3] Francis had recourse to his old tactics. He delivered himself of commonplaces about the usefulness of a General Council, but any tangible concession or an opinion on the places suggested by the Pope were carefully withheld. His motives are transparent. If he agreed to a Council in Italy, as proposed by the Pope, he would find himself at loggerheads with his virtual allies in Germany, the confederates of Schmalkalden. There was no risk in airing the latter's views, for he knew that the Pope would never agree to a Council on German soil nor the Emperor to one at Lyons or Turin. In any case he would prevent the assembly of the Council and the consequent strengthening of the Emperor's position. From the political point of view he was right; from the standpoint of religion and the Church his conduct could only cause grievous harm to the latter. Religion and the *raison d'Etat* were once again in irreconcilable opposition.

The attitude of the two paramount powers so incensed the Pope that he let fall a threat that he would proceed against them with ecclesiastical censures.[4] He cannot have meant it seriously. Paul III was convinced that it was the politician's not the hierarch's business to find a way out of the seemingly hopeless situation. The question was how the maintenance of neutrality could be reconciled with the pressing

[1] Report of 29 June 1537, *C.T.*, VOL. IV, p. 129.
[2] Nobili's reports of 16 June, Ferreri's of 20 June 1537, *C.T.*, VOL. IV, p. 130.
[3] Report of 31 July, *C.T.*, VOL. IV, p. 137. How tense the situation was at the time appears from Ferreri's report of 3 August on his conversation with Cardinal de Bourbon at Châlons, Vat. Arch., Nunz. di Francia I A, fols. 117ᵛ-119ᵛ. Ferreri threatened that the Pope would "pull other strings" against France, to which the cardinal replied with the counter-threat "si potria pensare a mettere in disputa le cose che possiede", whereupon Ferreri said, "But for this we must have a Council."
[4] Report of the French ambassador in Rome, 12 July 1537, Ribier, *Lettres*, VOL. I, p. 41; cf. the simultaneous threats of Ferreri in the preceding note.

need for a Council which, as Supreme Pontiff, he could not shelve. Reports from Germany left no room for hesitation; there was no escape from the alternative: either a General Council or a national one.[1] "If the General Council does not meet," Morone wrote on 16 July,[2] "there will be great upheavals in Germany." The power of the Lutherans was growing steadily. The childless Duke George of Saxony stood on the brink of the grave; no reliance could be placed on the new Elector of Brandenburg, Joachim II. If more ecclesiastical princes yielded to temptation and secularised their dioceses, almost the whole of north Germany would be lost. All the great imperial cities in the south had apostatised; mighty Augsburg was the most recent instance. Something had to be done, and as things were it could only be done by a Council, hence the Pope would not give up his plan for such a gathering. In view of the importance of the decisions that had to be taken the Pope summoned to Rome on 20 June 1537 those cardinals who did not reside in the city.[3] On the advice of the cardinals present in Curia he put off till 1 September [4] the final decision about the locality of the Council. The matter was urgent since the opening was announced for 1 November. In order to attenuate to some extent the bad impression that a further postponement of a decision was bound to create, the Pope caused a report to be spread that he intended to leave for Bologna about that date.[5] Thus it came about that it was only on 29 August that he formally requested the Doge to put one of the cities of the Venetian mainland at the disposal of the Council.[6] After some hesitation, due to bad news from Corfu which was being besieged by the Turks, the Signoria ended by putting Vicenza at the Pope's disposal.[7] The news reached Paul III on 29 September at Ronciglione. He immediately ordered Cardinal Piccolomini to summon a meeting of the cardinals for the next day so that he might inform the Sacred College and concert all necessary measures.[8] Under the impression that a

---

[1] Morone's reports of 6 and 12 July 1537, *N.B.*, VOL. I, PT ii, pp. 186 ff., 188 ff.
[2] *N.B.*, VOL. I, PT ii, p. 191 f.
[3] *C.T.*, VOL. IV, p. 125 f., cf. p. 132. The brief addressed to Cles was despatched by Sánchez on 8 July, St. Arch., Trent, Cles, Mazzo 10.
[4] The short notice in the consistorial acts, *C.T.*, VOL. IV, p. 131.
[5] Ribier, *Lettres*, VOL. I, p. 41. Filippo Trivulzio's summons to the Curia by brief of 31 July points in the same direction, *C.T.*, VOL. IV, p. 132 f.
[6] *C.T.*, VOL. IV, p. 134. For what follows, cf. B. Morsolin, "Il Concilio di Vicenza", in *Atti del R. Istituto Veneto*, 6th series, VOL. VII, i (1888-9), pp. 539-87.
[7] Instructions of 25 September, Morsolin, "Il Concilio di Vicenza", p. 583.
[8] Alessandro Farnese to the Maestro di Camera, 29 September, *C.T.*, VOL. IV, p. 134 f. Contarini's letter of 1 October to Ercole Gonzaga shows that the Pope was not at Nepi but at Ronciglione, a Farnese estate, *Q.F.*, II (1899), p. 174.

postponement until 1 January 1538 would suffice, the Pope gave them to understand that he would set out for the north about mid-October. However, the cardinals disapproved of such speed. At the consistory held immediately after the Pope's return to Rome on 8 October it was decided to postpone the opening of the Council for a full six months and to fix the new date for 1 May 1538.[1] On 18 October identical briefs to this effect were despatched to all princes.[2] This was the second postponement of a Council announced three years earlier.

The effect of the delay in Germany was terrible. Vergerio's sombre prophecies were being fulfilled. He himself had not rejoined his post in 1536, not, as Cardinal Cles's Roman agent surmised, because he was regarded as too keen a champion of the Council,[3] but because in consequence of his intrigues he had ended by forfeiting the confidence of Ferdinand I, who until then had been his staunchest supporter.[4] Vergerio's place was taken by Giovanni Morone,[5] the son of the former chancellor of Milan, a young man of only twenty-eight years of age. Paul III was an acute judge of character. This particularity of his enabled him to discern in the young man the uncommon aptitude for diplomacy which was to make of Morone the ablest diplomatist of the Curia within the space of a few years. When his nomination became known it was said: "At last the German nunciature is not being assigned to second and third-rate personalities, to men like Rorario and Pimpinella!" "The greater his modesty," Sánchez wrote to Vienna, "the more worthy he is of honour."[6] Modest he was indeed, even

[1] The consistorial acts and the Bull *Benedictus Deus*, *C.T.*, VOL. IV, pp. 135 ff. The Bull printed by Bladus is in *Catalogo delle edizioni romane di Antonio Blado Asolano* (1891), No. 1182.

[2] *C.T.*, VOL. IV, p. 138 f. Fabio Mignanelli, nuncio at a later date, went to the Emperor while the papal chamberlain Baldassare of Florence went to Francis I.

[3] Jacob Britius to Cles, 7 July 1536, in *A.R.G.*, x (1912), p. 74. On 27 July Britius added that the two "discorsi", viz. the memorials on the Bull, had done him a good deal of harm, *ibid.*, p. 75.

[4] In a letter to Cles, 8 May 1536, Sánchez compared Vergerio to a doctor who has never done treating a wealthy patient, St. Arch., Trent, Cles, Mazzo 10. On 5 June he wrote, "Vergerio cum quodam suo discursu manifeste deterret papam et collegium cardinalium a concilio." If the Pope were less determined to hold the Council it would be put off.

[5] Friedensburg's character-sketch of young Morone in *N.B.*, VOL. I, PT ii, pp. 7-18; a final appreciation of his personality and the literature about him will occupy us later. When Morone had acted as nuncio for three years Christoph Scheurl, who appears to have known his father, wrote to Johann Eck on 13 February 1540: "Is in universa aula bene audit, gratus est atque plausibilis, tum regi tum proceribus acceptus, humanitate et eruditione praeditus," *Briefbuch*, VOL. II, p. 233.

[6] Sánchez to Cles, 24 October 1536, St. Arch., Trent, Cles, Mazzo 10.

modesty itself, but this did not mean that he was not an extraordinarily shrewd observer and an accurate reporter. Within a few years no other Italian was more thoroughly acquainted with conditions in Germany. But from the first he was no mere reporter, or at best a mere agent; on the contrary, he was a real diplomatic counsellor, for he was able to see papal policy as a whole, in all its ramifications, while at the same time he had the courage to make a stand for his own views, even when they diverged from the official ones.

Thanks to his diplomatic skill, which was proverbial, Morone experienced no difficulty in justifying the double postponement in the eyes of a man so profoundly devoted to the Church and the Papacy as was Ferdinand, and in obtaining his promise to send his representatives.[1] But what he could not prevent was the sudden collapse of the exaggerated hopes which the German Catholics had at first set on the Farnese Pope. The few proctors who had set out for Mantua in the early summer of 1537 had retraced their steps.[2] Johann Eck, who in 1535 had been the mouthpiece of his countrymen's hopes,[3] now wrote to Aleander in a mood of profound discouragement: "Many people are scandalised when they see the Council gone with the wind." [4] He literally begged for information so as to enable him to keep the princes with whom he corresponded in good humour. Yet in mid-December 1537 he was still ignorant of the second postponement. He felt oppressed by sombre forebodings: "If there is no Council, then woe to England! woe to Denmark, Sweden and Norway! When will the apostasy end?" [5] Matthias Held told the nuncio to his face that by this time not one Catholic prince in Germany believed that a Council would ever take

---

[1] Statement by Ferdinand, 15 December 1537, *C.T.*, VOL. IV, p. 142, and Morone's report of the same day in *N.B.*, VOL. I, PT ii, pp. 241-4.

[2] During the few days that he spent at Trent the Bishop of Segni did not encounter a single visitor from Germany, *C.T.*, VOL. IV, p. 121, but we know that the Franciscan Kaspar Sager had started for the Council as the representative of the Archbishop of Bremen, B. Katterbach in *Franziskanische Studien*, XII (1925), p. 260, where the laudatory brief to the Archbishop dated 13 October already given in *C.T.*, VOL. IV, p. 137 f., is reprinted. Also on the way was the Carmelite provincial Andreas Stoss, son of the sculptor Veit Stoss, in the capacity of proctor of the Bishop of Bamberg, R. Schaffer, *Andreas Stoss, Sohn des Veit Stoss und seine gegenreformatorische Tätigkeit* (Breslau 1926), p. 102. The author, however, overlooks the fact that Scheurl (*Briefbuch*, VOL. II, p. 189) also mentions this mission. Sager went on to Rome, Stoss turned back somewhere between Innsbruck and Trent.

[3] Johann Eck to Paul III on 10 May 1535, *Z.K.G.*, XVI (1896), p. 219 f., but even at this time he was already tortured by the fear that the Council might be postponed; *id.*, to Vergerio on 2 July 1535, *ibid.*, p. 222.

[4] Johann Eck to Aleander, 8 October 1537, *ibid.*, p. 231.

[5] Johann Eck to Aleander, 5 September 1537, *ibid.*, p. 230; 11 December, *ibid.*, p. 232.

place.[1] When Morone begged King Ferdinand to write to some of the prominent princes in order to excuse the postponement he received the crushing reply: "It is useless; they believe me no more than they believe you." [2]

On the other hand the Lutherans were jubilant. Satires and lampoons about the Council sprang up like mushrooms. Luther himself brought out an edition of the first Bull of Convocation with a preface and sarcastic marginal notes.[3] In an essay on the Donation of Constantine he indulged in a particularly vicious attack on the Papacy.[4] In the spring of 1537 Antonius Corvinus in his "Conversation between Pasquillo and a German" (*Unterredung zwischen dem Pasquillen und dem Deutschen*) had described the Council of Mantua as mere bluff [5]; now, in a pamphlet probably printed at Wittenberg under the title of "Beelzebub to the Holy Papal Church" (*Beelzebub an die heilige bepstliche Kirche*), he asserted that all that Paul III aimed at with his plans for Council and reform was to hoax "the kings and the whole world" (*den königen und aller Welt eine nasen drehen*).[6] Henry VIII, in his *Sententia*, which circulated in Germany in pamphlet form,[7] also accused the Pope of fooling the kings with his Council and indulged in cheap jokes about the first postponement on the ground that it summoned the Council to "nowhere".

What was the good of the Roman jurist Antonio Massa and the Dutch divine Albert Pighius refuting the English lampoon in detail? Their tracts were never published.[8] Cochlaeus, who gave proof of a

---

[1] *N.B.*, VOL. I, PT ii, p. 220 (12 October 1537).

[2] *Ibid.*, p. 166 (10 May 1537).

[3] *L.W.*, VOL. L, pp. 92 ff. The preface to J. Kymeus, *Ein altchristliches Konzil zu Gangra gehalten* (*ibid.*, pp. 45 ff.), and the *Karnöffel* satire on pp. 131-4, also attack the Council of Mantua; cf. O. Menzel, "Johannes Kymeus, *Des Bapsts Hercules wider die Deutschen*, Wittenberg 1538", in *Heidelberger Sitzungsberichte philosophisch-historische Klasse*, 1940-1, *n.*6.

[4] *L.W.*, VOL. L, pp. 65 ff. Morone forwarded this tract and some other German anti-conciliar literature to Rome on 20 August 1537, *N.B.*, VOL. I, PT ii, p. 199.

[5] A. Corvinus, *Eine Unterredung zwischen dem Pasquillen und Deutschen von dem zukünftigen concilio zu Mantua* (1537), and a translation of the Latin tract by the same writer: *Pasquilli de concilii Mantuani iudicium* (1537). Description and index of contents in P. Tschackert, *Analecta Corviniana* (Leipzig 1910), pp. 26-30. I too am unable to ascertain what pamphlets van der Vorst forwarded to Ricalcati and Simonetta on 3 January 1537; de Ram, "Nonciature", p. 141. On the *Dialogus* of Urbanus Rhegius, cf. *C.T.*, VOL. XII, p. lxxvi.

[6] Schade, *Satiren*, VOL. II, pp. 102-4.

[7] Reprint in *C.T.*, VOL. XII, pp. 767-74; the passage quoted is on p. 772. The lampoon was distributed gratis at the Frankfurt Fair; for its effect in Germany, see Morone's report of 30 October 1537, *N.B.*, VOL. I, PT ii, p. 235.

[8] *C.T.*, VOL. XII, pp. 159-66, 774-810; cf. H. Jedin, *Studien über die Schriftstellertätigkeit Albert Pigges* (Münster 1931), pp. 22 ff.

truly touching zeal, published a whole series of tracts on the Council.[1] He even conceived the notion of using the printing press of his nephew Wolrab of Leipzig for publicity purposes on its behalf.[2] However, no one bought his books and before long Wolrab was faced with bankruptcy. Of the "Epistle about the Council" by Bishop Fabri of Vienna, which was printed in Rome,[3] Johann von Kampen said that "it was worthy of a blacksmith".[4]

Venice had placed Vicenza at the Pope's disposal, but many of the nobles shared the opinion of the envoy Soriano, who thought that a Council was the last thing Paul III really wanted. With caustic irony they suggested the Lido for its meeting: there would be plenty of room there![5] The Gonzagas' Roman agent, a man not entirely free from prejudice, wrote: "Whether Vicenza or any other town is chosen, one thing is certain—no one will come."[6] It would have been difficult to dispel this profound scepticism even if the Pope had taken immediate steps in preparation for the Council and had himself started on his journey as planned. But he did neither. The Curia remained in Rome and it was only on 19 December that Bishop Giberti of Verona and Ugo Rangoni, the conciliar nuncio under Clement VII, were instructed to betake themselves to Vicenza for the purpose of making all necessary arrangements for the reception of the Council.[7] Further measures followed at the beginning of the new year. On 7 January a commission of cardinals was set up to deal with all matters connected with the Council. It consisted of two cardinal-bishops, Cupis and Campeggio, five cardinal-priests, Ghinucci, Simonetta, Carafa, Contarini and Sadoleto, and two cardinal-deacons, Cesarini and Pole.[8] The

[1] Spahn, *Cochlaeus*, bibliography, Nos. 120-4.
[2] Cochlaeus to Ottonello Vida, Vergerio's secretary, 26 July 1536, *Z.K.G.*, XVIII (1896), pp. 267 ff.; to Morone, 31 August 1537, *ibid.*, p. 272. In the following year Wolrab actually published Nausea's *Rerum conciliarium libri V* (Leipzig 1538), with a preface addressed to Paul III, dated 1 February 1538.
[3] J. Fabri, *De necessitate et mera utilitate sacrosancti concilii epistola* (Rome 1537), 13 leaves; cf. *C.T.*, VOL. XII, p. lxiii f.
[4] Johann von Kampen to Dantiscus, 12 June 1537, in *Zeitschrift für Geschichte Ermlands*, IX (1891), p. 542.
[5] Agnello to Duke Federigo of Mantua, 31 August 1537; Morsolin, "Il Concilio di Vicenza", p. 546.
[6] Morsolin, "Il Concilio di Vicenza", p. 552 (20 September 1537).
[7] Brief to Giberti in Raynald, *Annales*, a. 1537, No. 34; also Giberti, *Opera*, ed. Ballerini (Verona 1733), p. xxxiii. Communication to the Doge, 12 December, *C.T.*, VOL. IV, p. 141.
[8] *C.T.*, VOL. IV, p. 142. On 28 January 1538 Sánchez mentions Cardinal Sanseverino instead of Pole and adds: "Frequenter de illis (rebus) consultant", St. Arch., Trent, Cles, Mazzo 10.

preliminary arrangements were entrusted to the experienced canonist Lorenzo Campeggio. We still possess the list of questions which the latter submitted for discussion by the plenary meeting: the choice of the presidents and officials of the Council, the question as to who had a claim to a vote and how to record it, the handling of the German Protestants and other dissidents.[1] Cardinal Contarini convened a group of theologians for a study of the dogmatic problems [2] and thus made a beginning of that scholarly preparation for the Council on which Bishop Fabri of Vienna had laid so much stress in a memorial handed in by him after the Mantuan convocation.[3] Antonius Bladus, printer to the Apostolic Camera, published Piero da Monte's treatise on the question of authority at the Council written during the Council of Basle, and a little later another work on the Council by the elder Cardinal Jacobazzi, composed during the fifth Lateran Council. Both these books were excellent in their way and full of useful information for the members of the Council, but they were not inspired by the problem of the hour. Bartolomeo Guidiccioni's treatise on the Council written at the Pope's request in the winter of 1535-6 was never printed.[4]

To ensure the presence at Vicenza of at least one patriarch, the Pope, on 3 January, ordered the Latin Patriarch of Alexandria, Cesare Riario, to present himself at the Curia within twenty days. On 4 February the King of Portugal was requested to despatch his bishops with all speed, above all the Infante Cardinal Alfonso whose prestige, it was hoped, would greatly contribute to the restoration of the unity of

---

[1] Campeggio's *questionnaire* in *C.T.*, VOL. IV, p. 143 f. This and the commission's concluding memorial, *ibid.*, pp. 151-5. I shall return to these important documents in the second Volume, when discussing procedure at the Council.

[2] Contarini to Ercole Gonzaga, 8 February 1538, *Q.F.*, II (1899), p. 188. During the winter of 1536-7 Contarini, while writing his *Summa conciliorum* (printed in his *Opera* (Paris 1571), pp. 546-63), had mastered the whole subject of the Council, Dittrich, *Gasparo Contarini*, pp. 333-40.

[3] Fabri's *Praeparatoria* of 6 July 1536, *C.T.*, VOL. IV, pp. 10-23; on 17 August Sánchez informed Cles that he had presented *Consilia et litteras* to the Pope, St. Arch., Trent, Cles, Mazzo 10; cf. L. Helbling, *Dr Johann Fabri* (Münster 1941), pp. 106-14. Of the activities of the Italian theologians whose convocation the Pope mentions in his *Responsio*, *C.T.*, VOL. IV, pp. 23-6, nothing is known. Fabri's reply of 14 December was forwarded to Rome by Morone on the 17th, *N.B.*, VOL. I, PT ii, pp. 77-84; the brief of acknowledgment of 3 January 1537 in *C.T.*, VOL. IV, p. 64 f.

[4] J. Haller, *Piero da Monte* (Rome 1941), p. 25.* Cristoforo Jacobazzi's edition of his uncle's work on the Council appeared in October 1538. For Fabri's *Epistola*, see above, p. 336, *n.* 3; for Guidiccioni, V. Schweitzer in *R.Q.*, XX (1906), *Geschichte*, pp. 51 ff., and my paper "Concilio e riforma nel pensiero del Card. B. Guidiccioni", in *Rivista di Storia della Chiesa in Italia*, II (1948), pp. 33-60.

the Church.[1] On 19 February he recalled Cardinal Quiñónez from Naples, where the latter was engaged in the reform of the Poor Clares, on the ground that he was thinking of making an early start (*propediem*) for the Council.[2] A month later, when it had become evident that the Pope would not go to Vicenza in person, three legates were appointed on 20 March.[3] Lorenzo Campeggio, an outstanding personality by reason of his experience and learning, was named president. He was to be assisted by Giacomo Simonetta, a canonist of the Curia, and by Aleander, recently raised to the cardinalate. The latter set out at once for Venice to collect his books and papers. This done he waited at Padua for the arrival of his colleagues.[4] However, Campeggio suffered an attack of gout at Loiano in the neighbourhood of Bologna, so that his progress was slow. Simonetta arrived at the near-by abbey of Praglia by mid-April, but the two legates decided to defer their entry into Vicenza from the first of May to the fourth or one of the following days.[5] Meanwhile the two commissaries, Giberti and Rangoni, had made a number of preparations. At this time Vicenza, "the Garden of Venice", had not yet been adorned with Palladio's buildings, but it was nevertheless a beautiful city and most suitable for the purposes of the Council. From this point of view there was no ground for a translation,[6] but the inhabitants showed little enthusiasm for the honour done to them. The golden stream which such an assembly was expected to direct towards their city seemed to them a long way off. On the initiative of the podestà, Francesco Contarini, the Council of the Hundred appointed a committee for the purpose of commandeering accommodation. However, those deputed twice declined the duty and only accepted after a third election.[7] Their hesitation was prompted

[1] *C.T.*, VOL. IV, p. 149 f. The brief of 31 March 1538 on the same subject in de Castro, *Portugal*, VOL. I, p. 467.

[2] *C.T.*, VOL. IV, p. 151.

[3] *Ibid.*, p. 156 f., brief of 20 March 1538.

[4] *Ibid.*, pp. 157-60, the legates' reports.

[5] According to Morsolin, "Il Concilio di Vicenza", p. 561, the commissaries left Venice on 23 January after expressing the Pope's thanks to the Signoria. Rangoni's first letter from Vicenza is dated 27 January, *C.T.*, VOL. IV, p. 145. In addition to Morsolin's work "Il Concilio di Vicenza", cf. also his "Nuovi particolari sul Concilio di Vicenza", in *Nuovo Archivio Veneto*, IV (1892), pp. 5-28; C. Capasso, "I Legati al Concilio di Vicenza del 1538", *ibid.*, III (1892), pp. 77-116. A. Casadei, "Proposte e trattative per l'apertura e per il trasferimento del Concilio a Ferrara", in *Il Concilio di Trento*, II (1943), pp. 243-71, discusses the plans for the transfer of the Council to Ferrara after the failure of Mantua, plans which were taken up once more at the time of the Tridentine convocation.

[6] *Q.F.*, II (1899), p. 183 (2 January 1538).

[7] The acts in Morsolin, "Il Concilio di Vicenza", pp. 584 ff.

by the not very encouraging reports about the prospects of the assembly which reached them from Venice and even from Rome itself.[1] The papal quartermaster for whom they had repeatedly asked in Rome for the purpose of allocating lodgings failed to arrive. As a matter of fact at the moment there would have been nothing for him to do. At the beginning of February a member of Cardinal Cles' household was seen in the town, looking for a suitable lodging for his master, but he soon vanished. Since then not a single member of the future Council had put in an appearance. Giovanni Ricci of Montepulciano, a large-scale contractor, engaged masons and carpenters for the enlargement of the cathedral chancel in accordance with a suggestion of the commissaries, but the work languished.[2] The papal master of ceremonies Gianbattista of Fermo who arrived on 14 April was recalled on the 24th; there was nothing for him to do at Vicenza. The two commissaries remained alone in the field.

However, one poor refugee turned up on 30 April. This was Bishop John Magnus, whom the Reformation had driven from his archdiocese of Upsala. Of the numerous prelates who were in the habit of spending some time at Venice, not one put in an appearance in spite of the summons of the nuncio Verallo.[3]

This then was the shattering result of the convocation of the Council. There is little doubt that, had he chosen to do so, it would have been an easy thing for the Pope to order two dozen Italian bishops, some abbots and the generals of Orders to proceed to the chosen city; they would have been about as many as were subsequently present at the opening session of the Council of Trent. The Pope took no such action. He was obviously determined to wait for the result of the meeting of the two monarchs at Nice which he had prepared and finally brought about through the exertions of his peace legates Jacobazzi and

---

[1] What follows is based on Rangoni's reports, *C.T.*, VOL. IV, pp. 150 f., 157, 160, 164 f.

[2] To the total cost of 700 scudi the chapter promised to contribute 200 sc. while the city promised another 100, Morsolin, in *Nuovo Archivio Veneto*, IV (1892), p. 22 f. The 400 sc. contributed by the Pope were paid by the treasurer Giovanni Ricci to the brothers Marangone of Bergamo on 7 April 1538, at Venice, Montepulciano, Bibl. Ricci, VOL. IX, fol. 281.

[3] Aleander to Verallo on 5 May 1538, *C.T.*, VOL. IV, p. 165 f. The city council of Strasbourg claimed to have information from Venice of another kind of "attendance" —that of certain "ladies" of doubtful reputation who were said to have betaken themselves to Vicenza, *Politische Correspondenz*, VOL. II, p. 500 (14 June 1538). There is no support whatever for the report, which is obviously a mischievous invention.

Carpi.[1] He himself was actually on the way to Nice. On 25 April 1538, from Piacenza, he directed the consistory to put off the opening of the Council for an unspecified period on the ground of the non-arrival of the prelates.[2] This was the third postponement, and this time it was made without indication of a time-limit.

The decisive motive for the postponement of the Council was not the non-arrival of the prelates but the forthcoming congress of Nice. Charles V and Francis I were about to lay down arms. The conclusion of peace would remove the chief obstacle to the Council so that there would be a solid prospect of its materialising. But even this hope proved delusive. Thanks to the Pope's mediation, the two monarchs concluded a ten years' truce, but no final peace treaty.[3] The question of the Council was no nearer a solution. In the course of the negotiations Francis I had declared that unless Milan were given up, he could not assent to a Council. At Nice he only laughed when asked for his assent. The Pope made the return journey in company with Charles V. At Genoa he agreed to postpone the opening of the Council of Vicenza until Easter, 6 April 1539. In the consistory of 28 June, in which this decision was taken, he revealed only one reason for this fresh delay, namely the two monarchs' wish to return to their dominions and to give their prelates time to make preparations for the journey.[4] However, the true motive was once more the desire to gain time, or more exactly a desire to await the result of the peace negotiations and to give a chance to the Emperor's policy of conciliation in Germany which, if successful, would immensely facilitate the Council, nay, might even render it superfluous.[5]

The immediate sequel of this fresh delay, the fourth, was the removal even of the modest pledge that the Council would take place,

---

[1] Pieper, *Zur Enstehungsgeschichte*, p. 13 f.; Pastor, VOL. v, p. 194: Eng. edn., VOL. XI, p. 275. The Emperor's letters to Aguilar show that Cristoforo Jacobazzi had promised that the Pope would see to it that, at the very least, Francis I would not obstruct the Council, *Cal. of St. Pap., Spain*, VOL. v, ii, pp. 424 ff., No. 179 f.

[2] *C.T.*, VOL. IV, p. 161.

[3] Sources and literature for the congress of Nice in Brandi, *Quellen*, p. 268 f.; also Dorez, *La Cour du Pape Paul III* (Paris 1932), pp. 293-300, and besides Pastor's account, VOL. v, pp. 197-205: Eng. edn., VOL. XI, pp. 287 ff., the political valuation in Rassow, *Die Kaiseridee Karls V*, pp. 352-70. For the agreement on the Council, cf. A. Korte, *Die Konzilspolitik Karls V in den Jahren 1538-43* (Halle 1905), pp. 15 ff.; for the preliminary negotiations see *Cal. of St. Pap., Spain*, VOL. v, ii, p. 396 (No. 172); p. 417 (No. 173, report of 4 January 1538).

[4] *C.T.*, VOL. IV, p. 167; also the Bull *Universi populi*, *ibid.*, p. 168.

[5] The "causae propter quas S.D.N. ad praesens prorogat celebrationem Concilii" which were most probably set down in writing only after 20 July, in *C.T.*, VOL. IV, pp. 171 ff.; cf. also the memorial of the year 1542 in *C.T.*, VOL. XII, p. 362 f.

namely the presence of the papal legates in the locality chosen for its celebration. On 12 May the three cardinals, accompanied by no more than five bishops, had made their entry into Vicenza. In compliance with the very definite orders of the Pope they had refrained from any act that could have been interpreted as the opening of the Council.[1] In June Simonetta betook himself to Verona for the purpose of presiding at a general chapter of the Augustinians.[2] At this time too a few visitors to the Council arrived from Germany. They were the proctors of the Archbishop of Mainz.[3] They were in complete ignorance of what had happened, and they came too late. On 7 July letters from Farnese and Ghinucci informed the legates of the latest postponement. They waited for another month, when they received the Bull of Prorogation drawn up in Rome on 2 August but dated 28 June. Its arrival at Vicenza on 9 August put an end to their mission. Campeggio, already a very sick man, and Simonetta returned to Rome, where the former succumbed on 20 July 1539. As for Aleander, he set out for Vienna in order to watch the Habsburg reunion policy. Once again the sceptics on the Rialto and elsewhere had been right, and they were to remain so for some time to come.

It soon became evident that the time-limit of nine months was too short for the purpose for which the postponement had been decided upon. Although the meeting of the monarchs at Aiguesmortes,[4] from 14 to 16 July 1538, took place amid such friendly demonstrations that

---

[1] According to the legates' report in Capasso, in *Nuovo Archivio Veneto*, III (1892), p. 111, the following made their entrance at the same time: Giberti, Rangoni, Tommaso Campeggio, Vergerio and the Bishop of Rethymo in Crete, who is described as "figlio del quondam Hieronimo Donato", that is probably Filippo Donato, but the latter was Bishop of Canea and is unconnected with Grechetto, cf. Buschbell, *Reformation und Inquisition in Italien*, pp. 36 ff. On 14 May the legates intervened with Farnese on behalf of Vergerio. They prayed him to prolong the time limit for the expedition of the Bull appointing him to the see of Capodistria. Farnese refused to comply with their request on 7 June, *A.R.G.*, x (1912), p. 78 f.

[2] *Analecta Augustiniana*, IX (1921), p. 48 f.; Jedin, *Seripando*, VOL. I, p. 147. On 29 May 1538 Seripando complained to Nausea: "Vincentiae iam ultra mensem sumus . . . concilium celebraturi nec quisquam comparet eorum qui tantas tragoedias excitarunt", *Epp. misc. ad Nauseam libri X* (Basle 1550), p. 225.

[3] *N.B.*, VOL. I, PT iii, p. 113 f.

[4] The chief result of Aiguesmortes, the Emperor wrote on 18 July to his sister Maria, was "de nous estre et demourer a toujours vrays bons freres, allyez et amys", Lanz, *Correspondenz*, VOL. II, p. 286. No one has expounded the political consequences of Nice more competently than L. Cardauns, *Nizza*, pp. 1-123. Capasso, *Paolo III*, VOL. II, pp. 1-91, 167-244, also has abundant documentation. For the negotiations of the League of Schmalkalden with France and England which began in the spring of 1538 but which we are not discussing in detail, John Frederick of Saxony's instructions are important, cf. Mentz, *Johann Friedrich der Grossmütige*, VOL. III, pp. 366-83.

it was described as a family party, the hope of peace was not fulfilled. Both parties were lavish with demonstrations of friendship. Queen Mary of Hungary paid a visit to Compiègne and the Emperor journeyed from Spain to the Netherlands, right across the territory of his opponent —an unheard-of occurrence—but the negotiations about the heart of the quarrel, viz. the duchy of Milan, did not advance one step. It had been arranged at Nice that Milan should be bestowed on the Duke of Orleans, who would marry a daughter of Ferdinand I, but no agreement had been arrived at on the conditions of the surrender. The Emperor now came forward with a fresh proposal which would have brought the houses of Valois and Habsburg even more closely together while preserving strategically irreplaceable Milan for the latter. This was that the Duke of Orleans should marry Charles's daughter Mary and receive the Netherlands, while Milan was to go to Ferdinand's second son, to whom Francis I would give the hand of his daughter Margaret: at the same time the French King would renounce all his claims to the duchy. However, this offer, in itself an attractive one for France, was bound up with so many conditions that Francis I refused to consider it. All this happened in the summer of 1540.

By that time the two monarchs had resumed their old attitude of mutual antagonism. Francis I had refused to join the defensive league against the Turks which the Pope, the Emperor and the Republic of Venice had formed some time before the Nice meeting (8 February 1538) and under the mask of a mediator for peace with the Porte the French King was actually doing his best, through his envoy Cantelmo, to smash this inconvenient alliance which, in point of fact, had already been loosened in consequence of the defeat of the allied fleet at Prevesa on 27 September 1538. The less his negotiations with the Emperor progressed, the more eagerly the King canvassed for allies for the impending conflict. To Venice, which had been compelled to conclude an unfavourable peace with the Porte, he offered his patronage. He also sought to win over as allies against Charles V the Dukes of Ferrara and Mantua, the German Protestants, and even some Catholic princes who were at variance with the Emperor. Before the Protestants—in view of the Emperor's plans for reunion—he posed as an opponent to any concessions by them, while before the Catholics he exhibited himself as a staunch upholder of Catholic principles. His only success was an alliance with Duke William of Cleves, who was on bad terms with the Emperor on account of the succession of Gelderland.

On the other hand Charles was consolidating his hold on Italy.

Filippo Strozzi's terrible end may be regarded as symbolic of the iron determination with which the Emperor was resolved to uphold Spanish rule not only over Naples and Milan, through his viceroys Pedro de Toledo and Alfonso del Vasto, but likewise over the secondary and small states immediately dependent on him. In Germany too he was able to register some decisive successes. While the attempt to attach the Elector John Frederick of Saxony to himself by a formal alliance proved a failure, the treaties of 1541 with Landgrave Philip of Hesse made a breach in the front of the potential enemies of the morrow and secured for him two valuable allies in the approaching conflict with France. But his greatest success was undoubtedly his *rapprochement* with England. Henry VIII had at first sought to prevent an *entente* between the two monarchs by every means in his power,[1] but after its realisation he paid court to both [2] while at the same time taking all necessary defensive measures against an attempt at invasion.[3] The return of the former tensions relieved him of further anxiety; once again he was a courted neutral. He enjoyed that position until the new fronts were set up, when he made overtures to the Emperor, whom he rightly regarded as the stronger of the two.

However, these details about the policies of the great powers have carried us far ahead of our story. For the moment it is enough to say that the peace which at the time of the prorogation of Genoa was thought to be at hand, was not achieved. The next chapter will show that the Emperor's policy of reunion, for the sake of which it had been made, was much slower in getting under way than had been expected. There was little likelihood that the Council would meet at the appointed time. All the same, throughout the second half of 1538, the Pope kept urging those whom it concerned to come to the rendezvous. Shortly before the decision to postpone the assembly, on 22 May 1538, he summoned

[1] The Council played a considerable role in these intrigues. Henry VIII began by announcing through his ambassador with Charles V that he would never accept a papal Council but only one convened by the Emperor, *Cal. of St. Pap., Spain*, VOL. v, ii, p. 500 f. (No. 212). He then demanded a delay and mentioned Cambrai as a suitable locality, *ibid.*, p. 429 f. (No. 182). In April it was reported that he intended to send two divines to Spain for the purpose of justifying his standpoint, *ibid.*, p. 526 (No. 223).

[2] For the proposals which Henry VIII made at this time to the French ambassador Castillon, see the latter's reports of 19 June and 18 July in J. Kaulek, *Correspondance politique de Castillon et de Marillac 1537-1542* (Paris 1885), pp. 61 ff., 70 ff.

[3] The two reports of the French ambassador Marillac dated 15 April 1539 in J. Kaulek, *Corresp. pol.*, pp. 90-3. Ribier, *Lettres*, VOL. I, pp. 437 ff., gives the text of one of the reports. The pact of friendship between the two monarchs, Marillac writes, is "le point principal qui trouble le cerveau de ces gens".

to Rome Miguel de Silva, Bishop of Viseu in Portugal, and on the same day he instructed his nuncio Capodiferro to inform King John that he definitely expected the arrival of the Portuguese prelates. In August he spoke in a similar strain to the Portuguese ambassador.[1] Sadoleto felt that the Pope's good-will justified the highest hopes.[2] But this optimism was without foundation, for while the old obstacles to a Council remained, a fresh one was now added; the fact, namely, that even the Emperor did not desire such an assembly as long as his efforts for reunion were in progress.

In the autumn of 1538 the French government forbade the publication of the Bull of Prorogation and refused to exercise its influence with a view to persuading the German Protestants to attend the Council.[3] When in the spring of 1539 the nuncio Ferreri officially requested the Connétable de Montmorency to urge the French bishops to attend, he was bluntly told that a Council was impossible just then because its composition would have an exclusively Italian character: it was necessary to await the result of the German policy of reunion.[4] To Latino Giovenale, the nuncio extraordinary, the King explained that his reason for rejecting Vicenza was that the German Protestants would never go there, and once again he mentioned Lyons.[5] France's attitude remained unchanged, her game being greatly facilitated by the fact that she was able to lay all the blame on the Emperor.

In Vienna the legate Aleander and the nuncio Fabio Mignanelli,[6] who had replaced Morone, had had the Bull of Postponement printed and distributed according to custom. King Ferdinand had gone so far as to say that the thought of the Council must be kept alive.[7] Yet at this moment a Council did not suit the Habsburg policy. When the nuncio Poggio mentioned the despatch of Spanish prelates to the

[1] *C.T.*, VOL. IV, pp. 166, 174, *n.*1; *Corpo diplomatico Portuguez*, VOL. III, p. 438. The Archbishop of Funchal alone was excused, *C.T.*, VOL. IV, p. 175; de Castro, *Portugal*, VOL. I, p. 473.

[2] *Sadoleti Epp.*; *Opera*, Verona 1737-8, VOL. III, pp. 32 ff.

[3] The brief in Raynald, *Annales, a.* 1538, No. 35; also Ferreri's report of 28 October 1538, *C.T.*, VOL. IV, p. 174 f.

[4] Ferreri's report of 9 May 1539, Vat. Arch. AA I-XVIII, 6530, fols. 157ʳ-159ʳ; on 13 June he writes: "lauda (the King) la prorogation del concilio", Nunz. di Francia, I A, fols. 198ʳ-200ʳ.

[5] *N.B.*, VOL. I, PT iv, p. 55; biographical information about Latino Giovenale in Dorez, *La Cour du Pape Paul III*, VOL. I, pp. 115-41.

[6] The briefs of 26 August with Farnese's covering letter of 30 August 1538, in *C.T.*, VOL. IV, p. 173 f.; *N.B.*, VOL. I, PT iii, pp. 215, 218. It was at this time that Mignanelli, till then a consistorial advocate and a married man, embraced the clerical state; short biography in *N.B.*, VOL. I, PT iv, pp. 41 ff.

[7] *N.B.*, VOL. I, PT iii, p. 198 and *passim*.

Council and requested a definite statement by the Emperor about the date of the opening of the assembly, he was kept waiting for weeks for an answer. We do not know the exact wording of the eventual reply, but it came to this: "At this moment a Council is impossible." The fact was that the Emperor could not send representatives to the Council without finding himself openly at variance with his policy of reunion within the Empire.[1]

As the date for the opening agreed upon at Genoa approached, it became ever more evident that there would be no Council. On the other hand the Pope knew only too well that he alone, and no one else, would be blamed for the failure. He accordingly did his utmost to prevent these suspicions from gathering strength. This explains his appointment on 21 April 1539, that is a fortnight after the expiration of the time-limit, of three new conciliar legates, namely Simonetta, Aleander and the uncle of the French nuncio, Ferreri, who replaced Campeggio, now stricken with mortal illness.[2] On 24 April Cervini informed Ferreri that everywhere prelates were being urged to set out for the Council.[3] However, in view of the negative attitude of the various courts, a consistory of 21 May took the unavoidable decision to postpone the Council, only this time it was not done in the form of a prorogation, but in that of a *suspensio ad beneplacitum*.[4] The Pope chose this formula because he feared, and with good reason, that if he fixed a time-limit which in the end would not be adhered to, he would expose himself to ridicule.[5] The information sent to the legate Aleander, to the effect that the suspension was only for a few months,[6] did not prevent the fact that in Germany the Council was regarded as done with and the blame laid on the Pope. Duke George of Saxony bluntly refused to listen to any further discussion of the subject.[7] The most

---

[1] Poggio to Pole on 2 May 1539, *N.B.*, VOL. I, PT iv, p. 40.

[2] *C.T.*, VOL. IV, p. 177. Ehses's statement (note 2) that Cardinal Quiñónez had urged the nomination of legates is due to a wrong reading of a passage in Ribier, *Lettres*, VOL. I, p. 445. The order to Aleander to repair to Vicenza (*N.B.*, VOL. I, PT iv, p. 53) was soon revoked. [3] *C.T.*, VOL. IV, p. 177, *n.*3.

[4] *Ibid.*, p. 178; also Aguilar's despatches of 13 and 19 April and 16 and 19 May 1539, in *Cal. of St. Pap., Spain*, VOL. VI, pp. 140-57 (Nos. 54, 57, 62, 64).

[5] This argument of Aleander's, which Ferdinand also made his own, *N.B.*, VOL. I, PT iv, pp. 100, 110, 130, is more illuminating than the Emperor's opinion, which Cardinal Alessandro Farnese countered with the remark that a fresh prorogation within a determined period would have been preferable, *C.T.*, VOL. IV, p. 180.

[6] *N.B.*, VOL. I, PT iv, p. 87 (3 June 1539).

[7] "Cum Pontifice nihil vellet habere agere" was George's sharp reply to the prelates of his territory on 31 July 1538, *Q.F.*, x (1907), p. 137. In May he had told Morone: "S.S.tà facendosi o non facendosi pace, doveva procedere al concilio et fare bona reformatione delli ecclesiastici", *N.B.*, VOL. I, PT ii, p. 290.

ardent protagonists of the Catholic cause were profoundly depressed. Cochlaeus sorrowfully asked: "What becomes of our Council?" [1] Eck expressed the general feeling when he wrote to Contarini on 13 March 1540: "People speak ill of the Pope on account of the Council." [2]

After four years of continuous talk and writing on the subject of a Council things had come to a point where people no longer trusted Paul III—the evidence of a fivefold postponement spoke too loudly against him. The Venetians' scorn and Francis I's sarcastic laughter at Nice were symptomatic of the profound distrust of the Pope's real intentions. The Emperor, who had made no mystery of his doubts at the time of Held's mission to Germany in 1536, now saw the Pope as the chief hindrance to a Council: of this fact we have irrefutable evidence.

In his Memoirs [3] Charles grants that at the beginning of his pontificate the Pope had announced his intention to hold a Council from which Clement VII had shrunk; however, with the passage of the years his zeal had cooled so that he ended by adopting the tactics of his predecessors, that is, a policy of fair promises while he put off and postponed the assembly again and again. The Emperor's whole policy for reunion rests on this conviction, from the Respite of Frankfurt to the Diet of Ratisbon. When on 23 April 1540, in order to counter the then impending religious convention, the nuncio Poggio suggested a solution by means of a Council Charles, usually so completely master of his feelings, could not restrain himself: "Do you want to stop me by talk about a Council? I have always wanted it! As far as I am concerned His Holiness may convoke it and open it at any time. I shall attend it and remain there for three, four, nay, six months. Only let him open it! Let him open it!—open it!" [4] The Emperor could hardly betray more clearly what he thought of the Pope's desire for a

---

[1] Z.K.G., XVIII (1897), p. 295 f. (24 June 1539). On 10 July, that is immediately after the fourth prorogation, Cochlaeus observed that with regard to the Council "altum silentium" prevailed in Germany, ibid., p. 287, and Witzel also wrote at this time (30 August 1538): "Sathan vicit, Sathan triumphat de impedito, neglecto, contempto, irriso concilio", Epp. misc. ad Nauseam, p. 229.

[2] Z.K.G., XIX (1899), p. 256 f.; during the whole of the winter Eck had been left without news so that he was unable to satisfy the prelates who turned to him for information, ibid., p. 235. On 9 February 1539 he wrote: "Hic nihil auditur; . . . simplices incipiunt nutare quia facile suadetur eis papam et Romanenses subterfugere causas et iudicium concilii", N.B., VOL. I, PT iv, p. 581 f.

[3] The passage in A. Morel-Fatio, Historiographie de Charles-Quint (Paris 1913), p. 256 f.; cf. also the thorough treatment by P. Leturia, "Paolo III e il Concilio di Trento nelle 'Memorie di Carlo V'", in Civiltà Cattolica, XCVII, ii (1946), pp. 12-23.

[4] N.B.. VOL. I, PT v, p. 194.

Council. Such weighty and widespread feelings cannot be lightly brushed aside. At the very least they must be accounted for. Public opinion might not see beyond the bare fact of the fivefold postponement, but informed persons like the Emperor, Francis I and the leading men of Venice could not avoid doing so. How did it come about that behind the avowed motives for these postponements they suspected others, unavowed ones, and that in spite of the unbroken series of papal gestures in favour of a Council, they did not believe that the Pope really wanted such an assembly? [1]

Our narrative has revealed the points where these doubts arose. After the convocation to Mantua the Pope had made it known, through his nuncios, that the Council would be held even if his efforts to bring about peace between the powers proved unsuccessful. But when war broke out anew, instead of opening the assembly he took advantage of the condition laid down by the Duke of Mantua—which, in point of fact, could scarcely have been accepted—to transfer it to Vicenza, a neutral city in Venetian territory. As the date for the opening drew near, military operations had come to an end and there was a prospect of an agreement between the two monarchs. Instead of presenting the world with a *fait accompli* by inaugurating the Council, the Pope adopted a waiting policy and allowed himself to be won over by the Emperor for the German programme of reunion from which previous experiences had taught him to expect but little good. In the spring of 1539 he finally suspended the Council without indication of a time-limit.

It must be granted that the simplest explanation of this series of facts is the one given in the Emperor's Memoirs. Yet it can hardly be the true one, for it not only charges the memory of a great pontiff with deliberate double-dealing, it also ignores facts and considerations which a contemporary could not weigh with the same impartiality as a historian who views them in the perspective of the centuries. There will always remain an element of uncertainty in any attempt to penetrate more deeply into the motives and ideas of so deep a politician as Paul III. Yet the attempt must be made, if we want to appraise accurately the decisive events.

[1] Besides Ehses and Pastor, Capasso also (*Paolo III*, VOL. I, pp. 382 ff., 663 f.) believes that Paul III was sincere with regard to the Council. The opposite view is upheld in particular by Friedensburg, *N.B.*, VOL. I, PT ii, pp. 47 ff., and *Kaiser Karl V und Papst Paul III* (Leipzig 1932), pp. 18 ff. This opinion is shared by Cardauns and by Korte, *Die Konzilspolitik Karls V*, p. 21, at least for the period following the meeting of Nice. In my opinion Leturia points the way to the right solution in the article referred to above, p. 346, *n.* 3; cf. the latter writer's observations in *Gregorianum*, XXVI (1945), p. 25 f. 40 ff.

There can be no doubt that at the beginning of his pontificate Paul III felt convinced of the need of a Council. During the sombre years preceding his elevation he had acquired the certainty that the Papacy could no longer evade the demand for such a gathering without further loss of prestige. Three solutions of the religious problem presented themselves: forcible subjection, a peaceful understanding, a Council. The first, in view of the power of the League of Schmalkalden, was fraught with grave risks; the second was by no means promising on account of Luther's obstinacy; the third alone—the conciliar solution—would be generally accepted while it might at the same time constitute a basis for future forcible measures against the rebels. That was why the new Pope judged a Council necessary. It was only as the years went by that he came to regard it as a necessary evil. In the course of the protracted negotiations on the subject the deep gap between his conception of a Council and the views of the Emperor and of many people beyond the Alps became evident, as did the risks involved in such an assembly.

After the Diet of Schmalkalden the Pope and his advisers became reconciled to the idea of holding a Council without the Protestants. In the Emperor's opinion the Council would only have a political significance if it succeeded in attracting the dissidents or, if they refused to appear at it, in putting them in the wrong in such a way that their condemnation could not be questioned and would meet with the approval of public opinion. This train of thought of the Emperor's was responsible not only for the endless difficulties in solving the problem of the locality of the Council but likewise for the grave difference about procedure to be observed at the assembly itself.

At the Curia it was felt that the condemnation of the heresies by the Council could be effected expeditiously enough. Since Luther's teaching merely revived heresies condemned long ago, all that was needed was to fulminate against him the condemnatory canons of earlier Councils. Great, therefore, was the surprise when Bishop Fabri of Vienna announced that prior to a discussion with the Protestants an extensive technical preparation was indispensable.[1] This included the

---

[1] *C.T.*, VOL. IV, pp. 10-26, see above, p. 337, *n.* 3; Campeggio's observations in *C.T.*, VOL. IV, p. 144, notes 10-12. The Franciscan Peter Crabbe was by this time engaged in a revision of the third edition of J. Merlin's *Quattuor conciliorum generalium* (on 12 August 1536 he sends corrections for Volume I to Nausea, *Epp. misc. ad Nauseam*, p. 179). The new edition was published in the autumn of 1538 by Peter Quentel at Cologne, cf. H. Quentin, *Les grandes collections conciliaires* (Paris 1900), p. 11 f.

purchase of five or six copies of all the books of their opponents and the drawing-up by a committee of theologians appointed by the Pope of a complete list of the errors they contained. This committee would sort out the old, previously condemned errors, from the new ones. The next step was an amended text of the Bible. Moreover, from fifty to a hundred copies of Merlin's *Collections of the Acts of the Councils* should be provided; these Acts should be completed by the purchase of manuscripts. A library should be provided for the benefit of the Council, containing all the works of the Fathers published within the last twenty years, as well as a printing press. Fabri's proposals were based on the assumption that there would be difficult and protracted discussions with the Protestants in which the new, positive theology would be on trial by the side of scholastic theology and would even be preferred to it. Nothing was further from the Pope's mind than a theological duel of this kind which might protract the Council for years while he was only prepared to devote a few months to it. The fact was that the Pope thought that the Council's second task, viz. the reform of the Church, was a comparatively simple affair. When we come to discuss his attempts at a reform of the Curia it will be seen that the precise purpose of his enactments against certain abuses among the Roman clergy and the officials of the Curia was to eliminate from the conciliar programme the most delicate point of the reform, the *reformatio in capite*. He was not afraid of the *reformatio in membris*. For the imperialists the *reformatio in capite et membris* was one of the essential tasks of the Council since it would do away with the grounds for the reformers' criticism of the Church and remove the *gravamina* against the Roman Curia and the abuses among the higher and lower clergy of Germany which were becoming more grievous with every passing year. The bitter complaints against clergy and hierarchy of such sincere Catholics as Ferdinand I and George of Saxony enable us to estimate the gigantic effort that reform would demand from the Council. Above all there came from beyond the Alps a unanimous demand for a reform of the Curia. In a memorial of 1536 [1] we read: "The Germans are not the only people who desire to restrict the Roman Church; the King of England also and many other princes, cities and nations seek to lower her and to secure advantages for themselves." With a sharpness all the more pitiless because it was courteous in tone, Guerrero, the president of the royal chamber of Naples, criticised the Curia's system of dispensations which had made it possible for a single Spanish curial

[1] *N.B.*, VOL. I, PT ii, p. 423.

official to hold one hundred and thirty benefices and to leave a fortune of 130,000 ducats at his death.[1] The French clergy's discontent with the wholesale bestowal of dioceses, abbeys and other benefices upon Italian cardinals and their familiars was well known and the complaint of the French bishops about the ordination in Rome of unworthy subjects [2] were not by any means the heaviest of the Gallican grievances.

What might not be expected from a Council at which all these hostile voices would blend in a single chorus of protests against Rome? On the basis of his observations in Spain, France and Flanders, Cervini wrote: "Unless we make haste to reform ourselves spontaneously reform will be forced upon us." [3] He was convinced that the Council would endeavour to enforce a reform of the Curia; at any rate it would seek to tie the Pope's hands with regard to the execution of reform decrees. The ideas of Constance and Basle were not yet dead. Luther's recent dictum [4] that effective reform was impossible as long as the Pope was not subjected to a Council and to the statutes of the Fathers found more secret than open adherents in the Catholic camp.[5] The importance attached to the fifteenth-century reform Councils in Germany may be gathered from the fact that Fabri declared with complete ingenuousness that the Acts of these Councils were indispensable for the conduct of the new Council,[6] as well as from the circumstance that the German bishops took it for granted that their representatives would enjoy full rights at the Council on the model of Basle,[7] while the Diet of Ratisbon did not hesitate to appeal to the decree Frequens.[8] Cardinal Erhard von der Mark of Liège warned the Pope in so many words not to risk a diminution of his authority by convoking a Council.[9] Cardinal Campeggio raised the question whether they should go back to the voting system of Constance, by nations, and whether scholars should be given a vote.[10] Earnest and convinced Catholics, not heretics, were

---

[1] C.T., VOL. XII, p. lx.
[2] N.B., VOL. I, PT V, p. 76. In February 1538 Cardinal Tournon warned Ferreri against calling a Council without the French, "il che quando accadasse, dice non si vorria trovar vivo, accennando che in questo regno si fariano cose inaudite", Vat. Arch., Nunz. di Francia, I A, fol. 156ᵛ (25 February 1538).
[3] N.B., VOL. I, PT V, p. 98.
[4] L.W., VOL. L, p. 516.
[5] Among these secret opponents I count Ugoni and his sympathisers of the school of Decius.
[6] C.T., VOL. IV, p. 17 (n.49); ibid., p. 25 (n.48) the rejection by the Pope.
[7] E.g. the provincial synod of Salzburg of 1537, Dalham, Concilia Salisburgensia (Augsburg 1788), p. 298 f.; the Bohemians, N.B., VOL. I, PT ii, p. 443.
[8] C.T., VOL. IV, p. 198, n.2.
[9] Ibid., p. 122 f.   [10] Ibid., p. 143 f. (n.6 and n.9).

of opinion that the Council would be useless and even harmful unless its decrees were insured against infringement by papal directives, viz. papal dispensations.[1] Even so pronounced an opponent of conciliar theory as the great Francisco de Vitoria was looking for ways and means to safeguard the future Council's decrees against the Curia's policy of dispensations.[2] As a matter of fact, in a memorial on the reform of the Church drawn up for his information by his most trusted advisers, the Pope had to read the terrible accusation that the curial teaching about the Pope's will being law was the Trojan horse out of which had come all the evils of the Church.[3]

The Pope was not merely having bad dreams when he saw these dangers. Hence his determination to hold the Council in Italy, where his personal presence and that of a great number of Italian bishops would more easily curb hostility to the Curia. For this reason too he entertained the idea of transferring the Council to Bologna or to some other town of the Papal States where he would be able, if not to thwart, at least to restrain the designs of people beyond the Alps and the influence of foreign powers. But even so a Council remained a risk. He had to ask himself seriously whether his hand would be strong enough to steer the ship firmly on the high seas or whether there was reason to fear that the tiller would slip from his hands.

The Emperor was the foreign helmsman whom the Pope feared the most. French diplomacy skilfully kept alive in his mind the fear of imperial "monarchy", that is, world-dominion, but that fear only became really overwhelming after the encounter of the two monarchs at Aiguesmortes. If a Council had been held at that time it would have been almost inevitably an "imperial" one. France could no longer be regarded as a real counterpoise. If a man like Charles V were to appear at the Council in the capacity of "Defender of the Church"—and a notion of this kind was an essential element of Charles's conception of the imperial dignity—he would have played a very different role from that of the Emperor Sigismund at Constance and Basle. There was no genuine mutual trust between the two heads; on the contrary, the Pope was suspicious because he had been excluded from the peace negotiations. He was also extremely annoyed because all this time the Emperor was condoning his daughter Margaret's resistance to her husband Ottavio Farnese. He accused Charles of

[1] *N.B.*, VOL. I, PT ii, p. 422.
[2] *Relectio IV* held in 1534; cf. V. Beltrán de Heredia, *Los mss. del Maestro F. de Vitoria* (Madrid 1928), p. 139 f. I shall revert to this most important matter.
[3] *C.T.*, VOL. XII, p. 135.

deliberately putting off the war against the Turks and even went so far as to say to the Venetian envoy: "The King of France has the interests of Christendom far more at heart than the Emperor." He seemed to breathe more freely when towards the end of 1540 a grave illness of Charles promised an early end of the awful oppression under which Rome laboured.[1] It is easy to understand that in these circumstances the Pope was unwilling to weaken his position through a Council and at the same time to strengthen that of the Emperor. It was this that led him to fall in with Charles's schemes for reunion, for thus he would at least gain time. He had no faith in a lasting peace between the two monarchs. He felt convinced, and with good reason, that Charles would never give up Milan. The new alignment of the powers that would then ensue was bound to improve his own position.

Paul III accordingly did not drop his plan for a Council in 1539, he merely put it off. He did so all the more willingly as the hope of taking strong measures against Henry VIII with the help of a Council was vanishing. As we have seen above, at the time of the Mantuan convocation some such action appeared to the Pope as one of the most important tasks of the future Council. On the basis of Carpi's reports from France it was thought in Rome at the close of 1536 that the Pilgrimage of Grace in the North of England would develop into a general rising of the Catholics against the King. Reginald Pole, Henry's cousin, for whom the King nursed a deadly hatred, was named cardinal legate for England.[2] By the time Pole reached Paris on 10 April 1537 the rising had been crushed. Francis I refused to receive the legate and ordered him to quit French territory. Even Pole's companion, Giberti, the determined exponent of Clement VII's francophil policy, failed to persuade the King to alter this decision in the course of a private interview at Hesdin. France's attitude led the Emperor to take corresponding measures. Pole was forced to leave imperial territory and to withdraw to ecclesiastical territory, viz. to Liège. After waiting there until the summer, he returned to Italy without having achieved anything. His first legation had proved a complete fiasco.

The armistice of Nice opened fresh prospects for the resumption of

[1] The best information on this mood of the Pope is derived from the despatches of the French envoys Grignan and Monluc, Ribier, *Lettres*, VOL. I, pp. 442 ff., 451, 557.

[2] G. M. Monti, *Studi sulla riforma cattolica e sul papato nei secoli XVI-XVII* (Trani 1941), pp. 3-20; the cardinal's letters in *Epp. Poli*, ed. Quirini, VOL. II, pp. 33-90. The declaration of the Anglican synod of Canterbury, 20 July 1536, against the Council of Mantua, in Wilkins, *Concilia Magnae Britanniae et Hiberniae* (London 1737), VOL. III, p. 808 f. Cf. also H. Boone, "L'infructueuse ambassade du Cardinal Pole", in *Mémoires de la société d'émulation de Cambrai*, LXXXV (1937), pp. 213-49.

the struggle against Henry VIII. It would seem that at this time the two monarchs led the Pope to think that they would lay an embargo on England's trade, on condition that he published the Bull of Excommunication which had been kept back for three years.[1] This was done on 17 December 1538. However, both Charles V and Francis I had long before pledged themselves to Henry VIII not to assent to any hostile measures that a future Council might take against him.[2] The Emperor refused to boycott English trade on the ground that it would injure the prosperity of the Netherlands, while Francis I made his action dependent on that of the Emperor; in this way nothing whatever happened. The Bull of Excommunication was not published in England. Pole, who had been named legate a second time, encountered the same obstacles as in 1537.[3] Henry VIII's fear that the Pope would rally the forces of Christendom against him was therefore without foundation.[4] Without in any way abating his hostility towards the Papacy,[5] Henry made a move back towards Catholicism when he compelled the clergy to subscribe to the Six Articles. He also destroyed the leaders of the Protestant party, Cromwell and Cranmer, broke off negotiations with the Schmalkaldic League and made overtures to Charles V.[6] In this

[1] I can find no certain proof of a firm guarantee. That discussions took place in the autumn of 1538 at the French court on the question of the Council, England, and the Lutherans—the grouping is highly significant—appears from Ferreri's reports, e.g., 22 October, Vat. Arch., AA, I-XVIII, 6538, fols. 91^r-94^v. The Bull of Excommunication in *Bullarium Romanum*, VOL. VI, pp. 203 ff.; cf. Pastor, VOL. V, p. 686 f.: Eng. edn., VOL. XII, p. 468 f.

[2] Carpi's reports of 24 February and 2 March 1538, Vat. Arch., AA I-XVIII, 6538, fols. 9^v, 14^r. When Henry VIII pressed Francis I to make his assent to the Council dependent on that of England and to make it one of the clauses of the peace treaty, the French King demanded in return such heavy subsidies that no agreement was come to, Kaulek, *Corresp. pol.*, p. 71. For Charles V's rather vague assurances to London, cf. *Cal. of St. Pap., Spain*, VOL. V, ii, p. 429 (No. 182); a written guarantee was flatly refused, *ibid.*, VOL. VI, i, p. 3 (No. 2).

[3] Pole's instructions and Farnese's reports from the imperial court in Quirini, *Epp. Poli*, VOL. II, pp. cclxxix ff.; *ibid.*, VOL. II, pp. 146-64, Pole's letters from Carpentras, where he had found a refuge with Sadoleto in the same way as during his first legation at Liège. Most of them are addressed to Contarini. On the Pope's complaints about the failure of the legation, cf. Aguilar's report of 10 August 1539, *Cal. of Letters*, VOL. XIV, ii, p. 8 (No. 32).

[4] Marillac's reports from London, 20 May and 9 June 1539, Kaulek, *Corresp. pol.*, pp. 98, 102; Ribier, *Lettres*, VOL. I, pp. 401 ff.

[5] At the beginning of June 1539 Henry VIII staged a warlike display in London in the course of which a royal galley beat a papal one whose crew, wearing the papal arms, were thrown into the river, Ribier, *Lettres*, VOL. I, p. 465; Kaulek, *Corresp. pol.*, p. 105.

[6] Prüser, *England und die Schmalkaldener 1535-40* (Leipzig 1929), pp. 176 ff. The Six Articles (the Real Presence, *Communio sub una specie*, clerical celibacy, monastic vows, private Masses, auricular confession) in Wilkins, *Concilia Magnae Britanniae et Hiberniae*, VOL. III, p. 845 f.

way the execution of the Bull against him dropped out of the programme of the future Council and one of the main reasons for promoting it vanished.

We may sum up the result of our survey in this way: in the course of the first five years of his pontificate Paul III was not unfaithful to his initial conviction of the need of a Council, but he never made up his mind to hold it at all costs. We may reproach him with avoiding, instead of overcoming, the obstacles that stood in the way of such an assembly during the first three years of his pontificate and for sticking too obstinately to his conception of a Council as a measure of preservation. Such a conception failed to meet the requirements of the time, with the result that those partners in the negotiations who did not share his views came to the conclusion that he did not want a Council at all. Even after 1538 his conciliar policy cannot be accused of double-dealing: it was more like a double track policy played with virtuosity, whose only fault was that it was no more than a policy! "He who conducts God's business must not be exclusively actuated by human considerations."[1] In these words Morone expressed the ultimate reason why we cannot but blame Paul III's conciliar policy during the first period of his pontificate.

[1] *N.B.*, VOL. I, PT V, p. 155.

CHAPTER VIII

The Dream of an Understanding and the Reality
of the Differences

THE Emperor's policy of an understanding which he pursued during the
years 1539-41 owed its origin to a proposal made by the young Elector
Joachim II of Brandenburg to King Ferdinand I in May 1538 at
Bautzen.[1] "The Protestants", Joachim explained, "will never send
their representatives to the Council. They will be condemned, therefore, in their absence; they will accordingly offer armed resistance to
the execution of its decisions; this means the dreaded war of religion.
Should not yet another effort be made before the Council to bring about
a friendly understanding with them—of course with the co-operation
of papal commissaries?"

Naturally enough Ferdinand hailed the proposal with delight. It
held out the prospect of obtaining from the Protestants sorely needed
help for the Turkish war. Even Morone did not reject the idea offhand,
but he thought that, lest the affair of the Council should suffer, the
negotiations for reunion should be taken to Vicenza when the Catholic
negotiators would receive their commission from the Council on the
lines adopted at Basle in the negotiations with the Hussites. The
Emperor, however, took up the proposal in its original form, won over
the Pope at Genoa and thus sealed the fate of the Council of Vicenza.
He was favoured by the circumstance that a considerable number of
princes of the Empire, among them four out of the seven Electors,
supported his plan.

How was it possible for so many thoughtful men to dream the dream
of an understanding as late as the year 1538?

We are acquainted with the Emperor's motives. He was anxious
to have behind him a religiously united empire during the impending

[1] Ferdinand's letter of 3 June, which arrived at Genoa on 24 June 1538, in *N.B.*,
VOL. I, PT iv, pp. 445-8. Morone's report from Breslau, *N.B.*, VOL. I, PT ii, pp. 293-6.
On Joachim's activity as a mediator, cf. G. Droysen, *Geschichte der preussischen Politik*,
VOL. II, ii (Leipzig 1870), pp. 167-97; H. Landwehr, "Joachims II Stellung zur
Konzilsfrage", in *Forschungen zur brandenburg-preussischen Geschichte*, VI (1893),
pp. 529-60; also the dissertation of F. Meine, *Die vermittelnde Stellung Joachims II
von Brandenburg zu den politischen und religiösen Parteien seiner Zeit* (Rostock 1898).

conflict with France. This was also the wish of the Electors who favoured reunion, but for a very different and even contrary reason. The Rhenish Electors, with the exception of the Elector of Mainz, gave their approval to Joachim's proposal in the summer of 1538 from fear of the ominous preponderance of the Emperor. War against Schmalkalden, they thought, would mean, if not the end, at least an irreparable curtailment of the liberty of all, even that of the Catholic princes of the Empire. So they supported the Emperor's policy of reunion in the hope of keeping the imperial power in check. An internal German accord promised to remove the fatal division of the German territorial powers into confessional federations, viz. those of Schmalkalden and Nuremberg, and to create a counterpoise to the power of the Habsburgs.

To this political consideration another, of a religious character, came to be added by many Catholics and by such as continued to shrink from the idea of a final religious cleavage. This was the threat of utter ruin for Catholicism as a result of the boundless confusion in the affairs of the Church in Germany. No one was more obviously inspired by this consideration than Duke George of Saxony.[1] His personal loyalty to the Church was unswerving, but his territory, Albertine Saxony, immediately adjoined the land that gave birth to the schism, Ernestine Saxony, with which it had sundry close relations. It was easy for those of his subjects who had leanings towards the new religion to hear the new doctrine preached in the neighbouring Protestant localities and to receive the sacraments, above all Communion in both kinds, for which many layfolk felt a keen desire. Wholesale expulsions of Lutherans proved useless and dangerous. The clergy, especially the regular clergy, left much to be desired. A visitation of the monasteries, which Duke George carried out through secular councillors, was uncanonical. It met with violent opposition and could not lead to reform from within. The monasteries gradually emptied for lack of fresh recruits, just as there were hardly any aspirants to the secular priesthood. It is easy to see how the Duke arrived at the conclusion that something had to be done to save his territory from a wholesale change over to Protestantism. This was bound to happen as soon as his brother Henry, an avowed Protestant, should succeed him.

For this reason, as early as April 1534, Duke George had made

[1] L. Cardauns, "Zur kirchenpolitischen Haltung Georgs von Sachsen", in *Q.F.*, x (1907), pp. 101-51. The memorial of the ducal councillors of 3 April 1539 is of particular interest, *ibid.*, pp. 144-51.

CHARLES V WITH A DOG
After the painting by Titian in the Museo del Prado, Madrid

arrangements for a religious conference at Leipzig, at which his councillors Carlowitz and Pflug had had a friendly discussion about the possibility of reunion with representatives of the Electors of Saxony and Mainz.[1] Though the meeting yielded no tangible result owing to the impossibility of arriving at an agreement on the doctrine of the sacrifice of the Mass, the attempt was repeated in January 1539, this time without the Elector of Mainz but with the participation of Philip of Hesse.[2] Once again nothing was achieved. The representatives of the Elector of Saxony, Melanchthon and Chancellor Brück, left the meeting after a few days. Both conferences had the approval of Duke George. Though personally averse to any concession to Lutheranism the Duke thought it would be in the interest of the Catholic cause to give free play to the councillors' efforts for reunion. Thus even the most faithful of the faithful had not completely shaken off the fatal delusion that there was no real schism! Is it any wonder then if Joachim II, who had become acquainted with Luther's teaching through his mother, still believed that it was possible to steer a middle course between the two parties—to be neither a "Papist" nor a Lutheran, and yet to remain a Catholic? In the Church-order [3] which he issued in 1540 for the Marches, until a General Council, a national assembly or a religious conference should decide otherwise, he obstinately stuck to the Lutheran formula of salvation by faith alone and together with the Canon of the Mass rejected its sacrificial character, while for the rest he retained many Catholic practices and the Catholic liturgy, as for instance, the feast of Corpus Christi, five feasts of Our Lady, and several feasts of Saints. With this Church-order he introduced Protestantism into Brandenburg, but this did not prevent him from reverently attending Mass during the Diet of Ratisbon in 1541 and from sending representatives to the Council of Trent ten years later.

Luther himself did not share the great delusion. At no time did he take part in a religious discussion with the Catholics and he sharply rejected every attempt to obscure the doctrinal differences for the sake of an accord. He likewise saw the danger for himself of the attitude of the "expectants", that is, the numerous Catholics and Protestants who

---

[1] The chief source is the report of 3 May 1534 to the Saxon Elector, *Corp. Ref.*, VOL. II, pp. 722-7; Paulus, *Dominikaner*, p. 217 f.

[2] L. Cardauns, *Bestrebungen*, pp. 1-31; Bucer's report of 2 January in M. Lenz, *Briefwechsel Landgraf Philipps von Hessen mit Bucer*, VOL. I (Leipzig 1880), pp. 63-8.

[3] Sehling, *Kirchenanordnungen*, VOL. III, pp. 39-90; J. Sonneck, *Die Beibehaltung katholischer Formen in der Reformation Joachims II von Brandenburg und ihre allmählige Beseitigung* (Dissertation, Rostock 1903).

hoped for a decision of the religious dispute by a Council.[1] When the
latter declared: "So long as the Council has not spoken we continue
in the old faith", they submitted to the authority of the universal
Church.[2] A timely conciliar sentence against Luther would have saved
most of them for the Church. This is why Morone, Fabri and all those
who were acquainted with the situation in Germany repeatedly urged
the convocation of such an assembly.

One thing, however, is certain: the "expectants" were no partisans
of a policy of agreement based on a compromise [3]; they were partisans
of a Council. They only welcomed and supported the former policy
when fifteen years of efforts to bring about such an assembly had proved
fruitless. Like the partisans of the policy of reunion the "expectants"
were on the look-out for a programme of union that would provide a
basis for the reunion they aimed at. Such a programme was actually
in existence: its author was none other than Erasmus. This is our
third encounter with the leader of humanism, whom public opinion in
the first years of the schism had closely linked with Luther and whose
ideas had been operative during the Augsburg attempt to achieve reunion. Now, in the era of the imperial policy of reconciliation, we meet
him again on the road to a Council.

In the famous controversy about the freedom of the will Erasmus
definitely parted company with Luther in 1524. In 1529 the introduction of the Reformation at Basle forced him to leave his second home.
In 1533, at Freiburg im Breisgau, where he found asylum in the last
years of his life, he published his book on the restoration of ecclesiastical
concord [4] which may fitly be described as his testament, for it only
affected the course of universal history after his death (12 July 1536).

In this book Erasmus places himself above the religious parties.
He impartially laments the radicalism which caused the innovators to

[1] Grouping of Luther's and other theologians' statements in L. Pastor, *Die
kirchlichen Reunionsbestrebungen während der Regierung Karls V* (Freiburg 1879),
pp. 115-20.
[2] The standpoint of the "expectants" is best formulated by Simon Pistoris in a
letter of 27 June 1530 to Erasmus (*Opus Epistolarum Desiderii Erasmi Roterodami*,
ed. Allen, Oxford 1906-47, VOL. VIII, p. 460): "Multi herent in eo quod quamvis
sentiant pleraque amplectenda (scil. Lutheranorum), attamen non liceat absque
universalis concilii auctoritate et assensu a patrum institutis discedere, etiam si Sedis
Apostolicae auctoritas accederet."
[3] It seems to me that Pastor has not taken this circumstance sufficiently into
account, *Reunionsbestrebungen*, pp. 115 ff.
[4] *De sarcienda ecclesiae concordia, Opera*, VOL. V, pp. 469-506; I use the edition in
Fasciculus rerum expet. ac fug. (Cologne 1535), pp. ccxxix ff. For what follows cf.
also R. Stupperich, *Der Humanismus und die Wiedervereinigung der Konfessionen*
(Leipzig 1936).

do away with ancient ecclesiastical institutions, the paradoxes in which Luther occasionally indulged and the excessive keenness of the theological zealots who were always ready to shout "heresy!" Cochlaeus was quite right when he observed [1] that materially, that is in detail, the book on reunion treats the Catholic side much more favourably than the Protestant. It defends good works as necessary for salvation, as well as the Mass and the intercession of the Saints against the destructive fury of the opponents. Not a few of the suggested reforms in the liturgical and disciplinary sphere were carried into effect in the course of the ensuing decades and centuries, while others were at least within the range of possibility. Erasmus's great mistake was that he persisted in regarding the Reformation only as a reform of the Church, regrettably violent yet still a reform which was only widened and deepened until it became a schism through the obstinate dogmatism of the theologians on both sides. In his opinion the ultimate cause of all the religious confusion was the absence of a live Christianity and the prevailing moral corruption. So he came to the conclusion that, given a measure of good-will, the sickness was by no means incurable. After all, both parties continued to believe in Christ!

From his scholar's study Erasmus failed to see that two ecclesiastical systems had long been in existence, separated the one from the other by a dogmatic chasm. The remedy of individual reform which a generation earlier might have started a great Catholic movement of reform was no longer adequate. The first requisite was to clear up the existing situation. This could only be done by a Council. Erasmus was not opposed to it, in fact he reserves the following four points for its decision, viz. obligatory auricular confession, the sacrifice of the Mass, the mode of Christ's presence in the Eucharist, the so-called "human statutes". "But", he asks, "who knows when the Council will take place? [2] Meanwhile we cannot remain idle; something must be done to bring the opponents together instead of inciting them against one another. Without an internal preparation of this kind no positive result, that is, no restoration of the Church's unity can be expected." As for the role of the Council, it was only that of an arbitration court which, once the reconciliation had taken place, would pronounce on the purely theological controversies.

The same ideas as those propounded in the 1533 book on concord

[1] *Z.K.G.*, XVIII (1897), p. 249; to Vergerio it seemed "ch'abbia voluto esso diffinire et farsi un sinodo a suo modo et a modo de suoi Germani", *N.B.*, VOL. I, PT i, p. 138.

[2] In 1527 Erasmus wrote: "Nec est quod spectemus concilium; sero veniet obstante principum dissidio." Erasmus, *Epist.*, VOL. VII, p. 200 (No. 1887).

are found in the "Letter of congratulation" addressed by Erasmus on 23 January 1535 to the newly elected Pope Paul III.[1] It breathes the same fatal optimism: "By far the greater part of Germany is still intact. If the Pope will only rise above the warring parties and meet the Lutherans' wishes by allowing them certain liturgical practices which can be tolerated without injury to the unity of the Church and grant them an amnesty for the past, then an accord remains within the realm of possibility. The only duty of the future Council will be to define certain dogmas. As for the opinions of the schools, the theologians should be allowed to discuss them freely." The "Letter of congratulation" confirms what we know already. Erasmus does not wish to dispense with a Council. What is alarming is the fact that he regards an authoritative clearing-up of the controversial points as of secondary importance. The primary fact in his opinion is that both parties continue to hold the substance of the Christian faith. Actually historical development took the opposite direction. Without considering what was jointly held by both parties, the Church acted as she has always acted throughout her history. The line of cleavage was clearly marked by her and Catholic dogma defined both accurately and in its full extent. Instead of abandoning private Masses or the veneration of the Saints and their images she asserted their importance with even greater emphasis. Not by toleration of the innovators' religious practices, but by an energetic tightening of its own Catholic observances was the battle of the counter-reformation won by the Papacy. In the light of this later evolution it is easy to see that the Church's organic laws of life had escaped Erasmus's observation. Many contemporaries were impressed by his programme, not only because it was sponsored by such a man, but also, and even chiefly, because it seemed to point the way out of the seemingly hopeless confusion of the contemporary ecclesiastical situation. The Erasmian "Programme" had long ago ceased to be a mere literary exercise. On the advice of Conrad von Heresbach, a disciple of Erasmus, Duke John of Jülich-Cleves had made it the basis of his ecclesiastical policy. The Church-order of 1532 [2] which he issued without the concurrence of the ecclesiastical authorities and which was to have force of law "until a future Council", enjoined preachers to leave controversial questions alone while at the same time it urged the pastoral clergy to be zealous in instructing the faithful in

[1] Published by Cardauns, in *Q.F.*, XI (1908), pp. 202-5.
[2] O. R. Redlich, *Jülich-bergische Kirchenpolitik*, VOL. I (Bonn 1907), pp. 246-51; *ibid.*, pp. 259-78, the "declaration" of 8 April 1533, valid "bis uf kunftig concilium, nationalversammlung ader unseren widern bescheid".

the faith, the commandments and the sacraments. The "explanation" of the Church-order which the Duke published in the following year had been submitted to Erasmus and had received his approval. It was the first experiment with the humanist's programme of reconciliation. Its general application led to the policy of reunion after the failure of the Council of Vicenza. In the meantime it had been further developed and had spread far beyond the German borders.

That able publicist George Witzel,[1] while still a young priest, had joined Luther's party and married. However, the moral and religious confusion that met his eyes and the study of the Church Fathers decided him to resign his Protestant parish and to return to the Catholic Church. Like a typical "expectant", he began by pleading for a Council,[2] but at a later date he became a protagonist of the Erasmian programme of reunion.[3] In his opinion an understanding between the orthodox and the adherents of the new religion must be arrived at on the basis of Christian antiquity. The belief and practice of the ancient Church are the "royal middle path" on which the disputants may and must meet.[4] This is the standpoint of the "orthodox" speaker in his *Gesprächbüchlein* (Little Book of Dialogues) who takes to task the thorough-going Lutheran "Teuto" for whom Luther is "the teacher above all teachers" no less sharply than the ultra-Catholic "Ausonius" who defends

---

[1] The literature on Witzel in Schottenloher, Nos. 22707-22737; the most valuable work is G. Richter's *Die Schriften George Witzels* (Fulda 1913); Döllinger, *Die Reformation*, VOL. I, (Ratisbon 1846), pp. 26-125, reproduces the exceedingly sombre picture drawn by Witzel of the moral consequences of Lutheranism. For his place among the peace-makers see P. Polman, *Elément historique dans la controverse théologique du XVIᵉ siècle* (Gembloux 1932), p. 380 f.

[2] In his letter to the Archbishop of Mainz, Goldast, *Monarchia*, VOL. I, pp. 653 ff., Witzel speaks of the council as "pharmacum reipublicae ecclesiasticae, asylum veritatis, extricatio atque enodatio difficilium causarum, assertio maiestatis scripturae sanctae, redintegratio divini cultus, recisio improbatorum morum, deletio Christo indignarum consuetudinum, excidium errorum, terror haereseon, consolatio spesque catholici populi, breviter certa sanitas ecclesiae Dei", and laments the non-observance of *Frequens*. In the spring of 1539 he had given up all hope of a Council and wrote to Nausea: "De concilio cogendo iam pridem spem abieci", *Epp. misc. ad Nauseam*, p. 246.

[3] On the policy of reunion the following works are the most notable: *Methodus concordiae ecclesiasticae* (1537), Richter, *Die Schriften Georg Witzels*, No. 35; *Drey Gesprächbüchlein* (1539), Richter, No. 49; *Typus ecclesiae prioris* (1540), Richter, No. 52; eight editions of the latter are in existence.

[4] Briefly summed up in Witzel's letter to Morone, 1 December 1540, *A.R.G.*, VI (1909), p. 239: "Illaesa nobis et salva omnino maneat doctrina primorum patrum quibus nihil aut sanctius aut doctius; . . . nolim removeri ritus atque observationes, quibus est usa tot iam saeculis sanctorum ubique congregatio; praesentes non tollantur, sed sicubi foret opus, corrigantur ac restituantur iuxta typum seu formam venerandae beataeque et victricis antiquitatis."

through thick and thin every use and abuse of the medieval Church. Though Witzel has parted company with Luther, he yet finds in the Catholic Church, as he sees it, much that cries for correction. The Church is in need of a thorough reform, but one in keeping with the principle: *tollatur abusus, non substantia*.[1]

Witzel was given an opportunity to attempt an understanding on these lines at the above-mentioned religious conference of Leipzig in 1539, in which he took part with Chancellor Carlowitz as the representative of Duke George of Saxony. Their opponents were the jurists Brück and Feige and the two most outspoken advocates of a policy of agreement of all the Protestant divines, viz. Melanchthon, the father of the *Confessio Augustana*, and Martin Bucer of Strasbourg, the most weighty as well as the most active of the south Germans and a confident of the Landgrave of Hesse on whose behalf he had most skilfully intervened in the course of Luther's and Zwingli's controversy over the Lord's Supper.[2] Bucer and Witzel jointly drew up a formula for a German accord [3] which, while it acknowledges the necessity of good works for salvation, does not state the doctrine of man's intrinsic justification with sufficient clearness. Individual communities were left free to decide whether they would have Mass daily or only on Sundays and feast days, "as was the custom in the days of the dear Augustine". The formula is silent about the sacrificial character of the Mass as well as on transubstantiation. There is not a word on the

---

[1] This principle is the inspiration of a "Modus concordandi inter catholicos et lutheranos" published by Cardauns in *Q.F.*, IX (1906), pp. 139-54, which may be an extract from Witzel's work on reunion composed, perhaps, in the entourage of the Bishop of Augsburg. O. Clemen has published it in *A.R.G.*, x (1913), pp. 101-5, and ascribed it to Witzel himself. It is not so much a formula for an agreement as a scheme of reform. The most dangerous statement is the following: "Canon missae reformetur; ab utraque parte missae extraordinariae prohibeantur."

[2] For Martin Bucer's (1491-1551) reunion policy which receives remarkably short treatment in *R.E.*, VOL. III, pp. 603 ff., I use the correspondence with Philip of Hesse and the letters to the brothers A. and Th. Blaurer of Constance; T. Schiess, *Briefwechsel der Brüder A. und Th. Blaurer*, VOL. II (Freiburg 1910), p. 60, 71 f., and *passim*; also W. Friedensburg, "Martin Butzer, Von der Wiedervereinigung der Kirchen", *A.R.G.*, XXXI (1934), pp. 105-91. The expression "apostle of concord" used by J. Ficker, *Martin Butzer* (Strasbourg 1917), p. 12, I would rather dispense with when speaking of this highly controversial personage. The remaining literature in Schottenloher, Nos. 2230-92; see also the monographs by H. Eells, *Martin Butzer* (New Haven 1931), and R. Stupperich, *Martin Butzer, der Reformator des Elsasses und Einiger des deutschen Protestantismus* (Berlin 1941), which I have not been able to consult.

[3] Text in Cardauns, *Bestrebungen*, pp. 85-108. *C.T.*, VOL. XII, pp. 259-71. The tract "Antwort und Repulsion" by the Carmelite Stoss, written by order of the Bishop of Bamberg, is found in R. Schaffer, *Andreas Stoss*, pp. 138-70.

Pope's primacy of jurisdiction. The precedence of the Bishop of Rome over the other patriarchs is traced back to the position of Rome as the capital of the Roman Empire. The Pope may interfere with the jurisdiction of the other bishops in order to suppress abuses, hence his powers are like those of a metropolitan in his province. The invocation of saints is dropped. The monasteries, whose inmates are no longer to take vows, are to be turned into schools. The law of fasting remains as a simple recommendation. The marriage of priests and Communion in both kinds are advocated.

The Leipzig draft for reunion remained an individual effort and as such it circulated in Germany, from where it reached the imperial court and even the Curia. As one reads it one realises what pressing need there was for an official clarification by a Council of the controversial doctrines and practices. The aim of the authors is so to trim the Church's life and teaching as to bring it in line with Christian antiquity. If the scheme had been carried through, it would have led to the Protestantising of the whole of Germany for it suppressed essential elements of the Catholic faith and in the guise of toleration gave free scope to the dynamics of Lutheranism.

The danger was great, chiefly because so many were unaware of its existence. Erasmian ideas continued to operate not so much on account of the number of those who held them as by reason of their intellectual and social standing. Among those who favoured them Witzel counted in 1536 Cardinal Sadoleto, Archbishop Critius of Gnesen, the Bishops of Basle and Augsburg, Stanislas Thurzo of Olmütz, John Dantiscus of Kulm, and finally Tunstall of Durham, the most distinguished among the English bishops and a friend of Erasmus of long standing.[1] Sadoleto could not be described as an Erasmian though he was an advocate of peace. All the others actually held Erasmus in veneration, though not with the same fervour as Bishop Stadion of Augsburg who spoke of him as his guide to true Christianity and ranked him above the greatest theologians of the past.[2]

The power and influence of Erasmian ideas were not due to the fact

---

[1] *Epp. theologicae* (Leipzig 1537), fols. 1, 1ᵛ. Most of the people mentioned by Witzel have figured before in these pages. On Dantiscus there is a good deal of information in the letters of the years 1537-43 published by F. Hipler in *Zeitschrift für Geschichte Ermlands*, IX (1891), pp. 471-572. The letters published in Erasmus, *Epist.*, VOL. VIII, pp. 299 ff., 343 ff., throw light on Tunstall's relations with Erasmus. For the entire group of "Henricians", see Constant, *La Réforme en Angleterre*, VOL. I, pp. 213 ff. (Eng. edn., ch. vii, pp. 341 ff.).

[2] "Is fuit qui veram pietatis ac religionis viam digito demonstraverit", Stadion to Nausea, 30 November 1537, *Epp. misc. ad Nauseam*, p. 202 f.

that they were held by bishops but by ecclesiastical politicians. Leaving the men of Schmalkalden on one side, there was scarcely a princely court without its Erasmians. At Dresden they were the jurist Simon Pistoris [1] and the above-mentioned Carlowitz, to whom must be added the dean of the cathedral of Meissen, Julius Pflug,[2] who had been won over to Erasmus's party by his teacher Petrus Mosellanus, a man of a conciliatory disposition. Conrad von Heresbach operated at the court of Cleves and Chancellor Hagen at that of the Elector of Cologne.[3] Erasmus's influence also made itself felt at Heidelberg, Koblenz and Aschaffenburg. At the Habsburg courts it was active through Cornelius Schepper, Johann von Weeze, who had been driven from his archiepiscopal see of Lund, Louis de Praët, whose benevolent attitude towards them earned him the praise of the Protestants; even Granvella, the Emperor's right-hand man for external affairs, was affected by it. The Erasmians did not form a secret society as did the freemasons in the era of Enlightenment; they were linked together by the same community of thought as were the ecclesiastical rationalists two centuries later, and just as the ideas of the latter coincided largely with those of the Jansenists—hence with a current which, at least in its beginnings, ran directly counter to theirs—so did the Erasmian mentality coincide with that of the "evangelicals".[4]

All over Europe during the fifteen-thirties theologians and laymen threw themselves into the study of Holy Writ and the Fathers—especially St Paul and St Augustine—and experienced in themselves the meaning of sin and grace, redemption in Christ and justification by faith in Him. Their heart's desire was to hear the words: "I am thy salvation"; passionately they wrestled with the greatest problem of the

[1] There is a good synthesis of the literature about Pistoris (1489-1562) in Erasmus, *Epist.*, VOL. IV, p. 308; Pistoris kept up a correspondence with Erasmus, see *ibid.*, VOL. VIII, pp. 86, 459 f., 475 f.; VOL. IX, p. 185 f. Luther regarded him as a genuine Catholic.
[2] Like Witzel, Pflug (1499-1564) also lacks a modern biography; the most informative is still A. Janssen in *Neue Mitteilungen aus dem Gebiet historisch-antiquarischer Forschungen*, XI (1863), pp. 1-110; II (1864), pp. 1-212; further literature in Schottenloher, Nos. 17222-32b.
[3] Van Gulik, *Johann Gropper* (Freiburg 1906), p. 43; there is a letter to Erasmus even from Medmann, Erasmus, *Epist.*, VOL. VIII, p. 413 f.
[4] I have applied Imbart de la Tour's conception of the transition period in France up to 1538, *Origines*, VOL. III, to the corresponding symptoms in Italy (*Seripando*, VOL. I, pp. 135 ff.; Eng. edn., p. 103). The best survey is D. Cantimori's contribution to E. Rota's *Problemi storici e orientamenti storiografici* (Como 1924), pp. 557-84. For Spain, cf. M. Bataillon, *Erasme en Espagne*, though in my opinion he exaggerates Erasmus's influence. Beltrán de Heredia's criticism of that work corrects it on many points but I cannot substantiate my own view here.

age. The German schism had roused men's minds. People searched the Bible and the Fathers for an answer to the questions that stirred their souls to the depths. Some book of the innovators may have come into the hands of this or that individual—may be a Biblical commentary. Actually there was no need for this to happen; questioning was in the air, or rather in men's hearts, all these searchers of the gospels had this in common; everything else—the answers to their queries and the influences that determined them—differs, so much so indeed that it seems almost rash to try to fasten a common label to such a riot of individualism.

Though a whole world would seem to divide Francis I's sister Margaret of Navarre, the authoress of the *Heptameron*,[1] from that most devout poetess Vittoria Colonna, the patroness of the first Capuchins,[2] the Frenchwoman nevertheless entered into a correspondence with one in whom she saw a kindred spirit while she herself called forth the admiration of a man like Seripando. The two Spaniards Alfonso and Juan Valdés were convinced Erasmians, but the basically unorthodox spirituality by which Juan, during his Neapolitan period, had attracted Giulia Gonzaga and her friends was permeated with a passion which the matter-of-fact Netherlander would never have recognised as spirit of his spirit. Gianpietro Carafa actually regarded it as no less diabolical than Erasmus's cold scepticism. Jacques Lefèvre's biblicism was no more Erasmian or Lutheran than that of the aging Cardinal Cajetan. The two men shared the misfortune of being condemned by the Sorbonne, yet what a contrast between the humanist who received a visit from Calvin and the great Thomist who was called to pass judgment on Luther! Bernardino Ochino, Italy's most popular preacher towards the close of the fifteen-thirties, ended as an anti-Trinitarian and was cast off even by the reformed divines of Switzerland, while Matteo Giberti, Bishop of Verona, in whose diocese Ochino had at one time won golden opinions, figures in the history of Catholic reform as a forerunner of St Charles Borromeo.

Though both their starting-point and their social position differed greatly, all these people had one thing in common, viz. a most acute awareness of the deepest problem of their time. The "religion of

---

[1] On the most recent biography of Margaret of Navarre, cf. L. Fèbvre, *Autour de l'Heptaméron* (Paris 1944), and D. Cantimori in *Società*, I (1945), pp. 261-73.

[2] Although in my opinion there can be no question of Vittoria's fundamentally Catholic attitude, the series of articles by Igino da Alatri in *Italia Francescana*, XXI (1946), pp. 84-93, 207-18, 280-95, does not fully solve the problem of the decisive years 1535-42.

justification by faith" was no longer a theological dispute fought out in Germany, it had become a preoccupation of the European mind. The movement was undoubtedly influenced, directly or at least indirectly, by the German schism. At Basle, in spite of every prohibition Italians, Frenchmen and Spaniards scrambled for Lutheran books.[1] On the other hand it is positively absurd for Oecolampadius to assert, because of this circumstance, that there were more "evangelicals" than Catholics in France, England and Italy.[2] The characteristic feature of the "evangelistic" movement was precisely that it was undefined, fluid and fraught with many possibilities for good and evil. Cardinal Pole cured Vittoria Colonna and the poet Marcantonio Flaminio of the Waldensian poison, yet his own teaching on justification was at one time thought to be tainted with Lutheranism.[3] It is not easy to detect any open heresies in the small book "On the benefit of Christ"—*Del beneficio di Christo*—which is typical of Italian evangelism; for all that the Roman Inquisition acted in the interests of the Church when it suppressed this work of the Benedictine monk Benedetto da Mantova, to such good effect indeed that scarcely a copy survives at this day. Even in strictly orthodox Spain it was a long time before the Inquisition took action against the "modern" preachers who had been trained at Alcalá.[4]

Granted that by comparison with the faithful masses the circles affected by the movement were relatively small, the fact remains that its adherents belonged for the most part to the educated classes, hence to the leading sections in the intellectual sphere. A glance at the literary products of the period, more particularly the commentaries on St Paul and the writings of St Augustine, gives us a good idea of the spread of evangelism. Lefèvre's Commentaries on St Paul saw no fewer than seven editions before 1540. St Thomas Aquinas's Commentary on the Epistles of St Paul, printed three times between 1522 and 1532, rivalled the popularity of a romance of chivalry.[5] It had become fashionable to study the Bible and to attend lectures on the Scriptures. The public lectures on St Paul of which we read in Italy

---

[1] "A bibliopolis Basiliensibus libros Lutheranos nulli iam avidius sibi comparant quam Galli, Itali, Hispani", Ber to Aleander on 24 April 1532, *Z.K.G.*, XVI (1896), p. 480.

[2] Laemmer, *Mon. Vat.*, p. 94.

[3] "Defendit et nititur probare," says the *Compendium processuum* of Pole, "doctrinam lutheranam de iustificatione esse veram", *Archiv. Soc. Romanae di storia patria*, III (1880), p. 284.

[4] Bataillon, *Erasme en Espagne*, p. 584.

[5] Imbart de la Tour, *Origines*, VOL. III, p. 338.

were not by any means forced upon the public: they met a demand. If it so happened that one Lenten preacher disagreed with another on such questions as justification and predestination, a whole city might get excited and split into two camps. Educated laymen like the diplomatist Lattanzio Tolomei and the poet Flaminio already mentioned sought information from their theological friends. Thus it came about that a whole series of tracts on St Augustine's teaching on predestination owes its origin to a quarrel of preachers over the person of the Augustinian Friar Musaeus.[1] Seripando, who intervened in the controversy with his "Epistle to Flaminio", also wrote at the same time for the benefit of the Prince of Salerno a treatise on the relation between God's fore-knowledge and man's free will.[2] In the course of the next few years he elaborated a doctrine of justification which led to lengthy discussions at the Council of Trent: it was evolved from St Augustine's wonderful work *De spiritu et littera*. The latter work, which had called forth Luther's enthusiasm during his formative years, was translated into Italian and was eventually followed by translations of Augustine's treatises on "Nature and Grace", "Faith and Works" and "Predestination".[3]

Perhaps the most amazing literary product of evangelism is the reformed Breviary of Cardinal Quiñónez, commonly called "Holy Cross Breviary" after the cardinal's titular church.[4] In an attempt to draw almost exclusively on Holy Scripture, Quiñónez suppressed almost all the non-Biblical parts of the existing Breviary, particularly in the first edition of 1535. In spite of these revolutionary alterations there was a rush for copies in Rome. The first edition was reprinted no less than ten times within one year; the second edition, in spite of a subsequent reaction, saw no fewer than eighty-two editions. The heresies which

---

[1] H. Jedin, "Ein Streit um den Augustinismus vor dem Tridentinum", in *R.Q.*, xxxv (1927), pp. 351-68. The forty-two "Theoremata catholica et Sanctissimi Patris Augustini . . . doctrina" in Vat. lat. 3913, fols. 232ʳ-236ʳ, which the Augustinian Ambrosius Quistellius presented to Cardinal Aleander, probably fall into the same period.

[2] Jedin, *Seripando*, VOL. II, pp. 468-73 (not in Eng. edn.); for the development of Seripando's teaching on grace, *ibid.*, VOL. I, pp. 95-131; Eng. edn., pp. 73 ff.

[3] P. Cherubelli, *Le edizioni volgari delle opere do S. Agostino nella Rinascita* (Florence 1940), pp. 30 ff.

[4] H. Jedin, "Das Konzil von Trient und die Reform der liturgischen Bücher", in *Ephemerides liturgicae*, LIX (1945), pp. 5-38, especially pp. 15 ff. On 26 March 1535 Cardinal Cles's Roman agent sent his master an unbound copy—the leaves were still wet—with the remark: "Hic certe incredibili fere aviditate ac festinatione huiusmodi breviaria a prelatis reliquisque curialibus expetuntur sive propter eorum commoditatem (ut predicant), sive quod re nova alliciuntur", St. Arch., Trent, Cles, Mazzo 10.

the Spanish Canon Juan Arze claimed to have discovered in the work of his fellow-countryman were non-existent, but he was right when he criticised it as a daring innovation. The same may be said of the evangelistic movement: it was a characteristic symptom of a period of transition—old, sound, traditional Catholic material lay thick by the side of what was new, questionable, false.

As long as a Council did not set up firm, universally recognised standards, it was not easy, even for the depositaries of the Church's authority, to "discern the spirits" in the difficult sphere of the doctrine of justification. On the whole, the gentle Master of the Sacred Palace, Tommaso Badia, dealt leniently with such preachers as were denounced to the Pope. He was satisfied with a simple retractation. Nothing happened when Sadoleto's commentary on the Epistle to the Romans, several passages of which had been criticised, was reprinted at Venice not from the amended second edition but from the original one.[1] Those dread instruments of the counter-reformation, the Roman Inquisition and the Index of prohibited books did not as yet exist.

In Germany, where direct contact with the schism was general, the number of evangelistic publications was legion. We single out only two. Johann Gropper,[2] cathedral-schoolmaster of Cologne, was by profession a jurist. Later on, "bewitched" by the study of the Fathers, he advocated in his *Enchiridion*—a summary of Christian dogmas published in 1538—a conception of the doctrine of justification which ignored scholastic theology altogether and rested upon St Augustine: faith formed the kernel of the theory. It is characteristic of the period that this book was hailed with enthusiasm by the Cardinals Contarini, Pole, Sadoleto and by Giberti and Cortese. Such was the demand for it in the bookshops of northern Italy that it was reprinted three times within two years. Eck, however, would have none of it, on the ground that it was semi-Lutheran. It certainly contained the germ of the doctrines which were rejected both by the Pope in his condemnation of the Ratisbon formula of union and by the Council of Trent in its condemnation of Seripando's teaching on justification. Yet the author of the book was the champion of the Catholic cause in the Rhineland,

---

[1] S. Ritter, *Jacopo Sadoleto* (Rome 1912), p. 66 f.

[2] W. van Gulik, *Johann Gropper*, Freiburg 1906, pp. 51 ff., though not conclusive. Cruciger's remark on Gropper's knowledge of the Fathers in *Corp. Ref.*, VOL. IV, p. 306; for his teaching on justification, Jedin, *Studien über die Schriftstellertätigkeit Albert Pigges*, pp. 117-21. For details on the reception of the *Enchiridion* in Italy, for which further research is required, cf. Jedin, *Seripando*, VOL. II, p. 264 (omitted in Eng. edn.). The future Cardinal Cortese expressed himself as "molto affezionato a quell' opera": *Opera*, VOL. I (Padua 1774), p. 136.

the man who resisted the Protestantising tendencies of the Archbishop of Cologne, Hermann von Wied, and who, as he neared the end of his life, received the red hat at the hands of such a Pope as Paul IV!

It is necessary to be quite clear about this appalling confusion [1] in the intellectual sphere if we would understand the history of the efforts for reunion and rightly appraise the work of the Council of Trent. The evangelistic type of man was not wanting even in the Protestant camp. The pious prince George of Anhalt [2] received a strict Catholic upbringing from his mother, Margaret von Münsterberg. Later on George Helt introduced him to the study of the Bible and the Fathers of the Church. He ended by adopting the Lutheran doctrine of justification and by inviting the preacher Hausmann into his territory he initiated the Protestantising process in the principality of Dessau over which he ruled jointly with his brother. For all that, when the Elector of Saxony appointed him ecclesiastical administrator of the diocese of Merseburg, he acted like a Catholic bishop, complied with the prescriptions of Canon Law and upheld the Catholic liturgy. The Lutherans claimed him as one of their own while he regarded himself as a "Catholic".

Evangelism, as we said at the beginning, and Erasmian tendencies met and frequently overlapped so that it is often difficult, if not altogether impossible, to disentangle motives in the conduct of

---

[1] The scheme for reunion proposed by the dean of the chapter of Passau, Rupert von Mosham, who in 1532 renounced the customary "thumbherrliches Leben" to take up a more serious mode of life, is symptomatic of the general confusion rather than of any real significance. Since 1537 he had been pressing both Morone and Ferdinand I with his proposals for an accommodation and reform in view of the Council. This imaginative personage actually came very near being summoned to Rome, *N.B.*, VOL. I, PT ii, p. 229 f.; Eck's warning against him is in *N.B.*, VOL. I, PT iv, p. 588. When he began to storm with impartial vehemence against the abuses in both religious camps the Bishop of Passau forbade him to preach. On 4 September 1539 he took to flight, whereupon he was deprived of his benefices. However, the preachers of Nuremberg were as little pleased with his "mediatrix doctrina" as were the authorities at Passau, so that he was compelled to leave Nuremberg also. He found a temporary asylum with the Archbishops of Mainz and Cologne, but his efforts for admission to the religious colloquies were in vain—it was generally realised that he was not normal; cf. M. Heuwieser, "Rupert von Mosham, Domdechant von Passau", in *Riezler-Festschrift* (Gotha 1913), pp. 115-92.

[2] *R.E.*, VOL. VI, p. 521 f., makes of him a Protestant saint, but his work at Merseburg shows how much Catholicism he retained; E. Sehling, *Die Kirchengesetzgebung unter Moritz von Sachsen und Georg von Anhalt* (Leipzig 1899), pp. 82 ff. A number of interesting points in O. Clemen, *Georg Helts Briefwechsel* (Leipzig 1907); further literature in Schottenloher, Nos. 28987a-29004. On the Augustinianism of Johann Honter of Siebenbürgen, who falls into this period, cf. K. K. Klein, *Der Humanist und Reformator Johann Honter* (Munich 1935), pp. 139 ff.

individuals.[1] Real life is infinitely more complex than the historical notions with the help of which we endeavour to group its manifold manifestations in the hope of interpreting them. To understand the reunion policy of the years 1539-41 it is enough to bear in mind that two ideas lay behind the political and the ecclesiastical-political motives that gave it birth, namely the Erasmian programme of reunion and evangelism, both of which were due to a tendency to seek an understanding with the Protestants on the basis of what both parties retained of the substance of Christianity. No one with any degree of insight can be blind to the fact that its chances of success were slender, but so splendid was the goal, namely the restoration of the religious unity of the West, that it seemed worth while to make the attempt. Success depended on whether all efforts in the direction of reunion were focused on one point. This actually happened when Paul III sent Cardinal Contarini as his legate to the Diet of Ratisbon in 1541. By comparison with this great event all previous negotiations for reunion were no more than preliminary tactics.[2]

In order to obtain the help of the League of Schmalkalden for the Turkish war, which was King Ferdinand's special concern—Sultan Soliman was making preparations for a fresh, large-scale attack on Hungary—a political truce, something like the Pacification of Nuremberg in 1532, would have sufficed. But the Emperor was out for more— for nothing less, in fact, than a fundamental understanding with the Protestants. By this means he hoped to heal the religious division and to remove the latent danger of war which in the last few years had been disquieting the Catholics, who were becoming ever weaker, while it paralysed the high policy of the Habsburgs. In order to pave the way for such an agreement the Emperor despatched the adroit Johann von Weeze first to the court of Ferdinand and from there to Germany. In February 1539 von Weeze began negotiations at Frankfurt with the Schmalkaldic League, in the presence of two councillors of the King of the Romans but without the participation of the other Catholic princes

[1] Thus, for instance, Julius Pflug's tract on justification, C.T., VOL. XII, pp. 290-5 is a genuine product of evangelism.

[2] In addition to his admirable work on the efforts for reunion, the first of his many books (1879), Pastor has provided a good deal of supplementary matter in his History of the Popes, VOL. V, pp. 253-347 (Eng. edn., VOL. XI, pp. 359 ff.), as well as in his new edition of Janssen VOL. III. (1917), pp. 460 ff., 521 ff., 557-69 (Eng. edn., VOL. VI, pp. 34 ff., 105 ff., 147 ff.), but the most important supplementary matter is in L. Cardauns, Bestrebungen. The more recent special literature will be noted with each religious colloquy. Cf. also C. Guttierez, "Un capitolo de Teologia pretridentina: el problema de la justificación en los primeros coloquios religiosos alemanes 1540-41", in Miscelanea Comillas, IV (1945), pp. 7-31.

or that of the Pope. The result was the Respite of Frankfurt of 19 April 1539.[1] Against a promise to send representatives to a Diet of princes which would provide the finances for the Turkish war the Schmalkaldic League was granted a suspension, for a period of fifteen months, of the suits against its members then pending with the supreme court of judicature. No agreement was come to with regard to their further demand for permission to admit new members into the confederation. For the purpose of paving the way for an accord, a religious conference was announced; it was to meet at Nuremberg and the Pope was expressly excluded. Behind this exceedingly ominous clause loomed the League's aim to secure for their confession a final, juridical recognition, one no longer subject to the judgment of a future Council. An accord such as this, from which the Pope was excluded, could only lead to the apostasy of the entire German nation from the Roman Church. This was the solution Rome was most afraid of.

In the Eternal City the Emperor's efforts on behalf of reunion were viewed with undisguised alarm. Prompted by this sentiment the Pope made choice of the most uncompromising member of the Sacred College, Aleander, for the post of delegate to the court of Vienna.[2] In point of fact, as a result of Aleander's persistent warnings, the Curia had disavowed the whole plan for an accord ever since 1538, and that in unmistakable terms. The Respite of Frankfurt seemed to justify the worst fears.

In a lengthy memorial[3] Aleander turned with extraordinary sharpness on von Weeze, the author of this "impious and criminal Recess", as he called it. Only the Emperor's presence, so he thought, offered any kind of guarantee against pernicious decisions by the prospective Diet. Morone expressed himself in calmer, more objective terms, but his language was equally firm. He likewise issued a warning against a project advocated by Matthias Held, von Weeze's opponent, for a simple "conference" of scholars, without the participation of the

---

[1] Text in Le Plat, VOL. II, pp. 625-30; P. Fuchtel, "Der Frankfurter Anstand", in *A.R.G.*, XXVIII (1931), pp. 145-206; the jubilee article of E. Ziehen, "Frankfurter Anstand und deutsch-evangelischer Reichsbund von Schmalkalden", in *Z.K.G.*, LIX (1940), pp. 324-51, exploits new Frankfurt sources. The passage about the exclusion of the Pope runs as follows: "Non placuit hunc (pontificem) ad istum conventum advocare neque utile videbatur eius oratores ad hanc collocutionem et compensationem admittere", Le Plat, VOL. II, p. 627.

[2] The acts and the diary in *N.B.*, VOL. I, PTS iii and iv; cf. also Friedensburg's preface, VOL. I, PT iii, pp. 67-84.

[3] *N.B.*, VOL. I, PT iv, pp. 519-33, and the despatch of 28 May, *ibid.*, pp. 80-4, together with the memorial of 29 June in Laemmer, *Mon. Vat.*, pp. 233-41. The letter to the Emperor, *N.B.*, VOL. I, PT iv, pp. 142-7.

Estates but under the presidency of the Pope, at which representatives of the Empire and of the King of France would also be present. "Experience has taught us", Morone wrote on 6 July 1539,[1] "that such conversations only tend to weaken the Catholics and to encourage their opponents. The only way to intimidate the Lutherans and to render them amenable to negotiation is a strong Catholic League supported by the two great powers and by the Pope."

On 18 August 1539 Giovanni Ricci of Montepulciano repaired to the imperial court in Spain in the hope of preventing the confirmation of the Respite of Frankfurt by the monarch and of procuring the fall of von Weeze.[2] The Farnesi's confidant succeeded in preventing a formal confirmation of the Respite, but the fall of von Weeze and still less the abandonment of the policy of reunion were not to be thought of.[3] Even Cardinal Farnese himself who, accompanied by his former tutor Cervini, visited the two courts in November 1539 in the capacity of peace-legate,[4] failed to dissuade the Emperor from his resolve to attempt a final settlement; all he could obtain was one solitary alteration in the plan, though an all-important one, namely the participation of the Pope in the prospective religious discussion. The worst danger was thus averted. After the break-down of the negotiations with Francis I in April 1540 and while great military preparations by the Turks brought the danger of war on two fronts ever nearer, the Emperor acted with surprising speed. On 18 April 1540 the Estates of the Empire were summoned to Speyer for a religious conference.

Papal diplomacy had vainly sought to arrest the course of the policy of reunion by means of a fresh offer of a Council. Farnese's programme: first peace with France, then a Council for the healing of the schism in Germany and England and, lastly, a joint military enterprise against the Turks, was by this time impossible.[5] In vain the nuncio Poggio drew the Emperor's attention to the intolerable situation which a compromise in the ecclesiastical sphere was bound to create. The Church in Germany would be following rites and customs wholly different from those in use in the French and Spanish Churches. Only through a

---

[1] N.B., VOL. I, PT iv, pp. 127 ff., similarly on 20 July, ibid., p. 137 f.

[2] Ricci's instructions, Laemmer, Mon. Vat., pp. 246-52; also the corrections in Pieper, Zur Entstehungsgeschichte, pp. 166 ff.

[3] The Emperor's reply in N.B., VOL. I, PT iv, pp. 537-40; more fully in the Emperor's instructions for Aguilar, Döllinger, Beiträge, VOL. I, pp. 22-8.

[4] N.B., VOL. I, PT v, pp. 39-246.

[5] Instructions in N.B., VOL. I, PT v, p. 42; cf. pp. 123, 184. The great memorial is in C.T., VOL. IV, pp. 182-7.

FRANÇOIS IER
After the painting by Titian in the Louvre, Paris,
dated 1538

General Council could the Church's unity be preserved.[1] Morone sought to influence Ferdinand I in the same sense. It was a piece of good fortune for the papal diplomatists that at this very time—February 1540—the King of Poland also made a proposal for a General Council through the Bishop of Caminiec.[2] Three German divines, Fabri, Cochlaeus and Nausea, worked in the same direction as the papal representatives. The Bishop of Vienna, Ferdinand's most influential adviser in matters of ecclesiastical policy since the death of Cardinal Cles, kept stressing the great Catholic principles in a whole series of memorials [3]: "What the Roman Church and the Apostolic See have condemned, is condemned. The Bull *Exsurge* and the Edict of Worms must form the basis of whatever discussions may take place. Nothing can be decided without the concurrence of the Pope. A Council is the supreme remedy for the many wounds from which the Church suffers and its most weighty task is to carry out a reform of the head and the members." "If it is not possible", he wrote at a later date, "to convoke a Council, let a conference be called at which all the nations are represented for the purpose of defining the controversial doctrines." [4] The greatest peril, in Fabri's opinion, would be a purely national solution without the concurrence of the Pope. In a memorial for King Ferdinand drawn up in the last days of June 1540 Cochlaeus wrote [5]: "We Germans cannot deny that the Roman Church is our mother in the faith, hence we may not differ from her on a single article of faith without imperilling the salvation of our souls. Abuses in the Church are much more easily and more effectively righted by a General Council than by a religious conference. A General Council is the object of the aspirations of all truly devout people." Even Nausea,[6] who was much more strongly influenced by Erasmian ideas than either Fabri or Cochlaeus, declared in the conclusion of a memorial on the *Confessio Augustana*: "On all these articles a Council would pronounce a

---

[1] *N.B.*, VOL. I, PT V, p. 192.

[2] *C.T.*, VOL. IV, p. 186; *N.B.*, VOL. I, PT V, p. 93 f.; cf. B. von Dembinski, *Die Beschickung des Tridentinums durch Polen* (Breslau 1883).

[3] Cardauns, *Bestrebungen*, pp. 25-31; *ibid.*, pp. 131-8, the text of the memorial drawn up in May 1540. The further elaboration of the *Preparatoria* in Laemmer, *Mantissa*, pp. 149-54; also Weiss, *Papiers*, VOL. II, pp. 590-5; its despatch to Rome on 22 April 1540, *N.B.*, VOL. I, PT V, p. 191. The memorial drawn up during the colloquy of Hagenau in Raynald, *Annales*, *a.* 1540, Nos. 34-8; new impression in Le Plat, VOL. II, pp. 647-50.

[4] Memorial of September 1540, Cardauns, *Bestrebungen*, pp. 141-5.

[5] Text in Cardauns, *Bestrebungen*, pp. 145-50; the passage quoted is on p. 149 f.

[6] Cardauns, *Bestrebungen*, p. 190; *ibid.*, pp. 150-7, the memorial to the Emperor.

clearer and more authoritative judgment." However, the Emperor had neither the will nor the power to draw back. Owing to an outbreak of an epidemic at Speyer the reunion conference met at Hagenau in June 1540.[1] The two leaders of the League of Schmalkalden, Saxony and Hesse, refused to attend, Melanchthon was taken ill on the journey and only a very small number of princes and prelates put in an appearance. Hence no positive result was arrived at. For the fiasco Ferdinand's many mistakes in the conduct of the meeting were largely responsible. No religious conference properly so called took place; the Recess fixed the opening of such a gathering for 28 October at Worms and suggested the participation of a papal representative.

For months both sides had argued about the procedure to be observed. Morone made a supreme bid to give the conference an international character [2] by means of an invitation to ten theologians, from each of the following nations, viz. Italy, France, Spain and Poland-Hungary, as against twenty Germans from both contending parties. His proposal was not acted upon; in any case a congress of divines would have lacked an essential qualification—authority. Another hotly debated point was: "On what text would the exchange of opinion be based?" Fabri's proposal had the merit of simplicity [3]: "Let a list be drawn up with the help of Crabbe's 'Collection of the Councils' of the pertinent doctrines already condemned and let them be submitted to the Protestants, point by point, in order to clarify their attitude, beginning with the specific tenets of Zwingli and the Anabaptists which the Lutherans rejected no less than the Catholics." Such a procedure would have safeguarded the Catholic position; it was, however, unacceptable to the Emperor because it would not lead to an accord but rather to a final rupture. In Fabri's and Cochlaeus's opinion [4] the *Confessio Augustana* on which the men of Schmalkalden were once more taking their stand, could not form a basis for negotiation, because even when it

---

[1] Schottenloher, Nos. 41323a-8; for us the most important documents are Morone's reports in F. Dittrich, *Nuntiaturberichte Giovanni Morones vom deutschen Königshofe 1539-40* (Paderborn 1892), pp. 130-79. The Recess of 28 July in Ranke, *Deutsche Geschichte im Zeitalter der Reformation* (Berlin 1839-43), VOL. VI, pp. 160-8; also *N.B.*, VOL. I, PT v, p. 448-51. It is remarkable that the electors' motion (*N.B.*, VOL. I, PT v, p. 448) speaks of a *modus vivendi* until the future Council and that Granvella reckons with the confirmation by the Council of eventual concessions, *ibid.*, p. 328. The Recess speaks of a "legitimate" Council (Ranke, VOL. VI, p. 162) for which the Protestants wished to substitute the words "christlich frei Konzil".

[2] Laemmer, *Mon. Vat.*, p. 286 (7 July 1540); Ferdinand thought of twenty to thirty theologians from Germany, Italy, France and Spain, *N.B.*, VOL. I, PT vi, p. 348.

[3] Laemmer, *Mantissa*, pp. 149 ff.

[4] Cardauns, *Bestrebungen*, p. 146.

was drafted it had not furnished an adequate definition of Lutheran teaching and now the Articles of Schmalkalden had rendered it super-fluous. If they started on such a basis they ran the risk of a sham agreement which would gloss over substantial doctrinal differences. If the Catholics insisted on alterations, as they needs must, they were faced with a rupture. The obstinacy with which the men of Schmalkalden stuck to their Confession was shown by their rejection of a proposal of Ferdinand's that they should simply accept the result of the Augsburg negotiations for reunion and limit themselves to a discussion of those points on which no agreement had been reached at that meeting.[1] As a matter of fact the Protestants were even less inclined to yield than the Curia. Their present position was very different from what it had been ten years earlier. At that time they faced the victorious, all-powerful Emperor as a religious body; now the League of Schmalkalden was the only compact political power in the Empire. In spite of the prohibition of Nuremberg the League was expanding year by year by the accession of new adherents and all the time its ecclesiastical organisation was being consolidated. On the Catholic side one state after another, one town after another crumbled away [2]—Württemberg, Pommerania, the greater part of Brunswick, Brandenburg and after the death of Duke George on 17 April 1539, Albertine Saxony. The Catholic Federation of Nuremberg, by means of which Vice-Chancellor Held had hoped to keep the Protestants in check, came to very little. The Rhenish Electors refused to join it and even the Pope hesitated. Internal dis-solution kept pace with external losses and Morone had good reason to complain of the supineness of the bishops.

In these circumstances Granvella's show of optimism failed to allay the anxiety felt by the papal diplomatists, that is the Cardinal-legate Cervini who had remained in the Low Countries after Farnese's departure, the nuncio Poggio and above all Morone. Every succeeding day brought fresh evidence of the Protestants' deep-seated aversion for the Papacy. "How can we hope to come to terms", Nausea and Coch-laeus asked,[3] "with people who regard the chief shepherd of Christ's flock as Antichrist? who ask us to accept the *Confessio Augustana*, an act that would be equivalent to apostasy from the Roman Catholic Church and throwing in our lot with them? Can anyone believe that the Protestant preachers will re-introduce Catholic teaching and practice

---

[1] Correspondence on the subject in *N.B.*, VOL. I, PT V, pp. 446-51.
[2] Eck's account, *N.B.*, VOL. I, PT iv, p. 588.
[3] Cardauns, *Bestrebungen*, pp. 146 f., 194 f.

which they have been fighting for decades and that princes will restore confiscated Church property?"

On 25 November 1540, nearly a full month after the date originally fixed, Granvella opened the negotiations for reunion at Worms.[1] Only after the Emperor had given a formal assurance that there would be no negotiations, still less would a decision be taken without the Pope's knowledge and approval,[2] did Paul III decide to send a special representative to Worms. Giberti was unacceptable to the Emperor on account of his notorious francophil attitude and Contarini's nomination had to be cancelled at the last moment. The Pope's choice then fell upon the Bishop of Feltre, Tommaso Campeggio,[3] who thus made his first appearance on the stage of history. Hitherto his influence had only been felt behind the scenes. There too, in time to come, he was to render signal service as an adviser to the Curia in all questions of Canon Law. However, his role was merely that of an observer. He was neither empowered to give his approval to any dogmatic formula of reunion—this goes without saying—nor could he on his own authority make any concessions in the disciplinary sphere.[4] His activity at Worms was further restricted in consequence of the personal tension between him and Morone, who was also present.[5] His address to the assembled representatives of the Estates on 8 December [6] was free from invectives against the Protestants and later also, in keeping with his promise, he endeavoured to act as a messenger of peace and reconciliation. For all that he did not escape the accusation of being an obstructionist, an accusation that might have been levelled with better reason at Morone. However, by maintaining contact with Granvella, the leader of the negotiations, as well as with the outstanding theologians of the Catholic party, Eck, Cochlaeus, Nausea and Hoetfilter, he

---

[1] The reports of Campeggio, Morone and Bernardo Sanzio, Bishop of Aquila, who were also present at Worms, in *N.B.*, VOL. I, PT vi, pp. 1-146, in part already in Laemmer; further literature in Schottenloher, Nos. 41404-16.

[2] *N.B.*, VOL. I, PT v, pp. 328, 332 ff.

[3] For Campeggio's life and writings (1481-1564), G. Fantuzzi, *Notizie degli Scrittori bolognesi* (Bologna 1781-4), VOL. III, pp. 67 ff., is the most exhaustive. Cardauns, *N.B.*, VOL. I, PT v, pp. xxx ff., has a sketch. Cf. also Hofmann, *Forschungen*, VOL. II, p. 76; Lauchert, *Literarische Gegner*, pp. 614-19. For his position within the movement, see next chapter.

[4] *N.B.*, VOL. I, PT vi, p. 13. Morone's proposals for an amendment of the Recess of Hagenau in *N.B.*, VOL. I, PT v, p. 449.

[5] Morone purposely avoided appearing jointly with Campeggio and subsequently reproached him with "insufficientia, poca memoria et maggior facilità nel parlare che non sarebbe bisogno a trattare negotii", *N.B.*, VOL. I, PT vi, p. 121, but we must bear in mind the opinion of the impartial Sanzio, *ibid.*, p. 66 f.

[6] *Corp. Ref.*, VOL. III, pp. 1192-5 (No. 2076).

376

repeatedly saved the situation when the uncertain attitude of the representatives of Brandenburg, the Palatinate and Cleves, who were reckoned among the Catholics, rendered it exceedingly critical. Campeggio was assisted by the following papal theologians: the Italian Badia, the Frenchman Gérard, the Scotsman Wauchope and the Dutchman Pighius.

Weeks were spent in controversy over the question of procedure at the conference—whether the discussion should be by word of mouth or in writing, the manner of voting, the number of speakers and so forth. All this goes to show that there could be no question of mutual trust.[1] The formal *colloquium* opened on 14 January 1541 on the basis of the *Confessio Augustana*, Eck and Melanchthon being the speakers. At the end of four days an agreed formula on the doctrine of original sin had been arrived at when an imperial command stopped the exchange of views and transfered it to the Diet of Ratisbon, which had been announced at Hagenau. At Ratisbon the Emperor was resolved to promote the work of reunion with all his might and by his personal presence. Cardinal Contarini, on whom all the hopes of the advocates of reunion were centred, was also to be present; on 10 January he had been named papal legate.

No one in the whole of the Sacred College was better qualified for such a task.[2] Sprung from one of the numerous branches of a noble Venetian family, which had given the Republic no less than six doges, Gasparo Contarini, at the conclusion of his philosophical studies at Padua, had entered on a strict religious mode of life together with his friends Tommaso Giustiniani and Vincenzo Quirini. But while his friends forsook the world to enter the solitude of Camaldoli near Arezzo, where they reformed the Order of St Romuald, Contarini, as a result of a spiritual experience connected with justification at the time of his Easter confession in the year 1511—an experience comparable with Luther's "tower experience"—resolved to remain in the world and there to lead a truly Christian life. He entered the service of the

---

[1] Campeggio's lengthy despatch of 15 December is to the point, *N.B.*, VOL. I, PT vi, pp. 68-79.

[2] Contarini's works were printed in Paris in 1572 and at Venice in 1578 and 1589; cf. also a critical edition of his counter-reform writings by F. Hünermann in *Corp. Cath.*, VOL. VII (Münster 1923), and F. Dittrich, *Regesten*. In the preface to an edition of thirty recently discovered letters of Contarini of the years 1510-23, which I published in De Luca's *Archivio per la storia della pietà*, I made some additions to the great biography by F. Dittrich, *Gasparo Contarini* (Braunsberg 1885), from Solmi, Friedensburg and others. Among more recent works H. Rückert's *Die theologische Entwicklung G. Contarini's* (Berlin 1926), is valuable for our purpose.

Republic and thus it came about that in 1521 he assisted at the Diet of Worms in the capacity of Venetian envoy. In this way he became acquainted with the Lutheran movement and perhaps even with some of Luther's writings. His own interior evolution, which was not without affinity with Luther's, led him to think that the latter's conception of salvation—though not its theological formulation and the conclusions he drew from it—had its roots in primitive Christianity. In a letter of 7 February 1523 he wrote to his friend Giustiniani: "No man is justified by his own works; we must have recourse to God's grace which we receive through faith in Christ." When he wrote these words Contarini did not take his stand by the side of Luther but with St Paul, St Augustine and St Thomas Aquinas. He also followed St Thomas when, a few years later, he drew up a short refutation of the fundamental tenets of Lutheranism. He started from the conviction that the religious dispute could be settled without either a Council or controversial exchanges and pamphlets—all that was required was good-will on both sides combined with charity and humility.[1] It was not long before he realised that this was not enough.

On 20 May 1535 Paul III raised Contarini, layman though he was, to the cardinalate. The Pope had probably come to know him more intimately during his term of office as Venetian ambassador to the Curia from 1528 to 1530. Before long Contarini became the heart and soul of the reform movement at the Curia as well as the acknowledged leader of a religious circle which had certain affinities with the evangelistic movement and included men like Pole, Gonzaga and Giberti. In Germany he, as well as Sadoleto, Fregoso and Pole, was thought to be sincerely in favour of an understanding with the Protestants.[2] This is why he had been considered for the duties of papal legate at the convention of Hagenau and subsequently at the conference of Worms.[3] Although he too was not empowered to come to an agreement at Ratisbon, or to make concessions even in the disciplinary sphere,[4] his nomination was a striking proof of the Pope's wish to meet the Emperor's aspirations for reunion. His personality was a guarantee that on the

---

[1] Corp. Cath., VOL. VII, p. 22.

[2] Campeggio's report of 23 December 1540 in N.B., VOL. I, PT vi, p. 90.

[3] Dittrich, Regesten, Nos. 460, 485, and the letter to Cervini, p. 312 f.; G. Cortese, Opera, VOL. I, p. 52 f.

[4] Contarini's instructions in Morandi, Monumenti, VOL. I, PT ii, pp. 112-22. The decisive passage is on p. 114: "Non fuit locus ut . . . cum ampla concordandi facultate mittere te potuerimus." Contarini's corresponding observations to Granvella in Z.K.G., III (1879), pp. 166 ff.

Catholic side the negotiations would be conducted in a most conciliatory spirit and that the German controversialists—Eck, Cochlaeus, Fabri and their followers, whom the Protestants loathed—would be kept in check.

Contarini made his entry into Ratisbon as legate on 12 March 1541.[1] Not for decades had a representative of the Pope been received with such enthusiasm in Germany. The oppressive, warlike tension which had envenomed relations between the two religious parties during recent years seemed to have lifted and hope revived. The Emperor and his minister Granvella showed so much concern for the Protestants that many Catholics felt slighted, while the crowd witnessed the extraordinary spectacle of the Elector of Brandenburg devoutly attending the celebration of the Catholic Mass.

However, all this was only on the surface: at bottom the sharp opposition between Rome and Wittenberg continued unabated. Neither Luther nor the Elector of Saxony came to Ratisbon, and Melanchthon had received strict orders not to depart from the *Confessio Augustana* and its Apologia. From Strasbourg, his temporary refuge, came the future arch-enemy of Rome, John Calvin. Shortly before the Diet the Curia, actuated as it was by distrust and anxiety, had replaced the nuncio Poggio, a man in complete sympathy with the Emperor, by Morone, who, as everyone knew, would have nothing to do with the policy of religious discussions. He was to counterbalance the peace-

---

[1] Bibliography of the Diet of Ratisbon in Schottenloher, Nos. 28073-82, 41376-89; best survey in Brandi, *Quellen*, p. 303 ff. Apart from the letters of Contarini already published by Quirini and Morandi, V. Schultze has published thirteen despatches in *Z.K.G.*, III (1879), pp. 150-83. The greater part of the remaining ones was published almost at the same time by L. Pastor in *H.J.*, I (1880), pp. 321-92, 473-500, and by F. Dittrich, *Regesten* (1881). Some supplementary matter may be found in *N.B.*, VOL. I, PT vii, pp. 3-26. Part of Morone's contemporary despatches was published by H. Laemmer, *Mon. Vat.* (1861), and another nine by V. Schultze in *Z.K.G.*, III (1879), pp. 609-41, the remaining ones by F. Dittrich in *H.J.*, IV (1883), pp. 395-472, 618-73. Additional matter by L. Cardauns, together with Sanzio's reports, in *N.B.*, VOL. I, PT vii, pp. 27-96. On the Protestant side Melanchthon's reports and those of the Saxon councillors, in *Corp. Ref.*, VOL. IV, pp. 142-637. Bucer's letters in Schiess, *Breifwechsel Blaurer*, VOL. II, pp. 71 ff. On Joachim II's attitude, cf. N. Müller, in *Jahrbuch für brandenburgische Kirchengeschichte*, IV (1907), pp. 175-248; also the reports of the envoys of the cities, viz. Strasbourg, *Politische Correspondenz*, VOL. III, pp. 177-205; Augsburg, edited by F. Roth in *A.R.G.*, II (1904), pp. 250-307; III (1905), pp. 18-64; IV (1906), pp. 65-98, 221-304; Frankfurt, Pastor, *Reunionsbestrebungen*, pp. 483-9. H. Nestler, in *Zeitschrift für bayrische Landesgeschichte*, VI (1933), pp. 389-414, supplies local colour especially after the chronicler Widmann. Extracts from the notes of the Swiss Hans von Hinwyl, who was present at Ratisbon, by L. Weiss in *Zeitschrift für schweizerische Kirchengeschichte*, XXVIII (1934), pp. 51-64, 81-104.

loving Contarini. Shortly before the opening of the Diet, on 9 March,[1] Cardinal Farnese gave the legate a final and most earnest warning against the Emperor's policy of lulling the parties to sleep. *Attenzione!* was the watchword of all Roman instructions.

The surest omen of success for the Emperor's plan was the circumstance that he had the support of the majority of the college of Electors, viz. Brandenburg, the Palatine, Trier and Cologne. The most active member of the Schmalkaldic League, Philip of Hesse, withdrew from the ranks of the opposition. Driven into a corner in consequence of his bigamous marriage, he sought to attach himself to the Emperor. Among the Protestant divines none worked harder for reunion than Bucer, Philip's friend. Viewed exclusively from the political standpoint the situation was such as to raise hopes of an understanding. Those who opposed it were few in number. They were Bavaria, Mainz and the pugnacious Duke Henry of Brunswick. The papal representatives were not taken in by the demonstrations of zeal for the Catholic religion of which the Bavarians were particularly lavish. They knew that this façade screened some exceedingly worldly aims and that their agitation in favour of war masked their desire to extend their power ("*farsi grandi*").[2] Was it not they who had started the intrigues which France was weaving in Rome against Contarini? Johann Eck was their spokesman among the theologians.

On the very day of the opening of the Diet, 4 April, it became evident that the question of a Council occupied people's mind as much as ever. In his "Proposition" the Emperor recapitulated the fruitless efforts made by him since his meeting with Clement VII at Bologna to bring about such an assembly.[3] In their reply of 9 April the Protestants maintained their previous standpoint. They had declined the Council of Mantua for "weighty and important reasons", but, they protested, "they were always ready to attend a free, Christian Council of the German nation" where they would account for their "reformation" which, so they claimed, was perfectly reconcilable with the customs of "the universal, Christian and apostolic Church".[4] The small

---

[1] Dittrich, *Regesten*, No. 601.

[2] Morone's despatches of 21 March, 28 April and 11 May: *H.J.*, IV (1883), pp. 438 ff.; 449 f., 459; also the despatches of 6 and 7 April: *Z.K.G.*, III (1879), pp. 625 f., 630.

[3] *Corp. Ref.*, VOL. IV, pp. 151-4 (No. 2179); also *Zeitschrift für schweizerische Kirchengeschichte*, XXVIII (1934), p. 60 f.

[4] Latin text in *Corp. Ref.*, VOL. IV, p. 158; German text in *Zeitschrift für schweizerische Kirchenschichte*, XXVIII (1934), p. 83.

committee exclusively composed of German theologians, which the Emperor set up on 21 April after the Easter pause, for the discussion of the disputed articles of the faith, was not intended to take the place of a future Council. It was not entitled to issue decisions; its only object was an exchange of ideas the result of which was to be submitted to the Emperor, the papal legate and the Estates. In view of the instructions of the Saxons, the basis of the discussions was not the *Confessio Augustana* but a new formula of reunion consisting of twenty-three articles and resting on a formula devised at Leipzig. This was the so-called *Book of Ratisbon*.[1] The book was the result of a secret conference at Worms between Gropper and Bucer and mainly Gropper's work. The confidants of the Emperor, Count Palatine Frederick and Granvella, were chosen as "mediators" or presidents of the conference. On 23 April six representatives of the Estates were adjoined to them as "hearers". The real leader was Granvella. The Curia's warnings against him were fully justified. Ecclesiastical scruples troubled him much less than the Emperor; his programme for reunion was inspired by Erasmus.[2] Two of the three Catholic collocutors, Gropper and Pflug—the latter had shortly before been appointed to the see of Naumburg—were convinced promoters of reunion. Eck on the other hand was an irreconcilable opponent. He longed to display his skill in debate on this occasion also, but had to yield the coveted leading role to Contarini, to whom the Catholic collocutors were obliged to report in the morning and evening of each day. Among the Protestants Bucer was regarded as practically won over to reunion.[3] On the other

---

[1] The original form of the "Book of Ratisbon", with the lengthy article 5—subsequently suppressed—in Lenz, *Briefwechsel*, VOL. III, pp. 31-72; final text in Le Plat, VOL. III, pp. 10-44, *Corp. Ref.*, VOL. IV, pp. 190-238 (No. 2207). H. Eells, "The Origin of the Regensburg Book", in *Princeton Theological Review*, XXVI (1928), pp. 355-72; R. Stupperich, "Der Ursprung des Regensburger Buches von 1541 und seine Rechtfertigungslehre", in *A.R.G.*, XXXVI (1939), pp. 88-116.

[2] Granvella's dependence on Erasmus is most clearly seen in the proposal made to Contarini previous to the colloquy, to the effect that the doctrine of transubstantiation should be referred to the Council, *Z.K.G.*, III (1879), p. 160. Granvella was also responsible for the suggestion of a compromise on this point in the course of the colloquy, *H.J.*, I (1880), p. 377. Even after the division of minds on the concept of transubstantiation Granvella stuck to his view that it was "una cosa sottile e pertinente solo alli dotti, non toccava al popolo", *H.J.*, IV (1883), p. 471. For a characterisation of the collocutors cf. Contarini's report of 28 April, *H.J.*, I (1880), p. 366 f., in which he also explains why the imperial statesmen excluded Pighius and Wauchope: both men were regarded as advocates of strong measures. Dittrich, *Regesten*, p. 324, gives a complete list of the participants in the colloquy.

[3] Granvella to Morone on 21 March, *H.J.*, IV (1883), p. 439; Morone subsequently acknowledged that the information was correct, *ibid.*, p. 454. "Without him", Morone wrote on 11 May, "la pratica era totalmente rotta", *ibid.*, p. 459.

hand Melanchthon, who had been its indefatigable advocate at Augsburg, tied as he now was by the strict instructions of his Elector, kept almost timidly in the background. When Eck was taken ill, the Hessian Pistorius withdrew from the conference.

The situation thus created was the best possible. The political and religious forces which pressed for reunion were all represented at the conference and its opponents were in the minority. The first results surpassed all expectations. In the course of a very few sessions agreement was reached on the first four articles of the *Book of Ratisbon* and on 2 May the Protestants accepted article 5 on justification as stated in the formula submitted by Contarini and approved by Badia and Eck, though reluctantly by the latter, to the effect that justification is by faith working through charity.[1] Contarini was highly gratified and informed Rome of the great event, while the Elector Joachim II ordered a serenade in honour of the legate of reconciliation.

The orthodoxy of the formula of reunion has been discussed for centuries. When it was submitted to the consistory of 27 May it was criticised as equivocal [2]; justly so if we compare its wording with that of the Tridentine decree on justification. The Council drew a much sharper line of demarcation between Catholic dogma and Protestant teaching. It rejected the doctrine of a "double justice" of the Ratisbon formula and devoted a whole dogmatic chapter to the concept of merit on which the Ratisbon formula was silent. But when we ask what meaning its authors attached to it the answers vary. As early as 25 May 1541 Contarini defended himself in the celebrated *Epistola de justificatione* against the objections raised by the Mantuan divine Messer

---

[1] Text of article 5 in Le Plat, VOL. III, p. 15; *Corp. Ref.*, VOL. IV, pp. 198-201. To this must be added the "scheda" which Contarini added to the formula of reunion by way of further clarification when forwarding it to Cardinal Gonzaga on 3 May: Th. Brieger in *Z.K.G.*, V (1882), pp. 593 ff.; also *C.T.*, VOL. XII, p. 313 f. The covering letter in Dittrich, *Regesten*, p. 324 f. The letter of Farnese under the same date in *H.J.*, I (1880), pp. 372 ff. Contarini at once detected the two critical points, viz. the "duplex iustitia" and the absence of the word "meritum".

[2] Pole had charged Aluise Priuli to influence the cardinals of Contarini's circle, namely Carafa, Bembo, Loreri, Fregoso and Aleander, in favour of the formula of reunion, Quirini, *Epp. Poli*, VOL. III, p. 25. However, Fregoso alone gave it serious support. Morandi, *Monumenti*, VOL. I, PT ii, p. 169, *n.*67, already conjectured that the opponent of the formula of whom Bembo speaks in his letter of 27 May, was Aleander. Farnese's official reply of 29 May, Quirini, *Epp. Poli*, ccxxxi-ccxl, states that the Pope had expressed no personal opinion but that he wished him to warn Contarini not to agree to an equivocal formula. The refusal of approbation was of course equivalent to a rejection.

Angelo.[1] The "Epistle" is therefore an authentic commentary on article 5 of the *Book of Ratisbon*. If we appraise its spirit and not merely every individual word, we are bound to agree with the doctors of the Sorbonne. In 1571, when asked for their opinion on the complete edition of Contarini's writings, these divines declared them to be orthodox.[2] Contarini was anxious to clear up the pernicious misunderstanding which had cumbered discussion with the Protestants from the beginning of Luther's activities, namely that the Catholic doctrine of salvation was Pelagian, was prejudicial to the merits of Jesus Christ as the sole source of salvation, diminished the significance of faith in the process of justification—in a word that it failed to uphold the all-sufficiency of divine grace. Ever since his Holy Saturday experience in the year 1511 Contarini's whole spiritual life had rested on this fundamental conception. He had stuck to it in spite of severe interior struggles and it constituted the very core of his religion. The conception is Catholic. Only ignorance of Catholic teaching could have prompted Theodore Brieger to say that the Epistle is "at heart genuinely Protestant", or lead Hans Rückert to assert that its greatest weakness lies in the fact that "ideas whose natural climate is Protestantism, whose main driving power they constitute, are there developed within the framework of a Catholic dogma which rests on a very different basis".[3] We grant that the formula lacks the Tridentine ring, but it does not emit a Protestant sound.

Agreement on article 5 of the *Book of Ratisbon* was reached because beneath the theological errors which controversial theology had discovered in Luther's notion of justification, Contarini saw the main religious consideration from which he had started. As the talks

[1] *Corp. Cath.*, VOL. VII, pp. 23-34. In the introduction Hünermann gives the list of previous publications. In the letters in which he defends his action, 9 June, *H.J.*, I (1880), pp. 478 ff., and 22 June, *N.B.*, VOL. I, PT vii, pp. 9-13, Contarini energetically rejects the accusation of ambiguity. In the letter of 22 July, Morandi, *Monumenti*, VOL. I, PT ii, pp. 186 ff., and *Z.K.G.*, III (1879), pp. 516 ff., probably addressed to Aleander, he defends the formula "nos iustificari fide efficaci per charitatem". H. Rückert, *Theologische Entwicklung Contarinis*, p. 81, gives a list of all the pertinent sources.

[2] Of the three conceptions listed by Hünermann, *Corp. Cath.*, VOL. VII, p. xxi f., the Catholic one is upheld, in addition to the above-mentioned, by Cardinal Quirini and by Morandi. The Protestant one was advocated in the eighteenth century by Kiesling, professor of theology at Leipzig and later on by the Church historians Gieseler and Weizsäcker—of the layman Ranke we prefer not to speak; the intermediary view, maintained by Laemmer, Pastor, Dittrich and others, is obviously untenable, for in the sphere of faith there can be no middle course, that is, there is no half-truth but only truth and error.

[3] Rückert, *Theologische Entwicklung Contarinis*, p. 105.

proceeded it became evident that reunion was impossible in view of the fact that the Protestants denied the sacramental nature of the Church and rejected her hierarchical constitution. Already in the discussion of articles 6 and 9, on the Church and her authority to interpret Scripture, the same Protestant conception showed itself which had led to the breakdown of the disputation of Leipzig, the notion, that is, that Councils were liable to error.[1] This was equivalent to the denial of a supreme teaching authority. In order to prevent an immediate rupture and in spite of Eck's protests, Contarini obtained the postponement of the discussion of this decisive question until the end of the *colloquium*. On 9 May he explained the reasons that prompted these tactics [2]: they are more to the credit of his theological insight than of his political acumen. He saw quite clearly what our narrative shows and what was abundantly confirmed by the course of the Council of Trent, namely that the discussions within the Church herself on the extent of the papal primacy and its relation to a General Council had not as yet led to such unanimity and clarity as to make it advisable to enter into details in a discussion with Protestants. The diversity of opinion among Catholics might indeed have produced the chaos Contarini was afraid of, quite apart from the circumstance that it would have been exceedingly unwise to wreck the agreement precisely on the article of papal supremacy. Contarini was determined, with the concurrence of Morone, to demand from the Protestants the recognition of the papal primacy of jurisdiction and the supreme authority of a Council in matters of faith, but only at the conclusion of the religious *colloquium*.[3]

The final rupture came with the discussion of article 14—the

---

[1] Contarini to Farnese, 4 and 9 May 1541, *H.J.*, 1 (1880), pp. 375 f., 376 ff.

[2] *Ibid.*, pp. 379 ff.

[3] Contarini drew attention to the fact that on the Catholic side Panormitanus and Pighius—of course for different reasons—taught that a Council was liable to error. He accordingly proposed the following text for the formula of reunion: "Quod quando incidit dubitatio rationabilis in expositione sacrae scripturae, eo quod non fuerit determinatum antea quicquam per concilium quodpiam legitime congregatum neque in scriptura habeatur sententia expressa, neque etiam existat consensus aut doctrina recepta ab universali ecclesia, tunc maiores nostri consuevere convocare concilia generalia quorum auctoritas in ecclesia cum fuerit (probably fuerint) legitime, recte in Spiritu Sancto congregata semper maxima fuit, cuique nullus ausus sit contradicere" (*ibid.*, p. 380, with Cardaun's corrections, *N.B.*, VOL. I, PT vii, p. 6). For the primacy Contarini proposed this formula: "Che Christo ha instituita questa gerarchia ponendo li vescovi nelle loro diocesi, li arcivescovi, li patriarchi e li primati, sopra li quali tutti per conservare l'unità della Chiesa ha constuito il Pontefice Romano, dandoli giurisditione universale sopra tutta la Chiesa" (*ibid.*). For Contarini's teaching on the primacy, see the tract *De potentia pontificis*, *Corp. Cath.*, VOL. VII, pp. 35-43.

Eucharist.[1] On this question the Protestants were bound to take into account the view that prevailed in north Germany—a view strongly influenced by Zwingli. They firmly declined to accept the concept of transubstantiation which Contarini had embodied in the text of the article and on whose acceptance—without any reservation whatsoever—he insisted, since it was a definition of the fourth Lateran Council. He also rejected the proposal, responsibility for which ultimately rested with Erasmus, that they might be content with a declaration that Christ is really and truly present in the Eucharist while leaving the discussion of the notion of transubstantiation to a General Council. Contarini's truly Catholic character was now seen in all its brightness. He was firmly resolved to forgo the desired agreement rather than permit the least whittling down of a dogma defined by the Church, nor would he cloak the divergence between the two doctrinal concepts with a sham agreement (concordia palliata). His sole concern now was the preservation of the truth (conservare la verità).

When on 14 May the Protestants declared their willingness to grant the usefulness of the confession of grave sins but not its necessity, there was no longer any doubt that the attempt at reunion had failed. Contarini explained the gravity of the situation to the Emperor.[2] The monarch must either compel the Protestants, in virtue of his imperial authority, to renounce those of their tenets which were irreconcilable with the fundamental dogmas of the Christian faith, or the reunion must not take place. The Emperor complied with Contarini's demand in that on 18 May he earnestly exhorted the Protestant leaders, that is the Grand Duke of Hesse, the Saxon councillors and Joachim II of Brandenburg, to make their submission,[3] but he refused to put an end to the conference which was kept going by Gropper and Pflug, Melanchthon and Bucer up to 22 May. They examined the remaining controversial points [4] and finally submitted the Book of Ratisbon with the

[1] For the discussions of 6-13 May, cf. Contarini's reports of 9, 11, 13 May, H.J., I (1880), pp. 376-87, the memorial in Dittrich, Regesten, p. 325 f., and the juxtaposition of the two opposite principles in Corp. Ref., VOL. IV, pp. 261 ff.

[2] Contarini's report of 15 May, H.J., I (1880), pp. 387-90.

[3] Contarini's report of 23 May, Dittrich, Regesten, pp. 326 ff. Text of the Emperor's exhortation in Corp. Ref., VOL. IV, pp. 293-8 (No. 2232).

[4] The chief points discussed were the Canon of the Mass, its sacrificial character and the invocation of the Holy Ghost, private Masses and Communion in both kinds. With regard to the primacy the Protestants made no difficulties at first, H.J., I (1880), p. 327, perhaps because the Catholics had not insisted on their recognising the primacy of jurisdiction, but even Zwingli's son-in-law Walthart, in his letter to Bullinger, Zeitschrift für schweizerische Kirchengeschichte, XXVIII (1934), pp. 98 ff., does not include the primacy among the points in dispute. Only at the conclusion did Contarini add to the Book of Ratisbon the formula of the primacy prescribed by the Pope.

glosses of both parties. On 31 May the Protestants submitted yet another document in which they summed up their attitude to the controversial points on which no agreement had been reached.[1] It was now for the Emperor to draw his own conclusions from the rupture.

As we survey the scene in retrospect we must conclude that the breakdown of the Ratisbon reunion was not due to the Curia's rejection of the formula of justification there agreed upon; the doctrine of the Eucharist and Penance had wrecked it long before the arrival on 8 June of Rome's unfavourable decision.[2]

On 28 May Granvella had a conversation with Morone about the immediate future [3]: "Was the war for which the firebrands were agitating really unavoidable? The imperial statesmen shrank from such a venture. Or should they be content with a partial accord and tolerate the articles not yet agreed upon until the Council met?" Toleration of this kind, partly religious and partly political, presented a very different aspect from the religious Pacification of Nuremberg—it was a step towards a legal if qualified recognition of the new teaching against which the Curia protested at once with the utmost energy. It proposed the immediate convocation of a General Council. The day of the above conversation between Granvella and Morone was the birthday of the Council of Trent.

On 15 June Contarini was instructed to make the following communication to the Emperor [4]: "The Pope", it said, "was firmly resolved to terminate the suspension of the Council and to convene that assembly at once." The first draft of the communication had actually mentioned the month of September. "The negotiations for reunion had only been tolerated out of regard for the person of the Emperor. Now that they had broken down no other remedy was left except a Council. Forcible means could hardly be thought of—they were far

---

[1] Le Plat, VOL. III, pp. 44-57; *Corp. Ref.*, VOL. IV, pp. 348-76 (No. 2254); these are the nine "articoli bestiali" of which Girolamo Negri speaks on 28 June, Dittrich, *Regesten*, No. 788. Distinct from these is the memorial of the Estates on the *Book of Ratisbon*, Le Plat, VOL. III, pp. 58-66; *Corp. Ref.*, VOL. IV, pp. 476-505 (Nos. 2300-02), comments on which were asked for from Melanchthon, Cruciger, Pistoris and Amsdorf, *Corp. Ref.*, VOL. IV, pp. 413 ff.

[2] Contarini's report of 9 June, *H.J.*, I (1880), pp. 478-81.

[3] *H.J.*, IV (1883), pp. 469-72; additional matter in Morone's report, Laemmer, *Mon. Vat.*, p. 372 f.

[4] Full text in Quirini, *Epp. Poli*, VOL. III, pp. ccxl-ccxlix; Laemmer, *Mon. Vat.*, pp. 376-82, but faulty; a better text for the part referring to the Council is in *C.T.*, VOL. IV, p. 195 f.; Th. Brieger has published Cervini's drafts in *Z.K.G.*, V (1882), pp. 595-604; Latin translation in Raynald, *Annales*, a. 1541, Nos. 20-4; cf. also Le Plat, VOL. III, pp. 118-23.

too risky." The proposed toleration was condemned in the sharpest terms; it was described as *illecitissima e dannosa.*

The legate executed his commission on 24 June.[1] The Emperor suggested they should wait until the Estates should demand a Council. Contarini insisted that the Pope's decision was irrevocable; to bring in the Estates would only lead to further complications. The impression that the Emperor was bent on putting off the Council was further strengthened when King Ferdinand, who arrived at Ratisbon on 21 June, as well as Granvella, took up the old refrain about the probability of the Lutherans, the French and the English holding aloof.[2] These fears turned out to be groundless. In the written answer which Granvella handed to the legate sometime before 27 June the Emperor left the solution of all the problems connected with the Council to the Pope.[3] The plan for an agreement was thus effectively buried and the struggle for a Council opened anew. The next chapter will describe its progress, but first we must cast a glance at the upshot of the Diet and its deeper causes.

We pass over the wearisome dispute about the acceptance of those points of the *Book of Ratisbon* which had been previously agreed upon, a dispute that lasted throughout the months of June and July. The moderates among the Electors—Brandenburg, the Palatinate and Cologne—favoured acceptance, but they were opposed by Schmalkalden, the Catholic action party of Bavaria and by Mainz and Trier. Actually neither party wanted to be bound by the agreement. When asked for his opinion by the Emperor, Contarini declared on 10 July, and even more clearly in writing on 19 July, that approval of the articles—even the agreed ones—must be left to the Pope and to the Council.[4] A declaration of this kind was needed in order to forestall the use of the *Book of Ratisbon* for propaganda purposes,[5] for a rumour had circulated even while the *colloquium* was still in progress that the Catholics had accepted the Protestant doctrine of salvation. On 7 July,

---

[1] Contarini's report of 24 June, *Z.K.G.*, III (1879), pp. 176-9.

[2] Morone's report of 27 June, *H.J.*, IV (1883), pp. 624-7.

[3] Contarini's report of 27 June, *H.J.*, I (1880), p. 487 f. On 29 June Contarini wrote to the French nuncio that the Emperor had accepted the Council "molto volontieri", Morandi, *Monumenti*, VOL. I, PT ii, p. 180.

[4] Both declarations, undated, in Morandi, *Monumenti*, VOL. I, PT ii, pp. 191-4; Le Plat, VOL. III, pp. 91, 95; *Corp. Ref.*, VOL. IV, pp. 506, 555. The first declaration was presented to the Estates on the 12th; for the second see the report of 19 July, *Z.K.G.*, III (1879), p. 180 f., with Pastor's additions, *H.J.*, I (1880), p. 497; detailed account in Dittrich, *Contarini*, pp. 700-77.

[5] "Per non dare occasione alli adversarii di interpretar le cose etiam ben dette in mal senso", says Contarini, 5 July. *H.J.*, I (1880), p. 489.

at the Emperor's request, the legate earnestly admonished the German bishops to avoid giving scandal themselves or to suffer scandal to be given by their entourage, to see to the proper discharge of the pastoral ministry in their dioceses, as became true shepherds, and to make provision for the preaching of the word of God and the instruction of youth.[1] Never before in the whole history of the German reformation had the whole episcopal body appeared before a papal legate. They took the admonition in good part though it was something of a humiliation for them; they even besought Contarini to exert himself for the immediate convocation of a Council, otherwise all Germany would turn Lutheran within a very short time. Yet almost in the same breath they mentioned the German *gravamina* and the decree *Frequens*. This shows that notions dating from the era of the Councils and which had been so injurious to the Catholic cause at the time of the Bull *Exsurge* were still at work in their minds.[2] Contarini's exhortation breathed the spirit of the Catholic reform. The Emperor communicated its text to the secular Estates without Contarini's knowledge. This could only weaken its effect. Relations between the Emperor and the legate, so cordial at first, were further troubled during the last days of the Diet by the circumstance that the draft of the Recess of the Diet[3] did not unconditionally leave the whole of the religious question to the forthcoming Council. To do so would only have been in keeping with the Emperor's reply to the papal instructions of 15 June, but instead of this the document even considered the possibility of a national council. In spite of previous assurances the draft had not been submitted to the legate, but Contarini nevertheless managed to ascertain its tenor. He accordingly warned the Estates through the Archbishop of Mainz, in the latter's capacity of Arch-Chancellor of the Empire, that no national council would be empowered to issue binding decisions in matters that were the concern of the universal Church.[4] He nevertheless failed to obtain

---

[1] Text in Morandi, *Monumenti*, VOL. I, PT ii, pp. 197 ff.; Le Plat, VOL. III, pp. 91 ff., and Contarini's above-mentioned report of 10 July. Granvella's complaint that up to this time Contarini had done nothing for reform (thus Morone on 21 June, *H.J.*, IV (1883), p. 622) needs no refutation—what opportunity was there during the colloquy? The reform tract presented by the Protestants (Le Plat, VOL. III, pp. 67-89; *Corp. Ref.*, VOL. IV, pp. 541 ff., No. 2317) will be discussed further on in a different context.

[2] *C.T.*, VOL. IV, pp. 197-200.

[3] *Ibid.*, p. 200 f., with Contarini's report of 26 June, *Z.K.G.*, III (1879), p. 183 f.

[4] Le Plat, VOL. III, p. 101 f. In their reply of 26 July (Le Plat, *ibid.*, p. 102; better text in *C.T.*, VOL. IV, p. 202 f.) the Protestant Estates point out with unconcealed irony that the simplest way to avoid a national council was to hold a general one; if this were convened there would be no question of the former.

any alteration in the text, in fact the final formula of the Recess of 29 July [1] was even more objectionable for there was question in it of the Council being held in Germany within the next eighteen months. By way of excusing this reversal of policy the Emperor told Contarini that a wise man must adapt his plans to circumstances.

In order to secure the help of the Protestants for the war against the Turks the Emperor took even a more disquieting step. In a secret "Declaration" [2] he permitted them, until a final settlement should be reached, to act on the interpretation which their own divines would put on the agreed articles. He also guaranteed to them the possession of secularised Church property and authorised them to admit into their communities adherents to the new teaching from territories other than their own. This secret "Declaration" implied a certain measure of toleration of Lutheranism even though its legal nature was not easy to define. By this means Charles V bought a momentary advantage, namely the help of Schmalkalden against the Turks, who had recently occupied Buda.

The issue of the great Diet of Ratisbon proved a disappointment for all parties. The Emperor was cheated of his hope of a religiously united Empire behind him in the approaching conflict with France. For such a misfortune his alliance with Brandenburg and Hesse were no adequate compensation. Most disturbing of all was the fact that the Catholic action party, above all Bavaria, had allied itself with the enemy of the morrow. This meant a shifting of fronts. If, as was to be expected, the Pope favoured the champions of the Catholic cause, the Emperor would accuse him of supporting the policy of France, while he himself viewed the Catholic federation, which the Curia did its best to strengthen, with a distrust that he did not seek to disguise.

The issue was even more painful for Contarini. When he left Ratisbon on 29 July at the same time as the Emperor, to return to Italy, he was aware that he was being decried as a Lutheran because he had worked for an accord. Like the great Christian that he was he accepted this fresh trial as part of his daily cross.[3] Contarini may not have been a constructive genius, but he was both a great Christian and

---

[1] The part of the Recess dealing with religion in *Corp. Ref.*, VOL. IV, pp. 625-30 (No. 2353), with Contarini's report of 27 July, *H.J.*, I (1880), p. 498 f.

[2] Latin text in Döllinger, *Beiträge*, VOL. I, pp. 36 ff.; German text in *Corp. Ref.*, VOL. IV, pp. 623 ff. (No. 2352).

[3] "Hora comincio ad essere buon Christiano patiendo nelle fatiche et pericoli", Contarini wrote on 22 July to Cervini, Morandi, *Monumenti*, VOL. I, PT ii, p. 185; *Z.K.G.*, III (1879), pp. 516 ff.

a great politician. We must admit that he sacrificed himself unselfishly for the Church and warded off from the Papacy the accusation that it did not desire the religious reunion of Germany, if it did not actually prevent it.[1] To accuse him of remissness where the interests of the Church and the Papacy were at stake was a gross injustice. The source of the calumny is known: it was a French intrigue instigated by Bavaria for the purpose of preventing reunion.[2] His unshakable firmness in upholding the concept of transubstantiation and the earnestness with which time and again he represented to the Emperor that this was not a question of words or of theological opinions but an essential dogma of the faith [3] make it abundantly clear that there can be no question of the Cardinal's Catholic attitude. In his mouth the protestation that he was prepared to sacrifice life itself for the preservation of the faith was no mere phrase. No professional diplomatist could have forwarded the Pope's true interests with greater skill or handled men—whether Emperor or statesmen, princes or theologians—with a shrewder regard for their individuality than he, seeing that he succeeded in taming even so difficult and pretentious an individual as Johann Eck.[4] As for the Protestants, they felt that here they dealt with a man who sought their souls, not their goods or some political advantage; they accordingly paid unstinted homage to his disinterestedness as well as to his theological acumen. Their protest against the above-mentioned declarations of 10 and 19 July,[5] after the failure of the *colloquium*, was not aimed at his person but against the cause for which he stood. They bore more readily with him than with that exasperating critic, Johann Eck.[6]

At Ratisbon Contarini attempted the impossible. History is wont to cast its blame on the men who misjudge hard realities or seek to prevent the inevitable. No such blame attaches to Contarini. Before the seamless coat of Christ, that is, the unity of the Western Church,

---

[1] Contarini himself thus conceived his mission, cf. letter to his brother-in-law, Matteo Dandolo, Venetian envoy to France, Morandi, *Monumenti*, VOL. I, PT ii, p. 200 ff.; *Z.K.G.*, III (1879), pp. 519 ff.
[2] Ercole Gonzaga to Contarini, 17 May 1541; Quirini, *Epp. Poli*, VOL. III, p. cclxxviii; Dittrich, *Regesten*, No. 720; Contarini to Capodiferro, 12 June, Morandi, *Monumenti*, VOL. I, PT ii, p. 177 f. and the report to Farnese of the same day, Dittrich, *Regesten*, p. 338 f. Contarini refutes with magnificent irony the accusation that he was "freddo", *H.J.*, I (1880), p. 480.
[3] *H.J.*, I (1880), p. 388 f.; cf. Dittrich, *Regesten*, p. 325 f.
[4] Morone on 24 April, *H.J.*, IV (1883), p. 449. Francesco Contarini informs the Signoria that the legate had given away benefices to the value of 1500 florins without demanding a penny in fees, Dittrich, *Regesten*, No. 718.
[5] Le Plat, VOL. III, pp. 103-7.
[6] Eck to Contarini, 20 January 1542, *Z.K.G.*, XIX (1899), p. 479.

was finally rent it was necessary to essay the impossible. Only the failure of the Ratisbon attempt at reunion could justify the drawing of the Tridentine line of demarcation.

Each party blamed the other for the unhappy issue.[1] In point of fact no single individual was responsible for a rupture that was due to an impersonal factor, viz. the irreconcilable opposition of contradictory doctrines. To have established this fact by dint of prolonged and arduous effort is the merit of pre-Tridentine controversial theology.[2]

On 30 August 1519 [3] the University of Cologne had condemned a whole series of errors propounded by Luther in the course of the controversy over indulgences. On 7 November of the same year Louvain acted in like manner.[4] The Bull *Exsurge* included in its forty-one propositions the result of the disputation of Leipzig, viz. the new concept of the Church. However, this pronouncement on Luther by the highest teaching authority—the only one right up to the Council of Trent—did not provide a complete survey of the doctrinal divergences. As a matter of fact this was impossible, for it was only after the publication of the Bull that Luther cast his conception of the sacraments, the sacrifice of the Mass, the priesthood, the Church and the Papacy into

[1] The controversial pamphlets exchanged between Melanchthon and Bucer on one side and Eck and Pighius on the other are catalogued by Schottenloher, Nos. 41376 ff.; Jedin, *Studien über die Schriftstellertätigkeit Albert Pigges*, pp. 43-6; W. Friedensburg in *A.R.G.*, XXXI (1934), pp. 145-91.

[2] I am of course well aware that what follows is no more than a first attempt to pose, rather than solve, the historical-dogmatic problem of pre-Tridentine controversial theology. It only carries the ideas expressed in my article "Die geschichtliche Bedeutung der katholischen Kontroverstheologie im Zeitalter der Glaubensspaltung", in *H.J.*, LIII (1933), pp. 70-97, a step further. Since the first survey of this field by H. Laemmer, *Die vortridentinisch-katholische Theologie des Reformationsalters* (Berlin 1858), a number of monographs on controversial theologians have been written by Nicholas Paulus, Joseph Greving and their collaborators and pupils, and not a few critical editions of controversial writings have been published in *Corp. Cath.* Moreover, increasing attention has been paid to controversial theology in historical-dogmatic works on the Council of Trent. But the central problem, the formation of the *Corpus Controversiarum* which was submitted to the Council, has scarcely been appreciated up to the present, hence much less solved. The most comprehensive modern work, P. Polman's *Elément historique dans la controverse religieuse du XVIème siècle* (Gembloux 1932), starts from a different angle of the problem; cf. my observations on it in *Theologische Revue*, XXXII (1933), pp. 305-11. The relevant section in Lortz, *Reformation*, VOL. II, pp. 154-98, is stimulating.

[3] Le Plat, VOL. II, pp. 45 ff.; P. Fredericq, *Corpus Inquisitionis Neerlandicae*, VOL. IV (Ghent 1900), p. 12; on the influence of the Dominicans, cf. P. Kalkoff in *Z.K.G.*, XXXII (1911), p. 30 f.

[4] Le Plat, VOL. II, pp. 47-50; Fredericq, *Corp. Inquis. Neerl.*, VOL. IV, pp. 14-16. On the "errores" forwarded to Cardinal Adrian in Spain, cf. P. Kalkoff, *Forschungen zu Luthers römischen Prozess* (Rome 1903), pp. 194-203.

a final mould. In February 1521 Glapion, the Emperor's confessor, extracted a list of thirty-two propositions from Luther's *De captivitate babylonica*.[1] In its censure of 15 April of the same year the University of Paris drew a substantially clearer picture of the heresiarch's teaching on the sacraments and the vows of religion, on the basis of his later writings.[2] Characteristically enough the theological faculty was silent on Luther's errors on the subject of the papal primacy; it took more than a decade before it filled up this lacuna. This it did in its censure of Melanchthon's twelve articles on reunion (1535) in which it declared that the Church's hierarchy and the Pope's authority exist by right divine.[3]

The condemnation by ecclesiastical authority of isolated erroneous propositions could not convey an adequate notion of the depth and extent of the doctrinal divergence: to do this was the task of technical theology. For the purpose of defending Catholic dogma it was imperative that theologians should make a systematic study of the new ideas and subject them to a minute analysis. This necessity gave birth to controversial theology. It was left to this new branch of the sacred science to fix with ever growing accuracy the boundaries beyond which lay Protestantism. This led to the systematisation of the disputed articles.

The new theology had to overcome two difficulties, one of which arose from its own nature. For some four hundred years technical theology had been synonymous with scholasticism, that is, the use in the study of dogma of the dialectical method evolved in the twelfth century. Now the turn of the fifteenth century witnessed the rise by its side, or rather in conflict with it, of positive theology based on the study of the Scriptures, the Fathers and the Councils in the original texts. The old was still in conflict with the new, for no satisfactory compromise had been reached at the moment when the innovators began to point new weapons at traditional scholasticism as well as at the ancient Church. While still in process of transformation theology saw itself compelled to defend not only its own existence and its methods but likewise the faith of which it had the guardianship. This accounts for the hesitation as to whether, and to what extent, one might tactically meet the opponents in the method of argumentation as well

---

[1] C. E. Förstemann, *Neues Urkundenbuch* (Hamburg 1842), pp. 34-41.

[2] Le Plat, VOL. II, pp. 98-114; Duplessis d'Argentré, *Coll. iud.*, VOL. I, ii, pp. 365-74.

[3] Duplessis d'Argentré, *Coll. iud.*, VOL. I, ii, pp. 397-400; cf. Feret, *La Faculté théologique*, VOL. II, pp. 152-63. Original sin, the seven sacraments and the principle of the Scriptures are missing.

as for the contrast between the "modern" and the "conservative" theologians which give to the Catholic defence a certain air of incoherence.[1]

The second difficulty was due to a widespread delusion about the relationship between the new errors and those of an earlier period. To regard Luther's teaching as no more than a rehash of all the old heresies was to block the approach to an understanding of their peculiarity and true nature. The fact that this or that particular proposition of Luther's had already been condemned by some earlier Council led all too easily to the conclusion that there was nothing new in what he taught; no need, therefore, of a searching examination of the logic of his ideas; all that was required was to put them by in the familiar pigeon-holes prepared for the purpose by such men as Epiphanius of Salamis and his successors! It was the task of controversial theology to correct these widely held notions [2] before it could enter upon its own characteristic task and so enable it to submit to a Council a full and accurate picture of the doctrinal divergence.

Pre-Tridentine controversial theology has long been looked at askance on account of its ill success in the field of propaganda. Up to 1525 the rising tide of Lutheranism owed much to the printing press. In fact, here we have the first instance of the use of the press for the purpose of directing public opinion and a consequent decisive influence on the course of history. The Catholic defence should have made use of this tool to the same extent in order to draw away from Luther the masses that flocked to him. This it failed to do. The one really popular writer in the Catholic camp, the Alsatian Franciscan Thomas Murner,[3] was unable to stem the flood-tide of hostile propaganda. Was his failure due to the lack of a genuinely popular style, or to the absence

[1] P. Polman, "La Méthode polémique des premiers adversaires de la réforme", in *R.H.E.*, xxv (1929), pp. 471-506.

[2] Under Clement VII in particular this notion was repeatedly advanced against the convocation of a Council, *C.T.*, VOL. IV, pp. xli, lii; Lorenzo Campeggio in Laemmer, *Mon. Vat.*, p. 64; the papal representatives at the negotiations of Bologna, Sanudo, *Diarii*, VOL. LVII, p. 499 f. Even Paul III himself was not wholly free from it, as is shown by his remark to Cifuentes, *N.B.*, VOL. I, PT i, p. 515.

[3] The publication of Murner's biography by Th. von Liebenau, *Der Franziskaner Dr Thomas Murner* (Freiburg 1913), makes a fresh synthesis desirable, for our knowledge of his literary work has been greatly increased, especially through the critical edition of his German writings (Strasbourg-Berlin 1918 ff.), the revision of the controversial section of which was entrusted to W. Pfeiffer-Belli and P. Merker, as well as the editions by J. Lefftz in *Archiv für elsässische Kirchengeschichte*, I (1926), pp. 141 ff.; III (1928), pp. 97 ff., summed up by W. Pfeiffer-Belli in his "Thomas Murner im Schweizer Glaubenskampf", *Corp. Cath.*, VOL. XXII (Münster 1939). Bibliography in Schottenloher, Nos. 16024-133.

of an appropriate organisation?[1] The experience of our own days discountenances the supposition: there are mass movements which are apparently irresistible.

It is doubtful whether a Görres, if such a man had been found among the sixteenth-century publicists, would have succeeded in arresting the Lutheran movement, hence we should not demand the impossible from controversial theology—it worked for the benefit of a later age. Although on the defensive and at first only a reaction, it prepared the way for and made a positive contribution to the dogmatic definitions of the Council of Trent. This preliminary work has not been adequately appreciated.

Before recounting the story of its achievement—the system of controversial articles—let us cast a glance at the men who contributed to it. It takes time before the eye is as it were able to distinguish the leading personalities in the confused hand-to-hand fighting of the first period. After the death in 1527 of Jerome Emser, court chaplain to Duke George of Saxony, the scene was dominated until 1550 by four men whom Johann von Kampen sarcastically described as Aleander's four evangelists[2] and for whom he nursed a particular hatred. They were Johann Eck, Johann Cochlaeus, Johann Fabri and Frederick Nausea.

Eck (d. 1543), the first of Luther's theological opponents,[3] was

[1] The suggestion of Jacob von Salza, Bishop of Breslau (1524), for the establishment of a Catholic centre of propaganda, perhaps at Leipzig, *Zeitschrift für Geschichte Schlesiens*, LXII (1928), p. 93, was not acted upon. In like manner the conversations in 1530 between Joachim I of Brandenburg, the Bishop of Lebus, Tommaso Campeggio, Wimpina and the Dominican Horst von Romberg, with a view to the systematic publication of Catholic books, led to no practical result, J. Greven, *Die Kölner Kartause und die Anfänge der katholischen Reform in Deutschland* (Münster 1935), p. 71 f. Aleander's proposal (1532) that the Apostolic Camera should contribute 500 scudi annually (thus according to Vat. Arch., Germania, 51, fol. 169ʳ, not 100 as Laemmer says in *Mon. Vat.*, p. 119) for the benefit of Catholic controversial theologians, was also made in vain. Cochlaeus's efforts to develop Wolrab's printing press at Cologne by means of private resources was doomed to failure, as were his attempts to counter the Lutheran propaganda in England, Scotland and Poland, *Z.K.G.*, XVIII (1897), pp. 245 f., 250, 283.
[2] *Z.K.G.*, XLIII (1924), p. 217, of the year 1536. In 1532 Aleander himself mentioned, in addition to these four, Ludwig Ber, a theologian of Freiburg, Laemmer, *Mon. Vat.*, p. 119. Cardinal Cles (1533) and Morone (1538) speak in the same terms of the above-mentioned four, *N.B.*, VOL. I, PT i, pp. 84, 88 f.; *A.R.G.*, I (1903), p. 378.
[3] The biography by Th. Wiedemann, *Dr Johann Eck*, is out of date (Ratisbon 1865). J. Greving had planned a new one, but died without having carried out his design. The list of his writings by J. Metzler in *Corp. Cath.*, VOL. XVI, pp. lxxi-cxxii; reprints of some of Eck's works in *Corp. Cath.*, VOLS. I, II, VI, XIII, XIV, and in W. Gussmann, *Quellen und Forsch.*, VOL. II (Kassel 1930). Further literature in Schottenloher, Nos. 5184-244. There is an excellent character-sketch of Eck by Morone in *H.J.*, IV (1883), p. 449. The details on his parochial activities are based on J.

passionately fond of controversy. He was well-read, sagacious, un-
beaten in dispute, endowed with an impeccable memory, but coarse,
sensual, a deep drinker, a witty conversationalist, sure of himself to the
extent of arrogance and an enemy of compromise. Through his
Enchiridion and his four volumes of sermons he achieved far more than
as a lecturer at Ingolstadt. However, our portrait of the man would be
incomplete did we not add that notwithstanding his many interests he
discharged his duties as parish priest of the church of Our Lady of
Ingolstadt zealously and conscientiously. Within a period of six years he
preached no less than four hundred and fifty-six sermons; he had at heart
the beauty and dignity of the liturgical services and nothing was too small
for him to attend to. The question has been asked, what might not such
a man have done for the Catholic cause had he occupied a bishop's chair?
But this raises another query, namely whether this theological gladiator
did not frequently deal more blows than was either useful or necessary?

Cochlaeus (d. 1552)[1] was a born schoolmaster, but the needs of the
Church drove him to journalism in which his output was unsurpassed
by any other publicist. His acquaintance with scholastic theology was
modest enough, but he was well read in humanistic literature. This
enabled him to quote many an ancient text with which to confute
Luther. His commentaries on the heresiarch's writings—the fruit of
his literary campaigning—influenced Catholic thought on Luther for
centuries. No one worked harder for the creation of a Catholic press;
no one surpassed this emotional Franconian's spirit of self-sacrifice and
selfless loyalty to the Catholic cause.

In contrast with the pretentious Eck the Swabian Fabri (d. 1541)[2]

Greving, *Johann Ecks Pfarrbuch für U. L. Frau in Ingolstadt* (Münster 1908). For
his significance for the Council of Trent, cf. H. Schauerte in *Theologie und Glaube*,
XIX (1918), pp. 133-8.
[1] Authoritative biography and list of writings by M. Spahn (Berlin 1898); for his
beginnings H. Jedin, *Des Johannes Cochlaeus Streitschrift "De libero arbitrio hominis"*
(Breslau 1927). A critical study of the Luther biography by A. Herte, *Die Luther-
kommentare des Johannes Cochlaeus* (Münster 1935); the same, *Das katholische
Lutherbild im Banne der Lutherkommentare des Cochlaeus*, 3 parts (Münster 1943).
Reprints of Cochlaeus's works in *Corp. Cath.*, VOLS. III, XV, XVII, XVIII, and *C.T.*,
VOL. XII, pp. 166-208. The letters published since Spahn wrote are grouped in
R.Q., XXXV (1927), p. 447. Two more have been published by H. Hoffmann in
Archiv für schlesische Kirchengeschichte, V (1940), pp. 217 ff. Further literature in
Schottenloher, Nos. 2986-3033.
[2] Jakob Ziegler's account of 16 February 1522 in Erasmus, *Epist.*, VOL. V,
p. 20 f. The most recent biography with list of writings is that by L. Helbling, *Dr
Johann Fabri* (Münster 1941). The "Malleus" edited by A. Naegele is in *Corp. Cath.*,
VOLS. XXIII and XXIV (Münster 1941). Outwardly, according to Scheurl (*Briefbuch*,
VOL. II, p. 234), Fabri had "nescio quid fabrile magis quam ingenii acumen; vestis
aliquantulum lacera ne dicam uncta", cf. Schottenloher, Nos. 5950-63.

impressed everyone he came in contact with during his stay in Rome by his discretion and reserve. Unlike Eck he was not on fire with hatred for Luther, and though he lacked the former's business ability his progress was all the more assured. As Vicar General of the extensive diocese of Constance he was Zwingli's most distinguished opponent. In 1530 he was raised to the See of Vienna. His influence as ecclesiastical-political adviser to King Ferdinand as well as to the Curia was greater than anyone else's. His writings are packed with erudition, but they cannot compare with those of Cochlaeus as regards quantity or with those of Eck in respect of their value.

Nausea (d. 1551),[1] a Franconian by birth and a good deal younger than the other three just mentioned, stands on the line of demarcation between pure controversial theology and Catholic reform. It is not just chance that he should have died at the Council of Trent. He is a preacher rather than a theologian, a humanist rather than a scholastic. He passes without harsh transition from a sharp polemical tone to a calm and even conciliatory examination of the opinions of his opponents. He entered the lists at a later period and was accordingly less handicapped than the others. As Fabri's successor in the See of Vienna he inherited his predecessor's ecclesiastical-political influence. He used it in order to convince the Roman authorities of the necessity of a thorough reform. By reason of his catechism he is one of the forerunners of St Peter Canisius.

The influence of these four men on the course of events was due to the fact that they worked in close association with the Curia and its representatives in Germany. As one peruses their numerous letters to Aleander, Campeggio, Cervini and Morone,[2] it is difficult to resist an impression that their writings, memorials and other suggestions were as a rule accepted with thanks but rarely acted upon. The Curia did

---

[1] Nausea still lacks a competent biography. That of J. Metzner, *Friedrich Nausea von Waischenfeld, Bischof von Wien* (Ratisbon 1884), is inadequate. There is copious material in Cardauns, *Bestrebungen*, pp. 39-52, 150-200. The great reform tract is in *C.T.*, VOL. XII, pp. 364-426; cf. Schottenloher, Nos. 16313-22.

[2] W. Friedensburg, "Beiträge zum Briefwechsel der katholischen Gelehrten Deutschlands im Reformationsalter", in *Z.K.G.*, XVI (1896), pp. 470-99—twelve instalments in *Z.K.G.*, the last in XXIII (1902), pp. 438-77. These 280 letters addressed to Eck, Cochlaeus, Fabri, Nausea, Ludwig Ber, Otto Brunfels, Wolfgang Capito, Albert Pighuis, Robert Wauchope are by far the most important publication on the joint activity of the controversial theologians and the Curia. Morone's list of 1536, *N.B.*, VOL. I, PT ii, p. 68, includes, besides the four, the Dominicans Köllin, Dietenberger, Bernhard von Lützelburg, the Franciscan Herborn, the Ingolstadt professor Leonhard Marstaller and the two converts Haner and Witzel. The list forwarded to Rome by Campeggio in 1540 also includes the names of Mensing, Pelargus, Helding, Kugele of Freiburg, Pighius and Hoetfilter. *N.B.*, VOL. I, PT VI, pp. 293-6.

very little to further their work or to improve their material situation.[1] The powerful prince-bishops and the wealthy abbots of Germany did even less. The man who plied his pen in the defence of the ancient Church was usually left to fend for himself as best he could.

The part played by the German theological faculties in the defence of orthodoxy is a modest one, though it would be unfair to say that the university divines proved a complete disappointment. Eck was a professor of theology and the faculty of Cologne was first in the field against Luther, while that of Tübingen sent as many as four of its members to the disputation of Baden.[2] In 1528 Conrad Wimpina, of the University of Frankfurt on the Oder, published a mighty folio entitled *Anacephalaeosis*,[3] the greater part of which is aimed at Luther. A perusal of the work shows quite clearly that Thomistic theology greatly facilitated the refutation of the new teaching. Recent research has once more demonstrated the fact that a study of the writings of controversial theologians of the nominalistic school may greatly contribute towards a better understanding of Luther.[4]

All the above-mentioned men were secular priests, but lay theologians were not wanting. Among the latter we must count Henry VIII by reason of his book on the Seven Sacraments, Duke George of Saxony who wrote in defence of the doctrine of the Eucharist,[5] Count Alberto Pio of Carpi, and Contarini. However, the great mass of

[1] Although a bishop, Fabri was so poor that his opponents pointed their fingers at him and mockingly asked: "Ubi est Deus eorum?" Vergerio, 13 March 1533, *N.B.*, VOL. I, PT i, p. 95. Four years later Morone established the fact that the majority of the controversial theologians were "veramente poveri" (*N.B.*, VOL. I, PT ii, p. 84) and obtained some material aid for them (*ibid.*, pp. 196, 209), but on 12 March 1540 Eck nevertheless wrote to Contarini (*Z.K.G.*, XIX (1899), p. 254): "Under Leo X a certain factotum (*scopetarius*) in Rome boasted that he held 39 benefices and a provostship. I have been a professor of theology for 39 years and of philosophy for 10, but I have never succeeded in obtaining even the most modest of provostships." Yet though he could not afford a secretary Eck was better off than Nausea, who had to face a four years' lawsuit with an Apostolic scriptor for the only benefice he enjoyed, *Z.K.G.*, XX (1900), p. 513, though his income from it was so slender that often enough, when on a journey, he literally starved (*ibid.*, p. 539).

[2] J. Haller, *Die Anfänge der Universität Tübingen*, VOL. I (Stuttgart 1927), p. 319. For Jakob Lemp, "the dear old sophist" whom the pamphlet *Die Lutherische Strebkatz* (Schade, *Satiren*, VOL. III, p. 124) names in the same breath as Emser, Eck, Fabri and others, see Haller, *Anfänge*, VOL. I, p. 195 f.; VOL. II, p. 71.* Other accusations against Lemp are in the *Schöner Dialogus*; Schade, *Satiren*, VOL. II, p. 119 f.

[3] Biography by J. Negwer, *Conrad Wimpina, ein katholischer Theologe aus der Reformationszeit*, 1460-1531 (Breslau 1909), with list of writings (62 items).

[4] O. Müller, *Die Rechtfertigungslehre nominalistischer Reformationsgegner* (Breslau 1940).

[5] H. Becker, "Herzog Georg von Sachsen als kirchlicher und theologischer Schriftsteller", in *A.R.G.*, XXIV (1927), pp. 161-269.

controversial theologians were members of the religious Orders, chiefly the mendicants—the Dominicans being in the front rank [1] in the persons of the Cologne professors Jacob Hochstraten and Conrad Köllin, the excellent and at the same time popular Johann Dietenberger of Frankfurt and the Hessian Ambrose Pelargus whom we shall meet again at the Council of Trent. Johann Faber of Augsburg, of whom we have already spoken, and men like Johann Mensing and Michael Vehe who took part in the religious "colloquies" prove that the Order of Friars Preachers was not by any means the citadel of intransigence of the popular imagination. The Franciscans produced one of the very first opponents of Luther in the person of Augustine Alveld and one of the most understanding in that of Caspar Schatzgeyer, a man of wide information and calm judgment.[2] Nicholas Herborn was also of more than local significance.[3] Prominent among the Hermits of St Augustine were Luther's former teacher Bartholomew Usingen and the Provincial Johannes Hoffmeister.[4] Outstanding personalities among the Carmelites were the two Provincials Eberhard Billick and Andreas Stoss.[5] Most of these men took up their pens on some local occasion, in defence of the Catholic cause against measures taken by heretical authorities or to ward off the attacks of the preachers, but by doing so they helped to clarify the whole theological situation.

From the standpoint of intrinsic value the Louvain group is unsurpassed. It included men like Jacob Latomus, an opponent of Luther

[1] Besides N. Paulus, *Dominikaner*, cf. H. Wilms, *Der Kölner Universitätsprofessor Konrad Köllin* (Cologne-Leipzig 1941).

[2] Biography of Alveld by L. Lemmens, *Pater Augustinus von Alfeld* (Freiburg 1899); G. Hesse in *Franziskanische Studien*, XVII (1930), pp. 160-78; two tracts in *Corp. Cath.*, VOL. XI (Münster 1926). Biography of Schatzgeyer by N. Paulus, *Konrad Schatzgeyer* (Freiburg 1899); his *Scrutinium*, edited by U. Schmidt in *Corp. Cath.*, VOL. V (Münster 1929); for an appreciation of his theological teaching, see O. Müller, *Die Rechtfertigungslehre nominalistischer Reformationsgegner*, pp. 74-161, and V. Heynck in *Franziskanische Studien*, XXVII (1941), pp. 129-51.

[3] L. Schmitt, *Der Kölner Theologe N. Stagefyr und der Franziskaner N. Herborn* (Freiburg 1899); *Confutatio Lutheranismi Danici*, ed. L. Schmitt (Quaracchi 1902); the *Loci communes*, newly published in *Corp. Cath.*, VOL. XII, will be discussed further on. For Konrad Kling, who worked at Erfurt, cf. H. Bücker in *Franziskanische Studien*, XVII (1930), pp. 273-97. The Franciscans' share in the work is summed up by H. Holzapfel, *Handbuch der Geschichte des Franziskanerordens* (Freiburg 1909), pp. 468-79.

[4] Biography of Usingen by N. Paulus, *Der Augustiner Bartholomäus Arnoldi von Usingen* (Freiburg 1893); also O. Müller, *Die Rechtfertigungslehre nominalistischer Reformationsgegner*, pp. 12-73; id., *Der Augustinermönch Johannes Hoffmeister* (Freiburg 1891).

[5] A. Postina, *Eberhard Billick* (Freiburg 1901); R. Schaffer, *Andreas Stoss, Sohn des Veit Stoss, und seine gegenreformatorische Tätigkeit* (Breslau 1926).

for whom the heresiarch himself had the greatest respect; John Driedo, noted both for his methodology and his teaching on grace, and lastly Ruard Tapper, who assisted at the Council of Trent in the capacity of dean of the university.[1] Albert Pighius (Pigge) was a graduate of Louvain but did not belong to the Louvain group. He made a name for himself by his book on the ecclesiastical hierarchy and by his teaching on grace.[2] However, as regards the influence they exerted all these writers were surpassed by the Martyr-Bishop John Fisher,[3] one of those rare controversialists who do not merely fight but persuade, because they look for the vein of gold even in an opponent. The bishop was deeply read in the Fathers. As early as 1523 he came to the conclusion that Luther was definitely lost to the Church. His books, the *Confutatio* of which we shall speak presently, and his defence of the Catholic doctrine of the Eucharist and a special priesthood were frequently quoted at Trent.

The imposing number of Italian controversial divines, whose life and work has been described by Lauchert,[4] was not uniformly matched by their intrinsic worth, but among them there is a star of the first magnitude, namely Thomas de Vio, better known as Cardinal Cajetan. Cajetan's bitter opponent, Ambrosius Catharinus of Siena, was one of the most prolific writers of the period. Cardinal Sadoleto was the perfect type of the peacemaker. France and Spain remained in the background during the pre-Tridentine period. The Fleming Jost Clichtove, who lived in Paris, is the author of a work entitled *Antilutherus*. He had but a small following in France,[5] where the

[1] H. de Jongh, *L'Ancienne Faculté de théologie de Louvain 1432-1560* (Louvain 1911), pp. 148-86; the older literature on Driedo in R. Draguet, "Le Maître louvaniste Driedo inspirateur du décret de Trente sur la Vulgate", in *Miscellanea historica, A. de Meyer*, VOL. II (Louvain 1946), pp. 836-57. H. Peeter, *Doctrina Johannis Driedonis a Turnhout de concordia gratiae et liberi arbitrii* (Malines 1938). F. Pijper, *Bibliotheca reformatoria Neerlandica*, VOL. III (The Hague 1905), two controversial works of Eustace of Sichem.

[2] H. Jedin, *Studien über die Schriftstellertätigkeit Albert Pigges* (Münster 1931).

[3] See BOOK II, Ch. vi, p. 303, *n.*3. The *Sacri sacerdotii defensio* ed. H. Klein-Schmeink in *Corp. Cath.*, VOL. IX (Münster 1925).

[4] F. Lauchert, *Literarische Gegner*, describes the life and writings of sixty-six theologians. See also J. Schweizer, *Ambrosius Catharinus Politus* (Münster 1910). M. J. Congar, *Bio-bibliographie de Cajétan* in the collection *Cajétan* (Paris 1935), pp. 3-49; the tract *De divina institutione pontificatus Romani pontificis*, ed. F. Lauchert, *Corp. Cath.*, VOL. X (Münster 1925). Th. Freudenberger, *Augustinus Steuchus und sein literarisches Lebenswerk* (Münster 1935).

[5] Biography by J. A. Clerval, *De J. Clichtovii Neoportuensis vita et operibus, 1472-1543* (Dissertation, Paris 1894). On the *Apologia* (1523) of the Dominican Lambertus Campester, cf. Jedin, *Des Johannes Cochlaeus Streitschrift*, p. 24 f.; the Sorbonnists Hieronymus Hangest and Robert Cenau also wrote against Luther and Bucer; Hurter,

theological defence only got under way at a later period when it became necessary to counter Calvinist propaganda. Alfonso de Castro's *Adversus haereses*, published some time before the Council, is an excellent product of Spanish theology whose greatest activity coincides with the actual progress of that assembly with such works as Domingo Soto's book on grace, Martin Perez's on tradition and Melchior Cano's *Loci theologici*. Only in the era of the Council of Trent did a regenerated scholasticism take a firm lead in Spanish controversial theology under the influence of Francisco de Vitoria.

In our account of the conciliar discussions we shall have occasion to describe what was done by the pre-Tridentines both for the refutation of Luther and for the establishment of the Catholic standpoint; for the moment we must be content with an examination of the process by which the system of the "controversial articles" as a whole came into being. As regards Luther, the system met with special difficulties because unlike Zwingli, and especially unlike Calvin, Luther never reduced his ideas to a system. Like all men of action he wrote under pressure of circumstances; even the *Assertio omnium articulorum*, which he published at the close of the year 1520 by way of a reply to the Bull *Exsurge*,[1] does not provide a complete presentation of his teaching, with the consequence that the Catholic refutations by Hochstraten, Cochlaeus and Wimpina often enough merely fasten on particular points. However, the most comprehensive of these works, namely John Fisher's *Confutatio*, actually served as a compendium of Lutheranism and as a manual for its refutation right up to the time of the Council of Trent, more particularly in Germany. On the other hand Melanchthon's *Loci communes*,[2] "the first dogmatic manual of Protestantism" published a year after the *Assertio*, received but little

Nomenclator, VOL. II, p. 1275; Feret, *La Faculté théologique*, VOL. II, pp. 42-51. The few Spanish writers who intervened in the controversy previous to the Council of Trent were moved to do so for the most part when they were out of Spain, for instance Alphonsus Ruiz Virvesius in Germany, Alphonsus de Herrera while in France, Hurter, *Nomenclator*, VOL. II, p. 1461.

[1] *L.W.*, VOL. VII, pp. 95-151. For the Catholic refutations, see Jedin, *Des Johannes Cochlaeus Streitschrift*, pp. 25 f., 32 ff. John Fisher's *Confutatio* in his *Opera* (Würzburg 1597), pp. 272-744.

[2] Besides the edition in *Corp. Ref.*, cf. Plitt-Th. Kolde, *Die loci communes Philipp Melanchthons in ihrer Urgestalt* (4th edn., Leipzig-Erlangen 1925). They were used, e.g. by Bart. Guidiccioni, in the draft for a new Bull against Luther, *C.T.*, VOL. XII, p. 234 f. (*ca.* 1538). It is most significant that the Italian translation published under a pseudonym could be sold in Italy—including Rome—for a whole year without interference; Tacchi Venturi, *Storia della Compagnia di Gesù in Italia*, (Rome 1910), VOL. I, i, p. 435.

attention and Cochlaeus's warning against the influence of the *Praeceptor Germaniae* fell on deaf ears. It was only in 1525 that Weissenhorn of Landshut published Eck's *Enchiridion*, a compendium of the Catholic controversial articles and a work free from polemics against any specific writing of Luther.[1] Inclusive of German, Flemish and French translations, the book appeared in ninety-one editions up to the year 1600. Its peculiarity consists in that it starts from the authority of the Church and the papal supremacy (articles 1-4) and treats rather briefly of justification (only the question of faith and works is touched upon) and the sacraments (5-11). It then proceeds to describe those doctrines and observances which most clearly marked the divergence between the Catholic Church and the Protestant communities then in process of formation, namely the Mass, the veneration of saints and their images, monastic vows, clerical celibacy, the doctrine of Purgatory, indulgences (art. 12-27). In this latter part there is a chapter on the cardinals, immunity, annates—hence a defence of the Curia against the German *gravamina*—and even a section on the war against the Turks. The *Enchiridion* thus provides a summary of all those things for which the Lutherans blamed the ancient Church while it clarifies the Catholic standpoint without losing itself in lengthy arguments. Each article is headed by a statement of the Catholic standpoint, the opponents' objections follow and their refutation concludes it.

By reason of its conciseness and lucid arrangement Eck's *Enchiridion* is superior to Fabri's *Malleus*, first published in Rome in 1522.[2] Fabri also starts from the doctrines of the Church and papal supremacy; his teaching on these points is even more emphatic than Eck's. He then gives lengthy extracts from Luther's writings which he proceeds to refute with a lavish display of patristic erudition, with the consequence that, much more than the *Enchiridion*, the *Malleus* bears the stamp of a mere polemical pamphlet.

It is matter for regret that the "German Theology" of Bishop Berthold Pirstinger of Chiemsee,[3] published in 1528 at the suggestion of Cardinal Lang of Salzburg, did not enjoy a wide circulation. The work presented a perfectly objective exposition of the nature of faith

---

[1] Some of the later editions have been considerably enlarged; complete list in *Corp. Cath.*, VOL. XVI, pp. xci-cii.

[2] Critical edition by A. Naegele, *Corp. Cath.*, VOLS. XXIII and XXIV; cf. Helbling, *Dr Johann Fabri*, p. 14 f.

[3] W. Reithmeier, *Bertholds, Bischofs von Chiemsee, Tewtsche Theologey* (Munich 1852).

and justification. Almost half of the fair-sized volume is devoted to the doctrine of creation, original sin, the merits of Christ, grace, while such subjects as the Church, the sacraments, the veneration of the saints and so forth are by no means omitted. This is also true of Herborn's *Enchiridion*,[1] a work of about the same size as Eck's. Herborn did not commit Eck's mistake of treating the question of salvation only incidentally; on the contrary, he provides an objective statement of the doctrinal divergences without involving himself in a discussion of the opponents' standpoint. But this was not enough. Moreover, the book only appeared in 1529—too late therefore to supersede the already popular manual of Luther's famous opponent.

Zwingli's rise at Zürich and that of Oecolampadius at Basle brought into the fray not only local champions such as Joachim am Grüt, Jacob Edlibach, Augustinus Marius,[2] but likewise celebrities like Eck, Fabri, John Fisher and Cardinal Cajetan. The Catholic party was not slow in realising that a new brand of Protestantism had made its appearance in Switzerland. No one pointed out the distinctive features of Zwingli's teaching, viz. the whittling down of original sin into a mere hereditary disease, the symbolic interpretation of the words of the institution of the Eucharist, the condemnation of images, with a surer finger than did Eck in the theses written for the Disputation of Baden (1526)—that "Diet of Worms" of the Swiss schism.[3] However, the fact remains that Zwingli's only comprehensive statement of his standpoint in his *Commentarius de vera et falsa religione* (1525)[4] did not receive the attention which the significance of its author called for. Even more surprising is the fact that controversial theologians ignored almost completely and for a considerable period the most outstanding systematic work of the whole Reformation period, namely Calvin's *Institutio* (1536), even after the appearance of the considerably enlarged second edition of 1539. They likewise failed to perceive that in this work

---

[1] Critical edition by P. Schlager, *Corp. Cath.*, VOL. XII (Münster 1927).

[2] J. Birkner, *Augustinus Marius* (Münster 1930), pp. 48-73.

[3] Eck's six theses in Gussmann, *Quellen und Forsch.*, VOL. II, p. 110; *ibid.*, p. 157, the pertinent literature; also Schottenloher, Nos. 41283c-97. Zwingli's controversial writings in *Corp. Ref.*, VOL. XCII, pp. 1-308. The second Zürich disputation (1523) had been about the Mass and the veneration of images; the acts are in *Corp. Ref.*, VOL. LXXXIX, pp. 651-803. Zwingli's sixty-seven final discourses for the first Zürich disputation (1523) and the ten discourses of Franz Kolb and Berthold Haller for that of Berne (1528) cover the entire ground but are formulated by Protestants. Texts in E. F. K. Müller, *Die Bekenntnisschriften der reformierten Kirche* (Leipzig 1903), pp. 1-6, 30 f.

[4] *Corp. Ref.*, VOL. XC, pp. 628-912, in twelve chapters.

Protestant thought had been cast into an entirely new mould.[1] For the Catholic controversialists the dispute over the Eucharist between the Swiss and Luther [2] was little more than a welcome opportunity for adding yet another item to the tally of Luther's inconsistencies— the Protestants' lack of unity among themselves.[3] The latter's fight against the Anabaptists was exploited by them in the same manner.

In addition to the attempts to define doctrinal divergence within the entire sphere of dogma described above, the method of extracts, which had been in use from the beginning, became an established practice. In 1526 Cochlaeus extracted no less than five hundred erroneous propositions from Luther's writings,[4] while Fabri boasted in 1530 that he had collected more than six hundred.[5] In his *Praeparatoria* he demanded that an official collection of the errors of Luther, Zwingli and the Anabaptists should be made and, if possible, printed for the benefit of the Council.[6] No such list was ever drawn up officially, but one private catalogue of the kind, namely the four hundred and four articles which Eck submitted to the Emperor previous to the Diet of Augsburg,[7] is of historic significance because it led Melanchthon to shape his apologia of the German reformation into a Lutheran profession

---

[1] The various editions of the *Institutio* in *Corp. Ref.*, VOLS. XXIX-XXXII. The new edition of the final formulation of 1559 in *J. Calvini Opera selecta*, edd. P. Barth and G. Niesel, VOLS. III-V (Munich 1928 ff.), is important for us because it endeavours to identify the Catholic authors quoted—that is, combated—by Calvin. I do not deny that some particular points of Calvin's teaching have been discussed by Catholic writers even in the pre-Tridentine period, for instance the doctrine of the freedom of the will, by Pighius; cf. Jedin, *Studien über die Schriftstellertätigkeit Albert Pigges*, pp. 40 ff.

[2] W. Köhler, *Zwingli und Luther: Ihr Streit über das Abendmahl nach seinen politischen und religiösen Beziehungen*, VOL. I (Leipzig 1924). This is a work of capital importance in which Catholic controversial literature receives adequate consideration.

[3] For Luther's self-contradictions, see e.g. Cochlaeus's *Lutherus Septiceps* (1527), Fabri's *Antilogiae* (1530), cf. Helbling, *Dr Johann Fabri*, p. 144 f. The Catholics' treatment of the Protestants' mutual contradictions would deserve a separate study. As an example, cf. Hoffmeister's confrontation of the views of Oecolampadius and Bucer on the Canon of the Mass with those of the Lutherans, *Corp. Cath.*, VOL. XVIII, p. 141.

[4] *Articuli CCCCC Martini Lutheri* (Cologne 1525); see Spahn, *Johannes Cochlaeus*, bibliography, No. 34.

[5] Helbling, *Dr Johannes Fabri*, p. 97; cf. *Z.K.G.*, XX (1900), p. 254 f.

[6] *C.T.*, VOL. IV, p. 11 f. (*n*.12 and *n*.17); Laemmer, *Mantissa*, p. 150, on the negotiations for reunion.

[7] Excellent edition by W. Gussmann, *Quellen und Forsch.*, VOL. II. The first part (1-65) includes the forty-one propositions of the Bull *Exsurge* and the theses of the disputations of Leipzig, Baden and Berne. The further division into dogmatic (66-168), ecclesiastical (169-331) and social and political errors is extremely questionable.

of faith under the title of *Confessio Augustana*.[1] The first part of that work, which is also the dogmatic section, mainly rests on the articles of Schwabach drawn up by Luther in 1529. It treats of sin and justification, defines the concept of the Church (arts. 7, 8, 14, 16), discusses the three sacraments—Baptism, Eucharist, Penance—(arts. 9-13), ritual (art. 15) and in the conclusion touches on three controversial points, viz. free will, the formula "faith and works" and the veneration of the saints (arts. 18-21). The whole of the second part (arts. 23-28) is a defence of the "reforms" based on the articles of Torgau, namely Communion in both kinds, the marriage of priests, the suppression of monasteries, the reduction of holy days, the alteration of the character of the Mass and the limitation of ecclesiastical authority to the ministry of preaching and the administration of the sacraments. The Dominican Peter Rauch's opinion of the adherents of the *Confessio* was not far wrong when he wrote in 1533 that they had "gemeiniglich in allen Artikeln anders geschrieben und gelehrt denn sie jetzund in ihrer Confessio bekennen" (in all their articles they have written and taught otherwise than they now profess in their *Confessio*).[2] The tendency of that document to attenuate differences made possible its use as a basis for reunion negotiations, but it had little to recommend it for the discussion of controversial questions. For this reason, apart from the official *Confutatio*, it was only rarely refuted by Catholic writers.[3]

A very different spirit breathes in the Articles of Schmalkalden. These were drawn up by Luther himself towards the end of 1536, by command of the Elector of Saxony in view of the convocation of the Council of Mantua and after thorough discussion with seven divines of repute.[4] Among these articles there were four of which Luther said

[1] Müller, *Die Bekenntnisschriften der evangelisch-luterischen Kirche* (Göttingen 1930), pp. 31-137.

[2] The passage from the *Antilutherus* (1533) in Paulus, *Dominikaner*, p. 47.

[3] Contarini's *Confutatio* in *Corp. Cath.*, VOL. VII, pp. 1-22. Nausea's memorial for the negotiations for reunion in Cardauns, *Bestrebungen*, pp. 157-93; for Hoffmeister's *Iudicium*, cf. Paulus, *Der Augustinermönch Johannes Hoffmeister* (Freiburg i.B. 1891), p. 390; on Peter Rauch's *Antithesis* (1533) and Johann Mensing's book against articles 3 and 4 (1535), see Paulus, *Dominikaner*, pp. 40 ff., 46 ff.

[4] Critical edition of the text in Müller, *Die Bekenntnisschriften*, pp. 405-68. For its origin, H. Volz, *Luthers Schmalkaldische Artikel und Melanchthons Traktat "De potestate papae"* (Gotha 1931). In *Corp. Cath.*, VOL. XVIII, Volz has given a critical edition of the refutations by Cochlaeus, Witzel and Hoffmeister. As soon as the Articles appeared Cochlaeus wrote to Morone (*Z.K.G.*, XVIII (1897), pp. 288): "Apertis itaque verbis praecidit nobis omnem concordiae spem, quantum in ipso est." Melanchthon's *Apologia* with its lengthy discussion of the concept of sacrifice, etc., had worked to the same end, Müller, *Die Bekenntnisschriften*, pp. 358-71. The

that from them "there must be no deviation, or yielding, though heaven and earth fall to pieces". They are (1) justification by faith alone; (2) the abolition of the sacrifice of the Mass since it is irreconcilable with the first and chief article and drags after it a dragon's tail of errors, such as the doctrine of Purgatory, prayers for the dead, veneration of the saints and their relics, indulgences; (3) the suppression of the monasteries, and (4) the abolition of the papal supremacy. On the remaining articles—the sacraments included—Luther was willing to "negotiate", that is to argue about, at a Council. Luther knew quite well where lay the kernel of the dogmatic divergence, much more clearly in fact than Melanchthon, who did not agree with the wording of the article on the Papacy and accordingly submitted an opinion of his own under the title *De potestate Papae*, which was subsequently embodied in the profession of faith of the Evangelical-Lutheran Church. The formulation of the article on the Lord's Supper caused Melanchthon to fear a recrudescence of the recently settled conflict with the North Germans and the Swiss. As a matter of fact, the latter had gone their own way in their "Confessions". To the "Confession of the four cities" (*Tetrapolitana*) which they had submitted at Augsburg there came to be added the "Confession of Basle" in 1534 and the first "Helvetic Confession" in 1536. These shared the fate of the *Confessio Augustana*—small attention was paid to them by controversial theology.

Towards the end of the fifteen-thirties controversial literature underwent an internal change. Mere polemics abated and the new positive theology (Verkündigungstheologie) emerged. The flood of publications subsided, the great oratorical and literary duels ended. Catholics realised at last that what the faithful needed was positive instruction. Catholic collections of sermons on questions in dispute appeared in considerable numbers.[1] The day of the catechism had dawned—that of the popular variety as well as the fuller one destined for the pastoral

---

Tetrapolitana in Müller, *Die Bekenntnisschriften*, pp. 55-78; *ibid.*, the Confession of Basle and the first Helvetic Confession, pp. 95-109.

[1] The most widespread was the collection of Eck's sermons in five volumes: Vols. I and II comment on the Sunday gospels (1530); Vol. III on those of the feast days (1531); Vol. IV treats of the sacraments (1534); Vol. V of the ten commandments (1539), *Corp. Cath.*, VOL. XVI, No. 68. For Nausea's *Quattuor Centuriae* (1532), Hurter, *Nomenclator*, VOL. II, p. 1405. In 1528 Fabri published sermons on the eight beatitudes and in 1529 on the Eucharist, see Helbling, *Dr Johann Fabri*, bibliography Nos. 33 and 35. Hoffmeister's homilies on the gospels in two volumes saw eleven editions, Paulus, *Hoffmeister*, p. 388 f. The widely diffused postils of Dietenberger and Wild belong to a later period.

clergy. There was no mistaking the influence of the Lutheran catechism. In 1535 the convert Witzel wrote the first German catechism. Two years later he was followed by Dietenberger, who had been admirably prepared for the task by the publication of a lengthy series of popular controversial writings and a German translation of the Bible.[1] Here we need only mention the larger compendiums for the clergy, drawn up in the main on the same lines as the popular catechisms and dealing with the usual doctrinal subjects, such as the Creed, the seven sacraments, the Lord's prayer and the ten commandments. Gropper's *Enchiridion*, which forms an appendix to the decrees of the Synod of Cologne of 1536, has been described as "the most complete dogmatic treatise of pre-Tridentine theology". This work was soon followed by Nausea's great catechism (1543) [2] and by Filippo Archinto's "Edict" (1545).[3] The traditional type of controversial writing, such as the *Controversiae* (1542) of Pighius and Hoffmeister's *Loci communes* (1547),[4] did not disappear altogether, but its character and aim took a definitely constructive turn.

The transition to positive teaching appears most clearly in the twenty-nine theses prescribed for the guidance of preachers by the University of Paris on 18 January 1542 [5] and in the thirty-two theses formulated with the same end in view by the University of Louvain in 1544.[6] Neither of these documents condemns any specific error; both state the Catholic standpoint so as to provide preachers with a solid basis for the proclamation of the word of God. Lastly, the fifty-nine theses to which the University of Louvain obliged its professors to subscribe on 8 December 1544 [7] constitute the most thorough and most logical summary of the doctrines in dispute of the whole of the pre-Tridentine era. From the doctrine of original sin (1-8) they go on to justification by Baptism and Penance—with special reference to the

[1] J. Wedewer, *Johann Dietenberger* (Freiburg 1888), p. 207; text in C. Moufang, *Katholische Katechismen des 16. Jahrhunderts in deutscher Sprache* (Mainz 1881), pp. 1-105. On Gropper, see above, p. 368, *n.2.*

[2] Metzner, *Friedrich Nausea*, p. 76 f.; Part VI is an introduction to the liturgy.

[3] Lauchert, *Literarische Gegner*, pp. 467-73. Strangely enough the Church and the primacy are not discussed.

[4] According to Paulus, *Hoffmeister*, p. 388, it was disseminated in thirteen editions. Pigge's *Controversiae* saw six editions, H. Jedin, *Studien über die Schriftstellertätigkeit Albert Pigges*, pp. 34 ff. In the preface Pighius explains his purpose: "Controversias ita explicavimus ut evidens faceremus ex qua parte in singulis staret orthodoxa catholicaque veritas."

[5] Duplessis d'Argentré, *Coll. iud.*, VOL. I, ii, pp. 413-15.

[6] Le Plat, VOL. III, pp. 250-4.

[7] There is no article on scripture and tradition. H. de Jongh, *L' Ancienne Faculté de théologie de Louvain*, pp. 81*, 89*.

role of faith and the doctrine of merit (13-27)—and to the other sacraments, the Church and the Pope's supremacy (40-49). The concluding propositions are the familiar ones about veneration of the saints and their relics, indulgences and the vows of religion. We have here substantially the framework of the decrees of Trent. From the point of view of the history of theology they are the result of the labours of the controversialists of the preceding period.

In their own camp the pre-Tridentine divines received but scant recognition while their opponents bespattered them with gross abuse. One of the latter accused Eck of handing over his people and country to the "Babylonian slaughter-house".[1] Fabri, they alleged, had written against the abolition of the law of celibacy because he feared the loss of the six thousand florins which priests living in concubinage were said to be paying annually in fines.[2] Cochlaeus, whose life had never been clouded by the least breath of scandal, had his name associated with a certain "kessen Anna" (a brazen woman of the name of Anne). His latinised name gave a chance to the punsters who sought to make him look ridiculous by nicknaming him "snail" and "ladle".[3] When one of them came to die it was rumoured that he had died in despair, by his own hand, or that the devil had made away with him.[4] Johann von Kampen said that his "four evangelists", Eck, Fabri, Cochlaeus and Nausea, would rather see the rise of three new Luthers than the conversion of the existing one. Even Morone reproached them with reducing their Catholicism to hatred and abuse of Luther.[5] As a matter of fact, in the eighteenth century a whole lexicon of invectives was extracted from the writings of Cochlaeus. At this day we find the coarseness of most of the other champions intolerable, but we should bear in mind that the other side repaid in kind. Eck blamed his fellow

---

[1] *Ein schöner Dialogus*, 1521, probably written by Urbanus Rhegius, Schade, *Satiren*, VOL. II, p. 125. The "Karsthans" asserted that for the Leipzig disputation Eck had received 500 florins from the Pope, Clemen, *Flugschriften*, VOL. IV, p. 83 f. Of the filthy stories in the *Eckius desolatus* and the parody of the 404 articles printed in Gussmann, *Quellen und Forsch.*, VOL. II, pp. 199-203, we prefer to say nothing although there is some foundation for them inasmuch as Eck's moral conduct was not altogether irreproachable.

[2] *Die lutherisch Strebkatz* was composed in 1524, Schade, *Satiren*, VOL. III, p. 130; cf. also O. Clemen in *A.R.G.*, II (1904), pp. 78-93.

[3] *Gesprächbüchlein*, according to A. Götze in *A.R.G.*, V (1908), pp. 48 ff., written by Erasmus Alberus (1524); text in O. Clemen, *Flugschriften*, VOL. I, p. 334; the other *epitheta* in Schade, *Satiren*, VOL. III, p. 127.

[4] Summed up in N. Paulus, *Luthers Lebensende* (Freiburg 1898), pp. 5-20.

[5] Morone to Sadoleto, 25 March 1538, *A.R.G.*, I (1903), p. 378. For Johann von Kampen's observation see above, p. 394, *n.*2.

pugilists for undue speed in publishing their lucubrations.[1] He forgot
that journalism must of necessity work at high speed. Pighius blamed
them for abandoning too hastily the standpoint on which Tertullian
had placed himself, an appeal, that is, to the fund of truth still held in
common, and for arguing too much.[2] In one sense he was right, but
in a discussion of any depth arguments from revelation could not be
dispensed with. When we blame these men for seeing only the things
that divided, and shutting their eyes to what was held by both parties,[3]
the answer of the history of dogma is that the controversialists' most
important duty was precisely to draw the line of demarcation. Did they
fulfil this duty?

At the beginning of the conflict Hochstraten, anticipating the
discoveries of his fellow-Dominican of our own time, Denifle, described
Luther's teaching on original sin and concupiscence as the stumbling-
block that caused him to trip.[4] This fundamental recognition was not
sufficiently elaborated by later theologians; all too often they forgot
that there was the source of every error in the doctrine of justification.
Eck's *Enchiridion* compresses the doctrinal divergences on justification
most one-sidedly into the formula "faith-works" and shifts the centre
of gravity into the sphere of ecclesiaticism, so much so indeed that when
van der Vorst, the conciliar nuncio, in the course of his travels in
Germany, inquired which were the main controversial points he was
given the following list [5]: (1) the papal supremacy; (2) the cult of the
saints; (3) auricular confession; (4) Purgatory; (5) the Mass; (6)
Communion in both kinds; (7) the veneration of images; (8) the
administration of Baptism in Latin; (9) the vows of religion and clerical
celibacy. Original sin and the doctrine of justification, that is the real
causes of disagreement, were not mentioned at all, external and obvious
divergences were alone considered.

It was the great merit of Gropper, Contarini and the rest of the

---

[1] *Z.K.G.*, xix (1898), p. 263. The record was broken by Cochlaeus when in the
summer of 1534 he published twelve pamphlets, eight in Latin and four in German,
each of them in an edition of 1000 copies, *Z.K.G.*, xviii (1897), p. 255 f.

[2] Jedin, *Studien über die Schriftstellertätigkeit Albert Pigges*, p. 124 f.; there also
Seripando's remark that they should not have met the opponents *in prove*. As early
as 1552 Luis Vives disapproved of the many small watchmen of Sion who rushed to
the defence of the Catholic cause in order to make a name for themselves or for the
sake of some financial advantage, C. Burmann, *Hadrianus VI* (Utrecht 1727), pp.
462 ff.

[3] Lortz, *Reformation*, VOL. II, p. 170.

[4] J. Hochstraten, *Colloquia cum divo Augustino* (Cologne 1522), fol. D 1ʳ: "Et hic
est lapis ille contradictionis ad quem Martinus allisus est."

[5] *C.T.*, VOL. IV, p. 62.

divines who worked for reunion that they placed the person of Christ, His merits and man's appropriation of them in the centre of the debate and strove to remove the dreadful misunderstanding that the Catholic faith prejudiced Our Lord's mediatorship and the universal efficaciousness of His grace. In this way they did yeoman service for apologetics, as Seripando did at a later date at Trent. It was precisely the negotiations for reunion at Augsburg and Ratisbon that made it perfectly clear that the ultimate and quite irreconcilable opposition between the Protestant ecclesiastical communities and Catholicism was due to a wholly different conception of the sacramental system and the juridical structure of the Church. The sacrificial character of the Mass, transubstantiation, the seven sacraments on the one hand, and the hierarchical structure of the Church and the Pope's primacy of jurisdiction on the other, constituted a chasm between the two parties which no amount of good-will and no political advantage could bridge over. When they discussed the Eucharist, the sacrifice of the Mass and the papal primacy more often and more fully than any other controversial question, Catholic apologists gave evident proof that they did not fasten on mere externals but were fully aware of the depth of the divergences. They not only furnished the Council of Trent with abundant material from the writings of the innovators and an arsenal of arguments for their refutation, they also provided that assembly with a fully worked-out system of controversial articles for use in the dogmatic definitions. The line of demarcation was clearly defined, the divergence in belief a reality.

CHAPTER IX

Reform Without a Council

In 1539, at a time when the failure of the convocation of the Council of Vicenza could already be foreseen, the Alsatian Augustinian Friar Johann Hoffmeister openly raised the question why the Council did not materialise. With remarkable impartiality this Friar of unimpeachable Catholic orthodoxy examined the arguments and motives of both religious parties.[1] "The Protestants", he writes, "are afraid that the Council will prove them in the wrong while their own pride will never suffer them to submit to an unfavourable sentence by the synod. As for the Catholics, they are indeed in possession of the true doctrine and valid sacraments, but a number of them defend 'with mistaken zeal' real abuses and fight shy of reform. Right is indeed on the side of the Papacy, but though aware of its own vices it is unwilling to amend."

Couched in these general terms, Hoffmeister's judgment is severe. However, the plain fact is that not only the Lutherans but many Catholics also felt that the main obstacle to the Council was the Roman Curia's unwillingness to reform. Belief in the existence of such a reluctance was widespread. In the light of this fact it is easy to understand how it came about that even thoughtful and responsible people came to the conclusion that an effective reform of the Curia, *previous* to the Council and *independently* of it, would best cut the ground from under the opponents' feet, convert the hesitant and guard the Papacy against the violent attacks of which it would surely be the object at a Council on the part of people north of the Alps.

Already during the pontificate of Adrian VI Johann Eck had suggested that since a Council was impossible for the time being, a papal reform Bull should take its place.[2] During the pontificate of Clement VII, when most people had given up all hope of a Council, there were those who thought that in order to disarm the Lutherans, Jacopo Salviati, the Pope's confidant, should propose a reform of the

[1] *Corp. Cath.*, VOL. XVIII, pp. 118 ff.
[2] *Beiträge zur bayrischen Kirchengeschichte*, VOL. II (1896), pp. 181 f., 189 f.

secular and regular clergy by means of Roman decrees.[1] During the
first years of Paul III's pontificate similar proposals came almost
simultaneously from various quarters.[2] At the Diet of Ratisbon King
Ferdinand I told Morone to his face that as long as he saw no reform
measures he could not believe that the Pope seriously intended to
convene a Council.[3] On the other hand a genuine reform in Rome
would render such an assembly superfluous [4]; if none took place, then
every papal attempt at reform would be met with the retort "Physician,
heal thyself!" On this point the nuncios van der Vorst,[5] Morone [6] and
Mignanelli [7] were in complete agreement. Cardinal Cervini never
ceased urging the Pope to do something in the matter of reform before
it was too late.[8] Everyone of those who had had occasion to see with
their own eyes the result of the German schism struck a similar note.
"As a result of evil example," the Scotsman Wauchope wrote on
5 January 1541 from Ratisbon, "things have come to such a pass that
people have abandoned the practice of good works together with the
true faith; but they are sure to come back as soon as they see holy

---

[1] Violi to Salviati, Florence, 6 October 1530, in *Carte Strozziane*, VOL. I (Florence
1884), p. 599. "Il più salutifero remedio e la più optima medicina ad questa voglia
bestiale luteriana saria rubare le mosse o far quello che tanto di là gridano, cioè cavare
fuori da N. S. una reformatione del Clero e de' religiosi e publicarla, per cominciare a
dare principio d'uno honesto vivere e d'una reformatione de' buoni costumi, e della
modificatione de' beni superflui delle Religioni: il che sarebbe per aventura . . . uno
serrare la boccha a chi così si dilecta di dire male."

[2] Memorial of an anonymous writer (1536), *N.B.*, VOL. I, PT ii, p. 424; Duke
George of Saxony (1538), *Q.F.*, x (1907), p. 107; Cardinal Ercole Gonzaga to Contarini,
2 January 1538, *Q.F.*, II (1899), p. 182.

[3] Morone on 27 June 1541, *H.J.*, IV (1883), p. 625; *id.*, on 7 March 1542, *N.B.*,
VOL. I, PT vii, p. 125. On 3 March Morone had reported (p. 120): "Altri dicono che
a Roma si doverebbe far prima la reformatione."

[4] *N.B.*, VOL. I, PT VII, p. 117 (15 February 1542); similarly to Verallo (31 January
1543): "Che N. S. potrebbe senza concilio reformare cominciando dalla corte sua",
ibid., p. 300. More threatening is the observation of the year 1545 in *N.B.*, VOL. I,
PT viii, p. 698.

[5] *C.T.*, VOL. IV, p. 97, l. 32 (1537).

[6] *N.B.*, VOL. I, PT v, p. 158 (1540). "Mi par necessario che senza alcun risguardo
di povertà et spese iminenti dal travagliato stato della Christianità o di qualch'altra
cosa . . . avanti che S. S.ta venghi al concilio, con effetto facesse la longamente
pratticata reformatione, acciocché iudicium inciperet a Domo Dei et non si potesse
dir' in un concilio: medice, cura te ipsum."

[7] *N.B.*, VOL. I, PT v, p. 362 (1540). "La S.ta V. sicondo il mio debil parere non
ha in sua mano altro che un solo remedio, ciò è far pigliare gl'otto concilii universali
con alcuni altri assai principali et decreti santi antichi et di quelli formare una
reformatione conveniente ala chiesa occidentale."

[8] *C.T.*, VOL. X, p. 170, l. 36; p. 186, l. 15 and *passim*, and the above-mentioned
accounts in *N.B.*, VOL. I, PT v, p. 408 f.; Vergerio's memorial in *C.T.*, VOL. XII, pp.
436 ff., agrees with this.

examples."[1] All these men shared a common conviction that a serious reform of the Roman Curia would initiate a renewal within the Church and would most surely prevent further apostasies; it would also considerably facilitate the meeting of a Council and might even take its place. In modern historical parlance the situation could be summed up thus: "Let the Papacy suffer itself to be caught in the movement of Catholic reform and it will solve at one and the same time the problem of the schism and that of the Council."

There was no lack of proper understanding of the situation, but the application of a remedy met with insuperable obstacles. The apostasy of the north and the catastrophe of the "Sack of Rome" were undoubtedly a rude shock for many who had familiarised themselves with the notion that everything could go on as before. This traditional attitude of mind was by no means overcome. Every attempt at a reform of the Curia between the Council of Basle and the fifth Lateran Council had failed (Bk. I, Ch. VI). The last stirrings of the conciliar theory had been successfully repressed and the misuse of the idea of a Council for political purposes had been countered with political means. But by this time the term "reformation" had become the watchword of those who accused the Papacy of perverting the truth of Christianity and the rallying-cry of men who saw in that institution the ultimate source of abuses the one-sided suppression of which had resulted in the disruption of religious unity by heresy. If anyone mentioned the word "reformation", he had first to furnish proof that he was not tampering with some essential article of the ancient faith and that his anxiety for a renewal of the Church was born of genuinely Catholic motives. The man who—outside the inner circle of the morally decadent—found fault with the abuses in the Church, or presumed to attack the traditional system by suggesting administrative reforms, came all too readily under suspicion of being in sympathy with the dissidents.[2] Any comment on the open wounds of ecclesiastical life—such as for instance the nuncio Chieregati's "confession" at Nuremberg—ran the risk of being pounced upon by the Lutheran press and hailed as a welcome confirmation of its own criticisms of the Papacy.[3] Criticism within the Catholic

[1] *Z.K.G.*, XXIII (1902), p. 446. Almost at the same time Poggio wrote: "Se verrà in tempo la pubblicatione della reformatione, sara una santa medicina", Laemmer, *Mon. Vat.*, p. 346.

[2] Cardinal Ghinucci's objection to the clause in the draft of the Bull of Approval of the Society of Jesus which forbade superiors to impose penitential practices on their subjects is significant: "per non dare ansa alli luterami", Dittrich, *Regesten*, p. 379.

[3] In the epistle to be mentioned below dated 3 April 1538, Johann Sturm addresses the authors of the *Consilium de emendanda ecclesia* in these terms: "Si vos

camp itself had become a matter of extreme delicacy now that a hostile army was in being.

Psychological difficulties were not the only ones that had increased; reform itself had become more difficult than in the era of the reform Councils. Historians warn us—not without reason—against accepting at their face value and as historically true every accusation against the curial system with which we meet in the writings of contemporary advocates of reform. Only a careful examination of every individual instance, if possible on a statistical basis, would enable us to form a just judgment of the effects of papal centralisation.[1] At the beginning of the religious rupture that system had assumed such proportions that on some aspects of curial practice there is hardly room for two opinions.

Indulgences had been so debased that they were widely regarded as little more than a financial transaction the yield of which was shared between the Curia and the secular princes. As a result of their enormous multiplication they had lost their spiritual significance, so much so indeed that Johann Eck tells of women who stoked their stoves with "certificates of confession".[2] The "compositions" which had come into use in the last three decades of the fifteenth century, that is, the collation to benefices and the grant of dispensations in return for an agreed tax to be paid to the Dataria or the Penitenzieria, could only be defended against the accusation of simony by means of an extremely precarious interpretation.[3] The sale of curial offices, now universally practised, was in itself no more than a capitalisation of state revenue such as was in use elsewhere, but one of its results was that when those who held these offices constituted a strongly organised body, they sought to increase the invested capital by arbitrarily raising taxes and by devising fresh charges. Moreover, as a result of the enormous increase of official posts—there were 2232 of them under Leo X—the

hoc admittitis, hoc nobis conceditis, sublata est inter nos maxima pars controversiae", *A.R.G.*, XXXIII (1936), p. 30. Johannes Sleidan, *Zwei Reden an Kaiser und Reich*, ed. Böhmer (Tübingen 1879), p. 84 f. asserts: "Confessionem hanc (of Roman abuses) superioribus annis nemo potuit eis extorquere, nunc tandem agnoscunt."

[1] E. F. Jacob, *Essays in the Conciliar Epoch* (Manchester 1943), pp. 20 ff.

[2] Quoted from Eck in *Beiträge zur bayrischen Kirchengeschichte*, II (1896), p. 222. For the financial side of indulgences cf. A. Schulte, *Die Fugger in Rom 1493-1523* (Leipzig 1904), VOL. I, pp. 176 ff.; N. Paulus, *Geschichte des Ablasses im Mittelalter*, VOL. III (Paderborn 1923), pp. 450-69.

[3] "Compositionum turpissimus quaestus", says Campeggio, *C.T.*, VOL. XII, p. 8, l. 19. Eck calls them "symoniacum vel symoniae velum", *Beiträge zur bayrischen Kirchengeschichte*, II (1896), p. 227. The tariff of 1519, in which the clause "ad arbitrio del datario" frequently recurs, in L. Célier, *Les Dataires du XVIe siècle* (Paris 1910), pp. 155-64.

Curia's system of taxation, uncontrolled, not to say arbitrary, as it was, had become an oppressive machine for the purpose of extorting contributions.[1] Outsiders were not the only people to complain of surcharges and the endless raising of taxes. Even men in the know, for instance Africano Severoli, freely admitted the existence of these abuses.[2] Given such conditions, it was almost inevitable that in the grant of dispensations the financial aspect should prevail over the spiritual one. Thus, to give but one example, the dispensation, so fatal to regular discipline, which permitted monks to live outside their monasteries had become a simple administrative measure granted without previous examination of the reasons alleged. Control of the administration was rendered more difficult by the circumstance that the two old-established central authorities, the Chancery and the Camera, had in practice become mere offices for the transaction of business while the powers of the Segnatura and the Dataria largely overlapped those of the Penitenzieria.[3]

The subterfuge by which the prescriptions of Canon Law against the union in one hand of several dioceses or parishes could be circumvented were without number. Thus a cardinal would get himself

[1] For the origin of the sale of offices in the fifteenth century: Hofmann, *Forschungen*, VOL. I, p. 162 ff.; E. Göller, "Hadrian VI und der Ämterverkauf an der päpstlichen Kurie", in *Festgabe Finke* (Münster 1925), pp. 375-407. According to Hofmann, *Forschungen*, VOL. I, pp. 277 ff.; VOL. II, pp. 209-26, the registration tax for supplicas, Bulls and the register of the Secretariat had increased three- and even five-fold. In the period between Pius II and Leo X the tax for briefs rose from one to five ducats; the tax for an episcopal appointment was doubled and even trebled. Hofmann's calculations (*Forschungen*, VOL. II, pp. 163-76) show the rise in the price of offices: the auditory of the Camera brought in 19,000 ducats, the office of the "magister plumbi" 6000; the sum paid for certain offices such as that of the notary of the Chancery or the notaries of the Rota yielded an interest of 20 per cent. and even 22 per cent., Hofmann, *Forschungen*, VOL. I, p. 286.
[2] In the *Formula reformationis imperfecta* of the period of Adrian VI, Vat. Arch., Borgh., VOL. IV, 216, fols. 2ʳ-19ᵛ, Severoli relates that after the death of Leo X the Camerario, instead of two carlini, demanded a ducat for the seal. The vicechancellor "postquam Leone vivente omnia sibi licere vidit", had been claiming, during the previous two years, half of the taxes levied by the Camera for the provisions (fol. 8ʳ). Severoli complains of the demand of "iocalia" by the clerics of the Camera (fol. 10ʳ), and of the non-execution of the tax reduction ordered by the Council of the Lateran (fol. 11ᵛ) both by the protonotaries (fol. 11ᵛ) and by the secretaries, scriptores and abbreviatores (fols. 14ʳ-15ʳ) as well as the "plumbatores", for "postquam histrionibus ac morionibus tam sanctum officium dari coeptum est in proximo pontificatu" (viz. Leo X's), that office, owing to "rapinis et extorsionibus per sordidissimos pueros familiares suos, cum ipsi per se ipsos huiusmodi officium exercere dedignarentur", has fallen into bad repute (fol. 12ᵛ). Severoli's statements are confirmed by the investigations and memorials printed by Hofmann, *Forschungen*, VOL. II, pp. 242-9.
[3] See the lists of taxes in Göller, *Pönitentiarie*, VOL. II, ii, pp. 141-80, with those in Célier, *Dataires*, pp. 152-64.

appointed administrator of a second or even a third diocese in addition to his own. If he ceded one of them to a nephew or secretary of his, he would secure for himself the "regress" and by this means keep it ultimately in his own hands and often enough continue to enjoy part of its revenues.[1] As for the benefice-hunter of a lower rank, he knew how by putting up a man of straw, or by the temporary union of several parishes, or their skilful combination with provostships, canonries and other benefices not tied to the cure of souls, to get so many benefices into his hands that he needed something like an alphabetical index to find his way among them.[2] The juridical institution of commendams made it possible to bestow upon secular clerics and even upon laymen the rich revenues of abbeys and priories.[3] The specific basis of the conveyance of benefices by the Pope—reservations—had been undermined by the possibility of annulling an already acquired claim by a simple process of ante-dating. But the climax of juridical uncertainty was reached when those who enjoyed the ordinary right of collation chose to dispute the validity of the reservation so as to prevent the Pope's nominee from entering upon his benefice. The imposition of ecclesiastical penalties and endless lawsuits before the Rota then became the order of the day.[4] Weary of the strife and unable to meet the cost,

---

[1] In *R.Q.*, XLII (1934), p. 315, I have shown the various ways in which the prohibition of the accumulation of benefices (cap. 28, *De multa*), x, III, 5, could be circumvented. In the course of the dispute over the appointment to the Venetian See of Concordia it was said at Venice that the three Venetian cardinals, Corner, Grimani and Pisani, sought to unite all the dioceses of the territory in their own hands, P. Paschini, "Il Card. Marino Grimani nella diocesi di Concordia", in *Memorie storiche Forogiuliesi*, XXXVII (1941), p. 80.

[2] Statement by Campeggio, *C.T.*, VOL. XII, p. 8, l. 10. Eck relates that certain traffickers in benefices would give up ten or twenty of them while retaining an equal number. One of them held fourteen and was given a provostship in addition to them. Eck's own parish of Ingolstadt was claimed by a certain Jacobus de Sanctis of Carpi, aged fourteen, a man of straw of course, *Beiträge zur bayrischen Kirchengeschichte*, II (1896), p. 224. Cf. the terribly long list of benefices held by Johannes Ingenwinkel, who was Datary at the time of his death in 1535, Schulte, *Die Fugger in Rom*, VOL. I, pp. 289-306.

[3] U. Berlière, in *Revue bénédictine*, XVII (1900), p. 30, describes commendams as "the canker of monasticism"; cf. Ulrich von Hutten's sarcastic remarks on the subject in the *Vadiscus*, *Opera*, ed. Böcking, VOL. IV, p. 248. Examples will be given later.

[4] The increase of suits with the Rota—the "litium meandri" as Campeggio put it (*C.T.*, VOL. XII, p. 9, l. 5)—appears from the statistics in N. Hilling, *Die römische Rota und das Bistum Hildesheim* (Münster 1908), p. 36 f. At this day the archives of the Rota contain twenty diaries of notaries for the years 1464-88 and seventy-four for the period from 1489 to 1513. The number of suits actually carried through is much greater since only about a sixth of the diaries has been preserved. For the first period Hilling counts twenty-one suits from the diocese of Hildesheim and eighty-two for the second. According to Imbart de la Tour, *Origines*, VOL. II, p. 229,

many a man would come to terms with his curial competitor and compound with him by means of a pension—the very thing the latter had been aiming at from the first.

There is no need to give instances of these abuses; the history of almost every diocese and cathedral chapter and that of many abbeys and parishes provides them in such numbers, and reform writings of curial origin confirm the accusations of non-Italian witnesses to such an extent that it would be hopeless either to deny or to minimise them. The fiscal system of the Curia had evolved along lines that constituted a danger for the Church, though this was by no means the unavoidable result of rules laid down in the decretals of the late Middle Ages or by the papal Chancery; rather was it due to their circumvention and infringement by crafty and unscrupulous speculators whose activities were tolerated or at least not checked by those in authority; thus Clement VII shut both eyes when, after the "Sack of Rome," officials sought to make good their losses by raising their fees.[1] A twofold menace lay in these fiscal abuses: they destroyed or obscured the true conception of the pastoral ministry—a vital one for the Church—the notion, that is, that an official position in the Church imposes pastoral duties; that ecclesiastical revenues must serve the salvation of souls, either through the performance of liturgical functions and the administration of the sacraments or by the preaching of the word of God and all other forms of instruction. The injury done to the life of the Church in every part of Christendom, of which there is undeniable evidence, may be largely traced to one single cause, namely the neglect of the duty of residence by bishops and parish priests who spent their time as officials at the Curia or at the court of some cardinal or secular prince. While they continued to enjoy the revenues of their benefices bishops relied for the discharge of their duties on auxiliaries while parish priests depended on vicars or substitutes—priests usually poorly remunerated and frequently changed. The inevitable consequence of such a system was the inadequate instruction of the people and the ruin and desolation of many monasteries whose revenues were being diverted from their

between the years 1498-1515, in each of ten French dioceses, two candidates fought for possession. The whole of the chapter entitled "Le Désordre des bénéfices" (pp. 213-41) presents a lurid picture of the chaotic conditions—though the Curia was not alone to blame.

[1] The statement in the memorial quoted by Hofmann, *Forschungen*, VOL. II, p. 249: "Alii sunt abusus qui post impiam Urbis direptionem magno impetu irrupere Clemente VII ex commiseratione suscepte calamitatis id officialibus permittente", is confirmed by recurrent remarks about the raising of the taxes "post urbis direptionem", *C.T.*, VOL. IV, p. 457, l. 27; p. 459, l. 14.

original purpose. This fiscal system constituted yet another danger for a different reason: it was a blind alley from which it was all the more difficult to find a way out as the revenues accruing from the sale of offices and from compositions met a substantial part of the commitments arising from the Pope's duties towards the universal Church. Under Leo X the monthly income from the Dataria averaged 12,000 ducats. Under Adrian VI it fell to not quite 70,000 ducats a year. During the pontificate of Clement VII the Venetian envoys Foscari (1526) and Soriano (1535) estimated it at 100,000 ducats, that is roughly a quarter of the total papal revenue. In 1537, under Paul III, it still amounted to 70,000 ducats.[1] It would have been difficult to make good the loss of sums of such magnitude. Moreover, the colleges of officials resisted every attempt to lower taxation on the plea that this would conflict with their legitimately acquired claims to the interest on their invested capital. Not one of the reform pamphlets had a practical suggestion to make as to how to satisfy these claims and to make good the loss that was bound to result from a strict reform of the various departments.[2] Thus the wish to reform stumbled against hard reality: it was less easy to find the road to Church reform than it appeared to superficial observers.

Two roads—both of them wrong ones—had to be avoided though they had been tried before. One was the road of conciliar theory, the advocates of which sought to reform the Church by curtailing the Pope's authority and subjecting it to an external control. This would have been equivalent to altering the Church's constitution. The other road was that of schism. Instead of restoring orthodoxy, as its advocates claimed, this would in reality have altered and reduced the very substance of the Catholic faith and established a new ecclesiastical discipline. On the latter road the Papacy had pronounced judgment. By their secession

---

[1] Göller's pertinent estimates in *Festgabe Finke*, p. 394 f.; the Venetian ones in Albèri, *Relazioni*, VOL. II, iii, p. 139 (120,000 out of 499,000), p. 327 (110,000). Pastor's observation (VOL. V, p. 124: Eng. edn., VOL. XI, p. 174), based on the latter statement, viz., that the Dataria yielded one-half of all the revenue, is accordingly inaccurate. Cf. the housekeeping accounts of the end of the fifteenth century in A. Gottlob, *Aus der Camera Apostolica des 15. Jahrhunderts* (Innsbruck 1889), pp. 253 ff. The result of C. Bauer's investigations "Die Epochen der Papstfinanz", in *H.Z.*, CXXXVIII (1928), pp. 457-503, viz. that the revenue from the States of the Church tended to exceed that from ecclesiastical sources, must be compared, for the period under consideration, with Soriano's remark in Albèri, *Relazioni*, VOL. II, iii, p. 315, that the failure of the income from the Dataria "saria torre il vivere a S. S.ta".

[2] Campeggio's proposals were the most illuminating (*C.T.*, VOL. XII, p. 16), but even of them Hofmann, *Forschungen*, VOL. I, p. 321, says that "not one of them was practicable". Guidiccioni's proposals in *C.T.*, VOL. XII, p. 248.

from the Roman Church Luther and his adherents had made it impossible, by their own act, for their proposals to bear fruit. But though strict conciliar theory had been rejected by the Popes, its advocates nevertheless hoped that it would maintain itself within the Church and by devious means they sought to keep its principles alive and operative. It exercised no real influence on the actual reform of the Curia, which was determined by three factors whose discussion and eventual combination gave birth to the Tridentine reform and in fact to the Catholic reformation.

The advocates of a reform from within and from below, that is, of a "personal reform of the members", as we called it above (Bk. I, Ch. VII), had long been working for the new spirit and the training of the new men without whom every effort for reform was bound to remain a dead letter. As a matter of fact the Church continued to produce zealous diocesan bishops, auxiliary bishops and parish priests. Efforts for a reform in the old monastic and the mendicant orders went on without interruption and were encouraged by Paul III in various ways.[1] Among the many and assuredly not undistinguished names recorded in the story of Catholic reform about the third and fourth decade of the sixteenth century there are two that stand for a whole programme. The term Chietinism described, not without a tinge of irony, the strict religious life of the company of priests founded by Gian Pietro Carafa, sometime Bishop of Chieti,[2] and Gaetano da Thiene, from whom they got their name of Theatines. The term Gibertalis disciplina [3] is Giovio's description of the efforts of Bishop Giberti of Verona to establish a truly up-to-date pastoral administration in his diocese, one suited to the requirements of the times, and to realise in his own person the new

[1] In addition to Paul III's briefs in favour of reform listed in Pastor, VOL. V, pp. 863-7, and his comments on pp. 348-73: Eng. edn., VOL. XI, pp. 589 ff., and pp. 503 ff., I may be permitted to refer to my article, "Ciò che la storia del Concilio si attende dalla storia ecclesiastica italiana", in Il Concilio di Trento, II (1943), pp. 163-75. For an instance of the activities of a zealous auxiliary bishop, cf. the decrees of Matthias Ugoni for Brescia (1531) edited by P. Guerrini: Atti della visita pastorale del vescovo Domenico Bollani alla diocesi di Brescia, VOL. II (Brescia 1936), pp. vii-xx. For the attempts at reform in the mendicant orders under Paul III, see R.Q., XLIV (1936), pp. 239-49; also the letters of Cardinal Gonzaga on the reform of the canons of the Lateran whose protector he was, Q.F., II (1899), pp. 196-209, and the lively description of the struggle for the recognition of the Capuchins in Cuthbert-Widlöcher's Die Kapuziner (Munich 1931), pp. 80, 104; further literature in BK. I, Ch. vii.
[2] The literature on the notion of "Chietinismo" in Pastor, VOL. V, pp. 138, 360; Eng. edn., VOL. XI, pp. 194, 520. The form "Chietinaria" occurs in an aviso of 30 July 1544, St. Arch., Modena, Roma, 27A.
[3] Giovio to Alessandro Farnese, 11 September 1545, ed. J. Buschbell, in Festgabe Finke (Münster 1926), p. 421.

conception of what a bishop should be. Up to this time very few people had heard of a Basque nobleman—one Ignatius of Loyola who in his "Spiritual Exercises" was opening out new ways for the spiritual life and who in Paris had gathered around him a small group of "reformed priests" with whose aid he devoted himself to apostolic and charitable activities first at Venice and later on in other cities of Italy. There was a deeply symbolic significance in Ignatius's resolve, about the beginning of November 1537, to journey to Rome. Unless the personal reform of the members affected the head also it would not be a Catholic reform in the true sense of the word. The struggle for papal approval of the young Society of Jesus brought to light the other two factors which had meanwhile taken shape in Rome. It is Paul III's undying merit that these reform groups were able to organise themselves in Rome. Nothing like it had been seen under Clement VII. In those days Giberti and Carafa had left Rome not only for personal reasons but because the Roman climate was not favourable to their ideas of reform. Not that there were no advocates of reform in the eternal city, but men like Cajetan, Quiñónez, Loaysa, Egidio Canisio received no support. It was the Farnese Pope who by raising the layman Gasparo Contarini to the College of Cardinals gave to the reform movement in Rome both a firm support and a solid centre. After the creation of 22 December 1536 several similarly minded cardinals grouped themselves around him, men like Pole, who was inspired by the same ideals as Contarini, the impetuous Carafa, the gentle Sadoleto, a man imbued with the spirit of Christian humanism. The promotions of 1538 and 1539 further strengthened the reform party by the addition of the Spanish Dominican Juan Alvárez de Toledo, the devout and learned Cervini and the eager Fregoso. In 1542 three more adherents of Contarini were added to the group—Morone, who had been won over to reform by what he had seen in Germany; the Benedictine Abbot Cortese and the Dominican Badia: the last two were products of monastic reform. These men did not constitute a faction; the link between them was an idea. From the point of view of the Curia they were outsiders. One thing they were agreed upon, that it was impossible to raise the level of the spiritual and moral life of the secular and regular clergy and to make a reality of the new pastoral ideal and the apostolate which was their aim otherwise than by a complete reorganisation of the system of clerical training and monastic discipline and by the application of stricter conditions for the ordination of candidates for the priesthood and the bestowal of benefices and offices. It was not enough to forbid the Roman clergy to wear fashionable silken clothes; what was needed was a radical change in the Roman Curia, in fact such a change was an essential prerequisite for reform. These demands were prompted by the spirit and the institutions of Christian antiquity. Biographers and other writers held up before the prelates the portrait of the ideal bishop —the bishop in the pulpit, the bishop as a guide of souls by means of spiritual letters, the bishop as a guardian of ecclesiastical discipline. It was inevitable that the contrast between idealised antiquity and existing conditions should be profoundly felt, with the result that the most incisive reforms were demanded. In a memorial to Adrian VI, Cardinal Cajetan had suggested that the cardinals of the Curia should resign their external dioceses and that they should have a fixed income out of the contributions of the countries of which they were the protectors. Bishops were to be chosen by representatives of the diocesan clergy. The age of ordination should be raised to thirty years and all conventuals (that is the relaxed branches of the mendicant orders) should be suppressed.[1] One anonymous writer thought that a change of procedure in the election of the Popes would provide a simple solution of all difficulties: let the bishops also have a say in it![2] Wise men would not hear of these day-dreams, but even the determined group of reformers around Contarini felt that a deep and incisive intervention in existing conditions was needed to enable the new spirit to assert itself.

This group was faced by a conservative party which one might be tempted to regard as reactionary and hostile to any reform; but it would be unfair to describe the whole party as such. It was made up for the most part by jurists who had run through the whole gamut of curial offices up to the cardinalate. Lorenzo Campeggio was in every respect its most distinguished and most enlightened representative. He had set down his ideas about reform in a carefully balanced memorial which he presented to Adrian VI at the same time as Cajetan submitted the one mentioned above.[3] That which his grave illness and his death on 19 July 1539 prevented him from accomplishing in his own person was done by his younger brother Tommaso during the whole period of the Tridentine labours for reform—namely the conciliation of the demands of the determined reformers with the tradition of the Curia. If the two brothers Campeggio and Cardinals Ghinucci, Cupis and Guidiccioni—of whom more presently—were conservative in the best sense of the word, the Pucci family of Florence which had directed the Penitenzieria during the two previous decades must be described as

[1] C.T., VOL. XII, pp. 32-9.   [2] Ibid., p. 44.   [3] Ibid., pp. 5-27.

representing a decidedly reactionary element. Antonio Pucci, who had succeeded his uncle Lorenzo in 1529 by means of a questionable financial transaction, was an adept in warding off every attack on the methods of his department; in the end he even succeeded in passing on his office to Roberto, another uncle of his.[1] It is an essential characteristic of Paul III that in almost all his promotions of cardinals besides the pronounced reformers he also invariably considered the claims of such curial jurists as were possessed of special business ability. Thus when he raised Contarini to the cardinalate he also raised Ghinucci, the auditor of the Camera, and the dean of the Rota Simonetta. Carafa received the red hat together with the Datary Cristoforo Jacobazzi and Del Monte, who had made his career in the administration of the Papal States. The last two were the nephews of jurists with a long record of service in the Curia. Bartolomeo Guidiccioni, created in 1539, had served the Pope for nineteen years in the capacity of vicar-general of Parma. His knowledge of the law was scarcely second to that of Parisio, who had been recalled to Rome from his chair at Padua. Marcello Crescenzio, whom the Pope raised to the Sacred College at the same time as Morone, had been dean of the Rota while Gianangelo Medici had served in the government of the Papal States. Many of these names will meet us again at a later date. This is yet one more proof that Tridentine reform was not exclusively the achievement of the reform movement but rather the result of its *entente* with the conservative forces.

The conservatives themselves could no longer afford to turn down every reform on the plea of superfluity, if only because the pressure of public opinion was too strong for such a course. However, in their opinion reform meant a return to the legislation of the decretals of the early Middle Ages. The basic elements of the organisation of the Roman Curia and its claims were to be preserved and only the obvious abuses removed—that is, those that infringed "the old law" as understood by them. They were opposed to the issue of new laws; it was enough to give effect to the old ones or to adapt them intelligently to present needs.[2] The various answers to the German *gravamina* that have come down to us are all formulated on these lines.[3]

---

[1] Göller, *Pönitentiarie*, vol. II, ii, pp. 91 ff.; Hofmann, *Forschungen*, vol. II, p. 97 f.

[2] The tract by an as yet unidentified author, but who signs himself M.F.C., is almost wholly devoted to this question, *C.T.*, vol. XII, pp. 48-52.

[3] The reply of the Sacred College in 1530, in the drafting of which Cajetan, Loaysa and Quiñónez took part with Monte, Cupis, Valle, Cesi and Cesarini, is in *C.T.*, vol. XII, pp. 58-66; Tommaso Campeggio's memorial of 1536 in *N.B.*, vol. I, PT i, pp. 341-421.

The curial officials, strongly organised in the colleges of the *scriptores, abbreviatores* and secretaries, were the real stronghold of reaction. These men had nothing to gain by a reform of the Curia, they only stood to lose by it; hence they fought with the utmost tenacity for privileges which provided them with an income. They took good care to avoid open resistance to reform and sedulously pleaded their justly acquired rights which, they insisted, must be respected in any circumstances. On no account must there be any yielding to the radicalism of the "Chietini" or to that of Contarini, and still less to the impudent demands of those beyond the Alps. "This affair of reform", they would add with a knowing smile, "must be settled between ourselves here in Rome", that is, ultimately everything must go on as before.[1] These circles utterly failed to read the signs of the times.

Purga Romam, purgatur mundus, Ferreri, the one-time secretary of the *conciliabulum* of Pisa, had written to Adrian VI.[2] The new "struggle for Rome" did not begin on the first day of the Farnese Pope's pontificate.[3] Paul III's initial reform measures did not go beyond the attempts by which his predecessors had sought to show proof of goodwill. In view of the Holy Year of 1525 Clement VII had formed a committee of cardinals for the purpose of reform. He had also ordered a visitation of the Roman churches and appointed Carafa as a commissary for the examination of candidates for ordination.[4] The committees of cardinals appointed by Paul III on 20 November 1534 with mission of "reforming morals" and of watching over the conduct of the officials of the Curia were so composed that no incisive proposals and effective measures could be looked for, especially as the Pope himself presently dropped them a hint that they should take into account the conditions of the times.[5] However, not even the reform Bull drafted by them was

---

[1] "Sgrossare quella parte in loco tuto et inter nostros", Bishop Giacomelli of Belcastro said in 1543, *C.T.*, VOL. X, p. 173, l. 27.

[2] *C.T.*, VOL. XII, p. 27, l. 4.

[3] To S. Ehses's basic essay, "Kirchliche Reformarbeiten unter Paul III vor dem Trienter Konzil", in *R.Q.*, XV (1901), pp. 153-74, 397-411, and the corresponding archival material in *C.T.*, VOL. IV, pp. 451-512, important supplementary matter has been added by Pastor, VOL. V, pp. 96-153; Eng. edn., VOL. XI, pp. 133 ff.; Göller, *Pönitentiarie*, VOL. II, i, pp. 112 ff.; VOL. II, ii, pp. 43-69; Hofmann, *Forschungen*, VOL. I, pp. 314 ff.; VOL. II, pp. 248-52, and finally V. Schweitzer in *C.T.*, VOL. XII, pp. 131-58, 208-56, 271-85. This material will be used in the sequel in its proper place. B. Llorca gives a resumé in "Antecedentes de la reforma tridentina" in *Estudios eclesiásticos*, XX (1946), pp. 9-32.

[4] Pastor, VOL. IV, ii, p. 577; Eng. edn. VOL. X, pp. 378 ff.; Pelliccia, *La Preparazione ed ammissione dei chierici ai santi ordini nella Roma del seculo XVI* (Rome 1946), pp. 88 ff.

[5] The relevant consistorial acts in *C.T.*, VOL. IV, pp. 451 ff.

ever published so that to this day its text remains unknown. The minutes of the consistory of 9 June 1535 give as a reason for this measure that no new laws were actually needed—all that was required was to enforce the existing ones. This proves up to the hilt that the conservative school dominated the situation. The conflict of the opposing forces became yet more apparent when the commission was further enlarged by the Bull of 23 August 1535 with a view to the reform of the city of Rome and the Curia in preparation for the forthcoming Council. It was obvious that with their experience of affairs long-service curial canonists like Ghinucci, Simonetta and Jacobazzi would at once gain the ascendancy over the other five members.[1] Their edict of 11 February 1536 [2] accordingly confined itself to regulations for the conduct and attire of the clergy of the city, ordinations, the duty of residence and the administration of parish priests and chapters; the management by officials of their respective departments was not mentioned.

Paul III's efforts for reform took on a very different appearance when in the summer of 1536, that is immediately after the convocation of the Council of Mantua, the Pope convened in Rome a commission for the study of the question of reform. The pontiff made it clear that he wished to be thoroughly informed about the programme for the future Council and to set the general reform of the Church in motion even before it assembled.[3] Those invited did not include a single curial canonist. With the sole exception of Aleander [4] they were all determined advocates of a thorough reform of the Church and the Curia. They were Cardinal Contarini, the reformers Carafa, Pole and Sadoleto—all three destined

---

[1] Cardinals Piccolomini, Sanseverino and Cesi had been members of the first reform committee; they were later joined by the conciliar nuncio Peter van der Vorst and Niccolò Dolce.

[2] Text in Pastor, VOL. V, pp. 823-7; Eng. edn. VOL. XI, p. 563.

[3] That such was the Pope's intention appears from the brief to Carafa, 23 July 1536, Q.F., II (1899), p. 221: "cunctaque interim (viz. up to the meeting of the Council) salubriter et pie dirigenda et ordinanda". The other briefs, for the most part in the same strain, in C.T., VOL. IV, p. 26 f.

[4] I do not include Aleander in Contarini's reform group, and on this point I am in agreement with P. Kalkoff, "Zur Charakteristik Aleanders", in Z.K.G., XLIII (1927), pp. 209-19. Aleander was a reformer from purely intellectual motives, without the inner urge which moved the members of that circle and untouched by the ideals of the reform movement. It is enough to study from this point of view his letters to the vicar-general, the factor and other personalities of his diocese of Brindisi, Vat. lat. 3913. By reason of this purely speculative attitude to the reform Aleander constituted the greatest possible contrast to Carafa, with whom the reform was a passion so that at times he was defeated by the arguments of an adroit opponent as was Antonio Pucci.

to be raised to the cardinalate in December 1536—Bishops Fregoso and Giberti; Abbot Cortese and the Master of the Palace Badia.[1] Its composition accounted both for the strength and the weakness of the new committee. Its deliberations, which were conducted in strict secrecy, began at the end of November 1536 with a discourse by Sadoleto and concluded at the end of February 1537. The result was a memorial entitled *Consilium de emendanda ecclesia*.[2] This document was presented to the Pope in the *Camera di Papagallo* on 9 March 1537 in presence of twelve cardinals, including those who had formed the reform committee of 1535.[3] Boldness in the presence of the wearer of the triple crown is even more difficult and more rare than courage before a king. Even a historian is fairly staggered when in a document destined for the eyes of a Pope he reads the terrible accusation that the root of the evil lay in an exaggerated theory of the papal power. "Flatterers", it says, "have led some Popes to imagine that their will is law; that they are the owners of all benefices so that they are free to dispose of them as they please without taint of simony. This conception is the Trojan horse by means of which numerous abuses have penetrated into the Church. These evils must be ruthlessly suppressed. Only such men must be ordained whose fitness has been carefully ascertained—in Rome by two or three prelates designated for the purpose and elsewhere by the bishop of the diocese. Bishoprics and benefices with cure of souls attached must not be granted for the purpose of providing a man with a livelihood but in order to secure shepherds for human souls. All contrary curial practices must be abolished, such as the charging of a benefice with a pension in favour of a third party who is not in need but by which the holder of the benefice is robbed, if not of the whole of his proper revenue, at least of a great part of it; resignations of

---

[1] Bartolomeo Guidiccioni did not attend with those who were invited in July 1536. The jurist Sigismondo Pappacoda, Bishop of Tropea, who had declined the cardinalate in 1527, was invited on 22 October but died on 3 November, *C.T.*, VOL. IV, p. 43.

[2] Text with exhaustive prolegomena which cover the whole of the literature up to 1930, by V. Schweitzer in *C.T.*, VOL. XII, pp. 131-45; also Friedensburg, "Das Consilium de emendanda ecclesia, Kard. Sadolet und Johann Sturm von Strassburg", in *A.R.G.*, XXXIII (1936), pp. 1-69.

[3] This important circumstance, which has not been sufficiently taken into account up to now, appears from Aleander's notes published by Friedensburg in *Q.F.*, VII (1904), pp. 260-3. Cf. also Schweitzer's observations in *R.Q.*, XXII (1908), pp. 132 ff. Besides Piccolomini, Sanseverino, Ghinucci and Simonetta, there were present Cupis, Quiñónez, Trivulzio and Cesarini. The latter had been a deputy in 1534. Campeggio was prevented by illness. Of the nine who signed, Pole and Giberti were absent, for they had set out for their legation to England. Fregoso too was absent.

bishoprics while their revenues are retained, the right of collation to benefices and regresses, since these practices make such dioceses practically hereditary; expectatives and reservations as a result of which it often happens that deserving men are excluded or one and the same benefice is bestowed on two candidates; the accumulation of several benefices in one hand and the concession of dioceses outside Rome to cardinals who as the Pope's official counsellors form his entourage and are therefore in no position to discharge their pastoral duties."

These incisive proposals for a reform of the curial system were inspired by the requirements of the pastoral ministry. The same motive suggested the demand for greater strictness in the concession of dispensations and absolutions, as for instance in the case of marriage dispensations from the impediment of the second degree; the absolution of simoniacs or dispensations from vows. Indulgences, certificates of confession and the right of testamentary disposal of revenues derived from benefices should only be granted in urgent cases. To achieve a higher standard in the pastoral ministry fidelity to the duty of residence on the part of bishops and parish priests is essential for—and here the memorial undoubtedly exaggerates—"almost all the shepherds have forsaken their flocks and entrusted them to hirelings". Furthermore, authority to punish the exempt must be entrusted to the bishops, regardless of privileges surreptitiously obtained or bought from the Dataria or the Penitenzieria. Ordinaries must have the right to examine confessors and preachers, even if they are members of religious Orders, as well as the right to watch over the universities and the press. Many scandals would come to an end if the conventual (relaxed) branches of the mendicant Orders were allowed to die out and if chaplaincies in convents of nuns were taken from them and handed over to the bishops. One of the worst sores of monastic discipline would be healed if every department of the Curia were to refuse permission for religious to live outside their monasteries and to lay aside the religious habit.

Both in the latter proposals as well as in the earlier ones about the examination of candidates for Holy Orders it is easy to detect Carafa's hand,[1] though it would be useless to try to ascertain the contribution of individual members of the committee to the final result or to ascribe the whole to one person in particular, even to Contarini himself, as has been done repeatedly. Even if Aleander, together with two others, were

---

[1] Cf. the account in *C.T.*, VOL. XII, pp. 136, ll. 4 ff.; 139, l. 26; 141, ll. 18 ff., with Carafa's reform tract of 1531, *C.T.*, VOL. XII, pp. 70, l. 8; p. 72, ll. 1 and 27; p. 75, ll. 2 ff.

responsible for the terse formulation of the memorial, as might be gathered from his report,[1] it remains a collective piece of work signed by all the members and for which all assumed and were in a position to assume responsibility precisely because it was the expression of the basic idea of the reform movement which they all held alike—the idea namely that the primacy of the pastoral ministry and the realisation of the apostolic ideal of a shepherd of souls were impossible without a radical change in the Curia's administrative system. It was this that constituted the kernel of the famous document, not the proposals for reforms in the city of Rome, such as the removal of certain scandals in St Peter's, which are only an appendix. With unheard-of boldness the document opened the offensive for the reform movement with a blow against the citadel of the Roman Curia on the conquest of which hung the fate of the Church.

In the session of 9 March Contarini read out the text of the *Consilium* together with some brief explanations. A separate opinion by Sadoleto was likewise brought to the notice of the meeting. The Pope then called upon Aleander to open the debate. He declined to do so on the plea that this was the privilege of the cardinals present. There was no mistaking the real motive of his action: it was prompted by disappointment at his having been passed over at the last creation. However, the cardinals remained silent. Cesi, who had taken notes during the reading, would not venture to offer any comment. Criticisms and objections only began after the text of the memorial had been handed out to the cardinals and when, at the request of Simonetta, they had obtained the Pope's permission to communicate it to their respective consultors. In this way the contents gradually seeped through to the general public, though even as late as the beginning of April Sánchez, Ferdinand I's resourceful agent, was unable to supply his employer with authentic information. All he had to report was a vague rumour to the effect that the bishops' duty of residence would be enforced, that the accumulation of benefices and regresses would be suppressed and that the taxes of the Chancery would be lowered.[2] We are in a position to ascertain the nature of the criticism of the memorial by circles which

[1] In any case Schweitzer's interpretation (*R.Q.*, XXII, p. 235), of Aleander's remarks in *Q.F.*, VII, p. 261, "nos tres deputatos esse minoris conditionis", as referring to the formulation by Aleander, Cortese and Badia is not cogent.

[2] Sánchez to Cles, 8 April 1537, St. Arch., Trent, Cles, Mazzo 10, or: "Qualis huiusmodi reformatio, plane ignoratur, quia secretissime tractatur. Verum fertur, quod episcopi teneantur residere personaliter, quod nullus non possit habere nisi unum beneficium cum animarum cura, quod regressus tollantur, taxae in cancellaria minuantur."

were conservative though by no means hostile to reform, from a discourse delivered in consistory by Cardinal Nicholas von Schönberg, the
text of which, however, has only been handed down to us by Sarpi, and
from a tract on reform drawn up in 1538 by the future cardinal Bartolomeo Guidiccioni. As a former member of the reformed Congregation
of San Marco, Schönberg could not be suspected of shying at reform; he
nevertheless observed that if a reform of the Curia were taken in hand
at that moment there was a danger that the Lutherans would regard it
as a confirmation of their accusations against the Papacy and would
exploit it as a success for their party.[1] The danger was real, but it was
no argument against reform. Guidiccioni deals much more radically
with the problem.[2] He regards the accusations of the memorial against
previous Popes and against the papalists as an intolerable presumption
while the desire to restore the Church to perfect purity and stainlessness
seems to him dangerously utopian. He puts up a vigorous defence of
curial practice as a live system that has superseded obsolete laws. It
was easy enough to abolish it but difficult to replace it by something
better. As a matter of fact, "where shall we get to if we attempt to
force the Church's life back to the rules of primitive Christianity and
the canons of the early Church? What the Church needs is not new
laws but the observance of the existing ones."

Guidiccioni further explained his principles in a criticism of some
specific proposals of the *Consilium*. The latter document proposes that
candidates for ordination at the Curia should be examined by two or
three prelates of good repute. "Why not stick to the old rule which
confers this right on the *Vicarius Urbis* and the clerics of the Camera?
Are not they *viri probi et docti*?" The memorial complains of the
inequitable distribution of benefices which was further intensified by
resignations and regresses while it denies to the cardinals the right to
hold external dioceses. But the Curia's system of dealing with benefices
rests on the Pope's supreme authority. All candidates enjoy the same
rights and are free to take advantage of the practices provided by
the curial system. Those who complain are like the labourers in the
vineyard who cast an envious eye upon the greater reward of their
fellow-workers. People who imagine that cardinals are incapable of

[1] Sarpi, *Istoria*, VOL. I, v, ed. Gambarin, VOL. I, p. 134 f. With Ehses, *H.J.*,
XXIX (1908), p. 603, I see no reason to regard Sarpi's further remarks about Sleidan
(*Commentarii*, VOL. XII, Strasbourg 1557) as an invention. The discourse has nothing
to do with the consistory of 20 April 1537 discussed by Ehses.

[2] *C.T.*, VOL. XII, pp. 227-33, supplemented by me from the preparatory work of
Guidiccioni in Vat. Lib., Barb. lat. 1173.

administering external dioceses must also deny them, if they wish to be logical, the right to hold any other dignities, abbeys or benefices with the cure of souls attached to them. How will it all end? The fight against the accumulation of benefices actually rests on an erroneous assumption: the obligations of the pastoral ministry are not linked with collation to a benefice but with the reception of Holy Orders. "Freely have you received, freely give", has nothing to do with benefices. Furthermore, it would be a dangerous mistake to try to abolish every dispensation that enables a man to enjoy incompatible benefices. The cure of souls is often far better discharged by a capable substitute than by an incapable rector of a church. Why make a clean sweep of all pensions, resignations, unions and *commendams* since Canon Law lays down the necessary safeguards against abuses as when, for instance, it makes provision for the maintenance of the holders of such benefices as may be burdened with pensions and for the proper service of churches united in one hand, or such as are given *in commendam*?

Guidiccioni concludes his critique with the statement that the *Consilium de emendanda ecclesia* would not conduce to the Church's reform but rather to her disruption: the radical principles contained in it would not issue in reform but in revolution.

The old man of Lucca was not out for the furtherance of his own interests; he no longer cherished any personal ambition. It took years before he consented to obey the Pope's summons to Rome. Nor was his defence of tradition without certain reservations. He too regarded the Dataria's compositions as irreconcilable with the principles of justice and equity.[1] He was in favour of reducing the College of Cardinals to twenty-four, equal consideration being given to every nation in their appointment. The sale of offices should be stopped. The various proposals for the reform of the Orders he regarded as inadequate and contradictory—uniformity should be introduced into the whole conventual system.[2] For the rest Guidiccioni maintains his standpoint that the reform of the Church must come about through existing laws and the actual practice of the Curia; while abuses must be removed existing conditions should be taken into consideration.

A composition with the existing order—which in practice meant the collaboration of the canonists and other officials of the Curia—could not be by-passed as soon as an attempt was made to cast the reform proposals into reform laws. To this end in the last days of

[1] Vat. Lib., Barb. lat. 1165, fol. 321ʳ.
[2] *C.T.*, VOL. XII, pp. 243 ff.

April 1537, with a courage to which we must pay homage, the Pope entered upon the task of reform at the most difficult point of all, viz. the Dataria. He accordingly adjoined to Cardinals Contarini and Carafa two experts in the persons of Ghinucci and Simonetta.[1] The department itself submitted, as a basis for reform, a schedule of the operations that came within its competence.[2] Thereupon the optimism which Contarini breathed in a letter to Pole of 12 May 1537[3] promptly veered round in the opposite direction. A long and hard struggle began. At the request of his colleagues Contarini drew up a report in which the compositions connected with regresses, coadjutorships and marriage dispensations were described as undoubtedly simoniacal; others, such as reservations of the revenues of benefices and pensions were qualified as extremely questionable, to say the very least. Contarini based his

[1] The fact of the nomination (previous to 30 April 1537) is based on the instruction for Giovanni Guidiccioni, *C.T.*, VOL. IV, p. 115, l. 22. The names are in Contarini's letter to Pole dated 12 May, Dittrich, *Regesten*, No. 325.

[2] The "scheda scripta"—which has not been preserved—was the basis of Contarini's report of which we shall speak presently (printed by Friedensburg, in *Q.F.*, VII (1904), pp. 263-7). This piece, as well as the rest of the memorials used for the history of the reform of the Dataria, are all undated. I have therefore endeavoured to establish an approximate chronology: (1) First Contarini's report already mentioned in the "scheda" submitted by the Datarius. (2) The divergences within the commission lead to the calling in of experts, that of Aleander and Badia by Contarini and that of Tommaso Campeggio by the opposite party. The latter's memorial (*C.T.*, VOL. XII, pp. 155 ff.) argues against the texts from St Thomas adduced by Contarini. (3) Contarini defends "in conventu nostro", viz. probably within the bosom of the commission, his view of the compositions, *C.T.*, VOL. XII, pp. 153 ff. (4) The Pope demands a memorial from Campeggio. The latter confesses that he is not yet in a position to make a clear statement ("modo huc, modo illuc distrahor") and concedes that the Pope is not "dominus" but "dispensator beneficiorum", though he is inclined to grant the lawfulness of the compositions on the ground of their being on a level with episcopal procurations and stole fees, *C.T.*, VOL. XII, p. 157 f. However, the insertion of the memorial at this point is not quite certain; it may be part of the conclusion of the controversy. (5) The reform party (Contarini, Carafa, Aleander, Badia) presents a separate report to the Pope—the *Consilium quattuor delectorum*, *C.T.*, VOL. XII, pp. 208-15, which must be dated after 24 September 1537, since Carafa signs as "Card. S. Sixti". (6) Counterproposals by the general of the Servites, Loreri, *C.T.*, VOL. XII, pp. 215-26, not drawn up before November 1537. (7) Memorial by Contarini on his attitude to the primacy, Le Plat, VOL. II, pp. 608-15. (8) Attempt by Contarini to win over the Pope for the views of the reform group (*C.T.*, VOL. XII, pp. 151 ff.) as a sequel to a "conventus R. morum cardinalium" held "hesterna die" and the question raised "in principio illorum capitulorum quae iussu S.tis T.confecimus". The date of this document—October 1538—is based on Dittrich, *Regesten*, No. 373. It is unlikely that the *capitula* are identical with the *Consilium quattuor delectorum* and No. 7 cannot be the "tractatulus" on the compositions.

[3] Dittrich, *Regesten*, p. 98. "Omnes fere R.mi Cardinales favent reformationi . . . adeo ut magnam spem, non dicam conceperim (quia nunquam desperavi), sed foveam, res nostras quotidie melius processuras."

judgment on St Thomas, for even in the latter instance the concept of simony was indirectly included, that is, there was an exchange or barter of something sacred for a material advantage.[1] This view led to a difference of opinion within the committee which had been further enlarged by the addition of several members of a lower rank, including Aleander and Badia, at a date which cannot be ascertained. Contarini accordingly sought to defend it by philosophical and theological arguments in a short address.[2]

The opposition party within the committee represented by Ghinucci and Simonetta and supported by that outstanding expert, Tommaso Campeggio, took the standpoint that compositions were nothing more than a tribute which the Pope demanded for his personal support from the recipients of certain favours, in much the same way as the parochial clergy demanded its stole fees. These contributions therefore were not prohibited by the Gospel (Matt. x, 8); on the contrary, they were justified by the apostolic axiom that "they that serve the altar partake with the altar".[3] When, therefore, the Datary withholds a marriage dispensation granted by the Pope when he signs the petition, until such time as the petitioner pays the composition (i.e. the fees), it is not his intention to sell a spiritual favour for money: the favour has already been granted gratuitously; all he does is to demand the fee for the execution of the document which enables the petitioner to make use of the dispensation.

When he saw that the discussions within the committee failed to reconcile the conflicting standpoints, Contarini drew up for the benefit of the Pope a memorial to which Carafa, Aleander and Badia also appended their signatures. This document is known as the *Consilium quatuor delectorum*.[4] It restates with the utmost clarity the views of the reform group [5] and ends with a refutation of the argument that a reform

---

[1] Text in *Q.F.*, VII (1904), pp. 263-7.

[2] *C.T.*, VOL. XII, pp. 153 ff.

[3] Campeggio's two memorials drawn up, the first for an unnamed cardinal, in *C.T.*, VOL. XII, pp. 155 ff.; the second composed at the Pope's request, *C.T.*, VOL. XII, p. 157 f. But Campeggio must not be regarded as unreservedly in favour of the compositions, for already in the first memorial he had arrived at the conclusion "compositiones tolerari et excusari posse censeo, approbare non audeo", *C.T.*, VOL. XII, p. 155, l. 16.

[4] *C.T.*, VOL. XII, pp. 208-15.

[5] The chief arguments against the pecuniary aspect of the compositions are: (1) the taxes are determined not by the resources of the petitioner but by their nature or object; (2) the refusal of the expedition of the document in case of non-payment, *C.T.*, VOL. XII, p. 213. The considerate treatment of the opposition party is remarkable, *ibid.*, p. 210, ll. 47 ff.

was equivalent to giving the Protestants an opening and injuring the memory of the Popes who had introduced or at least tolerated the compositions. "Rest assured", Contarini told the Pope, "that nothing will disarm the calumnies of the Lutherans and intimidate the King of England more effectively than a reform of the Curia and the clergy! The attempt to justify all the actions of all the Popes would be an arduous and in fact an endless undertaking.[1] We cast no stones at your predecessors, but from you the world expects better things!"

Thus the controversy was brought before the highest authority. With the full knowledge of those members of the committee who had not put their names to this document and undoubtedly at their request, the General of the Servites, Loreri, wrote a refutation of Contarini's memorial. This document, which rested on sound psychological principles, was also submitted to the Pope.[2] Its essential element was the claim that in themselves the compositions were not a barter—*mercatura*—since the poor were granted their requests gratuitously while those of the rich were rejected if they were contrary to the law. Even Adrian VI, speaking as a theologian, had defended their lawfulness and as Pope he had tolerated them. If Paul III were to forbid them now on the ground that they were simoniacal, the annals of his pontificate would one day contain the following item [3]: "During three years of his pontificate this Pope practised notorious simony; at the end of that period some learned and godly men"—the irony is unmistakable—"convinced him of his error; he accordingly suppressed simony though he made no restitution! On the other hand the Lutherans will triumph: 'We were right', they will say, 'when we spoke of Rome's tyranny and the Babylonish captivity of the Church!'"

This was a good hit. On 2 December 1537 the Bishop of Pavia wrote to Cardinal Gonzaga from Rome: "The reform of the Datary has gone up in smoke."[4] At a later date, when he himself had become Pope, Carafa described to the Venetian envoy Navagero an incident of

---

[1] The sentence, which is worth pondering in our own days, runs thus: "Magnum certe negotium et infinitum si quis voluerit omnia gesta omnium pontificum tueri" (*C.T.*, VOL. XII, p. 214, l. 42).

[2] *C.T.*, VOL. XII, pp. 215-26. Information on the author in A. M. Vicentini's brochure: *Il Cardinale B. Laurerio di Benevento nelle memorie raccolte dal suo concittadino e correligioso Giuseppe Romano* (Benevento 1925).

[3] *C.T.*, VOL. XII, p. 224, ll. 29 ff., somewhat compressed by myself.

[4] St. Arch., Mantua, Busta 1906, or: "La riforma del datario e ito in fumo"; the Pope is said to have assigned fresh revenues drawn from the Dataria to Carafa and Sadoleto, whereupon the Datary is reported to have said to the commissioners: "Signori, vedete quello che fate. Voi havete 700 scudi al mese sopra questo ufficio e lo volete rovinare, et il danno sara il vostro."

this period which, like a flash of lightning, lights up the background of the controversy. One day, while still a cardinal, he put his view of the compositions before Paul III by word of mouth. The Farnese Pope listened to him quietly, as was his habit, but the play of his features made it clear to Carafa that a decision unfavourable to the reform had already been taken, that in fact the battle was lost. As a matter of fact, everything went on as before.[1]

Meanwhile both Schönberg's and Loreri's forebodings were coming true. In April 1538 Johann Sturm, a pedagogue of Strasbourg, published the text of the *Consilium de emendenda ecclesia* recently printed in Italy with an introduction couched in relatively moderate terms. Soon afterwards Luther also published a German translation together with a number of sarcastic glosses.[2] Like Adrian VI's confession at the Diet of Nuremberg, this frank speech of a courageous man was greeted with derision as a stupid though cunning attempt to deceive the world. A caricature showed three cardinals engaged in sweeping a church with foxes' tails instead of brooms. Sturm regarded the memorial as a good beginning, but no more than a beginning which would have to be followed up by a fundamental change in the teaching and practice of the Roman Church, that is by a "reformation" as understood by the Protestants. Sadoleto and Cochlaeus defended the *Consilium* as best they could.[3] However, the mischief was done. Though the printing and sale of the memorial was forbidden by a decree published in Rome in the summer of 1538,[4] it was nevertheless

[1] Paul IV's communication to Navagero in 1555 is not chronologically certain, *C.T.*, VOL. XII, p. 208, *n.1*.

[2] Luther's advice in *L.W.*, VOL. L, pp. 288 ff.; for the illustrations see Grisar-Heege, *Lutherstudien*, VOL. v (Freiburg 1923), p. 57 ff. Sturm's letter of 3 April 1538, Sadoleto's reply of 15 July 1538 and Sturm's further communication of 18 July 1539 in Friedensburg, "Das Consilium de emendanda ecclesia", in *A.R.G.*, XXXIII (1936), pp. 28-68.

[3] Cochlaeus's *Aequitatis discussio super consilio delectorum cardinalium* (1538), ed. H. Walter, in *Corp. Cath.*, VOL. XVII (Münster 1931). On pp. 18 ff. and 23 f. Sturm's declarations are quoted together with Luther's gloss: "Also haben sie itzt aber ein Rank erdacht, von der ganzen Kirche Reformation, wie diesz Büchlein fuchsschwänzelt, auf dass, so man solcher Lügen gläubt, hinfurt keins Concilium noth sei", *ibid.* p. 3.

[4] On 3 June 1538 the Mantuan agent De Plotis forwarded the "Consiglio stampato circa la reformatione" and added "qui universalmente è molto biasmato che si sia lasciato stampare, perchè se non se exequisse poi, vengan li preti haver confessato li loro peccati e divulgatigli per tutto senza volere corregere li loro errori". On the same day the *governatore* of Rome forbade the sale of the publication, *Bolletino Senese*, xv (1908), p. 32. Only under Paul IV was the edition of the *Consilium* published by P. P. Vergerio in 1555 put on the Index (Reusch, *Index*, VOL. I, pp. 396 ff.). In consequence of the concise formula of the prohibition the opinion gained ground that all other editions were likewise forbidden.

published in thirteen editions within the next two decades. The question of the reform of the Curia, which by reason of its very nature should have been approached with the utmost delicacy, was expatiated upon by the press and was thereby dealt a heavy blow. That which the opponents of reform had dreaded had come to pass: the very authority of the Pope was being dragged into the discussion. Contarini accordingly judged it necessary to draw up for the information of the pontiff a well-reasoned memorial [1] in which he sought to convince him that his criticism of the papal extremists was neither inspired by an erroneous conception of the primacy nor was it an attempt to restrict the papal authority; on the contrary, its real aim was to strengthen that authority. The book of the "Babylonish Captivity" could not have been written had not the subject matter been supplied by the extremists and by the abuses which they sought to excuse.[2]

Meanwhile the autumn of 1538 had come. After the summer holidays reform was indeed mentioned at the consistory of 5 October, but nothing was done. Then came a day when the enchanting autumnal brightness of the Campagna lured the Pope to take a holiday in the neighbourhood of Ostia. While there he sent for Cardinal Contarini. The Pope told the cardinal that that very morning he had read the tract on the compositions which the latter, when almost despairing of the success of the cause he had at heart, had drawn up as a kind of supreme appeal to the pontiff.[3] In that document Contarini conjured the Pope not to stray from "the road of Christ" and to face the loss of the twenty or thirty thousand ducats which, it was feared, would result from a reform of the Dataria. The two men went once again over the whole ground. Contarini's heart throbbed with joy. But once again his hopes were destined to be dashed to the ground. When a few days later Vittoria Colonna asked him in the hearing of Cardinal Pole why the reform was not being carried through, he merely shrugged his shoulders: the poetess understood what he was unwilling to put into words.[4] The attack of the reform party against the citadel of the curial system—that is, the compositions of the Dataria—had failed.

[1] *De potestate pontificis in compositionibus epistola*, badly edited in Le Plat, VOL. II, pp. 608-15. Its dating in the autumn of 1538, on the basis of Dittrich, *Regesten*, p. 107, No. 373, seems wrong to me though it certainly falls in the last period of the struggle over the legality of compositions.

[2] On the allusion to the *De captivitate babylonica*, see Le Plat, VOL. II, p. 614; cf. Loreri's in *C.T.*, VOL. XII, pp. 223, l. 27, 255, l. 14.

[3] *C.T.*, VOL. XII, pp. 151 ff.; on the doubtful date, see above, p. 429, *n.*2.

[4] Report of De Plotis, an auricular witness, on 18 November 1538, *Bolletino Senese*, XV (1908), p. 33.

However, the Pope did not by any means intend to drop reform. While the conciliar attempt of Vicenza was drawing to a close and while the policy of reunion unfolded in Germany, Rome became the theatre of extensive preparations for reform. The radius of these preparations was extended still further when in addition to the Dataria the Chancery, the Penitenzieria and the Rota were also subjected to the reform committee although its driving power was weakened by the addition, at the beginning of 1539, of four new members none of whom belonged to Contarini's circle, namely Cupis, Campeggio, Cesarini and Ridolfi.[1] Two reformers were allotted to each of the four chief departments. The colleges of officials were given an opportunity to defend their interests in writing. This measure was the signal for a wearisome paper-war in which the conservative elements soon proved to have the upper hand. The second phase of Paul III's reforming activity—a general reform of the Curia on a conservative basis—had begun.

The many gaps in our information make it impossible to present a uniform and detailed account of the activities of the four sub-committees. The toughest struggle was that over the Penitenzieria. Here those determined reformers, Contarini and Carafa, were faced by the no less determined opponent of reform, Pucci the head of that department. Already there were those who lamented the fact that the poor "Madonna Penitenzieria" should have fallen into such evil hands, that is, into the hands of the two leaders of the reform party. But the latter had to deal with a cunning and tough opponent. On 1 December 1538 Pucci had taken the precaution of obtaining a fresh confirmation of the

[1] The chief source is Sernini's report to Ercole Gonzaga, 19 March 1539, Pastor, VOL. v, p. 132 f.; Eng. edn., VOL. XI, p. 186. The opinion reproduced above that the reform of the Dataria as proposed by Contarini was dropped at the end of 1538 seems to be at variance with Sernini's report that the Pope had declared at the time that "voleva che senza alcun rispetto si assettassano prima le compositioni del datariato" and that afterwards he sent for the Datary and commanded him to obey the orders of the commission. Of the signatories of the *Consilium de emendanda ecclesia* only Contarini and Carafa were present and thus in a hopeless minority. Aleander only reappears in the spring of 1540 (Vat. lat. 3913, fol. 152ᵛ). At his death his place was taken by Juan Alvárez de Toledo on 15 March 1542 (Pastor, VOL. v, p. 845; Eng. edn., VOL. XI, p. 584). Pole is only mentioned among the deputies when on 27 August 1540 their number was raised from eight to twelve, with the result that Cupis, Ghinucci and Pole represented the Camera while Cesarini, Monte and Guidiccioni stood for the Rota, Grimani, Aleander and Ridolfi for the Chancery and Contarini, Carafa and Loreri for the Penitenzieria, *C.T.*, VOL. IV, p. 454. On 1 February 1541 Sernini reports that Contarini and Carafa had left Rome so that the commission was reduced to ten members who were wont to meet at the house of Cardinal Cupis, Pastor, VOL. v, p. 841; Eng. edn., VOL. XI, p. 581.

privileges which Sixtus IV had granted to the Grand Penitentiary.[1]
True, the two reformers wrested a whole series of reform decrees from
the Pope,[2] and in spite of Pucci's extremely skilful defence they even
secured in the secret consistory of 6 August 1540 papal confirmation
for their own ordinances. However, they were frustrated in their
attempts to enforce a substantial curtailment of the powers of the
Grand Penitentiary. As a matter of fact, as Cardinal Gonzaga justly
observed,[3] such a curtailment would have had but little effect unless
similar measures had been taken in regard to the other offices, above all
the Dataria. The fact that in a consistory in February 1545 yet another
project for a reform of the Penitenzieria had to be read and approved [4]
showed that during Pucci's lifetime (he died on 12 October 1544) the
reform of that department had made but little headway.

While we know next to nothing about the reform of the Camera and
the Rota [5] we have abundant material about the reform of the Chancery.[6]
This circumstance enables us to get an extraordinarily clear idea of the
procedure adopted by the reform commission. The two reforming
cardinals, whose names we do not know, began by having a comprehensive report drawn up on the ordinances issued since the pontificate
of Martin V and Alexander VI and on the actual practice of the
Chancery, based on the available memorials of experts and the reports

[1] Göller, *Pönitentiarie*, VOL. II, ii, p. 93 f.; cf. VOL. II, i, p. 114 f., where the report
of the agent De Plotis, dated 14 July 1540, which had already been published by
E. Solmi in *Nuovo Archivio Veneto*, XIII (1907), p. 10 f., is used to complete that of
Sernini mentioned above. On 10 April 1540 Contarini himself wrote to Cardinal
Gonzaga: "Combatiamo cum Mons. Sanctiquattro", *Nuovo Archivio Veneto*, VII
(1904), p. 263. From De Plotis's report we learn the interesting detail that after
Carafa had succumbed to Pucci's arguments Contarini continued the fight alone
"a spada tratta".

[2] In the collection of Pucci's reform decrees, Göller, *Pönitentiarie*, VOL. II, ii,
pp. 43-69, starting from 23 January 1536, the first dated item (*Forma licentiae testandi*)
is of 5 November 1538 and the last of 5 May 1542. The doublets clearly show the
influence of the reform deputies.

[3] It is in this sense, that is as reservations, not as approval, as Göller, *Pönitentiarie*,
VOL. II, i, p. 116, would have it, that I think Gonzaga's representations to Contarini
dated 18 April 1540 are to be understood, *Q.F.*, II (1899), p. 204 f.

[4] *C.T.*, VOL. IV, p. 456 f.; Göller, *Pönitentiarie*, VOL. II, i, p. 119.

[5] A change could only come about by means of a detailed history of these offices
in keeping with modern historical methods. Cerchiari's repeatedly quoted work on
the Rota has in Part iii, pp. 281 ff., a few documents of the reform period, but it is
doubtful whether they are genuine products of the reform. The petition of the clerics
of the Camera mentioned by Ehses in *R.Q.*, XV (1901) p. 169, is too isolated an
instance to justify any considerable deductions.

[6] *C.T.*, VOL. IV, pp. 457-80, better arranged and completed by Hofmann,
Forschungen, VOL. II, pp. 248-52. The officials' reply there mentioned (Vat. lat. 6222)
has been published in the meantime in *C.T.*, VOL. XII, pp. 276-85.

of officials.[1] The next step was to give to each category of officials an opportunity to state their views.[2] None of them would plead guilty to any irregularity; all claimed that they did no more than insist on their just rights. The "calumnies" in the report were indignantly rejected: "Negligence there may have been, but no fraud", was as much as the regent of the Chancery, a man who had been in office since 1524, was prepared to admit while the notary of the department boasted of the moderation of his tariffs. "Relying on our just rights," the secretaries wrote, "we expect only one answer: 'Keep what you have!'" The college of abbreviators claimed that the committee's proposals for reform which, in the main, merely aimed at enforcing the fiscal rules laid down by the fifth Lateran Council, were at variance not only with Sixtus IV's charter of foundation but likewise with immemorial custom and the officials' right to emoluments acquired in good faith.[3] From their point of view they were right. The problem of finding a way out of the dilemma created by long-standing custom and the new requirements was well-nigh insoluble. As a matter of fact the economic situation of the officials was not a comfortable one. For various reasons the number of Chancery transactions had greatly diminished while the cost of living had gone up. "We wretched officials of the Curia are dying of hunger", one of them wrote on 20 February 1540.[4]

After the debate between the reform commission and the officials had dragged on for a whole year the Pope pressed for its termination.[5] On 1 July 1540 he assigned a new regent to the Chancery in the person of Tommaso Campeggio. On 27 August he charged Cardinals Grimani, Aleander and Ridolfi to give effect to the reform decrees.[6] We are unable to ascertain whether, or to what extent, this was actually done, but there are good reasons to doubt its having been successfully accomplished. It is enough to compare the various reports about the Bull on general reform which was to embody the reform of individual departments and tribunals. On 27 August 1540 the execution of the reform

---

[1] C.T., VOL. IV, pp. 457-67, without the Moderamina to be mentioned presently.

[2] Ibid., VOL. XII, pp. 276 ff.; VOL. IV, pp. 471-80.

[3] The Moderamina inserted by Ehses in the report of the commission, C.T., VOL. IV, pp. 457 ff., subsequently modified in view of the reply of the officials and the memorial of Tommaso Campeggio in C.T., VOL. IV, pp. 467 ff. The abbreviators' appeal to Sixtus IV, ibid., p. 474, l. 16.

[4] Cardauns, Bestrebungen, p. 62, n.1; on 21 January 1542, Pole's colleague Niño observed: "In cancelleria altra volte si facevano più facende in un giorno che hora in un mese", ibid., n.2.

[5] Consistorial acts of 10 and 21 April 1540 in C.T., VOL. IV, p. 454.

[6] All the acts mentioned hereafter are in C.T., VOL. IV, pp. 454 ff. For the composition of the commission, see above, p. 434, n. 1.

of the Chancery, the Camera, the Penitenzieria and the Rota, now definitely decided upon, was entrusted to three cardinals for each department respectively. On 21 November 1541 the Pope appointed several cardinals "for the execution of the reform". After the lapse of another six months, on 12 May 1542, that is shortly before the first convocation of the Council of Trent, the question of "concluding the reform of the officials" cropped up once more. On 14 July the heads of the three orders of the Sacred College, Cupis, Carafa and Ridolfi, were appointed executors and on 12 September a Bull was expedited to that effect. Now while it is quite certain that these men carried out their duties with energy, it is equally certain that by a Bull of 5 January 1543 the Pope trimmed their authority and enjoined moderation out of consideration for those cardinals and prelates who held important curial offices. "These prelates", the Bull stated, "must be approached with becoming discretion and dealt with only after mature deliberation." This counterstroke by officialdom dealt the cause of reform so heavy a blow that the Pope deemed it expedient, "in view of the forthcoming Council", to explain in the consistories of 19 March and 28 September 1543 that the January Bull did not imply that he was no longer resolved to carry out the reforms.

The reform of the official departments on a conservative basis initiated in the years 1540-2, with a lavish display of expert knowledge, failed to achieve its real purpose, as did the bold attack which Contarini's circle had launched against the whole administrative system of the Curia in the years 1536-8.[1] Many an improvement was undoubtedly introduced into the administration of the various departments and many an abuse countered by a shrewd policy in the choice of personnel,[2]

---

[1] The foregoing account makes it clear that the judgments of Ehses in *R.Q.*, xv (1901), pp. 171 ff.; Pastor, VOL. V, p. 150 f. (Eng. edn., VOL. XI, p. 212 f.); Capasso, *Paolo III*, VOL. II, p. 93, are too favourable at least as regards the genuine reform of the offices. With regard to the Segnatura's practice in respect of dispensations I have shown by examples (*R.Q.*, XLII (1934), pp. 311-32) that decisive progress was only made in the 1550's. As for the Penitenzieria, this only occurred under Pius V. On the other hand the verdicts of W. Friedensburg in his *Karl V und Paul III* (Leipzig 1933) and Cardauns, *Bestrebungen*, p. 58 f., appear to me too severe, so much so that I cannot now identify myself with them to the same extent as in my *Seripando*, VOL. II, p. 53 (Eng. edn., p. 510 f.).

[2] In addition to the above-mentioned appointment of Tommaso Campeggio as regent of the Chancery (1540), the present phase includes the attempt to secure the Dataria for Bart. Guidiccioni (1538), the latter's nomination as prefect of the *Signatura iustitiae* on 17 January 1540 and the dismissal of the Datary Durante on 21 February 1541, *C.T.*, VOL. IV, p. 454, l. 33. On the other hand it must be borne in mind that the efforts for reform were unfavourably affected by the circumstance that as a result of the legations undertaken by him Contarini was no longer available

but on the whole both with regard to the convocation of a Council and the reform of the Curia which was closely connected with it, those proved right who, like Thomas, would first see before they believed.[1] It must be granted that Paul III was at all times interested in reform and repeatedly promoted it by his personal intervention. Nevertheless, if he forwarded the work with one hand he hindered it with the other. The numerous confirmations of the privileges of officials which he granted during those critical years were an obstacle to any sort of reform.[2] There had been so much talk of reform that the meagre result was bound to prove disappointing.[3] In the eyes of those beyond the Alps it was nil.[4]

Yet had there been no advance at all?

In spite of the failures and the partial successes we have described the answer is that the battle for reform had not been fought in vain. When King Ferdinand I at Ratisbon drew the attention of Contarini, who died all too soon, to the need of reform of the Curia, the latter's

---

after 1541, while Giberti declined to comply with the call to Rome which he received on 27 April 1541, C.T., VOL. IV, p. 189 f. Moreover, a number of leading cardinals were removed by death, viz. Lorenzo Campeggio, 19 July 1539; Simonetta, 1 November 1539; Crist. Jacobazzi, 7 October 1540; Ghinucci, 3 July 1541; Fregoso, 22 July 1541. Aleander, 1 February 1542; Contarini, 24 August 1542; Loreri, 6 November 1542; In a letter of 23 October 1540 (Vat. lat. 3913, fol. 186ʳ) Aleander laments the fact that within the space of a year and two months eight cardinals had died, for to the above-named must be added Cles, Lang, Silva, Macon, Borgia and Manriquez.

[1] On 18 March 1539 the agent Lotti wrote to Cardinal Gonzaga: "Quest' aere d'hoggi da causa in tutti che voglian prima vedere che credere", Bolletino Senese, xv (1908), p. 35. The French ambassador goes surely too far when he writes on 22 February 1540: "Je suis seur qu'il ne s'en fera rien", Ribier, Lettres, VOL. I, p. 504. Niño's view comes nearer the truth (13 April 1540): "Non si verrà al vivo", Cardauns, Bestrebungen, p. 85, n.5.

[2] In addition to the confirmation of the privileges of the Grand Penitentiary (Göller, Pönitentiarie, VOL. II, ii, p. 93 f.) to this period also belongs the confirmation of the privileges of the auditors of the Rota, 17 August 1537 (Cerchiari, Rota, VOL. III, pp. 287 ff.) and those of the scriptores, referendaries and others, 1535-40, Hofmann, Forschungen, VOL. II, p. 67 f.

[3] As early as 25 September 1539, when the general reform of the offices came up for discussion, Ghinucci drew the Pope's attention to the danger of talking reform if it was not carried out, Sernini to Cardinal Gonzaga, 26 September 1539, Bolletino Senese, xv (1908), p. 37 f. This conversation should be remembered before we reject as a smart but unjust dictum Seripando's famous remark about Paul III's attempts at reform—"dixit et non fecit", C.T., VOL. II, p. 449, l. 3; also p. 405, l. 12. It is not the whole truth, but wrong it is not.

[4] On 5 February 1541 Poggio states that at the imperial court they did not believe in the publication of the reform Bull, Laemmer, Mon. Vat., p. 346. At the end of 1541 Granvella got the impression in Rome that there had been no substantial change in the conduct of affairs by the various departments, Cardauns, Bestrebungen, p. 63. He spoke in the same sense at Trent in 1543, C.T., VOL. IV, p. 304, l. 34; cf. also p. 301, ll. 32 ff. Pole's and Parisio's answers, ibid., p. 306, l. 5. The views of the German bishops, ibid., p. 198.

reply was a judicious and fundamentally accurate verdict on the situation. He readily granted that reform was as yet incomplete; as a matter of fact, it was impossible to carry it through with a single stroke; nor should it be forgotten how much had already been achieved through the elevation to the cardinalate of truly religious men, the insistence on the duty of residence and the general raising of the moral level.[1] With this judgment History is in complete agreement, for though individuals may be found wanting the movement of ideas is irresistible. The ideals of Catholic reform were about to conquer Rome and the Papacy, not indeed by a triumphant victory march, but slowly, amid many obstacles and set-backs and over a real way of the cross. It was symptomatic of the times that St Ignatius's preaching was criticised and denounced in Rome and that it was solely due to his indomitable energy that the incident was not merely quashed but ended with a formal acquittal. When the saint submitted the draft for the Bull of Approbation of his young Society two cardinals of the conservative party, Ghinucci and Guidiccioni, objected not only to this new form of ascetism but to the new foundation itself. Thanks to Contarini's intervention this difficulty also was overcome: the Bull *Regimini militantis ecclesiae* of 27 September 1540 was the first, and perhaps the greatest, success of the reform movement.[2]

Less easily assessed yet no less important was the raising in Rome of the moral and religious standard of conduct of the clergy, from the lowest ranks up to the cardinals. Moral lapses which would have been overlooked in the age of the Medici were now viewed as grievous scandals and every effort was made to hush them up.[3] No longer was the unaffected, disciplined piety of the youthful Archbishop of Naples, Francesco Carafa, sneered at as a display of "Chietinism".[4] The devout

[1] Report of 27 June 1541, *H.J.*, 1 (1880), p. 487.
[2] The earlier literature in Tacchi Venturi, *Storia della Compagnia di Gesù in Italia*, VOL. II, pp. 153 ff., 293-325. The most important document for our purpose is the report about Ghinucci's objection, Dittrich, *Regesten*, p. 379 f. On the persecution of 1538 see also M.H.S.J., *Fontes narrativi de S. Ignatio de Loyola*, VOL. I (Rome 1943), pp. 8 f., 500 ff. The Bull of Confirmation with the preliminary documents in M.H.S.J., *Constitutiones*, VOL. I (Rome 1934), pp. 1-32. The jubilee literature of 1940 is listed by E. Lamalle in *Archiv. hist. Soc. Jesu*, XIX (1941), p. 325 f.
[3] Very significant in this respect is the way Aleander dealt with the scandal that came to light after the death of his secretary Domenico Mussi (cf. *N.B.*, VOL. I, PT iv, pp. 3 ff.), viz. the disappearance of the money scraped together "Dio sa come in camera di quella donna che teneva", Vat. lat. 3913, fols. 145ᵛ, 201ᵛ (8 May and 15 December 1540).
[4] On 30 July 1544 the agent of Ferrara announced the impending death of the Archbishop and added "era assai meglior prelato di molti altri et con tutto che fosse molto giovine, ogni mese senza cerimonia et chietinaria si communicava et se ne muore molto christianamente", St. Arch., Modena, Roma 27A, or.

men, imbued with a truly ecclesiastical spirit, whom Paul III raised to the cardinalate—Contarini, Carafa, Pole, Cervini, Morone, Badia, Cortese, Sfondrato, Toledo, Mendoza, Silva—were not exceptions to the rule; on the contrary they set the standard of conduct. Even an observer like Granvella, a man who had but little love for the Curia, was forced to admit that the contemporary College of Cardinals presented a very different picture from that of the days of Clement VII.[1] The sixty-three cardinals that composed it at the opening of the year of the Council, 1545, constituted on the whole a truly worthy senate of the Church.[2]

Fraught with even greater consequences than this change in the moral and religious sphere was the fact that the ideals of reform were beginning to make themselves felt in the government of the Church. The ideal of the bishop as a shepherd, the primacy of the pastoral ministry, the spirit of the apostolate began to influence the Curia both in the choice of personnel and in its practical decisions. Fiscal considerations were being pushed into the background, though there was as yet no break with the system of accumulation of benefices in the hands of the cardinals.[3] In this respect the Pope's nephew Alessandro Farnese broke all records. However, a deep impression was made by Cardinal Pole's steady refusal, from conscientious motives, of the government of a diocese. Other advocates of a reform in the College of Cardinals, for similar reasons, took the greatest personal interest in their respective dioceses, as for instance Cervini, first at Reggio-Emilia and later at Gubbio,[4] and Sadoleto at Carpentras, while Morone would not regard his duties of nuncio or legate of the Romagna as absolving him from responsibility for his diocese of Modena.[5] While acting as regent of

---

[1] Report of 28 November 1541, Cardauns, *Bestrebungen*, p. 64, n.6.

[2] The list, based on a Roman broadsheet, is given by O. Clemen in *R.Q.*, xxv (1911), pp. 185*-8*.

[3] The Reform Bull granted the cardinals the right to hold two dioceses but obliged them to provide suitably paid auxiliaries, *C.T.*, vol. xii, p. 272, l. 14. The examples taken from the consistorial acts and which I have quoted in *R.Q.*, xlii (1934), p. 216, prove that even at the close of the pontificate of Paul III the ordinances against the accumulation of benefices by cardinals were still being circumvented.

[4] For Cervini's activity at Reggio see Pastor, vol. v, p. 854 f.: Eng. edn. vol. xi, p. 587 f.; at Gubbio, U. Pesci, *I vescovi di Gubbio* (Perugia 1919), pp. 106 ff., 111-19; Buschbell, *Reformation und Inquisition*, pp. 14, 207 ff.; A. Mercati, *Prescrizioni pel culto divino nella diocesi di Reggio-Emilia del Vescovo Card. M. Cervini* (Reggio-Emilia 1933). There is considerable information about Fregoso's work at Gubbio in the Archivio Armanni I D 8 of that city. Contarini's letters on the administration of Belluno in Dittrich, *Regesten*, pp. 297 ff.

[5] On 21 November 1541 Morone wrote to the Duke of Ferrara that he had been staying at Modena for eight days "per fare residentia alla mia Chiesia et vedere se con

the duchy of Mantua during the minority of his nephew, Bishop Gonzaga imitated the example set by his neighbour Giberti. "At Mantua", the Venetian Navagero reported,[1] "no one is admitted to Holy Orders or granted a benefice unless his manner of life has been found blameless." The ideal of a bishop as a shepherd delineated by Contarini a lifetime before inspired the *élite* and disturbed even the recalcitrant.

In the course of a meeting convened by the Pope on 13 December 1540 more than eighty absentee bishops then living in Rome were admonished by the pontiff in person to betake themselves to their respective dioceses and to carry out their pastoral duties.[2] The incident was of immense significance. The Pope was identifying himself with a demand which the reform party very properly regarded as the hall-mark of the new spirit. If he succeeded in enforcing the duty of residence reform would take a decisive step forward. However, it must be admitted that compliance with this duty—in itself the most natural in the world—had become a problem. Even before the conclusion of the meeting the bishops declared their readiness to comply with the Pope's exhortations provided he would first remove the obstacles to a fruitful activity in their respective dioceses. In a memorial handed in by them shortly afterwards[3] they pointed out that the numerous exempt corporations, such as monasteries, chapters, hospitals, as well as exempt persons—that is, familiars of the Pope and the cardinals and officials of the Curia—rendered an orderly administration of their dioceses almost impossible. Reservations and rights of patronage brought it about that a bishop had practically no say in the bestowal of benefices. He was forced to look on while legates and nuncios made use of their powers, whereas he himself could do little or nothing at all. Preachers and

l'aiuto di Dio e di Quella potea con carità disfamar questa città di V. E. del mal nome che ha pigliato non solo in Italia, ma anchor fuori de queste novità delle opinioni moderne", St. Arch., Modena, Giurisditione, eccl. Morone, filza 264, or. There is a great deal of material in these archives on the reform of monasteries and the bestowal of benefices at Modena in the years 1542 to 1544.

[1] Report of 1540, Albèri, *Relazioni*, VOL. II, ii, p. 16; A. Segarizzi, *Relazioni degli ambasciatori veneti*, VOL. I (Bari 1912), p. 56. The visitations of the years 1535, 1538 and 1544 ff. give a lively picture of the abuses, see R. Putelli, *Prime visite pastorali alla città e diocesi* (di Mantova) (Mantua 1934).

[2] *C.T.*, VOL. IV, p. 454, l. 25, and the report of Salazar, Bishop of Lanciano, an eye-witness, *C.T.*, VOL. I, p. 113.

[3] *C.T.*, VOL. IV, pp. 481-5, and the deputies' answers, *ibid.*, p. 485 f. The second memorial of 21 February 1541, with the deputies' answers, in *C.T.*, VOL. IV, pp. 486-9; also Ehses in *R.Q.*, XV (1901), pp. 397-403; Pastor, VOL. V, pp. 147 ff.: Eng. edn., VOL. XI, pp. 209 ff. Since the questions here touched upon were fully treated at the Council, I confine myself for the time being to essentials.

confessors of the exempt mendicant Orders, who had almost a monopoly of the cure of souls in the towns, were appointed by their own superiors and thus constituted a state within the state. It was the easiest thing in the world to circumvent the authority of the tribunal of the diocesan bishop by appealing to Rome or by invoking the secular power. In such cases the ordinary, who was best acquainted with local conditions, became himself liable to be cited to Rome or summoned before a higher secular court. In the South bishops were deprived of a considerable part of their modest income by pensions and tenths. It was no exaggertion to say that as soon as a prelate made up his mind to reside in his diocese and to carry out his pastoral duties he could be certain that a whole chain of annoyances, disappointments and lawsuits awaited him. Was there not every excuse, therefore, if many a bishop preferred to live in Rome, in the palace and under the patronage of some friendly cardinal who was in a position to improve his economic situation by obtaining further benefices for him while at the same time he enjoyed the amenities of life in the metropolis? After all, what could be done to retrieve the confused situation of a diocese in the depths of Apulia or in the Marches! The bishops' demands, on the whole, were not unreasonable. However, a number of the "obstacles" enumerated by them could not be removed by the Pope alone since they were created by the state or by laymen. The others, which were traceable to the administrative system of the Curia, he could in theory remove, but in practice he met with the same kind of resistance as that which was offered to the reform of the official departments. The cardinals charged with the study of the bishops' memorial—probably the same dozen who on 27 August 1540 had been entrusted with the reform of the officials—would have had to pull down entire wings of the extensive buildings in which they themselves lived. Exemption, now the butt of a violent attack, was at first a privilege granted by the Roman See to a chapter, an abbey or a whole religious Order, with a view to their free development. Those who benefited by the privilege fought for their independence of the bishops as a properly acquired right which secured sundry advantages for them while for the Papacy it was a trusty means with which to assert its universal authority. The commission of cardinals did not even consider the abolition of corporative exemptions but contented itself with limiting the personal ones.[1] Even then they were careful

---

[1] *C.T.*, VOL. IV, p. 485, l. 3 ff. (*protonotari participanti*) and actual familiars of cardinals. Thereupon the bishops demanded at least the right of correction, *ibid.* p. 486, l. 25.

not to touch the sensitive nerve. The reservation of the benefices of a familiar of a cardinal and his personal exemption were as good as ready money since they enabled the cardinals to remunerate their household without putting their hands into their pockets. It was too much to expect them to forgo of their own accord so great an advantage. Cardinal Ghinucci drew attention to a prohibition formerly issued for Flanders which forbade disputes about minor matters involving sums of less than twenty-five ducats to be taken to Rome. The result was that no lawsuits from that province were ever brought before the Roman tribunals, neither in the first instance nor in subsequent ones, even when the benefice in dispute was worth 10,000 ducats. "Means must be found", he said in the conclusion of his memorial,[1] "to meet the bishops, but without any undue curtailment of the interests of the Roman Curia."

The line of action thus traced out by Ghinucci was also the one laid down in the Bull *Superni dispositione consilii* [2] drawn up at the beginning of 1542. Its purpose was to make it easier for the bishops to comply with the duty of residence and to encourage them to do so. The Pope made important concessions to bishops in residence by which he strengthened their position in their dioceses and helped them to meet the demands of the pastoral ministry. Thus, for instance, parish priests who were also members of exempt Orders were to be completely subject to the ordinaries; vicars of incorporated parishes were likewise subject to their authority in so far as the cure of souls was concerned. In virtue of a special apostolic indult all the exempt were subjected to episcopal visitation—the actual familiars of the Pope and the cardinals alone being withdrawn from their jurisdiction. The privileges of the Orders with regard to preaching and the administration of the sacraments were curtailed in several respects. The Pope also fulfilled a promise made by him at the above-mentioned meeting of the bishops: to all residing bishops he gave the right to dispose of the benefices within their dioceses in the even months. He ended by protecting them against frivolous

---

[1] *C.T.*, VOL. IV, p. 489, l. 10. From a letter of Aleander, dated 20 June 1540, it appears that the reform of the courts of appeal had been considered even previous to the bishops' request. In connexion with an incident at Brindisi Aleander wrote to the archdeacon of that city: "Et perchè tra gli altri articoli della reformatione, la qual si tratta (essendo noi uno delli deputati) già siamo quasi del tutto resoluti che le cause beneficiali di qualunque somma si trattino in partibus in prima instantia, et per il Concilio Lateranense fu decreto che dette cause etiam di alquanto maggior somma di questa di Don Bilisario si debbano giudicare là dove sono nate, detto pover huomo facilmente harebbe ottenuto qui una commissione ad partes." Vat. lat. 3913, fol. 152ᵛ.

[2] *C.T.*, VOL. IV, pp. 489-98.

citations to Rome and the censures connected with them and admonished the secular powers to respect the Church's freedom.

The bishops might have been well satisfied with what they had secured if the Bull *Superni dispositione consilii* had been given force of law. This was never done. Consultation of the exempt Orders and their cardinal-protectors brought forth fresh objections, while the opposition of the secular powers to the part of the Bull dealing with the secular arm finally prevented its enforcement.[1] The Bull was only a gesture. On 11 February 1541 the Pope fixed the narrow time-limit of twenty days within which the eighty bishops whom he had reminded of their duty of residence were to return to their respective dioceses. We do not know how many complied with the injunction. The first papal measure to enforce the bishops' duty of residence proved a failure, though it was a real achievement for the reform movement that it should have been taken at all. Once taken up by the highest authority—and its consequences carefully calculated—the question of residence never came to rest. The ideal of the bishop as conceived by Catholic reform was on the march and was steadily gaining ground. Nothing throws a clearer light on this fact than the Pope's solicitude for his own diocese of Rome. The appointment as *Vicarius Urbis* of the trusty Guidiccioni, a man already marked for the cardinalate, is proof of a desire to invest this post, which until then had ranked far below that of the *Governatore*, with an importance in keeping with the new conditions.[2] The Milanese jurist Filippo Archinto who had held the post since 1542 had conceived his office as a pastoral task. He proved it by his labours on behalf of the clergy of Rome, his collaboration with the first Jesuits, and lastly, by his composition of a catechism.[3] Only a few more years were to elapse before the office of Vicar of Rome would be one of the most important of all the posts allotted to cardinals.

Paul III was not the first Pope of the Catholic reformation, but he

[1] In view of what happened later on at Trent the inquiries made from the procurators of orders and the cardinal-protectors on which Sernini reports on 3 December 1541 (Pastor, VOL. V, p. 843: Eng. edn., VOL. XI, p. 583) must be regarded as more weighty than the opposition of the governments which, in Contarini's opinion, had been almost completely overcome; cf. letter of 5 January 1542, *Q.F.*, II (1899), p. 218. Morone's remark of the year 1543, C.T., VOL. IV, p, 305, 1. 18, quoted by Ehses in *R.Q.*, XV (1901), p. 156, refers to Church reform in Germany.

[2] Guidiccioni's nomination on 22 November 1539, Schweitzer in *R.Q.*, XX (1906), p. 153.

[3] The nomination according to Eubel, *R.Q.*, VIII (1894), p. 499, who corrects G. Moroni, *Dizionario di Erudizione storico-ecclesiastica*, VOL. IC, p. 93 f. For Archinto's activities see Lauchert, *Literarische Gegner*, pp. 466 ff.; Pelliccia, *La Preparazione ed admissione dei chierici ai santi ordini nella Roma del seculo XVI*, pp. 112 f., 165 ff.

paved the way for it.[1] The sharp ear of this superior man heard the call for Council and reform, but the delicate, aristocratic hands of the old prelate which we admire in Titian's painting of 1543, lacked the strength to cut the threads which linked his whole being as well as the interests of the Curia with the Renaissance period of the Papacy. Between 1536 and 1538, on the suggestion of his best advisers—Contarini, Morone and Cervini—he courageously undertook a general reform of Church and Curia. This he did not only because he was convinced of its necessity but likewise in order to prevent the Council convened at Mantua and later transferred to Vicenza from meddling with so delicate a matter, one which, as was shown by the reform Councils, might even become dangerous. At any rate he was determined to restrict the area of attack. The large-scale reforming activity which he initiated between 1539 and 1541, after the ill-success of the first convocation of the Council, was conceived as a compensation for the prorogued assembly and as a counterpart of the contemporary negotiations for reunion. It is easy to see that the resumption of the plan for a Council in the summer of 1541 had some bearing on the formal conclusion of these reforming activities. "Reform without a Council" was no manœuvre to delude public opinion; nor was it merely a question of conscience; on the contrary, it was a carefully thought-out and fully justified attempt to strengthen the position of the Papacy both in general and in relation to a Council. The later development of the question of a Council to which we are about to revert shows that these considerations were only too well founded. More than once during the course of the Council appeal was made to principles laid down during this period.

[1] H. Jedin, *Katholische Reformation oder Gegenreformation?* (Lucerne 1946), p. 28 f.

CHAPTER X

The First Convocation of the Council of Trent

WHEN in the course of the summer of 1541 Paul III decided to propose a General Council to the German Estates, his determination was primarily inspired by the situation in Germany. The Ratisbon discussions for reunion had proved barren of result. The Pope accordingly reverted to the plan for a General Council which had been in abeyance since the meeting of Nice. By this means he hoped to counter both the fresh threat of a German national council and the no less objectionable policy of toleration. But it is more than a surmise that he was actuated by yet another motive, namely the encroachments of the new doctrines on Italian territory.

From Ratisbon Cardinal Contarini had raised a warning cry. The conflagration, he wrote, after spreading over the whole of northern Europe, was about to cross the Alps and set Italy aflame.[1] A few days later, as if to confirm Contarini's prognostication, the Pope received a report from the Marchese del Vasto in which the latter described the progress of heresy in the duchy of Milan and the inadequacy of the means with which it had been resisted until then.[2] The consistory of 15 July 1541 accordingly decided that the supreme direction of the Inquisition should be exercised from Rome. The duty was allotted to Cardinals Carafa and Aleander—both of them men whose character was a guarantee that an end would be put to the forbearance hitherto practised. This was the first step towards the establishment of the Roman Inquisition on 21 July 1542, almost exactly a year later.[3] The event marked the beginning of the parting of the ways within Italian evangelicalism. Bernardino Ochino, the Vicar General of the Capuchins

---

[1] Contarini to Farnese, 9 June 1541, *H.J.*, 1 (1880), p. 480.

[2] Ruggieri to the Duke of Ferrara, 16 July 1541, St. Arch., Modena, Roma, 27 A, or. Vasto's report of 28 June in Tacchi-Venturi, *Storia della Compagnia de Gesù in Italia*, VOL. I, ii, pp. 127 ff., together with his ordinances against the Protestants in Pavia, Cremona, etc., Chabod, *Storia religiosa dello Stato di Milano durante il dominio di Carlo V* (Bologna 1938), pp. 192 ff. On the Augustinian Agostino Mainardi who fled to Switzerland at this time, see H. Jedin, *Seripando*, VOL. I, p. 263.

[3] The second step towards the establishment of the Inquisition was the abolition by the brief *In Apostolici culminis* of all indults by means of which culprits had hitherto evaded responsibility, ed. Fontana, in *Archivio della Societa Romana di storia patria*, XV (1892), p. 283 f. The Bull of Foundation is in *Bull. Rom.*, VOL. VI, p. 344 f.

and a famous preacher, evaded examination by the Inquisition by flight to Geneva, just as his friend Vermigli fled to Strasbourg for the same reason. Evangelical circles were discovered not only at Milan and Venice—those natural avenues for an invasion of Italy by the German and Swiss reformation—but even at Modena and Lucca.[1]

These facts caused many people—doubtless the Pope among them—to appreciate the greatness of the peril. They were horrified as they realised that spiritual movements cannot be stopped by material barriers, that on the contrary they speed through space like waves of ether and find "receivers" everywhere. Evangelicalism had obscured the dogmatic divergences; apostasy had been far too generally regarded as a concern of the northern countries alone.

The encroachment of the movement on the Latin nations made it plain that the instinct of self-preservation laid upon the Church the inescapable duty of holding Protestantism at arm's length and of establishing universally binding rules of faith on the lines laid down by controversial theology, rules by which preachers and teachers would be bound no less than the Inquisitor himself. It was, of course, no less important that all the available forces of religious renewal should be harnessed so that the Church might carry out the reform which the dissidents claimed to have effected within their own camp, for though a reform on a Catholic basis had been started in Rome, it had never been completed. In view of the existing situation the first of these two problems could only be solved by a General Council; for the solution of the second a new possibility offered itself. Thus it came about that the discussion at the consistory of 15 July 1541 of the measures to be taken against heresy in Italy passed on almost spontaneously to a discussion of a plan for a Council. Though circumstances did not seem favourable for such a gathering, the Pope declared that he would nevertheless inform the princes of his intention to end the suspension of the Council of Vicenza. His language sounded none too resolute. The offer of a Council had been made, but from Ratisbon to Trent the road was exceedingly long. It required many more bitter experiences to steel the Pope's resolution and great tenacity and perseverance were

---

[1] To Pastor, VOL. V, pp. 337 ff., 705 ff.: Eng. edn., VOL. XI, pp. 488 ff., VOL. XII, pp. 492, and the literature quoted by him, must be added F. C. Church, *The Italian Reformers*, 2 Vols. (New York 1931); D. Cantimori, *Eretici italiani del Cinquecento* (Florence 1939), especially for the emigrants; F. Lemmi, *La riforma in Italia e i reformatori italiani all'Estero* (Milan 1939); for Ochino, see R. H. Bainton, *B. Ochino esule e riformatore senese del Cinquecento* (Florence 1941) and B. Nicolini, *B. Ochino e la riforma in Italia* (Naples 1935).

needed if he was to redeem his promise in spite of all obstacles and even in spite of a fresh failure.[1]

At the conclusion of the Diet of Ratisbon the Emperor had hastened to Italy in order to carry out the long-planned undertaking against Algiers in the autumn of the same year. A meeting between him and the Pope took place at Lucca from 12 to 18 September 1541, when they discussed the political situation in general as well as the projected Council and the reform of the Church in Germany which were so closely connected with it.[2]

The political horizon was darkened by ominous clouds. France's negotiations with the Porte left no room for any uncertainty that a fresh war on a large scale was imminent. The French court regarded the assassination, on Milanese territory, of Fregoso and Rincone, its envoys to Constantinople, as a breach of the truce of Nice. With a view to saving the armistice the Pope offered his arbitration. It was accepted by the Emperor, who by this means obtained at least a breathing space which would allow him to carry out without interference his African enterprise and to strengthen his whole position by a closer *rapprochement* with England. The issue of the ecclesiastical-political conversations was less satisfactory. It was decided that a prelate should be sent to Germany to promote the reform of the Church, but no agreement was come to on the crucial problem of the Council and of the place of its assembly. The Emperor favoured Trent. He stressed the fact that in that city, which was both ecclesiastical property and a strong place, the Pope would be no less safe than in his own territory. Paul III, however, declined Trent on account of the French. He also pointed out that it would be at variance with the ecclesiastical character of a Council if he were to appear there escorted by armed forces. The choice of a locality was accordingly left undecided. For the purpose of elucidating

---

[1] Best survey of the political history of the following years in Cardauns, *Nizza*, pp. 189-238, 266-308. Some of the documents not quoted in that work were subsequently published by W. Friedensburg in *A.R.G.*, XXIX (1932), pp. 35-66.

[2] For the Lucca conversations see the notes made by the papal side in *A.R.G.*, XXIX (1932), pp. 38-42. Ardinghello's instructions in *C.T.*, VOL. IV, p. 206 f., Verallo's in *N.B.*, VOL. I, PT vii, pp. 165 ff. The *Avisi* in the St. Arch., Modena, Lucca, are only concerned with ceremonial. For the literature, see Brandi, *Quellen*, p. 308; Cardauns, *Nizza*, pp. 191 ff.; Korte, *Die Konzilspolitik Karls V*, p. 48 ff. According to Poggio the imperial proposal for the locality of the Council was as follows: "Pare che non si possi trovare altro loco atto ad ciò che Trento, del quale si potrà N.S. assicurare, sì perchè è devoto a S.B. ne, sì etiam perchè è loco forte e lo potrà S.S.-ta munire et havere in sua potesta per tenerlo come loco proprio et come se ne fusse signore", *A.R.G.*, XXIX (1932), p. 39; Granvella's proposal in this sense and the above-quoted answer of the Pope, *ibid.*, p. 41 f.

it, as well as for the furtherance of such points as had not been settled at Lucca, Granvella, the Emperor's first minister, remained behind in Italy.

In a memorial drawn up in mid-October Contarini laid down a line of conduct for the papal side in the forthcoming negotiations.[1] His first demand was that the Council must be held without fail. Now that the offer had been made the Pope could not go back on his promise. Germany was out of the question for the actual meeting of the Council because the Pope's participation would then be impossible. France and Spain were likewise out of the running because the Germans would not go there, hence Italy alone remained. Imperial Milan would never be agreed to by the French; Ferrara and Bologna were papal cities; so the only acceptable locality for the Council was Mantua. The negotiations between Cardinals Farnese and Cervini on the one hand and the imperial representatives Granvella and Aguilar on the other opened at Bologna and ended in Rome. The result was not encouraging. The question of the Council had not been carried one step further.[2] The papal party insisted that there could be no question of a city of the Empire. Trent, which the imperial party urged, was too small, unhealthy and not easy to provision. To Granvella's plea that no German prince, whether Catholic or Protestant, would attend a Council outside the Empire, Farnese replied that even if it were true that the Protestants would refuse to be represented at a Council convoked by the Pope, the Catholics would undoubtedly go to wherever the Pope might summon them. The written acceptance of several bishops was there to prove it.[3] Instead of Trent the papal negotiators first proposed Mantua and Ferrara and eventually Cambrai, which, like Trent, was situated within the Empire though it had long ago become a French town. None of these proposals proved acceptable to the imperial party. Ferrara, they argued, was a papal fief, hence even less suitable than Mantua, while the cardinals would refuse to travel to distant Cambrai. As a matter of fact Cambrai was situated in the very centre of the future theatre of war. Its choice was inspired by a desire to please the French. In the end the Pope himself dropped it at the last audience granted to Granvella and Aguilar on 19 November. In its place mention was made of

---

[1] *C.T.*, VOL. IV, p. 208 f.

[2] Chief sources: Farnese's letters of 15 and 21 November, *C.T.*, VOL. IV, pp. 210 ff.; reports of the imperial negotiators, 14 and 22 November, *Cal. of St. Pap., Spain*, VOL. IV, i, pp. 386-93, 396-406 (Nos. 206 and 208).

[3] Farnese is probably thinking of the memorial drawn up towards the close of the Diet of Ratisbon by Cardinal Albrecht of Mainz, *C.T.*, VOL. IV, p. 203 f.

Modena, which, though subject like Ferrara to Duke Ercole II, was not a fief of the Papal States. However, like all other localities proposed by the Pope's side, the choice of Modena could not be reconciled with the obstinately maintained thesis of the imperialists, which, at bottom, was nothing else but the old formula of "a council in German lands".

As in the affair of the Council, so no understanding was arrived at on the other subjects of negotiation. Meanwhile Francis I had declined the Pope's arbitration on the plea that he was unwilling to have his hands tied. So the only thing the Pope could do was to resume, on his own initiative, the thankless role of a mediator, which he had played before and during the last war.[1] He rejected the imperialists' demand for the reinstatement of his rebellious vassal Ascanio Colonna, nor would he hear of making himself responsible for a quarter of the eventual war expenditure to be incurred by the Catholic League of Nuremberg. He only yielded to the imperialists' pressure to the extent of naming a specified figure for his contribution to the war against the Turks. Granvella left Rome on 22 November an embittered man. His final report and the great memorial in which he summed up his impressions [2] contributed very largely to the mutual distrust which continued to poison the relations between Pope and Emperor during the ensuing years and to paralyse the progress of the affair of the Council. Granvella stated his conviction that there would be no Council and that it was useless to bring pressure to bear on the Pope both on this point and on that of Church reform since the pontiff shrank from any real sacrifice for either cause. This conviction became also that of the Emperor. The Pope was justified in regarding the secret declaration of Ratisbon as a deception both of his legate and of himself and he reproached the Emperor for his dealings with Henry VIII even more severely than Francis I for his alliance with the Porte. In the course of the negotiations Cardinal Farnese gathered the impression that for the time being the imperialists were not greatly interested in a Council.

The only practical result of the Roman negotiations was the despatch of Morone to Germany. He was assigned a threefold task [3]: (1) he was

---

[1] Survey of the papal efforts for peace in Pastor, VOL. V, pp. 470-7: Eng. edn., VOL. XII, pp. 147 ff.; Cardauns, *Nizza*, pp. 266-75.

[2] Both pieces, dated 28 November, published by W. Friedensburg in *A.R.G.*, XXIX (1932), pp. 45-62; the passages referring to the Council and reform, pp. 46, 50, 58.

[3] The instructions of 8 January 1542 in Raynald, *Annales*, a. 1542, Nos. 2-8; corrections and previously settled guiding principles in *N.B.*, VOL. I, PT vii, pp. 99 ff. The part referring to the Council also in *C.T.*, VOL. IV, p. 214 f. The reports from Speyer in part already in Laemmer, *Mon. Vat.*, pp. 399-428; additions in *N.B.*, VOL. I, PT vii, pp. 111-45.

to discuss the Pope's joining the Catholic League and his contribution to the Turkish war; (2) to further the execution of the reforms to which Contarini had obliged the German bishops to consent at the Diet of Ratisbon; (3) to sound the attitude of the Estates in regard to the locality of the Council. Morone entered on his task of a reformer while still on the way, during a stay with Cristoforo Madruzzo, the newly appointed Bishop of Trent. He also made sure of the active assistance of Duke William of Bavaria, on whom he called at Munich. While at Dillingen he studied the prospects of reform with the Bishop of Augsburg.

Christoph von Stadion stood on the brink of the grave (d. 1543). The gaze of that shrewd and experienced prelate lingered on the past, on the long sequence of lost opportunities.[1] The retrospect filled him with deep pessimism. If only Rome had furthered the reform of the Church twenty years ago, as she was doing now, much could have been achieved and even more could have been prevented! But now? "Now", he told Morone, "things have come to such a pass that, as a result of the collapse of ecclesiastical discipline during two decades, the continual encroachments of secular princes and the terrible lack of priests, even if the bishops were willing to do what is right they would not have the power."

Morone was not the man to allow himself to be discouraged by this attitude of resignation of a weary old man, even though there were some justification for it. "The consciousness of past mistakes", he told Stadion, "must not paralyse the activity of the bishops in their respective dioceses." This was the only right attitude, to it belonged the future; but for the moment Stadion's pessimism was justified. The hour for a large-scale reform of the German Church had not yet struck. The energies which within and without were working for a renewal were not yet strong enough for a mighty counter-offensive against the Reformation.

From the moment of his arrival at Speyer, Morone began to discuss reform with the bishops gathered in that city. He quickly perceived that not one of them was prepared to begin with himself. Some suggested, not without a touch of irony, that he had better start his reform work in Rome; others, among them the well-disposed but weak Cardinal of Mainz, were of opinion that a reform *before* the Council would be premature; others told him that the Lutheran districts were the best field for his missionary zeal; some even went so far as to

[1] Laemmer, *Mon. Vat.*, p. 402 f. (8 February 1542).

threaten to go over to Lutheranism if they were bothered with reforms.[1] All that Morone could do was to admonish them individually. This he did with the utmost kindness. The Archbishop of Bremen had vanished from Speyer four days after the nuncio's arrival so that Morone had no chance to speak to him on the subject of reform. Those who were most in need of reform took good care not to put in an appearance. Morone admonished them by letter, among them the Archbishop of Cologne, Hermann von Wied, but all his efforts did not avail to restrain that prelate's leanings towards the new religion.[2] The best disposed of them all was actually the Bishop of Constance, Johann von Weeze, on whom Aleander had been so hard only three years earlier. Cardinal Albrecht of Mainz submitted a comprehensive scheme for reform which was to serve as a basis of discussion at a future provincial Council. Morone saw clearly that it would never be carried into effect; as a matter of fact it never got beyond the blue-print stage.

The only tangible results of these first efforts for a Catholic reform in Germany were due to the Jesuits Faber, Bobadilla and Jajus, who accompanied and assisted Morone. In the course of their pastoral work in South Germany and in Austria during the following years, these zealous priests scattered seeds which eventually sprang up and grew to maturity, but the requisite conditions for a reform on a grand scale were lacking, above all in the episcopate. Robert Wauchope, Morone's Scottish assistant, who had settled at Ratisbon with Jajus, was expelled by the city council at the beginning of 1543.[3]

What made Morone's extraordinary mission to Speyer memorable was not so much his fruitless efforts for Church reform, or the Pope's prospective adhesion to the Catholic League, as his success in getting Trent accepted as the locality for the Council. The question of locality had entered a new stage when Mantua, the first of the four cities mentioned in Morone's instructions, was definitely ruled out. Cardinal Gonzaga, who jointly with his sister-in-law was acting as regent during the minority of his nephew, had informed Contarini that, after consultation with his brother Ferrante, he felt bound by the will of his deceased brother, hence he could not make Mantua available for the Council. In any case the German Protestants would regard his government as

---

[1] *N.B.*, VOL. I, PT vii, p. 119 f. (3 March 1542).

[2] Laemmer, *Mon. Vat.*, p. 418 f.

[3] Wauchope's and Jajus's letters publ. by B. Duhr in *Z.K.Th.*, XXI (1897), pp. 593-621; the same on Bobadilla's activity, in *R.Q.*, XI (1897), pp. 565-93; summary by the same in *Geschichte der Jesuiten in den Ländern deutscher Zunge* VOL. I, (Freiburg 1907), pp. 3-32.

suspect and he himself might easily find himself at variance with the Emperor if, as was to be expected, Francis I were to come to the Council with an armed escort.. There was something to be said for these arguments, but they were not the decisive ones. The Gonzagas' decision was chiefly prompted by financial considerations. What they feared was that the expenses in connexion with the inescapable duties of hospitality would interfere with the restoration of the finances of their house which had been thrown into confusion by the late duke.[1]

With Ercole II of Ferrara the Pope apparently never entered into any negotiations. When the Duke inquired from Morone before the latter's departure how the question of the locality of the Council stood, the cardinal told him that besides Ferrara, Modena was also being considered but that no final decision had as yet been arrived at.[2] It was precisely with a view to securing such a decision that Morone was going to Germany.

As was to be expected, Ferdinand I received the announcement of the Council with scepticism, in fact even the Pope's sincerity was called in question.[3] Morone did his best to dispel these clouds of mistrust. On the other hand Farnese's claim that the German Catholics had abandoned the Recesses of the imperial Diets and were prepared to agree to any locality designated by the Pope, even outside Germany, proved unsound. The Archbishops of Trier and Cologne refused to commit themselves. King Ferdinand, though personally indifferent, warmly supported the choice of Trent, and even Duke William of Bavaria was of opinion that this was the best solution in the event of Mantua falling through.[4] This was also Morone's personal view. On the strength of the latter's reports the Pope decided on 6 March 1542 to modify his previous instructions in the sense that if none of the four Italian cities mentioned in them met with the approval of the Estates, the nuncio was to propose Trent.[5] The

---

[1] Gonzaga to Contarini, 18 January 1542, Vat. Lib., Barb. lat. 5790, fols. 112ᵛ-113ᵛ; cop., letter of the same to Ferrante, 12 January, *ibid.*, fol. 108ᵛ.

[2] Morone to the Duke of Ferrara, 18 December 1541, St. Arch., Modena, Giurisdit. eccl., filza 264 or, publ. in part in *N.B.*, VOL. I, PT vii, p. 105 f.

[3] At Ratisbon the Emperor said: "Quando io il vedrò, il crederò", Contarini on 10 July 1541, *H.J.*, I (1880), p. 493. Stadion was of the same opinion, cf. Laemmer, *Mon. Vat.*, p. 403. On 19 January Eck wrote to Alessandro Farnese; "De universali concilio agite ut orbis christianus videat non stare per pontificem quominus concilium fiat"; *Z.K.G.*, XIX (1899), p. 478 f.

[4] *N.B.*, VOL. I, PT vii, pp. 119 f., 186; Laemmer, *Mon. Vat.*, pp. 406 ff.

[5] *C.T.*, VOL. IV, p. 217 f. Korte's view, *Die Konzilspolitik Karls V*, p. 54, that the Pope only agreed to Trent, which he had hitherto obstinately declined, because he counted on the Council not materialising, finds no support in the sources to which I have access, but there is no doubt that his assent was reluctantly given.

prospective date for the convocation was to be Pentecost 1542. This would have been a very short time-limit indeed. However, Morone assured King Ferdinand that though the Council would be inaugurated at Whitsun, the opening would be followed by a period of waiting.

Such were the proposals with which Morone presented himself before the Catholic Estates on 23 March.[1] However, even before he could get a reply, he found himself in a most painful predicament as a result of fresh instructions from Farnese, dated 21 March. They were to the effect that at the consistory of 15 March, Cambrai had once more been spoken of as the most suitable locality for the Council. The proposal of 23 March was thus nullified. What was to be done? After consultation with Verallo, the ordinary nuncio, with King Ferdinand, and with the leaders of the Catholics—Mainz, Trier, Bavaria—Morone came to the conclusion that for the moment the best thing was to wait for the reply of the Estates. They accepted Trent. But now, whether he liked it or not, Morone was compelled to come out with the fresh proposal of Cambrai. The effect was shattering. No one was prepared to believe that the motive alleged for the choice of Cambrai, namely that in the event of war that city would be less exposed than Trent, was the true one. It was obvious that the Franco-Netherlandish frontier was much more likely to become a theatre of war than Trent, which was remote from any possible Italian theatre of war. Many people had the impression that the new proposal was no more than a diplomatic manœuvre—an intrigue of those cardinals who opposed the Council and were accordingly resolved to sabotage it.[2] Once again the sceptics were triumphant: had they not always said so! Even Morone's sincerity was called in question. A general distrust, mixed with a secret fear of the Italians' diplomatic subtlety, gained the upper hand. Was not the whole proposal a cunningly laid trap which would make it possible to lay the blame for the failure of the Council on the Germans?

Thanks to his diplomatic skill, Morone succeeded in extricating himself from an awkward situation without injury to his reputation. He persuaded King Ferdinand to agree to the oral reply of 1 April being regarded as non-extant, on the ground that it had been given without his formal participation. This manœuvre would leave the way open for second thoughts by the Estates. On 4 April the latter informed

---

[1] Morone's proposition in *C.T.*, VOL. IV, p. 218; his report of 28 March in Laemmer, *Mon. Vat.*, pp. 419 ff.
[2] *Ibid.*, pp. 424 ff. (3 April 1542).

the nuncio of their decision. It was in writing [1] and was identical with the first: they accepted Trent. The proposal of Cambrai was passed over in silence. In a postscript to his despatch of 3 April Morone observed with an indignation which may have been partly simulated,[2] that this silent omission constituted an affront to the authors of the new project. Yet that answer was better than a refusal. The meeting of the Council at Trent, which Morone had advocated from the first, was thus assured. But if out of consideration for France some town in the West appeared preferable, he suggested either Trier or Liège. He also pointed out that the Lutherans' protest which repeated the old formula "a free Christian council in German lands", did not finally close the door on further negotiations.

Thereupon Morone returned to Rome, where, on 2 June, he received the well-earned red hat. Meanwhile the Bull of Convocation was being drafted. The consistory of 26 April had finally decided in favour of Trent. The date of Whitsunday could no longer be maintained. The feast of the Assumption of Our Lady (15 August), that of St Luke (18 October) and All Saints (1 November) were proposed in turn. The latter date was eventually agreed upon. On 22 May the text of the Bull of Convocation *Initio nostri huius pontificatus* was read in consistory. This date was retained although the Bull was only published in the traditional manner on 29 June.[3]

The introduction recounts in detail the story of the Mantua and Vicenza convocations and fixes with historical accuracy the Ratisbon offer of a Council as the starting-point of the present convocation. The Pope goes on, almost apologetically, to explain that he had not been able to wait for the assent of Christian princes because the Turkish peril and the threatening situation in Germany demanded the utmost speed. For the same reason a whole year's interval required by a certain decree—the decree *Frequens* was meant—if a change of locality was made, could not be adhered to, hence 1 November of the current year was decided upon. The choice of a border town was justified by its favourable geographical situation. The Pope does not shut his eyes to the fact that great difficulties must be expected and that the result of the convocation is uncertain. However, what human planning cannot achieve, God's power will bring about. Trusting in divine assistance,

---

[1] *C.T.*, VOL. IV, p. 221. The Estates, however, declared that they would have preferred Ratisbon or Cologne.

[2] Full report of 4 April 1542, *N.B.*, VOL. I, PT vii, pp. 136 ff., in part already in *C.T.*, VOL. IV, p. 221, *n.*1.

[3] *C.T.*, VOL. IV, pp. 226-31.

he summons all bishops, abbots and other prelates entitled to be present to come to Trent for the opening on 1 November. He further invites the Emperor, the King of France and other princes to take part in the assembly either in person or at least through their representatives.

Long before the publication and even before the drafting of the Bull, diplomacy had been at work with a view to securing a proper representation at the Council. The Emperor had signified his assent, at least in principle, as early as the summer of 1541. In February 1542 Poggio, the nuncio at the imperial court, was instructed to announce that the Pope would hold the Council at all costs—*ad ogni modo*. At that date there was still talk of one of the four cities, Mantua, Ferrara, Piacenza, Bologna, as possible localities for the gathering.[1] The decision taken not long afterwards in favour of Trent was undoubtedly inspired by a desire to meet the Emperor's wishes. Poggio pointed out [2] that though the promotions to the cardinalate of 2 June might not have satisfied the Emperor's wish for a strengthening of the imperial element, it had enriched the Sacred College by the addition of men who would render outstanding service in the course of the Council—men like Morone, Cortese, Badia, all of them members of Contarini's reform circle, and the canonist Crescenzio. The first and the last of the above trio were eventually destined to preside over the Council. On 10 July 1542 Farnese entrusted Luigi Lippomani, who was going to Portugal as nuncio, with an authentic copy of the Bull of Convocation which he was to hand to Poggio. The latter had three hundred copies printed for distribution to the Spanish bishops. All was to no purpose, for on that same day, 10 July 1542, Francis I declared war against the Emperor.[3]

The declaration of war was the last link in the long chain of attempts, conspiracies and incidents engineered by the French during the preceding six months in the Netherlands and in Lorraine, in Piedmont and at Milan and even in the territory of Venice. Relying on his splendid armaments and on his alliance with the Porte, the King of France meant to settle accounts once for all with his old opponent. He immediately took the offensive in the Netherlands and on the Spanish frontier. A combined grand attack from west and east, with the co-operation of the Turkish fleet in the western basin of the

[1] *Ibid.*, p. 216 f. (5 February 1542).
[2] Farnese to Poggio on 4 June 1542, *C.T.*, VOL. IV, p. 231 f.
[3] Cardauns, *Nizza*, pp. 203-38, supplies the fullest account of the negotiations and the incidents that preceded the war as well as of the course of the campaign in the Netherlands and before Perpignan.

Mediterranean, was planned for the spring of 1543. All the Pope's efforts to prevent the outbreak of war had been in vain. In a period of six months Giovanni Ricci, the Farnesi's confidential agent, had travelled no less than four times to and fro between Rome and the imperial and the French courts with proposals for a settlement which were never either directly rejected or acted upon.[1] As at the time of the Mantuan convocation, so now the clash of arms drowned the call to the Council. Now, as then, the Pope remained neutral in the contest between the two great powers.

In his famous address to the Roman consistory in 1536 the Emperor had sought to persuade the Pope to abandon neutrality and to side with him. On 25 August 1542 he appealed to him once more for the same purpose in an impassioned letter.[2] He drew up a veritable catalogue of Francis I's crimes, reproached him for his understanding with the Turks and accused him of continual sabotage of the Council from selfish motives. If the calamities and the division of Christendom, for which King Francis was responsible, touched the Pope's heart, he must declare himself openly against the French King. Only victory over the disturber of the peace jointly won by Pope and Emperor would make it possible to hold a Council and to restore the unity of the Church. For the duration of the war it would not be possible to send delegates to the Council either from the Empire or from the hereditary states.

The letter was a flat rejection of the invitation to the Council and, what was worse, it called in question the Pope's sincerity with regard to it. Was the convocation at this moment really more than a gesture? Was it not evident that once hostilities had broken out an assembly of this kind could not be held?

The Emperor overlooked the fact that the Bull of Convocation had been drawn up with full knowledge of the existing tension but previous to the declaration of war. It did not conceal the difficulties that would be encountered and it was fully aware of the boldness of a venture undertaken under pressure of the gravest motives. But in Charles's eyes it was not a venture but a feint. In papal neutrality, which put

---

[1] Summary account by Ricci in Vat. Arch., Arm. 64, VOL. 32, fol. 184ʳ-189ʳ, cop., does not mention the Council, but his despatch of 15 June 1542, Vat. Arch., lettere di Principi, 12, fol. 334ʳ, shows that he apologised to Francis I for the choice of Trent. He was told "che là non seria mai per venire".

[2] C.T., VOL. IV, pp. 238-45, with the date 25 August; the section referring to the Council on p. 244. Cf. also Charles V's observations in the Memoirs, Morel-Fatio, Historiographie de Charles-Quint, p. 255. According to Brandi the draft is at Vienna, Quellen, p. 327.

him on a level with the aggressor, he saw an enormous injustice against which he protested with passionate vehemence.

The imperial ambassador Count Aguilar was not the only one to criticise the policy of neutrality. The shrewd envoy of Cosimo of Florence, Averardo Serristori, represented to the Pope in the best Macchiavellian tradition that he only stood to lose by his neutrality.[1] He would be in the hands of whichever party won a decisive victory and if the war ended in a stalemate the Turk would become the master of a weakened Christendom. The Pope's place was therefore by the side of the prospective victor—and this was none other than the Emperor! "You are right," Paul replied, "it is as in the days of Caesar and Pompey. Lorenzo the Magnificent once said: 'Better a wise enemy than a foolish friend.'" The Pope nevertheless hesitated to side with his shrewd but too powerful enemy—for he had come to regard Charles V more and more as an enemy. Apart from all other considerations, his fear of a French schism was only too well founded. He stayed neutral.

The Emperor's resentment knew no bounds. When towards the end of September the Portuguese Cardinal Silva presented himself at court to offer his mediation for peace and to urge the Emperor to attend the Council he met with an exceedingly cold reception.[2] The legate was told to present his proposals in writing and, having done so, to return at once whence he had come. The two ministers Granvella and Cobos created a veritable scene. However, Silva refused to withdraw without the Pope's leave and by his prudent and firm attitude he eventually induced even the Emperor to adopt a milder tone though without in any way abandoning his standpoint. Charles V deprecated any mediation for peace and assumed full responsibility for whatever was to come. Neither he himself nor any envoy or bishop of his took the road to Trent.[3]

In France the cause of the Council fared no better—in fact it fared

[1] Serristori, 12 June 1542, G. Canestrini, *Legazioni di A. Serristori* (Florence 1853), pp. 124 ff.

[2] Briefs of 26 August 1542, Lanz, *Correspondenz*, VOL. II, p. 357; Silva's final report, Vat. Arch., Arm. 64, VOL. 32, fols. 7ʳ-10ʳ. The Emperor's reply, 29 September, Latin text in Lanz, *Correspondenz*, VOL. II, pp. 378-81, with wrong date—the right date is given in the French text in Weiss, *Papiers*, VOL. II, pp. 645-9. Extracts from Poggio's report in *N.B.*, VOL. I, PT vii, pp. 439 ff.; Cardauns, *Nizza*, pp. 272 ff.; de Castro, *Portugal*, VOL. I, pp. 418 ff.

[3] In Silva's report the following passage is not quite clear: "In Monzone parlai anchora del concilio. S.M.ta si rimesse e quello che havea risposto, poi con la venuta di Granvella mutò consiglio et si fece quello che V. S.R.ma sa", Silva's reports, Vat. Arch., Principi 12, fols. 44ʳ-63ᵛ.

much worse. While the Diet of Ratisbon was still in session Paul III had despatched to that country, in the capacity of nuncio, a man of his immediate entourage, the Datary Jerome Capodiferro. And lest the French court should grow suspicious, as well as for the purpose of keeping in close touch with it, he accredited his secretary Dandino as envoy extraordinary to Francis I immediately after the conclusion of the conference of Lucca. After Granvella's departure in the last days of November, Ardinghello, Capodiferro's successor in the Dataria, was despatched to Paris in a similar capacity. However, neither of them succeeded in preventing either France's approaches to the Porte or the outbreak of war.[1] On the question of the Council Francis I stuck to his old tactics: he refrained from a categorical refusal while crossing by devious devices the measures that would bring it about. Thus he agreed to Cambrai or Metz, on condition that peace was first restored. None knew better than he that the two things were illusory.[2] He also saw to it that French cardinals did not obey the papal summons to Rome.[3]

In May 1542 Capodiferro sought to make the selection of Trent acceptable to the King by pointing out that such a choice in no way met the real wishes of the Germans, that it was a compromise with which the French might very well be satisfied. In any case they could get to Trent through the neutral territories of Switzerland and Venice. On 17 May 1542 Francis I nevertheless rejected Trent, though he wrapped his refusal in the customary formula that he agreed in principle.[4] Farnese's attempt to treat this answer as susceptible of a constructive and even a favourable interpretation was quite hopeless.[5] Capodiferro felt it incumbent on him to shatter this delusion in ruthless fashion.[6] To this end he once more approached the King, very tactfully and not in person but through his secretary, with a request for a favourable decision. The King bluntly refused to send a representative to the

---

[1] Capodiferro's original reports for 1541-3 in Vat. Arch., AA I-XVIII, 6532, fols. 1-180. On 27 December 1541 he observes: "Non volendo rompere", we must proceed with the policy hitherto pursued in spite of all disappointments, ibid., fol. 71.

[2] C.T., VOL. IV, p. 222 (17 April 1542).

[3] Ibid., p. 215 f., the almost identical briefs of 17 December 1541; ibid., p. 212 f., Sadoleto's excuses from Carpentras dated 3 January 1542 for his inability to comply with the summons to Rome "a causa del concilio" that had reached him the day before, by reason of his age, the season of the year and his lack of money, A. Ronchini, "Lettere del Card. J. Sadoleto e di Paolo suo nipote", in Atti e memorie delle R.Dep. di storia patria modenese e parmese, VI (1872), p. 89.

[4] Farnese to Capodiferro, 28 and 29 April 1542, C.T., VOL. IV, pp. 222 ff.

[5] Farnese to Capodiferro, 4 June 1542, ibid., p. 232.

[6] Capodiferro's report, 24 July 1542, ibid., p. 233.

Council on the plea that it was nothing but a one-sided action in favour of the Emperor. He also refused to permit the publication of the Bull of Convocation. The secretary asked him at least to tolerate it. Thereupon the King flew into a rage and told him not to bother him with the affair. Sadoleto, who was despatched to Montpellier in September as a peace legate, did not even venture to broach the question of the Council at the audiences of 2 and 4 October.[1] In view of the attitude of the two great powers it was of small consequence that Portugal authorised the nuncio Lippomani to communicate the Bull of Convocation to the bishops of that country,[2] that its publication met with no difficulties in Hungary and in Poland, and that the Catholic Estates of the Empire promised to send representatives to the Council.

With a view to gratifying German national sentiment the task of delivering the Bull was entrusted to the youthful Otto Truchsess of Waldburg, son of William Truchsess, a man highly esteemed for his Catholic sentiments.[3] Educated in Italy, where he had made friends with Madruzzo, the future Bishop of Trent, Otto was destined, even in a larger measure than Madruzzo, to become the instrument and right hand of papal policy in Germany and the promoter of the Catholic effort for reform during the ensuing decades, first as Bishop of Augsburg in succession to Bishop Stadion and finally as a cardinal (1544). On 13 August 1542, in company with the nuncio Verallo, he presented himself before the Diet assembled at Nuremberg. The Bull was read, and though the Protestants withdrew immediately and even the majority

---

[1] Brief of 17 August 1542, Raynald, *Annales, a.* 1542, No. 27; Sadoleto's reports of 7 September to 30 November 1542 in Vat. Arch., Germania, 59, fols. 279ʳ-310ʳ, cop.; Cardauns, *Nizza*, p. 268 f. On 27 October Sadoleto writes: "Non vorrei mescolare altre proposte con quella (della pace) che non fussero grate al Re, come questa del concilio" (fol. 295ᵛ). Further correspondence of Sadoleto during the period of the legation in Ronchini, in *Atti e memorie . . . modenese e parmese*, VI (1872), pp. 92-107.

[2] Brief of 21 May 1542 for Lippomani in *C.T.*, VOL. IV, p. 225. Lippomani was told to persuade the King of Portugal to get his theologians to study the controverted doctrines. However, in view of the fact that the nuncio was not *persona grata* at the Portuguese court on account of his friendship with Silva, he was recalled in the autumn on the plea that he was wanted at the Council.

[3] F. Siebert's biography of Otto, the printing of which had been completed in 1944, was destroyed by fire except for a very few copies. So for the time being we depend on Siebert's article in *L.Th.K.*, VOL. X, pp. 723 ff., and on the preparatory work of B. Duhr in *H.J.*, VII (1886), pp. 177-209, 369-91; XX (1899), pp. 71-4. B. Schwarz's work *Otto Truchsess* (Hildesheim 1932), Tübingen phil dissertation (Hildesheim 1923), only goes as far as the year 1543. Further literature in Schottenloher, Nos. 29199-223. Otto's reports of the year 1542 in *N.B.*, VOL. I, PT vii, pp. 566-79. The decree granting him the revenues of his deanery of Trent and his canonry of Speyer for the duration of his mission is in *C.T.*, VOL. IV, p. 234.

of the Catholics made no secret of the fact that they doubted whether the assembly would ever materialise, the orthodox Estates gave their adhesion on 17 August.[1] Verallo expressed the hope that the new Diet which was to be held at Nuremberg in November would not prevent the prelates from putting in a personal appearance at Trent, or at least from sending their representatives. But if this time also the Council was to be transferred, suspended or prevented, no one would believe any longer that the Pope was in earnest about it.[2] In view of such a state of mind Protestant propaganda against the Council had an easy task. The German bishops could allege a number of excuses for their refusal to attend the Council, such as war, the wintry season, the inconveniences of the locality. "Though one or more Germans may have shown themselves at Vicenza," they roundly declared, "not one of them would go to Trent." For the prince-bishops, above all for the sceptical Stadion, the recent expulsion of the Catholic Duke Henry of Brunswick by the Protestants provided a particularly strong motive for not leaving their dioceses. On the other hand Wauchope found the Bishops of Ratisbon and Eichstätt and even the Archbishop of Salzburg prepared to attend the Council provided the Pope took steps to open it and to take a personal part in it.[3] King Ferdinand habitually followed the political line of his brother and accordingly urged the Pope to abandon his neutrality,[4] but he accepted the invitation to the Council in spite of his misgivings about the final issue of the undertaking. On 21 September [5] he informed the Pope that owing to the pressure of the Turks he was unable to repair to Trent in person but that he would have himself represented by trusty legates and in other respects also would not fail to do his duty. As a matter of fact the King invited his advisers to draw up a list of the various measures by which he could

---

[1] Verallo and Truchsess report (N.B., VOL. I, PT vii, pp. 243 ff., 566 ff.) that after leaving the hall where the session had taken place the Protestants derisively exclaimed: "What a Council!" On account of the French war and the campaign against the Turks, as well as by reason of the feud in Brunswick, the Catholics reckoned even at this time with a prorogation of the Council. The nuncio's proposition and the reply of the Estates in C.T., VOL. IV, pp. 234-8.

[2] On 18 August Verallo wrote: "Io vedo certissimamente che se per caso N. S. prorogasse, o sospendesse, o facesse qualche atto che s'impedisse di farsi questa volta el concilio, che la religione in Germania sarebbe in tutto perduta, et quelli Catholici che vi sonno, veniranno in una tal diffidenza di S. S.tà et di quella santa sede che non crederanno mai più", N.B., VOL. I, PT vii, p. 245. Truchsess expresses a similar opinion, ibid., p. 568.

[3] Wauchope to Cervini, 1 October 1542, C.T., VOL. IV, pp. 248 ff.

[4] N.B., VOL. I, PT vii, pp. 231, 242, 278 ff.

[5] Ferdinand's observations to Morone, H.J., IV (1883), pp. 625; N.B., VOL. I, PT vii, p. 125; to Verallo, ibid., pp. 154, 198.

further the cause of the Council.[1] Among various proposals we find the following:—diplomatic steps to assure the food-supply from Ferrara, Mantua, Milan and Bavaria; a safe-conduct and exemption from toll for members of the Council; the appointment of a prince of the Empire—perhaps one of the Bavarian dukes—as the Emperor's personal representative at the Council; the enrolment of a conciliar guard; lastly, a declaration that the Diet fixed for 14 November would not stand in the way of the bishops' attendance at the Council.

In the course of the autumn Verallo and Truchsess completed their mission. At the beginning of September the former despatched the conciliar Bull and personal briefs to the Archbishop of Gran and his suffragans [2] while Truchsess distributed these documents to the prelates of Swabia and the Rhineland. This done, he set out for Poland. At Cracow, on 15 October, he presented the invitation to the Council to the King and to the Archbishop of Gnesen. The latter promised to publish it at the forthcoming provincial Council and either to appear at the Council in person or to send learned representatives.[3] However, in this instance also words were one thing, deeds another. The Hungarians pleaded the Turkish war as an excuse. As for the Poles, Truchsess thought that at most only one or two would send representatives; probably not one of them would attend in person. Towards the end of December Ferdinand I yielded to Verallo's repeated representations that he should bring pressure to bear on the bishops of the hereditary states, but even his most earnest efforts were unable to dispel the ever-growing doubts of the success of the conciliar convocation. Clement VII's reluctance to hold a Council and the failure of Vicenza cast their shadow over the latest convocation.[4]

The negative or at least hesitating attitude of the powers did not prevent the Pope from taking a number of measures in preparation for the actual opening of the Council. On 18 September the Bishop of Verona and Bishop Tommaso Sanfelice of La Cava were named com-

---

[1] Ferdinand's letter to Paul III dated 21 September 1542 (*C.T.*, VOL. IV, p. 248) is the answer to the brief of 29 July (*C.T.*, VOL. IV, p. 233 f.). Cf. also Verallo's report of 11 August, *N.B.*, VOL. I, PT vii, p. 241 f. The very cautious *Consultatio* of the royal councillors on 13 October in *C.T.*, VOL. IV, p. 257 f.

[2] *N.B.*, VOL. I, PT vii, p. 253 (10 September). Verallo personally handed the documents to the Bishop of Colocs.

[3] *C.T.*, VOL. IV, pp. 259 ff., 279 ff., also Theiner, *Mon. Pol.*, VOL. II, p. 541 f.; *N.B.*, VOL. I, PT vii, pp. 257, 570 ff., for the adhesion of the Bishop of Olmütz dated 16 November; Truchsess had called on him on his return journey, *C.T.*, VOL. IV, p. 280, *n.*1.

[4] *N.B.*, VOL. I, PT vii, pp. 263, 269, 285, 292 ff., 296 f.

missaries of the Council. Their task was to make immediate preparations for the reception of the prelates at Trent. Orlando Ricci, who until then had held the post of inspector of the fortresses of the Papal States, was adjoined to them in the capacity of billeting officer.[1] Sanfelice reached Trent on 5 October, but as the Prince-Bishop was absent he was forced to await his return before he could enter upon his task.[2] Madruzzo showed himself most helpful. It was agreed that separate accommodation should be assigned to each nation; the suites were to be billeted, at least in part, in the neighbouring localities. The Bishop's residence of Castel del Buon Consiglio was provisionally reserved for the Pope's accommodation. Such was the magnificence of that palace that when Ricci saw it he exclaimed: "There is nothing like it in the whole world! By comparison with it the Vatican is only a shop-keeper's dwelling!" A number of topics were discussed, such as the guard of the Council which was to consist of from 200 to 300 men, if the Pope did not attend in person, but if he should come in person their number would be increased. A fixed price for provisions and animal fodder was agreed upon and arrangements were made for getting supplies from Lombardy, the Romagna and Bavaria. A regular postal service between Rome and Trent was to be assured and an information bureau on events in Germany set up. The conciliar commissary forwarded plans of the city, the cathedral and the episcopal palace to Rome. By reason of its completeness his detailed list of the accommodation at Trent, which was drawn up with the assistance of a local committee, was far superior to the arrangements made for the Council of Vicenza.

A census of the male population of the diocese showed that the number of men able to bear arms and who might be called up for the defence of the Council reached the remarkable total of 13,211. In order to prevent a rise in the price of provisions, on which Sanfelice had also sent a brief report, their export was prohibited. Enterprising tradesmen were soon on the scene with their offers. When the prohibition of the export of grain from Venetian territory began to force up prices, King Ferdinand's counsel examined ways and means for obtaining from the Signoria a free transit over the main supply-routes, viz. the Val Sugana, the defile of Verona and Lake Garda, for the transport of corn from the States of the Church and the duchies of

---

[1] The briefs of 18 September 1542 in *C.T.*, VOL. IV, p. 246. Giberti was unable to execute the commission on account of his having been cited to Venice on a charge of high treason. He was only set at liberty on 17 November, *ibid.*, p. 251, *n.*5.

[2] What follows is based on Sanfelice's reports of 6, 9, 13, 19 and 25 October, *ibid.*, pp. 251-68.

Ferrara, Mantua and Milan. The possibility of obtaining corn and fodder from Bavaria and cattle from Hungary was also examined.

Preparations for the reception of the prelates were thus in full swing at Trent. But while the conciliar commissary did his best to convince the doubtful ones by deeds, Rome remained silent. October was drawing to a close; within a week the Council should be opened; yet not a word of encouragement from Rome; no Italian bishop to be seen, above all no legate! In the preliminary negotiations the Pope's presence at the Council had been taken for granted, but the pontiff made no move to transfer his residence to the neighbourhood of the place of assembly—to Bologna.[1] On the contrary, on 14 October, he asked the cardinals whether in view of the obstacles that had arisen in the meantime it was practicable to appoint a legate. He only made up his mind to do so after an affirmative reply had been given in the next consistory.[2]

On 16 October three legates were appointed. This time also the senior in rank was a jurist, Pierpaolo Parisio, a brilliant professor of civil law at Padua and later on, until his elevation to the cardinalate in 1539, an auditor of the Apostolic Camera.[3] In the world of high politics his name was practically unknown. In that sphere the leading role was undoubtedly reserved for Morone, who could be regarded as an expert on the German schism in the same way as Aleander on a former occasion. Cardinal Pole represented the nations beyond the Alps and the reform movement. None of them ranked among the well-tried leading figures of the Sacred College or among the Pope's intimates. It was therefore all the more surprising that on their departure from Rome on 26, 27 and 28 October, the pontiff, instead of uniform written instructions, merely handed them three memorials

---

[1] On 6 November 1542 the Pope mentioned this plan for the first time in consistory, C.T., VOL. IV, p. 247, n.2, but without making any arrangements for his departure though he had warned the governor of the Marches as early as 18 October to see to the collecting of the taxes in view of the additional expenditure that would arise from his journey, ibid., p. 276, n.4.

[2] Ibid., p. 261 f., and Sernini's report in Pastor, VOL. V, p. 849: Eng. edn., VOL. XII, p. 665.

[3] For Parisio see, in addition to Ciaconius, Vitae et res gestae, VOL. III, p. 667, Cardella, Memorie storiche de' Cardinali, VOL. IV, p. 224. f. For the list of his law writings, cf. Schulte, Quellen, VOL. III, p. 444; Katterbach, Referendarii, pp. 91, 101. Giovio, Historia sui temporis, VOL. XLII (Venice edn. 1553, VOL. II, ii, p. 418), describes him as "divini ac humani iuris professione insignis". In this and in the next chapter the biographical literature is only given in the case of those personalities which we shall not meet again in the course of the Council; for the others this will be found in subsequent volumes.

drawn up by the canonists Del Monte, Guidiccioni and Tommaso Campeggio.[1]

The memorials of the two cardinals contain more or less important suggestions of a general character. Del Monte kept closest to the traditional style of papal instructions. His worst anxiety was lest the legates should open the Council prematurely and without the Pope's leave or allow themselves to be drawn into negotiations with the Protestants. Guidiccioni was even more anxious to steady them against all attempts to introduce innovations in the sphere of faith and worship or to discuss anew former conciliar decisions; above all the reform of the Roman Curia was to be strictly kept out of any discussion. We know Guidiccioni's conception of such a reform.

Campeggio alone put the burning question—and that with disconcerting frankness: "Does the Pope really wish to hold the Council, or does he not?" Uncertain as he was himself about the ultimate intentions of his master, he reckoned with both possibilities. If there was a serious intention to hold the Council, and if there was a desire to further it actively, then a week after their arrival at Trent the legates should convene the local clergy in the cathedral in order to explain to them the object of their mission. If, as was to be expected, only a small number of foreign prelates arrived in the course of the ensuing months, a public protest against their remissness should be made before another assembly of the clergy and a time-limit of three months fixed within which the prelates must put in an appearance. Meanwhile some six or eight cardinals and between twenty and twenty-five bishops should be sent to Trent from Rome, to be joined by the bishops of the neighbourhood of Trent. The universities should be pressed to send their representatives; indigent prelates and scholars should be given financial assistance and an official invitation to attend the Council should be addressed to the dissidents, such as the Hussites, the Swiss, the northern kings and the King of England. His study of the history of the Councils had convinced Campeggio of the importance of an inviolable safe-conduct. Nor did he overlook such practical matters as the Council's exemption from taxation, its jurisdiction over its own members, the accommodation of so many persons and, lastly, the price of commodities.

However, these proposals would be meaningless if there were no real intention to hold a Council. If the only aim was to save appearances

---

[1] *C.T.*, VOL. IV, pp. 267-75; the last piece is also in Döllinger, *Beiträge*, VOL. III, pp. 304-09.

while another solution at some future date was being sought, the holding of a Council being judged impossible, or if there was no clear decision as to what should be done, then the proposed measures need not be given a moment's thought. In that case it would be enough if the legates repaired to Trent and there waited for the arrival of the prelates. They should be on guard against some rash individual declaring the Council open against their will, or actually inaugurating it. To prevent such an occurrence it might be advisable to draw up a secret protestation, previous to their solemn entry into the conciliar city, to the effect that their entry did not by itself constitute a conciliar act and that the assembly was only to be regarded as inaugurated after a solemn session had been held.

The "other solution" to which Campeggio alludes is precisely the one which the Popes had invariably fallen back upon ever since the Council of Basle as often as they were faced with a demand for a Council,[1] namely an international convention convoked by the Pope and consisting of some two hundred bishops, scholars and delegates. Such an assembly would decide dogmatic controversies, initiate a "reform of the members" and examine all pending questions, but without the legal formalities proper to a General Council. Its role would be an advisory one, for it would depend exclusively on the Pope and its deliberations would be held by his authority. Such a gathering would eliminate by a single stroke all the risks inherent in a General Council, such as the reopening of the question of the superiority of the Council, discussions on procedure, more particularly on the right to vote and the method of voting by nations, and last, but not least, the attacks that would surely be made against the Roman Curia's administrative methods. A convention of this kind could be held in spite of the political tension between the great powers. Of course, the Protestants would not be represented, but neither would they put in an appearance at a General Council, and they could be condemned without such an assembly in the same way as Simon Magus was condemned by the Apostle Peter and the heresies of the early Middle Ages were anathematised by Popes Alexander III, Innocent III and Gregory IX.

---

[1] Campeggio's tract *Quae timenda sint pericula ex Concilio Tridentino*, C.T., VOL. XII, pp. 301-06, in view of the mention of Trent as the locality of the Council, falls not in the year 1541 but in the period between April and July 1542, that is, in the interval between the decision in favour of Trent and the outbreak of war, otherwise Campeggio would hardly have described the relations between Charles V and Francis I in these terms: "nemo est qui nesciat quam male inter se animorum consensione conveniant", p. 303, l. 1.

There was no reason to fear that they would convene a national Council; neither the Emperor nor the Catholic princes would ever recognise the decisions of an assembly of that kind. For Campeggio a papal reform convention was like Columbus's trick with the egg—a surprisingly simple solution of the seemingly insoluble question of the Council.

It was necessary to expound Campeggio's arguments at length because they represent, if not the personal thought of the Pope, at least the wishes of influential circles of the Curia. It is matter for surprise that so important an official and so valued a counsellor as Campeggio should not have been clear in his own mind about the Pope's ultimate intentions on the question of the Council, and it is even more surprising that the latter should have done nothing to dispel the prevailing uncertainty. All he actually did was to hand to the legates the memorial of the regent of the Chancery together with the two other instructions. It would be an excess of simplicity were we to shut our eyes to so weighty a fact. We are bound to infer that by the autumn of 1542 Paul III had begun to waver in his resolve to hold the Council in any circumstances. The official version was as before, that he was determined to convoke the Council, and on 1 November Farnese wrote to the conciliar commissary in this sense; "those who doubt will be put to shame", he observed with unwarranted assurance.[1]

Madruzzo and Sanfelice were instructed to welcome such visitors to the Council as arrived previous to the legates' arrival.[2] Poggio, Capodiferro and Verallo made fresh representations at the courts to which they were accredited on the subject of the departure for Trent of the Spanish, French and German bishops. Sadoleto, the peace-legate, worked in the same sense previous to his definitive departure from the French court.[3] In the last days of the year the Swiss were admonished to send representatives to the Council. The invitation was sent not only to the Catholic Cantons but likewise to Protestant Zürich, Basle and Schaffhausen.[4] Twenty cardinals not resident in

[1] *C.T.*, vol. IV, p. 276, "perchè in ogni evento S.Stà è deliberata".
[2] Vat. Arch., Concilio, 132, fol. 170 f. or (25 October).
[3] Instructions for Poggio, 3 November, *C.T.*, vol. IV, p. 277; Verallo's report of 10 December, *N.B.*, vol. I, PT vii, p. 292; cf. pp. 294, 299. The informative report of Capodiferro's secretary dated 10 November, on his conversations with Cardinals Este and Tournon as well as Sadoleto's report of 14 November, are in *C.T.*, vol. IV, pp. 281-4.
[4] The briefs addressed to Lucerne, Fribourg, Uri, Solothurn and Appenzell under date of 22 December 1542 merely request that "velitis quantum in vobis fuerit ad prosecutionem promotionemque dicti universalis concilii intendere"; those addressed to the Protestants on 23 December contain the demand "vestros mittere non differatis", *C.T.*, vol. IV, p. 295 f.

Rome received a fresh summons to repair thither. In briefs dated 16 October and couched in almost identical terms they were told that no one could hold himself excused now that the date for the opening had arrived.[1]

All these appeals of the Pope died away on the empty air. One-half of the non-Roman cardinals were Frenchmen; these either took cover behind their King or pleaded sickness. Farnese instructed the nuncio to inform the Emperor that the Pope would not object to his retaining in the country the only two cardinals then in Spain, viz. those of Toledo and Seville.[2] When the three legates made their solemn entry into Trent on 21 November 1542 there was not a single bishop there apart from Madruzzo and Sanfelice.[3] The reports of the dean of the chapter of Salzburg, Ambrose von Lamberg, who had gone to Trent by order of his Archbishop for the purpose of seeking information, were not encouraging: Trent was empty. It was natural enough that the Archbishop of Salzburg and the other German bishops who had sent messengers to Trent [4] were not prepared to undertake the journey themselves before the presence of Italian bishops held out a solid prospect that the assembly would really take place. So long as none of these was to be seen at Trent, all the earnestness of the conciliar commissary failed to convince the hesitating.[5] The commissary was negotiating with the civic authorities to secure a lowering of the standard rent they had fixed for every kind of accommodation. In this effort he was actively supported by Madruzzo. The latter scarcely disguised his disappointment that the legates had not brought him the red biretta, especially as a report had long ago seeped through to the public and had even reached Germany that he was one of the two cardinals reserved *in petto* at the last creation by the Pope.

This all too peaceful idyll was rudely shattered by the arrival on 7 January 1543, without previous warning, of a pompous imperial embassy composed of Granvella, his son the Bishop of Arras, and Diego Hurtado de Mendoza, the imperial ambassador at Venice. The legates had of course heard rumours of their impending arrival; they

[1] *C.T.*, VOL. IV, p. 262.
[2] *Ibid.*, p. 277, *n.*4, Lenoncourt's and Gaddi's excuses.
[3] *Ibid.*, p. 286 f., the first report of the legates from Trent, 24 November 1542.
[4] *Ibid.*, pp. 284, 287 f. The list of envoys from Germany given in the legates' report of 24 November has been lost, but it certainly included Ewald Kreutznacher, the Bishop of Würzburg's secretary, *ibid.*, p. 299, *n.*3.
[5] *Ibid.*, pp. 290-3, Sanfelice's report of 30 November and 6, 9, 15 December. Pole's suite included the exiled Bishop of Worcester, Richard Pate, *ibid.*, p. 303, *n.*3.

imagined, however, that Granvella would only be passing through Trent on his way to the Diet of Nuremberg; they had no inkling that these three and Aguilar, the imperial ambassador in Rome, had been named envoys to the Council as early as 18 October.[1] In Rome, too, nothing was known of Granvella's mission; Thomas de Chantonnay, Granvella's other son, had not breathed a word of it in the course of a visit of courtesy he had paid the Pope on 24 December.[2] Parisio and Morone were thunderstruck when on the evening of his arrival Granvella informed them, with all due formality, that he had come as the Emperor's representative at the Council. To Pole he expressed his surprise that, contrary to His Majesty's expectations, the preparations were not being pushed more actively.[3] Yet the Emperor had let it be clearly known in the course of the summer that he regarded the Council as inopportune!

From a purely political point of view Granvella's arrival at Trent was a master-stroke.[4] By this sudden show of zeal for the Council the Emperor stole a march not only on his opponent Francis I but even on the Pope himself: this act of his would help to fix responsibilities! Paul III felt cheated and compromised; he was made to look as if his convocation of the Council were a mere gesture for the purpose of exculpating himself in the eyes of the public. The legates only saw

[1] Ibid., p. 263 f.

[2] Aguilar to the Emperor, 4 January 1543, Cal. of St. Pap., Spain, VOL. VI, ii, p. 200 (No. 93).

[3] The legates' report of 9 January (C.T., VOL. IV, pp. 297-300) makes it clear that Granvella must have arrived at Trent not on the 8th, as might appear from the introductory remarks and from other reports, but on the evening of the 7th. Sanfelice was sent to call on Granvella on the 8th, after which the latter presented himself before the legates when the ceremonial of the audience was discussed. This took place in the forenoon of the 9th (ibid., pp. 300-3). In the notaries' instrument drawn up on the occasion the following names appear among the witnesses: Count Sigismund Arco, Niccolò and Aliprando Madruzzo, Francesco di Castelalto, Sigismund von Thun. I was unfortunately unable to see Granvella's letter to Aguilar dated 14 January (St. Arch., Vienna, Belgica A 49) which Cardauns, Nizza, p. 279, was able to study.

[4] At the meeting with Ercole Gonzaga, Granvella stated the purpose of his mission in these terms: "Che la ragione perchè va nella Magna principalmente è perchè il Papa secondo ch'a inteso S.M.ta s'è sforzato mostrar di là per chè lei (viz. the Emperor) et non per lui (viz. the Pope) si resta di far il concilio, et perciò lo manda con l'occasione della dieta di Norimberga per chiarir ognuno che non manca dall' Imperatore che l'concilio non si faccia, et cosi se n'andrà a Trento et intendera se son comparsi i procuratori di Francia et d'altri potentati christiani. Et quando non ve ne truovi alcuno, se ne passera più oltra alla dieta", Ercole Gonzaga to Ferrante, 6 January 1543, Vat. Lib., Barb. lat. 5791, fols. 94ᵛ-95ʳ, cop. Hence Granvella's question to the legates, "se tutte le nationi havevano accettato di venir a questo concilio", C.T., VOL. IV, p. 298, l. 23.

through the manœuvre on the following day when Granvella came out with a demand for a solemn public audience in the cathedral. An audience marked by so much solemnity might very well be construed as a conciliar act—as a *de facto* opening of the Council. In accordance with their instructions the legates unhesitatingly rejected the demand though they declared themselves willing to receive the envoys with the customary ceremonial and to draw up a duly authenticated document on the subject. Granvella was furious and threatened to lodge a protest while the legates maintained their standpoint that in no circumstances would the audience take place in the cathedral. Thereupon the imperialists gave way. On the morning of 9 January, accompanied by a large suite, they presented themselves before the legates at Parisio's palace. After an address by the Bishop of Arras they presented their credentials and excused the absence of the Spanish bishops on the plea that the French rendered the roads and the sea unsafe. In the course of the conversation which followed the audience the envoys announced that during the night a courier had brought King Ferdinand's credentials for Madruzzo. This made it quite clear that the King of the Romans made common cause with his brother.

In the course of the negotiations which were resumed on 10 January Granvella did his utmost to weaken the strongest objection that might be adduced against the Emperor's willingness to further the Council, namely the absence of the Spanish bishops. This was put down to the arrest by the French eighteen months earlier of the Archbishop of Valencia.[1] On the other hand he promised the French prelates, in the Emperor's name, a safe-conduct for their journey to the Council, on condition that they travelled solely in order to attend the assembly and had no other aim in view. He roundly declared that at the imperial court no one believed that the Pope really wanted a Council; if he did, he would be much more concerned to reform the Curia and would not tolerate a state of things that was bound to give rise to painful discussions at the Council. Parisio and Pole vainly sought to weaken this argument by pointing to the reforms actually in progress at the Curia. On the other hand Granvella's fresh attack on the Pope's policy of neutrality failed to impress the legates.

On 11 January Granvella left Trent together with his sons for Nuremberg, for which he was actually bound. As for the legates, they

---

[1] On these reprisals by Francis I for the assassination of the envoys at Pavia and on the Pope's efforts for the release of the Archbishop, see Ehses, *C.T.*, VOL. IV, p. 208, *n.*1.

were no longer in any uncertainty about the purpose of this diplomatic stroke and they feared even worse for the future.[1] The time-limit of eighteen months for the meeting of the Council which had been agreed upon at the Diet of Ratisbon of the year 1541 had now been reached. There was reason to fear that in the hope of buying the help of the Lutherans against the Turks and the French Granvella would present himself before the Diet of Nuremberg with a statement in something like the following terms: "I have personally ascertained that the Council has not been opened and that there is no prospect of its beginning within a measurable time. That this should be so is no fault of the Emperor's. Nor has the reform of the Church, which he demands, and which was promised at Lucca, been carried out. The Emperor accordingly feels obliged to allow the holding of the national Council promised by him in precisely such an eventuality and to give his assent to the Protestant demands, namely, freedom to preach, Communion in both kinds, the marriage of priests, the 'reform' of the imperial dioceses and the admission of Protestant judges to the supreme court of judicature." The legates were of opinion that Rome was faced with two alternatives—either to hold the Council or to lose Germany altogether. In their view the only means of averting imminent disaster were the following: first of all stern measures should be taken to compel the bishops to attend the Council, those of Italy to begin with, and then those of Germany, France and Spain; secondly, a nuncio extraordinary should be sent to Nuremberg to prevent the developments referred to above. The first of these proposals was already being complied with in Rome, at least in part, no doubt in consequence of Sanfelice's and Verallo's earlier reports, for before his departure from Rome for the Farnese estates on 10 January the Pope had ordered a number of bishops to betake themselves to Trent.[2] However, not one of them seems to have made a start, on the plea that no subsidy was forthcoming to assist the indigent. Cervini and Dandino personally pressed the prelates residing in Rome to set out for Trent; the latter was actually drafting briefs for those outside Rome, but the matter was only seriously pressed in February after the Pope's return to the eternal city.

The pontiff was exceedingly worried.[3] Granvella's conduct at Trent and certain military movements in the Kingdom of Naples gave rise in

---

[1] *Ibid.*, undated report of the legates (12 January 1543), pp. 306 ff.
[2] *Ibid.*, p. 300, *n.*1; 308 f., Farnese to the legates on 20 and 22 January 1543.
[3] "Mirabilmente teme dell' Imperatore", Cardinal Gonzaga writes to Mendoza, 16 February, Vat. Lib., Barb. lat. 5791, fol. 102ᵛ.

his mind to an exaggerated suspicion that after his diplomatic stroke the Emperor was busy preparing a military one in order to intimidate him and thus to win him over to his side. The Pope accordingly ordered the defences of the Borgo to be attended to. He also got in touch with Venice and more urgently than ever pressed the bishops to set out for the Council. As a matter of fact a number of prelates complied with his wishes. The bishops of Sardinia were urged by briefs couched in the most pressing terms. The nuncio in Venice admonished the bishops of that territory of their duty. King Sigismund of Poland was reminded of his promise to send envoys and prelates. Otto von Truchsess was despatched on a second mission to Germany with a whole packet of briefs. He was charged to express to the bishops gathered at Nuremberg the Pope's pained surprise at their refusal to set out for Trent, especially as it was for their sake that the Council had been convoked in the first instance. Their example was put forward by the bishops of other countries as an excuse for staying away.[1] Otto's and Verallo's chief task was to prevent the religious question from being put on the agenda, for in that event the danger of the whole of Germany becoming Protestant would have become acute. On 26 February the Pope set out for Bologna. Through the nuncio Poggio he informed the Emperor that he held him to his promise to allow the Spanish bishops to go to Trent. If they did, the Portuguese prelates would not fail to follow their example.

From France nothing was to be expected. Francis I sent word that he stuck to his earlier point of view, that at the moment a Council at Trent was not practicable. He rejected the compromise proposed by Farnese, that he should at least put a few bishops at the Pope's disposal for purposes connected with the Council; he also declined a meeting with the Pope.[2] The Emperor's acceptance of a similar invitation and

---

[1] The briefs mentioned in the text, the instructions for Truchsess and Poggio and other material in *C.T.*, VOL. IV, pp. 309-17. Admonition to other prelates, e.g. John Magnus, Archbishop of Upsala, *ibid.*, p. 314, *n.*7.

[2] *Ibid.*, p. 310, *n.*1; p. 337, l. 40, on the mission of the French agent Siney, who arrived in Rome on 20 February 1543; Aguilar on 28 February, *Cal. of St. Pap., Spain*, VOL. VI, ii, p. 258, No. 108. There is no evidence that by his refusal to send representatives to Trent Francis I met the Pope's secret wishes and that he was in a clandestine agreement with him, as Cardinal Gonzaga suspected at the time (Gonzaga to the Duke of Ferrara, 7 March 1543, Barb. lat. 5791, fol. 109ʳ). Even more fantastic was the project ascribed to the Pope by Gonzaga in the event of the non-appearance of the Protestants at Trent, viz. the holding of a sham Council with the French and the Italians in some other locality, "persuadendosi dover haver li prelati di Francia al suo commando et con quelli et questi di qua far tutto quello che prima haveva disegnato, cioè serrar il concilio reformando solamente alcuna cosetta di poco

his readiness to meet the Pope in the course of his journey to Germany by way of northern Italy decided the fate of the Council. The Pope's journey to Bologna was actually connected with the proposed meeting.

While Granvella's flying visit to Trent continued to cause a great stir elsewhere, calm returned to the seat of the Council. On 17 January Mendoza left for Venice though the legate had refused him permission to do so, but his departure was compensated for by the arrival, on 10 and 11 March, of the first Roman prelates, Tommaso Campeggio and Cornelio Musso.[1] They found the city both congested and expensive. In their opinion it was inadvisable to open the Council at Trent since it would eventually have to be transferred to some other locality. The measures suggested by Sanfelice in the autumn for securing food supplies had not been acted upon with the result that the arrival of the first prelates led to an immediate rise in the price of grain, wine and animal fodder. Between the last days of March and the beginning of May the Archbishops of Corfu and Otranto, the Bishops of Belcastro and Melopotamos and the proctors of three German bishops arrived at Trent [2] and 10 May witnessed the arrival of the first German prelate in the person of Valentine von Tetleben, Bishop of Hildesheim, with his auxiliary the Dominican Balthasar Fanneman. Both these prelates, as well as the jurist and controversialist Konrad Braun and Jodocus Hoetfilter, also a noted writer, were the accredited proctors of Cardinal Albrecht for the three dioceses of Mainz, Magdeburg and Halberstadt. However, the legates refused to recognise the proctors as fully qualified

---

relievo". But should the Lutherans come "non pensa di lasciarvisi accoglier in alcun modo, ma bene armarsi et solicitare Francia a tutto suo poter che rompa guerra", that is, that France should prevent the Council by invading Italy, Gonzaga to Vivaldino, 25 February and 1 March 1543, Barb. lat. 5791, fols. 103ʳ, 107ᵛ.

[1] In recommending him to Madruzzo, 18 February 1543 (St. Arch., Trent, Madruzzo 1543 or) Farnese calls the latter, who was Bishop of Bertinoro at the time, "mio molto domestico". Campeggio's report of 15 March, *C.T.*, VOL. IV, p. 318 f.

[2] The legates' reports of 20-29 March, 11-16 May, in *C.T.*, VOL. IV, pp. 319, 329 ff.; Madruzzo to Farnese, 30 April, *ibid.*, p. 327 f.; *ibid.*, the laudatory brief for Tetleben dated 2 June, *ibid.*, p. 343. Tetleben's chief object was to obtain help against Hildesheim, which had turned Protestant, A. Bertram, *Geschichte des Bistums Hildesheim*, VOL. II (Hildesheim-Leipzig 1916), pp. 137-43. On Fannemann, whom the legates erroneously describe as "ep. Misnensis" instead of "Mysiensis", see Paulus, *Dominikaner*, pp. 84 ff. Braun, who had resigned his post as chancellor of the supreme imperial court of judicature at Speyer in 1542, from conscientious motives, began at this time his work *De concilio universali*, which he did not complete and which was never published, N. Paulus in *H.J.*, XIV (1893), p. 533. One of the three German proctors mentioned was undoubtedly Ewald Kreutzenacher, a canon of the collegiate church of Haug and a native of Würzburg, *C.T.*, VOL. IV, p. 342, *n.3*.

representatives of their superiors for they were anxious to secure the latter's personal presence.

All in all the result of the convocation of the Council was truly pitiful. Seven months after the date fixed for the opening only ten bishops were present at Trent! Exactly ten bishops—an insignificant fraction of the entire hierarchy had complied with the pressing, oft-repeated appeal of the Pope! Nothing throws a more lurid light on the crisis of papal authority—not of course of the primatial authority—than this fact which demands an explanation. It is easy enough to explain it in the case of the episcopate of the already consolidated national states and of those of Italy. In France, by the King's command, the Bull was never published. Not only the bishops of Spain but those of Portugal also waited in vain for their sovereigns' command to set out for the Council. The Italian bishops were unwilling to run into expense before the opening of the Council was assured, while on their part the Swiss and the Germans were waiting for the Italians, though in their case other factors were also at work.

In Switzerland neither Catholics nor Protestants had taken the invitation to the Council seriously. On 15 June 1543 the thirteen Cantons ended by replying to the briefs of invitation presented to them by the papal agent Rosin. They declared that the Council which was to meet at Trent could not be a general one as long as peace was not restored in Christendom. As soon as an undoubted General Council (*uno indubitato generale concilio*) should meet, they would do their duty.[1] This was an open challenge to the oecumenicity of the Council.

In Germany the cause of the Council had been grievously injured by the wide publicity given to the Emperor's letter of rejection of 25 August 1542, of which we have already spoken.[2] People in Germany

---

[1] Rosin to Farnese, 22 June 1543, C. Wirz, *Akten über die diplomatischen Beziehungen der römischen Kurie zu der Schweiz 1512-53* (Basle 1895), pp. 384 ff. In a letter of 1 May to the Strasbourgers the men of Basle based their hesitation on the fact that no time-limit had been fixed for their appearance at Trent. Very significant too are the negotiations of the Abbot of St Gall with Schwyz and Lucerne, *Eidgenössische Abschiede*, VOL. IV, i (d), pp. 239, 272 f.

[2] On the publication of the imperial letter of 28 August 1542 in Latin, Spanish and German, together with the brief of 12 November (Raynald, *Annales, a.* 1542, No. 31 f.), and the imperial reply of 16 December, see *C.T.*, VOL. IV, p. 294 f. and p. 238, *n.*5; p. 321, l. 37; *N.B.*, VOL. I, PT vii, pp. 299 f., 314, 340, 573. Schottenloher, Nos. 43207c-08 lists one Latin and three German printed editions. The French answer of 10 March 1543 in Le Plat, VOL. III, pp. 159-94, also found in *Storia italiana* of Melchiorre Cresci published by U. G. Oxilia in *Miscellanea di storia italiana*, III (1907), pp. 153-84, does not take up a decisive position with regard to the accusation that France had sabotaged the Council but contents itself with the assertion that that assembly was nothing more than a means for satisfying Charles V's lust of domination.

were only too ready to regard the convocation of the Council as a mere gesture. If at this moment the Emperor also declared himself unfavourable to such a gathering it was evident that the whole affair was a sham. Could there be a more forcible argument than this dilemma: "If the Pope really meant to hold a Council he would long ago have ordered the Italian bishops to Trent; if the Emperor desired it the Spanish bishops would have put in an appearance?"[1] What guarantee was there that during the absence of the prince-bishops their Protestant neighbours would not carry out a *coup-de-main* against their ecclesiastical territories? The Catholic League offered but a slender protection since it was only loosely knit together and without strength, and the Pope had refused to join it.[2] Bucer's summons to Cologne and the hesitations of the Bishops of Münster and Strasbourg were ominous symptoms that the episcopal front was beginning to crack. The episcopal cities of Ratisbon and Hildesheim had but recently declared themselves in favour of the new teaching. Lutheranism was advancing along the whole line while timidity and passivity paralysed the Catholics. The apostasy of the whole country, so often foretold by Morone, Contarini and other experts, appeared to be only a question of time.

For a while the peril threatening from Germany made the proceedings of the Diet of Nuremberg the centre of interest. Verallo and Truchsess did all they could to convince the hesitant and the doubtful that the papal convocation was made in good earnest and to prevent a development of the religious question along the lines which the legates feared it would take. Thanks to Ferdinand I's intervention, the result was better than could have been expected. True, the Protestants refused to have anything to do with the "papal" Council of Trent, but they no longer insisted on a national one. The Catholics maintained their earlier approval. They declared that since the Pope had met their wishes and suggestions by summoning the Council to Trent, that assembly could not be boycotted under any pretext whatsoever.[3] Truchsess handed to the bishops personally present or to their representatives the briefs of which he was the bearer. On the archbishops he called in person in accordance with his instructions. He got the impression that the German bishops were obviously taking a livelier interest in the cause of the Council. Like the Apostle Thomas they

---

[1] These ideas are most clearly developed by Verallo on 26 February 1543, *N.B.*, VOL. I, PT vii, p. 317; cf. also pp. 297, 299.

[2] Verallo, 18 February, *N.B.*, VOL. I, PT vii, pp. 310-14, and *passim*, with the documents of pp. 513-50.

[3] *Ibid.*, pp. 317 21, 327, Verallo on 26 February, 1 and 13 March.

felt that at last they had tangible evidence of the Pope's good-will. This revulsion of feeling was no doubt due to the predicament in which they found themselves—either to submit to the Council and its Catholic reform or to allow themselves to be "reformed" by the Protestants.[1]

Truchsess's view of the situation was far too rosy. Before long he was to have experience of the obstacles that stood in the way of German representation at the Council. Bishop Stadion of Augsburg was carried off by sudden death while the Diet was in session.[2] On 10 May the cathedral chapter's choice of a successor fell on Truchsess. Thus it came about that he too found himself prevented from undertaking the journey to Trent by pressing obligations to the cathedral chapter. Most of the other bishops were paralysed by fear or a sense of uncertainty; the mere despatch of proctors by the Archbishops of Mainz and Trier and by the Bishop of Bamberg was a sign of good-will. Bishop Maurice of Eichstätt alone fulfilled his promise to Verallo: on 22 June he arrived at Trent, provided with powers of attorney for his neighbour, the Bishop of Würzburg where he held the post of provost of the cathedral chapter.[3]

---

[1] Truchsess on 31 March, *C.T.*, VOL. IV, pp. 319-25; 6 and 8 April, *N.B.*, VOL. I, PT vii, pp. 572-9. More critical than Truchsess, Verallo, on 8 April (*N.B.*, VOL. I, PT vii, p. 352), distinguishes between three groups at the Diet: (1) The first group regards the Council as impossible on account of the war and favours a national council or an equivalent imperial gathering; (2) The second group considers the Tridentine convocation as "una pastura et cosa più presto finta che vera"; (3) The third group is prepared to believe that the Council will materialise provided the Pope repairs to Trent in person; if he refuses to do so "senza dubbio reputeriano ogni cosa vana et inutile". The well-meant suggestions for the success of the Council by an anonymous writer (*C.T.*, VOL. XII, pp. 426 ff.) betray the counsellor's inexperience.

[2] On the evening before his death (15 April) Stadion told his companions at table: "They want me to go to the Council, but I do not know whether I shall get as far as Dillingen whole and sound", *N.B.*, VOL. I, PT vii, p. 356; *ibid.*, p. 361, on Otto's election.

[3] Morone on 30 June, *C.T.*, VOL. IV, p. 346; the Würzburger's letter, *ibid.*, p. 342. According to K. Ried, "Fürstbischof Moritz von Hutten und seine Stellung zur Konzilsfrage", *Festgabe Joseph Schlecht* (Munich-Freising 1917), pp. 281-99, and *id.*, *Moritz von Hutten und die Glaubensspaltung* (Münster 1925), pp. 67 ff., Hutten left Eichstätt on 4 June. The day of his arrival is uncertain. He stayed at the house of Canon Christoph Nagelbeck. His contest with the Italian bishops over precedence in *C.T.*, VOL. I, p. 181. Truchsess had handed the invitations to Konrad von Bibra, Bishop of Würzburg on 7 September 1542. On 26 May 1543 Bibra informed his chapter that he intended to send the licentiate Armbruster to Trent; see A. Amrhein, *Reformationsgeschichtliche Mitteilungen aus dem Bistum Würzburg* (Münster 1923), p. 64. On the four proctors of Trier Johann Count Isenburg, Ambrose Pelargus, Nicolaus Mondrichius and Jacob Pergner cf. *C.T.*, VOL. IV, p. 352, *n.*3, VOL. V, p. 142; Ehses in *Pastor bonus*, 1897, p. 324 f. The Archbishop's correspondence with the chapter (12 May-8 June 1543) in St. Arch., Koblenz, C 1 16293. From a letter of provost Paul Neydecker to Nausea dated 3 February 1543 (*Epp. misc. ad Nauseam*,

The one man who needed no goading and who was all on fire to participate in the Council was kept back against his will. Bishop Nausea of Vienna had been chosen by King Ferdinand as his personal representative at the Council. Such was that prelate's keenness that as early as November 1542 he had instructed Canon Erasmus Strenberger to secure accommodation for him at Trent in the house of Stephen Rosin. In his eagerness he ignored the warning of his confidential agent against undue haste. His departure was fixed for 3 February when a royal ordinance dated 20 January came to damp his ardour. He was not to set out until ordered by the King. There was nothing for it but to wait. Then came the monitory brief of 18 February together with a letter from Truchsess with a formal assurance that the Pope would not allow himself to be diverted from his purpose. Thereupon Nausea announced his readiness to set out at once and besought King Ferdinand to allow him to do so and to supply him with the necessary funds. Verallo supported his request. On 12 May Ferdinand replied coldly that he stood by his decision. If Nausea was summoned by the Pope he could, of course, set out for Trent, but not as his envoy and consequently not at his expense. Urged by a second admonition from the Pope, Nausea set out, not for Trent but for the Curia. He reached Parma in mid-June when he presented to the Pope his most recently published works—his great Catechism and an extensive work on the reform entitled *Sylvae Synodales*.[1] However, by this time the fate of the Council had been decided—it was already at its last gasp.

On 25 May 1543 Charles V entered the harbour of Genoa with a powerful fleet. From Genoa he intended to march into South Germany for the purpose of chastising the Duke of Cleves, who had allied himself with France. Once rid of this thorn in his side he intended to launch a great counter-offensive against France from the Netherlands. The Emperor's march through northern Italy provided an opportunity for the meeting with the Pope which the latter had long desired. Such an interview was more necessary than ever, for the tension between the

p. 356) we learn that the Bishop of Bamberg had appointed the cathedral preacher Johannes Eckelsheim as his proctor. The Bishop of Breslau had intended to appoint Cochlaeus as his proctor, but while he was still discussing the matter with his chapter the Council was suspended, *Archiv für schlesische Kirchengeschichte*, I (1936), p. 64.

[1] *C.T.*, VOL. IV, p. 326 f.; the copious correspondence is in *Epp. misc. ad Nauseam*, pp. 354-65. From Farnese's letter of 26 May to Nausea we gather that the fresh brief of convocation desired by Nausea was actually despatched, *N.B.*, VOL. I, PT vii, p. 365, *n*.1, but his travelling expenses were not refunded, *Z.K.G.*, XXI (1901), p. 539. Extract of *Miscellanea* in *C.T.*, VOL. XII, pp. 364-426; soon afterwards Nausea handed to Cardinal Cervini the memorial printed *ibid.*, pp. 428 ff.

two rulers had been intensified rather than eased. Quite recently at Nuremberg Verallo and Truchsess had had to listen to Granvella's accusation that the Pope favoured France.[1] The Turkish fleet operated quite openly with the French in the Tyrrhenian Sea and ravaged the coast of Italy with the sole exception of the States of the Church. All this was done under the expert leadership of a French Knight of St John. Yet the Pope refused to abandon his neutrality for he was more than ever afraid of the Emperor's preponderance. However, the Franco-Turkish full-scale aggression failed on all fronts. If France were completely defeated and reduced to impotence Charles V would be the unquestioned monarch of the West and the weight of his authority would be more than could be borne by the head of the Church, the Papal States and the house of Farnese. Even apart from these considerations, it is incontestable that France's reply to the abandonment of neutrality by the Pope would have been a schism. A Council dominated by the Emperor or at least subservient to him and in which the French took no part would constitute a positive danger for the Church. Its oecumenicity would be called in question while it would be but an extremely doubtful remedy against the German schism. On the other hand, if the Pope maintained his neutrality and allowed things to go on as before, the Council of Trent would inevitably be an almost exclusively Italian rump-Council. Papal policy stood at the cross-roads; whichever turning it took, a truly oecumenical Council was beyond attainment.

On 5 May, in view of the decision that must be taken, Paul III summoned the conciliar legate Pole to Bologna to report.[2] The day after the cardinal's arrival, 11 May, the consistory discussed the question whether the other legates should be recalled.[3] It had become known that the Emperor's suite included two bishops provided with powers of attorney for several other prelates. Was the monarch planning another sudden stroke? Or was it his intention to force the opening of the Council on the plea of at least a token-participation of the Spanish hierarchy? Or was the presence of these prelates to be the

---

[1] *C.T.*, VOL. IV, p. 321; *N.B.*, VOL. I, PT vii, p. 575. At Trent Castelalto spoke to Campeggio of his fear that the movements of the papal troops were directed against the Emperor and warned him against taking sides against the monarch, *C.T.*, VOL. IV, p. 332.

[2] *C.T.*, VOL. IV, pp. 328 ff.

[3] What follows is based on the despatches of the agents of Ferrara, Ruggieri and Nobili, of 12 and 13 May, St. Arch., Modena, Roma 27A orr. The "congregatione de heri" mentioned in the despatch of the 13th is surely the consistory of 11 May. The two Spanish prelates who accompanied the Emperor were the Archbishop of Compostella and the Bishop of Huesca, *C.T.*, VOL. IV, p. 351, *n*.3.

means of prolonging the present situation? The Pope was determined not to allow himself to be caught unawares as in January. The recall of the legates could be accounted for by the necessity of hearing their report, though this measure meant the dissolution of the Council since the legates' departure rendered the assembly incapable of action. With the legates' recall the Pope would create a *fait accompli* and forestall any plan the Emperor might entertain.

The recall of the legates had been decided [1] when the Cardinal of Burgos rose in the consistory and as spokesman of the imperial cardinals emphatically opposed a measure which the Emperor would regard as an attempt to force his hand. The question was accordingly left open. On 13 May the Pope recalled Parisio, leaving Morone alone at Trent, but since the latter had full legatine authority even though alone the dissolution of the Council was avoided for the time being. The discussion of the problem then passed from the consistory to the conciliar committee [2] consisting of Cupis, dean of the Sacred College, the authors of the legates' instructions, Del Monte and Guidiccioni, Crescenzio and Badia to whom the Pope now adjoined Grimani, Cervini and Cortese. On 11 May these eight men were instructed to study the question carefully and to submit a report at the next consistory.

No minutes of the deliberations of the members of the committee among themselves and later on with the Pope and the two legates have been preserved, but it is not difficult to imagine on what points they turned. If they eschewed the solution of a prorogation—a contrivance somehow overdone at Vicenza—there remained three other possibilities. In view of the small attendance the Council might be suspended until the conclusion of peace, that is for a few months or for an indefinite period; or it might be transferred to some city of the Papal States such as Bologna or Piacenza; or, finally, an attempt might be made to maintain for a time the existing state of suspense. The latter possibility was the one that met the Emperor's wishes as we gather from Morone's reports [3] of his lengthy conferences with Granvella between 26 May and

---

[1] On 13 May Nobili wrote: "Nella congregatione de heri se intende che s'era determinato che li legati tornassero, ma sotto colore di voler relatione delle cose pertinenti al concilio, con dechiaratione quod in absentia legatorum quicquid fuerit, esset irritum et inane. Et per questa via intende S. S.tà de risolverlo. Alche opponendosi il Rev.mo di Burgos et altri imperiali con dire che non li parea honesto che sulla faccia dell'Imperatore ipso inscio se resolvesse il concilio. Non si è però restato di fare questo di sopra." See previous note.

[2] *C.T.*, VOL. IV, p. 329, *n.*2.

[3] Morone on 26 and 28 May, *ibid.*, pp. 335-42, especially pp. 337, l. 29 and 341, l. 43.

2 June during the chancellor's passage through Trent while on his way to rejoin the Emperor. Granvella urged the latter solution with the utmost energy, for the Council was a trump-card which made it much easier for him to counter the Protestants' demands in the religious sphere. On the other hand one objection to this solution was that a further postponement of the opening of the Council was scarcely reconcilable with the dignity and authority of the Apostolic See. A translation to the States of the Church was undoubtedly the solution that would best please the Pope and the majority of the cardinals; it would also meet France's wishes; on the other hand it would cut across the Emperor's plans and it was doubtful whether the Germans would attend and recognise such a Council. In that eventuality and in the light of certain remarks of Granvella, there was a possibility of a fresh agitation in favour of a German city, such as Mainz or Speyer.

There remained the alternative of a suspension. However, if the Pope took this step after his many protestations that he would hold the Council in any case he ran the risk of being accused that the convocation was no more than a gesture. A suspension was equivalent to a dissolution and a provisional abandonment. Like a translation, it was at variance with the Emperor's wishes. In either case, Tommaso Campeggio wrote to Farnese on 21 May,[1] they would have to reckon with serious difficulties either in the shape of a formal protest by the Emperor or a renewal of discussions as to whether the Pope was empowered to dissolve or to transfer a General Council once convoked similar to those which had arisen on the occasion of the translation of the Council of Constance to Ferrara, not to speak of the Emperor's claim that he was entitled to call a General Council in a state of emergency—a claim supported by a number of canonists. Once again the scene was darkened by the fatal question of authority of Pope and Council. Would the Pope's personal influence with the Emperor enable him to counter the latter's objections to either of the two solutions that he himself favoured?

We can gauge the depth of mutual distrust of the two rulers by the preliminary discussions about the place and the conditions of their prospective meeting. Charles V did not wish to go too far out of his way while proceeding to Germany. He insisted on coming with a strong military escort. On his part, for reasons of personal security and prestige, Paul III insisted on Bologna or Parma, and a small suite, with the result that up to the last moment it was doubtful whether the

[1] *Ibid.*, p. 334 (21 May).

meeting would take place. In the end both sides yielded. On 21 June the Pope made his entry into the small town of Busseto near Parma; the Emperor followed him with an escort of only five hundred men.[1]

The conference which ensued lasted five days but failed to ease the tension. Not one of the questions pending was settled to the parties' mutual satisfaction, in fact it was precisely on the most important points that they failed to come to an understanding. Charles V declined to enter into peace negotiations with France, while Paul III refused to abandon his neutrality. The compromise proposed by the Pope, that the duchy of Milan should be bestowed on Ottavio, the Pope's grandson, against payment of a large sum of money, was not openly and definitely rejected by the Emperor, but the proposal roused his strongest indignation and strengthened his conviction that papal policy was largely determined by the interests of the Farnese family. The question of the Council also remained unsolved. In view of the Recess of Ratisbon the Emperor wished it to be kept open while the Pope desired either its translation or its suspension, since in the existing conditions it lacked that character of universality which was essential for dogmatic definitions. While not directly opposing

---

[1] On the conference of Busseto at which, among other topics, there was question of the nomination of imperial cardinals, the reinstatement of Ascanio Colonna and the Turkish war, see Farnese's report to Verallo, 22 and 28 June, *N.B.*, VOL. I, PT vii, pp. 370-4, the letters of Charles V to Ferdinand I and Maria of Hungary dated 29 June, used by Korte, *Die Konzilspolitik Karls V*, p. 87, and by Brandi, *Kaiser Karl V*, p. 426 f.: Eng. edn., p. 494, and the instructions for the new ambassador to Rome, Juan de Vega, 4 July, in *Cal. of St. Pap.*, *Spain*, VOL. VI, ii, p. 560 f. The part that concerns the Council, with wrong date, is in Ferrandis-Bordonau, *El concilio de Trento*, p. 26. We get a lively picture of the confusion before the meeting in the letters of the agent of Ferrara, Niccolò Bendidio of Parma, 14-19 June, St. Arch., Modena, Parma. Another agent, Francesco Villa, writes on 16 June: "Alcuni dubitano che questo abboccamento non si faccia poichè S.M.ta vuole venir tanto ben accompagnato che anchorche venga in casa di S.S.ta venendole il capriccio si potria far patrone di lei" (*ibid.*). To the literature listed in Pastor, VOL. V, pp. 486-93: Eng. edn., VOL. XII, pp. 174 ff., must be added Cardauns, *Nizza*, pp. 281-93; Brandi, *Quellen*, pp. 331-5. The best thing on the *Pratica di Milano* which Pallavicino, *Historia del Concilio di Trento* (Rome 1656), VOL. V, iii, pp. 1-11, as against Sarpi, VOL. I, vi (ed. Gambarin, VOL. I, p. 166 f.) considers to cast an unfair suspicion on Paul III, is in Chabod, *Lo stato di Milano nell' Impero di Carlo V* (Rome 1934), pp. 35 ff. From Ruggieri's report of 20 August, to be quoted at the end of this chapter, it appears that the Milanese project was the chief cause of the misunderstanding between Alessandro Farnese and Cervini because the latter "ricercato da lui e dal Duca Ottavio a persoader a N.S. la pratica di Milano l'habbia piutosto dissuaso". The fact was that Cervini was thinking of the consequences which were thus summed up by Ferdinand I for the benefit of Verallo: "Questa era cosa di far perder al tutto la religione in Germania e la buona opinione del concilio perchè li Lutherani se ne ralegrano grandemente et li Catholici si perderanno affatto", *N.B.*, VOL. I, PT vii, p. 374.

this wish, Charles V avoided a clear-cut answer and so left the responsibility of a decision to the Pope, who was thus compelled to assume it.

The decision was a heavy one and fraught with tremendous consequences. Before taking it the cautious Farnese Pope consulted not only the cardinals but likewise the bishops who had remained at Trent, especially the legate Morone, by whose frank opinion he set great store.

Morone's unenviable task it was to keep up appearances by continuing to hold a position which was as good as abandoned. With Pole and Parisio gone, no one at Trent believed any longer that the Council would ever meet. Imperial partisans, men like Captain Francesco di Castelalto and the Bishop of Hildesheim, confided their anxiety for the immediate future to Campeggio. What they feared was that the Pope would go over to the French side, a step that would lead to a German national Council.[1] Morone himself had to listen to representations of a similar kind by Granvella. Each of the two men sought to convince the other that so far no decisive step had been taken, but they were unable to soften the bad impression made by the recall of the two legates.

But a final decision had to be made. In compliance with his instructions Morone asked the Italian bishops assembled at Trent for their opinion as to what should be done with regard to the Council. The consultation was little more than a formality but the answers are nevertheless of great interest since they reflect the state of mind at the highest level. Almost all the answers were against a suspension and advocated a translation on the ground that for various reasons Trent was unsuitable and, from the canonical point of view, just then insecure. A Council held in such conditions would not be a truly oecumenical assembly on account of the absence of the French. Campeggio, Zanettini and Musso openly expressed the opinion that in order to avoid such a danger they should be prepared to run even the risk of a German national Council. Any compromise that such an assembly might arrive at would be more easily disposed of than an accord— including the secularisation of Church property, Communion in both kinds and the marriage of priests—which the Germans might extort from a Council. In any case the translation must be carried out forthwith, *in continenti*, before the arrival of the Germans at Trent and without previous consultation with them, otherwise it would be

[1] *C.T.*, VOL. IV, pp. 332 f., 337.

exceedingly difficult to effect it and they might be faced with a worse situation than at Basle.[1]

The only one to voice any misgivings about such a solution was the Archbishop of Otranto, Pietro Antonio di Capua, a well-known figure in the history of Italian evangelism. This prelate was convinced that in the existing circumstances no General Council could successfully be held either at Trent or anywhere else; hence a translation would be meaningless and might easily become dangerous because it would lead to a national Council and the consequent loss of Germany. The only thing to do was to keep the convocation in suspense in accordance with Granvella's proposal. The Archbishop of Otranto's observations received support from a remark of the Bishop of Hildesheim, who, it would seem, had not been directly consulted. It was to the effect that a translation would drive the German Catholics to despair. These considerations impressed Morone, who shuddered at the light-heartedness with which the prelates of the Curia accepted the notion that Germany was lost already. He saw clearly—and history bears him out —that that country, situated as it is in the very heart of Europe, is decisive for the fate of the whole of Europe.[2] Morone accordingly rejected a translation, advocated though it was by the majority, without previous consultation with the German Estates. He nevertheless hesitated to advise such a step for fear of the latter demanding a translation into the interior of Germany, for even an imperial guarantee would not constitute an effective safeguard against the complications that were to be expected in such an eventuality. In view of the German situation Morone also rejected another way out, one to which he had evidently given a great deal of thought: namely that instead of a suspension there should be a kind of *restitutio in integrum*, in the sense that the Pope should declare, with all the solemnity of a Bull, that circumstances compelled him to refrain from a Council but that he was resolved to convene one at the appropriate time and in a locality acceptable to all nations and in particular to Germany. But such a declaration should be followed up by immediate action, nothing less in fact than a general reform of the Church.

---

[1] Morone's report of 28 June, *ibid.*, pp. 345-8. T. Campeggio's illuminating letter to Cardinal Pucci, 30 June, *Carte Strozziane* VOL. I (Florence 1884), pp. 580 ff. Campeggio writes: "Trent, non solo non è sicuro per li francesi, ma anco non è sicuro per l'altre natione per il transito de' soldati che de Italia vanno alla guerra di Ungheria et a quella di Fiandra, per lo quale le hostarie se abandonano ne vi si trova da vivere."

[2] "Quando la Germania sara caduta totalmente, che tutto 'l resto de la Christianità sara in periculo manifesto." *C.T.*, VOL. IV, p. 347.

Morone knew Germany too well not to realise that a withdrawal of the convocation of the Council, even in the above form and accompanied by so unmistakable a proof of good-will, would do almost irreparable injury to the whole notion of a Council, especially among the German Catholics. Such a responsibility he was unwilling to take on himself. Prolonged and anxious consideration of the problem led him to favour a solution which more than any other took account of the German situation, the one proposed by Granvella and the Archbishop of Otranto. He knew that the Pope felt that further delay was not in keeping with his dignity, while he regarded Trent as a not very suitable locality for the Council. But what were these drawbacks by comparison with the fact that he would be redeeming his promise to hold the Council in any circumstances? Morone thought little of the dangers arising out of the position of Trent. He felt that it would be possible, even at Trent, to keep the situation well in hand and to prevent its domination by the imperialists.

The course of the Council of Trent was to show that Morone's assessment of the ecclesiastical and political forces was substantially correct. Exactly twenty years later, in the capacity of president of the Council, he himself gave effect to these suggestions when he successfully steered the assembly through the most grievous of all the crises it experienced. In 1543 his advice was ignored.

During the Emperor's stay at Trent between 2 and 5 July in the course of his progress to Germany, Morone had occasion to observe that the tension between the two rulers had not been eased in the least. His own treatment by the Emperor was extremely chilly; of the results of the conference of Busseto the monarch spoke in slighting terms. In the hope of breaking the ice, Morone spoke of the help the Pope was giving to King Ferdinand for the Turkish war [1] and of the measures taken against the Turkish fleet. "They are useless," the Emperor coldly observed. "That pirate Barbarossa allies himself with his brother, the King of France, but the Pope chooses not to notice it." With calculated irony he proceeded to express his sympathy with the legate for his being compelled to stay on at Trent. "Actually," he observed, "the question of the Council was no concern of his; it was the Pope's own affair." In order to refute this assertion Morone recounted briefly and with perfect courtesy the antecedents of the

---

[1] Granvella complained of the slow progress of the papal troops. Giovio had foretold that they would not reach Linz by the time the Turks had captured Vienna, C.T., VOL. IV, p. 350.

convocation; nor did he neglect to remind the Emperor that he himself had sent envoys to Trent. "Yes," the Emperor replied significantly, "they arrived all too soon for your convenience! It is useless to speak of the Council at present; I am only waiting to hear what His Holiness has decided!" [1]

Morone was ignorant of the Pope's decision, nor did Poggio, who rejoined the court at Trent on 3 July, bring any information. This was all the more embarrassing as the Emperor had obviously arranged to stop at Trent for the purpose of informing Morone of his German plans. Only on 6 July, the day after the departure of the court, did the Pope take the expected decision at a secret consistory held at Bologna. The Council was suspended. The Bull of Suspension *Etsi cunctis*,[2] of the same date but only published on 29 September, gave a fairly detailed account of its convocation. It spoke of the Pope's efforts with the great powers, his repeated admonitions to the bishops for whose arrival the legates had waited in vain—*non sine aliqua dictae Sedis indignitate*—of the pontiff's journey to Bologna and of the encounter of Busseto. The Bull then drew this conclusion: In view of the fact that there was no peace and that the attendance was inadequate, the plan for the Council could not be put into effect for the time being. After hearing the report of the legates who had been recalled to Bologna, and the opinion of the bishops still at Trent, he felt convinced that the Council must be prorogued until a more favourable time. There was no mention of the Emperor's approval of the suspension, for Granvella had expressly deprecated any such reference.[3] In terms obviously aimed at the Emperor's proposal to leave the convocation in suspense for a further period the Bull proceeds: "Since the Pope feels compelled to return to Rome on account of the Turkish menace and since, on the other hand, he is anxious to ease the conscience of the prelates whose duty it is to attend the Council, he has decided, on the advice and with the consent of the cardinals, to suspend the assembly until such time as shall be determined by the Apostolic See, to recall the legates and to allow the prelates who have come to Trent to take their departure." It was no mere formality but a calculated precaution

[1] Free rendering after *C.T.*, VOL. IV, p. 349, l. 9-13. On Charles's great plan in particular, cf. his instructions for his son Philip, whom he had named Regent of Spain, Brandi, *Karl V*, p. 415: Eng. edn., p. 484; *id.*, *Quellen*, p. 329.

[2] *C.T.*, VOL. IV, pp. 352-5. The long delay of the publication may have been due to Granvella's request that the conclusion of the Diet of Schmalkalden should be awaited. *N.B.*, VOL. I, PT vii, p. 447.

[3] Poggio on 13 July, *N.B.*, VOL. I, PT vii, p. 446.

485

when the Bull declared any act contrary to this disposition to be null and void.

No such act was to be feared on the part of the prelates at Trent: they were glad to get away. Morone was informed of the suspension by a brief and a covering letter.[1] However, he thought it his duty to await the arrival of the promised Bull of Suspension; when that document failed to arrive he left Trent, but only after he had received formal leave to do so on 25 July.

Thus the latest attempt to summon a Council—the first Tridentine one—ended in failure. It must be granted that it was beyond the Pope's power to remove the chief cause of the failure, namely the war between the two great powers. His offers to act as a peace mediator had been rejected by both sides. The major responsibility lay undoubtedly with the aggressor, Francis I, but Charles V cannot be completely absolved from blame. Angered by the Pope's political neutrality and actuated by his ever-growing suspicion of the latter's ultimate aims, Charles V prevented the Spanish bishops from journeying to Trent and thereby provided the other nations with a plausible pretext for holding back. Lastly, Paul III himself waited far too long before taking the two measures which would have convinced the world of the sincerity of his intentions with regard to the Council, namely the ordering of the Italian bishops to Trent and his own departure for Bologna.

The first Tridentine convocation was nevertheless no mere comedy, as has been said; it was also more than a gesture the hopelessness of which was obvious from the first, as the Emperor imagined.[2] The Pope was well aware that the religious destiny of Germany, and not hers alone, but the fate of Italy and perhaps that of all Europe, would be at stake if the Council, the clarification of dogma, and the reform of the Church were still further delayed. However, fear of anti-Roman feeling and of conciliar theory—which his advisers did their best to foster—led him to stick obstinately to his notion of a preservative Council and to the idea that if a Council was to be held without injury to papal authority it must needs be convened within the immediate

---

[1] The brief of 6 July in *C.T.*, VOL. IV, p. 352. The covering letter of the 7th (*N.B.*, VOL. I, PT vii, p. 379) is missing as well as the permission to leave, which, however, may be deduced from the letter of the Archbishop of Corcyra, but of which Morone had no knowledge when he wrote his last report on 25 July, *C.T.*, VOL. IV, p. 356.

[2] The phrase "Comedy of the Council" in Cardauns, *Nizza*, p. 284. On the Emperor's observation in his Memoirs, cf. the pertinent remarks of P. Leturia in *Civiltà Cattolica*, XCVII, ii (1946), pp. 19 ff.

domains of the Church, that is, within the Papal States or in the territory of some small Italian state, or at the very least within the territory of the Republic of St Mark. In his opinion Trent marked an extreme concession which it would hardly be possible to uphold in the long run should the Emperor choose to make a display of authority at the Council and the Protestants—against all expectation—decide to take part in it. The idea of transferring the Council into central Italy had been contemplated from the first. Hence the frequent complaints of the bishops of the high cost of living, the restricted space and the climate of the city of Trent—complaints which later on were seen to have been without foundation, or at least greatly exaggerated. The Pope was prepared to do his share in bringing about a Council, but to a Council at Trent he only gave a half-hearted support.

Nor could he overlook the fact that if the state of war continued, France's participation was practically ruled out, while an inadequately attended Council, or one attended by only one party, would never command the incontestable authority in matters of faith which was essential for the condemnation of Protestantism. Instead of healing the wound, the decisions of a rump-Council might easily conjure up incalculable complications. This consideration was a decisive argument against the opening of the Council in the prevailing circumstances. The Pope had convoked it at an unpropitious moment in order to redeem the promise made at Ratisbon. There were weighty reasons against its being opened at Trent, but its translation, desired by many, the Pope himself included, was fraught with no less danger. Thus it came about that it was finally decided to suspend it. It may be that things would not have got so far, or that the Pope would have continued the waiting policy advocated by Morone and desired by the Emperor, if the latter had fallen in with the pontiff's wishes by resolving the question of Milan in a sense favourable to the house of Farnese. Here we come up against a disturbing factor, one that fatally upset the magnetic needle of Paul III's political compass which pointed to the Council and Church reform—namely his family policy, whose keenest exponent was Alessandro Farnese. There can be no doubt that during the decisive years of the Catholic reform the builder of the Gesù, the Palazzo Farnese, the Villa Caprarola, and the patron of artists and humanists showed neither interest in nor understanding of the forces at work for a renewal within the Church, and that he hindered their development as soon as they stood in the way of his dynastic policy and his personal covetousness. Up to the beginning of the fifteen-forties, by reason of his youth and inexperience, the cardinal-nephew had not been in a position to pursue a personal policy. In his legations he had been accompanied by Cervini in the capacity of adviser, for though the Pope did not regard the latter as a great politician or as a creative genius, he knew him as a conscientious, wise and loyal counsellor. But now the twenty-three-year-old young man ruthlessly shook himself free of a yoke which had hitherto checked his unrestrained ambition and his unscrupulous family policy. Cervini was an opponent of the Milan transaction. Alessandro resented Cervini's influence with the Pope which enabled him to cross his designs. He accordingly refused to work with him any longer. He maintained this attitude even when the Pope suggested a compromise by the terms of which the nephew would have dealt with political affairs while Cervini would have handled ecclesiastical matters. The rupture was so complete that during the whole of the journey from Bologna to Perugia the two men did not exchange a single word. Their arrival was marked by a most humiliating scene for the elder of the two.[1] With a view to hushing up the conflict, Cervini withdrew for a while to his native Montepulciano. During his absence the Farnese clan, Alessandro, Ottavio and their father Pierluigi, worked upon the Pope for two whole days at Ronciglione in order to bring him round to their views. Their pains did not go unrewarded. Cervini returned to the Curia, but for a long time his political influence could not make itself felt. He devoted himself to the administration of his diocese of Gubbio, which had been bestowed on him at the beginning of 1544, to his learned studies and to ecclesiastical affairs. But it was not long before his conciliar legation removed him from Rome. At last Alessandro was rid of the tiresome monitor; at last he had a free hand for his ambitious plans. When towards the end of his life the Pope became aware of the intrigues of his nephews, it was too late: the mistakes that had been made were beyond repair.

Impartial history, whose duty it is to serve truth, cannot absolve the Pope from the reproach of excessive weakness towards his own family, but the severity of its judgment may be softened by taking into

[1] Particulars about the rupture between Farnese and Cervini (cf. p. 481, n.1) in Ruggieri's despatch in cypher, 20 August 1543, St. Arch., Modena, Roma 27A, confirmed by the despatch of the Venetian envoy Venier, C.T., VOL. IV, p. 351, n.4. At first the Pope did not by any means take Alessandro's side without further consideration. At Perugia he called him a devil on account of his obstinacy. Ruggieri ascribes Cervini's fall to three influences: "Prima, i principi et poi alcuni Rev.mi et ultimamente gente del suo paese, volendo insinuare di Mons. Ardinghello e di Montepulciano (Ricci)."

account the pontiff's great age. All the more grievous are its charges against a cardinal who, once he had secured the most influential post in the Curia while still in youthful years, induced the Pope to abandon the genuine ecclesiastical policy upon which he had entered. In this way Farnese cast away a role which, two decades later, another equally youthful nephew—Charles Borromeo—was to play for the good of the Church. The blame for the profound estrangement between Paul III and Charles V, which hampered conciliar policy almost continuously up to the very end of the pontificate must be ascribed in large measure to the dynastic intrigues of Alessandro Farnese.

CHAPTER XI

The Peace of Crépy and the Second Tridentine Convocation

THE effect of the suspension of the Council on the German Catholics was crushing: too often they had been assured that it would be held in any circumstances. Those zealous prelates who, on the strength of these assurances, had despatched their representatives to Trent felt disappointed. They saw themselves in a false position. On top of all this the proctors of the Archbishops of Mainz and Salzburg complained in vehement terms to Granvella of the treatment they had met with at Trent.[1] As for the representatives of Trier, they discovered on their arrival on 8 July that the Council had already been suspended. The event appeared so enormous that in many places the report met with incredulity. This alone accounts for the fact that as late as the first days of August several abbots and Augustinian priors of the diocese of Freising designated Erasmus Strenberger, a canon of Trent, and Provost Stephen Rosin, as their proctors.[2]

Nausea had foretold that a fresh failure of the conciliar convocation would inevitably lead to a German national Council or at least to a deliberate apostasy of the princes who, up till then, had remained Catholics.[3] Like Morone and other people acquainted with German conditions, he took too gloomy a view of the future, though the situation north of the Alps was serious enough.

King Ferdinand took the news of the suspension like the simple, loyal Catholic that he had so often shown himself to be. Though he was critical of Church and Pope, his was a childlike devotion to both.[4]

---

[1] Poggio, 13 and 19 July 1543, *N.B.*, VOL. I, PT vii, pp. 446, 449, 451.

[2] St. Arch., Munich, Haus und Familiensachen, Conc. Trid., fasc. 1: Nominations of proctors by Abbot Maurus of Ettal, 4 August, the Augustinian provost Wilhelm von Rayttenpuech, 3 August, the Augustinian provost Ambrose of Understorf, 31 July, Abbot Andrew of Scheyern, 30 July, Abbot Leonhard of St Sebastian at Ebersberg, 15 August, Abbot Leonhard of Sts Peter and Paul at Beylberg, 6 August, and the prelates of Weihenstephan, Weiern and Beiharting. The Abbot of the Schotten at Vienna and provost Francis of St Dorothea had prayed Nausea as early as 20 June to excuse their absence from the Council, *Epp. misc. ad Nauseam*, p. 362 f.

[3] *C.T.*, VOL. XII, p. 430.

[4] *N.B.*, VOL. I, PT vii, p. 381.

He granted that though there was a pressing need of a Council, circumstances made its assembly impossible. He accordingly submitted to the papal decision on the one condition, that his brother—after consultation with the Estates of the Empire—did not take up a different standpoint.

It was not long before he learned that though he preferred a suspension to a translation, the Emperor was exceedingly put out by the Bull of Suspension.[1] Charles V missed any reference in that document to the fact that he had concurred with the convocation by the despatch of envoys, and he was indignant at being put on a level with Francis I at the very time when the French King was allowing the Turkish fleet to winter in the harbour of Toulon, thereby removing the last doubt about his alliance with the Turks. More than ever the Emperor felt that on the plea of official neutrality the Pope was actually favouring France. His ambassador in Venice observed that "the Pope had six lilies in his escutcheon but six thousand fleurs-de-lis in his heart", while his ambassador in Rome, Juan de Vega, when kept waiting while the French ambassador was closeted with the Pope, left the ante-chamber with the pointed remark that "in there they are evidently busy with the affairs of Christendom, so he would not interrupt".[2]

England's entry into the war against France on 22 June and the Emperor's quick defeat of the Duke of Cleves gave Charles V a decided advantage over his opponent. As a matter of fact the possibility of his decisive victory was already apparent, as Serristori had prophesied to the Pope. On the other hand the Farnesi were greatly angered by the final rejection of their ambitions in respect of Milan and were unmistakably working for a *rapprochement* with France. They were planning the marriage of Vittoria Farnese, the sister of Alessandro and Ottavio, with the Duke of Orleans, when Milan would be bestowed on the couple. This was not to be thought of in the event of the Emperor's victory; hence it was necessary to secure a tolerable peace for France before a decision in favour of the Emperor should lay the whole of Europe at his feet. Besides these dynastic considerations there were other, more weighty reasons why the Pope should make a further effort for peace, namely the Turkish successes in Hungary and the need of a

---

[1] Poggio to Farnese, 11 July 1543, *N.B.*, VOL. I, PT vii, p. 446; Charles V to Ferdinand, 19 November 1543, Druffel, *Karl V und die römische Kurie*, VOL. I, p. 197; similarly in the course of the conversation with Farnese, Lanz, *Staatspapiere*, p. 353.

[2] Canestrini, *Legazioni di A. Serristori*, pp. 130 ff. (13 October 1543).

Council. "Peace and Council" was the keynote of the Pope's instructions for Cardinal Farnese when, towards the end of 1543, the latter visited first Francis I and then Charles V as peace-legate.[1] On the advice of Morone and in the hope of securing the support of the princes of the Empire for the papal peace-offensive, the jurist Francesco Sfondrato, who had but recently embraced the clerical state and who until 1541 had been in the service of the Emperor, set out for Germany at the same time.[2] Farnese personally called on Truchsess, the newly appointed Bishop of Augsburg, the Dukes of Bavaria, the Count Palatine and the Archbishop of Trier. Other princes, such as the Elector Joachim II of Brandenburg and the Archbishops of Cologne and Salzburg, he exhorted by letter to do their utmost at the forthcoming Diet with a view to paving the way for peace, or at least for a long-term armistice which would make it possible to hold the Council and to organise a joint offensive against the Turks.[3] On 23 January 1544 Sfondrato and the legate Farnese met at Worms.

As was to be expected the latter had met with a much more friendly reception at the court of Francis I than Sadoleto the year before. The King discussed the peace conditions with him; he was even prepared to consider a partition of the duchy of Milan, nor was he unwilling to conclude an armistice. The Farnese family plans were submitted to an exhaustive examination. In an attempt to induce the Pope to take his side the King held out the prospect of the marriage of the Duke of Orleans with Vittoria Farnese. The magnificence of the reception extended to the youthful cardinal—who was extremely sensitive to

[1] The preparatory memorials by Morone in Pieper, *Zur Enstehungsgeschichte*, pp. 183 ff., and *N.B.*, VOL. I, PT vii, pp. 483 ff. The instructions for Sfondrato are partly in *C.T.*, VOL. IV, p. 357 f.; the parts omitted there are in *N.B.*, VOL. I, PT vii, pp. 485-91. Druffels's account, "Kaiser Karl V und die römische Kurie 1544-46", in *Abhandlungen der Münchener Akad., historische Klasse*, XIII (1877), p. 2, is full of information but decidedly anti-Roman. J. Müller's sagacious study, "Die Konzilspolitik Karls V am Trienter Konzil im Jahre 1545", in *Z.K.G.*, XLIV (1925), pp. 225-75, 338-427, to which I shall often refer in the sequel, also fails to do justice to the ecclesiastical side of Paul III's policy.

[2] Short biography of Sfondrato in *N.B.*, VOL. I, PT x, p. xxi f. He became Bishop of Sarno on 12 October and a cardinal on 19 December 1544. By his wife Anna Visconti he had had six children. His son Niccolò was raised to the Chair of St Peter under the name of Gregory XIV, Pastor, VOL. X, p. 531: Eng. edn., VOL. XXII, p. 351. The singleness of character of which he gave proof as a senator of Milan and in the settlement of the disputes with Siena is a guarantee that he fulfilled his German mission without injury to his loyalty to the Emperor.

[3] Sfondrato's reports of 25 December 1543, 9 and 22 January 1544, and the identical Latin letter to the six princes, in *N.B.*, VOL. I, PT vii, pp. 493-503; Joachim II's reply in Döllinger, *Beiträge*, VOL. I, p. 38 f.

such things—and the friendliness of the gallant court left nothing to be desired.[1]

A very different atmosphere prevailed at the imperial court. Charles V had told the nuncio Poggio in plain terms that a peace-legate would not be welcome. When Farnese nevertheless presented himself before him at Kreuznach, on 21 January, the Emperor poured out a torrent of complaints. "The Pope", he said, "favoured France; he had not a word to say about the King's far-reaching offers to the League of Schmalkalden, the original text of which had been shown to Granvella by the Landgrave Philip, while he blamed the Emperor for his alliance with England." He flatly rejected Francis I's peace conditions as well as an armistice which "as a matter of fact, would not advance the cause of the Council since the French state council had long ago arrived at the conclusion that such an assembly would not be in the interests of France and must therefore be prevented." [2] In the Emperor's view Farnese's legation and Sfondrato's mission to Germany were nothing but an attempt to rescue France in her hour of peril. He quoted a remark of Wotton's, the English ambassador, who had observed that "as long as there are apostolic nuncios, the King of France is not without his agents here".[3]

This suspiciousness, though not wholly groundless, was nevertheless excessive. While it cannot be denied that the Pope's sympathies were with France and that his efforts for peace were most acceptable to that country in the critical condition in which it found itself, these efforts were undoubtedly in the best interests of the Church. Peace alone, or a long-term armistice, would make it possible to hold a Council; if the Emperor rejected both alternatives he rendered the meeting of

[1] From the final report on Farnese's mission, which may be ascribed to one of his companions (Ardinghello or Ricci), Vat. Arch., Arm. 64, VOL. 32, fols. 11ʳ-13ʳ, it appears that the Council was not discussed either at the French or at the imperial court. The hopelessness of his efforts for peace wrung from Dandino the sigh: "Piaccia Dio metterci la mano a questa volta, perchè . . . questa cura è totalmente reservata a S.M.tà divina", Vat. Arch., Francia, 2, fol. 217ʳ (9 January 1544).

[2] The Emperor's statements to Poggio in N.B., VOL. I, PT vii, pp. 460, 476 ff. The Emperor's views of the negotiations with Farnese in the "Information" for Juan de Vega, probably of 25 January, Lanz, Staatspapiere, pp. 346-58. The invectives against the Farnesi which Cardinal Gonzaga says he heard from the Emperor's lips (including a warning of the fate of Clement VII) are not incredible, but the letter of 18 March (Pastor, VOL. V, p. 852 f.; Eng. edn., VOL. XII, p. 670) to Ferrante betrays once more an inclination for "combinazioni", which was so characteristic of the cardinal. For Este's mission at Venice and Rome, see V. Pacifici, Ippolito II d'Este (Tivoli 1920), pp. 77-89, and the reports of the English agent Harvel, Cal. of Letters, VOL. XIX, PT i, pp. 312, 346, 409. We hear an echo of the feelings at the imperial court in the complaints of the "Papa francese" which Verallo heard at the court of Ferdinand I, N.B., VOL. I, PT vii, pp. 414, 431.

[3] Cal. of Letters, VOL. XIX, i, p. 94 (No. 161).

the Council impossible, just as Francis I had rendered it impossible the year before by his declaration of war.

The tension between Pope and Emperor became so acute in the course of the ensuing months that many people believed a rupture was unavoidable.[1] Paul III was very angry at the Emperor's treatment of Alessandro Farnese. He was prepared to proclaim null and void the Spanish Concordat by which foreigners were debarred from all Spanish benefices.[2] He welcomed the French victory of Ceresole (14 April 1544) with a sigh of relief. He allowed Pierluigi Farnese to support by every means in his power the Florentine emigrant Pietro Strozzi, an adventurer in the pay of France, and his recruiting activities in Italy. He nevertheless shrank from the last step: he refrained from openly siding with France—the risk was too great. Cardinal Ippolito d'Este pressed him in vain to enter into a triple alliance with France and Venice. The Republic of St Mark was not prepared to come out into the open until the Pope should have done so too. Paul III shrank from such a step—officially he remained neutral.

The imperialists watched the Pope's growing intimacy with the French with ever mounting bitterness. Relentless *raison d'état* had forced the Emperor's daughter Margaret into a matrimonial alliance with the Farnese family. Womanlike, and torn between anger and despair, she vented her dislike of that family without the least restraint. The imperial ambassador Vega went so far as to indulge in covert and even open threats. In May 1544 he left Rome without taking leave of the Pope. The tension reached its climax during the summer, when Paul III felt compelled to protest against the decisions of the Diet of Speyer.[3]

[1] The most vivid account is in the reports of Serristori who was in close association with Vega and Margaret during March and May 1544, Canestrini, *Legazioni di A. Serristori*, pp. 133-40. I was not able to consult *La embajada a Roma de Juan de Vega*, by M. Lasso de la Vega y de Taejada (Saragossa 1944).

[2] *C.T.*, VOL. IV, p. 377, *n.9*. The Venetian envoy relates an interesting incident at the consistory of 18 December 1543, St. Arch., Venice, Senato, Roma 1543-44: The Pope proposed that a declaration be issued to the effect that "la pragmatica di Spagna s'intendesse nulla"; whereupon Cardinal Parisio demanded that the minute be submitted to himself and to the other deputies. To this the Pope assented. In the course of the ensuing discussions the Cardinal of Burgos demanded that similar action be taken in regard to France and Venice.

[3] The best account of the Diet of Speyer is that of F. Heidrich, *Karl V und die deutschen Protestanten am Vorabend des Schmalkaldischen Krieges*, VOL. II (Frankfurt 1912), pp. 3-50, already used by Janssen, VOL. III, pp. 637-48 (Eng. edn., VOL. VI, pp. 247 ff); Brandi, *Karl V*, pp. 438 ff. (Eng. edn., pp. 509 ff). The dissatisfaction of the representatives of the cities is illustrated by Sturm's reports, *Politische Correspondenz*, VOL. III, pp. 452-517, and Sailer's letters in Roth, "Aus dem Briefwechsel Gereon Sailers mit den Augsburger Bürgermeistern Georg Herwart und Lamprecht Hofer", in *A.R.G.*, I (1903), pp. 101-71. The Estates' reply in view of the declaration

The Emperor had given Farnese a hint to the effect that the religious question would come up for discussion at Speyer and this without the participation of a papal representative. There was talk of concessions to the Protestants. Though Luther and Melanchthon were rather in the dark about the aims of high politics they nevertheless looked forward to the forthcoming Diet with joyful anticipation. The Protestants were in a position to urge that the promised Council, which was to have been held within a period of eighteen months, had not materialised; they were therefore entitled to demand the national Council which had been held out to them as a substitute. On the other hand the Emperor was in need of the assistance of the Empire for the great offensive against France which he planned to carry out in conjunction with England in the course of the summer of 1544.

On 20 February 1544 he delivered his proposition to the Diet. A decisive success against the external enemy, that is, the Turk, he explained to the Estates, was only possible if the internal enemy was first disposed of, viz. Francis I. To crush him utterly he needed the help of the Empire.

The German princes were still under the impact of the catastrophic defeat of the Duke of Cleves. They were therefore in a pliant mood, in fact even the men of Schmalkalden had turned a deaf ear to French solicitations, and whereas at previous Diets French envoys had freely mingled with them, none were suffered to show themselves at Speyer. For all that, it was by no means certain that the Emperor's proposals would be accepted. Bavaria urged that the Estates should mediate with France. This was wholly in keeping with the Pope's ideas. The suggestion was not acted upon. The princes yielded to the Emperor's arguments—not to say his threats. On 12 March 1544 Francis I was declared an enemy of the Empire.

The Emperor bought this great success at the cost of far-reaching concessions to the Protestants in the ecclesiastical-political sphere.[1]

---

against France, in Weiss, *Papiers*, VOL. III, pp. 21-5. The French envoys' "Orationes" in Le Plat, VOL. III, pp. 210-34, are pure propaganda, as is the "supplex exhortatio ad Caesarem Carolum V et principes aliosque ordines Spirae nunc Imperii conventum agentes" drawn up at this time by Calvin, *Corp. Ref.*, VOL. XXXIV, pp. 453-534.

[1] The part of the Recess of 10 June affecting religion in *C.T.*, VOL. IV, pp. 358-62; the whole text in Lünig, *Reichsarchiv*, VOL. II, pp. 721-44. From the instruction for the Bavarian councillors dated 7 January 1544, printed by Druffel, *Karl V*, VOL. I, pp. 108-11, it appears that though Bavaria desired a temporary religious peace, she was opposed to a particularist settlement of the religious question on the ground that there was "kein ander weg sollich zwispalt in der religion christlich abzulegen dann durch ein gemain concili" which should be "jetzt von stund an widerumb ausgeschrieben". *Ibid.*, pp. 119 ff., the envoys' report of 27 May on the protest by Bavaria, the three archbishops and the Bishop of Augsburg.

He held out the prospect of another Diet in the autumn or winter at which the religious question would be discussed anew. At that Diet "devout, learned and peace-loving men" would submit a plan for a "Christian reformation". Until then, or until the opening of the General Council, no one was to use either force or coercion in the religious sphere. The enjoyment of ecclesiastical revenues was guaranteed to all, hence even to Protestant holders of benefices. Provided these revenues were applied to such purposes as the founding of schools and so forth, Protestants might retain them: all previous dispositions in this respect were to remain valid. Lawsuits against Protestants actually in progress at the supreme court of justice were suspended and the prospect of the eventual admission of Protestant judges was held out. All recesses against Protestants passed by previous Diets were likewise suspended.

These concessions of the Emperor in respect of Church property and the supreme court of justice were almost identical with the secret declaration of Ratisbon. The annulment of the previous recesses practically amounted to a declaration of toleration. However, all these concessions were only temporary; a final settlement would be made by the new Diet by means of a "reformation" worked out without the Pope's concurrence. Here was the chief stumbling-block, for the whole of this recess had not been extorted from the Emperor by means of prolonged haggling and bargaining; on the contrary, something unprecedented had happened, inasmuch as the Estates had left the drafting of the recess to the Emperor himself. This was Charles V's "greatest diplomatic victory" (Cardauns); but he also bore the sole responsibility for the fateful decision.

Thus it seemed that Morone's and the German bishops' fears as to the result of the suspension were about to be realised. All the Curia's efforts to keep the religious question out of the agenda of the Diet of Speyer, or at least to make sure that it would not be discussed without its participation through its delegate, had been in vain.[1] Whereas at Ratisbon the Emperor had given up important Catholic

---

[1] Morone's arguments in the instructions already quoted, in *N.B.*, VOL. I, PT vii, pp. 483 ff. Granvella made no secret of his opposition when Poggio mentioned the despatch of a legate to Speyer, *N.B.*, VOL. I, PT vii, p. 463. To Farnese he said that at previous Diets the papal legates had done more harm than good, Lanz, *Staatspapiere*, p. 358. With a view to defending himself against the accusation that he favoured the Turks, Paul III, on 26 February, addressed a brief to the Estates at Speyer (Raynald, *Annales, a.* 1544, No. 3, and Le Plat, VOL. III, p. 208 f.) which caused Luther to exclaim: "O christianissimum regem! O Sanctissimum patrem! O Catholicissimos Venetos!" Brandi, *Quellen*, p. 344.

positions in deepest secrecy, he now yielded them openly and in due legal form for the sake of a momentary political success. He lent himself to an arbitrary settlement of the ecclesiastical situation at some future date which, in view of the state of things, might easily lead— was perhaps bound to lead—to the whole of Germany becoming Protestant. There is little doubt that the monarch—of whose sincerely Catholic sentiments none were more firmly convinced than his keenest critics, viz. the Lutheran divines—was even then resolved not to carry out engagements which did violence to his conscience but, on the contrary, to have recourse to forcible measures. Rome, however, only considered the actual situation and acted accordingly.

The contents of the Recess of the Empire became known in Rome on 4 June. The Pope had his version of the text read out in consistory together with a brief criticism. Each cardinal was handed a copy.[1] As soon as the final version became available the pontiff instructed Cardinals Crescenzio, Cortese and Pole to draw up a comprehensive warning brief for the Emperor, one in keeping with the gravity of the matter.[2] A first draft, couched in extraordinarily sharp terms, was

[1] The "Advertenda" in Raynald, *Annales*, a. 1544, No. 5, used by Ehses in his notes on the Recess.

[2] The complicated antecedents of the admonitory brief have been cleared up, after Ehses, chiefly through the texts published by Cardauns, *N.B.*, VOL. I, PT vii, pp. 579-86, and the researches of J. Müller, *Z.K.G.*, XLIV (1925), pp. 399-411; Capasso, *Paolo III*, VOL. II, pp. 386 ff., marks a retrogade step. We thus get the following picture: (1) Draft A, last printed in *C.T.*, VOL. IV, pp. 374-9—a set of invectives which would justify the title of "Brief of blame"; (2) Draft B, in *N.B.*, VOL. I, PT vii, pp. 582-6—milder in tone and based on historical reminiscences, in keeping with the memorial printed *ibid.*, pp. 579-82, and which Müller rightly connects with Ricci's instructions (*C.T.*, VOL. IV, pp. 362 ff.), but wrongly dates after 30 July, for the word "cesserà" on p. 363, l. 44, shows that 27 July is a tenable date; (3) Final text C, in *C.T.*, VOL. IV, pp. 364-73. To this clarification of the origin I am in a position to add the following despatch of Ruggieri, the Este agent, dated 16 July, which has hitherto remained unnoticed: "Intendo che in questo ultimo consistorio si è fatta gran doglienza di questo altro recesso di Spira. Et parlandosi delle cose de la religione non si facci alcuna mentione di qua. Di che pensando S.S.tà di dolersi con l'Imperatore havea data la cura a li R.mi Crescentio, Cortese et Inghilterra di formar ciascuni da se una minuta di lettera. Il che essendosi fatto è restata poi l'ultima cura a M. Marco Antonio Flaminio di formar la lettera latina del modo ch'ella dee restare. Intendo anco che si è parlato per contraminar al concilio nationale di Germania di convocarne uno in Italia et forse in Bologna", St. Arch., Modena, Roma 27A or. The existence of several drafts seems therefore due to the instructions given by the Pope at the beginning of July to the above-mentioned three cardinals. Whether the memorial in question was a directive elaborated in the papal private secretariate for the benefit of the three cardinals or for Flaminio, I dare not decide. In the latter case draft B would have to be regarded as the first formulation of the final text which was further altered and even amplified with Cervini's concurrence and thus became text C. It is impossible to ascertain with any degree of certainty which text was read at the consistory of 30 July.

rejected. The definitive text, completed on 24 August, appears to owe its literary form to the humanist Marcantonio Flaminio, one of Pole's intimate friends. On 27 July Giovanni Ricci, who was going to Portugal in the capacity of nuncio, was instructed to inform that court of the basic ideas of the brief in the hope that it would exert its influence with the Emperor in the same sense.[1]

The brief, couched in grave but fatherly terms, comes to the essential point at the very outset: "The Emperor has promised to decide the ecclesiastical affairs of Germany at an imperial Diet with the co-operation of laymen and even that of heretics while excluding the Pope, nay he even speaks of a future General Council or a national Council without mentioning the Pope.[2] His action is an encroachment on the rights of the Apostolic See and is bound to meet with the same divine judgment as the encroachment of Oza, Core and Ozias on the privileges of the priesthood of the Old Law, or the attempts of the Roman emperors and those of King Henry IV and the Emperor Frederick II against the Papacy. In the ecclesiastical sphere the Emperor's role is that of the arm, not that of the head." With obvious reference to the accusation that he had prevented the Council by underhand practices, the Pope insists that he himself had clung to the project as long as there remained a spark of hope. Out of consideration for the Germans he had designated Trent for its assembly and had sent his legates there. However, "we came, and there was not a man: we called, and there was none that would hear" (Isa. L, 2). Yet in spite of everything he stands by his plan for a Council; the Council is not dissolved, it is only suspended. But one preliminary condition for its meeting is indispensable—there must be peace. The reader has an impression that he listens to an echo of Alessandro Farnese's unsuccessful peace-legation as he reads the Pope's appeal to the Emperor: "Prepare the way for the Council, make peace!" The brief ends with certain specific demands. The Emperor must refrain from encroaching on the ecclesiastical sphere, from discussing religious questions at the Diet and from disposing of Church property. If peace cannot be brought about by any other means he must accept the arbitration of

---

[1] C.T., VOL. IV, pp. 362 ff. (27 July).

[2] In my opinion the decisive motive for the brief seems to have been the fear lest the Emperor should take into his own hands not only the ordering of the Church in Germany but the affair of the Council as well; hence the reference to Constantine, cf. C.T., VOL. IV, p. 370, l. 29, and even better in N.B., VOL. I, PT vii, p. 580, with note e, and draft A in C.T., VOL. IV, p. 378, l. 3. This point of view is very much to the fore in Calvin's and Luther's polemical writings.

the Council.[1] The concessions made to the Protestants must be revoked. In the event of the Emperor refusing to comply with these demands he will be sternly dealt with. The careful elaboration of the brief, its tone and its comprehensiveness, as well as its vast array of Biblical and historical parallels, clearly shows that it was meant to be an authoritative statement of the principles which inspired the Pope's attitude towards the imperial policy in respect of religion and a Council. Conscious as he was of his responsibility to the Church, the Pope takes to task, in grave but fatherly terms, the ruler of the first world-wide empire of modern times who still saw himself in the role of a medieval Emperor. The brief lays down fundamental principles, hence it may be set side by side with those weighty pronouncements which were wont to issue from the chancery of the medieval Popes in the course of the struggle between *sacerdotium* and *imperium*. The Pope protests against the injury done to his primatial rights and the threat to the unity of the Church implicit in a purely national solution of the religious controversy and without the concurrence of the Apostolic See. He protests with equal energy against having a General Council forced on him, though he is in favour of it, provided it conforms to the laws of the Church. The brief repeats the watchword: "Peace and Council." The warning brief is therefore in line with the traditional policy of the Papacy, except that it stresses its guiding principles with extraordinary solemnity. But this was only one of its purposes—the purely ecclesiastical one. Whether intentionally or otherwise it had yet another aim— a political one—in that it dealt a heavy blow to the moral authority of the Emperor and to that extent assisted his hard-pressed opponent. However, if such was its purpose the blow missed the mark.

In view of the fact that the Emperor had deprecated the despatch of Morone as peace-legate, a measure which had been decided upon in the consistory of 30 July, the original text of the brief was taken to the imperial court, then in residence at Brussels, at the beginning of October by an official of lower rank, the Chamberlain David Odasio. However, as a result of the intervention of the nuncio Poggio, the document was never presented, for reasons to be discussed presently. The Emperor only learnt its contents from a copy [2]; other copies were

---

[1] This fresh proposal of arbitration by the Council, which stood but a slender chance of being acted upon, is found not only in draft C (*C.T.*, VOL. IV, p. 372, l. 36, but likewise in draft A (*ibid.*, p. 379, l. 43). It was based on the earlier proposal—at least an armistice, then a Council!

[2] Refusal of Morone's legation according to Poggio's report of 25 August, Vat. Arch., Concilio 38, fol. 85ʳ: "Per hora non venghi qua, che non potrian riceverlo

distributed by the Bishop of La Cava,[1] who had been despatched to the court of King Ferdinand I on 27 August. The bishop's journey took less time than that of Odasio, hence it was inevitable that the text should become known in Germany before the imperial court became acquainted with it. The Protestants also got hold of it and, owing to an indiscretion, the earlier, sharper and later on disavowed text found its way to Wittenberg by way of Venice. It roused Luther to fury and inspired his last and most virulent pamphlet against the Papacy.[2] Calvin published the brief with sarcastic glosses of his own.[3] The two leaders of Protestantism vied with each other in their attempt to pillory the Pope's efforts for a Council as lies and hypocrisy. One may well wonder which was more offensive—Luther's vulgar abuse or the cutting sarcasm which Calvin, as the better informed of the two, poured on the conduct of Pierluigi Farnese and his sons. Basing themselves

meglio che il R. mo Viseo, ma peggio." On receipt of this information Farnese directed Morone on 8 September to interrupt his journey, which he did, stopping at Lyons on 14 September (Morone to the Emperor, *ibid.*, fol. 88ʳ). Besides the monitory brief, Odasio was also the bearer of the briefs of 24 and 25 August (cf. *C.T.*, VOL. IV, p. 364, *n.*2) addressed to Granvella and Pedro Soto, the Emperor's confessor (the brief to the latter is also in V. Carro, *El Maestro Fr. P. de Soto y las controversias politico-teológicas en el siglo XVI*, Salamanca 1931, VOL. I, p. 362), in which both men were urged to work in the sense of the papal admonition to the Emperor (Raynald, *Annales, a.* 1544, No. 9; Le Plat, VOL. III, p. 347 f.). On Poggio's intervention, see Navagero's report of 7 October, *Z.K.G.*, XLIV (1925), p. 408. Ehses's view based on Massarelli (*C.T.*, VOL. I, p. 163, l. 16) that the original brief of admonition had been presented by Savelli at the beginning of 1545, can hardly be maintained—there is an obvious misreading of Massarelli.

[1] Brief of 27 August 1544 in Raynald, *Annales, a.* 1544, No. 9; Le Plat, VOL. III, p. 248. The contemporary brief on the peace legations of Morone and Grimani (No. 21) was now superfluous. The assertion six months later by some of the German princes at the Diet of Worms, that they had got hold of the brief even before it reached the Emperor (Druffel, *Karl V*, VOL. II, p. 49), may be true, but it does not prove that the Curia deliberately took a step which in our days would be the same as the publication of a diplomatic note before it was handed to the person to whom it was addressed. Druffel's view, VOL. I, pp. 76 ff., 87 f., that Granvella allowed a copy to fall into the hands of the Wittenbergers is untenable.

[2] *L.W.*, VOL. LIV, pp. 206-99, with the introduction, pp. 195-202. The considerations on the Council of which Grisar scarcely took any notice (*Luther*, VOL. III, pp. 322 ff.: Eng. edn., VOL V, pp. 381 ff.) will demand our attention later on. For the illustrations see Grisar-Heege, *Lutherstudien*, VOL. V (Freiburg 1923), pp. 62 ff., VOL. VI (Freiburg 1923), pp. 30 ff.

[3] *Corp. Ref.*, VOL. XXXV, pp. 253-88. On the genesis of Calvin's letter to Myconius, 27 March 1545, see *ibid.*, VOL. XL, p. 56. Calvin takes it for granted that Paul III never wanted a Council: "Qui serio eum (scil. Papam) cogitasse unquam de habendo concilio putat, micam sani cerebri non habet", *ibid.*, VOL. XXXV, p. 279. Of the first Tridentine convocation he says: "Quasi vero vocaverit spe colligendi, ac non potius de industria tempus elegerit, quod esset ab omni pacata consultatione alienissimum. Quum satis compertum haberet, bello distineri duos praecipuos christiani orbis monarchas, . . . concilium se velle simulavit."

on the history of the early Councils, the pamphleteers took it for granted that it was the Emperor's prerogative to convoke a Council, not the Pope's, hence there was no point in the latter's protest if the Emperor made use of his right.

The Emperor declined to answer the brief. As a matter of fact by the time it reached him it had been out-paced by military and political events. An exchange of notes could only thwart his new plans and diminish the authority of both rulers.[1] The brief was out of date because the long-desired peace had come.

During the summer months the Emperor had taken the offensive against France and was actually advancing on Paris. Exhausted and war-weary, Francis I desired peace. In the course of August the Spanish Dominican Gabriel de Guzmán, the confessor of Charles V's sister Queen Eleanor, repeatedly presented himself at the headquarters of the two monarchs. Owing to difficulties in obtaining supplies and the lack of discipline in his army, the Emperor lowered his demands. An agreement on the chief points was arrived at on 6 September and on the 18th peace was concluded at Crépy.[2] The Emperor consented to the marriage of his daughter or one of his nieces with the Duke of Orleans and the cession of the Netherlands or Milan as her dowry. Francis I on his part undertook to restore Savoy, to assist in the war against the Turks, and to make reparation to England, which, for the time being, continued the war. But of far greater consequence than these open conditions, which were never executed owing to the unexpected demise of the Duke of Orleans, was the secret clause of the peace treaty by which Francis I agreed to the Council being opened at Trent, Cambrai or Metz, at a date to be determined by the Emperor. He also undertook to send bishops and theologians to whichever locality should be decided upon.[3]

[1] The Emperor's reply to Odasio in Druffel, *Karl V*, VOL. I, p. 79. The last clause, which Ehses understands to refer to Francis I (*C.T.*, VOL. IV, p. 371, n.2), surely refers to Clement VII: "Si cadauno huviesse hecho segun su grado y estado y cualidad lo mismo, no havrian sucedido los inconvenientes en que al presente se halla la christianidad."

[2] The literature on Crépy in Brandi, *Quellen*, pp. 346-51. The original French text of the secret clause, with which Müller was not acquainted (*Excursus, Z.K.G.*, XLIV (1925), pp. 411-17), has been published by A. Hasenclever in *Z.K.G.*, XLV (1927), pp. 418 ff.; Italian translation in *C.T.*, VOL. X, p. 262, n.3.

[3] The passage about the Council runs as follows: "Et quant au Concille general desmaintenant consentons et accordons, quil se tienne et celebre ou en la cite de Trente, ou en celle de Cambray ou Metz au choix de predit frere et en tel temps, quil advisera, et y envoyerons noz procureurs et ambassadeurs et gens doctz et peu d'hommes de bonne vue et zele pour avec les commis et ambassadeurs de nos dits freres entendre par ensemble et unanimement a la celebration dicelluy concille et de tout ce que sera treuve requis et convenable en traicte."

The treaty of Crépy thus removed the greatest obstacle to the Council. It was the Emperor who forced open the door that had barred the road to it; it was due to his pressure that Francis I, in the secret clause, abandoned an opposition inspired by political considerations. The fact that the clause was kept secret puts it beyond a doubt that by extorting this one-sided declaration from his partner in the treaty the Emperor wished to forestall the Pope, to remove the pontiff's alleged opposition to a Council on imperial territory and in general to secure for himself the initiative in the question of the Council. He was even then meditating the great plan with which he intended to influence profoundly both the character and the course of the Council.

Until this time Charles V had regarded a Council as the surest road to a peaceable settlement of the German schism. The refusal of the Protestant Estates to attend a Council convoked by the Pope thwarted this hope. There could be no doubt that they would never submit to the decrees of such an assembly; Ratisbon had demonstrated the impossibility of an alternative peaceful solution by means of a mutual understanding. The policy of concessions lay heavily on the Emperor's conscience and was bound to bring him into conflict with the Pope. He accordingly asked himself whether it would not be possible, as a first step, to break the political power of the Protestants, particularly that of the League of Schmalkalden, and so to compel them to send representatives to the Council and to accept its decisions.

For a long time he had not felt strong enough for such an undertaking, but now he thought himself equal to it. He had crushed the Duke of Cleves without the latter's Protestant relations and allies moving a finger to help him. The Elector John Frederick of Saxony, the head of the League, was wholly passive and could easily be kept in check with the help of his ambitious cousin, Duke Maurice of Saxony. The most active member of the League, the Landgrave Philip of Hesse, politically paralysed as he was by his bigamous marriage, was in the Emperor's power. The League of Schmalkalden had lost some of its cohesion and with it some of its strength. Thus it came about that though outwardly Protestantism continued to spread—the Palatinate had recently seceded and the Archbishop of Cologne, Hermann von Wied, was only restrained by his clergy and his Estates from a similar step—its military and political power was no longer what it had been. The great imperial cities which provided it with funds were incensed by the selfish conduct of the princes; moreover, their economic position was extremely vulnerable. The weakness of the German opposition and the peace of Crépy, which secured his rear, brought to maturity an idea which the Emperor, now at the height of his powers, had long repressed, the idea namely of paving the way for the Council and the return of the dissidents by forcible measures against the Protestants. In this scheme the Council would play an entirely new function. With their military and political power broken, the Protestants would not dare to refuse to attend the assembly and to submit to its decrees. The unity of the Church—the Emperor's supreme aspiration—might yet be restored. This could only be brought about with the Pope's concurrence. The great plan could not be put into effect without the closest co-operation between the two rulers. For these reasons the Emperor refrained from a discussion of the warning brief but took immediate steps to persuade the Pope to revoke the suspension of the Council of Trent.

The pontiff built golden bridges for him and met the monarch half way. When informed of the conclusion of the peace of Crépy, he repressed his annoyance at having been deliberately excluded from the preliminary discussions and congratulated the two monarchs on the result.[1] Nuncios were despatched to both: Sfondrato to the Emperor, Dandino to Francis I. The most important information they had to impart put to shame those who had doubted the sincerity of the Pope's intentions with regard to the Council. In Sfondrato's instructions the Pope declared that the fairest fruit of the peace was the Council. He was determined to revoke its suspension and to hold it without delay. Moreover, so as to put an end to further discussions about the locality, he declared that it would be held at Trent although the peculiar status of that city precluded his personal presence. By this means Paul III hoped to eliminate the danger to the unity of the Church implicit in a partisan solution by a German national Council or a corresponding imperial Diet. One of his conditions, however, was that the religious question should be kept out of the agenda of the future Diet which the Emperor had promised at Speyer.[2]

It is easy to see that the Pope had not departed from the basic line of the warning brief. The speedy convocation of the Council was meant to ward off the peril which his best advisers had on the whole accurately foreseen previous to the suspension. The Pope's

[1] Brief to Francis I, 13 October; to the Emperor, 16 October, Raynald, *Annales*, a. 1544, Nos. 24 and 26; Le Plat, VOL. III, p. 249 f.
[2] Sfondrato's instructions dated 27 October, by Ehses, *C.T.*, VOL. IV, pp. 380 ff.; those of Dandino are unknown to me; his reports are missing in Vat. Arch., Francia, 2.

action crossed that of the two monarchs. In accordance with the secret clause of Crépy, both Charles V and Francis I informed the nuncios accredited to them of their wish that the Council should be opened forthwith at Trent.[1] In the consistory of 7 November the French envoy in Rome, Georges d'Armagnac, Bishop of Rodez, read a letter from the King to the Pope in which besides a request for pecuniary assistance for the war against England Francis I prayed the pontiff to open the Council at Trent within a period of three months so that the necessary arrangements for a coalition war against Henry VIII might be made there.[2] This linking of the convocation of the Council with a military undertaking against England was a cleverly calculated manœuvre for it was a pet notion of the Pope to make the Council the starting-point of armed action against the Papacy's most powerful enemy.

The fact that the action by both parties coincided accounts for the rapidity of the decisions that followed. As early as 14 November the consistory unanimously resolved that the General Council should be convoked for 25 March 1545. A consideration of a liturgical kind, namely the fact that in that year the feast of the Annunciation fell in Passion Week, led to a slight alteration of the time-limit of the convocation, with the result that the Bull of Convocation which was read in the consistories of 19 and 22 November, fixed the opening for 15 March—*Laetare* Sunday.

Laetare Jerusalem [3]—these words of Isaias (LXVI, 10) taken from the Introit of the Mass of the opening day, are the keynote of the Bull of

---

[1] The relevant reports of Poggio and Alessandro Guidiccioni—the latter had been in charge of the French nunciature since May 1544—(Pieper, *Zur Entstehungsgeschichte*, p. 103) are not available to me, but the fact is confirmed by Poggio's instructions of 14 November, *C.T.*, VOL. IV, p. 383 f. An *aviso* from Brussels dated 17 October (St. Arch., Modena, Busta 3) reports: "Assolutamente sara concilio col quale si spera rimediar a tutto." Corresponding instructions for Vega dated 16 October in J. L. Villanueva, *Vida literaria* VOL. II (London 1825), p. 409).

[2] The connexion between the English problem and that of the Council does not emerge in the extract in *C.T.*, VOL. IV, p. 328 f., as it does in the complete text in Raynald, *Annales*, a. 1544, No. 28. On 15 November Farnese wrote to Poggio that he should do everything in his power "che la Ces. M.ta sia per volgersi etiam con le forze scoperte alla reduttione et al castigo di un tal rebello", Vat. Arch., Spagna, 1A, fol. 94ʳ.

[3] Preliminary acts, and text of the Bull in *C.T.*, VOL. IV, pp. 385-8. Of the consistory of 22 November, of which Ehses makes no mention, Carlo Gualteruzzi writes on the same day to Giovanni della Casa (Montepulciano, Bibl. Ricci, 4, fol. 21ᵛ or): "Alli 12 si fece consistorio dove fu letta la bolla del concilio". According to him it originally began thus: "Tempus est iam nos de somno surgere"; however "ciò fu ripreso, ne videremur hactenus dormivisse"; cf. also Capasso, *Paolo III*, VOL. II, pp. 392 ff.

Convocation. In it the Pope expresses his joy that his protracted efforts on behalf of peace and the Council were at length being crowned with success. No obstacles had deterred him from his sacred task; at no time had he given up hope; at no time had he lost sight of the goal. Now the happy day had dawned which promises to restore the unity of Christendom! The Bull goes on to recapitulate the reasons for the suspension, announces its revocation and appoints the fourth Sunday in Lent for the opening. The objects of the assembly are the following: the removal of religious discord, the reform of the Christian people and the liberation of the Christians under the yoke of the Turks. As on former occasions of this kind, bishops and abbots and all persons entitled to take part in the assembly, or under obligation to do so, are exhorted to attend in person. Christian princes are similarly requested to take a personal part in the proceedings, or at least to have themselves represented.

Unlike the Bulls of 1536 and 1542, the Bull *Laetare Jerusalem* was drawn up in great haste; for all that, and again unlike the previous ones, it is of historical importance both on account of the success it achieved and the events in which it resulted. It is nevertheless necessary to guard against the notion that the favourable circumstances to which it owed its origin already bore in themselves the germ of its success. In the present instance also, between the publication of the Bull announcing the opening of the Council and its actual inauguration there occurred a much longer lapse of time than most people had expected.

At first events succeeded each other with unwonted speed. The Bull was published on 30 November by the *cursor* Jean Roillard in front of St Peter's, the Lateran and the Cancelleria. The papal private secretariate drew up the customary covering letters. Thus on 3 December letters were drawn up for the Emperor, the King of Portugal and the Portuguese bishops, the Swiss and the Duke of Bavaria. On the same day the Pope summoned to Rome those cardinals who lived outside the eternal city for a discussion of matters connected with the forthcoming Council.[1] The committee of cardinals for questions connected with the great assembly was reconstructed. Its constitution remained substantially the same as before the conference of Busseto except for the addition of the former legates Parisio, Morone and Pole and that

---

[1] The relevant volume of the register of briefs is badly damaged (*C.T.*, VOL. IV, p. 384, *n.*1), hence the Roman tradition only enables us to know some of the briefs drawn up at that time, Raynald, *Annales, a.* 1544, No. 30 f.; *Corpo diplomatico Portuguez*, VOL. V, p. 318; de Castro, *Portugal*, VOL. II, p. 457.

of Carafa, who replaced Badia.[1] On 19 December the Sacred College was reinforced by the creation of thirteen new members. Among them were three Spaniards [2] and four diplomatists who had taken a leading part in the earlier negotiations connected with the Council, namely Truchsess, Sfondrato, Ardinghello and Capodiferro. Finally the Pope took a precautionary measure which, while it had not been overlooked on the occasion of the previous convocation, had nevertheless not been given the same solemnity. By the Bull *Ad prudentis patrisfamilias officium*, also dated 19 November,[3] the Pope secured for the College of Cardinals the exclusive right of electing a successor in the event of his death. He likewise decreed that even if he should die in the locality where the Council was being held, the conclave must be held at Rome or in some strong city of the Papal States, such as Civita Castellana, Orvieto or Perugia. There was to be no repetition of the occurrences at Constance and Basle.

It was less easy, and it took a longer time, to tie up the severed threads between the Curia and the imperial court and to co-ordinate the plans of the two parties. Serious differences remained and it was much too soon to speak of mutual trust, though such a relationship was an essential requisite for the success of the undertaking. Juan de Vega, the imperial envoy, returned to Rome while Poggio, the nuncio at the imperial court, was replaced first (at the beginning of February 1545) by Sfondrato and later on by Verallo, who until then had represented the Curia at the court of King Ferdinand.[4] Quite independently of them, Cardinals Truchsess and Madruzzo also did their best to mediate between the two rulers. While the latter exerted himself in Rome in order to secure help for the Turkish war, the former did so at the Diet of Worms, which had opened on 21 January, in his capacity as imperial

---

[1] The consistorial acts of 19 November in *C.T.*, VOL. IV, p. 385. Both Grimani and Morone were absent, the former as legate at Piacenza, the latter at Bologna, as we learn from Farnese's letter of 17 November, *ibid.*, p. 384 f., and from Morone's correspondence with the Duke of Ferrara, St. Arch., Modena, Giurisd. eccl., filza 264. On 17 November the Pope had a conversation with the general of the Augustinians, Seripando, whose elevation to the cardinalate was being considered at the time, Calenzio, *Doc. ined.*, p. 185.

[2] The nomination of three Spaniards met the wishes of the Emperor but did not yield the hoped-for result on account of the exclusion of Pacheco which was due to his having been one of the authors of the Pragmatic Sanction, *N.B.*, VOL. I, PT viii, p. 18.

[3] *C.T.*, VOL. IV, p. 388 f. In 1536 and 1542 a decision had been come to in consistory, but no Bull was drawn up.

[4] In any case Vega's return to Rome and Poggio's recall were of doubtful value for a *rapprochement*. Vega was unpopular with the Farnesi on account of his bluntness, while Poggio was "in grossem gesehen" (highly esteemed) by the Emperor and as "guet bayrisch" he was acceptable to the Catholic action group, Gryn to Duke William, 22 November 1544, Druffel, *Karl V*, VOL. II, p. 42.

commissary. As to the programme of this Diet, the views of the two parties differed fundamentally. Through Sfondrato the Pope had let it be known that the religious question must on no account be discussed by that assembly. At first he had even refused to appoint a legate on the ground that the Diet was not competent to deal with a subject which must be reserved for the Council.[1] On the other hand the Emperor felt bound by the Recess of Speyer which held out to the Protestants the prospect of an interim reform.[2] The monarch greatly desired the presence of a legate.[3] Though his mind was even then engrossed in his great plan for warlike action against the Protestants, he intended for the present to make at least a show of carrying out the Speyer policy of compromise so as to lull his opponents into a sense of security and thus to secure for himself a surprise victory. In this scheme the Council was allotted a decisive role. The Protestants' refusal to attend would be the pretext for forcible action. Thus his policy was running along a double track: on the one hand he took steps to further the Council[4]; thus on 24 March 1545, through King Ferdinand, he warned the Estates to refer the religious question to the Council,[5] while on the other, in the course of the negotiations, he made a show of continuing the Speyer policy. He reckoned with the possibility of a delay, or even the failure, of the latest convocation, as a result of the Pope's lack of initiative [6]

---

[1] Verallo's explanations of 15 February 1545 in *N.B.*, VOL. I, PT viii, p. 71, and the brief accrediting Mignanelli (*ibid.*, p. 83) are in keeping with the monitory brief to which the legates also appeal, *C.T.*, VOL. X, p. 7.

[2] The information of vice-chancellor Naves to Gryn, the Bavarian agent, on the likelihood of a reform being granted, which the latter communicated to Duke William in a letter of 24 January is in Druffel, *Karl V*, VOL. II, p. 45; cf. the instructions for the imperial commissaries of the Diet in Lenz, *Staatspapiere*, p. 384.

[3] Truchsess to Farnese, 21 March 1545, Druffel, *Karl V*, VOL. II, pp. 48 ff.

[4] Mendoza's commission as envoy to the Council, *C.T.*, VOL. IV, p. 392 f. On 28 February Verallo reports about directions to the Viceroys of Sicily and Naples to promote attendance at the Council, *N.B.*, VOL. I, PT viii, pp. 8, 80. On 18 March Queen Mary urged the Bishop of Cambrai to attend the assembly, Le Plat, VOL. III, p. 264. That the Spanish government took appropriate steps appears from the replies of the Bishop of Pampeluna and others, *C.T.*, VOL. IV, p. 400, l. 17.

[5] Weiss, *Papiers*, VOL. III, p. 100 f.; *N.B.*, VOL. I, PT viii, p. 86 f. Granvella's counter-manœuvres are described by J. Müller, in *Z.K.G.*, XLIV (1925), pp. 254 ff.

[6] Light is thrown upon the Emperor's remark to his brother that the Pope showed "peu de volonté au remède des affaires publiques" (Druffel, *Karl V*, VOL. II, p. 48) by his letter of 3 April to Vega in which he says that in Germany Protestants and Catholics alike thought "que todo lo que el papa hace por este efeto (viz. the Council) sea fingido", *ibid.*, p. 51. However, the accusation which the Emperor is alleged to have proffered against the Farnesi (that Pierluigi was a "vigliaccio", that the Pope would have to give an account to the Council of the way the money for the Turkish war had been spent) are not sufficiently supported by the Roman *aviso* of 18 March, *N.B.*, VOL. I, PT viii, p. 638.

and France's secret obstruction. Certain facts seemed to lend substance to his suspicions.

In the above-mentioned letter which Francis I had addressed to the Pope in the course of the autumn, the King had underlined his acceptance of a Council in a remarkable manner; he had even made immediate preparations for it by convoking an advisory assembly of theologians.[1] On the other hand he did not hesitate to use the conciliar project as a wedge with which he hoped to split the Anglo-Imperial alliance. In the course of the peace negotiations at Calais, Cardinal du Bellay confidentially informed Paget, the English delegate, of the impending convocation. He was well aware of the effect of such a piece of news on Henry VIII, especially if it was accompanied by a hint that the possibility of armed action against Britain was the real object of the negotiations for an anti-English league now in progress between the Pope, France and the Emperor. By this means it was hoped to bring pressure to bear on Henry so as to render him more accommodating.[2]

Another cause of delay was the slowness, not to say the state of apathy into which the Curia relapsed after the publication of the Bull of Convocation. While the nuncios abroad were busy, as in duty, bound, making the Bull known,[3] a hush fell upon Rome in respect to

---

[1] The invitation to the Sorbonnist Claude d'Espence, dated 15 November 1544 in Le Plat, VOL. III, p. 254. At a later date the imperial ambassador, St Maurice, puts the number at 12 and gives Melun as the place of assembly, *Cal. of St. Pap., Spain*, VOL. VIII, p. 149, No. 82. On 31 December the Florentine envoy, Bernardo de' Medici, informed Duke Cosimo that ten scholars, including the tutor of the Dauphine, had come together in the neighbourhood of Paris in order to "disputare sopra i articoli del concilio, acciochè comparischino resoluti sopra essi ogni volta che il concilio si facessi, che qui non si crede", A. Desjardins, *Négociations*, VOL. III, p. 141. As to the duration of the conference the nuncio Della Casa writes to the legates from Venice on 17 April 1545: "I theologi . . . essendo stati ben 4 mesi insieme ciascun di loro era tornato a casa sua", Montepulciano, Bibl. Ricci, 4, fol. 4ʳ or. Della Casa adds that from one of their former fellow-students he had learnt that they were "pieni di queste opinioni nove et reprobe" (viz. conciliarist ideas), *ibid.*, fol. 6ᵛ (30 April).

[2] Report of the English agents, 18 and 21 October 1544, *Cal. of Letters*, VOL. XIX, ii, p. 260 (Nos. 456 and 470). Henry ordered this answer to be returned: "Quid ad Regiam Majestatem?" (*ibid.*, p. 273).

[3] On 2 March Poggio, now a collector in Spain, wrote from Valladolid that he had had 400 copies of the Bull printed and distributed "perche ognun diceva di non sapere che (il concilio) si farebbe e lo ponevano quasi in dubbio". Transcripts had already been sent from Rome to the metropolitans, *C.T.*, VOL. X, p. 15 f.; see extract in Druffel, *Monumenta Tridentina*, VOL. I (Munich 1884), p. 15 f. Since the documents published by Druffel are now available in a much better textual edition in *C.T.*, VOL. X, and *N.B.*, VOL. I, PT viii, I shall not refer to his edition whenever I use it later. It was a valuable publication at the time in spite of its pronounced partisan spirit.

the Council. The Pope's only action was to inform the bishops resident in Rome, on 3 January, that they must either be ready to set out for Trent by Candlemas Day or state their reasons for not doing so.[1] The Pope seemed in no particular hurry to appoint legates; only half-heartedly did he take the measures which a memorial of Campeggio's had described as indispensable.[2] The cardinals who were to preside at the Council were only appointed on 22 February 1545, that is a bare three weeks before the date fixed for the opening.[3] Cardinals Del Monte, Cervini and Pole were empowered to preside, in such wise that if one of them happened to be absent or to be in any way prevented, the other two were to have full authority; eventually a brief of 6 March gave full powers to each of the three legates. A second Bull, also dated 22 February but kept secret, empowered them to transfer the Council to some other locality should they judge it necessary and either to continue it there or even to dissolve it altogether, and if necessary, to inflict ecclesiastical censures upon the recalcitrant. The Bishop of La Cava resumed his duties as a conciliar commissary, assisted by Antonio Pighetti of Bergamo, one of the Pope's familiars. Both men were instructed to get in touch with Madruzzo who in the meantime had been placated by the announcement of his elevation to the cardinalate. When making this announcement the Pope had also requested him, in a brief couched in the most gracious terms, to make all the necessary preparations.

However, all these measures failed to convince the Emperor of the earnestness of the Pope's intentions with regard to the Council, for similar things had happened both after the Mantuan convocation and after the first Tridentine one. So deep-rooted was Charles V's distrust of the Farnese Pope and his entire family that he put an utterly

[1] Gualteruzzi to Della Casa, 3 January 1545, Montepulciano, Bibl. Ricci, 4, fol. 37ʳ or.

[2] "Quae censeat ep. Feltrensis velut praeparatoria quaedam providenda ante inchoationem concilii Tridentini", Rome, Arch. of Gregorian University, 632, pp. 151-6, drawn up after the decision for the convocation but previous to Sanfelice's return from Germany, viz. in November or December 1544. Several of Campeggio's proposals, such as the invitations to the universities of Cologne, Louvain, Paris and Orleans, the immediate putting at the disposal of the poorer members of the Council of a sum of 1000 ducats a month (p. 155), the study of old conciliar acts preserved among the literary remains of Cardinal Aleander (p. 156), were not acted upon even at a later date.

[3] All the documents are in C.T., VOL. IV, pp. 393-7. The Bull of Nomination and the brief were forwarded to the legates on 7 March (C.T., VOL. X, p. 4). At a later date and at Del Monte's request they were redrafted because in the original form the translation or the dissolution of the Council was made to depend on the Council's assent, C.T., VOL. X, p. 7, l. 42; p. 13, l. 28; p. 15, l. 8; p. 35, l. 8.

unwarranted construction on the wholly trivial circumstance that Cardinal Pole remained at Viterbo, his official residence as legate of the Papal States, while his colleagues set out for Trent. That keen promoter of the Council, the Emperor imagined, was being purposely kept back so that the other two, whom he regarded as mere tools of the papal policy, might have a free hand.[1] If he had known that these cardinals were empowered to transfer the Council, his distrust would have been greater still.

On 22 February the legatine cross was handed to Cervini and Del Monte. Thereupon both left the Eternal City, the one on the 23rd, the other on the 24th.[2] By-passing Siena and Florence, Cervini journeyed through Montepulciano, his home-town, and Pontassieve, and reached Bologna on 5 March. After only a day's rest he continued his journey, by-passing both Mantua and Verona so as to reach Trent within the time-limit fixed for the opening. Del Monte followed him one day later, for he was plagued by the gout which he ascribed to the wine of Montepulciano. On 12 March the two legates met at Rovereto. There they were met by Angelo Massarelli, Cervini's secretary, who in company with Gianbattista Palmerio, one of Cervini's familiars, had left the party at Monterosi on 24 February to go ahead in order to make the necessary arrangements for its accommodation at Trent. Cervini was to lodge in the Palazzo Giroldi while Del Monte was to stay at the house of the jurist Queta. Provisions had been bought and everything was ready.

On 13 March the legates made their solemn entry into Trent. Torrential rain restricted the display which usually accompanied such occasions. Cardinal Madruzzo, surrounded by his whole court, came to meet the Pope's representatives at the monastery of the *Crocifisso*, outside the city walls. Shortly after two o'clock the procession got under way and entered through the Porta S. Croce, where a triumphal arch had been erected, until it came to a halt in front of the cathedral, at the portals of which Madruzzo, in his capacity of ordinary of the place, offered the legates a liturgical welcome. This done, everyone hastened to his own quarters. Apart from the Bishop of La Cava there

---

[1] The Emperor to Vega, 9 April 1545, Druffel, *Karl V*, VOL. II, p. 51. Pole's fear of Henry VIII was by no means groundless, as we learn from the Pope's protests against the conduct of the condottiere Ludovico delle Arme and that of the Conte di S. Bonifacio, both of whom were supplied with funds from Venice, *Cal. of St. Pap.*, *Venice*, VOL. V, pp. 135 ff (No. 335); Montepulciano, Bibl. Ricci, 4 (17 April, 25 June, 21 July), Della Casa's reports.

[2] Massarelli's account of his journey, *C.T.*, VOL. I, pp. 151-9; Cervini's and Del Monte's letters during their journey, *ibid.*, VOL. X, pp. 3 ff., 8 f.

was as yet not a single prelate from any other place at Trent. Tommaso Campeggio only arrived from Rome on the evening of 14 March. It was evident that there could be no question of opening the Council on the appointed date. *Laetare* Sunday went by without any of those present stirring from their residences: it rained in torrents from morning till night. Would there be a repetition of the situation described in the papal brief of admonition: "We came, and there was not a man; we called and there was none that would hear"? The events of the weeks immediately following were to prove that times had changed. The *orbis catholicus* was stirring. At the beginning of March the Pope had charged Cardinals Cupis and Parisio to make all the necessary arrangements for the assembly of the Council.[1] Towards the end of the month the bishops at the Curia and the generals of Orders were admonished to set out for Trent. The committee of cardinals showed great unwillingness to listen to excuses [2]; but they all took their time. Until then, apart from Campeggio, only the Bishops of Belcastro, Bitonto and Bertinoro had actually started. They reached Trent in the last days of March and the first of April.[3] This was also the time when Pole set out for that city, plagued though he was by fear of the snares of Henry VIII.[4] Ludovico Beccadelli, an excellent man and a former secretary of Contarini, was named secretary to the Council after Marcantonio Flaminio, who had been selected for the post, had declined it.[5]

---

[1] Farnese to the legates, 12 March 1545, *ibid.*, VOL. X, p. 6.

[2] Gualteruzzi to Della Casa, 28 March, Montepulciano, Bibl. Ricci, 4, fol. 63ʳ: "Questi prelati hanno ordine di dover andar tutti indifferentemente, et quelli che si scusano sono poco intesi"; *C.T.*, VOL. X, p. 13, l. 18. Seripando was invited by Cardinal Cupis on 27 March (*C.T.*, VOL. II, p. 406) but he only set out on 19 April. For his itinerary see *Analecta Augustiniana*, IX (1921), p. 299. He reached Trent on 19 May, at the same time as the general of the Carmelites Audet (*C.T.*, VOL. I, p. 190 f.). Of the Roman prelates Gualteruzzi writes on 29 April (Montepulciano, Bibl. Ricci 4, fol. 71ʳ) "Questi prelati si solicitano di mettersi in ordine, pur vanno anchor molto adagio."

[3] Bitonto arrived on 24 March, *C.T.*, VOL. I, p. 162, l. 21; Bertinoro on 4 April, *ibid.*, VOL. I, p. 168, l. 36; Belcastro on 10 April, *ibid.*, VOL. I, p. 172, l. 25.

[4] Del Monte and Cervini repeatedly urged Pole to make a start and to overcome his fears of an attempt on his life, *Epp. Poli*, ed. Quirini, VOL. IV, pp. 184 ff. For reasons of security he was to travel with Farnese, but the plan was abandoned because Pole was not prepared to keep pace with the latter "come quello che corre malvolontieri", Gualteruzzi on 18 April, Montepulciano, Bibl. Ricci, 4, fol. 69ʳ. On 6 April Pole was still at Viterbo, G. Signorelli, *Viterbo nella storia della Chiesa*, VOL. II, ii (Viterbo 1940), p. 165; on 28 April he was at Bologna and on 4 May he reached Trent, *C.T.*, VOL. I, p. 183.

[5] Gualteruzzi on 18 April: "Il nostro M. Ludovico Beccadelli e stato eletto secretario del concilio et gli e stato Triphone per scrivano. Il Flaminio non ha voluto accettare che sogliono esser dui et alcuna volta quattro", cf. *C.T.*, VOL. X, p. 36; Beccadelli reached Trent on 24 April, *ibid.*, VOL. I, p. 178.

Some bishops of northern Italy also made preparations for the journey. The auxiliary of Vicenza, Ludovico Chieregati, a brother of the nuncio who had served in Germany under Adrian VI, apologised through a representative for his temporary absence. The auxiliary of Brescia, Ferretti, promised on 15 April that he would make an early start.[1] For all that it was not until May that the repeated exhortations of the legates for the immediate despatch to Trent of Italian prelates, theologians and canonists began to yield visible results.[2]

However, the first envoy to the Council had arrived before that date. Accompanied by his secretary Domenico Gaztelù, Diego Hurtado de Mendoza came over from Venice, and since the legates, like their predecessors in 1543, declined his request for a reception in the cathedral, he delivered his inaugural address as imperial ambassador in Del Monte's reception-room on 26 March.[3] He made excuses for his own belated arrival and prayed that for the time being no canonical proceedings should be instituted against those Spanish bishops who had not yet come to the Council. In their oral reply, and subsequently in their written answer of 27 March, the legates made no reference to this point, but they seized the opportunity to stress the papal demand that, in view of the convocation of the Council, the Diet of Worms should remove the religious question from its agenda. Shortly after Easter Francesco di Castelalto, the King's captain at Trent, and the jurist Antonio Queta presented themselves as envoys of Ferdinand I, though they produced no credentials to that effect.[4] Much more important than the presence of these envoys would have been that of the bishops. On this point a serious cleavage of opinion soon made itself felt.

By the terms of the Bull of Convocation all bishops and abbots

[1] C.T., VOL. I, p. 161, l. 24; ibid., VOL. X, p. 34, n.5. From a letter of Farnese from Bologna the legates learnt that the Bishop of Fano was on his way to Trent, ibid., VOL. X, p. 54, n.1.

[2] C.T., VOL. X, p. 24, l. 33. There was not a little exaggeration when Maffeo wrote to Nausea on 9 May: "Confluunt eo iam Italiae episcopi . . . nonnulli ex Gallia iam advenerunt."

[3] Gaztelù reached Trent on 17 March, Mendoza on the 23rd, C.T., VOL. I, pp. 160 ff. The notaries' instruments on the reception in C.T., VOL. IV, pp. 399-402; the legates' report, ibid., VOL. X, pp. 17 ff. Venice's criticism of the attitude of the legates, ibid., VOL. IV, p. 401, l. 35. Della Casa's remarks to the legates, 30 April (Montepulciano, Bibl. Ricci, 4, fol. 6ᵛ) must be traced back to Mendoza himself. On 5 May the latter was back at Venice, on the 6th he delivered a message of the Emperor to the senate, Montepulciano, Bibl. Ricci, 4, fol. 7ʳ (8 May).

[4] C.T., VOL. I, p. 171; according to the legates' report, ibid., VOL. X, p. 17, Ferdinand informed them that later on he would send "persone più idonee et instrutte".

were bound to attend the Council. In spite of this fact the Emperor
and his son Philip had only requested seven prelates out of the entire
Spanish hierarchy, together with a number of jurists and theologians,
to prepare for an early departure for Trent.[1] From among the many
bishops of the kingdom of Naples the viceroy had only singled out four
prelates for this duty, whilst ordering the others to give these four
their powers of attorney.[2] The basic argument against this artificial
restriction of the attendance at the Council was the principle that the
bishops' authority to bear witness to the faith and to establish ecclesiastical discipline at a Council is ultimately rooted in the episcopal order
and is therefore vested in their own persons. They are not free to
delegate this authority at their own good pleasure, as Canon Law
permits in respect of other juridical matters. Such a policy had nevertheless been followed at the reform Councils, especially at the Council
of Basle, which in practice had been little more than a gathering of
deputies. It was precisely this recollection that threw light on the
possible consequences of the present situation. If the viceroy's arbitrary
action was acquiesced in, not only was the normal representation of the
kingdom of Naples at the Council in jeopardy, but there was a danger
that the chosen prelates—all of them reliable partisans of the Emperor
—would claim as many votes as they had powers of attorney, that is,
over a hundred. They would thus constitute a majority in the Council.
If the Spaniards were also possessed of powers of attorney for the

---

[1] The Spanish Privy Council had proposed to send five or six bishops, *Cal. of
St. Pap., Spain*, VOL. VII, p. 494 f. (No. 260). According to Poggio the list submitted
to it included the names of the Cardinals of Compostella and Coria and the Bishops of
Jaén, Astorga, Malaga, Huesca and Lérida (*C.T.*, VOL. x, p. 16). The acceptance of
Jaén and Lérida, 13 March, in Ferrandis-Bordonau, *El Concilio de Trento*, pp. 27 ff.;
ibid., p. 36 f. Compostella's change of mind, 20 March; Pacheco's excuses for
delaying his departure, 7 May, *ibid.*, p. 39; the jurists Vargas, Velasco and Quintana
signified their acceptance, *ibid.*, pp. 32, 35, 37; Domingo Soto accepted on 19 March,
ibid., p. 33, but Francisco de Vitoria declined, *ibid.*, p. 31.

[2] Pedro de Toledo's ordinance of 27 March for powers of attorney to be made
out for the Bishops of Castellamare, Gaeta, San Marco and Lanciano in *C.T.*, VOL.
x, p. 36, *n.1*. In mid-April the Cappellano Maggiore called together all the bishops
then at Naples and repeated the viceroy's command. He met with unanimous
opposition, *ibid.*, p. 69. On 20 April the Bishop of Capaccio was nominated in
the place of the Bishop of Gaeta, who had been taken ill, *C.T.*, VOL. IV, p. 406 f.
These powers were not to be made out for the whole duration of the Council but only
"durante nostra absentia". The Pope had his suspicions because "tutti 4 delli
riservati a S.M.tà" and were therefore nominees of the Emperor, Gualteruzzi on 11
April, Montepulciano, Bibl. Ricci, 4, fol. 67ʳ. In the duchy of Milan the viceroy left
the nomination of the prelates who were to repair to the Council to the bishops,
C.T., VOL. x, p. 33, l. 27. There is nothing to show that he followed the precedent
set by the viceroy of Naples.

bishops who had remained at home,[1] the imperial influence would be increased to an alarming degree.

To forestall such a development the Pope, not content with counter-proposals through his nuncios, intervened in person and applied an effective brake. By the Bull *Decet nos* of 17 April he forbade the nomination of representatives to the Council without adequate reasons and once again reminded the bishops in pressing terms of their duty to attend in person.[2] By a brief of 25 April he summoned the viceroy, Pedro de Toledo, not only to recall his ordinance but to do his best to persuade the bishops of the realm to take a personal part in the Council. Both the Emperor and the viceroy gave way: thus this danger to the attendance at the Council was averted.[3]

Representatives from other countries were slow in coming. The bishops of the Empire were temporarily detained at the Diet of Worms.[4]

[1] Thomas de Villanueva's letter of 20 March to Prince Philip shows that the bishops who remained in Spain were ordered to give powers of attorney to the Emperor's nominees, Ferrandis-Bordonau, *El Concilio de Trento*, p. 34 f. Further evidence is to be found in many letters of the period, *C.T.*, VOL. XI, p. 3 f.

[2] *C.T.*, VOL. IV, p. 404. The nomination of a proxy is only permitted "ad se in eodem concilio excusandum et de eorum legitimo impedimento fidem legitimam faciendam". From Blosius's instructions, *ibid.*, p. 407 f., we are able to infer the contents of the brief; for the canonical justification, cf. Campeggio, *C.T.*, VOL. X, p. 416 f. The conciliar legates thought the Bull was too exacting, they accordingly resisted its publication, *ibid.*, p. 81, but it was too late, *ibid.*, p. 87, *n.*4. Diego de Mendoza saw in it nothing but a means for keeping the prelates from beyond the Alps in a minority, *C.T.*, VOL. XI, p. xxxvii.

[3] Pedro de Toledo was exceedingly annoyed by the brief and revenged himself by delaying the permit for the transport of Greek wines for the papal household, *C.T.*, VOL. X, p. 87, *n.*8, though he ended by allowing the four prelates to proceed to Trent without powers of attorney. They reached Trent at the beginning of June, *C.T.*, VOL. I, p. 198; VOL. X, p. 118. There is information from Spain that as from April all the prelates had been mobilised, e.g. Palencia and Valencia, Ferrandis-Bordonau, *El Concilio de Trento*, p. 41; L. Fullana, "Por que Santo Tomás de Villanueva no assistió al concilio de Trento", in *Verdad y Vida*, III (1945), pp. 217-25. On the summons to the Benedictine Malvenda, see *C.T.*, VOL. IV, p. 434, and R. Angé in *Analecta Montserratensia*, VII (1928), pp. 303-07.

[4] Mignanelli repeatedly approves this excuse of the German bishops, *N.B.*, VOL. I, PT viii, p. 699; *C.T.*, VOL. X, p. 41, l. 43. It is found in the mandate of the Bishop of Hildesheim, 12 January, *C.T.*, VOL. IV, pp. 389 ff. (with the names of the following proxies, viz. Latorff, Hoyer, Rosin and Marsaner); the excuse of the Bishop of Cambrai in *C.T.*, VOL. IV, p. 403, VOL. X, p. 32 f. That the latter made serious preparations we learn from the directions he gave to his auxiliary on 26 March, Le Plat, VOL. III, pp. 265 ff., and from the latter's circular to the deans, *ibid.*, p. 271 f. The Bishop of Eichstätt designated Cochlaeus as his proxy as the latter informed Camillo Capilupi on 25 April. He was to be assisted by the abbot of a near-by monastery, but the two men decided not to set out until they were assured of the arrival of bishops from Spain and France by a messenger whom they had despatched to Trent, G. Kupke in *Q.F.*, III (1900), pp. 137-41. Cochlaeus wrote to Cervini in this sense on 26 April, *Z.K.G.*, XVIII (1897), p. 457.

As for the bishops of his hereditary states, King Ferdinand said that little was to be expected from them [1]: the Turkish peril and the financial effort to avert it swallowed their resources. So far not one French prelate had put in an appearance either at Vicenza or at Trent, but on 12 April the legates were surprised by the simultaneous arrival of two of them in the persons of the abbots of Cîteaux and La Boussière.[2] True, their immediate intention was to go to Rome, where they wished to lodge a protest against the excessive ease with which privileges were granted to Cistercian monasteries as well as to individual monks. It was actually on the plea of such privileges that they had been refused hospitality in two Milanese houses. There was indeed a prospect of a wider French representation, but so far it had not materialised. Francis I had designated several French bishops and scholars for the Council, but their departure depended on the result of the Diet of Worms and the Protestants' reaction to the invitation to the Council.[3] The legates accordingly endeavoured to speed their journey through Grignan, the French envoy at Worms, but only by the end of June did it become known that six bishops—among them Cardinal Lenoncourt —twelve theologians and six jurists had been ordered by the King to set out for Trent.[4]

On the basis of this information the prospects for the success of the assembly were, on the whole, substantially better than on the occasion of the earlier attempts. In the first days of April a bare half-dozen bishops were actually present at Trent. The question had to be faced whether so small an attendance justified the opening of the Council. On 24 March the legates had been instructed by Cardinal Farnese to delay the opening until after Easter (5 April), that is, until the nuncio Mignanelli's first reports from Worms should be available.[5] These

---

[1] The Bishop of Breslau, who in his capacity as a territorial captain was the last feeble support of Catholicism in Silesia, also named Cochlaeus his proxy, *Archiv für schlesische Kirchengeschichte*, I (1936), p. 64, and the Bishop's letter to Nausea, 27 January 1546, *Epp. misc. ad Nauseam*, p. 388 f. This letter I overlooked. As regards Austria, Nausea was without resources and the abbots were hard pressed by the Turkish war, *C.T.*, VOL. X, p. 25 f.

[2] *C.T.*, VOL. I, p. 173; VOL. IV, p. 403 f.

[3] The reports of St Maurice, the imperial ambassador to France, to Cobos, dated 31 March and 7 May 1545, in *Cal. of St. Pap., Spain*, VOL. VIII, pp. 78, 101 (Nos. 36 and 49); the nuncio Alessandro Guidiccioni on 29 April, *C.T.*, VOL. IV, p. 412.

[4] The legates to Mignanelli on 10 May 1545, *C.T.*, VOL. X, p. 75; *aviso* of 22 May, *C.T.*, VOL. X, p. 127; St Maurice on 29 June, *Cal. of St. Pap., Spain*, VOL. VIII, p. 149 (No. 82).

[5] *C.T.*, VOL. X, p. 15 (24 March); on Mignanelli's passage through Trent, 23-25 March, *ibid.*, VOL. I, p. 162 f.

reports gave no clear picture of the situation. The nuncio hesitated to declare himself definitely either for or against the opening. In the end he came to the conclusion that it would be better to wait for a larger attendance and for developments at the Diet.[1] Only in one eventuality were the legates given a clear direction by the Pope. On 11 April they were told that as soon as the assembly at Worms began to discuss the religious question, the Council was to be opened at once, regardless of the number of those present.[2]

However, the legates felt that the Pope's decision failed to take into account the situation created by the imperial Proposition of 24 March as well as the dignity of the Apostolic See. In his Proposition the Emperor had put the question of assistance for the Turkish war at the head of the agenda. He had also suggested that the discussion of Church reform, on which the Protestants insisted, should be held over until the closing stages of the Diet when the course of the Council would show whether there was any prospect of real reform. Should none be in sight by the end of the Diet, the Emperor would make arrangements for another Diet, for the discussion of the reform. If the Council was not opened, the Emperor would have a plausible motive for continuing the Speyer policy. It was also to be expected that the Protestants would not be prepared to concur in a war against the Turks unless he gave them a solemn guarantee, in due legal form, that their refusal to attend the Council would not be visited upon them. Such a declaration would have rendered it impossible for the imperial authority to give effect later on to the decisions of the Council.

Of even greater weight was another consideration which the legates set down in a strictly confidential letter exclusively intended for the Pope's eyes. Their suspicions about the Emperor's intentions with regard to the Council were not less than the latter's misgivings about the Pope's determination to hold it. In the legates' opinion the purpose of the Emperor's preparations for the Council was to make a show of zeal before the world for the cause of the Council so as to put the Pope in the wrong. The Pope should forestall the Emperor and act independently. They accordingly proposed that the Council should be opened at once, before the Emperor's arrival at Worms. If this was done, no one would be able to say that the Pope had only resolved to act under pressure from the Emperor.[3]

The legates' proposal was prompted by a very natural desire to put an end to the painful uncertainty in which they found themselves.

[1] *C.T.*, VOL. X, pp. 28, 41.   [2] *Ibid.*, p. 35.   [3] *Ibid.*, pp. 44 ff.

POPE PAUL III
After the painting by Titian, in the Pinacoteca Nazionale, Naples,
painted about 1543

However, by the time their suggestion reached Rome it had been nullified by a piece of information which had come to their knowledge two days before their letter was written, but the import of which they had failed to grasp and, indeed, could not have grasped. This was that in his letter of 12 April Cardinal Farnese had informed them that the Pope had decided that he should go as legate to Worms, where the Emperor's arrival from the Netherlands was expected at this very time.[1]

This information was somewhat surprising. Up to this time the Pope had repeatedly and emphatically refused to send a representative to Worms. Now he suddenly decided to despatch one. This change of mind was due not so much to Mignanelli's reports about the danger of the religious question being discussed and the Council being circumvented,[2] as to certain hints concerning the Emperor's ulterior plans which Cardinal Truchsess passed on to Rome through his secretary Annibale.[3] It was probably in this way that the Pope got his first, though as yet incomplete insight into the Emperor's great plan. He saw at once that it completely altered the political situation. Should the Emperor at length venture upon an enterprise which Cardinal Campeggio had regarded as inevitable fifteen years earlier, namely an attack on the Schmalkaldic League—that state within a state—he would require the Pope's assistance on account of his chronic financial straits. In this way the pontiff rose from the equivocal position into which he had been manœuvred by the Peace of Crépy to the role of a courted

---

[1] *Ibid.*, p. 37.

[2] Mignanelli's first report from Worms dated 4 April, in *C.T.*, VOL. X, pp. 21 ff. *N.B.*, VOL. I, PT viii, pp. 89-93, cannot possibly have influenced, as Friedensburg assumes (*ibid.*, p. 28), the decision to send Farnese. This must have been arrived at between 6 and 12 April. Neither this report, nor the next of 6 April (*C.T.*, VOL. x, p. 25 f.), contained any disquieting information; in fact, as late as 12 April Verallo sets the Curia at rest with regard to the attitude of the Catholic princes, *C.T.*, VOL. x, p. 38. Only in his later despatches, especially in that of 20 April, did Mignanelli become more insistent, obviously under pressure from King Ferdinand.

[3] Farnese to the legates on 12 April, *C.T.*, VOL. x, p. 37. I do not think that Cardinal Truchsess's letter of 21 March, Druffel, *Karl V*, VOL. II, pp. 8 ff., can have contained all the information Annibale Bellagais was charged to take to Rome. Truchsess may have left Worms before 21 March since on the evening of the 24th he was at Trent, *C.T.*, VOL. I, p. 163; on the other hand the Pope's action at the consistory of 13 April, *N.B.*, VOL. I, PT viii, p. 106, and his hesitation on the question of the opening of the Council, show that there can only have been hints rather than positive information. This view agrees with the legates' statement that Cardinal Truchsess's action was "nata e proceduta de più alto". On the much-discussed mission of Flaminio Savelli to the imperial court (Müller in *Z.K.G.*, XLIV (1925), pp. 408 ff.) I have no new information, but the possibility remains that he too may have imparted information of the same kind as above.

ally. If the power of the Protestants was broken, the Council lost for him one of its most threatening aspects. Even more important was the fact that a close agreement between Pope and Emperor promised to dispel the atmosphere of mutual distrust in which Mignanelli—quite accurately—saw the chief obstacle to the success of the Council.[1]

Cardinal Farnese left Rome on 17 April for Trent, where his arrival was awaited with an anxiety which it is easy to understand. The splendour of his ceremonial entry into the city of the Council completely eclipsed that of the legates.[2] Del Monte, Cervini and Madruzzo went out to meet him at Riva, on Lake Garda. On 25 April Farnese made his solemn entry into Trent. All the bishops present, the imperial ambassador Mendoza and the leading members of the local nobility took part in the procession, together with the numerous suite of the papal nephew, making in all two hundred and fifty persons on horseback. Mortars thundered a welcome from Dos Trento, from the tower of the Adige bridge and from the city tower near the cathedral. On the following day, a Sunday, Madruzzo gave a splendid banquet in the castle, and on the Monday he personally conducted his guest through the city. The rest of the time was taken up by discussions. Farnese had long conferences with Cervini alone and afterwards with the two legates, when Madruzzo and Mendoza were also present. The fact that the imperial representatives took part in these conversations was a symptom of the change in papal policy that was preparing, but how radical the change was appeared only on the day of Farnese's departure.

The Pope, by nature cautious and inclined to be suspicious, had been so impressed by the considerations submitted by the legates that without any more ado, on 23 April, he fixed the opening of the Council for 3 May, feast of the Invention of the Holy Cross.[3] The bearer of these instructions reached Trent on the morning of 28 April, at the very moment when Farnese, booted and spurred, was about to continue his journey. The legates hastened at once to the castle to examine the new situation with him. The result was that Farnese took full responsibility for putting off the opening of the Council until he should have seen the Emperor at Worms.[4]

[1] *C.T.*, VOL. X, p. 41, ll. 19 and 48.

[2] *Ibid.*, VOL. I, pp. 178 ff.; VOL. X, p. 44. Report on the journey, *N.B.*, VOL. I, PT viii, pp. 106 ff., 119 ff., in between *C.T.*, VOL. X, p. 54, *n.*1.

[3] *C.T.*, VOL. X, p. 53, repeated on 27 April, VOL. X, p. 56 f.

[4] In their report of 28 April, *C.T.*, VOL. X, pp. 60 ff., the legates also assume responsibility. However, Massarelli's version is obviously accurate (*C.T.*, VOL. I, p. 180); it does not conflict with Cervini's memorial which the latter entrusted to Farnese, *C.T.*, VOL. X, p. 55 f.

The cardinal was unwilling to compromise in advance the success of his mission. From the reports of the nuncios he had learnt that the court was "like a land flowing with milk and honey". Was this the moment to provoke fresh bitterness by inaugurating the Council without previous announcement? It was certain that the Emperor would not reach Worms before the middle of May. This meant the postponement of a decision concerning the discussion of the religious question. Thus the legates' strongest objections to the postponement of the inauguration lost some of their force. Moreover, Farnese had received fresh reports from Worms which put him in a very hopeful mood.[1] He was a good deal more optimistic than the Pope about his chances at the imperial court.

As a matter of fact his reception by the Emperor surpassed all his expectations. Every effort was evidently being made to prevent an impression that the court interpreted the arrival of the legate as a capitulation by the Curia to the victorious monarch. Old accounts were apparently wiped out, a new chapter was opening. Only now was the cardinal fully enlightened about the Emperor's great plan and consequently able to gauge the full import of his mission. If it proved completely successful—if it marked the beginning of a sincere collaboration between Pope and Emperor—there was no cause for anxiety about a successful Council.

However, for the time being the decision to put off the opening was maintained. The Pope gave his approval to the steps taken by Farnese in conjunction with the legates and countermanded a service of intercession for which arrangements had been made.[2] On the other hand the legates were not blind to the fact that a continuation of a passive waiting policy could not fail to affect adversely those who had already come to the Council. Accordingly on 3 May, with a view to giving them information as well as occupation, they summoned the prelates, who of late had been arriving in increasing numbers[3] to the great hall of the Palazzo Giroldi. After explaining in general terms why

---

[1] Cardinal Truchsess's letter is not in, *N.B.*, VOL. I, PT viii, p. 121, but on 20 and 22 April Mignanelli repeatedly spoke of the "nota confidentia" between the two heads, *C.T.*, VOL. X, p. 49, l. 8; p. 51, l. 13. At the moment of leaving Rome Farnese was still very uncertain about his reception at court, *N.B.*, VOL. I, PT viii, p. 639.

[2] *C.T.*, VOL. X, p. 70 f.

[3] The following arrivals are reported: on 24 April the Bishop of Mallorca; on the 28th the Bishop of Accia; on 2 May the Bishop of Piacenza; on 3 May the Bishops of Pesaro and Cadiz—the latter was also an Italian, *C.T.*, VOL. I, pp. 178, 180, 182. On 25 April Della Casa informed the legates of the impending arrival of the Archbishop of Corfu, Montepulciano, Bibl. Ricci, 4, fol. 6ʳ.

it had been found necessary to put off the opening, they passed on to questions of ceremonial, the decoration of the cathedral choir and the liturgical vestments to be worn at the conciliar sessions.[1] A *questionnaire* on these matters was also submitted to the papal master of ceremonies.[2]

Prelates continued to arrive from Italy during the ensuing weeks, so that on Whitsun Eve, 23 May, seventeen bishops and five generals of Orders were present at the liturgical function of the day.[3] But their state of mind was anything but optimistic. The first question of every fresh arrival was: "When will the Council be opened?" No one knew the answer, not even the legates. "Even if we open the Council," Tommaso Campeggio observed, "it will not be easy to convince the prelates that it will run its normal course: there are too few of them for regular discussions. Better no decrees than invalid ones!"[4] The feast of the Ascension and that of Pentecost went by, though both days would have been most suitable for the opening, without the decisive word having come from Farnese. At last, on 25 May, a courtier arrived from Worms, but only to announce yet another heavy disappointment.[5]

For reasons of security Farnese had by-passed Protestant Württemberg and had reached Worms on 17 May, one day after the Emperor's arrival. In his audience on 18 May he at once broached the subject of the inauguration of the Council. The evident hesitation with which Charles V approached the matter was accounted for—as was shown by the subsequent negotiations with Granvella—by the Emperor's

---

[1] *C.T.*, VOL. I, p. 183; VOL. IV, p. 413; VOL. X, pp. 63 f., 72 f. The question of the seating was not without political significance. Thus on Easter Sunday Mendoza demanded a place in the choir immediately behind the legates and before all the cardinals and other prelates. The legates refused to comply with the demand and referred him to the place of the imperial ambassador in the *capella papale* while the masters of ceremonies described the request as one that could not even be discussed, *C.T.*, VOL. I, pp. 167 ff.; VOL. IV, pp. 418, 421. Another worry for the legates was the claim (supported by Campeggio, *C.T.*, VOL. I, pp. 414-17) of the German prince-bishops to precedence over all the other bishops on the plea of their rank as Electors, dukes or princes, *C.T.*, VOL. X, p. 64. Their pretension was also rejected by the Pope, *C.T.*, VOL. IV, p. 418, l. 25.

[2] *C.T.*, VOL. IV, p. 419.

[3] *C.T.*, VOL. I, p. 192. The only non-Italians were the Archbishop of Armagh and the Bishop of Worcester. Helding was not present because he had no vestments, *C.T.*, VOL. X, p. 88 f.

[4] *C.T.*, VOL. IV, p. 414, ll. 25 and 31; also VOL. X, p. 80.

[5] Farnese's letter from Worms, 22 May, *C.T.*, VOL. X, pp. 91-6. On his letter to the Pope which he instructed Cervini to keep back for the time being, Friedensburg observes, *N.B.*, VOL. I, PT viii, p. 164, *n.*1, that he continued to misjudge the situation, hence Dandino did his best to render him innocuous. On the whole subject, see J. Müller, in *Z.K.G.*, XLIV (1925), pp. 338 ff.

desire to put off the opening until after the Diet because there was reason to fear that the Protestants would withdraw from it and start warlike preparations. Granvella obviously exaggerated the danger that threatened from that quarter in order not to upset the progress of the negotiations about their contribution to the Turkish war. For the time being the Emperor was unwilling to commit himself to a definite policy. The opening of the Council would force him to show his hand prematurely and so compromise the success of his great plan.

This fresh postponement was bound to jeopardise the actual assembly of the Council, for the longer the opening was delayed, the stronger became the doubts about its successful realisation, and in the eyes of the world the culprit would be the Pope. It was comparatively easy, from the ecclesiastical point of view, to refute the Emperor's arguments,[1] but impossible to act in opposition to his wishes. What kind of Council would that be at which none of his bishops were present? Against their will and under protest the legates bowed to the imperial dictate. Depression was universal when, on 31 May, they informed the members of the Council of the nature of the instructions they had received.[2] Two days later, when Farnese, accompanied by a small suite, touched Trent on his return journey from Worms, they were at last initiated into the complex scheme of which the decision which hurt them so profoundly was a part. Only now did they learn of the big things that were preparing in Germany. War against Schmalkalden was decided while an offensive alliance between Pope and Emperor was in the making.[3] Naturally enough, so important a piece of information could not be divulged since the success of the undertaking depended on the secrecy of the preliminary negotiations. To the twenty prelates then present at Trent the legates could only

---

[1] *C.T.*, VOL. X, p. 99, ll. 11 and 29; p. 102, l. 13. Reports were coming in at this very time to the effect that the Turks would undertake no large-scale offensive that year, *C.T.*, VOL. I, p. 195. Shortly after this the imperial secretary Veltwyck visited the Porte for the purpose of negotiations.

[2] "Quod licet omnes grave ferrent", *C.T.*, VOL. IV, p. 423, l. 6.

[3] The nuncios' notes on the communications made by the Emperor to Farnese as well as a Spanish memorial for Vega on the subject are not known (*N.B.*, VOL. I, PT viii, p. 171, *n.*1), but from certain remarks, e.g. that after his conversations with the Emperor and Granvella Farnese showed signs of great satisfaction (*N.B.*, VOL. I, PT viii, p. 630), the Italian diplomatists at Worms, such as Capilupi, drew some accurate conclusions, as they did from some hints thrown out by Cardinal Truchsess (*ibid.*, p. 632). Navagero was given some information (*ibid.*, p. 660 f.), but the Florentine envoy was put off by Granvella with generalities, though he too somehow succeeded in learning something about the "segreta intelligentia", *ibid.*, pp. 613 f., 616.

communicate the broad outlines of the scheme in vague and general terms.[1]

In spite of these precautions, partly as a result of this very communication and partly through indiscretions on the part of Farnese's companions, so much of the true facts seeped through that voices made themselves heard among the prelates insisting on an alteration in the role assigned to them.

One of them, probably the Bishop of Belcastro, suggested that the Council should be suspended and in its place an international reform committee set up in Rome, while to save appearances, and for the sole purpose of deluding the Protestants, a religious debate would be arranged in Germany between Catholic and Protestant divines.[2] The proposal was not a novel one. If it was adopted, the projected Council was doomed to go up in smoke. More deserving of consideration was the suggestion of Pietro Bertano, Bishop of Fano.[3] This prelate, whose sympathies were with the imperial party, uttered a grave warning against opening the Council at Trent. There was a danger, he urged, that it would drag on for years and slip from the Pope's control, especially if contrary to expectation the Protestants should decide to send their representatives. In that event even a translation, which he had regarded at one time as possible and had even advocated, could not be easily effected. On the other hand the bishop was convinced that the interests of Christendom would only be served by a Council personally presided over by the Pope. He accordingly pressed the pontiff to summon the prelates actually at Trent to Rome for the purpose of initiating a "reform of Christian life" as well as to clarify the controverted doctrines by means of a new formulary of the faith. At the same time the Pope should have himself represented at the conference which the Emperor had promised to hold in Germany and thereby recognise it as a substitute for a Council.

However the political inspiration of these proposals may have differed, they were prompted by a common motive, none other in fact

---

[1] Massarelli's *Diarium* evidently contains all he heard, *C.T.*, VOL. I, p. 199, hence undoubtedly more than the legates allowed the bishops to know. On the other hand his report in the acts, *C.T.*, VOL. IV, p. 423, l. 17, is far too concise. On 11 July Diruta, a Friar Minor, openly spoke of the impending war against the Protestants, *C.T.*, VOL. XI, p. 9.

[2] The letter of 2 June which Buschbell originally ascribed to the Bishop of Fano, and later, on more solid grounds, to the Bishop of Belcastro, is in *C.T.*, VOL. X, pp. 108 ff. The latter repeated the same proposal on 13 August, *ibid.*, p. 172 f.

[3] *C.T.*, VOL. X, pp. 159 ff. (25 July). I only take into account Bertano's earlier letter of 3 July (*ibid.*, pp. 132 ff.) in so far as it diverges from the later one.

than that of once again preventing a General Council by procuring the postponement of its opening. Such a step would have meant an abrupt break in the course of a papal policy whose beginning was so recent. The resumption of a policy of reunion, even though not seriously meant, would give rise to grave misgivings since it would give fresh substance to the dream of an understanding. The futility of such a course had been proved at Ratisbon and could only prejudice that "testing of the spirits" which was so urgently needed. The Pope remained firm in his resolve to hold the Council and turned a deaf ear, at least for the time being, to the proposal for a reform conference in Rome as a substitute. All the same, it is surprising that the idea of a Roman reform conference, with which the history of the fifteenth century and the pontificate of Clement VII have familiarised us, should crop up in the story of the Council of Trent even before the actual opening of that assembly and that it should raise its head whenever the continuation of the Council met with difficulties.

The last word on the war-plan as well as on the fate of the Council was spoken in Rome after Farnese's return on 8 June.[1] Paul III was in a state of deep distress just then on account of the death of his daughter Constanza, but he seized the proferred hand. He declared his willingness to grant Charles V a subsidy of 200,000 ducats for the war against Schmalkalden, a body of 12,500 auxiliaries for a period of four months, and one-half of the ecclesiastical revenue of Spain together with the right to alienate for the same purpose Spanish Church property up to the value of half a million ducats. In the last days of June an *entente* was concluded on these conditions. At the Emperor's request the opening of the Council was put off until more prelates from foreign parts should have arrived.

Thus, after twenty years of opposition—sometimes covert, at other times overt—Pope and Emperor joined forces against the Protestants. The Pope threw off the suspicion and fear which until then had so largely conditioned his relations with the Emperor, in the hope of dealing the renegades a decisive blow in conjunction with the monarch. The decision had not been an easy one: the pontiff had not overcome

---

[1] The Pope's proposal is in Farnese's letter to Granvella, 17 June, *N.B.*, VOL. I, PT viii, pp. 198 ff.; information about it for the legates in *C.T.*, VOL. X, pp. 142 ff. On its reception by the Emperor, cf. Mignanelli, 27-28 June, Verallo on 24 June, *N.B.*, VOL. I, PT viii, pp. 202-13. I consider that Brandi (*Karl V*, pp. 450 ff.: Eng. edn., pp. 525 ff.) is wrong when he suggests that Paul III sought to rid himself of the Council by means of a war against the Protestants. On the opponents of war against the heretics in the imperial camp, see Brandi, *Quellen*, p. 356 f.

his misgivings, he had only put them on one side. Both parties were far from trusting each other, as the future was to reveal.

From a purely ecclesiastical point of view the new political orientation could not but inspire anxiety, and the situation was not perfectly clear, as the legates in their capacity as advocates of the Council did not hesitate to point out to the pontiff.[1] For one thing, the role of the Council in the whole scheme had not been specified. Were the Pope and the Emperor about to have recourse to arms in order to compel the Protestants to send delegates to the Council? Quite recently, at Worms, they had once more refused to do so while on the other hand the Council had not been inaugurated, hence any action against the recalcitrants would be premature. Or was it the Council's task to convict the Protestants of heresy in order that its sentence might be carried into effect by means of armed force, as was in its time the sentence of Constance against the Hussites? This presupposed a formal judicial procedure by the Council against the heretics. In either hypothesis it was advisable that the assembly should be opened at once and at Trent. At a later date, when these proceedings had been concluded, it would be easy to transfer it to some city within the Papal States, there to deal with the problem of reform.

This suggestion came undoubtedly from the canonist Del Monte. From the point of view of Canon Law it could be considered, but on political grounds it was not practicable. The immediate result of the opening of proceedings for heresy at Trent would have been an armed rising by the Protestants at a time when the Emperor's military preparations were still quite inadequate. Rome made no comment on the suggestion.

Even more pressing were the last-minute warnings addressed to Rome by Cervini,[2] after the bearer of the Pope's reply to the Emperor's proposal had left Trent. "Beware of the selfish and unlimited schemes of the Emperor in general," he wrote, "and of his intentions with regard to the Council in particular! Do not on any account commit yourself to anything until it is agreed that the Pope is absolute master of the Council!" The Bishop of Fano sounded a similar note.[3]

The Pope refused to listen to these warnings. He fell in with the

---

[1] C.T., VOL. X, p. 114 f. (7 June), only signed by Del Monte and Pole; Cervini was indisposed, C.T., VOL. I, p. 202.

[2] The secret letter of 20 June in C.T., VOL. X, p. 123. *Plus ultra* (p. 124, l. 19) was Charles V's motto. Cervini also entertained some unjustified misgivings in regard to Ferdinand I, cf. C.T., VOL. X, p. 127, l. 1, and p. 131, ll. 10 and 166.

[3] C.T., VOL. X, pp. 132 ff. (3 July).

ideas which the nuncio Mignanelli had summed up in a memorial at the time of Farnese's departure for Worms.[1] Mignanelli granted that war against the Protestants was a plunge into the unknown; he nevertheless urged the Pope to trust the Emperor, "whose thoughts were fixed on God". He was therefore quite logical when he advocated an alliance, since otherwise Germany would be definitely lost and relations with the Habsburg brothers troubled for ever. Like his colleague, Verallo also urged the Pope to avoid every appearance of a lack of confidence in the Emperor.

In this way an *entente* was brought about and eventually a formal alliance. The arrangement gave neither party a sense of real security or unalloyed satisfaction; in fact, it contained the germs of fresh disagreements. The treaty was meant to harmonise two irreconcilable ideologies and to bring together for joint action two equally important but mutually opposed personalities. In the Emperor's estimation the alliance did no more than restore the normal conditions which corresponded to his wholly medieval conception of the Christian commonwealth of Western nations and of his own position as its secular head. He had always resented the Pope's policy of neutrality and his support of the "disturber of the peace" and "the friend of the Protestants and the Turks" as a violation of what he regarded as the normal political situation in the West. The feature of the alliance against the German Protestants to which he attached perhaps the greatest importance was the resumption of close collaboration with the Pope. The suggestion that what he proposed to the Pope implied nothing less than the pontiff's subordination to his plans, hence the sacrifice of his independence, would have appeared absurd to him. In his eyes victory over the disturbers of the established order in Church and Empire was also a triumph for the Church.

Paul III, on his part, concluded the alliance in the spirit in which every modern statesman enters upon similar compacts, viz. for one definite purpose, none other, in fact, than the overthrow of the Protestants. It was not his intention to issue a blank cheque out of sheer benevolence. The thought of yielding on any point in which the interests of the Papacy and his responsibility as head of the Church were at stake did not enter his mind for a moment. He never really trusted Charles V. He was prepared to do what he could in the hope

---

[1] *N.B.*, VOL. I, PT viii, pp. 170-7; Verallo's report, p. 223. Ferdinand in particular did his utmost to convince the nuncios that "la Ces. M.tà et lei vogliano in ogni modo il concilio", *ibid.*, p. 189.

that by means of the ultimate, bloody instrument of war the disrupted unity of the Church might yet be restored. It was this higher consideration that induced him to consent to the postponement of the opening of the Council. What a heavy burden he thus laid upon its presidents and its members was to be seen in the coming weeks and months.

While couriers journeyed to and fro between Rome and Worms, it needed all the legates' skill and energy to prevent the dispersal of that gathering. A few more prelates arrived indeed in the course of June,[1] but those already at Trent were looking for pretexts to take their departure, one for Milan, another for Venice and a third for his diocese. They found Trent inconvenient and expensive and not a few were in financial straits as the funds promised by the Pope for the benefit of needy prelates were not yet available. Rumour had it that several Neapolitan bishops had broken their journey to the Council at Rome, where they intended to await developments. In these circumstances it was some comfort when the Bishop of Termoli arrived on 22 June. It was thought that he would be well informed for he was a nephew of Cardinal Durante. In any case, in the opinion of the legates a word of encouragement from Rome was needed to raise the drooping spirits of the prelates, not to speak of the greatly needed ducats.[2]

In this atmosphere of uncertainty and hesitation the feast of St Vigilius, Patron of the diocese of Trent, was celebrated on 26 June with a solemn pontifical High Mass. This was followed by a great banquet at the castle, to which Madruzzo invited all the prelates. On the feast of St Peter and St Paul the pontifical Mass was sung by Del Monte in the presence, according to Massarelli, of twenty-seven bishops, six generals of Orders, three abbots and an imposing number of theologians and jurists, who had come to Trent by order of the Pope.[3]

---

[1] The arrival took place on 7 June of the Bishops of Ivrea and Nice, in the company of the young Duke of Savoy, Philip Emmanuel, *C.T.*, VOL. I, p. 202 f.; on the 12th that of the proxy of the aged Bishop of Reggio-Emilia, *ibid.*, p. 205, and on the 18th that of three abbots of the Congregation of St Justina, p. 206 f.

[2] *C.T.*, VOL. X, p. 118, l. 19; p. 128, l. 1; on the available funds, see *ibid.*, pp. 81, 118 and *passim*.

[3] *C.T.*, VOL. I, p. 211 f. For a judgment on the list—subsequently completed— see J. Müller in *Z.K.G.*, XLIV (1925), p. 357. Massarelli, for instance, includes among those present the Archbishop of Corfu (*ibid.*, p. 206), because his absence was thought to be merely temporary. The report of the Florentine agent Duretti, of 3 June, may serve as a means of checking these statements—on that day he counted 25 prelates at Trent, St. Arch., Florence, Med. 376, fol. 388ʳ or.

There was no lack of able men in a company that included men like Pighino, auditor of the Rota and a future president of the Council; Severoli, a promoter of the Council and author of the most reliable diary that we possess for the first period of its existence; Domingo Soto, that luminary among Spanish theologians, and Bartolomeo Carranza, subsequently Archbishop of Toledo—both of them Dominicans. Among the prelates there were men of outstanding learning and literary ability, such as Olaus Magnus, the exiled Archbishop of Upsala and brother of the historian; the jurist Tommaso Campeggio with whom the reader is by now well acquainted; Bertano, the wise and learned Bishop of Fano; Seripando, the general of the Augustinians who was to be the mainstay of the legates in the discussions about justification; the exegete Isidoro Chiari, Abbot of Santa Maria of Cesena; the preacher Musso; the poet Vida; the humanist Beccadelli. The men of the opposition, round whom controversy was to be busy at a later stage, were also there: Nacchianti of Chioggia, Martelli of Fiesole, Abbot Luciano degli Ottoni.

The Italians were in an overwhelming majority, but it was reported that prelates from Spain and France were on the way.[1] They arrived in the last week of July and the first of August. The party consisted of four Frenchmen, viz. the Archbishop of Aix, accompanied by the Bishops of Clermont, Agde and Rennes; two Spaniards, namely the Bishops of Jaén and Astorga; and lastly, two Sicilians, the Bishops of Palermo and Syracuse. This gave the gathering a certain air of universality which, for the sake of prestige, it greatly needed. With some exaggeration Peter Merbel, a secretary employed by the government of Milan, wrote to Beatus Rhenanus [2]: "Every day witnesses the arrival at Trent of bishops of every nation, but no Germans."

At Worms the German Protestants obstinately maintained their standpoint that the Council of Trent was not "the Christian council in German lands" they had been promised.[3] In countless pamphlets they

---

[1] *C.T.*, VOL. x, p. 153, l. 17; p. 157, l. 9. Arrival of three Spanish jurists, p. 147, l. 24. The Bishop of Astorga arrived on 23 July, the Bishop of Pampeluna on the 24th, *C.T.*, VOL. I, p. 224 f.; the French prelates reached Trent on 5 August, *ibid.*, p. 230.

[2] A. Horawitz and K. Hartfelder, *Der Briefwechsel des Beatus Rhenanus* (Leipzig 1886), p. 532 (12 May 1545).

[3] Bucer's attitude in Lenz, *Briefwechsel*, VOL. II, pp. 297, 299, 321 (the Council "lauter gespött"). In his pamphlet against the Papacy Luther describes it as a "gaukelspiel", *L.W.*, VOL. LIV, pp. 206 ff. *Politische Correspondenz*, VOL. III, pp. 584, 586 f., throws further light on the Protestant Estates' unanimity in rejecting the Council.

attacked an assembly of which, in spite of the disparaging terms in which they spoke of it, they were yet afraid.[1] They were actually engaged in drawing up an official document of rejection.[2] So badly were they informed about the happenings at Trent that in the course of the summer Count Mansfeld despatched a scout to Trent with mission to reconnoitre.[3]

Catholic opinion swayed between hope and fear.[4] "Too often", Cochlaeus wrote to Cervini, "have I packed my trunks for the journey to the Council, only to unpack again, amid the jeers of friend and foe!"[5] In view of the tense political situation it was not to be expected—in fact it was hardly advisable—that bishops should leave their dioceses, hence there could only be question of the appointment of representatives. Mignanelli advised the legates to invite the German bishops once more to put in an appearance.[6] However, these prelates hesitated

---

[1] In addition to Luther's tract, which was soon translated into Latin by Justus Jonas, Bucer too wrote a book, *De Concilio* (Strasbourg 1545), against Cochlaeus's open letter *Ad principes ac status Romani Imperii*, *C.T.*, VOL. XII, p. lxxvi; VOL. X, p. 121, l. 1; *Z.K.G.*, XVIII (1897), pp. 460, 601 f.; Druffel, *Mon. Trid.*, VOL. I, p. 110 f. Sleidan's *Zwei Reden*, though published in 1544 (new edition ed. Böhmer, Tübingen 1879), belongs to this period in view of the historical background of the Council to be found in its pages (pp. 110-21). Another work, *Radtschlag des allerheiligsten Vaters Bapsts Pauli des Dritten mit dem Collegio cardinalium gehalten, wie das angesatzte Concilium zu Trient furzunemen sey* (1545 *sine loco*), is sheer satire, Schottenloher, No. 43208c; *C.T.*, VOL. XII, p. lxxix.

[2] Bucer did not agree with the Wittenbergers on the opportuneness of a refusal based on Canon Law, Lenz, *Briefwechsel*, VOL. III, pp. 337 f., 342 ff., but cf. *Corp. Ref.*, VOL. VI, pp. 7 ff. (No. 3352); also the Strasbourg memorials, *Politische Correspondenz*, VOL. III, pp. 590, 600, Schottenloher, Nos. 43209a-c. On 27 June the Jesuit Bobadilla suggested to Farnese that a fresh attempt be made through the Emperor to win over the Protestants, M.H.S.J., *Mon. Bobadillae*, VOL. I (Madrid 1903), p. 70 f.

[3] Justus Jonas to Duke George of Anhalt, 16 July 1545, G. Kawerau, *Der Briefwechsel des Justus Jonas*, VOL. II (Halle 1885), p. 165. The statement there made that Helding's companion was a "venter Franciscanus" is wrong—Necrosius was a Dominican. That Protestants in general were badly informed about the Council appears from the frequent requests for information on the part of Protestant divines. Thus Jonas had nothing better to report than wild rumours about the arrival at Trent in the near future of the Emperor and the Kings of France and England, about the translation of the Council to a city in Burgundy, and so forth, *ibid.*, VOL. II, p. 162 f.

[4] Cochlaeus's observation to Cervini on 26 April is significant: "Concilium oecumenicum Tridentinum, de cuius sane felici progressu et dubitant apud nos multi et ego anxie sollicitus sum", *Z.K.G.*, XVIII (1897), p. 457. On 25 April he wrote in the same strain to Capilupi, *Q.F.*, III (1900), p. 138. More later on about Cochlaeus's tract, *De auctoritate et potestate generalis concilii* (Mainz 1545), dedicated to Madruzzo.

[5] Cochlaeus to Cervini, 24 September 1545, *Z.K.G.*, XVIII (1887), pp. 460 ff. This time Nausea made no arrangements for a journey to the Council but made repeated efforts to get himself summoned to Rome, *ibid.*, XXI (1901), p. 541.

[6] *C.T.*, VOL. X, p. 121, l. 33; p. 130, l. 7.

to comply with the advice, if only because they felt uncertain about the fate of the assembly. This explains why the despatch of delegates from Germany was so slow in getting under way.[1] Michael Helding, coadjutor to the Archbishop of Mainz and his delegate to the Council, together with his two companions, the Dominican Necrosius and the jurist Kauf, and Canon Johann Armbruster, the proctor of the Bishops of Würzburg and Eichstätt, were the only representatives of the German nation at Trent up to the day of the opening of the Council.[2] As for the Swiss, the efforts of nuncio Rosin at the convention of Baden yielded no practical result either with the Protestants or the Catholics [3]; the former followed in the wake of Schmalkalden,[4] while the latter refused to take action for the time being.[5]

The absence of the German Protestants and the majority of the German bishops was regrettable on many grounds though it did not rob the gathering of its character of a General Council,[6] hence there was no reason why it should not be inaugurated, except that the Emperor's warlike plan stood in the way. The situation was further

[1] Thus, e.g., the Bishop of Constance writes on 27 June 1545 to Abbot Gerwig of Weingarten that on his (the abbot's) return from the Diet he would discuss with him the question of attendance at the Council, H. Günter, *G. Blarers Briefe und Akten*, VOL. I (Stuttgart 1914), p. 520 f.

[2] Helding arrived on 18 May, *C.T.*, VOL. I, p. 189; VOL. IV, p. 421 f.; VOL. X, p. 88 f. His powers, dated 27 April, *ibid.*, VOL. IV, p. 410 f. Biography of Helding by N. Paulus in *Katholik*, LXXIV, ii (1894), pp. 410-30, 461-502. Arrival of Armbruster on 2 September, *C.T.*, VOL. I, p. 256; VOL. IV, p. 428; VOL. X, p. 189. On 21 September the Jesuit Jajus (Lejay) wrote to Ignatius Loyola that Cardinal Truchsess pressed him day by day to set out for Trent, M.H.S.J., *Mon. Jaji*, VOL. I (Madrid 1903), p. 295. For the whole question, see H. Jedin, "Die deutschen Teilnehmer am Trienter Konzil", in *T.Q.*, CXXII (1941), pp. 238-61; CXXIII (1942), pp. 21-37, where p. 22 f., the question of the proctors—is touched upon; cf. J. Schlecht, *Kilian Leibs Briefwechsel und Diarien* (Münster 1909), p. 133.

[3] *Eidgenössische Abschiede*, VOL. IV, i (*d*), pp. 456 f., 462 f.; Rosin's report in C. Wirz, *Akten*, pp. 398 ff. Rosin handed to each of the cantonal representatives a brief and a copy of the Bull of Indiction.

[4] Communication by Basle to Strasbourg about the Diet of Baden, 11 March, *Politische Correspondenz*, VOL. III, p. 565; justification of the rejection of the Council by the League of Schmalkalden, by the town clerk of Constance, 7 September 1545, *Eidgenössische Abschiede*, VOL. IV, I (*d*), p. 528 f.

[5] Fresh summons by Rosin, Lucerne, 4 April 1545, *Eidgenössische Abschiede*, VOL. IV, I (*d*), p. 472; C. Wirz, *Akten*, pp. 403 ff.; H. Förster, "Die Vertretung des Bischofs von Basel auf dem Konzil von Trient", in *Basler Zeitschrift*, XLI (1942), p. 33.

[6] This erroneous view is found in a tract composed by Vergerio at the turn of the year 1544-5 (*C.T.*, VOL. XII, pp. 431-9), which Döllinger (*Beiträge*, VOL. III, p. 291) ascribes to Morone. Vergerio indicates the real motives of the Protestants' refusal.

complicated when, at the beginning of July it became clear that the campaign could not begin in the course of the late summer, as originally planned, but would have to be put off until the following spring when funds would be available and recruiting completed. It was clearly impossible to defer the opening until then. By way of a solution of the dilemma the Emperor suggested to the Pope on 15 July, through Jean d'Andelot,[1] that he should open the Council but that the assembly should confine itself to the discussion of reform and hold over that of the controverted doctrines until the termination of the war. On his part the Emperor gave the Pope a guarantee that the authority of the Apostolic See would not be interfered with.

Cardinal Truchsess and the nuncios Verallo and Mignanelli greatly feared lest the whole laboriously erected structure of the *entente* between Pope and Emperor should topple over as a result of this suggestion. The very opposite happened. The Pope displayed extraordinary friendliness towards d'Andelot. Though he insisted on the Council being inaugurated in any case, he agreed in the same breath to a postponement of a few weeks, that is until the Emperor should have left Worms. He did not even reject out of hand the restriction of the programme of the Council to reform, though he let Verallo know that he failed to see how the main point of that programme, namely the discussions of the controverted doctrines, could be held over indefinitely. As for the proposed *colloquium*, he contented himself with a warning that nothing must be done there to prejudice religion and the Apostolic See.

The Pope's remarkable willingness to meet the Emperor's wishes— which meant the continuation of an exceedingly dangerous uncertainty about the unfolding of the conciliar programme—is not adequately accounted for by the pontiff's paramount anxiety not to jeopardise the success of the enterprise against the Protestants. There can be no doubt that yet another motive was at work, none other in fact than that of securing the Emperor's good-will for a long-cherished aspiration of the Farnese family. On 26 August, against strong opposition within the Sacred College, Paul III had bestowed the duchies of Parma and Piacenza on Pierluigi Farnese. This act of nepotism was only thinly

---

[1] Both the nuncios and Truchsess speak of the Emperor's resolve to postpone the war against the Protestants until the spring of 1546 as early as 5 and 6 July, *N.B.*, VOL. I, PT viii, pp. 226-36. D'Andelot's address and the Pope's reply in Farnese's letters to the legates and to Verallo, 19 July, *C.T.*, VOL. x, pp. 152-8. According to J. Müller, *Z.K.G.*, XLIV (1925), p. 345 f., the decisive reasons were the influence of Ferdinand and the wish to detach some of the Protestant states from Schmalkalden.

camouflaged by the circumstance that the investitures with these rich territories could be represented as an exchange for the modest Farnese fiefs of Camerino and Nepi.[1] However, as soon as that stroke had been brought off successfully the Pope showed clearly that in the long run he was not prepared to subordinate the great interests of the Church to the Emperor's political schemes. He displayed both energy and skill in his efforts to set the Council in motion. It was no easy task and his own legates began to despair of a successful solution of the problem that confronted them.

With growing uneasiness they had seen the management of affairs taken out of their hands. Weighty decisions were being taken in Rome and at the imperial court, while at Trent theirs was the thankless task, day after day, of comforting prelates weary of waiting with the prospect of a future which even for them was full of uncertainty. Like the captain of a ship riding idly at anchor they had repeatedly cheered the passengers with a promise of putting to sea, first in the spring, then in the summer, and now in the autumn. Nothing had happened and, worse still, there was no hope for the immediate future. "We are caught like quails in a net," they wrote on 19 July, "and are unable to extricate ourselves. Must we perish here, or must we be transferred to Germany, as people are whispering?"[2] The mere thought of such a translation was depressing enough, but it became a nightmare when Madruzzo, exasperated by the ceaseless carping of some of the prelates at the discomforts of his episcopal city, asked them in angry and threatening tones whether they imagined they would feel more comfortable at Worms.[3] The Pope's reply to d'Andelot, of which they were informed on 24 July, could not but fill the legates with the gravest misgivings. Cervini vented his vexation at the pontiff's apparent surrender in a letter to the private secretary Bernardino Maffeo which

---

[1] Particulars in Pastor, VOL. V, pp. 525 ff.: Eng. edn., VOL. XII, pp. 229 ff. Capasso, *Paolo III*, VOL. II, pp. 450 ff., admits that the investiture created an impression "nettamente sfavorevole", but he justifies the creation of the new duchy on political grounds, for it had become a "forte baluardo tutto italiano contro la politica assorbitrice di Carlo V", *ibid.*, p. 457. Verallo only heard of the transaction when all was over, *N.B.*, VOL. I, PT viii, pp. 286, 289.

[2] *C.T.*, VOL. X, p. 151, l. 26. The legates were put out by the fact that the "lettere mostrabili", for which they had prayed, had not yet arrived, *ibid.*, p. 149, l. 34.

[3] Madruzzo to the legates on 17 July, *C.T.*, VOL. X, p. 149, l. 18; *ibid.*, Madruzzo's earlier protest, p. 145 f. In *C.T.*, VOL. I, p. 218, l. 28, Massarelli lists the grievances which had so greatly angered Madruzzo—the rise of prices, the lack of fruit, the rudeness of the natives, the tremendous heat. For the rumour then current at Trent that the Council was to be transferred to Germany, see *N.B.*, VOL. I. PT viii. p. 240. n.3; *C.T.*, VOL. X, p. 151, l. 5; p. 160, l. 14.

was never despatched.[1] Both he and his colleagues were convinced that a further postponement of the inauguration of the Council would create great confusion while a *colloquium* in Germany would completely undermine its authority. They were equally of one mind on the fact that it was not possible to discuss a reform without reference to the dogmas on which it was based. More precisely even than in the legates' joint letter to Farnese, Cervini formulated the alternative: "either a Council or a *colloquium*". If, relying on specious promises, the latter is granted, the only thing to do is to hold a papal convention, but one that will enforce a real and thorough reform. Thus Cervini fell in line with Bertano's and Giacomelli's proposals.

How low the barometer of the Council stood appears even more clearly from a memorial submitted by Cervini on 8 August at Farnese's request.[2] In this document the cardinal maintains the principle that for the healing of religious dissension the Council was "the right remedy, the one indicated both by tradition and by the existing situation". He saw no less clearly the obstacles that stood in the way: "The love of the various nations for the Apostolic See has grown cold," he wrote, "bishops depend too much on princes, while the latter are mainly concerned with their own interests. Yet in spite of everything and trusting in the divine assistance the great undertaking must be risked, for the eventual triumph of truth is not in doubt. But if the Pope is unable to make up his mind to hold a Council because he feels it cannot be realised, the only alternative is reform without a Council. But if this path is to be taken without grievous loss of prestige, it is essential that a carefully planned reform Bull, one that takes into account the grievances of foreign nations, shall be published at once, before the dissolution of the Council. Such a Bull must be carried into effect immediately, for nothing but effective reform will prove any sort of substitute for a Council."

Cervini's memorial is not only informative about current views on the subject of the Council, it also makes it perfectly clear that he was inclined to regard its cause as lost. The Pope refused to act as requested. He was not inclined to give his opponents the satisfaction of boasting

---

[1] Letter of Cervini and general report of 26-9 July in *C.T.*, VOL. X, pp. 161 ff. Bertano also expressed himself in sharp terms against the *colloquium*, *C.T.*, VOL. X, p. 159, *n.*3. To the legates (*ibid.*, p. 145, l. 8) the nuncios spoke in a much more decided tone than to Farnese, *N.B.*, VOL. I, PT viii, pp. 240, 246.

[2] *C.T.*, VOL. X, p. 170 f., and the legates' report on the table-talk of 7 August, *ibid.*, pp. 167 ff. A fragment of Farnese's answer to Cervini's proposals is in *C.T.*, VOL. IV, p. 427. In view of Mendoza's hint that a translation to the south would not be regarded with disfavour, Brandi's opinion (*Karl V*, p. 456: Eng. edn., p. 531) that the imperial diplomacy made game with the legate is not without foundation.

CARDINAL CRISTOFORO MADRUZZO
*After the painting by Titian in the Museu de Arte, São Paulo,
dated 1542*

that he had dropped, on the very eve of its realisation, the main item of his programme, the one which ten years earlier he had declared to be the chief aim of his pontificate. He accordingly rejected Cervini's proposal for a reform Bull and the Roman reform convention that would follow its publication. He had his own plan for saving the Council, but he was not yet quite clear in his mind about its execution.

The legates on their part felt convinced that the Emperor wished the existing state of suspense to go on, not only for a few weeks, as d'Andelot had requested, but for many months; they even thought they had tangible proofs of such an intention. At a banquet which they gave on the occasion of the birth of Don Carlos, the heir to the Spanish throne, Del Monte sat next to Mendoza. The latter enlarged on the advantages which both parties would derive from a temporising policy. With all the assurance of the layman turned theologian he went on to explain that, with regard to the faith, they knew all there was to know; all the bishops and doctors of the Council together could not say anything new on such a theme. At the moment reform was not in the interest of either Pope or Emperor. The latter's first concern was to empty the gold bags of the Spanish prelates so as to enable him to meet the expenses of the war! "How often", Mendoza exclaimed, "have I not made it clear to the Emperor that he must ally himself with the Pope. At last the moment has come! Cardinal Farnese has done his job well, very well indeed!"

About such an encomium, from such a speaker, opinions may differ. Farnese could scarcely take it as a compliment. After these remarks the conversation drifted on to a discussion of various wines. Niccolò Madruzzo praised the vintage of Trent which the company was sampling at that moment. Del Monte, the host, was gratified by the compliment but slyly observed that "it was only good in summer". Thereupon Mendoza whispered in his ear: "During the winter you shall drink Greek wines in Rome."

Cervini commanded excellent sources of information so that he had no difficulty in sensing the purport of these hints. He felt that the Emperor would more readily agree to a translation of the Council to Rome than to its opening, for his supreme anxiety was to gain time. "Translation"—this was the watchword the Pope had long had in readiness, and in August he came out with it.[1]

---

[1] On 1 August Gualteruzzi informed Della Casa that "si parla della translation del concilio et dicesi di Milano, ma la cosa è di molta considerazione". On 8 August "N.S. partira verso la fin del mese per Perugia. In questo mezzo si fara un consistorio nel qual si parlera del concilio o aperiendo o transferendo, il quale ingrossa a maraviglia per quello s'intende", Montepulciano, Bibl. Ricci, 4, fols. 98ᵛ, 100ᵛ.

The summoning of the Council to Trent was a concession to the Germans which the Pope had only made under duress. He still felt convinced that a Council would only be free from grievous risk for the Papacy if it were held in the Papal States or in one of the states of central Italy. As early as mid-July he had sounded the legates on the possibility of a translation.[1] They replied that it was feasible, but only to a place in Italy and subject to the consent of the Emperor. This answer did not satisfy the Pope. He had not sought information about the possibility of a translation but about the means of effecting it. In order to satisfy this desire, and in general for the purpose of laying before the Pope their anxiety with regard to the Council, the legates despatched the secretary of the Council, Beccadelli, to Rome on 13 August to report. In their instructions for Beccadelli[2] they stated that a translation to Rome would be the best solution of the existing crisis. However, in order to avoid a fresh convocation and the necessity of fixing a new time-limit, it would be advisable to have a formal opening at Trent followed by an immediate translation, both measures being carried out in virtue of a papal commission.[3] There were any number of reasons for a translation—the conditions in regard to supplies at Trent, the smallness of the town, the severe Alpine winter, the proximity to Germany, the danger of anti-papal agitation. On the other hand the Emperor's consent was an unavoidable condition for a translation. If he agreed to it his action might be rewarded by some concession on their part; for instance the assembly might occupy itself with a discussion of reform projects until he was ready to strike. But the suggestion that such tactics should be adopted at Trent and that a *colloquium* should be held simultaneously in Germany was wholly

---

[1] *C.T.*, VOL. X, p. 144, l. 22; p. 151, l. 9.

[2] *Ibid.*, VOL. X, pp. 174 ff., Beccadelli's instructions. His mission followed Farnese's refusal to send a trusted person from the Curia to Trent. On 20 August he was in Rome, *ibid.*, p. 188, "ottimamente visto da N.S. e da Mons. R.mo Farnese", Gualteruzzi reports on 22 August, Montepulciano, Bibl. Ricci, 4, fol. 104ᵛ. He took a week to recover from his journey; on 4 September he accompanied the Pope on his journey north (fols. 106ᵛ-108ʳ). He was sent off at Orvieto on 16 September and on the 24th he was back at Trent, *C.T.*, VOL. X, pp. 193, 198.

[3] At a later date the legates came to doubt the opportuneness of this proposal. They feared lest a translation after the opening should meet with opposition within the Council itself, an opposition that would be fostered by the Emperor. They accordingly altered the instructions in the sense that it would be advisable to transfer the Council before the opening, *C.T.*, VOL. X, p. 177 f. A third way out was suggested by the Bishop of Belcastro in a letter of 13 August to his brother, the Pope's physician, but which was meant to be seen by the pontiff. He suggested that as soon as the Council was inaugurated the majority should approach the Pope with a request for its translation, *ibid.*, p. 173.

unacceptable. But so was any further waiting for the arrival of prelates from abroad. "Here no one is prepared to listen to such a suggestion," they wrote; "if the Council must be inaugurated at Trent, the road must be cleared for it and it must be in a position to cite the Lutherans and to prevent the *colloquium*!"

The legates were likewise disposed to agree to a translation to Ferrara, but not to Mantua or Milan, on the ground that these cities were within the Emperor's sphere of influence. The whole of their scheme was well thought out, but the one condition for its execution—the Emperor's consent—was not fulfilled and could not be fulfilled.

On 19 July Cardinal Farnese had instructed the nuncio Verallo to try to ascertain what would be the imperial court's reaction to a translation.[1] At that time the nuncio failed to obtain any definite information; the Emperor merely confirmed the statement made by d'Andelot, viz. that he had no objection to the inauguration of the Council on the feast of the Assumption or that of the Nativity of the Blessed Virgin, but he insisted that for the present the assembly should not pass judgment on the Protestants but concern itself exclusively with the reform of the clergy; otherwise there was reason to fear that Schmalkalden would forthwith rush to arms and so jeopardise the successful issue of the whole undertaking. As for the *colloquium*, the Emperor repeated that it was no more than a manœuvre which could not in any way trench upon the Pope's authority. In a subsequent conversation Granvella stressed once more the need of mutual trust.[2] A few days later, on 4 August, the Recess of the Diet of Worms fixed the beginning of the *colloquium* for 30 November at Ratisbon. After this the Emperor withdrew to the Netherlands and Granvella to his estates in Burgundy. The affair of the Council remained in abeyance for over a month, pending the arrival of Dandino, the nuncio extraordinary, which had been announced some time before.

Previous to the despatch of Dandino on 11 September[3] the Pope

---

[1] *N.B.*, VOL. I, PT viii, p. 254.

[2] *Ibid.*, p. 265 f. (3 August), more briefly on 1 August, to the legates, *ibid.*, p. 165, l. 21. For the literature on the Recess of Worms, see Brandi, *Quellen*, p. 358 f. In Müller's account, in *Z.K.G.*, XLIV (1925), p. 348, Granvella had wrested the *colloquium* from the Emperor by way of compensation for the national assembly he had promised.

[3] Dandino's instructions, *C.T.*, VOL. IV, pp. 430 ff.; his itinerary, *N.B.*, VOL. I, PT viii, p. 314, *n*.3; report of 5 October, *ibid.*, p. 320 f.; more briefly to the legates, VOL. X, p. 205; cf. VOL. I, p. 277; VOL. X, pp. 184, 188, 192. The fullest account is in Müller, "Die Konzilspolitik Karls V, etc.", in *Z.K.G.*, XLIV (1925), pp. 368-82. Vega's instructions for Marquina, Dandino's companion, in *Spanische Forschungen der Görresgesellschaft*, IV (1933), pp. 331-44.

had also listened to Mignanelli, who had recently returned to Rome. The latter strengthened the pontiff in his view that there was not a single valid reason for holding the Council at Trent and that a translation was not only desirable but necessary. Dandino was detained at Bologna by illness so that he only reached Brussels on 3 October, without having touched Trent. When on the following day he submitted to the Emperor the plan for a translation he met with a refusal couched at first in courteous terms but which eventually hardened to an emphatic rejection. Repeated discussions with the regent Figueroa and the secretary Idiaquez, as well as yet another audience with the Emperor on 7 October, failed to shake this determination.[1]

The monarch insisted that he must redeem the promise made to the Estates of the Empire as a whole, hence to the Catholics as well as to the Protestants. If he insisted on Trent, it was not from any undue readiness to meet the latter; on the contrary, he meant to make their refusal to attend the reason for going to war with them. The Emperor also observed that a translation of the Council to Italy would necessarily create the impression that the Pope was seeking to rid himself of it by means of a subterfuge; that in fact he had no wish for a free, independent Council. In the last resort it was also in the Pope's interest that the Council should be held at Trent. The prelates' complaints of the discomforts of the conciliar city he brushed aside with the ironical remark that during the congress of Nice the Pope had stayed in a monastery and he himself in the small town of Villafranca. Was it really asking too much from the prelates that for the sake of a great and sacred purpose they should be satisfied with one room instead of a whole house? The Emperor showed some irritation against the legates because they laid the blame for the delay on him. Dandino felt that this irritation and the fear that he would be held responsible for the translation, should he give his consent to it, contributed not a little to the stiffening of the monarch's opposition.[2]

A translation of the Council against the express will of the Emperor

---

[1] The Emperor's reply in writing, dated 10 October and brought by Pedro Marquina, Vega's secretary, in *C.T.*, VOL. X, p. 213 f. For the background, cf. *N.B.*, VOL. I, PT viii, p. 351 f., and the reports of Dandino and Verallo to Farnese, dated 8 and 10 October, which were also forwarded by Marquina, *ibid.*, pp. 323-53. The latter's letters to the legates of the same dates, in *C.T.*, VOL. X, pp. 210-13. On the mediating role played by Marquina and Vega in the course of the negotiations of that period, see G. Buschbell, "Die Sendungen des Pedro de Marquina an den Hof Karls V, Sept.-Dez. 1545 und Sept. 1546", in *Spanische Forschungen*, IV (1933), pp. 311-53.

[2] *N.B.*, VOL. I, PT viii, p. 345; *C.T.*, VOL. X, p. 211 f.

would have meant the rupture of the alliance and the abandonment of the war against the Protestants. The nuncio Verallo granted that the Emperor's arguments could not be rejected out of hand, but he also clearly perceived what the monarch's confessor, Domingo Soto, would not admit,[1] namely that a Council inaugurated at Trent could not escape the Emperor's influence and that it would be difficult to transfer it, at a later date, to some other locality.[2] An "open Council", especially one on imperial territory, would prove a constant temptation for the Emperor to use the opposition that was to be expected there as a weapon against the Pope. True, the Emperor was willing that the Council should be opened at Trent, yet in the same breath he sought to restrict its freedom of action by laying down the condition that for the time being it should confine itself to Church reform. Against such a restriction of its programme the legates had lodged a protest on a former occasion in the sharpest terms. In their letter of 19 October to Farnese they described a condition of this kind as dishonourable and at variance with the freedom and the prestige of the Council. On the other hand the present state of inactivity could not be allowed to go on. After weighing the pros and cons, only one road remained open, and this road the legates urged the Pope to take. Let him put his trust in God and open the Council immediately! Having done so, let him tackle the two problems for which the Council had been convened with complete freedom and regardless of the wishes of out-siders. A remark of Marquina's to Pacheco led the legates to conclude that eventually the Emperor would not insist on a deferment of the dogmatic discussions as strongly as it appeared just then.[3]

In point of fact the adoption of this plain, courageous and truly Christian advice was the only way to end an almost hopeless deadlock. The Pope took it. After consultation with the conciliar committee, and with Beccadelli he announced in the consistory of 30 October that

---

[1] *N.B.*, VOL. I, PT viii, p. 334, and Dandino's remark to Cervini, *C.T.*, VOL. X, p. 212, and *N.B.*, VOL. I, PT viii, p. 352.

[2] Verallo (*N.B.*, VOL. I, PT viii, p. 336 f.), in my opinion, appreciated the divergent views much more impartially than Dandino who was unable to shake off his notorious anti-imperial attitude while on this mission. Whereas Bertano urged the translation of the Council, regardless of the Emperor's wishes (*C.T.*, VOL. X, p. 206 f.), Madruzzo regretted that the plan should have matured so far as to have become a subject on which the monarch was to be consulted, *C.T.*, VOL. I, p. 289, l. 4.

[3] *C.T.*, VOL. X, p. 219 f. The reaction to the information which Marquina brought from the imperial court on 19 October, in *C.T.*, VOL. I, p. 291 f. According to what we read on p. 293, l. 13, Madruzzo sponsored Marquina's observations. On 24 October the legates stressed anew the importance of the matter, *C.T.*, VOL. X, p. 221.

he intended to open the Council before Christmas. In the next consistory, on 6 November, the date of the opening was definitely fixed for the third Sunday in Advent.[1] The decision was communicated to the Roman prelates on the following day. Their refusal to regard it as final was only too natural, and they were in no hurry to make preparations for their departure. When Cardinal Farnese put before them the alternative of Trent or Castel Sant' Angelo, many of them took the threat as a bad joke.[2] They were mistaken; this time it was serious. The key with which the Council was to be opened and which Giovio thought had been irretrievably lost in a deep well [3] had been recovered. It was high time too, for in the period of three months which had been taken up with the missions of Beccadelli and Dandino, not only had new arrivals almost completely ceased, but the assembly was on the point of dissolving of its own accord. Up to 12 September a dozen prelates had left Trent on one pretext or another without formal authorisation of the legates.[4] Francis I gave the French bishops leave to take their departure, though only if the opening of the Council was still further delayed. However, when Del Monte explained to the Bishop of Rennes that the delay was due to the legates' efforts to secure

---

[1] *C.T.*, VOL. IV, p. 435, *n.5*; VOL. X, pp. 226 f., 231 f., supplemented by Beccadelli's letters, pp. 227 ff., which record the Pope's remark that throws so much light on his motives: "Noi faremo si che il mondo conoscera se da noi manca o da altri" (p. 228, l. 8, also l. 1). To Vega he spoke in the same terms as to the legates, viz. "che lo voleva aprir ad ogni modo, volendosi piutosto confidare in Dio che ne gli huomini", Gualteruzzi to Della Casa, 7 November, Montepulciano, Bibl. Ricci, 4, fol. 126ʳ. This observation shows that Müller, in *Z.K.G.*, XLIV (1925), pp. 382 ff., draws exaggerated conclusions from the delay of an official communication to the Emperor (cf. *C.T.*, VOL. X, p. 227, l. 10). The ever cautious pontiff was anxious not to cut off the possibility of retreat should this become necessary, though there was no "unworthy irresolution" (p. 386) in his conduct. Vega, on the other hand, persisted in his belief that the Pope recoiled from the very idea of a Council, *C.T.*, VOL. XI, p. 14.

[2] Gualteruzzi to Della Casa, 21 November, Montepulciano, Bibl. Ricci, 4, fol. 130ᵛ: "Questi Signori clerici (di Camera) hanno ordine di andare a Trento et credesi che alla perfine andaranno, perciochè ultimamente fu intimato molto bravamente: O a Trento o in Castello, qualchuno credette che Mons. Rev.mo Farnese burlasse, ma poi si è veduto che la cosa va da dovero."

[3] *C.T.*, VOL. X, p. 216, l. 11; the effect at Trent, *C.T.*, VOL. I, p. 287, l. 16.

[4] *C.T.*, VOL. X, p. 191. Examples: Fano's departure for Mantua, *ibid.*, p. 180, *n.*4; Bitonto's for Padua, where his brother lay sick, *ibid.*, p. 189 f. The consequence was that the rumour spread in Protestant circles that the Council had already dissolved, Renato to Bullinger, 10 August, and the latter's reply of 18 December, in W. Schiess, *Bullingers Korrespondenz mit den Graubündern*, VOL. I (Basle 1903), pp. 79, 85. But the accusation (*N.B.*, VOL. I, PT viii, p. 310) that the legates were "ad dar licentia ad chiunque la dimandava" was not justified. Girolamo Vida wrote from Cremona (no date) that he no longer counted on the Council assembling and that the existing situation was unseemly, *Arch. storico Lombardo*, XXI (1894), pp. 21-5.

the freedom of the assembly, they consented to wait for fresh instructions from Paris. In the meantime, until the return of the couriers, they took a holiday on their own authority and left the city.[1] The fact that at the conclusion of his mission in Rome Beccadelli did not resume his post as secretary to the Council but took up once more his functions of tutor to Ranuccio Farnese, the Pope's young nephew,[2] was not encouraging. A command of the Pope, issued through Cardinal Cupis, ordering the Roman prelates to set out for Trent within eight days, was not complied with,[3] for rumour had it that the Council would be translated at an early date, probably to Rome.[4] Why should anyone start out on an expensive journey to Trent?

At Trent itself there was nothing to do for the prelates, who were weary of waiting and irritated by reason of the expenses they were forced to incur. Small wonder that parties began to form and intrigues were spun. At the beginning of September two Milanese, Trivulzio of Piacenza and Simonetta of Pesaro, perhaps at the instigation of the French, sought to induce their discontented colleagues to take a collective step in Rome for the purpose of forcing a decision.[5] The Bishop of Belcastro boasted that he had at his disposal a bodyguard of twenty prelates, wholly devoted to the Pope, who were prepared to follow him through thick and thin. Others pointed an accusing finger at the black sheep which they claimed to have discovered among the prelates present at Trent and whom they suspected of holding conciliarist or even Lutheran opinions.[6] Their intrigues were of course reported to the suspects and called forth their resentment. Was it any wonder that the Curia kept them in the dark about the fate of the Council when such reports reached Rome? With a view to rendering the informers harmless the Bishop of Fiesole drew up a protest to the Pope for which he sought the signatures of a number of prelates. They refused to put their names to the document. Bishop Martelli nevertheless forwarded his protest to the Pope on 18 August.

---

[1] *C.T.*, VOL. X, p. 199f.

[2] *Ibid.*, p. 192 f.

[3] *Ibid.*, VOL. IV, p. 429.

[4] Gualteruzzi to Della Casa, 29 August, Montepulciano, Bibl. Ricci, 4, fol. 106ᵛ: "Si crede et tien per fermo che si habbia ad aprire et transferire, et è chi parla di Roma."

[5] *C.T.*, VOL. I, p. 261 f. The legates' attempt to bring about a collective step by the prelates assembled at Trent in favour of a translation, which Müller (in *Z.K.G.*, XLIV (1925), pp. 359 ff.) places at the beginning of August, is pure surmise.

[6] *C.T.*, VOL. X, p. 139 f. (Romeo); p. 133, l. 30; p. 160, l. 42 (Bertano). Belcastro's "body-guard", p. 173, l. 35.

He received a courteous reply to the effect that Rome was not to blame for the delay. Martelli's indignation was inspired by yet another, wholly personal motive; an official of the Apostolic Camera had recently excommunicated him because he had failed to pay his tenth in full.[1] Of all people the legates were the least to be envied. Rumours reached them from all sides while they themselves were condemned to inactivity and all the time they had a feeling that their self-sacrificing efforts were not properly appreciated in Rome. Only after strong representation to the Pope did the College of Cardinals grant them a share of the "dues" to which they were entitled as papal legates.[2] Del Monte had been feeling unwell since mid-August: he suffered from bouts of fever and toothache. Head, throat, back, his whole body was in pain, and for all this, he felt convinced, the climate of Trent was responsible. Later on it was found that he suffered from a form of jaundice, the real cause of which was irritation at being condemned to prolonged idle waiting. He was indignant that an adventurer like Ludovico delle Arme, a leader of a band of mercenaries and actually in the service of England, should dare to insult him from the street while he stood at the window of his apartment.[3] His colleague Cervini, deeply depressed by Pierluigi Farnese's nepotistic investiture with Parma and Piacenza,[4] took up his learned studies, made plans for his villa at Montepulciano and practised the virtue of patience. Cardinal Pole spent his days in deep retirement and in constant fear of an attempt on his life by his enemy Henry VIII.

When, therefore, on 7 November the first though vague report of the forthcoming opening of the Council reached Trent, the effect on the depressed gathering was that of a deliverance. For a while the legates kept the report secret.[5] They only communicated the news to

---

[1] Text of Martelli's address and the letter in which he sharply condemns "falsas ineptasque calumnias . . . irridendas potius quam pertimescendas", in Vat. lat. 6208, fols. 171ʳ-177ᵛ, in *C.T.*, VOL. XII, pp. 439-44; the remainder in *C.T.*, VOL. IV, p. 439, n.1; VOL. X, pp. 178 f., 195.

[2] *C.T.*, VOL. X, p. 138 f., 209 and VOL. IV, p. 433, also VOL. I, pp. 240 ff. The decision in favour of the legates was only taken at the consistory of 30 October, in the teeth of some opposition, *C.T.*, VOL. X, p. 257, l. 5.

[3] *C.T.*, VOL. X, p. 182 f.; p. 193 f. Del Monte accordingly left for Lake Garda on 15 September, to recuperate, *C.T.*, VOL. I, p. 267, l. 30; he returned on the 19th, *ibid.*, p. 269, l. 32.

[4] *C.T.*, VOL. X, p. 186 f.; Massarelli's observations on Paul III's nepotism in *C.T.*, VOL. I, p. 290, l. 25, are undoubtedly an echo of Cervini's feelings.

[5] *C.T.*, VOL. I, p. 310; Farnese's letter of 31 October, ordering the recall of the absentees to Trent in *C.T.*, VOL. X, p. 226 f. The legates thereupon recalled the Bishops of Feltre, Fano, Alba and Belcastro by letter, *C.T.*, VOL. X, p. 319, l. 4.

the prelates on 13 November. On the same day a letter of Farnese, dated 7 November, informed them that 13 December was the date fixed for the opening.[1] Everybody was jubilant; at last the period of torturing uncertainty was at an end. Only a few days earlier Madruzzo had explained at great length to Massarelli why there was no prospect of an early inauguration of the Council; if it were otherwise the Pope would not persevere in his nepotism and endeavour to secure for his family both Modena and Reggio in exchange for Ravenna and Cervia, which were part of the Papal States, while the Emperor would take good care not to provoke the Protestants by such an act.[2] Even after the arrival of the good news from Rome there were sceptics who felt unable to give it credence; as a matter of fact they came very near to being in the right, for an unforeseen incident put the opening once more in jeopardy at the last moment.[3]

On 14 November the three Frenchmen who had remained at Trent informed the legates that a royal letter of 26 October recalled them to France. The fatal letter had actually been in their hands since 9 November. In accordance with custom they had informed the legates of the nature of its contents with the exception of this all-important item. The impression made by this announcement was all the more painful as they only made it at the moment when the date of the opening had become known. Was it France's intention to sabotage the Council by recalling its prelates? Cervini, ever distrustful, feared that such was her intention, while Pole took a calmer view. In his dismay Madruzzo went so far as to announce his intention to prevent the departure of the Frenchmen by force. It goes without saying that the legates would not hear of so foolish a proposal. On Del Monte's advice they refrained from drawing up a written protest against their departure, as they had at first intended, and contented themselves with negotiations, with the result that at least two Bishops—those of Aix and Agde —decided to remain at Trent until the courier should have returned with fresh instructions. The Bishop of Rennes alone left the conciliar city. Thus the danger of the French nation withdrawing as a whole

---

[1] C.T., VOL. I, p. 317 f.; Farnese, 7 November, in C.T., VOL. X, p. 231 f.; the legates' report of 16 November, C.T., VOL. X, pp. 242 ff.

[2] C.T., VOL. I, p. 313, l. 3; as late as 30 November the legates mention casually that "alcuni dichino liberamente di non poterlo credere", C.T., VOL. X, p. 258, l. 36.

[3] Particulars of the negotiations in Massarelli's Diarium, C.T., VOL. I, pp. 319-27; Massarelli was frequently sent, now here, now there, with messages so that his diary is much more informative than the legates' reports, C.T., VOL. X, pp. 242-5; cf. also Zorilla's letter, C.T., VOL. XI, p. 15 f.

was averted. The legates, however, were powerless to prevent the departure of the Bishop of Rennes, who, on 26 November, withdrew to Venice without taking leave of them. Pacheco, as spokesman of a deputation of Spanish and Neapolitan prelates, appealed in vain to the Peace of Crépy and to the agreement between King and Emperor [1]; in vain the legates, in a letter couched in grave but fatherly terms, reminded the Bishop of Rennes of his episcopal oath. The prelate justified his action by pleading that he had come to Trent not so much as a bishop than as a representative of his King, hence he felt bound to obey the latter's order for his recall, but he nevertheless remained in Italy. The Bishop of Clermont also stayed on in the neighbourhood while awaiting developments.[2] The Archbishop of Aix continued to reside at Trent.

The great question was how to account for this strange behaviour of the Frenchmen: it was a matter of the utmost gravity. In the course of the last few months the political sky had become very much overcast. The execution of the Peace of Crépy, which a year earlier had opened the road to the Council, had been jeopardised by the sudden death of the Duke of Orleans on 9 September 1545. Fresh negotiations were taking place, but progress was slow.[3] The League of Schmalkalden had but recently foiled the Catholic Duke Henry of Brandenburg's attempt to reconquer his territory and had even seized his person. They had likewise resumed relations with their old supporter in the West. Their immediate aim was to pave the way for peace between France and England.[4] If Francis I's rear was once more protected and if, as certain symptoms seemed to show,[5] he resumed his

---

[1] Audience of the imperialists, 25 November, C.T., VOL. I, p. 332; VOL. X, pp. 251 ff.; letter to the Bishop of Agde, C.T., VOL. I, p. 335. Madruzzo also drew attention to the secret clause of Crépy, C.T., VOL. I, p. 325, l. 5.

[2] The Bishop of Clermont's stay at Venice is mentioned by Mendoza on 5 October, Cal. of St. Pap., Spain, VOL. VIII, p. 258 (No. 144); later on we find him at Ferrara and on 28 November he was at Bologna, C.T., VOL. I, p. 338, l. 10.

[3] Verallo's and Dandino's reports of 8 and 12 November to Farnese and to the legates (N.B., VOL. I, PT viii, pp. 409-20) are still optimistic. When France refused to give up Piedmont, Dandino began to despair of the issue, N.B., VOL. I, PT viii, p. 421; C.T., VOL. X, p. 241, l. 10 (16 November); on 1 December he had the impression that things were taking "mala piega", C.T., VOL. X, p. 263, l. 29. At the consistory of 9 October the Pope had stated that a fresh rupture with France would render the Council impossible. In Rome the opinion prevailed at the time—it was premature —that "li Tridentini si richiameranno et si fara una altra prorogatione", Gualteruzzi to Della Casa, 10 October, Montepulciano, Bibl. Ricci, 4, fol. 118ᵛ.

[4] Johann Sturm's report on his negotiations in France, Politische Correspondenz, VOL. III, pp. 635-9 (21 September); Lenz, Briefwechsel, VOL. II, p. 357.

[5] C.T., VOL. X, p. 263, l. 31; cf. VOL. I, p. 333, l. 30; p. 337, l. 10; VOL. X, p. 256, l. 7. In October Zorilla learnt at Trent that "Su Sᵈ tiene ya por cierta la gerra entre el emperador y el rey de Francia", ibid., VOL. XI, p. 13.

activities at Constantinople, the conditions which had enabled the Emperor to plan war against the Protestants would be at an end; such a war would be impossible and the holding of the Council in the balance.

"The condition of Christendom is worse than ever", Cervini wrote on 6 December.[1] Like his colleagues he trembled lest the opening should be prevented at the last moment for at the imperial court signs of disapproval could be detected. The nuncios had the impression that Granvella was none too pleased with the decision to open the assembly. If the French were to thwart the plan, the legates thought, the minister would welcome their action.[2] Suspicion was further increased by the recall of Helding, the auxiliary of the Archbishop of Mainz. Helding was the only German bishop at Trent. It was with difficulty that the prelates prevailed upon him, in mid-November, to ignore the order for his recall issued by Sebastian von Heusenstamm, the new Archbishop.[3] If he were to leave for the Ratisbon *colloquium* there would not remain a single representative of the German nation on the bishops' benches. Thus the position was identical with that of the French; yet the imperial party, above all Pacheco, insisted that the legates should grant Helding formal permission to leave. "If the Pope were here," Pacheco asserted, "he would undoubtedly grant it." "If you were to ask for a hundred years, you would get no other answer than 'No'!" Del Monte replied. The legates were not to be shaken— Helding did not leave.[4]

While the legates were thus engaged in a supreme effort for the success of the conciliar convocation, they were left for a whole fortnight without any message from Rome. They were kept waiting for the brief formally ordering them to open the Council for which they had twice prayed. Not one of the Roman prelates was to be seen, though the Pope himself, and after him Cardinal Cupis, as chairman of the conciliar committee, had urged them to speed their departure for Trent. Only from the neighbourhood did one or two put in an

[1] *C.T.*, VOL. X, p. 267, l. 24, like Massarelli, *ibid.*, VOL. I, p. 344, l. 18. On 14 November Gualteruzzi wrote to Della Casa, Montepulciano, Bibl. Ricci, 4, fol. 128ᵛ: "Se l'aviso della presa di Brunsvic si conferma si stima che si fara qualche nuova deliberatione intorno alle cose del concilio."

[2] *C.T.*, VOL. X, p. 247, l. 3; p. 254, l. 27. On 29 November Verallo and Dandino report "ci ha mostrato che sia stato ben fatto", p. 257, l. 20. For further information on the state of tension at this time between Pope and Emperor, mainly on account of the delay in concluding an alliance, see Müller in *Z.K.G.*, XLIV (1925), pp. 388 ff.

[3] *C.T.*, VOL. X, p. 243 f.; Helding's confirmation by the cathedral chapter (*C.T.*, VOL. I, p. 308, l. 4; VOL. IV, p. 434), was thus made superfluous.

[4] Here too Massarelli (*C.T.*, VOL. I, p. 341, l. 18; pp. 342-8) is more informative than the legates' report (*C.T.*, VOL. X, p. 266).

appearance, together with a Dominican theologian who came as the vanguard of the Portuguese bishops.[1] In the end Cervini judged it expedient to make it perfectly clear to the Pope's secretary Maffeo that there could be no going back, otherwise the Pope would expose himself to the accusation so often mooted by the canonists, that it was he who prevented the Council.[2]

Those in a position of responsibility felt as if a weight had been taken off their shoulders when in the afternoon of 11 December a courier arrived bearing the longed-for brief and the formal order for the opening of the Council.[3] The final preparations in the cathedral chancel and in the great hall of the Palazzo Giroldo were completed.[4] By the light of torches the following day was proclaimed a fast-day. Madruzzo's auxiliary improvised a procession of intercession by the clergy of the city on the morning of 12 December and the prelates were invited to a preparatory conference in the afternoon in the Palazzo Giroldi. In spite of the haste with which these arrangements were made, everything went according to plan. The procession of intercession took place; at the conference the legates submitted the brief of inauguration; but they rejected Pacheco's proposal that the Bull accrediting them should also be read. They did so in terms of such sharpness that Seripando felt compelled to appeal to the spirit of Christian charity. All the shops in the city were closed. In silence, prayer and fasting clergy and people awaited the great moment. But before we ourselves relive it with them it will be well to cast a glance at the stage on which the great event was enacted—the city of Trent as the theatre of the Council.

[1] Admonitions to the Roman prelates in *C.T.*, VOL. X, p. 232, ll. 9 and 24; p. 251, l. 4; p. 262, l. 2. The following prelates returned to Trent: on 19 November, the general of the Servites (*C.T.*, VOL. X, p. 248, l. 11); on 21 November, the Bishops of Belcastro and Termoli (*ibid.*, VOL. I, p. 330, l. 22); on 3 December the Bishop of Feltre (*ibid.*, VOL. I, p. 342, l. 11); on 11 December the Archbishop of Armagh (*ibid.*, p. 350, l. 33). The Portuguese Hieronymus ab Oleastro, whose arrival had been announced some time before (*C.T.*, VOL. X, p. 248, l. 24), reached Trent on 5 December (*ibid.*, VOL. I, p. 347, l. 34; VOL. IV, p. 443).

[2] *C.T.*, VOL. X, p. 260, l. 31.

[3] *C.T.*, VOL. I, p. 350, l. 36. The delay was due to the Roman courier having broken a leg and the messenger who took his place having been held up by a swollen river. He was the bearer of the brief of inauguration of 4 December and one dated 5 December which empowered the proxies of the German bishops to vote at the Council, *C.T.*, VOL. IV, pp. 442 ff., and Farnese's letter of 7 December, *ibid.*, VOL. X, p. 267 f.

[4] For the preparations in the cathedral see *C.T.*, VOL. I, p. 315, l. 16; p. 342, l. 20; p. 348, l. 28. The legates' decision with regard to the Palazzo Giroldi, *ibid.*, p. 338, l. 31. On the congregation of 12 December, Severoli, *C.T.*, VOL I, p. 1 ff.; Seripando, *ibid.*, VOL. II, p. 408 f.; Massarelli, *ibid.*, VOL. I, pp. 400 ff.; VOL. IV, p. 445 f.

CHAPTER XII

The Theatre and the Inauguration

TRENT owed its choice as the theatre of the Council both to its geographical situation and to its juridical status. Situated at the gate of
Italy and even then a predominantly Italian city, it nevertheless
belonged to the Holy Roman Empire of the German nation and was
subject to the territorial overlordship of its bishop, so that it answered
both the express wish of the Curia that the Council should be held in
an Italian city and the demand of the German Estates for a Council
in "German lands". It may well be that it was the future Cardinal
Cles who as early as 1524 first drew the Emperor's attention to these
peculiarities of his episcopal city.[1] When Paul III convoked the
Council in 1536 Trent was again mentioned,[2] though it had to yield
to Mantua, which was at least an imperial fief and with its 25,000
inhabitants was able to offer far better accommodation, while its situation in the fertile plain of the Po and its waterways greatly eased the
problem of supplies for the considerable number of people whom the
Council was bound to draw thither. When Mantua was dropped,
similar advantages recommended Vicenza, a Venetian, hence a neutral
city. For years it was regarded as the chosen locality until the Republic
withdrew its consent. Milan, also an imperial fief, would have been
even more suitable, but when it became an apple of discord between
Charles V and Francis I the latter's consent could not be hoped
for. As for Ferrara, Piacenza and Bologna, they belonged either
indirectly or immediately to the Papal States, and thus could not be
considered on account of the German Protestants. So it was once
more the Emperor who on the occasion of his meeting with the Pope
at Lucca proposed Trent [3] in preference not only to the above-named
cities of northern Italy, but even to Cambrai, which had in its favour
a similar juridical status. His choice was eventually agreed to by

---

[1] Charles V to the Duke of Sessa, 23 July 1524, Heine, *Briefe*, p. 618 f.; Balan,
Monumenta, p. 356 f.; *Cal. of St. Pap.*, *Spain*, VOL. II, p. 649.
[2] Albèri, *Relazioni*, VOL. II, iii, p. 316. Vergerio's reports show that at this time
Cardinal Cles and Duke Henry of Brunswick had suggested Trent, *N.B.*, VOL. I,
PT i, pp. 343, 346.
[3] *C.T.*, VOL. IV, p. 207, *n.1*.

Rome.[1] This compromise solution was necessitated by circumstances but was firmly adhered to in spite of endless objections to the choice. These objections were inspired less by the teaching of the canonists,[2] than by another consideration, i.e. that the city chosen for the seat of a Council should not only be able to guarantee the personal safety and the freedom of vote of those attending the Council, but that it should also be in a position to provide food and accommodation for them. For months the legates had been waiting at Trent for the order to open the Council, yet all the time both they and their master took it for granted that the city was unequal to the demands that would be made upon it.[3] Even the bishop of the place agreed that the city was "inadequate" and "not very suitable".[4] Before long it became evident that he allowed himself to be unduly influenced by the wishes of the Italian prelates, who desired a translation to central Italy. However, in spite of all objections, Trent remained the conciliar city. Its choice was a compromise which solved the long-drawn controversy about the locality of the Council, and in the end the city was found to be far better adapted to the purpose than its own bishop had been prepared to believe.

Situated in the valley of the Adige, on the Brenner route which since the fifteenth century had become increasingly important for traffic between North and South, at a point where the Pass of Pergine opens direct communication with the Val Sugana and thence with Venice,[5]

---

[1] *C.T.*, VOL. IV, pp. 217 f., 224, hinted at in the convocation Bull, p. 229, l. 43. However, in 1543 and even in 1545 Frederick Nausea, in his work *Super deligendo futurae in Germania synodi loco catacrisis* (Vienna 1545), recommended Cologne or Ratisbon for the Council, Metzner, *Friedrich Nausea*, p. 87 f.; *Epp. misc. ad Nauseam*, p. 364.

[2] D. Jacobazzi, *De Concilio*, VOL. I, BK ii, art. I (fol. 74); Ugoni, *De Conciliis*, fol. 60 or, designates as suitable for a Council "civitates et loca insignia quae annona et rebus ad victum convenientem necessariis abundant . . . habito in primis respectu quod ea in provincia concilium convocaretur in qua haereses et causae alie propter quas congregabantur, vigebant". In his *De auctoritate conciliorum*, cap. 4, fol. 14ᵛ, Campeggio requires that the locality of the Council should be free of "difficultates annonae", have a wholesome climate, easy and safe of access and able to assure the freedom of the vote. In his *Rerum conciliarium libri V* (Leipzig 1538), Nausea (BK III, ch. 13, fol. xxii), adds the further condition that the place should be easy to defend and that there be a supply of books for the members of the assembly. Nausea thought that Mantua would meet nearly all these conditions.

[3] *C.T.*, VOL. I, p. 239; VOL. X, pp. 175, 183; so also Dandino's instructions, *ibid.*, VOL. IV, p. 430.

[4] *C.T.*, VOL. I, pp. 288, 297. On the rumours of a translation to Metz, Mainz or Cologne, cf. *Cal. of St. Pap.*, *Spain*, VOL. VIII, p. 210.

[5] Short descriptions of the city by members of the Council: Sanfelice, *C.T.*, VOL. IV, pp. 254 ff.; Massarelli, *C.T.*, VOL. I, p. 156 f.; Vega, in the appendix to the

Trent could boast a favourable position for communications, though in this respect it was not equal to the other cities, such as Verona, Milan, Lyons and Basle, which had been considered as possible localities for the Council. Its markets,[1] chiefly of cattle and horses, had been thrown in the shade by the fairs of Bozen, but they were nevertheless of more than merely local importance, thanks to the attendance of merchants from Venice, Ferrara, Mantua, Brescia and even from Germany. Communications with Italy were facilitated by the circumstance that both goods and persons could easily be transported on Lake Garda and on the Adige, which at that time was navigable.[2]

At a time when men's health was believed to depend on climate and atmospheric conditions to an even greater extent than today, the climatic conditions of the city had an importance which should not be underestimated. It was easy—much easier than at Mantua—to escape from the summer heat of the deep valley of the Adige, which was often oppressive,[3] by retiring to the surrounding villa and vineyard-dotted

Brescia edition of the decrees of the Council of the year 1563, and frequently re-printed; Milledonne, in A. Baschet, *Journal du Concile de Trente* (Paris 1870), pp. 31 ff.; Torelli, Le Plat, VOL. VII, ii, p. 161 f. These writers confine themselves to general impressions, hence Michelangelo Marini's book, *Trento con il suo Sacro Concilio* (Trent 1673), though written a whole century after the Council, nevertheless retains its value, especially because of the account it gives of ecclesiastical conditions. The best modern description is that of C. De Giuliani, "Trento al tempo del Concilio", in *Archivio Trentino*, I (1882), pp. 145-202; II (1883), pp. 129-45; III (1884), pp. 3-82; also reprinted separately under the title *Trento* (1884); brief resumé by V. Casagrande in H. Swaboda's collective work, *Das Konzil von Trient, sein Schauplatz, Verlauf und Ertrag* (Vienna 1912), pp. 9-28; supplemented on the historical and artistic side by G. Fogolari, *Trento* (Bergamo, undated). G. Cuchetti's *Storia di Trento* (Palermo 1939), for the sections treating of the sixteenth century (pp. 133 ff.), is based on second-hand material and of no value. A. Gallante, *Trento ed il Concilio Ecumenico tridentino* (Rome 1922), offers surprisingly little from the point of view of local history.

[1] Massarelli, a diligent visitor of the market, supplies useful information. For the fair of St Vigilius, which lasted ten days, 3000 to 4000 horses and other cattle had been collected in pens outside the city walls, *C.T.*, VOL. I, p. 209. At the Michaelmas fair which also lasted eight days, Cervini bought two horses while Massarelli acquired several dozen spoons, mirrors, etc., *C.T.*, VOL. I, pp. 277 f., 280 f. The Fair of the Dedication began on 18 November, *C.T.*, VOL. I, p. 329. On the improvement of the Brenner road, by carrying it from Ritten to the valley of Eisack—an operation executed by Sigismund of Tirol, see O. Wanka von Rodlow, *Die Brennerstrasse im Altertum und Mittelalter* (Prague 1900), pp. 140-70.

[2] Mendoza left on 11 September 1545 by boat down the Adige, *C.T.*, VOL. I, p. 265. After the translation many prelates despatched their luggage by "zattere", *C.T.*, VOL. XI, p. 136. The corn bought in Bavaria in 1562 was transported from Bronzolo on the Adige; see below, p. 550, *n.*4.

[3] Thus, e.g., the legates did not attend the banquet at the castle on 26 June 1545 on account of the heat, *C.T.*, VOL. I, p. 210. On 6 July Massarelli reports that by that date the terrible heat had lasted a whole month, *ibid.*, p. 210.

hills until towards the end of August, when the first falls of snow on the Alpine peaks brought relief.[1] The severe Alpine winter, which began about the end of November,[2] was of course a sore trial for the southerners, who found it hard to put up with the local earthenware stoves and the consequently overheated rooms. Cardinal Cervini installed an iron stove in his study; the two Portuguese Dominicans at San Lorenzo were given a stove at the expense of the Council; some prelates ordered fur coats from Venice. The less exacting secretary of the Council, Massarelli, was satisfied at first with a fur cap which he bought at a fair on the occasion of the anniversary of the dedication of the cathedral church,[3] but as the cold became ever sharper he had a fur-lined doublet made.[4] The South Italians found the icy *tramontana* of the valley of the Adige unbearable. To them it seemed incredible that it should be necessary as late as 7 May 1545 to light fires in the Palazzo Prato, and that a few days later the mountain peaks should be powdered with fresh snow.[5] Before long a number of prelates complained that the climate of Trent did not agree with them. Mendoza, the imperial ambassador, left the city on 11 September 1545, on the plea that his physicians recommended a change of air.[6] When Cardinal Del Monte complained to Fracastoro, the official physician of the Council, of pains in the throat, the latter told him bluntly: "You commit suicide if you remain here any longer", and his medical colleague Fregimellica of Padua asserted with the utmost conviction that his brief stay at Trent had ruined his health. In the autumn of 1546 the legates drew up a long list of prelates who had arrived in good health and had left as sick men: Cardinal Pole's name headed the catalogue.[7] In the autumn of 1562 the Bishop of Bergamo refused to return to the Council on the plea that in the opinion of medical men the cold air of Trent was extremely injurious to his eyes.[8] We shall

[1] *C.T.*, VOL. I, p. 246 (20 August). On 20 October the mountains were covered with snow down to within two miles (3 km.) of the city and the next day to within one mile, *ibid.*, p. 294 f.

[2] On 18 November 1545 the snow had reached the near-by Sardagna. On the 27th there prevailed "grandissimo freddo" and on the 29th, when the legates came out of church, the street was covered with a carpet of snow of three fingers' thickness, *C.T.*, VOL. I, pp. 328 f., 338. For repairs to the chimney in the Palazzo Prato and the erection of a stove in San Lorenzo in November 1546, cf. Calenzio, *Doc. ined.*, pp. 26, 30.

[3] *C.T.*, VOL. I, p. 392.   [4] *Ibid.*, p. 367.
[5] *Ibid.*, pp. 185, 188.   [6] *Ibid.*, p. 265.
[7] Report of the legates, 20 September 1546, *C.T.*, VOL. X, p. 654 f.; cf. p. 183, l. 4.
[8] St. Arch., Mantua, Busta 1942 (8 October 1562) or.

see later on to what extent the climate of Trent influenced the translation of the Council to Bologna.

While an adequate quantity of meat and fish,[1] butter and cheese, fruit and wine was available, the supply of wheat for bread and oats for the horses was unsatisfactory. The district scarcely produced one-half of its own requirements and was accordingly obliged to obtain the remainder from Germany in exchange for its native produce, chiefly wine.[2] During the Council any surplus produce was consumed on the spot, so that shortages had to be made good by imports from the neighbouring districts. However, the necessary export and transit permits were only granted when there was a good harvest. As early as the autumn of 1545 the commissary of the Council found it difficult to obtain grain for bread from Mantua and Cremona, where bad weather had damaged the crops. On 22 September he reported to Rome that unless wheat could be procured from the Papal States before the onset of winter it would be impossible to prevent shortages and high prices.[3] In the spring of 1546 Venice accordingly granted the free transit of 6000 loads of corn and 3000 loads of oats from the Papal States, but from its own territory it only allowed the export of 500 small loads of oats from the districts of Vicenza and Verona.[4] In the winter of 1546 Ferrara supplied 3000 loads of wheat.[5] Soon afterwards the commissary of the Council asked the Duke of Mantua for 2000 loads of oats, for the transit of which the consent of Venice was required.[6]

Similar difficulties reappeared during the second period of the Council. In May 1551 Madruzzo, evidently from fear of not being able to hold out until the harvest, asked the Duke of Mantua for 300 sacks of corn.[7] Shortly before the opening of the third period of the Council the Curia, taught by previous experience, approached the

---

[1] At the banquet on St Martin's Day 1545 each meat dish was followed by fish, *C.T.*, VOL. I, p. 316. In the winter of 1551, when fishing at Trent came to an early termination owing to the cold, Madruzzo requested Cardinal Gonzaga to despatch four or five loads of fish every week, St. Arch., Mantua, Busta 1404 (27 November 1551) or.

[2] Thus Milledonne in Baschet, *Journal du Concile de Trente*, p. 32. In 1542 Sanfelice said that the available provisions in the city and neighbourhood would only last three months, *C.T.*, VOL. IV, p. 264.

[3] *C.T.*, VOL. IV, p. 432 f.; VOL. X, p. 199, l. 5.

[4] The papal nuncio at Venice, Giovanni della Casa, paid 60 scudi for the issuing of the required documents; this sum had to be refunded by the merchants, Montepulciano, Bibl., Ricci, 4, fol. 13 (24 April 1546); *ibid.*, fol. 70ʳ, the legates' reply of 10 May. These are probably the deliveries mentioned in *C.T.*, VOL. X, p. 411.

[5] St. Arch., Mantua, Busta 1409 (22 November 1546) or.

[6] *Ibid.*, 7 January 1547, or.

[7] *Ibid.*, Busta 1404 (5 May 1551) or. On 5 September the Emperor promised to have wheat sent from Spain via Genoa and meat from Hungary, *C.T.*, VOL. XI, p. 643.

Republic of Venice, the Dukes of Ferrara and Mantua and the governor of Milan for the purpose of securing licences for the export of corn.[1] Owing to the failure of the harvest that year the replies were either in the negative or the amount granted was inadequate.[2] It became therefore necessary in the autumn of 1561 to import from the Papal States— actually from the Marches—at the expense of the Apostolic Camera, 1000 loads of corn. The grain was transported on barges from Ancona to Riva by way of the Po and the Mincio. From Riva, Francesco Manelli, the nephew of the Depositary, had it taken to Trent in fifteen convoys of twenty-three to twenty-five carts each between April and September 1562. On 1 February the legates fixed the price at thirty-eight *carentani* per *staro*.[3]

For the following economic year the legates appealed for help to King Ferdinand and the Duke of Bavaria. Through Michele Borzella (Barcella), a corn dealer of Torboli, a considerable quantity of grain (10,000 *stari*) was bought at the fair of Wasserburg. In the spring of 1563, as soon as navigation on the Adige reopened, the grain was transported in barges from Bronzoll to Trent, where it was stored. The German corn was a good deal dearer than the Italian; its price was fifty *carentani* per *staro*. On this the members of the Council lived until the conclusion of the assembly. The remnant was sold at half-price (twenty-six *carentani*).[4]

[1] J. Šusta, *Die römische Curie und das Konzil von Trient unter Pius IV* (Vienna 1904-14), VOL. I, p. 67 f. Brief of 17 January 1561 to the Duke of Mantua, St. Arch., Mantua, Busta 3356.

[2] On 18 and 24 August Cardinal Gonzaga personally inquired from his nephew how much wheat he would be able to send to Trent, St. Arch., Mantua, Busta 1409 orr.

[3] Vat. Arch., Concilio, 146, fol. 448^r; *ibid.*, the pass dated 3 March 1562, for Ser Berardino Camerutio and Giovan Paulo Ungini dalla Piro della Marca, fol. 451^r. The documents relating to transport (e.g. the agreements with skippers Simon di Giovanni of Ancona and Niccolò de Marco of Ragusa, and with the merchant Francesco Ambrosi of Florence, the customs' receipts of Count Arco, etc.) are in Rome, Bibl. Vallicelliana, Cod. L. 40, fols. 178^r-247^v, cop.; *ibid.*, fols. 229^r-247^v, Francesco Manelli's account book.

[4] The contract with Borzella, 27 September 1562, and other documents in Bibl. Vallicell., Cod. L. 40, fols. 194^r-220^v; *ibid.*, fols. 267^r-279, Francesco Manelli's account book between December 1562 and October 1563. In the course of the preliminary negotiations, 7 September 1562, Girolamo Faleti informed Cardinal Gonzaga from Prague that the Duke of Bavaria had delivered the "tratta" for 1000 sacks of corn. On 14 September the Archbishop of Prague wrote that the Emperor had instructed the government of Innsbruck to deliver the required corn at Trent free of duty, St. Arch., Mantua, Busta 1943 or. The legates' correspondence with the government of Innsbruck about the purchase of 3000 "stara" of oats for the horses at Hall (Ala) "perchè si patisce assai di biada de cavalli", Vat. Arch., Concilio, 146, fol. 461^r (1 November 1562); *ibid.*, fol. 464^r (3 January 1563), a letter of thanks for 100 barrels of corn, a request for another 100 and for 50 barrels of oats for the horses.

As an ecclesiastical corporation the Council claimed immunity. Whereas the city of Basle had refused to exempt the members of the Council from the charges laid upon the rest of the population and only agreed to a compromise after several years, it was in the nature of things that the ecclesiastical overlord of Trent would grant to the members of the Council immunity from taxation,[1] but prolonged negotiations were required before immunity from customs' dues for supplies to the Council could be obtained from the secular lords: the toughest of them all were the Counts of Arco.[2] With regard to other articles of food the prophecy of the commissary of the Council, that there would only be a rise in the price of poultry, game, eggs and perhaps wine, was unfortunately not fulfilled.[3] The authorities of Trent forbade all exports, but this prohibition could not by itself stem the rise in prices for the simple reason that the amount of food available in the country was not equal to the increased demand. Imports at the proper time would have kept down prices; but the provision merchants hesitated to lay in large stocks before the actual opening of the Council, and even after its inauguration there was no guarantee against its premature translation or its dissolution.[4] Supply remained therefore substantially the same while demand kept rising—hence prices also. On his arrival at Trent Massarelli found many items, such as beef and salt, imported from Hall near Innsbruck, extremely cheap.[5] But before long hoarding began. Four French prelates laid in a large stock of wine with the result that the price of wine rose at once by 20-30 per cent.[6] Beef rose from eight to eleven *quattrini* and a load of hay from six to ten *lire*.[7] The worst feature was the dearth of fodder. Canon Strenberger accordingly advised Nausea, Bishop of Vienna, to come with as few

---

[1] *C.T.*, VOL. I, p. 654; for the situation at Basle, see R. Wackernagel, *Geschichte der Stadt Basel*, VOL. I (Basle 1907), p. 486.

[2] On 11 February 1562 the legates requested Julio, Battista, Oliviero, Francesco and Orsola, Counts of Arco, through Gabriele Calzoni, not to create further difficulties for the transport of grain, "cosa che da ogni altra persona havremmo aspettato che da lei", Vat. Arch., Concilio, 146, fol. 448ʳ. In a memorial which accompanied their letter they stated that the corn had been kept back by the Arcos "tanti giorni". Further details on the incident in Calzoni's letters to the castellan of Mantua, 12 and 16 February 1562, St. Arch., Mantua, Busta 1409 or.

[3] *C.T.*, VOL. IV, p. 256.

[4] In 1542 Sanfelice proposed that tradespeople should be encouraged to lay in betimes a considerable stock of goods, *C.T.*, VOL. IV, p. 264, but his advice was not acted upon. Losses were of course incurred in the purchase of grain by the Apostolic Camera in 1562.

[5] *C.T.*, VOL. I, p. 156 f.

[6] *Ibid.*, p. 233.

[7] Giuliani, *Trento*, p. 8.

horses as possible [1] and in 1562 so exalted a personage as Cardinal Hohenembs kept only two horses for his personal use. [2]

The maximum prices agreed upon by the commissary of the Council and the civic authorities [3] were of course circumvented as soon as supplies became scarce. In order to increase meat supplies, butchers were ordered in 1561 to import four hundred oxen and three thousand fattened cattle from Germany, [4] but it is not possible to ascertain whether this attempt to regulate the market proved successful. At any rate, laments over the shortage never ended. We may unhesitatingly ignore the complaints during the waiting period of 1545, for they must be traced back to the wish for a translation of the Council. At a later date they were undoubtedly justified to some extent and the lament of Hohenwarter, the representative of Basle [5]—"everything is exceedingly dear" —was re-echoed by the Fathers of the Council with rare unanimity.

With its 1500 houses Trent offered adequate accommodation for a gathering of moderate size, [6] and the better class burghers were in a position to evacuate their town houses and to retire to their villas and vineyards in the neighbourhood. [7] Nevertheless the finding and

---

[1] *Z.K.G.*, XXI (1901), p. 558 (15 July 1551); on 29 November 1551 Sleidan wrote that the costliest items were bread and oats, H. Baumgarten, *Sleidans Briefwechsel* (Strasbourg 1881), p. 177.

[2] Hohenwarter to Rebstock, 6 August 1562, *Basler Zeitschrift*, XLI (1942), p. 79. However, from the list of members of the Council printed at Riva in 1562 we learn that the cardinal had 22 horses, so that 20 must have been stabled outside the city.

[3] Giuliani prints several price lists in *Archivio Trentino*, III (1884), pp. 5 ff., but undated. I know of two, the date of which is certain, viz. (1) "Prezzi delle vettogaglie mandati dal Rev. Vescovo di Cava con le lettere de 13 di ottobre 1542", Vat. Arch., Concilio, 77, fols. 40^r-41^r, the result, according to *C.T.*, VOL. IV, pp. 291-3, of an agreement between the commissary of the Council and the city council; (2) The price list for provisions and house rents of the year 1561, *ibid.*, 12, fols. 127^r-128^v, printed in *C.T.*, VOL. VIII, p. 985 f. The "Memoriale della valuta delle robbe in Trento che non mancano mai", Vat. Lib., Vat. lat. 3944, fol. 156^v, must be dated in December 1561. It only includes provisions. The prices are somewhat lower than in the foregoing list, thus we read "circa li frutti l'havemo meglio mercato al doppio che non avete a Roma". The rate of exchange of the various currencies at Trent is noted in a table printed at Brescia in 1563 as an appendix to a "provinciale". There is a copy in the Vat. Lib., Racc. gen. Concilio, VOL. IV, 269, int. 31.

[4] Giuliani, *Trento*, p. 83.

[5] *Basler Zeitschrift*, XLI (1942), p. 80 (31 August 1562).

[6] *C.T.*, VOL. I, p. 156. In my opinion 1500 is an exaggeration. Equally exaggerated is Milledonne's statement (Baschet, *Journal du Concile de Trente*, p. 32) that Trent had accommodation for 300 prelates and their suites as well as for 20 "autres personnages"—viz. probably diplomatists.

[7] For instance the Trent notary Malpaga. In 1546 he let his house in the S. Maria quarter, with 2 beds and stabling for 6 horses, to one of the bishops and betook himself to Cognola, G. Ciccolini, *Riflessi del Concilio di Trento nei registri del notario Giorgio Malpaga* (Rovereto 1929), p. 8.

allocation of lodgings was the most anxious problem with which the commissary of the Council had to deal in conjunction with the civic committee set up for that purpose.[1] It was at first intended to lodge the various nations in separate quarters. Statistics of the available accommodation drawn up on this basis in the autumn of 1542 [2] showed that in the quarter of San Benedetto there was accommodation for 15 cardinals, 10 bishops, 18 persons of rank and 71 domestics: a total of 252 beds and stables for 399 horses being available. In the quarter of S. Maria Maggiore there was accommodation for the same number of persons of rank and for 93 domestics. Beds numbered 170 and there was stabling for 626 horses. It was hoped that in the quarter of San Pietro accommodation would be found for 13 cardinals, 14 prelates, 10 persons of rank, 128 domestics and stabling for 827 horses. In the quarter of S. Vigilio it was thought that 18 cardinals, 17 prelates, 7 persons of rank and 56 servants could be put up and stabling found for 515 horses. The number of beds available in the former district was 311 and in the latter 221. The details concerning the accommodation for cardinals show that the organisers reckoned with the presence of the whole of the Sacred College, though this depended on whether the Pope would take part in the Council, an eventuality which was at first considered. The episcopal palace was reserved for the pontiff's residence.

The plan for the allocation of lodgings drawn up in 1542 was eventually dropped, no doubt from a fear lest the separate accommodation of the nations should prove a pretext for their isolation and above all for the objectionable voting system that had been adopted at Constance. In point of fact the numerical preponderance of the Italians made this impossible; it was also too optimistic. There was room indeed for 100 prelates and a corresponding number of diplomatists, but accommodation was not only required for the permanent members of the Council but likewise for visiting princes and courtiers, jurists and theologians. Where were they to be put up if the inns were also

---

[1] There were actually two commissions, one of four members, whose duty it was to make an inventory of lodgings (*C.T.*, VOL. IV, p. 255) in the direction of the four city gates, Aquila, Ponte, S. Martino, S. Croce; another commission of eight members, two for each quarter, was to fix prices. They were, for S. Benedetto, Enrico di Povo and Tommaso Cazuffo; for S. Pietro, Girolamo Tono (Thun) and Domenico Slosser; for S. Maria, Girolamo Balduino and Battista Galasso; for Borgo Nuovo, viz. S. Vigilio, Bonaventura Calepino and Dr Calvete: Giuliano, *Trento*, p. 5.

[2] Vat. Arch., Concilio, 77, fols. 45[v]-59[v]; the date is inferred from *C.T.*, VOL. IV, p. 265.

commandeered?[1] This explains how it came about that when Cardinal Alessandro Farnese passed through Trent with a large suite in November 1546, Ludovico Strozzi, his companion, was unable to find lodgings and would have had to camp in the open street if the house of the Bishop of Fano, who happened to be away, had not been put at his disposal.[2]

Moreover, inadequate allowance had been made for the circumstance that many foreign prelates, such as the three Rhenish archbishops[3] and most of the French and Spanish bishops,[4] were accompanied by suites of between 25 and 50 persons, not to speak of the courts of the cardinals. Ercole Gonzaga's following, for instance, comprised no less than 160 persons.[5] This explains why as early as November 1561, when the number of bishops present was still far below 100, only 12 houses were available for the accommodation of "great" prelates.[6] Later on, when the number of those entitled to vote rose to nearly 200, it became necessary to fall back upon the neighbouring localities for the accommodation of the servants and the animals. This eventuality had been considered from the beginning. In the above-mentioned statistics of accommodation of the year 1542 it was estimated that within a radius of 15 kilometres (c. 10 miles), some 2200 beds and stabling for 6591 horses were available. Another survey ordered by Madruzzo,

[1] The statistics of accommodation given above include 16 hostelries, 9 of which were in the quarter of S. Pietro, viz, Pesce, Rosa, Cavaletto, Corona, Cervia, Torre, Sole and two unnamed "osterie". The first two of the above named were elegant and spacious, with 25 beds each and stabling, the first for 50 horses, the second for 48. The remaining hostelries were more modest but the Cavaletto had 12 beds and stabling for 66 horses; Torre had 25 beds and stabling for 24 horses. The quarter of S. Benedetto had only 2 "osti", S. Maria had 3, S. Vigilio only boasted the "oste Antonio de la buona ventura"; immediately before the Porta S. Croce stood the Hosteria del Moro with 10 beds and stabling for 30 horses. The inn of the Two Swords in which Massarelli lodged (C.T., VOL. I, p. 156) is not included in this list. The Archbishop of Sassari also stayed at this inn for a while, and when he left he owed the innkeeper 10 florins, Calenzio, Doc. ined., p. 8 (19 March 1546).

[2] St. Arch., Mantua, Busta 1409 (12 November 1546) or.

[3] The lists of their "gentiluomini", each of whom again had his own servants, were published by me in T.Q., CXXII (1941), p. 247.

[4] In 1561 the Bishops of Oviedo, Coimbra and Salamanca had each a suite of 30 persons, Vat. lat. 3944, fols. 154^r-156^v.

[5] Sickel, Römische Berichte, VOL. I (Vienna 1896), p. 21. Hohenembs's "familia" consisted of 70 persons, that of Hosius and Simonetta of 60 each, and that of Seripando of 50. On the other hand, in 1545 Cervini's household counted only 37 persons, C.T., VOL. I, p. 168.

[6] Calzoni to the castellan of Mantua, 10 November 1561, St. Arch., Mantua, Busta 1409 or. On 13 November 1561 the Bishop of Fiesole reports that lodgings had been found for 70 "famiglie", so that the "migliori allogiamenti" were nearly all taken. It might be possible, though not easy, to find accommodation for another 100 "famiglie", St. Arch., Florence, Med. 490 to fol. 1073 or.

admittedly over a wider area, yielded even more favourable results: 24 localities on the right bank of the Adige would alone provide lodgings for 2699 persons and stabling for 3746 horses,[1] Though the lodging of the servants in the neighbouring localities entailed a number of inconveniences, it provided at least a partial solution of the housing problem, which towards the end became more and more pressing.

One consequence of the shortage of houses was a fantastic rise in rents. By the autumn of 1546 rents alone were as high at Trent as the total cost of living elsewhere. Thus it came about that by the end of one year's stay at Trent Mignanelli had run through all the money he had put by for the Council.[2] In 1551 for one living and sleeping-room, including two meals a day, the historian Sleidan had to pay 12 Italian crowns (florins) a week at the inn of "The Golden Rose".[3] A price list, drawn up in the year 1561 [4] by a committee of burghers, put the rent of a prelate's three-roomed apartment with only the most indispensable furniture, but including bed-clothes, at 3 scudi a month, and for each additional bed-sitting-room another scudo, according to requirements. To this was added the rent of stabling, payment for the use of kitchen utensils and other items of this kind. These prices were still tolerable; the only danger for the lodger was the practice of charging for special services. The commissary of the Council accordingly proposed fixed prices, as, for instance, 16 florins a month for a large apartment with six to eight rooms with a corresponding number of beds, and stabling for eight horses. He represented to the committee that if the Council went on for some three or four years those who let their houses would be able to recover all the money they had originally spent on them, and as for beds and other furniture, they would get their value two or three times over.[5] The prices actually paid soon outran every prearranged limit. Melchior Lussy, the Swiss envoy, was obliged to pay for his quarters—not very spacious ones to be sure—as much as 18 scudi a month,[6] while Hohenwarter paid 6 crowns a month for his one room. The rent of the Palazzo Roccabruna in which

---

[1] C.T., VOL. IV, p. 255; Giuliano, Trento, p. 7.

[2] C.T., VOL. X, p. 654. At the beginning of August 1545 Massarelli had rented a house for him for the sum of 11 scudi, ibid., VOL. I, p. 231.

[3] Baumgarten, Sleidans Briefwechsel, p. 177.

[4] C.T., VOL. VIII, p. 986.

[5] Giuliano, Trento, p. 9 f.

[6] K. Fry, J.A. (Ulpius) Volpe, Documente, VOL. I, (Florence 1935), p. 324; the Florentine envoy, Giovanni Strozzi, paid 16 scudi, cf. Mellini to Cosimo, 17 June 1563, St. Arch., Florence, Med. 500, fol. 236ʳ or.

Count Luna resided, amounted to 50 scudi a month.[1] The cost of living as a whole—that is food and lodging—according to the Archbishop of Zara in the autumn of 1561, amounted to 61 scudi a month for a prelate whose household consisted of four persons and who kept only one mount.[2] The historian Giovio arrived at much higher figures —but he was a journalist.[3] It follows that the sum of 25 scudi, which at that time was granted to needy prelates, was hardly adequate. Girolamo Muzio complained that he was unable to feed his household of ten persons with the 20 scudi granted to him.[4]

It was in the nature of things that the scarcity should affect relations between the members of the Council and the local population. At this time the inhabitants of Trent numbered between seven and eight thousand souls,[5] the majority of them Italians. Many of them were acquainted with the German language.[6] The Tuscan Torelli describes them as rough, suspicious, inordinately addicted to wine; he even suggests that Trent had become a city of refuge for the shady characters of both nations.[7] However, Torelli is alone in passing these unfriendly criticisms; as a rule the members of the Council merely complain of

[1] Hohenwarter to Lichtenfels, 31 August 1562, *Basler Zeitschrift*, XLI (1942), p. 80; *Archivio Trentino*, III (1884), p. 51.

[2] Baluze-Mansi, *Miscellanea*, VOL. IV, p. 200.

[3] *Archivio Trentino*, III (1884), p. 35. The Archbishop of Prague, who had a household of 30 persons and who was also under obligation to maintain Ferdinand's second envoy, Sigismund Thun, spent each month the enormous sum of 800 ducats, that is 200 ducats more than his total income, S. Steinherz, *Briefe des Prager Erzbischofs Anton Brus von Müglitz* (Prague 1907), p. 47.

[4] Muzio to Gonzaga, 14 March 1562, St Arch., Mantua, Busta 1939 or.

[5] That the number of 10,000 usually given is too high is shown by Massarelli's report (*C.T.*, VOL. I, p. 197), in which he says that on the feast of the Blessed Trinity when, thanks to a charity, bread and cheese were distributed to all who visited the cathedral, 7800 portions had been prepared but only 4400 were actually asked for.

[6] Torelli writes: "Promiscuam habet linguam Teutonicam et Italicam, sed Itali omnes etiam, cum placet, Teutonice loquuntur", Le Plat, VOL. VII, ii, p. 161. This is confirmed by Massarelli, who says (*C.T.*, VOL. I, p. 169) that on Easter Day Madruzzo's servants, most of them Italians, sang the hymn "Christ ist erstanden" before dinner. It must be remembered that at this time the language frontier passed by Lavisio, as we learn again from Massarelli, *C.T.*, VOL. I, p. 286. In his description of his journey in 1517, Antonio de Beatis writes: "In la Magna se entra ad uno miglio Tedesco da Trento, passato un ponte de un fiume che intra in Atice", L. Pastor, *Die Reise des Kardinals Luigi d'Aragona* (Freiburg 1905), p. 92. Utterly wrong is the assertion of the Dominican Peter Faber that the Germans were at the helm. The list of the "podestàs" of Trent given by C. Perini, *Il Concilio di Trento* (Trent 1863), p. 149, only mentions Italians for the period that concerns us though even for this period the unreliable Faber speaks of the Germans as "urbis rectores", *Evagatorium*, ed. C. D. Hassler, VOL. I, p. 75.

[7] "Tridentinum Germanorum sentina, Italorum vero refugium est", Le Plat, VOL. VII, ii, p. 161.

the covetousness of the citizens of Trent, but they overlook the fact that it was exceedingly rare that the causes of the scarcity were due to a single individual and that most of the inhabitants also suffered from the rise in prices. On their part the people of Trent frequently overlooked the great material advantages they derived from the Council and the munificence which the legates, to mention them alone, displayed towards the poor of the city.[1]

Occasions of friction between natives and strangers were of course bound to arise. Again and again the carrying of arms was either restricted or completely forbidden, though never entirely suppressed. As early as 1545 brawls occurred on the occasion of dances, so that it became necessary to forbid amusements of this kind both in the city and in the neighbouring villages.[2] Occasional acts of violence were also committed by the servants.[3] Such incidents were perhaps inevitable, but when it happened that even one of the prelates fell short of the standard of conduct that one would expect from a person of his standing, a painful impression was bound to be created. In spite of repeated requests by Madruzzo and the instant prayers of the family, the Bishop of Bertinoro, a Dominican, refused to give up in favour of his hostess who had fallen grievously sick during the bitter cold of the winter, the only room of the house that could be warmed. Thereupon the indignant neighbours resolved to deal with the case in their own way. They seized the room by force and threw the prelates' effects

---

[1] A glance through Antonio Manelli's account books in Calenzio is enough to show that actually every section of the population profited by the Council. The merchants Zerletta and Ronchini provided velvet and other material for the members of the assembly. The tailor Francesco made cushions for the chairs of the five cardinals; candles were bought in the shop of the "spetiali" Bernardino and Ceschi; the mason Giovanni got 3½ scudi for repairs to the chimney in the hall of the Council; a joiner of the name of Giovanni earned 5½ scudi by making footstools with a view to protecting the prelates' feet against the cold; Baldassare, a smith, made an iron pipe for the stove; the bookseller Battista provided three Missals for the sum of 3 scudi and 35 baiocchi. The convent of the Observants of San Bernardino received an alms of 12 scudi from the legates each month, Calenzio, *Doc. ined.*, pp. 3, 5 and *passim*. During the first period of the Council there was a daily distribution of bread to the poor at Santa Maria Maggiore, which cost the legates 60 scudi a month, *C.T.*, VOL. I, p. 338; however, the number of recipients, which Massarelli puts at 700 to 800, appears to me excessive. The Jesuits Lainez and Salmeron were able to clothe 76 poor people with alms collected by them from the prelates; Salmeron to St Ignatius, 30 September 1546, M.H.S.J., *Epistolae P. Alphonsi Salmeronis*, VOL. I (Madrid 1906), p. 29.

[2] *C.T.*, VOL. I, p. 217 f.

[3] On 1 August 1545 the Bishop of Cadiz's cook was arrested for attempted rape, *C.T.*, VOL. I, p. 228 f.; on 30 December a familiar of the Archbishop of Aix kicked a servant girl in the open street, *ibid.*, p. 365.

into the street. When he complained to the legates, Cervini gave him the only appropriate piece of advice—to hold his tongue.[1]

To regard incidents of this kind as the rule and to picture the relations between natives and strangers as a permanent warfare would be contrary not only to the simple reflection that unpleasant incidents never fail to be chronicled whereas pleasing ones are only rarely recorded, it would also be at variance with what actually happened, as for instance the rich donations which the Bishop of Verdun, on his departure from Trent, left to his host and family and to a merchant—probably the one who had supplied goods to him—to a painter and to several poor priests and lay people.[2] Nor should we allow ourselves to be unduly impressed by the laments about the scarcity of supplies and the climate; least of all should we judge conditions by modern standards. Otherwise would it have been possible, as late as 1562, that is at a time when the Council underwent its most serious crisis, for a bishop to state in open session that there was an abundance of food at Trent and that the health of the members of the Council left nothing to be desired?[3] In his description of the city Vega not only praises its cleanliness and the comfort of its houses and extols the excellence of its wines and its bread but, as regards the inhabitants, he testifies that they were humane, decent and easy to get on with. There can be no question but that he is nearer the truth than Torelli.

The traveller who approached Trent from the south would enter the city by the Porta S. Croce, which owed its name to the monastery of the same name outside the walls. Anyone coming from Venice, through the Val Sugana, entered through the Porta d'Aquila, hard by the bishop's castle; the traveller from the north passed through the Porta S. Martino and the suburb of the same name, along the road to Bozen. The city itself was divided into the above-mentioned quarters. The centre of the town, between the Adige and the Contrada Larga (the present Via Belenzani) which leads to the *duomo*, included the quarter of S. Benedetto. Contiguous to this were, towards the west the rather poor quarter of S. Maria, towards the south-east the aristocratic cathedral-close of S. Vigilio, where the gentry and the canons of the cathedral resided, and towards the north and below the bishop's castle, the German quarter of S. Pietro.[4]

[1] *C.T.*, VOL. I, pp. 363, 365.
[2] *Ibid.*, VOL. II, p. 877 f.   [3] *Ibid.*, VOL. VIII, p. 525.
[4] *Ibid.*, VOL. IV, p. 255. The plan of the city which Sanfelice forwarded to Rome in 1542 has unfortunately been lost—I use the one of 1563 reproduced by Merkle in *C.T.*, VOL. I.

This position of the German quarter was not fortuitous. From the end of the fourteenth century the bishops of Trent had all been Germans. Some of them had been the bearers of high-sounding names, such as Frundsberg and Liechtenstein. As for learning, none of them equalled the jurist Johannes Hinderbach of Hesse (1465-86), whose somewhat soft features are reproduced with lifelike fidelity on his monument in the *duomo*. The influence of the German bishops, but even more so the growing importance of the Brenner pass for the traffic between North Germany and Venice, had strengthened the German minority. It preserved its own manners and customs.[1] In the parish church of S. Pietro, a late Gothic edifice of comparatively modest proportions but famous on account of the relics of the child-martyr Simon, they had an altar and a preacher of their own [2]; they also had a hospital and a confraternity.

Among the ecclesiastical bodies the cathedral chapter with its eighteen well-endowed canonries (200 florins) and its three dignitaries (dean, provost and archdeacon) was the most important by reason of its right to elect the bishop. Though not exclusively aristocratic in its composition, it was nevertheless the instrument by means of which the nobility of town and chapter—the Thuns, Trautmannsdorfs, Lodrons, Roccabrunas, Sardagnas, Tabarellis, Albertis—shared in the government of the principality, though there can be no question in this case of a far-reaching independence like that enjoyed by the great imperial dioceses. The presence of an imperial captain was a constant reminder to bishop and chapter that the Counts of Tirol would not tolerate a really independent territorial authority within the boundaries of their domains. But in one respect the chapter of Trent resembled the chapters of the imperial dioceses—the moral and religious conduct of a number of its members left much to be desired.[3] The obligation of residence was not complied with and the liturgical services in the cathedral were carried out by twenty-six beneficed clergy. Built in the late romanesque style and consecrated by Bishop Vanga, the cathedral was dedicated to St Vigilius, patron of the city. Its chancel provided ample space for great pontifical functions.

[1] *C.T.*, VOL. I, pp. 186, 235, 315. Massarelli was also struck by the Germans' bad drinking habits during his stay as the guest of Secretary Oittinger (Etinger), *ibid.*, p. 224.

[2] At Easter there was a sermon in Italian in the cathedral and another in German at S. Pietro, *C.T.*, VOL. I, p. 170.

[3] In 1542 Morone spoke very earnestly to some of the canons who were living in concubinage, *N.B.*, VOL. I, PT vii, p. 106.

Only two religious Orders were established within the city walls, the Hermits of St Augustine near S. Marco, memorable for the sojourn as well as the sepulchre of the unforgettable Seripando, and the Poor Clares near S. Trinità, not far from the *duomo*. The Franciscan Conventuals' house of San Francesco, situated not far from the present residence of the archbishop, counted fewer members than that of the Observants of S. Bernardino, which stood in a delightful part of the valley of Fersina and recalled the stay at Trent of the Sienese saint. In 1235 the Dominicans obtained possession of the former Benedictine abbey of S. Lorenzo, at that time situated beyond the Adige but since the regulation of the course of the river in the last century on the near side, by the railway station.[1] While the Council was in session the two Sotos and the Venerable Bartolomeo de' Martiri were wont to ponder their votes in its cool gardens and Pedro Soto found a grave in the now almost completely ruinous romanesque church. The prelates and theologians of the Franciscan Order, among them Alfonso de Castro and Andrew de Vega, found refreshment in the gardens of S. Francesco and S. Bernardino. The library of the Observants, already of considerable size at the beginning of the sixteenth century, was further enriched in 1549 by the collection of their General Lunello and in 1558 by that of Canon Erasmus Strenberger.[2] At the time of the Council the Carmelites and the Servites were not yet established at Trent.[3]

One drawback was the lack of a local printing press, though this deficiency favoured the secrecy of the negotiations. In 1478 and 1528 two books had been published by printers who made a short stay in the town, namely the story of the boy-martyr St Simon and Cardinal Cles's *Statutum tridentium*. It was only in 1584 that a printing press was permanently set up. During the third period of the Council the lack of a printing press was made good to some extent by a press set up at Riva by a Jewish physician of the name of Nino Jacob, who printed not only thirty-four Hebrew books but likewise fifty-seven works connected with the Council, mainly lectures and sermons. The latter works were commissioned by two publishers, Bozzola of Brescia and Alciati of Padua. These two publishers kept bookshops at Trent.

[1] S. Weber, *I Domenicani nel monastero di S. Lorenzo a Trento* (Trent 1938), p. 17. The abbey continued at S. Apollinare up to the fifteenth century, when the mensal revenues of the abbot were applied to the endowment of the cathedral provost, S. Weber, *L'Abbazia benedettina di S. Lorenzo a Trento* (Trent 1936), p. 56.

[2] *Contributi alla storia dei Frati Minori della Provincia di Trento* (Trent 1926), p. 189 f.

[3] The great Carmelite convent "alle Laste", situated near Cognola, was founded at a later date by Gallas, one of Wallenstein's generals.

We know the name of one bookseller during the first period of the Council, a certain Battista, from whom Antonio Manelli bought three Missals for use during the Council.[1]

At the beginning of the century, when Albrecht Dürer, coming from Bozen, drew the famous Indian ink sketch of Trent now preserved in the Albertina at Vienna, the city, seen from the direction of the Adige, with Torre Verde near the Porta San Martino, the mighty Torre Vanga by the one hundred and forty feet long wooden bridge over the Adige and the many towers of the houses of the nobles, still retained the aspect of a wholly medieval town. But by the time the Fathers of the Council entered it, it presented an entirely new aspect; what they saw was a town profoundly affected by the new artistic orientation of the Renaissance. This was due to the activities of the late Bishop of Trent, Cardinal Bernard Cles (1514-39).[2]

Born of a noble provincial family in the Val di Non, the son of an Italian father and a German mother—Dorothea Fuchs—Cles combined in his person the keen intelligence, the sober realism and the strong artistic sense of the Italian with German thoroughness and perseverance. The early death of his father was for him, the eldest of seven brothers, an incentive to make the most of his abilities. The study of law at Bologna enabled him within the space of a few years to make his way in the ecclesiastical administration of the diocese. He successively became archdeacon and counsellor to the Emperor Maximilian and at the death of Bishop Neudeck he succeeded him at the early age of twenty-nine. The heavy features in the Roman portrait of him by an anonymous Flemish master betray a character of unusual energy. The prominent chin, especially marked on the coins and medals of the Palazzo Tabarelli, further enhances the impression of an enterprising and indomitable spirit. A burning ambition, concealed but not

---

[1] G. Bampi, "Della Stampa e degli stampatori nel principato di Trento fino al 1564", in *Archivio Trentino*, II (1883), pp. 202-21; Calenzio, *Doc. ined.*, p. 10. However, Messer Niccolò, a Trent citizen, was one of the first representatives of his craft at Venice, as Ippolito Chizzola informed Cardinal Gonzaga on 15 August 1562, St. Arch., Mantua, Busta 1942 or.

[2] The biography by Janus Pyrrhus Pincius, *De vitis pontificum Tridentinorum libri XII* (Mantua 1546), from Book VI onwards, is a panegyric in the humanist manner. B. Bonelli, *Notizie istorico-critiche della Chiesa di Trento*, VOL. III, (Trent 1762) pp. 366-98; VOL. IV, (Trent 1765) pp. 175-95. A modern biography, based on the copious archival material, is still wanting. The fourth centenary of Cles's death saw the publication of the popular booklet: *Bernardo Clesio vescovo e cardinale* (Cles 1939), and G. B. Emert's "Un elogio in onore di B. Clesio", in *Studi Trentini*, XX (1939), pp. 134-7. Fogolari, *Trento*, pp. 91-133, sums up the cardinal's building activities.

repressed by cautious restraint, urged him onward and upward. He became successively Ferdinand I's leading minister, then a cardinal, and even the tiara did not seem beyond his reach. He did not demur when before the conclave of 1534 the King of the Romans put forward his minister as a candidate for the Papacy.[1] In the religious contest he invariably fought with courage for the Catholic cause. Vergerio and Morone with one accord describe him as a pillar of the Catholic faith not only in the hereditary states of the Habsburgs but in the whole Empire.[2] In his own diocese he suppressed with inflexible severity any Lutheran movement as soon as it showed itself in the German districts, as, for instance, at Bozen and Egna, and in 1526 he sought a decision of the theological faculty of Tübingen on the teaching of a preacher who was making Tramina the theatre of his activities. A visitation carried out in the years 1537 and 1538 by Canon Alberto d'Alberti and George Ackerle, parish priest of S. Maria Maddalena, brought to light isolated cases of Lutheranism and Anabaptism in the German parts of the diocese, while the Italian section was entirely free from heresy. As regards moral conduct, the German clergy was, on the whole, superior to the Italian. The blameless priests of S. Pietro of Trent presented a pleasing contrast to certain clerics of the cathedral parish and those of S. Maria Maggiore. Here too, as in the Empire, the German section suffered from a great shortage of priests.[3]

Nor was the temporal side neglected. Cles succeeded in recovering a number of possessions and privileges which had been alienated under his predecessors. It is no exaggeration to say that he restored the temporal sovereignty of the diocese. In 1527 he issued a constitution for his episcopal territory. But the dearest wish of his heart was the reconstruction of his episcopal city. He was the real founder of the city as it presented itself to the prelates who came to Trent in 1545, the year of the Council. Building was one of the passions of this great man. He gratified it by drawing on the revenues of the diocese, which were estimated at 12,000 scudi, and on other rich sources of income

---

[1] H. Ausserer, "Kardinal Bernhard von Cles und die Papstwahl des Jahres 1534", in *M.Ö.I.G.*, XXXV (1914), pp. 114-39.

[2] *N.B.*, VOL. I, PT i, p. 270; PT ii, p. 124. His death, Cardinal Farnese wrote, is "di grandissimo danno e iattura alla religione", *ibid.*, PT iv, p. 162.

[3] V. Zanolini, "Appunti e documenti per una storia dell' eresia luterana nella diocesi di Trento", in *Ottavo Annuario del Ginnasio pareggiato di Trento* (Trent 1909), pp. 10-30. For the visitation of 1537-8, on the basis of the acts, see A. Cetto, "Condizioni morali e religiose della diocesi di Trento alla vigilia del Concilio di Trento", in *Il Concilio di Trento*, III (1947), pp. 58-77.

which his growing influence opened for him. The latter were estimated at 50,000 scudi. Soon after entering upon office he began the task of modernising the city.[1] He ordered the removal of the outbuildings, most of them wooden structures, which narrowed the two main streets Contrada longa and Contrada larga (now Via Roma and Via Belenzani) and shut out light and air. All the more important streets were paved and the Fersina, a tributary of the Adige, was diverted and made to run through the city in a number of runnels, with a view to improving public hygiene and facilitating the fight of the frequent outbreaks of fire.[2] The *Statuto Clesiano* laid down stringent regulations for all new constructions; thereafter no new building was to be undertaken without the approval of the city council. The actual execution of these measures in the building sphere was entrusted to the city architect, Antonio da Vigolo. But the cardinal found time, even while at the court of Ferdinand I, personally to attend to the smallest details and to breathe something of his own energy into their execution. In the building sphere he himself set a shining example. In the western quarter there stood since 1520 the one-aisled Renaissance church of S. Maria Maggiore, where during the last session of the Council the general congregations were held. One of the ornaments of the building was Vincenzo Grandi's magnificent organ-loft. In accordance with the taste of the period the *duomo* was given an octagonal cupola. The year 1536 saw the erection in near-by Civezzano of the church *delle Grazie*, which at a later date the members of the Council loved to visit.[3] The episcopal castle of Selva, on the shore of Lake Levico, underwent so sumptuous a restoration as to call forth the admiration of Cervini and Massarelli when they came to inspect it, familiar though they were with the palaces of Rome.[4] The ancestral castle at Cles and Castel Toblino, on the northern shore of Lake Garda, were similarly restored.

But the cardinal's most important construction and the one in which he indulged his passion for building to the fullest was the *Magno Palazzo*, the magnificent Renaissance castle erected for him by Andrea Crivelli with the assistance of a number of Italian artists between 1528

---

[1] L. Bonfioli, "B. Clesio e il rinnovamento edilizio di Trento", in *Studi trentini*, XX (1939), pp. 269-99.

[2] Antonio de Beatis saw the new layout as early as 1517, Pastor, *Die Reise des Kardinals Luigi d'Aragona*, p. 92.

[3] Massarelli's pilgrimages to Civezzano in execution of a vow made during his illness, in *C.T.*, VOL. I, pp. 247, 274 f.

[4] *C.T.*, VOL. I, p. 266.

and 1536,[1] by the side of the old "Castel del buon Consiglio" which had been the residence of the bishops of Trent since the middle of the thirteenth century.[2] He thus acquired a residence which complied with every requirement for his personal safety as well as with the exacting demands of the refined taste of the Renaissance.[3] The audience-hall on the first floor was adorned with the portrait of Charles V, who on his return from the coronation at Bologna had stayed in the as yet unfinished palace, and that of Ferdinand I, who soon after its completion in September 1536 was received within its walls with truly regal splendour.[4] The spacious banqueting-hall on the second floor, with its coffered ceiling, was designed as a worthy setting for the entertainments which, as bishop and territorial lord of the conciliar city, he planned for the princes, cardinals, prelates and diplomatists who were to attend the Council. The adjoining circular room was adorned with the seven famous Flemish tapestries representing New Testament scenes which are now the property of the cathedral. A lateral wing housed the library, most of the manuscript contents of which had been acquired by Bishop Hinderbach [5]; to these Cles added more than a thousand printed works. The portraits of twenty-four eminent divines, philosophers, jurists, physicians and poets in the lunettes above the shelves bore witness to the breadth of mind of the founder of the library. It is not possible to ascertain whether the transfer of this collection, which we know to have taken place under his successor, and its eventual dispersal, were solely due to neglect or to the fact that the library was used by the members of the Council who, naturally enough, found it extremely convenient to have at hand the many controversial writings that filled its shelves.

Long before he undertook the construction of the palace the cardinal had awakened and encouraged a taste for building among the patricians

---

[1] S. Weber, "Le residenze dei vescovi di Trento", in *Studi trentini*, v (1924), also as a separate reprint.

[2] The earliest description by Andrea Mattioli, *Il Magno Palazzo del Cardinal di Trento* (Venice 1539). For the story of the building, C. Ausserer–G. Gerola, *I documenti Clesiani del Buonconsiglio* (Venice 1925), with list of earlier writings (Woelzl, Schmölzer, etc.).

[3] In 1542 Sanfelice thought the castle was so strong and so well equipped with defensive armour that a small garrison would be able to hold it for many days, even for months, *C.T.*, VOL. IV, p. 253.

[4] Pincius describes the preparations for the feast, *De vitis pont. Trid.*, fols. 99ᵛ-100ᵛ.

[5] G. Tarugi Secchi, *La biblioteca vescovile di Trento* (Trent 1930), pp. 18 ff., 55 ff. It must have included the codex mentioned in *C.T.*, VOL. II, p. 742.

of Trent.[1] The Palazzo Giroldi-Prato, of which only a few remains survived a destructive fire in the year 1845 and whose site is now occupied by the Post Office, was already of ancient date. During the first two periods of the Council it housed the legates, and the main hall was used for the general congregations. Various aristocratic dwellings, fortresslike and flanked by towers, were made more habitable by the opening of new windows and the construction of balconies in keeping with the taste of the period, as, for instance, the house of Archdeacon Martin von Neydeck, known to-day as Torre Massarelli, after its occupant during the Council,[2] and the house now known as No. 15 Via Santa Trinità. But the most characteristic products of the new building era were the charming palaces in the Venetian style which, with their pretty balconies and their splendid frescoes on the side facing the street, constitute to this day the chief ornament of the city. In these palaces, with their moderately sized though commodious rooms, cardinals and other eminent personages were accommodated during the Council; thus, for instance the Palazzo Salvadori in the Contrada larga, erected by Cles as early as 1515, was occupied by Cardinal Seripando. A few paces further on stood the Palazzo Geremia, where Cardinal Simonetta lodged; Palazzo Pedrozzi in the Contrada longa; Palazzo Monte (now Rohr), situated near the city's busiest cross-roads in the direction of the castle. In 1551 Vargas, the imperial envoy, stayed in the Casa Cazzuffi in the street now called Oss Mazzorana. Emulating the cardinal, Antony, dean of the cathedral, and Canon Donato Tabarelli erected their family palace in the same street. The façades of these edifices, built of huge blocks of freestone, are inspired by Bolognese models. Canon Roccabruna erected in the Via S. Trinità the palace which eventually came into the possession of the Sardagna family. Count Luna, Philip II's envoy, lodged and died within its walls. Queta, the cardinal's secretary, built for himself a house, probably in the Contrada larga, which was occupied for a time by Cardinal Del Monte. The most spacious were the two connected houses of the influential family of Thun, now the municipio. This was the residence of Gonzaga and later on of Morone during the last period of the Council.

At the time of Cardinal Cles's unexpected death in 1539, at the early age of 54 and only a short time after he had taken over the

---

[1] S. Weber, "Le abitazioni dei Padri a Trento durante il Concilio", in *Il Concilio di Trento*, I (1942), pp. 57-64; II (1943), pp. 139-46. For what follows I must observe that all the lodgings mentioned in contemporary sources are far from having been identified with absolute certainty on a cadastral basis.

[2] *C.T.*, VOL. I, p. 182.

neighbouring diocese of Brixen, the city of Trent had assumed a new aspect. His successor, Cristoforo Madruzzo, reaped the fruits of his labours. Whereas Cles was on the whole a self-made man, Madruzzo owed his easy and rapid rise to the influence of his father, Giovanni Gaudenzio, president of the episcopal council.[1] His father's second son by his wife Euphemia von Sporenberg, he was born on 5 July 1512 at Castel Nano. While still in his early youth he was given a canonry at Trent together with the parishes of Meran and Lienz. At a later date he became dean of the cathedral chapter of Trent and a canon of Augsburg, Salzburg and Brixen. While pursuing his studies at Bologna (1532-7) he made a friend for life in the person of the future Cardinal Otto Truchsess of Augsburg. He also made many other contacts which greatly affected his future career, including the Pope's nephew Alessandro Farnese and Ugo Buoncompagni, who taught him law. Finally, at the early age of twenty-six Madruzzo was raised to the see of Trent.

Handsome, tall, of elegant appearance, the young man charmed the Nuremberg jurist Christopher Scheurl, with whom he lodged in 1540 while on his way to the imperial court in Flanders, no less than the ladies of that imperial city. His pale, only very slightly coloured countenance and his small eyes created an impression of mysteriousness. His modest demeanour was not due to embarrassment; it actually went with a ready wit. Scheurl was immensely gratified by the opportunity of parading his knowledge of Italian before such a man and the large suite that accompanied him.[2]

The young man thus described by Scheurl also meets us in the portrait, now in New York, dating from the year 1542 and ascribed to Titian.[3] At that time he was about to exchange the neat, black dress

[1] Madruzzo, too, has not found a modern biographer. There is valuable material in B. Bonelli, *Notizie istorico-critiche della Chiesa di Trento*, VOL. III, pp. 399-448; VOL. IV, pp. 195-211. For the period up to 1515, see C. de Giuliani, "Cristoforo Madruzzo", in *Archivio trentino*, xx (1905), pp. 52-88. Codices 2914-2917 of the Giuliani Collection now preserved in the Biblioteca Communale of Trent, with notes on books, pictures and drawings, might be useful for a full-length biography such as that planned by Giuliani. For the correspondence, formerly kept at Innsbruck and now in the State Archives of Trent, see A. Galante, *La corrispondenza del Card. Madruzzo nell' Archivio di Innsbruck* (Innsbruck 1911), and *Miscellanea Attilio Hortis*, VOL. II (Trieste 1910), pp. 787-805. Out of the rich printed and MS material at my disposal I have only selected such information as appears important for the portrayal of Madruzzo's personality.

[2] Scheurl to Johann Eck, 13 February 1540, *Briefbuch*, VOL. II, p. 236.

[3] When one compares the New York portrait (frequently reproduced, e.g. by Fogolari, *Trento*, p. 137) with the medal struck in 1546 (*ibid.*, p. 139), one asks oneself how it was possible that four years should have worked so marked a change in a man. The fleshy face, framed by a beard, is that of a man of fifty rather than that of one of thirty.

that became him so well for the purple of a cardinal. At the consistory of 2 June 1542 he was created a cardinal in *petto*. He was informed of his nomination but was made to give a written assurance that he would not style himself a cardinal until the publication,[1] which only took place on 7 January 1545, shortly after his friend Truchsess, who in the meantime had become Bishop of Augsburg, had also received the red hat. Since 11 December 1542 Madruzzo was likewise Bishop of Brixen. Honours rained upon this spoilt child of fortune. But, we may well ask, was the youthful cardinal-bishop and territorial prince equal to the historic mission that devolved on him?

Fate seemed indeed to have destined him for the role of an intermediary between the two highest authorities, the Papacy and the Empire. Born on the dividing line of two cultures and as a bishop and territorial lord placed over Italians and Germans, he had something in common with both races. German was his mother tongue. "As a child", he declared at the Council, "I learnt the Lord's Prayer, the Creed and other pieces that are usually committed to memory, in our German tongue." [2] There can be no doubt that he learnt them from his mother Euphemia, for whom he cherished a filial veneration and whom he frequently visited. "Since I am a German", he once told Massarelli,[3] "I am able to treat with the German princes as one of them in their own tongue, not as a foreigner." Italian was the language of his choice. His studies at Padua and Bologna, the friendships there contracted, the almost exclusively Italian society that surrounded him at Trent, the superior culture of the Renaissance and its humanism combined to attach him to Italy. At a later period Ippolito Capilupi fostered the aging cardinal's secret aspirations to the tiara, though not without subtle irony, by reminding him that after all he was an Italian, not a German.[4]

By reason of his position as an imperial bishop and his family connexions his place was naturally in the imperial camp. His father, Gaudenzio, was governor of the sons of Ferdinand I, and his brothers Niccolò, the future *custos* of the Council, and Aliprando who died in

---

[1] Sfondrato's report of 10 December 1543, *N.B.*, VOL. I, PT vii, p. 491.

[2] *C.T.*, VOL. I, p. 37. For Euphemia, see the remark in *C.T.*, VOL. I, p. 497. In 1532 at Bologna, Madruzzo registered with the proctor of the German nation, Martin von Neydeck, the future Archdeacon of Trent. In 1534 Cristoforo acted himself as proctor, C. Malagola–E. Friedländer, *Acta nationis Germanicae universitatis Bononiensis* (Berlin 1887), pp. 303, 308; G. C. Knod, *Deutsche Studenten in Bologna* (Berlin 1899), No. 2225 (p. 325).

[3] *C.T.*, VOL. I, p. 251. On another occasion Massarelli speaks of the "favori todeschi" shown him by the cardinal, *C.T.*, VOL. I, p. 364.

[4] Capilupi to Ercole Gonzaga, 28 February 1560, St. Arch., Mantua, Busta 1933 or.

1547 at the early age of twenty-five, were officers in the service of the Emperor. Truchsess was his best friend. He was likewise on excellent terms with the Dukes of Bavaria, the Bishop of Eichstätt and other imperial princes. His attendance at the imperial Diets helped to widen the circle of his friends. Even the Elector Maurice of Saxony had recourse to him and used him as an intermediary with Rome.[1] And he was a cardinal! He attached great importance to his being regarded as a friend of the house of Farnese,[2] and his Italian friendships were more numerous than his German ones.

It had been the dream of Madruzzo's youth to restore, in the capacity of papal legate in Germany, harmony between the two heads and, if possible, to pave the way for the return of those who had seceded from the Church. On no less than three occasions within the space of a few months he proposed himself to Massarelli for the post of legate.[3] He failed to measure the width of the breach and was unaware of his own limitations. Paul III was too sound a judge of men to employ him on missions of high politics; he even denied him the coveted dignity of legate at the Council. Charles V did not entrust the leadership of his party to him, but rather to the astute Pacheco, and when he did send him to Rome as a mediator in the desperate situation which arose towards the close of 1547, the issue of the mission only confirmed the Emperor's earlier opinion of the man.

Like Cles, Madruzzo was actuated by a burning ambition, but an ambition as devoid of greatness as it was free of any sinister feature—in fact, he displayed this weakness in so uninhibited and naive a fashion as to make it look almost like childish vanity at which one could afford to smile. He completely lacked the statesmanship, the cool shrewdness and the resourceful astuteness by which his predecessor had risen to greatness and his political naivety was at times astonishing.[4] As a matter of fact, he aimed neither at power nor at actual achievement;

---

[1] A. von Druffel, *Beiträge zur Reichsgeschichte 1546-1551* (Munich 1873), VOL. I, Nos. 116, 348; letters of Madruzzo to Christoph von Carlowitz, *ibid.*, Nos. 431, 527; for Gaudenzio, *N.B.*, VOL. I, PT iii, p. 208.

[2] In 1540 Tommaso Campeggio describes him to Cardinal Farnese as a "gran servitore suo", *N.B.*, VOL. I, PT vi, p. 16; at a later date when Madruzzo made no secret of his criticism of Paul III's nepotism (e.g. *C.T.*, VOL. I, p. 313, and still later, when he condemned the nomination of the astrologer Gauricus to a bishopric, *ibid.*, p. 362), and when on the other hand the Pope became increasingly estranged from the Emperor, some very unfavourable remarks were passed on Madruzzo at Rome, *C.T.*, VOL. X, p. 903 f.   [3] *C.T.*, VOL. I, pp. 251, 308, 363.

[4] How was it possible for Madruzzo to imagine that Paul III would ever transfer the Council to central Germany? *C.T.*, VOL. I, pp. 271 f., 288, 297, 372. What would have happened if the legates had acted on his advice to keep the French bishops at Trent by force?

what he desired was honours, titles, revenues. It was his ambition either to become Elector of Mainz or Trier, or to obtain the wealthy archdiocese of Salzburg.[1] He was immensely gratified when in July 1548 he was invited to officiate at the magnificent wedding at Genoa of Maximilian II and empowered to exercise authority in the duchy of Milan as Philip II's governor,[2] but neither the viceroyalty of Naples nor the dignity of protector of the German and Spanish nations came his way. When he finally settled in Rome in 1560, the magnificence of his establishment—it was said that his monthly expenditure amounted to 2000 scudi—roused the envy of Truchsess, a prelate for ever in debt, and the displeasure of Pope Pius IV.[3] The latter made him legate of the Marches, but any real influence on the policy of the Curia he gained neither under that Pope nor under his successors. In spite of all his striving he proved unequal to the role of a political-ecclesiastical mediator for which he seemed predestined. He was neither a Morone nor a Contarini. Of the sincerity of his personal piety there can be no question. Nor can there be any doubt that he was pained by the lack of understanding of the German character and of the religious background of the German reformation shown by many Italian prelates and that he sought contact and friendship with the more enlightened among them. Cardinals Gonzaga, Sadoleto, Morone and Pole were friends of his: Nacchianti was his guest. The latter—as well as Carnesecchi—found in him an advocate when they stood their trial before the Inquisition.[4] He lacked a theological training of any depth

[1] *C.T.*, VOL. I, pp. 301, 303; on his aspirations to Salzburg, see G. Wolf in *Beiträge zur bayrischen Kirchengeschichte*, VI (1900), pp. 194 ff.

[2] This is not to deny that Madruzzo enjoyed the personal confidence of Ferdinand I and Philip II. In the conclaves of the fifteen-fifties he was charged with the interests of the Habsburgs; cf. Ferdinand's letters to Madruzzo in *Studien und Mitteilungen aus dem Benediktiner und Cisterzienser Orden*, v (1884), i, pp. 199 ff., 473 ff.; ii, pp. 457 ff.; Druffel, *Beiträge*, VOL. IV, No. 679, quotes a declaration of confidence by Philip II. It was due to this Habsburg orientation that the Venetians regarded him and his brother Niccolò, as well as the other "semi-Italians"—Arco, Lodron and others—as enemies of the Republic, Albèri, *Relazioni*, VOL. I, i, p. 464.

[3] A. Steichele in *Archiv für Geschichte des Bistums Augsburg*, II (1859), pp. 150, 155, 157, gives all the letters of Cardinal Truchsess to Duke Albrecht of Bavaria. Pius IV took Madruzzo to task because "il modo del vivere suo haveva più del temporale che del spirituale" and for running into debt, Capilupi to the Camerlengo, 21 September 1562, St. Arch., Florence, Med. 3727, fol. 406ᵛ or.

[4] His close relations with Ercole Gonzaga are attested by numerous letters in the St Arch., Mantua. This was yet another reason why Madruzzo incurred the displeasure of the Farnesi; cf. two letters of Sadoleto in Bonelli, *Notizie istorico-critiche, della Chiesa di Trento*, VOL. III, pp. 441-4; *ibid.*, a letter from Pole, VOL. IV, p. 198 f. For his relations with Nacchianti, see Buschbell, *Reformation und Inquisition in Italien*, pp. 156 ff. Letters of recommendation for Carnesecchi, dated 11 April 1558, in *Z.K.G.*, v (1882), p. 612 f.

and was accordingly betrayed into more than one false step. The Augustinian Nicholas of Verona, who enjoyed his favour for a time, was a Lutheran at heart and Vergerio's apostasy got his patron into a most awkward situation.[1] By advocating the translation of the Bible into the vernacular and by his attitude in the debate on justification at the Council he came under suspicion of being the head of the German party, that is, the party that favoured Luther.[2]

The suspicion was unjustified. Madruzzo's Catholic sentiments were no more open to doubt than those of his predecessor. As a bishop he frequently held pontifical functions in person, a thing his colleagues in Germany did but seldom, and during the greater part of his reign he dispensed with the assistance of an auxiliary.[3] Isidoro Chiari regarded him as a supporter of those members of the Council who were in earnest about reform.[4] For all that he cannot be described as a "bishop of the Catholic reform". Salmeron succeeded in interesting him in the establishment of a Jesuit College either at Trent or at Brixen, but he lacked the necessary perseverance for the execution of the plan.[5] He stands on the watershed of two streams, on the frontier of the old and the new age between which we moderns seek to draw a dividing line but which in actual fact interpenetrate like light and darkness.

As a lover of letters and a patron of the *literati* Madruzzo harvested many a literary dedication[6] and many a eulogy.[7] He was a keen collector of antiquities[8]; he even thought of founding a university at

[1] Jedin, *Seripando*, VOL. I, p. 264 f.: Eng. edn., p. 221; *ibid.*, p. 268: Eng. edn., p. 225, for Andrea da Volterra. For Madruzzo's attitude in the proceedings against Vergerio, see Buschbell, *Reformation und Inquisition in Italien*, pp. 110 ff., 288.

[2] Grechetto to Santa Fiora, 31 August 1546; Buschbell, *Reformation und Inquisition in Italien*, p. 256 f.

[3] S. Weber, *I Vescovi suffraganei della Chiesa di Trento* (Trent 1932), pp. 103-15; the attempt to get the conventual Diruta appointed an auxiliary bishop proved unsuccessful, *C.T.*, VOL. I, pp. 213, 362 f., 543.

[4] Chiari to Madruzzo, 10 June 1546; Bonelli, *Notizie istorico-critiche della Chiesa di Trento*, VOL. III, p. 408 f.

[5] J. A. de Polanco, *Chronicon Societatis Jesu*, VOL. II (Madrid 1894), p. 469; M.H.S.J., *Lainii Monumenta* (Madrid 1912-17), VOL. I, pp. 206 ff.; *ibid.*, VOL. VII, p. 109, Lainez's significant remark about Madruzzo, "se contenta de dar buenas palabres".

[6] List of dedications in Bonelli, *Notizie istorico-critiche della Chiesa di Trento*, VOL. IV, p. 203 f.: Trent, Biblioteca Communale, Cod. 2917. On the Augustinian Nicholas Scultellius, who enjoyed Madruzzo's favour, and his studies on Plato, cf. Jedin, *Seripando*, VOL. I, pp. 82 ff.: Eng. edn., p. 58 f.

[7] Collection of poems, among them one by Niccolò d'Arco, in Bonelli, *Notizie istorico-critiche della Chiesa di Trento*, VOL. III, pp. 424-31. Leonardo Colombino's *Trionfo tridentino* composed for 3 May 1547, in A. Galante, *Il Concilio di Trento* (Trent 1908), pp. 49-62.

[8] *C.T.*, VOL. I, p. 289.

Trent.[1] However, these varied interests were not backed by solid and deep scholarship. They produced nothing permanent; music alone seems to have affected him deeply.[2] With their violins, lutes and harps an orchestra directed by Giovanni Contini of Brescia used to contribute to the gaiety and splendour of the entertainments which, as a lover of company, he gave in the magnificent rooms of his castle. He found healing in music when sickness or failure lay heavy on him. At the princely wedding-feast at Genoa his singers distinguished themselves above all others.

Cristoforo Madruzzo is no outstanding figure of history. The many pleasing characteristics which made him so popular with his contemporaries would not have secured for him a place in history had he not played the role of host to the Council of Trent. He seemed to have been made for that task; in fact, it was a good thing that during the Council the See of Trent was not occupied by so forceful a personality as Cardinal Cles, for in that case the imperial pressure which could not but be felt during the first two periods would have been increased to a dangerous degree.

Madruzzo welcomed the Council to his episcopal city without any kind of previous bargaining with the Pope, as was done at the earlier Councils.[3] Whatever he did to ensure the smooth running of the assembly and for the welfare of its members was done spontaneously and out of sheer good-will. The legates and the conciliar commissary Sanfelice, who more than anyone else might have had cause to complain, never tired of extolling his solicitude and his willingness to be of service.[4] He was happy in the role of a princely host and, we must grant him this much, his hospitality was on a truly magnificent scale.

When Sanfelice was entertained by him in 1542 for the first time he expressed his astonishment at the combination of German lavishness with Italian refinement and courtesy that met him.[5] The banquet

---

[1] G. B. Trener, "Notizie sul progetto del Cardinale Madruzzo di erigere in Trento un ginnasio et uno studio generale 1552-53", in *Tridentum*, III (1900)—also separate publication; S. Weber, "La cattedra di giurisprudenza a Trento", in *Studi trentini*, XXIII (1942), pp. 137-54.

[2] M. Levri, "La Cappella musicale del Madruzzo e i cantori del Concilio", in *Il Concilio di Trento*, II (1943), pp. 393-405.

[3] The 27 *Capitula et conventiones* which Martin V concluded in 1423 with the city of Siena, in view of the proposed Council, in John of Ragusa, *Mon. con. gen.*, VOL. I, pp. 14-20. For the Basle agreement, cf. Wackernagel, *Geschichte der Stadt Basel*, VOL. I, pp. 484 ff.

[4] E.g. *C.T.*, VOL. IV, p. 252; *ibid.*, VOL. X, p. 476.

[5] "Mi dette un desinare non meno ricco d'abbondanza todesca che servito di politia italiana", *C.T.*, VOL. IV, p. 253.

which Madruzzo gave in honour of the legates on Easter Tuesday 1545 lasted three whole hours and no fewer than seventy-four dishes were served.[1] Princely personages who happened to pass through Trent, such as Cardinal Alessandro Farnese and the youthful Emmanuel Philibert of Savoy, were splendidly entertained even in his absence. Massarelli never ceased wondering at the sumptuous luncheons to which he and his colleagues were treated by the Cardinal's secretaries and his steward.[2] Hardly a week went by without his sending some present to the house of the legates. One day it would be a huge sixty-pound sturgeon, another day some magnificent melons and artichokes, partridges and quails. On one occasion he treated Cervini to a hundred-year-old Valtellina wine.[3] There were times when the stern legate felt compelled to apply the brake lest it should be said in Rome that the legates' only occupation at Trent was to attend banquets.[4] When on the occasion of the celebration of a wedding at the bishop's residence Madruzzo went so far as to induce the bishops present to join in the bridal quadrille, according to local custom, the legate was grievously shocked.[5]

That promoter of Catholic reform could not reconcile himself to the fact that Castel Buonconsiglio was not only a bishop's residence but likewise a prince's palace, while Madruzzo delighted in stressing his princely rank and in displaying it in his outward appearance. He usually wore the red velvet dress of a prince, and only the scarlet biretta betrayed the fact that he was a cardinal of the Roman Church.[6]

Notwithstanding his declaration that for the duration of the Council he did not regard himself as the ruler of the city, but that the legates were its masters, in spite also of his instructions to his officials that they were to obey their commands as if they were his own,[7] he was ever mindful of his responsibility. Thus he solved single-handed and at his own expense the problem of the conciliar guard which had

[1] *C.T.*, VOL. I, p. 170 f.; cf. *ibid.*, pp. 179, 202, 316. In view of this extravagance Giovio called him "gran Lucullo", *C.T.*, VOL. X, p. 216, l. 40.

[2] *C.T.*, VOL. I, pp. 206, 224, 228 and *passim*.

[3] *C.T.*, VOL. I, pp. 175, 210, 290, 328. He even paid for the mourning apparel made for the Farnesi at Trent, *C.T.*, VOL. X, p. 125.

[4] *C.T.*, VOL. I, p. 316; cf. p. 210.

[5] *C.T.*, VOL. I, p. 507; Vergerio's letter of 5 March 1546 to Gonzaga gives further details, St. Arch., Mantua, Busta 1915 or.

[6] *C.T.*, VOL. I, pp. 159, 168. The incident with Cardinal Del Monte, when Madruzzo strongly asserted his princely rank, will be recounted in Vol. II.

[7] *C.T.*, VOL. I, p. 271; *ibid.*, VOL. X, p. 145. Thus it came about that, e.g. Madruzzo's vicar received direct orders from the legates, *ibid.*, VOL. I, p. 351.

wrecked the Mantuan convocation.[1] In addition to all this he did everything in his power to make the prelates' stay at Trent as pleasant as possible. Not only the episcopal castle, but the Palazzo delle Albere which he had erected on the banks of the Adige, south of the city, with its magnificent gardens, as well as his villa at the entrance of the defile of Fersina were at all times open to them. He had good reason therefore to resent the complaints of the everlasting grumblers who had not a good word to say for the city of Trent and its inhabitants: "They should be made to feel how they would fare at Augsburg, Nuremberg or Ratisbon!" he once observed to Massarelli.[2] It must have been a matter for profound satisfaction to him when, after the translation of the Council to Bologna, the echo of a sigh reached him from that far bigger and wealthier city: "Ah! if only we were sitting by the flesh pots of Trent!"[3]

The grand scale on which Madruzzo practised hospitality brought him to the verge of ruin. While the Council enriched the citizens of Trent, it impoverished its bishop. His income was considerably reduced by the fact that he now missed the taxes levied at Trent, Klausen and Brixen on the wine formerly exported to Germany. Expenditure kept rising, not only because of the sums spent on hospitality, but also on account of indispensable security measures.[4] As early as August 1546 he saw himself compelled to request Cardinal Gonzaga for the loan of 4000 scudi.[5] The legates, at his request, suggested to the Pope that the pontiff should pay the cardinal a sum of 10,000 scudi by way of indemnity.[6] We do not know whether that sum was ever paid; it was only after Cardinal Del Monte had become Pope that he paid him 20,000 scudi, that is, double the sum Madruzzo had suggested. To this sum Cervini, as Pope Marcellus II, added a further 10,000 scudi, probably in view of the second session of the Council, which had taken place in the meantime, as well as by way of consoling

---

[1] As long as the Pope's personal appearance had to be reckoned with, the enlisting of a considerable force from the men of the district had to be kept in mind. If he did not come to Trent, Madruzzo thought at first that some 200 or 300 men would be required (*C.T.*, VOL. IV, p. 253), but subsequently he was satisfied with 150, *ibid.*, VOL. X, p. 32. It would seem that even this number was not reached, for the additional expenditure amounted to no more than 100 scudi a month (*ibid.*, p. 439); Niccolò Madruzzo, as guardian of the Council, was the commander of the force.

[2] *C.T.*, VOL. I, pp. 218, 271; *ibid.*, VOL. X, p. 145 f.

[3] J. P. Ferretti to Madruzzo, 5 April 1547, Bonelli, *Notizie istorico-critiche della Chiesa di Trento*, VOL. III, p. 417.

[4] *C.T.*, VOL. X, pp. 145 f., 438.

[5] Madruzzo to Gonzaga, 24 August 1546, St. Arch., Mantua, Busta 1915 or.

[6] *C.T.*, VOL. X, p. 552 (6 July 1546); cf. pp. 32, 395 f., 421 f.

Madruzzo for the denial of the legation of the Romagna which the cardinal had vainly sought to obtain.[1]

During the last period of the Council Madruzzo handed over the duties of hospitality at Trent to his nephew Ludovico, who had also been raised to the purple by Pius IV on 26 February 1561. In 1567 he resigned the See of Trent in Ludovico's favour when he himself was promoted to the suburbicarian See of Porto. He died on his sixty-sixth birthday, 5 July 1578, while a guest of Cardinal d'Este at the latter's villa at Tivoli. By that date the Council of Trent had become a historical fact. Though it had failed to bring about the return of the dissidents it had strengthened Catholicism and the Papacy to a degree which Madruzzo could not have foreseen. More in keeping with his temperament was the new culture which was even then taking shape in that courtly baroque age. The Cardinal found his last resting-place at a spot of surpassing beauty. His tomb is in the little church of S. Onufrio on the Gianicolo, in the Madruzzo chapel erected by his nephew, and facing the grave of the courtly poet Torquato Tasso.

The hands of the clock which Madruzzo had put up on the wall of his old episcopal residence next to the cathedral were pointing to the first hour of the day—about 9.30 by our reckoning—as the members of the Council assembled in the church of the Most Holy Trinity for the opening procession.[2] The day was 13 December 1545. The cardinals put on their vestments—mitres of white damask and copes of red material embroidered with gold thread which had arrived from Venice on the previous evening. The bishops wore linen mitres and copes of plainer material. The cathedral chaplain Domenico intoned

---

[1] Pastor, VOL. VI, pp. 41, 349; Eng. edn., VOL. XIV, p. 46.

[2] The description of the opening session is based on the following documents: the notaries' instrument included in the acts of the Council, C.T., VOL. IV, pp. 515-32; the description in C.T., VOL. I, pp. 402 ff., omitted in Massarelli's *Diarium*, VOL. I, but transmitted independently. The latter account should be checked by that of Severoli, C.T., VOL. I, p. 4 f., and Prée, C.T., VOL. II, p. 368 f., who is inaccurate here and there, as when he says that besides the two Bulls Campeggio also read the Brief of Inauguration. The legates' reports of 13 and 14 December, C.T., VOL. X, pp. 274-8, give only a summary account of the proceedings. There is a description of the ceremonies in a pamphlet entitled "Was für ordnung unnd Cerimonien des Bapst Legation Cardinele und Bischoffe zu Trient versamlet in der eroffnung des Concilii doselbst gebraucht und gehalten haben", 4°, 6 leaves, without place and date, with Paul III's arms on the title-page. There is a copy at Vienna, St. Arch., Religions-akten 13, with the rubric: "Famos libell Trientisch Concilium anno 1545 betreff"; cf. also J. Hortleder, *Handlungen und Ausschreiben von den Ursachen des deutschen Krieges*, VOL. I (Gotha 1645), pp. 606 ff. Strangely enough the pamphlet, which derives from an Italian source, puts the conclusion of the session at three o'clock in the afternoon.

the hymn *Veni Creator Spiritus*. The second strophe was taken up by all the clergy and the procession got under way. First came the secular and regular clergy of the city and the cathedral chapter; after them came the prelates of the Council and the envoys of King Ferdinand I, followed by the nobility and a great crowd of people from the city and the neighbourhood who had come to witness the great event.

In the cathedral the spacious chancel above the crypt of St Vigilius, at the entrance of which the high altar stood at that time, had been arranged as a council hall. It formed a square, the side facing the nave being boarded off by a wooden partition. At the east end stood an altar above which was suspended a magnificent Flemish tapestry representing the resurrection of Christ. On the right of the altar were the red velvet-covered seats reserved for the four cardinals and on the left the credence table with the requisites for Mass. On either side there were three rows of seats for the members of the Council. The benches on the left, that is the gospel side, were reserved for the prelates who took their places according to the date of their promotion. They included four archbishops representing four nations, viz. Aix, Palermo, Upsala and Armagh, and twenty-one bishops, all of them Italians, with the exception of two Spaniards, one Frenchman, one Englishman and one German. Last came the generals of the two branches of the Franciscan Order and those of the Hermits of St Augustine, the Carmelites and the Servites. Two prelates of the Curia had their places among these as they had no vote; they were the auditor of the Rota Pighino and the promoter of the Council Severoli.

When one bears in mind that, after counting out England, the Scandinavian countries and those German dioceses which had gone over to Lutheranism, the number of diocesan bishops considerably exceeded four hundred, and when one recalls the numbers present at the four General Councils of antiquity and at the medieval Councils,[1] the attendance was modest enough. For all that, if we remember the

---

[1] According to Hefele the number of those present at the Council of Nicea oscillates between 250 and 320 and for Chalcedon between 520 and 630. For the Council of Constantinople he puts the number at 186 (including the Macedonians) and at 200 for Ephesus. At the third Lateran Council, according to Tangl, *Die Teilnehmer an den allgemeinen Konzilien des Mittelalters* (Weimar 1922), pp. 212 ff., there were roughly 300 prelates, while there were 404 at the fourth. According to Müller (*Das Konzil von Vienne*, Münster 1938, p. 69) there were 114 bishops at Vienne. However, these figures cover the whole period of these Councils, not the first day. At the opening of the Council of Constance Ulrich von Richental, *Chronik des Constanzer Concils* (ed. M. R. Buck, Stuttgart 1843), counted 23 cardinals, about 37 bishops and archbishops, besides the abbots and other prelates. At the opening of the fifth Council of the Lateran 83 prelates were present according to Paris de Grassis,

pitiful results of the two previous convocations of Mantua and Vicenza, it was a genuine success.

The imperial envoy Mendoza was detained at Venice by illness.[1] The two envoys of King Ferdinand I, the royal captain of Trent Francesco di Castelalto and the jurist Antonio Queta were the only diplomatists present. They sat on a bench placed across the upper end of the bishops' benches. The seats on the right—the epistle side— were occupied by the theologians, forty-two in number, all of them members of the mendicant Orders with the exception of four Spanish secular priests. Next to the Italians, the Spaniards were the most strongly represented: there were thirteen of them. There still remained a good deal of room, so members of the Trent nobility—even some ladies—successfully pushed their way into the chancel.

A conciliar session is not only a legal or canonical act; on the contrary, like the coronation of a Pope or a canonisation it partakes of the nature of a liturgical function. The liturgical setting is not something purely external, it is of its very essence for when a Council discharges its proper function, which is to define the Church's faith and discipline, it performs acts that appertain to the worship of the divine majesty. The ceremonial of the Roman Church in use at the time [2]

the master of the ceremonies (Döllinger, *Beiträge*, VOL. III, p. 417); at the next session—reckoned as the first—there were present 100 persons entitled to vote, cf. Acts in Mansi, VOL. XXXII, pp. 676 ff.

[1] That Mendoza did not sham illness appears from Della Casa's report to the legates, 17 November, Montepulciano, Bibl. Ricci 4, fol. 11ʳ: "Non ho potuto ben negotiar col Signor Don Diego, che S.S. è forte melancolico e sta ritirato per le sue quartane che le molestano assai."

[2] The *Ceremoniale Romanum* was observed at Trent, as has been pointed out by Ehses, *C.T.*, VOL. IV, p. 516, *n.*2, and by M. del Alamo, "Trento y la Liturgia", *El Concilio de Trento* (Madrid 1945), p. 305. Marginal notes in the manuscript Ceremonial, Vat. lat. 12349, fols. 89ʳ-94ʳ, seem to me to point to the fact that this manuscript was the very Ceremonial used at Trent since the one printed in 1516 by Cristoforo Marcello, which had been put together by Agostino Patrizio, was not regarded as authoritative. One point of the Ceremonial was not observed—Del Monte gave his short address not immediately after the gospel but before putting the question "Placetne?" On the other hand the *Pontificale Romanum* (ed. Catalani (1738), VOL. III, pp. 96 ff.) places the address otherwise, viz. after the *Veni Creator*. The use of the Ceremonial had already been recommended by Jacobazzi, *De concilio libri V*, art. 2 (pp. 260-3), by Ugoni, *Synodia* (Venice 1532), fols. 89ᵛ-90ʳ, and by Guidiccioni in his treatise on the Council written in 1536, Barb. lat. 1165, fols. 228ʳ- 229ᵛ. At the fifth Lateran Council there was at first some uncertainty as to whether the *Ceremoniale reformatum* or the *Libri antiqui*, that is, probably the *Pontificale Romanum*, should be drawn upon (cf. the master of the ceremonies' *questionnaire*, Vat. Arch., Concilio, 6, fols. 429ʳ-430ʳ, more especially questions 8 and 9; see also Raynald, *Annales, a.* 1512, No. 32). In the end it was decided to use the Ceremonial, though in the account in Mansi (VOL. XXXII, pp. 665 ff.) the *Veni Creator* was sung before the gospel *Designavit* was chanted.

contained a complete conciliar liturgy which had been observed at the fifth Council of the Lateran and, as far as we are able to ascertain, also at the reform Councils of the fifteenth century. The master of ceremonies, Pompeius de Spiritibus, was guided by the texts and rubrics laid down in that liturgy. The solemn function began with the Mass of the Holy Ghost, celebrated by the senior legate Del Monte, Cardinal-Bishop of Palestrina. At its conclusion he imparted to all present a plenary indulgence. This done, the Minorite Cornelio Musso, Bishop of Bitonto, entered the pulpit erected on the right of the entrance to the hall and delivered an oft-quoted and much discussed discourse the text of which was taken from the Introit of the Mass of that day: *Gaudete in Domino*.[1]

Starting with the joy at the opening of the Council which filled the hearts of all present, Musso expatiated on the blessings which the Catholic Church had derived from General Councils throughout the centuries. It was the task of the present Council to defend the faith and the sacraments, to restore charity among Christians, to eliminate from the body of the Church the poison of covetousness and ambition, and to ward off the "scourge of God", the Turks. It was meet and right that he should mention all those who had helped to bring about this gathering; first of all the Pope, then the Emperor, King Francis I, King Ferdinand, the King of Portugal. Nor did he forget to praise the three legates and the lord of the city, Madruzzo. He ended with a prayer for the synod. "Gathered as it is at the gate of the Empire, may it effect the reunion of Germany with the Roman Church. To the realisation of so high a purpose all must contribute—Latins and Greeks, Spaniards and Frenchmen, Germans and Italians, every one must give of his very best. May St Vigilius, the patron of the diocese of Trent, also watch over the Council until its successful conclusion, until it could be said of it: 'Great are the works of the Lord'." (Ps. cx, 2).

---

[1] For Musso's life (1511-74) and personality, see H. Jedin, "Der Franziskaner Cornelio Musso", in *R.Q.*, XLI (1933), pp. 207-75. G. Cantini, "Cornelio Musso dei Frati Minori Conventuali, Predicatore, Scrittore, e Teologo al Concilio di Trento", in *Miscellanea Franciscana*, XLI (1941), pp. 145-74, 424-63. Sarpi's unfair verdict on the sermon (*Istoria*, VOL. II, ii, ed. Gambarin, VOL. I, pp. 209 ff.) has been refuted by Pallavicino, VOL. v, p. 18, but it should be noted that as against Massarelli's and Severoli's reports about the deep impression made by the discourse there is the profound silence of Seripando, *C.T.*, VOL. I, p. 4, l. 40; p. 440, l. 8; VOL. II, p. 409. For a comprehensive judgment on Musso as an orator, see the literature compiled by myself (p. 253 f.) and by Cantini (pp. 170 ff.) as well as the observations of Ottaviano Lotti on his sermons in the year 1539, in *Bolletino Senese*, XV (1908), p. 46.

Cornelio Musso was one of the most popular pulpit orators of Italy. In his conciliar sermon he forgot no one and left out no topic worth mentioning. His familiarity with the text of Holy Scripture and his dexterity in the use of words fills us with astonishment. The modern reader of the sermon may get the impression that here there is too much of a good thing; that more than one parallel is rather forced. Such a reader should bear in mind that like every other sermon this one too was intended for a particular audience and that Musso's hearers were children of a humanistic age for whom the tricks of rhetoric were in their very blood. As a matter of fact the listeners were profoundly stirred by the spirited delivery of the sermon and many were actually moved to tears.

The Mass of the Holy Ghost and the sermon were only the preliminaries of the formal opening of the Council. The master of ceremonies first invited the assembly to pray in silence. After this Del Monte recited the collect of the Holy Ghost *Adsumus, Domine, Sancte Spiritus*—that prayer so full of doctrine and so profoundly moving.[1] After the choir had sung the antiphon *Exaudi nos, Domine* (Ps. LXVIII, 17), no doubt to a polyphonic setting, Del Monte recited yet another shorter prayer to invoke the assistance of the Holy Spirit. There followed the Litany of the Saints in which, after the invocation for the Pope, a thrice-repeated invocation for the Council was interpolated: *Ut hanc sanctam synodum et omnes gradus ecclesiasticos benedicere et regere digneris.* At each invocation the presiding legate made the sign of the cross over the assembly.

The chanting of the passage of the Gospel which recounts the mission of the disciples (Luke x, 1-9), and of the hymn *Veni Creator Spiritus* with its versicles and prayers finally led up to the act by which the Council was formally inaugurated. The Bishop of Feltre, in cope and mitre, entered the pulpit to read the Bull *Laetare Jerusalem* convoking the Council as well as the Bull accrediting the legates. This should have been followed by a formal statement by the president declaring the Council open. Instead of such a declaration there followed an incident which reminds us of the vitality, even then, of the

---

[1] The prayer "Adsumus" is missing in the *Pontificale* of Durandus, M. Andrieu, *Le Pontificale Romanum*, 4 Vols., Città del Vaticano 1938-41, VOL. III, pp. 596-602. It was not said at Vienne; Müller, *Das Konzil von Vienne*, pp. 673 ff. I am unable to state at what period it got into the *Pontificale Romanum* (ed. Catalani, VOL. III, p. 97) and into the Ceremonial. Jacobazzi bears witness to its use in the Segnatura and the Rota, *De concilio*, p. 262. L. Gomez, *Comment. in regulas cancellariae iudiciales* (Paris 1547), fol. 155ᵛ, shows that in his time it was no longer in use in the Segnatura.

medieval conception of a Council as the representation of the _corpus christianum._ In that view the Pope and the Emperor were the heads of Christendom. After the reading of the Bull accrediting the legates the credentials of the imperial representatives should have been read. But Mendoza was absent. In his place the Spanish theologian Alphonsus Zorilla advanced towards the seats of the legates and after apologising for the absence of the imperial ambassador in his own words, read a letter of excuse and finally presented the credentials to the president. Only then did Del Monte rise to point out in a few moving words the significance of the moment and to ask the assent of the Fathers of the Council to the opening of the assembly in the terms of the traditional formula: _placetne vobis . . . decernere et declarare sacrum Tridentinum et generale concilium incipere et inceptum esse?_ It was in this fashion too that it was decided that the next session would be held on 7 January 1546. The president then pronounced a blessing and the promoter of the Council Severoli charged the two notaries present, Claudius della Casa and Nicholas Driel, to draw up a legal instrument about the act of inauguration. The choir then intoned the _Te Deum._ Overcome with emotion, Madruzzo embraced the three legates and, with tears of joy in their eyes, the Fathers of the Council followed their example and embraced one another. It was two o'clock in the afternoon when the session came to an end.

"The door is now open," Seripando noted in his diary,[1] "the mouth is open that only utters unadulterated truth; the tribunal is set up which alone can examine and decide all controversies; it is for this purpose that the Council has been demanded and convoked." The General Council, longed for and prayed for, feared and delayed for more than a hundred years, had opened its doors. But before we begin to attend to what was said and done in this sacred drama it behoves us to cast a glance backward and to survey the road over which we have travelled.

The struggle for a Council had gone on for exactly twenty-five years. That it should have lasted so long was an "immense calamity"[2] for the Church. For a whole quarter of a century bishops and faithful in the countries affected by the religious schism had been waiting for a decisive pronouncement on an innovation which claimed to be the long-desired reform. "Only a general assembly of all the Christian estates,

---

[1] _C.T._, VOL. II, p. 409.
[2] Pastor, _Reunionsbestrebungen_, p. 121.

by favour of the Holy Spirit," the Bishop of Constance had told the
men of Zürich in 1523,[1] "would be able to pronounce a definitive
judgment on doctrinal differences of so fundamental a nature as those
propounded by Zwingli." Twenty years later the sisters of Heiligen-
grab in the March of Brandenburg only accepted Lutheran preachers
who were forced upon them with the reservation "until the convocation
of a General Council".[2] With this reservation "until the General
Council", numerous compromises had been agreed to which, though
many did not realise it, replaced the Catholic way of life by another.[3]
A confusion of ideas such as Catholics of today are scarcely able to
imagine made it possible for a generation reared in the Catholic faith
to die out and for another to grow up, fashioned by the teaching, the
worship, and the propaganda of Protestantism. The opening of the
Council came only just in time to preserve the Latin nations from a
similar calamity; for the northern ones it was too late.

It is not within the competence of the historian to speculate on the
course history would have taken if some particular event had not
occurred or if it had happened at some other period. For all that, no
one can prevent him from suggesting with due modesty which factors,
humanly speaking, would have been eliminated in such an eventuality
and which would have proved more effective. If the Council of Trent
had met in 1525 instead of 1545 it would only have been faced with a
heresy and a popular movement instigated by it. At the former date
Lutheran churches were not yet organised, the princes and towns who
had embraced the new faith did not as yet constitute a political power,
the mass of the people were still moulded by Catholic teaching and
piety. A conciliar condemnation of Luther's teaching would probably
have been accepted by the great majority of the German people and a
reform decreed by the Council might yet have prevailed over the
Lutheran one. Harnack's query whether the Reformation would have
developed as it did if the Tridentine decree on justification had been
promulgated by the fifth Lateran Council is not entirely gratuitous;
it is possible to doubt whether, in that event, we should have to witness
the present religious division of the West.

[1] *Eidgenössische Abschiede*, VOL. VI, 1 (*a*), p. 343 f. (17 October 1523), and the
representations of the Bishops of Constance, Basle and Lausanne at the Diet of
Lucerne, 1 April 1524, *ibid.*, p. 397.

[2] F. Curschmann in *Forschungen zur brandenburgisch-preussischen Geschichte*, xxv,
ii (1912), p. 68.

[3] Letter of the preacher Hausmann to Bishop John of Meissen, 28 October
1538, O. Clemen, *Georg Helts Briefwechsel* (Leipzig 1907), p. 118 f.; O. Redlich,
Jülich-bergische Kirchenpolitik, VOL. I, pp. 232 ff.

But events took a different turn. As a result of a calamitous concatenation of circumstances the Council became a mirage which invariably faded out before the eyes of those who had lost their way as often as they seemed to come up to it. In order to understand why the Council only materialised at so late a date it was necessary to go over the futile and unsuccessful efforts of a quarter of a century. Yet no one with a sense of history will presume to assert that what actually happened was bound to happen. The ideas which—as presented in these pages—determined the course of events, the various conceptions of the idea of a Council, the idea of reform as formulated by Catholic reformers and its Protestant counterfeit, the contradictory conceptions of justification and the nature of the Church—all these things were not necessitated by a natural law, they worked themselves out in and through free agents. Luther's appearance during the pontificate of Leo X, Clement VII's rejection of the proposed Council, the burial of the *corpus christianum* of the Middle Ages by Paul III and Charles V by a reversal of their respective roles, are contingent events. Contingency of events and freedom of the agents preclude every possibility of the latter evading responsibility before history. Our exposition did not presume to summon to judgment those who bear responsibility—either to condemn them or to absolve them. Our first step was to explain, to understand. This done, it was necessary to appraise, that is, to assess the conduct of men in the light of the historical mission allotted to them. For the appreciations thus arrived at we claim no absolute validity; no such claim can be made, for though based on a firm Catholic view of events all such estimates are none the less conditioned by the writer's personal conception of history. The stream of history flows on uninterruptedly. In another hundred years another historian of the Council of Trent will appraise many a personality and many an event otherwise than we do in our day. Lastly, the creative mind of God which so uses human error as to cause divine truth to shine forth more brightly, which obliterates, and compensates for, the failure of some by the holiness of others—this all-controlling mind which ordains all things to its own ends also constitutes the ultimate and true meaning of history while it remains a mystery which we may dimly sense but can only reverently adore.

Bibliography
and
Abbreviations

Bibliography and Abbreviations

Acta Comitiorum = Acta Comitiorum Augustae ex litteris Philippi, Jonae et aliorum ad Martinum Lutherum, ed. Berbig, Halle 1907.

Acta Conc. Const. = Acta Concilii Constantiensis, edd. Finke, Heimpel and Hollnsteiner, 4 Vols., Münster 1896-1928.

Acta Tomiciana = Epistole, legationes, responsa, actiones, res geste . . . Sigismundi, ejus nominis primi, regis Polonie . ., edd. Count A. T. Dzialynski and L. Koenigk, 9 Vols., Posen 1852-76.

A.F.P. = Archivum fratrum Praedicatorum, Berlin 1931 ff.

A.K.R. = Archiv für katholisches Kirchenrecht, 1857 ff.

Albèri E., *Relazioni = Relazioni degli ambasciatori Veneti al Senato durante il secolo XVI*, Series I-III, Florence 1839-55.

Ammanati, *see* Pius II.

A.R.G. = Archiv für Reformationsgeschichte, 1903 ff.

Bachmann A., *Reichsgeschichte = Deutsche Reichsgeschichte im Zeitalter Friedrichs III und Maximilians I*, 2 Vols., Leipzig 1884-94.

Balan P., *Monumenta = Monumenta reformationis Lutheranae ex tabulariis S. Sedis secretis*, Ratisbon, 1881-4.

——, *Mon. saec. XVI = Monumenta saeculi XVI historiam illustrantia*, Innsbruck 1885.

Baluze S.-Mansi J. D., *Miscellanea novo ordine digesta*, 4 Vols., Lucca 1761-4.

Bataillon M., *Erasme en Espagne*, Paris 1937.

Böcking E. (ed.), *Ulrici Hutteni opera*, 5 Vols., Leipzig 1859-62.

Bonelli B., *Notizie istorico-critiche della Chiesa di Trento*, VOLS. III and IV, Trent 1762, 1765.

Brandi K., *Berichte = Berichte und Studien zur Geschichte Karls V: Nachrichten der Gesellschaft der Wissenschaften zu Göttingen, philosophische-historische Klasse*, Berlin 1930 ff.

——, *Kaiser Karl V*, VOL. I, Munich 1937; Eng. edn., *The Emperor Charles V*, London 1939.

——, *Quellen = Quellen und Erörterungen*, Munich 1941.

Brieger Th., *Aleander und Luther*, Gotha 1884.

Bucholtz F. W. von, *Ferdinand I = Geschichte der Regierung Ferdinands I*, 9 Vols., Vienna 1831-8.

Bull. Rom. = Bullarium Romanum, VOLS. IV and V, Turin 1859-60.

Burchard of Strasbourg, *see* Celani *and* Thuasne.

585

Buschbell G., *Reformation und Inquisition in Italien*, Paderborn 1910.

Calenzio G., *Doc. ined.=Documenti inediti e nuovi lavori letterarii sul Concilio di Trento*, Rome 1874.

Cal. of Letters=Calendar of Letters, foreign and domestic, relating to the reign of Henry VIII, edd. J. S. Brewer, J. Gairdner etc., 21 Vols., London 1875 ff.

Cal. of St. Pap., *Spain=Calendar of Letters, Despatches and State Papers relating to the Negotiations between England and Spain*, ed. G. A. Bergenroth and (from VOL. v) P. G. Gayangos, VOLS. II-VIII, London 1862-1904.

Canestrini L., *Legazioni di Averardo Serristori*, Florence 1853.

Capasso C., *Paolo III*, 2 Vols., Messina 1924.

Cardauns L., *Bestrebungen=Zur Geschichte der kirchlichen Unions- und Reformbestrebungen, 1538-42*: Bibliothek des preussischen historischen Instituts in Rom, VOL. IX, Rome 1910.

——, *Nizza=Von Nizza bis Crépy:* Bibliothek des preussischen historischen Instituts in Rom, VOL. XV, Rome 1923.

——, "Paul III"="Paul III und Franz I in den Jahren 1535-36", in *Quellen und Forschungen aus italienischen Archiven und Bibliotheken*, XI (1908), pp. 147-244; XII (1909), pp. 181-211, 321-67.

Cardella L., *Memorie storiche de' Cardinali della S. Romana Chiesa*, VOL. IV, Rome 1793.

Castro J. de, *Portugal=Portugal no Concilio de Trento*, Lisbon 1944.

Celani L., *J. Burchardi Argent. Liber notarum*, 3 Vols., Città di Castello 1910 ff.

Célier L., *Dataires=Les Dataires du XVIe siècle*, Paris 1910.

Cerchiari E., *Sacra Romana Rota*, 4 Vols., Rome 1919-21.

Ciaconius-Oldoinus, *Vitae et res gestae Pontificum Romanorum et S.R.E. cardinalium*, VOL. III, Rome 1677.

Clemen O., *Flugschriften=Flugschriften aus den ersten Jahren der Reformation*, 4 Vols., Leipzig 1907-11.

Coll. doc. inéd.=Colleccion de documentos inéditos para la Historia de España, Madrid 1842 ff.

Combet J., *Louis XI=Louis XI et le Saint-Siège*, Paris 1903.

Conc. Bas.=Concilium Basiliense, edd. J. Haller, H. Herre and G. Beckmann, 8 Vols., Basle 1896-1936.

Constant G., *La Réforme en Angleterre*, VOL. I, Paris 1930; Eng. edn., *The Reformation in England*, London 1934.

Corpus Catholicorum. Werke katholischer Schriftsteller im Zeitalter der Glaubensspaltung, Münster 1919 ff.

Corp. Ref.=Corpus Reformatorum, Halle 1834.

Crabbe P., *Conc. omnia=Concilia omnia tam generalia quam particularia ab apostolorum temporibus in hunc usque diem a sanctissimis patribus celebrata*, Cologne 1538.

C.T.=Concilium Tridentinum: Diariorum, actorum, epistolarum, tractatuum nova collectio, ed. Görres-Gesellschaft, Freiburg 1901 ff.

Desjardins A., *Négociations diplomatiques de la France avec la Toscane*, 3 Vols., Paris 1859-75.

Dittrich F., *Gasparo Contarini*, Braunsberg 1885.

——, *Regesten=Regesten und Briefe des Kardinals Gasparo Contarini*, Braunsberg 1881.

Döllinger J. J. I., *Beiträge=Beiträge zur politischen, kirchlichen und Kulturgeschichte der sechs letzten Jahrhunderte*, 3 Vols., Munich 1862-82.

Druffel A. von, *Beiträge=Beiträge zur Reichsgeschichte*, VOLS. I-III, Munich 1873-82.

——, *Karl V und die römische Kurie*, 4 parts, Munich 1877-91.

D.Th.C.=Dictionnaire de théologie Catholique, Paris 1909 ff.

Dupin L. E. (ed.), *Gersoni opera*, 5 Vols., Antwerp 1706.

Duplessis d'Argentré Ch., *Coll. iud.=Collectio iudiciorum de novis erroribus*, 3 Vols., Paris 1724 ff.

Eckermann K., *Studien=Studien zur Geschichte des monarchischen Gedankens im 15. Jahrhundert*, Berlin-Grünewald 1933.

Eidgenössische Abschiede, Lucerne 1839 ff.

Erasmus, *Epist.=Opus Epistolarum Desiderii Erasmi Roterodami*, ed. P. S. Allen, 11 Vols., Oxford 1906-47.

Eubel K.-Gulik W. van, *Hierarchia catholica medii aevi*, VOL. III, Münster 1910; 2nd edn. ed. L. Schmitz-Kallenberg, 1923.

Evagatorium=Fratris Felicis Evagatorium, ed. C. D. Hassler, VOL. I, Stuttgart 1843.

Feret P., *La Faculté de théologie de Paris et ses docteurs les plus célèbres. Epoque moderne*, 7 Vols., Paris 1900-10.

Ferrandis M.- Bordonau M., *El Concilio de Trento*, VOL. I., Valladolid 1928.

Förstemann C. E., *Neues Urkundenbuch zur Geschichte der evangelischen Kirchenreformation*, Hamburg 1842.

Fredericq P., *Corpus Inquis.=Corpus Inquisitionis Neerlandicae*, Ghent 1927.

Freher M.-Struve B. G., *Germ. rerum script.=Germanicarum rerum scriptores*, 3 parts, Strasbourg 1717.

Gebhardt B., *Gravamina=Die Gravamina der deutschen Nation*, 2nd edn., Breslau 1895.

Gerson, *see* Dupin.

Gess F., *Akten und Briefe=Akten und Briefe zur Kirchenpolitik Herzog Georgs von Sachsen*, 2 Vols., Leipzig 1905-17.

Giberti, *Opera*, ed. Ballerini, Verona 1733.

Giovio, *Hist.=Historia sui temporis*, Venice 1553.

Goldast M., *Monarchia=Monarchia Romani Imperii*, 3 Vols., Hanover-Frankfurt 1611-13.

Göller E., *Die päpstliche Pönitentiarie*, 2 Vols. in 4 parts, Rome 1907-11.

Grisar H., *Luther*, 3 Vols., 8th edn. Freiburg 1925: Eng. edn., 6 Vols., London 1913-17.

Gussmann W., *Quellen und Forsch.=Quellen und Forschungen zur Geschichte des Augsburger Glaubensbekenntnisses*, 2 Vols., Leipzig 1911, Kassel 1930.

Hain L.,*=Repertorium bibliographicum*, 4 Vols., Stuttgart-Paris 1826-38.

Haller J., *Anfänge=Die Anfänge der Universität Tübingen*, Stuttgart 1927.

——, *Papsttum und Kirchenreform*, VOL. I, Berlin 1903.

——, *Piero da Monte*, Rome 1941.

Hardt H. von, *Conc. Const.=Magnum oecumenicum Constantiense concilium*, 6 Vols., Frankfurt-Leipzig 1697-1700.

Hefele C. J. von, *Conziliengeschichte* (VOLS. VIII and IX by J. Hergenröther), 9 Vols., 2nd edn. Freiburg 1873-90; Eng. edn., Edinburgh 1872-96, incomplete.

Heine G., *Briefe=Briefe an Karl V, geschrieben von seinem Beichtvater Loaysa in den Jahren 1530-32*, Berlin 1848.

H.J.=Historisches Jahrbuch der Görres-Gesellschaft, 1880 ff.

Hofmann K., *Die Konzilsfrage auf den deutschen Reichstagen von 1521 bis 1524*, Theological dissertation, Heidelberg 1932.

Hofmann W. von, *Forschungen=Forschungen zur Geschichte der kurialen Behörden*, 2 Vols., Rome 1914.

Horawitz A.-Hartfelder K., *Briefwechsel des Beatus Rhenanus*, Leipzig 1886.

Hottinger J. H., *Historia ecclesiastica Novi Testamenti*, 9 Vols., Zurich 1651-7.

Hübler B., *Constanzer Reformation=Die Constanzer Reformation und die Konkordate von 1418*, Leipzig 1867.

Hurter F., *Nomenclator=Nomenclator litterarius theologiae catholicae*, 6 Vols., Innsbruck 1903-13.

H. Z.=Historische Zeitschrift, 1859 ff.

Imbart de la Tour P., *Origines=Les Origines de la Réforme*, VOLS. I-III, Paris 1905-14; VOL. II, 2nd edn. Melun 1944.

Janssen J., *Geschichte des deutschen Volkes seit dem Ausgang des Mittelalters*, VOLS. I-III, 19th and 20th edns. Freiburg 1913-17; Eng. edn., London 1896-1925.

Jedin H., *Seripando=Girolamo Seripando*, 2 Vols., Würzburg 1937: Eng. edn., St Louis, U.S.A., and London 1947.

——, *Der Quellenapparat der Konzilsgeschichte Pallavicinos*, Rome 1940.

Kalkoff P., *Aleander gegen Luther*, Leipzig-New York 1908.

——, *Forschungen zu Luthers römischen Prozess*, Rome 1905.

Katterbach B., *Referendarii=Refendarii utriusque signaturae*, Vatican City 1931.

Kaulek J., *Corresp. pol.=Correspondance politique de Castillon et de Marillac*, Paris 1885.

Labbé P.-Cossart G., *Sacrosancta Concilia*, 16 Vols., Paris 1671-2.

Laemmer, H., *Mantissa=Meletematum Romanorum mantissa*, Ratisbon 1875.

——, *Mon. Vat.=Monumenta Vaticana historiam ecclesiasticam saeculi XVI illustrantia*, Freiburg 1861.

Lanz K., *Correspondenz=Correspondenz des Kaisers Karl V*, 3 Vols., Leipzig 1844-6.

——, *Staatspapiere=Staatspapiere zur Geschichte Kaiser Karls V*, 3 Vols., Stuttgart 1845.

Lauchert F., *Literarische Gegner=Die italienischen literarischen Gegner Luthers*, Freiburg 1912.

Lenz M., *Briefwechsel=Briefwechsel Landgraf Philipps von Hessen mit Bucer*, 3 Vols., Leipzig 1880-91.

Le Plat J.,=*Monumentorum ad historiam Concilii Tridentini potissimum illustrandam spectantium amplissima collectio*, 7 Vols., Louvain 1781-7.

Lettere di principi, 3 Vols., Venice 1570-7.

Lortz J., *Die Reformation in Deutschland*, 2 Vols., 2nd edn. Freiburg 1941.

L.Th.K.=Lexikon für Theologie und Kirche, ed. M. Buchberger, 10 Vols., Freiburg 1930-8.

Lünig J. Ch., *Deutsches Reichsarchiv*, 24 Vols., Leipzig 1710-22.

L.W.=Martin Luthers Werke. Kritische Gesamtausgabe, Weimar 1883 ff.

Mansi J. D.=*Sacrorum conciliorum nova et amplissima collectio*, 31 Vols., Florence-Venice 1759-98.

Martin V., *Gallicanisme=Les Origines du Gallicanisme*, 2 Vols., Paris 1939.

Mercati A., *Raccolta=Raccolta di concordati in materia ecclesiastica tra la Santa Sede e le autorità civili*, Rome 1919.

M.H.S.J.=Monumenta historica Societatis Jesu, Madrid 1894 ff.

M.Ö.I.G.=Mitteilungen des Instituts für österreichische Geschichtsforschung, 1880 ff.

Mon. conc. gen.=Monumenta conciliorum generalium saeculi XV, ed. Akademie der Wissenschaften, 2 Vols. in 3 parts, Vienna 1857-73.

Morandi L., *Monumenti=Monumenti di varia letteratura tratti dai manoscritti di Mons. L. Beccadelli*, 2 Vols. in 3 parts, Bologna 1797-1804.

Morsolin B., "Il Concilio de Vicenza," in *Atti del R. Istituto Veneto*, Ser. VI, VII, I (1888-9), pp. 539-87.

Müller E. F. K., *Die Bekenntnisschriften der reformierten Kirche*, Leipzig 1903.

Müller P. Ewald, *Das Konzil von Vienne 1311-12, seine Quellen und Geschichte,* Münster 1934.

N.B.=Nuntiaturberichte aus Deutschland, PT I, 1534-59, ed. Preussisches historisches Institut in Rom, 12 Vols. Gotha 1892 ff.

Panzer G. W., *Annales=Annales typographici*, 11 Vols., Nuremberg 1793-1803.

Pastor L., *Geschichte der Päpste*, 16 Vols., Freiburg 1885-1933, VOLS. I, III, IV, in new edn. 1924-6; Eng. edn., London 1923 ff.

——, *Reunionsbestrebungen=Die kirchlichen Reunionsbestrebungen während der Regierung Karls V*, Freiburg 1879.

——, *Ungedr. Akten=Ungedruckte Akten zur Geschichte der Päpste*, VOL. I, Freiburg 1904.

Paulus N., *Dominikaner=Die deutschen Dominikaner im Kampfe gegen Luther*, Freiburg 1903.

Pez-Hueber, *Thesaurus anecd.*=*Thesaurus anecdotorum novissimus*, 6 Vols., Augsburg 1721-9.

Pieper A., *Entstehungsgeschichte*=*Zur Entstehungsgeschichte der ständigen Nuntiaturen*, Freiburg 1894.

Pius II (Aeneas Silvius Piccolomini), *Commentarii rerum memorabilium*, with the letters of Cardinal Ammanati, Frankfurt 1614.

——, Correspondence, *see* Wolkan.

——, *Opera*, Basle 1551.

——, *Opera inedita*, ed. J. Cugnoni, Rome 1883.

Politische Correspondenz=*Politische Correspondenz der Stadt Strassburg im Zeitalter der Reformation*, edd. H. Virck, O. Winckelmann and J. Bernays, VOLS. I-III, Strasbourg 1881-98.

Posch A., *Concordantia catholica*=*Die Concordantia catholica des Nikolaus von Cues*, Paderborn 1930.

Q.F.=*Quellen und Forschungen aus italienischen Archiven und Bibliotheken*, ed. Preussisches historisches Institut, Rome 1898 ff.

Quirini A. M., *Epistolae Reginaldi Poli S.R.E. cardinalis et aliorum ad ipsum*, 5 Vols., Brescia 1744-57.

Ram F. X. de, "Documents"="Documents relatifs à la nonciature de Pierre van der Vorst," in *Bulletin de la Commission Royale de Belgique*, Ser. III, VOL. VI (1864).

——, "Nonciature"="Nonciature de Pierre van der Vorst, évêque d'Acqui, en Allemagne et dans les Pays-Bas," in *Nouveaux mémoires de l'Académie Royale de Bruxelles*, XII (1839).

Rassow P., *Kaiseridee*=*Die Kaiseridee Karls V*, Berlin 1932.

Raynaldus O., *Annales*=*Annales ecclesiastici*, Rome 1646 ff., quoted according to year and number.

R.E.=*Realencyklopädie für protestantische Theologie und Kirche*, 3rd edn., 24 Vols., Leipzig 1896 ff.

Reusch H., *Der Index der verbotenen Bücher*, 2 Vols., Bonn 1883-5.

R.H.=*Revue Historique*, 1876 ff.

R.H.E.=*Revue d'histoire ecclésiastique*, 1900 ff

Ribier G., *Lettres*=*Lettres et Memoires d'Estat des roys, princes, ambassadeurs et autres ministres sous les regnes de François I, Henri II et François II*, 2 Vols., Paris 1666.

R.Q.=*Römische Quartalschrift*, 1889 ff.

R.Q.H.=*Revue des questions historiques*, 1867 ff.

R.S.T.=*Reformationsgeschichtliche Studien und Texte*, edd. J. Greving and others, Münster 1905 ff.

R.T.A.=*Deutsche Reichstagsakten*, ed. Historische Kommission, Munich, 16 Vols., Munich-Gotha 1867 ff.; new series, VOLS. I-IV, VII, Gotha 1893 ff.

Sadoleto J., *J. Sadoleti opera*, 4 Vols., Verona 1737-8.

Sägmüller J. B., *Kardinäle*=*Die Tätigkeit und Stellung der Kardinäle bis Papst Bonifaz VIII*, Freiburg 1896.

Sanudo M., *Diarii=I Diarii* 1496-1535, 58 Vols., Venice 1879-1903.

Sarpi P., *Istoria=Istoria del Concilio tridentino*, ed. G. Gambarin, 3 Vols., Bari 1935.

Schade O., *Satiren=Satiren und Pasquille der Reformationszeit*, 3 Vols., Hanover 1856-8.

Scheurl Ch., *Briefbuch*, edd. F. von Soden and J. K. Knaake, 2 Vols., Potsdam 1867-72.

Schirrmacher F. W., *Briefe und Akten=Briefe und Akten zur Geschichte des Religionsgesprächs zu Marburg 1529 und des Reichstags zu Augsburg 1530*, Gütersloh 1876.

Schlecht J. *Zamometič=Andrea Zamometič und der Basler Konzilsversuch von 1482*, Paderborn 1903.

Scholz R., *Publizistik=Die Publizistik zur Zeit Philipps des Schönen und Bonifaz' VIII*, Stuttgart 1906.

Schottenloher K., *Bibliographie zur deutschen Geschichte im Zeitalter der Glaubensspaltung*, 6 Vols., Leipzig 1933-40, quoted "Schottenloher" with number.

Schulte J. F. von, *Quellen=Die Geschichte der Quellen und der Literatur des kanonischen Rechts von Gratian bis auf die Gegenwart*, 3 Vols., Stuttgart 1875-80.

Sehling E., *Kirchenanordnungen=Die evangelische Kirchenanordnungen des 16. Jahrhunderts*, 5 Vols., Leipzig 1902-13.

Spahn M., *Johannes Cochlaeus*, Berlin 1898, with bibliography.

St. Arch.=State Archives: in this volume use has been made of the State Archives of Basle, Florence, Mantua, Modena, Munich, Trent and Venice.

Stoecklin A., *Der Basler Konzilsversuch des Andrea Zamometič*, Basle 1938.

Tangl M., *Kanzleiordnungen=Die päpstlichen Kanzleiordnungen von 1200 bis 1500*, Innsbruck 1894.

Theiner A., *Mon. Pol.=Vetera monumenta Poloniae et Lithuaniae*, VOL. II, Rome 1861.

Thuasne L., *J. Burchardi diarium*, 3 Vols., Paris 1883-5.

T.Q.=Theologische Quartalschrift, Tübingen 1819 ff.

Tract. ill. iuriscons.=Tractatus illustrium iurisconsultorum ex universo iure, Venice 1584.

Valois N., *Le Pape=Le Pape et le Concile*, 2 Vols., Paris 1909.

——, *Pragmatique Sanction=Histoire de la Pragmatique Sanction de Bourges sous Charles VII*, Paris 1906.

Vat. Arch.=Vatican Secret Archives.

Vat. Lib.=Vatican Library.

Walch C. W. F., *Monumenta medii aevi*, 2 Vols., Göttingen 1757-63.

Weiss Ch., *Papiers=Papiers d'Etat du Cardinal de Granvelle*, 9 Vols., Paris 1841-52.

Wirz C., *Akten=Briefe und Akten über die diplomatischen Beziehungen der römischen Kurie zur Schweiz*, Basle 1895.

Wolkan R., *Der Briefwechsel des Eneas Silvius Piccolomini:* Fontes rerum Austriacarum, Series II, VOLS. LXI, LXII, LXVII, LXVIII, 4 Vols., Vienna 1909-18.

Z.K.G.=Zeitschrift für Kirchengeschichte, 1876 ff.

Z.K.Th.=Zeitschrift für katholische Theologie, 1877 ff.

Z.Sav.R.G.K.A.=Zeitschrift der Savignystiftung für Rechtsgeschichte, kanonistische Abteilung 1912 ff.

Index

Index

No entries are given for *Emperor, King of England, King of France, Pope* etc. when these persons are referred to by their general titles.

Pio, Alberto, of Carpi *see* Carpi
— Rodolfo, of Carpi *see* Carpi
Piombo, Sebastiano del 221*n*
Piro della Marca, Giovan Paulo Ungini
dalla 550*n*
Pirstinger, Berthold, Bishop of Chiemsee,
author of *Tewtsche Theologey* 401
Pisa, Archbishop of 72
— Assembly of 14, 31, 78, 98ff
— *Conciliabulum* of (1511) 34, 39, 58,
106, 113, 116, 422
— General Council of 53, 107, 110
Pisani, Francesco, Cardinal 415*n*
Pistoia, Antonio da, Sforza's Roman
agent 82*n*
Pistoris, Simon, jurist 358*n*, 364, 386*n*
Pistorius 251*n*, 382
Pius II (Aeneas Silvius Piccolomini) 19,
24, 32*n*, 36, 43, 46, 48ff, 55, 63ff, 67f,
70f, 84f, 91, 95*n*, 121, 123f, 127, 162,
173, 175, 201, 235, 284, 414*n*
— III (Francesco Piccolomini) 51, 71,
75, 84, 126
— IV (Giangelo de' Medici) 28*n*,
569, 574
— V (Michele Ghislieri) 130, 437*n*
Planitz, Hans von der, jurist, Saxon
Councillor 197, 211*n*
Platina 71
Plotis, de, Mantuan agent 432, 433*n*,
435*n*
Podiebrad, George, of Bohemia 49ff
Podio, Auxias de, Cardinal, legate 69*n*,
74
Podocataro, Ludovico, Papal secretary
127
Poggio (the humanist) 115
— Gianfrancesco, son of Poggio the
humanist 114
— Giovanni, nuncio 307*n*, 314*n*, 344,
345*n*, 346, 372, 375, 379, 412*n*, 438*n*,
448*n*, 456, 458*n*, 467, 472, 485, 490*n*,
491*n*, 493, 496*n*, 499, 500*n*, 504*n*,
506, 508*n*, 513
Poitiers, University of 110
Poland, King of *see* Sigismund
— envoy of King of *see* Tarnowski
Pole, Reginald, Cardinal, deacon 336,
345*n*, 352f, 366, 368, 378, 382*n*, 419,
423, 424*n*, 429, 433, 434*n*, 436*n*,
438*n*, 440, 464, 468*n*, 469f, 478, 482,
497f, 505, 509ff, 524*n*, 540f, 548, 569
Pommerania, Duke of 318
Poncher, Archbishop of Paris 149
Pontano, Ludovico 25, 39
Pornaxio, Raphael de, OP 26
Porta, Ardicinus de, Cardinal 119
Portugal, King of 240, 280, 314, 327*n*,
337
— envoys of King of 40
— Cardinal of 88
Porzio, Girolamo 111

Posen, Bishop of 16
Povo, Enrico di, commissioner to fix
prices in Trent 553*n*
Praeparatoria (Fabri) 403
Praët, Louis de, Emperor's agent 270,
272, 280*n*, 364
Pragmatic Sanction of Bourges 20f, 45,
54f, 132f, 154, 506*n*
Prague, Archbishop of 550*n*, 556*n*
Praise of Folly (Erasmus) 160
Prée 574*n*
Prevesa, battle at (1538) 342
Prie, de, Cardinal 107, 112
Prierias, Sylvester, OP, Master of Sacred
Palace 28*n*, 170, 172, 185, 190f
Priuli, Aluise 382*n*
Probus, Philip, of Bourges 77*n*
Procuratorium (Louis XII) 108
Professio Fidei Adriani VI 207
Professio Fidei (Boniface VIII) 15*n*, 80,
83
Provisiorium (Truchsess) 261
Prussia, Dominic of, Prior of the Charter-
house of Trier 144
Pseudo-Dionysius 22
Pucci, family 420
— Antonio, Cardinal, adviser of Clement
VII 283*n*, 421, 423*n*, 434f, 483*n*
— Lorenzo, uncle of Antonio 131*n*, 421
— Roberto, uncle of Antonio 421
Pulka, Peter von 17

Quentel, Peter, printer 348*n*
Queta, Antonio, jurist, secretary to Cles
510, 512, 565, 576
Quiñónez, Francisco de, Cardinal, Emperor's chargé d'affaires, General of
the Franciscans 181*n*, 238f, 242,
265, 266*n*, 338, 345*n*, 367, 419, 421*n*,
424*n*
Quintana, jurist, Emperor's confessor
276, 513*n*
Quintuplex psalterium 1509 (Lefèvre) 157
Quirini, Vincenzo Pietro, OCamald,
author of *Tractatus super concilium
generale* 28*n*, 61, 114*n*, 115*n*, 128ff,
132, 135*n*, 147, 157f, 164, 353*n*, 377,
382*n*, 383*n*, 386*n*, 390*n*
Quistellius, Ambrosius, OESA 367*n*

Radinus 190
Ramung, Matthias, Bishop of Speyer
151
Randegg, Burkhard von, Bishop of Con-
stance 151
Rangoni, Guido, condottiere, cousin of
Ugo 281*n*
— Ugo, Bishop of Reggio-Emilia, nuncio
281, 283, 285*n*, 296, 308, 311, 336,
338, 339*n*, 341*n*, 526*n*
Raphael 137

Printed in Great Britain
by T. and A. Constable Ltd., Edinburgh,